SKETCHES

OF

VIRGINIA

HISTORICAL

AND

BIOGRAPHICAL.

(First Series)

WILLIAM HENRY FOOTE

JOHN KNOX PRESS
Richmond, Virginia

Originally published 1850. New edition with Index published 1966.
Library of Congress Catalog Card Number: 66-26775
© M. E. Bratcher 1966
Printed in the United States

CHAPTER OF CONTENTS.

CHAPTER IX.

CHAPTER X.

CHAPTER XI.

CHAPTER XII.

CHAPTER XIII.

CHAPTER XIV.

CHAPTER XV.

CHAPTER XVI.

CHAPTER XVII.

CHAPTER XVIII.

CHAPTER XIX.

ABOUT THE INDEX

The decision of John Knox Press to respond favorably to a suggestion of the Committee on History of the Synod of Virginia has made available again this hard-to-get treasure-house of Presbyterian history usually known as "Foote's Sketches." Without question this will be a source of rejoicing to a host of historians and librarians across the country.

The Library of Union Theological Seminary hopes that the Index to this monumental work will also cause rejoicing. Heretofore there has been no easy way to lay hold of a fact in Foote's voluminous record of people and churches, and state and national affairs. The Library has transferred all of its rights in the Index to John Knox Press in the belief that it will make Foote's *Sketches of Virginia* more sought after and more widely used.

A fortunate combination of circumstances made possible the production of the Index. The first stages were compiled by Miss Karen Cowsert of Mary Baldwin College, who worked in the Seminary Library during the summer months of 1965. Miss Cowsert was given substantial assistance by Mrs. T. N. Elliott, Jr., and Mrs. John Callaway, both of whom are wives of Seminary students and members of the Library staff. The work was put in its final form by the Reverend Lennart Pearson, who had the benefit of extensive suggestions and counsel from Mr. William M. E. Rachal, Editor of the *Virginia Magazine of History and Biography;* Dr. Howard M. Wilson, Director of the Historical Records Project of the Synod of Virginia; and Dr. George Apperson, Professor of History at Southwestern at Memphis. To this entire company, the Library wishes to offer its great thanks and appreciation for a task well done.

H. M. Brimm, Librarian
Union Theological Seminary in Virginia

ADVERTISEMENT.

—◇—

IT was in contemplation that the Sketches in this volume should be continued to a later period. Materials were procured in abundance; and a number of sketches prepared, viz: James Turner—Cary Allen—The old Churches and Church Yards in the Valley—List of all the members of Hanover Presbytery, from its formation to the year 1786, with short notices of many of the brethren—and Cornstalk, the Shawanee Chief. But the size of the volume forbids their insertion. The appearance of a second volume will depend upon the reception the present volume may meet with from an indulgent public.

ROMNEY, *Hampshire Co., Virginia,*
    December 1849.

SKETCHES

OF

VIRGINIA.

———o———

INTRODUCTORY CHAPTER.

THERE have lived men, in Virginia, whose names are worthy
of everlasting remembrance. There have been events that
should never be forgotten. There have been principles avowed,
whose influence will be felt through all time. There have been
historians of Virginia—there have been volumes of Biography worthy of the writers, and of the men whose lives they
record. The materials for these volumes have been found
abundant, and are not yet exhausted. Mines of literary wealth
remain untouched.

Virginia claims the veneration and love of her children.
Situated in the medium latitude between the extremes of the
Union, she borders on the Atlantic, and six of her sister States.
In her bosom was the first of those colonies, that have in-
creased and multiplied into the United States of America. As
the mother of great men, and theatre of great events, in
Church and State, all posterity will acknowledge her claims.

While political events have had their historians, and political
men their biographers, the great struggle for *Religious Liberty*
which preceded the Bill for Religious Freedom, has never been
set forth. It has been but slightly referred to in the record of
those very events over which it had a controlling influence.
And while it remains unknown, Virginia, both past and present, remains unknown. The power of the religious principle
in moulding the civil and political institutions in Virginia has
not been appreciated. The law for religious freedom, in the
Statute book, cannot be duly estimated, while the history of
the men, that thought and laboured and suffered for the unrestrained liberty we enjoy, remains unwritten. This liberty
was not the offspring of mere greatness of mind, or of political

sagacity. It was a child of principle, cradled in sufferings, and fed on tears. Afflicted beyond endurance, it fled from the old world, and suffered, and toiled in patience, and gained the victory in the new. It is the glory of Virginia that the contest for civil and religious liberty began so early in her borders, and was so soon followed by that phenomenon, entire freedom of conscience, novel to herself and strange to the old world.

The object of the following sketches is to delineate some of the scenes witnessed in Virginia, and portray the characters of some of her children, and of some, who captivated by her beauty and fertility, cast in their lot, for life or for death, for glory and wealth, or poverty and suffering, and aided in the working out the system of things which has been, and is, the glory of Virginia. These have not been given in any volume of History or Biography presented to the public; and their omission has rendered the history of Virginia enigmatical. Effects have been delineated for which no sufficient cause has been given. And readers of voluminous histories of Virginia have risen from this enjoyment, or task, with very imperfect, if not utterly erroneous views of the principles and doings of the past. CONTRIBUTIONS TO ECCLESIASTICAL HISTORY have been made to illustrate the character, doings, and fate, of that denomination, which, established by law, with the settlement of the province, was sustained by the legislature with paramount, and almost uncontrolled, influence, for nearly a century and a half. Some reference has been made in history to classes of people that, at different times, previous to 1700, appeared, were opposed, persecuted, in part put down, in part driven away, but not annihilated; but history has not said that they finally wrought a change in the sentiments of the freeholders of Virginia, and consequently in her constitution. These sketches will attempt to set forth these men and their doings. And if they appear to be sketches of a denomination, it is because the men whose acts have been worthy of something better than vituperation and forgetfulness were of that denomination.

The materials for these sketches have been gathered in every section of the State. Records of Civil Courts and Ecclesiastical Judicatories, in manuscript, have been examined, volume after volume. Private journals, diaries, memoranda, and family genealogies have been fully consulted and freely used. Magazines of unquestioned standing, and pamphlets to be relied on, have contributed largely. Comparatively little has been taken from any political history, in general circulation. The events described in such history are supposed to be known; and are here introduced only to show the reader whereabouts in the civil history of the State, the events, here recorded, find their place and give their moulding influence. The writings of Captain John Smith are an exception. The sources of traditionary information have been examined. Over these the grave is rapidly closing; already the memory of what was done and said in the Revolution speaks out, at distant intervals, from here and there a solitary representative of the last century. Traditions have been compared with written documents, and nothing has been received from conjecture, or preconcieved hypothesis. The sources of information are faithfully given, in all cases, where the knowledge of the source is supposed to be of any importance.

No invidious comparisons are designed in these sketches, whose object is to rescue from oblivion the names and virtues of noble men,—" Sons of Liberty"—of that liberty which rejoices all good men. In making this rescue, facts and characters will be brought into view worthy of the study of the aged and the young, of the minister of the gospel and the statesman. The principles of liberty, in matters of religion and the State, will be seen struggling against error and misconceptions, gaining the ascendency step by step, conflict by conflict,—" the blood of the slain multiplying the martyrs,"—till at last the groans are lost in the shouts of victory. And if in doing this, the names of men not yet recorded in their proper place in history, and the relation of events, not hitherto noticed, or slightly passed over, hold a prominent place, there can be no complaint. Truth is stronger and more strange than fiction. Every writer gives what he supposes, or wishes others to suppose, the most important in the past. Political writers seem to labour under a great difficulty in making record of the principles and doings of religious men,—at least of some religious men,—and also in stating the proper influence of religion, either in principle or in practice. It has of late years become a matter of earnest inquiry,—What has the religious principle done? That strange, abused, inexplicable Carlyle has turned the current of English history for generations. The obscure past outshines the present. The clouds that overhung the Puritans are dissolving, and long defamed names are resplendent in letters of glory.

The labours of the man, who uncheered by any companions, through many years of toil and suffering, unstimulated by applause, in the colony or the mother land, laid the corner stone of a majestic spiritual building to the honour of the Lord Jesus, in the New World, are not now appreciated, because unknown. The importance of the congregations, gathered by his sufferings and solitary labours, is not felt because not understood. To understand these, and to appreciate the labours of such men as

Davies, Robinson, Waddel, Craig, Brown, Henry, and Todd, and the congregations gathered by them, and multiplied by the Smiths and Grahams and Hoge, and the men trained by their teaching and their example, it will be necessary to take a view of the civil and religious condition of Virginia during the first seventy years of her colonial existence. Reference must be made to the condition of Ulster, Ireland, during the same period, and some preceding and some succeeding years, because so many Virginia families and Virginia principles claim *Ireland*, and through her *Scotland*, as their *Mother Land*.

The cavaliers of Virginia and the Puritans of New England agreed in thinking religion an essential part of the State; and that the will of the majority should decide in all ecclesiastical concerns. They each established their forms, and resolutely defended them. They each drove out from their borders, as far as practicable, all dissenters, and called it self-defence, the liberty of the majority. The emigrant from Ulster, contended for the liberty of the minority, and in this differed from the Cavaliers and the Puritans. On the subject of civil liberty, the Puritan and the Presbyterian agreed, and both for a time disagreed with the Cavalier. The union of the three wrought the American Revolution, and established the liberty of law. The part of history, not yet written, contains the developement of the principles of these people, modified by education and circumstances. And if these sketches shall throw any light on important facts hitherto imperfectly known, they will have fulfilled the object for which they were designed.

To a great extent, and generally as far as practicable, or useful, the important facts are given in the words of the original writer, or author of the tradition, that the reader may make his own construction. By this means numerous footnotes are avoided, the searching out authorities for verification less necessary, and the liability to misconstruction greatly lessened. Due acknowledgment is made, or intended to be made, of the assistance rendered by friends of truth, in the chapters in which their assistance was given. The reader will perceive that the treasury, from which these sketches have been drawn, is not exhausted. Whether another volume shall follow in succession will depend, other things being equal, much upon the reception this may meet with from an indulgent public.

It is proper to state that great use has been made of Hening's Statutes at large. The laws of Virginia that appear in the following sketches have been taken from that work. They are quoted by their number, and the year. It will be understood without continual reference, that the Extracts are from the laborious collections of W. W. Hening.

I have also made frequent use of the labours of the Rev.

Richard Webster, where an acknowledgment of the obligation was inconvenient. His collections are a treasury of facts for an American Ecclesiastical historian. It is not impossible there may be valuable papers, illustrating particular facts, hereafter brought to light, which may modify or strengthen the statements made in these sketches. All things bow to the majesty of truth.

CHAPTER I.

VIRGINIA IN SIXTEEN HUNDRED AND EIGHTY-EIGHT.

THE year 1688 is an epoch in English history. The protestant succession was then secured to the crown of England. The protestant religion was established as the religion of the State; in England, under the form of prelacy, in Scotland, of presbytery. Civil liberty made a great advance, and the anglo-saxon race ascended in the sight of all Europe, regaining what had been lost after Cromwell, and thenceforward holding the balance of power.

The civil and ecclesiastical condition of Virginia, at that time, cannot fail to be interesting to those, who take pleasure in noticing the progress of the human race, in the discovery, the possession, and the defence of the rights of man. Virginia, as she was then, and as she is now, exhibits strongly by contrast, colonial dependence on arbitrary power, and republican liberty. About that time, commenced in Virginia, a contest for religious liberty, which, after a hundred years of conflict, ended in the famous law entered on her statute book in 1785, declaring the citizens of the commonwealth as free in mind as in body, in religion as in politics. Four score and two years had passed since the little fleet of three ships, whose whole capacity for burden did not exceed one hundred and sixty tons, set sail from Blackwall in England on the 19th of December, 1606, under the command of that experienced navigator, Christopher Newport, bearing a company of adventurers to the wilderness of Virginia. Three of these enterprising men will be famous to all posterity, Bartholomew Gosnold, Rev. Robert Hunt, and Captain John Smith. The names of the others have been saved from absolute oblivion by the famous Smith in his history of Virginia.

On the 26th of April 1607, the fleet, driven by a storm, entered the Chesapeake. On the 30th they cast anchor at a

point well known in modern times. The voyagers named it
Point Comfort, because after their long voyage and the late
storm it had—"put them in good comfort." On the 13th of
May the colony was landed on a peninsula, on the north side
of James' river, about forty miles from its mouth. There they
commenced the first permanent colony in North America. In
honour of the king, James I., the place was called Jamestown.
Here was a theatre, on which the enterprise, courage, and
magnanimity of Smith, and the piety and patriotic devotion of
Hunt displayed themselves. Here was the residence of the
Governor, and the place of the meeting of the Burgesses, who
claimed and exercised in the wilderness all the privileges of
Englishmen. Here at the time of the accession of the Prince
of Orange, in 1688, was the only place in the colony that
might be called a town.

In 1688 the plantations in Virginia were scattered along
the shores of the Chesapeake,—across the narrow strip of land,
that separates the bay from the ocean,—along the banks of the
rivers and creeks that fall into that noble bay, and on their
tributary streams to the head of tide water. No settlement
had been made above the falls where the river Powhatan,
"falleth from the rockes farre west." The neighbourhood of
some navigable water being esteemed essential to the successful operations of planters, the most fertile portions of land
between the rivers, were occupied only in scattered positions.
The expectation of finding abundant mines of the precious
metals had allured multitudes, of the early adventurers, to
Virginia. This had passed away, and the more sober, and
ultimately more enriching, pursuits of agriculture occupied the
public mind. The colony had become permanent in its inhabitants, and in its occupations. Few emigrants came, as at first,
with the expectation of sudden wealth, and a speedy return to
England. A cheerful independence, in the new country, in
preference to poverty in the old, was the more reasonable
expectation and desire. The emigrants also came in families,
or sought to unite themselves, by marriage, with the older colonists. They were encouraged to do this, by the patrons in
England, to give importance to the colony and increase their
income; and by the colonists, to add to their numbers, their
pecuniary strength and warlike means. The importation of
wives by the cargo, that stroke of policy in the patrons, had
long ceased, and men wooed and won their wives, according to
the usages of civilized life. Children, grand children, and
great grand children claimed Virginia as their home, England
as the fatherland.

Of all the productions, which the earth brought forth in
abundance, tobacco received the greatest attention. The first

specimen of this plant peculiar to America was taken to England, from Carolina, by Ralph Lane, in 1586. It met the entire reprobation of the Queen. In less than ten years after the settlement of the colony, at Jamestown, tobacco was the principle article of export. The demand increased with the consumption, and the cultivation with the demand. The making of tar, pitch, and turpentine, and the hunting of mines, the objects of the first emigrants, were abandoned for the occupation of the planter. Governor Berkely says, in 1671, "commodities of the growth of our own country we never had any, but tobacco, which yet is considerable that it yields his Majesty a great revenue." The planters, being absorbed in the cultivation of tobacco, repeatedly suffered the evils of famine through their neglect to cultivate corn in sufficient quantities for home consumption. The supply from the savages, always scanty and precarious, became wilfully less, as the wants of the planters increased. The Indians desired by all, and every means, to drive the intruders from their fields and rivers. Laws were passed by the House of Burgesses to enforce the production of corn, and limit the amount of tobacco. In 1624, at the first Assembly, whose records have been preserved, it was resolved, by act 16th—"That three sufficient men of every parish shall be sworne to see that every man shall plant and tende sufficient corne for his family. Those men that have neglected so to do are to be by the said three men presented to be censured by the Governour and Counsell." By act 18th—"Every freeman shall fence in a quarter of an acre of ground before Whitsuntide next to make a garden for planting vines, herbs, roots, &c. sub pœna ten pounds of tobacco a man." The evil not being remedied by these enactments, it was ordered, in the year 1630, by act 6th—"That two acres of corne or neere thereabouts bee planted for every head that worketh in the ground, and the same to bee sufficiently tended weeded and preserved from hoggs cattell and other inconveniences. And if any planter shall be found delinquent therein, hee shall forfeit all his tobacco, which bee made of his cropp that yeare the one halfe to the informer, the other to bee employed to publique uses for the good of the country." In the revisal of the laws in 1632 the wording of this law was altered, but the spirit retained. In the revisal of 1642, Act 8th, the penalty was changed to—"five hundred pounds of tobacco per acre defective." In 1647 the act for enforcing the planting of two acres,—"either in Indian or English grayne"—is renewed. Act 6th with the additional penalty—"and for the neglect of any constables in not presenting both the planting and sufficient tending thereof, that the commissioners of the county doe impose a fine of five hundred pounds of tob'o upon each constable so defaulting—and in case the commissioners do not take a strict care in taking accompt of the constables in the execution of this act, that then the said commissioners shall be fined at the discretion of the Gov'r and Council." In the same year the exportation of corn was forbidden on penalty of five hundred pounds of tobacco; and the price, at home, was limited to one hundred pounds of tobacco per barrel containing five Winchester bushels. In 1657, during the Commonwealth of England, the act for planting two acres of corn was renewed, with the same penalty on the planters; the constables not being mentioned.

Tobacco became the standard of value, and supplied, in part at least, the place of a circulating medium of the precious metals. By act 64, in 1632—"The Secretaries fees shall be as followeth, viz—ffor a warrant 05lbs of tobacco,—ffor a passe 10lbs,—ffor a freedom 20,—ffor Commission of Administration 20,—The Marshalls fees shall be, ffor an arrest 10lbs of Tobacco,—ffor warning the cort 02,—imprisonment, coming in 10, going out 10,—Laying by the heels 5,—whippinge 10,—Pillory 10,—Duckinge 10.—The Prisoner lying in prison, Marshalls attendance per day 5,—ffor every 5lbs of tobacco the Marshall may require 1 bushel of corne." By act 61st 1642, Attorney's fees, in the county court, for any kind of service, was not to exceed 20lbs of tobacco, upon penalty of 500 lbs of tobacco; and in the quarter court not to exceed 50lbs, upon penalty of 2000lbs of tobacco. The house of Burgesses was slow in admitting Lawyers to plead in the courts, on any terms. One of the charges,—"Duckinge 10lbs,"—refers to the English law for the punishment of turbulent women.

The price of tobacco was always fluctuating on account of the varying quantity and quality of the crops. Some years, immense crops were tended, and the supply of good tobacco was greater than the demand; in other years the quantity was less, and the quality inferior. Keeping accounts in tobacco became inconvenient, especially if payment were delayed for a length of time. It was therefore enacted 1633, Act 4th—"Whereas it hath beene the usuall custome of marchants and others dealinge intermutually in this colony to make all bargains, contracts, and to keep all accounts in tobacco and not in money, contrary to the former custome of this plantation and manner of England, and other places within the Kings dominions, which thinge hath bredd many inconvenienceys in the trade, and occasioned many troubles as well to the marchants as to the planters, and inhabitants amongst themselves. *It is thought fitt by the Governor and Councill and the Burgesses of this Grand Assembly*, That all accounts and contracts be usually made and kept in money and not in Tobacco,

That all pleas and actions of debt or trespass be commenced and sett downe in lawful money of England onlie, and in no other commoditie." In order to preserve an equality in the price of tobacco the Legislature frequently attempted to regulate the quantity of the crops, by determining, by Statute, how many hills of tobacco might be tended for each poll on a plantation.

In 1688 there were no large towns in Virginia, nor any number of small ones, or even villages. The Legislature, in conformity to the wishes of the mother country, encouraged the gathering of numerous families, in close community, for the purpose of traffic and mechanical trades. It layed out towns and made regulations for them. It directed that foreign traffic should be carried on, exclusively at these towns. Ports of entry were made in sufficient numbers to accommodate the country, and secure the revenue. But the places, called towns, or ports of entry often consisted of a single dwelling-house with a store, or office; and not a single flourishing town was to be found in the whole province, Jamestown, the capital, not excepted. The trade now collected in cities, as centres, was then scattered over the whole country. The planters preferred making sale of their own tobacco directly to the foreign trader; and welcomed the vessels that cast anchor, for the purpose of trade, in the nearest river, or at the most convenient landing, not very scupulous whether the port was established by law or chosen for convenience. A statute of Assembly required the planters to report, on pain of fines, the number of hogsheads they sold these foreign vessels. Whether the change effected, by transferring the principal business of the whole country to a few cities, either within or without the state, has proved beneficial to community at large, by confining to a few hands the business once shared by all, is a matter for discussion. The popular feeling is, however, in favour of cities, and the course of trade is settled on the principle, the more merchants the more traffic, and the better business.

The inhabitants of the colony were all planters. Scattered over the country as suited their interest or convenience, they lived unrestrained, fed by their plantations and the abundance of the sea. Their first exposure had been to the pressure of famine; and the next to massacre from savage hands. The plentiful crops gathered, in consequence of the watchful care of the legislature, and the remembrance of past sufferings from their improvidence, had removed the fears of want; and their increasing numbers, and the wasting strength of the Indian tribes, had relieved them from the alarms of midnight attacks. Governor Berkeley says, in 1671,—" We suppose, and I am very sure we do not much miscount, that there are in Virginia above

forty thousand persons, men, women, and children, and of
which there are two thousand black slaves, six thousand Christian servants for a short time, the rest are borne in the country
or have come in to settle and seat in bettering their condition
in a growing country. Yearly, we suppose, there comes, of
servants, about fifteen hundred, of which most are English, few
Scotch, and fewer Irish, and not above two or three ships of
negroes in seven years. Eight thousand horse could be easily
called together on alarm." These planters cherished a spirit
of personal independence, in all their communications. Each
lived on his own freehold, and could draw from the soil abundant provisions; and from the neighbouring streams and
marshes, fish and fowl in variety; and from the surrounding
forests, the wild deer, and innumerable smaller game. Captivated with this kind of life, few mechanics, that came to the
colony would continue to carry on their trade. The planters
purchased in England, or from vessels direct from the motherland, what their necessities required; and indulged in luxuries as
far as their tastes demanded, or their resources permitted. They
delighted in an isolated life. The aversion to living in contiguous dwellings, or even in neighbourhoods, was carried to an
extent, that required legislative interference. Act 5th, 1667,
says—"Whereas the despatch of business in this country is
much obstructed for want of bridle wayes to the severall houses
and plantations, *It is enacted by the Grand Assembly and the
authority thereof*, that every person having a plantation shall
at the most plaine and convenient path that leades to his house
make a gate in his ffence for the convenience of passage of
man and horse to his house about their occasions at the discretion of the owner." To this may be added an enactment expressive of indignant hospitality. Act 16th, 1663—"Whereas it
is frequent with diverse inhabitants of this country to entertaine
strangers into their houses without making any agreement with
the party what he shall pay for his accommodations, which (if
the party live) causeth many litigious suites, and if the stranger
dye lays a gap open to many avaricious persons to ruyne the
estate of the person deceased, ffor remedy whereof for the
future,—Be it enacted that noe person not making a positive
agreement with any one he shall entertayne into his house for
dyett or storeage shall recover any thing against any one soe
entertayned or against his estate, but that every one shall be
reputed to entertayne those of curtesie with whom they make
not a certain agreement."

This predeliction of the Planters for isolated life raised an
almost insuperable barrier to the instruction of the mass of the
people. Neither the King in Council, nor the Legislature
of the Province had taken any effective steps for the education

of even a portion of the people.   Some preparatory movements had been made for the erection of a college, in the early days of the colony; some donations were made for that purpose; and the subject had been repeatedly agitated in succeeding years, without success.   Efforts had been made by individuals to establish free schools, as appears from Act 18th, 1642, 3— " Be it also enacted and confirmed upon consideration had of the Godly disposition and good intent of Benjamin Symme, deceased, in founding by his last will and testament a free school in Elizabeth county, for the encouragement of all others in the like pious performances, that the said will and testament with all donations therein contained concerning the free school and the situation thereof in the said county and the land appertaining to the same, shall be confirmed according to the true meaning and godly intent of the said testator without any alienation or conversion thereof to any place or county."   That this plan failed of its designed good, appears from Governor Berkeley's letter about thirty years after.   He says, in 1671— in answer to the inquiry what was done in education—"The same course that is taken in England out of the towns; every man according to his ability instructing his children.   But I thank God there are no free schools nor printing, and I hope we shall not have these hundred years; for learning has brought disobedience and heresy, and sects, into the world, and printing has divulged them, and libels against the best government, God keep us from them both."   This opinion of the Governor was no idle abstraction; for in February, 1682, according to Hening, vol. 2d, p. 518—"John Buckner was called before Lord Culpepper and his Council for printing the laws of 1680 without his Excellency's license, and he and the printer ordered to enter into bonds in £100 not to print any thing thereafter until his majestie's pleasure should be known." Without a printing press, college, or free schools, or public schools of any kind, it is not to be supposed that the benefits of education were diffused further than the piety and enterprise of the different families, or some members of them, found opportunity.   Instruction of children was a domestic duty.

The government of the colony, in 1668, was the same as Berkeley tells us it was in 1671, being in—"a Governor and sixteen Counsellors, who have, from his sacred majestie, a commission of Oyer and Terminer, who judge and determine all causes that are above fifteen pounds sterling; for what is under there are particular courts in every county, which are twenty in number.   Every year, at least, the Assembly is called, before whom lye appeals, and this Assembly is composed of two Burgesses out of every county.   These lay the necessary taxes, as the necessity of the war with the Indians, or other exigencies require."

Captain Smith in his History of Virginia, pp. 38, 39, vol. 2d, has preserved the concise account given by John Rolfe, of the meeting of the Burgesses in the year 1619, under Governor Yeardly;—"Then our Governour and Councell caused Burgesses to be chosen in all places, and met at a Generall Assembly, where all matters were debated thought expedient for the good of the colony." This meeting was called on the authority of the Company in London; but its powers were not fully defined. Previously to the year 1645, the number of Burgesses to be sent by each neighbourhood, or plantation, as the settlements were called, or by shires after they were formed, was indefinite.

The first Assembly, whose records have been preserved, was held in 1624. Ten years afterwards, by act of Assembly, the country was divided into eight shires—"which are to be governed as the shires in England. The names of the shires are, James City, Henrico, Charles City, Elizabeth City, Warwick River, Warrosquyoake, Charles River, Accawmack. And as in England, sheriffs shall be elected to have the same power as there; and serjeants, and bailiffs where need requires." In the year 1643, the number of shires was ten. The burgesses were sent from,—Henrico 3, Charles City 3, James City 6, Warwick 2, Elizabeth City 2, Isle of Wight 2, Upper Norfolk 2, Lower Norfolk 2, York 3, Northampton 2. At the time Berkeley wrote, in 1671, there were twenty counties, or shires, Henrico, Charles City, York, New Kent, James City, James County, Warwick, Surry, Isle of Wight, Nansemond, Lower Norfolk, Elizabeth City, Gloster, Lancaster, Rappahannock, Stafford, Westmoreland, Northumberland, Northampton, and Accomack.

In the year 1645, the number of burgesses from each county, was limited to four, except James City county, which might send five, and the city one. Act 84th, in the year 1662, declares—"that hereafter noe county shall send above two burgesses who shal be elected at those places in each county where the county courts are usually kept." By the same law the metropolis was entitled to one burgesse; and the counties severally were empowered—"to lay out one hundred acres of land, and people it with one hundred tithable persons"—and the place, thus laid out, was entitled to one burgesse. By the 85th Act of the same year—"Whereas, the immoderate expences of the burgessesses causing diverse heartburnings between them and the people occasioned an injunction to make agreement for the allowance before the election which

may hereafter probably induce interested persons to purchase votes by offering to serve at low rates, by which
means the candour and ffreedome which should be in the
choice of persons credited with soe honorable and greate a
trust might be very much prejudiced and that place itself
become mercenary and comtemptable,—*Be it therefore enacted*
that the maintenance of every burgesse shal be one hundred
and fifty pounds of tobacco and caske per day, besides the
necessary charge of goeing to the Assembly and retorning."
Each county paid its own delegates from the county levy.

All freemen, at first exercised the right of suffrage. They
sent their suffrage to the place of election, in writing, when it
was most convenient not to attend personally. Neither the
place of election, or the qualifications of candidates for the
Assembly were established by law, till necessity compelled.
Act 8th, 1654, declares—"The persons who shall be elected to
serve in Assembly shall be such and no other than such as are
persons of known integrity and of good conversation and of
the age of one and twenty years." By the same act the Right
of Suffrage was restricted—"all housekeepers whether ffreeholders, leaseholders, or otherwise tenants, shall onely be
capable to elect Burgesses—Provided that this word house-
keeper repeated in this act extend no further than to one
person in a ffamily." The next year this restriction was
repealed. In the Revisal of 1657, 8, the right of suffrage was
extended to—"all persons inhabiting in the colony that are
freemen." But by Act 3d, 1670 the right of suffrage was
confined to freeholders—"Whereas the usuall way of chuseing
burgesses by the votes of all persons who having served their
time are ffreemen of this country who having little interest in
the country doe oftener make tumults at the election to the
disturbance of his majestie's peace, then by their discretions in
their votes provide for the conservative thereof, by making
choyce of persons fitly qualified for the discharge of soe great
a trust, and whereas the lawes of England grant a voyce in
such election only to such as by their estates real or personall
have interest enough to tye them to the endeavour of the publique good:—*it is hereby enacted* that none but ffreeholders and
housekeepers who only are answerable to the publique for the
levies shall hereafter have a voice in the election of any burgesses in this country; and that the election be at the Court-
house." This restriction was enforced by the instructions from
King Charles 2d to Governor Berkeley in 1676. In article 2d,
he says—"You shall take care that the members of the Assembly be elected only by Freeholders as being more agreeable to
the custome of England, to which you are as nigh as conveniently you can to conforme yourselfe."

In 1688 the Indians in Virginia were a subdued people. They never welcomed the English to a permanent settlement. They met, with warlike demonstrations, the little band that stepped on shore at Cape Henry the 26th of April, 1607, and wounded them with arrows. For about seventy years, they resisted the English at every advance into the country, as ene- mies whose destruction they would gladly compass at all hazards. Their power and spirits were broken by Nathaniel Bacon in 1676. Powhatan never loved the whitemen. He made every effort, a sagacious savage could devise, for their destruction. The influence of that admirable girl, Pocahontas, was wonderful and extensive but temporary. It is an exhibition of the power of loveliness and gentleness over barbarians. She was the beauty of her tribe,—of Virginia; as gentle and kind as she was beau- tiful. Her father loved her passionately. The nation admired her. The father's love, and the nation's admiration were the Englishman's shield. The Virginia Indians, in their almost numberless tribes, had, from the head of tide water to the ocean, been brought under the dominion of the warlike Pow- hatan. The fierce Opechankanough, in his implacable enmity, breathed the true spirit of the savages. Brave in war, open in his enmity, he carried the hearts of the redmen with him. He knew well there could be no divided empire with the English. He turned the chafed spirits of the subjugated tribes against these intruders. The fires of exterminating war burned in every savage breast. They asked no peace while the habitation of a whiteman encumbered their cornfields, or his footsteps were traced in their forests. Opechankanough died as he lived, a brave, implacable savage.

The doings of the English, in the early years of their settle- ment, were not calculated to win the confidence of the natives, or break their courage. The ease with which they would be surprised, provoked the depredations of the savages. And the unwise and feeble revenge of the colonists embittered the already aggravated and cruel spirits of barbarous men, that fought for their forest fields and comfortless homes. The sea- captains, and traders, and explorers seemed to forget that the Natives had rights or feelings, and that revenge is the darling passion of the savage. Corn grew luxuriously, in the Indians' fields, along the river banks, yielding abundance for the tribes, but not enough to supply the colonists, and the vessels visiting the coast. When traffic and persuasion, and threats, failed to procure the wished supply, resort was had to violence. Rolfe's narrative, as given by Smith, says,—"In December (1619) Captain Ward returned from Patawomeek the people there dealt falsely with him, so that he took eight hundred bushels of corne from them by force." One man alone was more terrible to them than all the colony beside, in its early years, Captain John Smith. They trembled at his very name. His bravery, his strength, his power of command, his excellence in every thing a savage admired, united to his accomplishments as an Englishman, entirely overawed their fierce spirits. Ardently desiring his death, they knew not how to kill him when in their power. The rest they hated, and murdered as occasion offered.

The early charters speak of christainizing the savages as part of the objects designed in making settlements in Virginia. In the letters patent to Sir Thomas Gates, 1606, the beginning of a plantation in America, between thirty-eight and five and forty degrees of north latitude, is spoken of as—"a work which may, by the Providence of Almighty God, hereafter tend to the glory of his divine majesty, in propagating Christian religion to such people as yet live in darkness and miserable ignorance of the true knowledge and worship of God, and may in time bring the infidels and savages living in those parts, to human civility, and to a settled quiet government." In the third charter dated March 12th, 1611–12—"and for the propagation of Christian religion, and reclaiming of people barbarous to civility and humanity we have by our letters patent, &c." In the commission, to Sir Francis Wyatt and his Council, dated July 24th, 1621,—"which said Council are to assist the Governor in the administration of justice, to advance christianity among Indians, to erect the colony in obedience, &c." In the instructions given him, the third is— "To use means to convert the heathen, viz. to converse with some; each town to teach some children fit for the college intended to be built." The history of this college shows kind and benevolent designs which were not successful and is worthy of remembrance.

Efforts, for the conversion of the savages, were early made, by some ministers, and some pious laymen. Opechankanough pretended a desire to become a christian. He beguiled the pious head of the college, Mr. Thorpe, to take much pains in instructing him, in hopes of numerous converts, till the fatal Friday, March 22d, 1622. That good man, with multitudes of others, was horribly massacred, according to the secret plans of this wily chief, who under the mask of religion plotted the complete and sudden destruction of the English.

Rev. Robert Hunt is one of the few of that company who landed at Jamestown on the 18th of May, 1607, whose biography posterity will desire. He appears to have been equal to his station as pastor of the colonists. Whatever may have been his desires for the conversion of the savages, the difficulties of his situation and his short life prevented the accomplish-

ment of any good. Mr. Whitaker instructed and baptized
Pocahontas, in preparation for her marriage; but neither the
baptism nor the marriage exercised any happy influence towards
the conversion of her nation to Christianity. Capt. Smith, in
vol. 1st, p. 58, gives us—"the opinion of Master Jonas Stock-
ham a minister in Virginia, who even at this time when all
things were so prosperous, and the salvages at the point of conversion, against all their governours and councels opinion, writ
to the councell & company in England to this effect, May 28th,
1621. As for those lasie servants who had rather stand all
day idle, than worke, though but an houre in this Vineyard, &
spend their substance riotously, than cast the superfluity of their
wealth into your treasury, I leave them as they are to the eter-
nall judge of the world. But you right worthy that hath
adventured so freely, I will not examine, if it were for the
glory of God, or your desire of gaine, which it may be you
expect should flow unto you with a full tide, for the conversion
of the Salvages: I wonder you use not the means. I confess
you say well to have them converted by faire means, but they
scorne to acknowledge it, as for the gifts bestowed on them
they devoured them, and so they would the givers if they could,
and though many have endeavoured by all means they could
by kindnesse to convert them, they find nothing from them but
derision and ridiculous answers. We have sent boies amongst
them to learne their language, but they return worse than they
went; but I am no Statesman, nor love I to meddle with any
thing but my bookes, but I can find no probability by this
course to draw them to goodnesse; and I am persuaded if Mars
and Minerva goe hand in hand they will effect more good in
one houre than these verbal Mercurians in their lives, and till
priests and ancients have their throats cut, there is no hope to
bring them to conversion." Smith appears to have adopted
this opinion. It spread over the colony, and through England;
and efforts for the conversion of the Indians were few previous
to the eighteenth century. That individuals felt deeply interested for the salvation of this unhappy race is unquestionable;
but public sympathy was not with them for a century after the
fatal massacre of 1622.

The Acts of Legislature passed in 1623, 4, show the terror of
the colonists and their hostile feelings towards the authors of
their sufferings. Act 23d says, "that every dwelling house
shall be pallizaded in for defence against the Indians." Act
24th—"that no man go or send abroad without a sufficient
party well armed." In 1632 the citizens were required to
carry their arms to church. Act 25th—"that men go not to
worke in the ground without their arms (and a centenell upon
them.) Act 26 says—"that the inhabitants go not aboard

ships or upon any other occasions in such numbers, as thereby to weaken and endanger the plantations." Act 27th—"that the commander of every plantation take care that there be sufficient powder and ammunition within the plantation under his command and their pieces fixt and their arms complete." Act 29—"that no commander of any plantation do either him-selfe or suffer others to spend powder unnecessarily in drinking or entertainments." Act 32d contemplates the entire destruc-tion of the Indians—"that at the beginning of July next the inhabitants of every corporation shall fall upon their adjoyning salvages, as we did last yeare, those that shall be hurt upon service, to be cured at the public charge; in case any to be lamed to be maintained by the country according to his person and quality."

This war of extermination was carried on, with spirit, for years. At last it became disgusting. The savages were less spirited in their attacks and defence, and the colonists began to feel the savages were men, barbarous indeed, but men pos-sessed of rights. The 1st Act of the Session 1655, 6, was in their favour;—"Whereas wee have bin often putt into great dangers by the invasions of our neighboring and bordering Indians which humanely have been only caused by these two particulars our extreme pressures on them and theire wanting of something to hazard and loose beside their lives; Therefore this Grand Assembly on mature advice doth make these three ensuing acts, which by the blessing of God may prevent our dangers for the future and may be a sensible benefitt to the whole country for the present: ffirst, for every eight wolves heads brought us by the Indians, the king or great man (as they call him) shall have a cow delivered him at the charge of the publick. This will be a step to civilizing them and to making them Christians, besides it will certainly make the com-manding Indians watch over their own men that they do us no injuries, knowing that by their default they may be in danger of losing their estates, and therefore be it enacted as aforesaid only with this exception that Accomack shall pay for no more than what are killed in their own county."

"Secondly—If the Indians shall bring in any children as gages of their good and quiet intentions to us and amity with us, then the parents of such children shall choose the persons to whom the care of such children shall be entrusted, and the countrey by us their representatives do engage that wee will not use them as slaves but do their best to bring them up in Chris-tianity, civility, and the knowledge of necessary trades: And on the report of the commissioners of each respective county that those under whose tuition they are, do really intend the bettering of the children in these particulars then a salary shall be allowed to such men as shall deserve and require it."

Thirdly—"What lands the Indians shall be possessed of by order of this or other ensuing assemblyes, such land shall not be alienable by them the Indians to any man de futuro, for this will putt us to a continuall necessity of allotting them new lands and possessions, and they will be alwaies in feare of what they hold not being able to distinguish between our desires to buy or enforcement to have, in case their grants and sales be desired: Therefore be it enacted that for the future no such alienations or bargaines and sales be valid without the assent of the Assembly. This act not to prejudice any Christian who hath land allready granted by patent."

In the session of 1657, 8, acts were passed forbidding any person, to whom an Indian child had been committed, assigning or any way transferring that child; and that the child should be free at twenty-five years of age:—also to prevent the stealing of Indian children, or the buying them from the Indians or others for traffic, or the selling them in any condition by the English, on penalty of five hundred pounds of tobacco.

But in 1676, in consequence of the exasperation arising from Bacon's war, the Assembly resolved—"and bee it further enacted by the authority aforesaid, that all Indians taken in warr shall be held and accounted slaves during life." This act was repealed by the general act setting aside all the acts of Assembly that sat in 1676 under the auspices of Bacon. But it is believed that there are slaves living who are descended from Indian captives, in this, or previous wars.

Nothing had been done for Christianizing the Indians, that produced any effect, from the settlement of the colony till the English Revolution in 1688. Besides Pocahontas, no name of an individual is given that embraced Christianity. Their numbers had decreased; their power and spirits were broken. While they ceased to make war upon the English, they hated them no less, and loved their religion and desired their civilization no more. After the death of the famous Powhatan, and the fierce Opechankanough, no warrior or statesman of eminence arose among the Indians east of the mountains. The feeble tribes after Bacon's war were esteemed helpless enemies rather than terrible foes, for whose civilization or conversion there was no hope. Among all the Indian women of Virginia, Pocahontas had no rival, and posterity will love to think that few of any race either in England or America could claim to be her superior.

The names and power of the tribes that hunted on the banks and fished in the streams of the beautiful rivers occupied by the colony in 1688 is thus given by Smith, Vol. 1st, pp. 116—118. He begins with the James, which—"falleth from rockes

farre west in a country inhabited by a nation they call Mona-
cans—but where it commeth into our discovery it is Powhatan.
In a peninsula on the North side of this river are the English
planted in a place they call James Towne. The first, and next
the river's mouth are the Kecoughtans, who besides their women and children have not past 20 fighting men. The Paspa-
heghes (on whose land is seated James Towne some 40 myles
from the Bay) have not past 40. The river called Chickaha-
wania, the backe river of James Towne neare 250. The
Weanocks 100. The Arrowhatocks 30. The place called
Powhatan, some 40. On the south side this river the Ap-
pamatuchs have 60 fighting men. The Quiyoughcohanocks
25. The Nansamunds 200. The Cheropeacks 100. Fourteen myles northward from the river Powhatan is the river
Pamounkee. On the south side inhabit the people of Yough-
tenund, who have about 60 men for warres. On the north
branch Mattapament, who have 30 men. Where the river is
divided the country is called Pamounkee, and nourisheth neare
300 able men. About 25 myles lower on the north side of this
river is Werawocomico, where their king inhabited when I was
delivered him prisoner; yet they are not past 40 able men.
Ten or twelve myles lower on the south side of this river, is
Chiskeack, which hath some 40 or 50 men. These, as also
Apamatuck, Irrohatuck and Powhatan, are the great King's
chief alliance, and inhabitants. The rest his conquests. There
is another river, some 30 myles navagable that commeth from
inland, called Payankatanke, the inhabitants are about 50 or 60
servicable men. The third navigable river is called Tappaha-
nock, this is navigable some 130 myles. At the top of it inhabit
the people called Mannahoacks amongst the mountaines. Upon
this river on the north side are the people Cuttatawomen, with
30 fighting men. Higher are the Moraughtacunds, with 80.
Beyond them Rappahanock with 100. Far above is another
Cuttatawomen with 20. On the south is the pleasant seat of
Nantaughtacund having 150 men. The fourth river is called
Patawomeke. It is inhabited on both sides. First on the
south side at the very entrance is Wighcocomico and hath
some 130 men, beyond them Sekacawone with 30. The
Onawmanient with 100. And the Patawmokes more than
200."

On the eastern shore in Accomac, he reckons on the river
Tants Wicomico with 100 men; the Acohanock with 40; Accomack 80. Southward, the Chawonocks and Mangoags.
There were numberless small divisions of these tribes whose
names are occasionally mentioned in history.

The effort to convert the Indians was made in good faith.
Stith tells us, pp. 1623, that the king had formerly issued

letters to the bishops in his kingdom—"for collecting money to erect and build a college in Virginia, for the training up and educating infidel children in the true knowledge of God. And according there had been paid near fifteen hundred pounds towards it." The Bishop of Litchfield promised Sir Edwin Landys that a collection should be made in his diocese for the purpose. And he (Sir Edward) likewise moved and obtained, that ten thousand acres of land should be laid off for the University at Henrico, a place formerly resolved on for that purpose. This was intended, as well for the college for the education of Indians, as also to lay the foundation of a seminary of learning for the English." Fifty men were sent in 1619 and fifty more the next summer to work these lands— "as tenants at halves." From each of these hundred hands it was expected that five pounds would be gained. Thus five hundred pounds a year would be secured to the college. Mr. George Thorpe, a kinsman of Sir Thomas Dale, and a gentleman of his Majesty's privy chamber, and one of the Council in England for Virginia, was sent over in 1620 as the company's deputy and superintendent of the colony. For his support the company allowed three hundred acres with ten tenants. "And (p. 166) he particularly mentioned one unknown gentleman alone, who promised five hundred pounds, on demand, for the conversion and education of threescore Indian children. There had been (p. 171) presented, by an unknown person the former year (1619) a communion cup, with a cover and case, a trencher plate for the bread, a carpet of crimson velvet, and a damask table-cloth, for the use of the college. And now in the beginning of this year (1620) another unknown person sent five hundred pounds directed, To Sir Edwin Landys, the faithful Treasurer of Virginia. This was for the maintenance of a convenient number of young Indians, from seven or under to twelve years of age, to be instructed in reading and the principles of the Christian religion, and then to be trained and brought up in some lawful trade, with all gentleness and humanity, till they attained the age of twenty-one; and after that to have and enjoy the like privileges with the native English in Virginia." The company ordered a treaty to be made with Opechankanough in order to promote the design, and also that presents be made him. "Mr. Nicholas Farrar who bequeathed three hundred pounds for converting the infidel children in Virginia, to be paid at such time as it should appear by certificate that ten Indian children were placed in college." Mr. Thorpe entered upon his office with spirit; made the treaty, gave the presents, and as he supposed won the confidence of the savage chief. In the fearful massacre

perpetrated by the savage chief in 1622, this friend of the
Indians was cruelly murdered. With him expired the college
for the civilization of the Indians.

Servants of the African race, in 1688, composed about one
twentieth of the population. The first company of Negroes
were brought into the colony in the month of August succeeding the first meeting of the Burgesses, under Governor Yeardly.
Beverly, in his history of Virginia, says that the introduction of
Negroes was in the summer after the first meeting of the house
of Burgesses, and that these two events took place in 1620.
Smith in his history of Virginia says the two events took place
in 1619: vol. 2, pp. 37, 38, 39—"For to begin with the
yeare of our Lord 1619 there arrived a little pinnace privately
from England about Easter for Captain Argall, who taking
order for his affairs, within four or five daies returned in her,
and left for his deputy Captain Nathaniel Powell. On the
eighteenth of Aprill, which was ten or twelve daies after,
arrived Sir George Yearly, by whom we understood Sir Edward Sands was chosen Treasurer, and Master John Farrar
his deputy. Sir George Yearly to beginne his government
added to be of his Councell Captaine Francis West, Captain
Nathaniel Powell, Master John Porey, Master John Rolfe and
Master William Wickham and Master Samuel Macoike, and
propounded to have a Generall Assembly with all expedition.
In May came in the Margaret of Bristoll, with four and thirty
men, all well and in health, and also many devout gifts, and
we were much troubled in examining some scandalous letters
sent to England, to disgrace this country with barrennesse, to
discourage the adventurers. The 25th of June came in the
Triall with corne and cattell all in safety, which took from us
cleerely all feare of famine; then our Governor and Councell
caused Burgesses to be chosen in all places, and met at a
Generall Assembly, where all matters were debated thought
expedient for the good of the colony. About the last of
August came in a Dutch man-of-warre that sold us twenty
Negroes." Stith in his history of Virginia says on the fourth
page of his preface—" the inquisitive reader will easily perceive how much of this volume is founded on Captain Smith's
materials. They are large and good and of unquestionable
authority, for what is related while he staid in the country.
The latter part of his history especially from Captain Argall's
government is liable to some just suspicions. Not that I question Captain Smith's integrity; for I take him to have been a
very honest man and a strenuous lover of truth." In his 182d
page of history Mr. Stith relating the doings of 1620 says—
" In May this year, there was held another General Assembly,
which has through mistake, and the indolence and negligence

of our historians, in searching such ancient records as are still
extant in the country, been commonly reputed the first General
Assembly of Virginia.   But the privilege was granted sooner,
&c."; and in his history of the doings of 1619. he follows
Smith's account of the calling the Assembly.   At the close of
the sentence he adds—"And we are likewise told by Mr.
Beverly, that a Dutch ship putting in this year sold twenty
Negroes to the colony, which were the first of that generation,
that were ever brought to America;"—but he does not give
the reason why he follows Beverly in this matter and Smith in
the other.   Modern historians have followed Beverly without
giving a reason.   The oldest authority is for placing the introduction of Negroes in 1619.

Until the introduction of Negroes the labours of the plantation were thrown as much as possible on hired servants, as in
England; or on bought servants, persons, who by previous
agreement with ship-owners, were sold to planters for a term of
years sufficient to pay for their transportation.   The tending
tobacco is particularly irksome and was gladly consigned to
redemptioners and heathen Africans.   In 1619, says Stith—
p. 167-8, "the Treasurer and Council received a letter from
his Majesty, commanding them forthwith to send away to
Virginia a hundred dissolute persons, which Sir Edward Zouch
the Knight Marshal would deliver to them.   In obedience to
his Majesty's command, it was resolved to send them over with
all conveniency to be servants, which the Treasurer understood, would be very acceptable to the colony.   And I cannot
but remark, how early that custom arose of transporting loose
and dissolute persons to Virginia as a place of punishment and
disgrace.   It hath laid one of the finest countries in British
America under the unjust scandal of being a mere hell upon
earth."   These dissolute persons arrived in the year 1620.

Those servants who were sold for their passage commanded
different prices at different times.   We are told by Smith, vol.
2, pp. 104, 5, that the passage money was six, eight, or ten
pounds; but that the demand for them was so great in a few
years, that they were sold in Virginia for forty, fifty, and sixty
pounds.   In page 38 he tells us—"an industrious man not
otherwies imploied may well tend four akers of corne, and
1000 plants of tobacco."   The produce of corn on new ground,
he says was—"thirty or forty bushels an aker, and a barrell
of pease and beanes, which we esteem as good as two of corne,
so that one man may provide corne for five and apparell for
two by the profit of his tobacco."   The price of the Afreans
at their introduction is not given.   The thousand plants of
tobacco would produce about one hundred weight of merchantable tobacco.   In 1672 the price of a servant to serve five

years was about ten, and of an African, according to Bancroft, vol. 1, p. 115, about twenty-five pounds.

In 1688 about one in twenty of the inhabitants of Virginia were of the African race. Vigorous efforts were made by pains and penalties to prevent the intermingling of the white and black races. The Anglo Saxon and the African was to be kept pure, the one as master, and the other as slave. The result of servitude, beyond the present gain, and the possible intermingling, of the two races, in some small degree, appears never to have been anticipated. The gain from the African labour outweighed all fears of evil from the intermixture. There appears to have been no question about the morality and right of purchasing them for life, any more than of purchasing for a term of years those servants that come from England, who ultimately became freemen.

When a mixed breed appeared, it was enacted in 1662, in order to render all such connexion opprobrious, that—"Negro womens children serve according to the condition of their mother." Greater severity in the management of Negroes was judged advisable, and in 1669 it was enacted—"Whereas the only law in force for the punishment of refractory servants resisting their master, mistress or overseer cannot be inflicted upon Negroes, nor the obstinacy of many of them by other than violent means supprest,—Be it enacted and declared by this Grand Assembly, if any slave resist his master (or other by his masters order correcting them) and by the extremity of the correction should chance to die, that his death shall not be accompted ffelony, but the master (or that other person appointed by the master to punish him) be acquit from molestation, since it cannot be presumed that prepensed malice (which alone makes murther ffelony) should induce any man to destroy his own estate."

Act 3d, 1667 declares that—"Whereas some doubts have arisen whether children that are slaves by birth, and by the charity and piety of their owners, made partakers of the blessed sacrament of baptisme, should in virtue of their baptisme be made ffree. It is enacted and declared by the Grand Assembly, and the authority therof, that the conferring of baptisme doth not alter the condition of the person as to his bondage or ffreedom; that divers masters ffreed from this doubt may more carefully endeavour the propagation of Christianity by permitting children, though slaves, or those of greater growth if capable to be admitted to that sacrament."

What persons were to be held as slaves is thus set forth by Act 12th, 1670—"Whereas some dispute having arisen whether the Indians taken in warr by any other nation, and by that nation that taketh them sold to the English, are servants for life or term, of years,—It is resolved and enacted that all servants not being Christians imported into this colony by shipping shall be slaves for their lives; but what shall come by land shall serve, if boyes or girles until thirty yeares of age; if men or women twelve yeares and no longer."

But in the year 1682 the Legislature went at length into this subject, and determined what persons shall be held slaves for life in Virginia. Act 1st, after reciting the act of 1670, goes on to say—"and forasmuch as many negroes, moores, mullatoes and others borne of and in heathenish, idollatrous, pagan, and mahometan parentage and country have heretofore, and may hereafter be purchased, procured or otherwise obtained of, from or out of such their heathenish country by some well disposed christians, who after such their obtaining and purchasing such negroe moor or molatto as their slave, out of a pious zeale have wrought the conversion of such slaves to the christian faith, which by the laws of the country doth not manumit them or make them free, and afterwards seeck their conversion, it hath and may often happen that such master or owner of such slaves being by some reason inforced to bring or send such slaves into this country to sell or dispose of for his necessity or advantage, he the said master or owner of such servant which notwithstanding his conversion is really his slave, or his factor or agent must be constrained either to carry back or export againe the said slave to some other place where they may sell him for a slave, or else depart from their just right and tytle to such slave, and sell him here for no longer time than the English, or other christians are to serve, to the great losse and damage of such masters or owners; and the great discouragement of bringing in such slaves for the future and to no advantage at all to the planter or buyer;—and whereas also those Indians that are taken in warre or otherwise by our neighboring Indians confederates or tributaries to his majestie, and this his plantation of Virginia are slaves to the neighbouring Indians that soe take them and by them are likewise sold to his majesties subjects here as slaves,—Bee it therefore enacted &c.—that all the said recited act of the 5th of September 1670 be, and is hereby repealed and made utterly voyd to all intents and purposes whatsoever. And be it enacted &c.—that all servants except Turkes and Moores whilst in Amity with his majesty which from and after the publication of this act shall be brought or imported into this country, either by sea or land, whether Moores, Molattoes or Indians, who and whose parentage and native country are not christian at the time of the first purchase of such servant by some christian although afterwards and before such their importation and bringing into this country, they shall be converted to the christian faith; and all Indians which shall hereafter be sold by our neighbouring Indians or any other trafiqueing with us as for slaves are hereby adjudged deemed and taken, and shall be adjudged deemed and taken to be slaves to all intents and purposes, any law usage or customs to the contrary notwithstanding.

By the 3d Act of the same legislature, masters and overseers were forbidden to—"permitt or suffer, without leave or license of his or their master or overseer, any negroe or slave not properly belonging to him or them, to remain or be upon his or their plantation above the space of four houres at any one time." The penalty was two hundred pounds of tobacco. This act was intended as a safeguard against insurrection. It made the plantation of the master both the home, and the world, to the slave.

So the state of servitude stood in 1688. There were indented servants, redemptioners or those sold for a term of time for their passage, the dissolute and convicts and rebels sent away from England, and the African slaves. The last finally became predominant. They have done the hard work, and have in a measure moulded the habits and manners of Virginia.

Toleration, in the forms of Religion, was unknown in Virginia in 1688. From the commencement of the colony, the necessity of the religious element was felt. The company knew not how to control the members composing the colony, but by religion and law. They exercised a despotism in both. The colonist left England from no ecclesiastical or political grievance. The advantages they expected to gain was a release from poverty and debt. The hope of improving their condition cheered them to undertake the perilous enterprise.

In their habits, manners, tastes, and style of living, they as nearly resembled England, as their possessions, and the soil, climate and productions of their new home, would permit. By force of circumstances they changed much, intentionally nothing. They had been educated in the Church of England. They chose her forms, and her creed. The minister, Robert Hunt, that came with them, had been set apart by Diocesan authority.

That many of the colonists disliked the restraints of that religion, all required for their well being, is evident from Smith. He says, vol. 1st, p. 150—"On the 19th of December, 1606, we set sayle from Blackwall, but by unprosperous winds were kept six weeks in the sight of England; all which time, Mr. Hunt our preacher was so weake and sicke, that few expected his recovery. Yet although he was but twentie myles from his habitation (the time we were in the Downes) and notwithstanding the stormy weather, nor the scandalous imputations (of some few little better than Atheists, of the greatest rank amongst us) suggested against him, all this could never force from him so much as a seeming desire to leave the business, but preferred the service of God, in so good a voyage, before any affection to contest with his godlesse foes, whose disasterous designs (could they have prevailed) had even then overthrown the businesse, so many discontents did there arise, had he not with the water of patience, and his godly exhortations (but chiefly by his true devoted example) quenched those flowers of envie and dissention."

At first the adventurers laboured and lived and traded in common stock. This state of things was to continue for five years, by the King's order. The King in his directions in 1606, according to Stith, pp. 37, and 40, required—"that the said presidents, councils, and the ministers, should provide, that the true word and service of God be preached, planted, and used, not only in the said colonies but also, as much as might be, among the savages bordering upon them, according to the Rites and Doctrine of the Church of England. That all persons should kindly treat the savage and heathen people in those parts, and use all proper means to draw them to the true service and knowledge of God, and that all just and charitable courses should be taken with such of them, as would conform themselves to any good and sociable traffick, thereby the sooner to bring them to the knowledge of God and the obedience of the King."

Sir Thomas Dale who came over as high marshal of Virginia, introduced rules and regulations drawn up for him by Sir Thomas Smith, under the title of "Lawes, divine, morall, and marshall for Virginia." The first section of this document says—"I do strictly command and charge all captaines and officers of what qualitie or nature soever, whether commanding in the field, or in towne, or townes, forts, or fortresses, to have care that the Almighty God bee duly and daily served, and that they call upon their people to hear sermons; as that also they diligently frequent morning and evening prayer themselves, by their own exemplar and daily life and duty, herein encouraging others thereunto; and that such who shall often and wilfully absent themselves, be duly punished according to the marshall law in that case provided." By the second law, death was the penalty of speaking "impiously" against the Trinity, or the known articles of religion. By the third law, boring the tongue with a bodkin was the penalty for profanity, the second offence. And for blaspheming God, the third offence was death by sentence of "Martiall Court." By the fifth law unbecoming treatment of ministers of religion was punished by whipping the offender three times publicly, and he "aske public forgiveness in the assemblie of the congregation three several Sabbath daies." By the sixth, absence from church "on the first towling of the bell upon the working daies to heare divine service"—for the second offence, whipping,—for the third, six months in the gallies. For neglecting divine service on the Sabbath,—the third offence, death. By the thirty-third law, a failure to give satisfactory account of religious knowledge to the minister,—whipping; the second offence, two whippings and public acknowledgment; for the third offence whipping every day till the offender comply with the law. While Stith exclaims against these laws as subversive of the rights of Englishmen, he admits that—"had not these military laws been so strictly executed at this time, there were little hopes or probability of preventing the utter subversion of the colony."

The little we know of the first ministers that came to Virginia makes us wish we knew more. Rev. Robert Hunt, that saved the first colony from a mutiny while yet in sight of England, has left scarce a memorial. After the burning of Jamestown in 1607, 8, Smith says of him,—"Master Hunt our preacher lost all his library and all he had but the cloathes on his backe; yet none never heard him repine at his loss." We know not the time of his death.

A brief but honourable testimony is borne of Mr. Whitaker, minister of Bermuda Hundred, who instructed Pocahontas in the principles of the Christian religion, administered to her the ordinance of baptism, and performed for her the marriage ceremony. Smith, vol. 2d, p. 32, says—"Master Whitaker their preacher—(under date of June 18th 1614) complaineth, and much museth, that so few of our English ministers, that were so hot against the surplice and subscription come hither, where neether is spoken of. Doe they not wilfully hide their talents, or keep themselves at home for feare of losing a few pleasures; be there not any among them of Moses his minde, and the Apostles, that forsook all to follow Christ, but I refer them to the Judge of all hearts, and to the King that shall reward every one according to his talent." Mr. Whitaker had the charge of the town of Henrico, built in the year 1611. He enclosed a hundred acres of land, and built a parsonage which he called Rockhall. In the Epistle dedicatorie of W. Crashawe to the "Good Newes from Virginia" there is this eulogium. "I hereby let all men know that a schollar, a graduate, a preacher, well borne and friended in England; not in debt, nor disgrace, but competently provided for, and liked and beloved where he lived; not in want, but (for a schollar and as these days may be) rich in possession, and more in possibilitie; of himself, without any persuasion (but God's and his own heart) did voluntarily leave his warme nest; and to the wonder of his kindred and amazement of them that knew him, undertooke this hard, but, in my judgement, heroicall resolution to go to Virginia, and helpe to beare the name of God unto the Gentiles." A memoir of this man would find readers every where.

In 1619—the year the first colonial assembly was held—the year African servants were brought into the colony—the year that the king determined to send dissolute persons to Virginia, and the company determined to send the colonists wives, Mr. Stith tells us there were about six hundred persons in the colony divided into eleven parishes, and for the supply of these there were five preachers. The doings of the colonial assembly before the year 1623, 4, are not known; but from after reference it appears the salary of the ministers was ten pounds of tobacco per poll and a bushel of corn, provided it did not exceed fifteen hundred pounds of tobacco and sixteen barrels of corn.

In 1623, 4, the first assembly, whose records have been preserved, held its meeting in the month of March. The first Act says—"There shall be in every plantation, where the people use to meete for the worship of God, a house or room sequestered for that purpose, and not to be for any temporal use whatever, and a place empaled in, sequestered only for the buryal of the dead."

"Act 2d. That whosoever shall absent himselfe from divine service any Sunday without an allowable excuse shall forfeite a pound of tobacco, and he that absenteth himselfe a month shall forfeite 50 pounds of tobacco."

"Act 3d. That there be an uniformity in our church as neere as may be to the canons in England, both in substance and circumstances, and that all persons yield readie obedience to them under paine of censure."

"Act 5th. That no minister be absent from his church above two months in all the yeare upon penalty of forfeiting halfe his means, and whosoever shall absent above foure months in the yeare shall forfeit his whole means and cure."

"Act 7th. That no man dispose of any of his tobacco before the minister be satisfied, upon pain of forfeiture double his part of the ministers means, and one man of every plantation to collect his means out of the first and best tobacco."

The meaning of the word "poll" is defined in Act 1st, 1642, 3—"be it also enacted and confirmed, that there be ten pounds of tob'o per poll and a bushell of corne per poll paid to the ministers within the severall parishes of the collony for all titheable persons, that is to say, as well for youths of sixteen years of age as upwards, as also for all negro women at the age of sixteen years." By Act 8th, 1662, the tithables were intended to include all males imported and all negroes males or females imported.

In the year 1632, there was a revisal of the laws. The act for conformity was re-enacted, somewhat varying in words but not in spirit. The penalty for non-attendance at church was changed to "one shillinge for every tyme of any person's absence from church having no lawfull or reasonable excuse to bee absent." By Act 6th, The minister was required to preach one sermon every Sunday in the year—"havinge no lawfull impediment." By Act 7th, The ministers were required to catechise the youth and others every Sabbath "halfe an houre or more before evening prayer." By Act 13th, "All preachinge, administeringe of the communion baptizinge of children and marriages shall be done in the church except in cases of necessilie."

Act 11th, 1632—"Ministers shall not give themselves to excesse in drinkinge or ryott, spending their tyme idelie by day or by night playinge at dice, cards, or any other unlawfull game, but at all tymes convenient they shall heare or reade somewhat of the holy scriptures or shall occupie themselves with some other honest studies, or exercise, always doinge the things which shall appertayne to honestie and endeavour to profitt the church of God, havinge alwayes in mynd that they ought to excell all others in puritie of life, and should be examples to the people, to live well and christianlie."

By Act 56, 1632—"It is ordered, That no person or persons shall depart out of this colony to inhabit or abide within any other plantations of New England or elsewhere, unlesse he obtayne a lysense or passe for his departure under the Governor's hand."

In the Revisal of 1642, the Act for conformity was made more severe on ministers. "Ffor the preservation of the puritie of doctrine and unitie of the church, It is enacted that all ministers whatsoever which shall reside in the collony are to be conformable to the orders and constitutions of the church of England, and the laws therein established, and not otherwise to be admitted to teach or preach publicly or privately, And that the Gov. and Counsel do take care that all nonconformists upon notice of them shall be compelled to depart the collony with all convenience."

This law was not a dead letter as will be seen in the treatment of the Puritans. These people began early to emigrate to Virginia hoping to find a resting place. And although in 1614 Mr. Whitaker—"complaineth and museth much, that so few of our English ministers that were so hot against the surplice and subscriptions come hither where neither is spoken off"—in ten years the colonial Legislature resolved to con-

form the Church—"as neere as may be to the forms and
ceremonies of the Church of England. There is no intimation
given by historians of any persons in the colony to whom this
law could apply but the Puritans. Cotton Mather in his
Magnalia, vol. 1st, pp. 538, 539, tells us—"In the year 1741,
one Mr. Bennet, a gentleman from Virginia, arrived at Boston,
with letters from well disposed persons there, unto the ministers
of New England, bewailing their said condition, for the want
of the glorious gospel, and entreating that they might hence
be supplied with ministers of that gospel. These letters were
openly read at Boston, upon a lecture day; whereupon the
ministers agreed upon setting apart a day for fasting and
prayer, to implore the direction of God about this business;
and then the churches of Watertown, Braintree and Rowley,
having each of them two ministers apiece, Mr. Philips of Watertown, Mr. Thompson of Braintree, and Mr. Miller of Rowley
were pitched upon for the intended services, whereof the General Court so approved, that it was ordered the Governor should
recommend these persons by his letters to the Governor and
council of Virginia. Mr. Philips being indisposed to the
voyage, Mr. Knowles went in his room; and Mr. Miller's
bodily weakness caused him also to decline the voyage. But
the two churches of Watertown and Braintree, though they
loved their ministers very well, yet cheerfully dismissed them
unto this great concern; accounting it their honour that they
had such desirable persons, by whom they might make a mission of the gospel, unto a people that sat in the region and
shadow of death. On October 7th, 1642, they began their
voyage:—at Rhode Island they lay long wind bound; and
they met with so many other difficulties, that they made it
eleven weeks of dangerous passage before they arrived at Virginia; nevertheless they had this advantage on the way, that
they took in a third minister for their assistance, namely Mr.
James then at New Haven.

"Though their hazardous retardation in this voyage, made
them sometimes to suspect whether they had a clear call of
God unto their undertaking, yet the success of their ministry,
when they came to Virginia, did sufficiently extinguish that
suspicion. They had little encouragement from the rulers of
the place, but they had a kind entertainment with the people;
and in the several parts of the country where they were bestowed, there were many persons brought home to God. But
as Austin told mankind, the devil was never turned Christian
yet; the powers of darkness could not count it for their interest,
that the light of the gospel powerfully preached, should reach
those dark places of the Earth. The rulers of that province
did not allow of their publick preaching; but instead thereof

an order was made,—That such as would not conform to the ceremonies of the Church of England, should by such a day depart the country. By which order, these holy, faithful, painsful ministers, were driven away from the Virginia coast. But when they returned, as they left behind them not a few seals of their ministry, so they brought with them some who afterwards proved blessings to New England." Mr. Winthrop tells us, that two years previous some Emigrants from Massachusetts had sought a residence in Virginia. It is not improbable that the messenger Mr. Bennet was one of these. Or he might have been sent in their behalf. He also remarks— "that though the state did silence the ministers, because they would not conform to the order of England, yet the people resorted to them in private houses to hear them." This mission from Massachusetts took place about the time of the last war of Opechankanough, which resulted in his capture. About this time also a great sickness prevailed in the colony, which Mather connects with the driving away of the missionaries.

Mr. Calamy in his life of Baxter tells us—in a sketch of the life of Mr. Knowles—that in Virginia, "Mr. Harrison, that was the Governor's Chaplain, openly moved they might have full liberty, but secretly endeavoured they might be dismissed, as he owned afterwards with concern and sorrow. This was that Mr. Harrison that was afterwards so useful a man in England and Ireland. Mr. Knowles and Mr. Thomson being discharged from public preaching in Virginia, continued a while preaching, privately and did much good." After having referred to the massacre in the Indian war that followed—he says—"five hundred are reported to have been murdered on this occasion. Among those that escaped this miserable massacre, some were gathered into church order by Mr. Harrison, who became quite another man after this providence than he was before. But the Governor dismissed his chaplain who was now grown too serious for him."

In 1648, as Mr. Holmes tells us in his annals, the Puritans were still numerous. About one hundred and eighteen were associated in church fellowship under the Pastoral care of Mr. Harrison. The greatest numbers were in Nansemond County. This year Mr. Harrison, being driven from the colony, went to New England and thence to England. Mr. Durand one of its Elders having been banished by the Governor, retreated to North Carolina and took his abode on a neck of land which still bears his name. The Congregation was scattered, and nothing more is heard of any puritan preacher from New England, or elsewhere, unless some that came over in the time of Cromwell were such. John Hammond, the author of a

pamphlet called Leah and Rachel, published in 1656, says—
"And there was in Virginia a certaine people Congregated into
a church calling themselves Independents, which daily increasing, severall consultations were had by the State of that colony,
how to suppress and extinguish them, which was duely put in
execution; as first their pastor was banished; next their other
teachers; then many by information clapt up in prison, then
generally disarmed (which was very harsh in such a country
where the heathen live round about them) by one Colonel
Samuel Matthews, then a Counsellor of Virginia, so that they
knew not in those straights how to dispose of themselves."
Mr. Winthrop tells us—that Mr. Harrison reported that many
of the council were favourable to him and his opinions, and
that by conjecture about a thousand of the people were of a
similar mind. Mr. Hubbard tells us that Mr. Harrison after
spending a year or two in New England, went to England and
received the degree of Doctor of Divinity, and finally settled in
Ireland. These events signalized the early part of Sir William
Berkeley's administration.

During the protectorate of Cromwell the legislature of Virginia made efforts that were in part successful, to obtain a
supply of proper ministers. Act 5th 1656 declared—"Whereas many congregations in this colony are destitute of ministers
whereby religion and devotion cannot but suffer much impair-
ment and decay, which want of the destitute Congregations
ought to be supplied by all means possible to be used, As also
to invite and encourage ministers to repaire hither and merchants to bring them in, Bee it therefore hereby Enacted for
the reasons aforesaid that what person or persons soever shall
at his or their proper cost and charge transport a sufficient
minister into this collony without agreement made with him
shall receive for satisfaction of his or their said charges of him
the said minister or they that shall entertain him for their
minister, twenty pounds sterling by bill of exchange or two
thousand pounds of tobacco, and also for what money shall be
disbursed for them besides their transportation to be allowed
for." By act 1st the power of managing the affairs of the
parish was lodged in the hands of the vestry. This was productive both of good and evil. The vestry were supposed to
consult the wishes of the parishioners, and thus was there an
approach to freedom of conscience. But the power of oppress-
ing the whole parish in the choice of a minister was lodged in
the hands of the vestry. "Be it enacted by this present
Grand Assembly concerning church Government as followeth,
that all matters concerning the vestry, their agreement with
the minister, touching the Church Wardens, the poore, and
other things concerning the parishes or parishioners respec-

tively be referred to their owne ordering and disposeing from time to time as they shall think fit."

These efforts to bring over proper ministers were in part successful. Berkeley says—"the persecution in Cromwells tiranny drove divers worthy men hither." But in general the clergy were little better than before. Hammond in his Leah and Rachel, says—"Many came such as wore black coats, and could babble in a pulpit, roare in a tavern, exact from their parishioners, and rather by their dissolutenesse, destroy than feed their flocks. Loath was the country to be wholly without teachers, and therefore rather retain them, than be destitute; yet still endeavours for better in their places, which were obtained and those wolves in sheeps clothing by their assemblies questioned, silenced, and some forced to depart the country."

Stith tells us, p. 173—that the company as early as 1620 "had ordered an hundred acres of land, in each of the Burroughs, to be laid off for a glebe." In 1656, Act 9th says— "Whereas there are many places destitute of ministers, and like to continue soe, the people content not payinge their accustomed dues, which makes them negligent to procure those which should teach and instruct them, soe by this improvident saving they loose the greatest benefitt and comfort a Christian can have, by hearing the word and use of the blessed sacraments,—therefore be it enacted &c. that all countys not yet laid out into parishes shall be divided into parishes &c.—and that all tithable persons in every parish within this collony, respectively, in the vacancy of their minister, pay 15 lbs of tobacco per poll yearly &c.—this to go to building a parish church and purchasing a glebe and stock—for the next minister that shall be settled there." After this particular care was taken by the Legislature that glebes should be provided for all the parishes.

By the revisal of 1662 the uniformity of worship was guarded with much circumspection. By act 2d, "twelve of the most able men were to be chosen as vestry men in each parish. None shall be admitted to be of the vestry that doe not take the oath of allegeance to his Majesty and subscribe to be conformable to the doctrines and discipline of the Church of England." By act 3d, glebes were to be laid out in every parish, "and a convenient house built upon them for the reception and abode of the minister; and that such provision be made for his maintenance in the valuable and current commodityes of the country as may be really worth at least fourescore pounds per annum, besides his perquisites and glebe." Act 4th says—"Noe minister be admitted to officiate in this country but such as shall produce to the Governour a testimoniall that he hath received his ordination from some Bishopp in England; and if any person pretending himself a minister shall contrary to this act presume to teach or preach publiquely or privately, the Governour and councell are desired and impowered to suspend and silence the person soe offending, and upon his obstinate persistance to compell him to depart the country with the first conveniency, as it hath been formerly provided by the 77th act made at James Citty the second of March 1642." By act 9th, persons absent from the prayers and preachings of the parish churches on the Sabbath and the four holidays were subject to a fine of fifty pounds of tobacco. By act 4th, December 1662—"Whereas many scismaticall persons out of their aversenesse to the orthodox established religion, or out of the new fangled conceits of their owne hereticall inventions refuse to have their children baptized, be it &c. that all persons that, in contempt of the divine sacrament of baptisme, shall refuse when they may carry their child to a lawfull minister in that county to have them baptized, shall be amerced two thousand pounds of tobacco; halfe to the informer, halfe to the publique."

Governor Berkeley in 1671, in answer to the inquiry, "What course is taken about the instructing the people within your government in the Christian religion?" says—"We have forty-eight parishes, and our ministers are well paid, and by my consent should be better, *if they would pray oftener and preach less*. But of all other commodities, so of this, *the worst are sent to us*, and we had few that we could boast of since the persecution in Cromwell's tyranny drove divers worthy men hither."

There is an excuse however, or rather a palliation for the condition of the established church. The executive officer of the Episcopal Church did not reside in Virginia; nor till after the revolution in England, in 1688, did a commissary reside in the province. Proper discipline therefore could not be kept up. Multitudes of cases, that could not be judged in England, required attention on the spot; and in their neglect the church suffered.

The Quakers came in for their share of legislative opposition. Uniformity in religion, after the manner of the Church of England, was the determined purpose of the majority of the colony. The estimation in which the Qakers were held, by the Legislature, can be best understood from the preamble of Act 6th, 1659, 60—"Whereas there is an unreasonable and turbulent sort of people, commonly called Quakers, who contrary to the law do dayly gather together unto them unlaw'll assemblies and congregations of people, teaching and publishing lies, miracles, false visions, prophecies and doctrines, which have influence upon the communities of men both ecclesiasticall and civil endeavouring and attempting thereby to destroy religion, lawes, comunities and all bonds of civil societie, leaving arbitrarie to everie vaine and vicious person whether men shall be safe, lawes established, offenders punished, and governours rule, hereby disturbing the publique peace and just interest, to prevent and restraine which mischiefe be it enacted" &c. 1st— that any master of a vessel bringing a Quaker into the colony should be subject to a fine of one hundred pounds sterling: 2d—that all Quakers be arrested and imprisoned without bail, " till they do adjure the country, or putt in security with all speed to depart the colonie and not to return again;" 3d—if a Quaker returned, he was to be punished and sent away; 4th— if he returned the third time he was to be proceeded against as a felon; 5th—that no one should entertain a Quaker or permit their assemblies at his house under the penalty of one hundred pounds sterling; and 6th—" that no person do presume on their peril to dispose or publish their bookes, pamphlets or libells bearing the title of their tenets and opinions."

Act 9th of 1661, 2 after forbidding all unnecessary journeys on the Sabbath—" And that noe other thing, be used or done that may tend to the prophanation of that day,—but that all and every person and persons inhabiting in this country diligently resort to their parish church or chappell,"—imposes a fine of fifty pounds of tobacco for absence from the church on Sabbath,—"and the fower holy days," but excepts Quakers and others for a greater punishment—" Quakers or other recusants who out of noncomformitie to the church totally absent themselves,—shall be liable to such fines and punishments as by the statue of 23d of Elizabeth are imposed on them, being for every months absence twenty pounds sterling, and if they forbeare a twelvemonth then to give good security for their good behaviour besides their payment for their monthly absences, according to the tenure of said statute.   And that all Quakers for assembling in unlawfull assemblyes and conventicles be fined and pay each of them there taken, two hundred pounds of tobacco for each time they shall be for such unlawfull meeting taken or presented by the church wardens to the county court and in case of the insolvency of any person among them, the more able then taken to pay for them."

More severity was, in the opinion of the legislature called for against Separatists. Act 1st, 1663, declares—" that certain persons under the name of Quakers and other names of separation have taken up and maintained sundry dangerous opinions and tenets, and—under pretence of religious worship, doe often assemble themselves in great numbers,—separating and dividing themselves from the rest of his Majesties good and

loyall subjects—Be it enacted,—that if any person or persons
called Quakers, or any other separatists whatsoever in this
colony,—shall departe from the places of their severall habitations and assemble themselves to the number of five or more
of the age of sixteen yeares or upwards at any one tyme in
any place under pretence of joyning in a religious worship
not authorized by the laws of England nor this country,—shall
for the ffirst offence fforfeit and pay two hundred pounds of
tobacco,—for the second offence forfeit and pay five hundred
pounds of tobacco." Quakers or Separatists of ability were
held responsible for those that were poor. For the third
offence, the punishment was banishment "to the places the
Governor and Councell shall appoint." The penalty for bringing in a Quaker was increased; and all persons were forbidden to—"entertaine any Quakers in or near their houses, that
is, to teach or preach"—on penalty of five thousand pounds of
tobacco. A proviso concluded the law—"if Quakers or other
Separatists shall after such conviction as aforesaid give security that he, she, or they, shall for the time to come forbeare
to meet in any such unlawfull assemblies"—then they were
to be discharged from all penalties.

These laws were not dead letters. The Quakers suffered as
the Puritans years before. Their historians complain much of
fines levied under these laws. That their complaints are not
without foundation will appear from the record of the House
of Burgesses given by Hening, Sept'r 12, 1663—" Whereas
Mr. John Hill high sheriff of Lower Norfolk hath represented to the House that Mr. John Porter, one of the Burgesses of that county was loving to the Quakers and stood well
affected to them and had been at their meetings, and was so far
an Anabaptist as to be against the baptizing of children, upon
which representation the said Porter confessed himself to have
and be well affected to the Quakers, but conceived his being at
their meetings could not be proved, upon which the oaths of
Allegiance and Supremacy were tendered to him which he
refused to take; whereupon it is ordered that the said Porter
be dismissed this house." The refusal to swear allegiance to
the King, or to acknowledge him as head of the Church
visible, in the English dominions, was a political offence, of
which all the nonconformists in Virginia might be made guilty.

Others besides Puritans and Quakers, or for other offences
than Puritanism or Quakerism, suffered under the laws of
Virginia as will appear from Hening, vol. 1st,. " Oct. 7th, 1634,
Henry Coleman excommunicated forty days, for using scornful
speeches and putting on his hat in church, when according to
an order of court, he was to acknowledge and ask forgiveness
for an offence. In 1640, Stephen Reekers put in pillory two

hours with a paper on his head expressing his offence, fined £50 sterling and imprisoned during pleasure for saying that his Majesty was at confession with the Lord of Canterbury. March 25th, 1630, Thos. Tindall to be pillory'd two hours for giving my Lord Baltimore the lye and threatening to knock him down. 1640, Francis Wildes, clerk of Charles River Court, turned out of his place and fined for speaking against the laws of the last Assembly and the persons concerned in making them." A State religion can be maintained only by severe laws.

The Governor and Council acted out to the extent of their ability, the state and parade of the King and his Lords. The House of Burgesses filled, in the colony, the place of the House of Commons in the mother land, and the wealthy planters according to their means, that of the nobility and gentry. The more wealthy planters flocked to the seat of government, particularly during the meeting of the House of Burgesses, and sessions of the General Court, and learned to imitate the profusion and elegance of the Governor. All the elements of the Virginia character, in its excellencies and follies, were in operation in 1688, wealth, love of ease, profusion of expense, generosity, unrestrained passions, chivalric attention to the fair, high sense of honor, personal independence, carelessness of money, sense of superiority and easy manners. These governed by devoted attachment to the crown, and the religion of the State because it was the religion of the State, and of their fathers, and of the King, formed a state of society interesting and peculiar. It exhibited in strong contrast the scholar and the unlearned; the vulgar and the gentleman; the African slave and his Anglo-Saxon master. Compelled by their location, and the nature of their society, to the daily use of the horse, the Virginians became lovers of that noble animal, and daring in his exercise. Self-possessed from their daily exposures, they were in danger of over-confidence in their own judgment and capabilities. They knew nothing in America greater and grander than their own beautiful and luxuriant colony. They talked independently to the mother country, bowing to the majesty of the crown, from whose splendor the ocean alone separated them.

In civil matters, there was, in 1688, the idea and the exercise of Liberty. From the first meeting of the Legislature in 1619 the colonists enjoyed all the priviliges of Englishmen. They were Royalists. They were loyal to the king. The inconveniences, arising from their distance from the throne, were counterbalanced by advantages resulting from the same distance and their wilderness home. The king could raise a revenue only through the house of Burgesses. They were always slow to load their fellow-citizens and themselves with duties and imports. Act 8th of the first assembly, whose records are preserved, 1623, 4, declares—"The Governor shall not lay any taxes or ympositions upon the colony their lands or commodities other way than by the authority of the General Assembly, to be levyed and employed as the said assembly shall appoynt." And by the next act they declare that the Governor should not withdraw the inhabitants from their labours for his own services—"and in case the publick service require ymployments of many hands before the holding a General Assemblie to give order for the same, in that case the levying of men shall be done by order of the Governor and whole body of the counsell and that in such sorte as to be least burthensome to the people and most free from partiality." To save the expense of calling the assembly—"the charge of which doth most times equal itt, if not exceed all other taxes of the country"—the house gave permission in the years 1660 and 1661, to the governor and council to lay the taxes, provided he did not exceed twenty pounds of tobacco per poll. "November 9th, 1666, Die Jovis—The honourable Governour sent knowledge of his pleasure to the house that two or more of the councel might join with the house in granting and confirming the sums of the levy. The humble answer of the house is, that they conceive it their privilege to lay the levy in the house, and that the house will admit nothing without reference from the honourable Governour and councel unless it be before adjudged and confirmed by act or order, and after passing in the house shall be humbly presented to their honors for approbation or dissent. Mr. Ballard, major Weir and captain Bridger are appointed to present this answer to the honourable Governour and councel. This is willingly assented to and desired to remain on record for a rule to walk by for the future, which will be satisfactory to all. William Berkeley."

The Legislature of Virginia early showed respect to age and enterprise. Act 10th, 1623, 4, says—"That all the old planters that were here before or came in at the last coming of Sir Thomas Gates they and their posterity shall be exempted from their personal service to the warrs and any public charge (church duties excepted) that belong particularly to their persons (not exempting their families) except such as shall be ymployd to command in chief." In 1631 this act was amended by leaving out the words—"they and their posterity." The spirit of this exemption law reserved an aged Quaker from the penalties of the law enacted against that sect,—as the Quaker accounts say that the first born male that grew to adult years became a Quaker, and in compliment to his birth was liberated from the penalties of the law.

Thus Virginia appeared in 1688. The inhabitants occupied but a small portion of her immense territories. They were rapidly increasing in wealth, and slowly extending their plantations toward the mountains. The protestant religion was universal. The forms of the church of England as general as the supply of ministers from England would allow; and were guarded by penal laws. The dissenters from the forms and creed of the State religion, oppressed by fines, and in some cases uncompromisingly driven from the colony. The rights of men in civil matters better understood than the rights of conscience. The Indian tribes East of the Blue Ridge broken in spirit and wasted. Not a congregation of them gathered for the worship of God, or civilization, from all the numerous tribes that once dwelt along the bay shore and the river banks. No college in the colony; and education but partially diffused. The citizens independent in their thoughts, habits and actions, enjoying the privileges of Englishmen, in their distant wilderness. With all the imperfections of society a foundation was laid for a great and noble State, that retains many traits of its colonial infancy. The community at large were sensible of some great defect in their religious matters, and desirous of a change. Averse to any fundamental revolution in creed or forms or State patronage, they longed for a purer ministry, and many desired more effect in ordinances, and more spiritual exposition of Scripture. In the preamble to the Revisal of 1661, 2, they say—"And because it is impossible to honor the king as we should unlesse wee serve and feare God, as wee ought, and that they might show their equall care of church and state they have set downe certaine rules to be observed in the Government of the church, until God shall please to turne his majesties pious thoughts towards us and provide a better supply of ministers among us." And in the 18th Act entitled *"provisions for a colledge,"* they say—"Whereas the want of able and faithful ministers in this country deprives us of those great blessings and mercies that always attend upon the service of God; which want by reason of our great distance from our nation, cannot in probability be always supplied from thence: Bee it enacted that for the advance of learning, education of youth, supply of the ministry, and promotion of piety, there be land taken up or purchased for a colledge and free school." From the first source, the king, they never obtained "a better supply." From the second, the college, which was soon after reared by Commissary Blair, the State has been drinking, as from a fountain of pearls; she has gathered gems that sparkle in her crown as an independent State. Relief in matters of Religion and Conscience was sought in vain from England; help came from another quarter.

The causes that has wrought most strongly to make Virginia what she is, have been partly moral and partly physical. Those that made her what she was in 1688 were all in operation in 1619. Previous to that date, tobacco planting became the absorbing occupation of the colonists, and in its operation was hostile to towns and villages and mechanical arts. In 1619, the Company in London at the instance of Sir Edward Landys, took steps to make the colony permanent by sending the colonists wives. In the same year the King determined to send a company of dissolute persons to act as servants to the colonists, making labour disreputable, and rendering Virginia for a time the receptacle of malefactors. In 1619 the first cargo of Africans was brought to Virginia and sold to the colonists as slaves for life. The servitude of Englishmen had a bound; that of the Africans no limits, as his children were slaves. In 1619 the most vigorous efforts were made to christianize the Indians, and erect a college for the use of the colony. All these influences acting under the moulding power of a state religion made Virginia what she was on the accession of the Prince of Orange to the crown of England. After that event another element was infused, whose influence though last was not least, the Republicanism of the Religious principle. Its influence will be portrayed in the following sketches.

CHAPTER II.

REV. FRANCIS MAKEMIE AND HIS ASSOCIATES.

THE first minister, dissenting from the Church of England, that had leave, from the constituted authorities, to preach in Virginia, was a Presbyterian. He is the first, on the Geneva model, that is known to have taken his residence in Virginia, or the United States of America. This was Francis Makemie. The churches gathered by his labors, were in Barbadoes, in the West Indies,—in that part of Maryland between the Atlantic and the Chesapeake,—and in Accomac county, Virginia. He has no lineal descendant on earth. Not a sermon, or a page of a diary, and but a single letter, from his hand, is in existence. No biographical sketch, drawn by a cotemporary, has given a portraiture of the man, or a connected history of his services. What remains of him,—and there are remains,—is like the ruins of an ancient temple, that awakes admiration by the beauty of the fragments, and the symmetry of the particular parts, while the uniqueness of the sculpture almost forbids an imagination of the grandeur of the whole.

Perhaps however it is not a matter of disquietude, that all that Makemie possessed in common with his race has passed away to the compend of all history,—he was born, he lived, and died; or that all he possessed in common with preachers of the Gospel in every age, is preserved only in meager notices in the records of Ecclesiastical bodies. We are left to suppose that he had his share of the troubles and joys of life, in his person and his family; that he knew the perplexities and excitements of the ministerial race, and came to his end with hope triumphant over the fears, and troubles, and doubts, which beset the human soul in his course of purification for heaven. The history of a man's life becomes interesting to his own generation, or to posterity, only as he has done uncommon things well, or common things better than his compeers. The interest attached to the name, birth place, and labours of Makemie arises from the circumstance, that he was, in all probability, the first consistent Presbyterian minister in the United States; certainly the first in Virginia. The Presbyterian ministers, mentioned by Mather and others as residing in Massachusetts, at an early date, were more or less Congregational in their forms and discipline. They were intermingled with Congregationalists, and ultimately became entirely blended with that denomination. Had Makemie been a man of less than mediocrity of talent, and had he been called only to the trials incident to a church of emigrants, his being first in a series of ministers, whose progression has been so noble, would encircle him with a halo bright from surrounding darkness.

First in the series of worthies is not the only honor of Makemie. Called to pass through scenes of trial and perplexity, such as cannot be the lot of the present generation, he acquitted himself with honor. His imitators were clothed with honor. "The Attorney has met his match to-day"—was the exclamation of the bar, when Davies stood before the Governor and Council of Virginia and plead, as Makemie did in Virginia and before Lord Cornbury in New York, the true meaning and extent of the Act of Toleration, and vindicated the rights of conscience as acknowledged, imperfectly indeed, yet acknowledged by the English law. Makemie established the great truth, that it was no crime against the State, or known law, for him to preach the gospel to those who desired to hear, and avowed that desire to the magistrates. Davies followed his example, and the bar said he was a "capital lawyer spoiled."

Reed, in his history of the Presbyterian Church in Ireland, tells us that Makemie was from the neighborhood of Ramilton in Donegal. His name, which has been spelled differently, by different writers evidently meaning the same man,—Mackamy, —Mackamie,—and McKemie,—was, as appears from the records of Accomac Court, spelled by himself, Makemie. It indicates his origin from that race which emigrating from Scotland to Ireland and from Ireland to America, bears, in America, the appellation, *Scotch Irish.* There is no record of the condition or baptismal names of his parents. His mental exercises, in his early days are unknown, with one single exception. In reply to a charge brought against him in Virginia, of denying the influence of the Holy Spirit, because he rejected baptismal regeneration, he declared, that so far from denying the influence of the Spirit, he fully believed them to be indispensable to all religion; and that he had reason to thank God that at the age of fourteen, under the instruction of a pious schoolmaster, he felt their power on his own soul.

Mr. Reed informs us that he was introduced to the Presbytery of Lagan, by his pastor, the Rev. T. Drummond, in the year 1680, and that he was licensed by that Presbytery in the year 1681. Application had been made to that body, in 1678, by a Captain Archibald Johnson, for assistance in procuring a minister for Barbadoes. In December, 1680, Colonel Stevens from Maryland, "near Virginia," applied to the same Presbytery for a minister to settle in that colony. In consequence of these applications, Makemie was ordained as Evangelist for America. The precise date of his ordination is not known. There is a deficiency in the records of the Presbytery of Lagan arising from the imprisonment of the Stated Clerk and some other members. Their crime had been the holding a fast on account of the peculiar situation of the country. They were fined, they suffered imprisonment for months, and then gave security for good behaviour for an act which could be an offence only to a tyrant. Mr. Reed tells us that Makemie removed to America, resided for a time on the Eastern shore of Virginia; that the ministers from Europe uniting with him in the formation of the first Presbytery in America according to the Westminster Confession, were from the Province of Ulster, Ireland; and there he pauses.

From the circumstances of the case, it appears that he must have been ordained for his mission to America as early as 1682 or 3. He laboured in Barbadoes, in Maryland and Virginia. Mr. Spence in his Letters tells us, that the churches in Somerset county, Maryland, were organized at a period of time when there was no other Presbyterian minister to organize than Francis Makemie. Snowhill was established by act of the provincial assembly, 1684, then in Somerset, now in Worcester, the latter having been set off as a county in 1742. "It was,—Mr. Spence tells us,—settled by English Episcopalians, and Scotch and Irish Presbyterians, and it is certain that persons resided there at the time, or soon after the time, in which the town was laid out, who were afterwards members of the Presbyterian church. My ancestor was a ruling elder in that church,—he was the father of five children, all of them natives of Snowhill, or its neighbourhood, the youngest of whom was born in 1698. I am persuaded that he lived in Maryland the last twenty years of the seventeenth century." To this church at Snow Hill Mr. Makemie performed the duties of a minister, after he had assisted in its organization. "I doubt"—says Mr. Spence—"whether the memory of any gospel minister was ever held in higher honour by an American congregation, than was that of Makemie by the people of Snow Hill. His praises have not yet left the church, although he has rested from his labours almost a hundred and thirty years. Tradition has made a record of his labours and many excellencies of his character; one generation has uttered his praises in the ears of its successor, and you may even yet hear its echo. Parents made his surname the Christian name of their children, until in the neighbourhood of Snow Hill it has become a common one. Information derived from aged lips, which it was once my pleasure to listen to, and my duty to honour, produces peculiar feelings whenever I hear the name of Francis Makemie." The "ancestor" of whom Mr. Spence speaks, was Adam Spence, an emigrant from Scotland,—"who had probably affixed his name to the Solemn League Covenant,"—and had settled at or near Snow Hill, as a merchant about the year 1680.

Mr. Makemie preached in Barbadoes. He declared, on his trial in New York, that he had certificates according to law, both for Barbadoes and for Virginia. He does not mention the date of his certificate; that was not called for. The records of Accomac Court mention the fact of his preaching in Barbadoes, but does not give the date. Long after Makemie's death the Presbytery and the Synod of Philadelphia, gave the congregation in Barbadoes their assistance, but their records make no mention of the time of his labours there.

The first mention of Makemie's name by any record in the United States, is found in the county of Accomac, Virginia, and bears date Feb. 17th, 1690. It is in the record of a suit brought by him to recover from one William Finney, the amount due him for molasses sold. He had other suits, in the same court, to recover debts, from careless or unjust debtors. These debts were the consequence of his being engaged in commerce. There is also a record of a certificate for four hundred acres of land bearing date Feb. 21st, 1692.

Mr. Makemie was united in marriage to Naomi, the eldest daughter of William Anderson, a wealthy merchant of Accomac. Mr. Anderson, by will admitted to record Oct. 16, 1698, gave to Francis Makemie and his wife Naomi, a tract of land, containing one thousand acres, at Matchatouk, a creek that empties into the Chesapeake, a little south of the village of Onancock, the county seat, and made a port of entry in 1680. Near this village they had their residence, five or six miles from Drummondstown the present county seat. He also gave them the "plantation at Pocomoke, containing nine hundred and fifty acres, for and during their or either of their natural lives; in remainder to the child or heir of my daughter Naomi, if such she have, and its hereditable issue forever. But for want of such, then to revert and descend to my grand daughters, by my daughter Comfort Taylor, and to her heirs forever." The will goes on to say—"Item, my Lotts being three at Onancock town, I give unto Mr. Francis Makemie and his heirs and assigns forever. Item, I give and bequeath to my daughter Naomi Makemie, four Negro Slaves, viz:—Dollae, Hannah the Elder, Darkeih, young Sarah. Item, I make, constitute, ordain, and appoint my son in law, Mr. Francis Makemie ***** to be my joint and several executors of this my last will and testament, desiring them to be kind and assisting to my wife." In his will Mr. Anderson makes mention of three sisters, by the names of Barons, Hope, and Nock, to each of whom he makes a small legacy. No other person is named as executor with Makemie.

How Mr. Makemie became engaged in trade, and whether before or after his marriage, are questions not now to be answered. Mr. Anderson's will says—"I also give, unto said Makemie, all the money lent him, in full of all or any accounts, that may be between us, upon consignments or any other ways; and my will is, that he may have his sloope with what may appertain to her at my death. Likewise whatever my daughter can claim as hers in my house,—without let or delay, and all—on both sides to be ballanced."

The next important notice, in the records of Accomac bears date Oct. 15th, 1699. "Whereas Mr. Francis Makemie made application by petition to this court, that being ready to fulfill what the law enjoynes to dissenters, that he might be qualified according to law, and prayed that his own dwelling house at Pocomoke, also his own house at Ononcock, next to Captain Jonathan Liveley's, might be the places recorded for meeting, and having taken the oaths enjoyned by act of Parliament instead of the oaths of allegiance and supremacy, and subscribed the Test as likewise that he did in compliance with what the said Law enjoynes, produce certificate from Barbadoes of his qualifications there, did declare in open court, of the said county and owned the articles of religion mentioned in the statute made in the 13th year of Queen Elizabeth, except the 34th, 35th and 36th and those words of the 20th article, viz: the church hath power to decide rites and ceremonies, and authority in controversies of faith, which the court have ordered to be registered and recorded, and that the Clerk of the court give certificate thereof to the said Makemie according as the Law enjoynes." This is the first certificate of qualification under the Toleration Act, known to be on record. The two places mentioned in the preceding certificate were his own property under the will of his father in law. The dwelling house at Pocomoke was in Virginia, not far from the present Village of Rehoboth, which is on the Maryland side of the river. In that village Makemie owned property. There was a meeting house. And there, at this day, is a Presbyterian church, organized in the time of Makemie. In his will which bears date April 27th 1708, Makemie says—"as also my lot joining the new meeting house lot in Pocomoketown, called Rehoboth, empowering my executrix to make over and alienate that lot on which the meeting house is built, in as ample a manner, to all intents and purposes as shall be required for the ends and uses of a Presbyterian congregation, as if I were personally present, and to their successors forever, and none else, but to such of the same persuasion in matters of religion." After the death of Makemie, his dwelling house on Pocomoke ceased to be a place of worship; the public ministrations being confined to "Pocomoketown," or Rehoboth.

Mr. Makemie mentions two other places in his will,—"my house and lot in the new town in Princess Anne county, on the Eastern branch of Elizabeth River; as also my lot and house, or frame of a house, in the new town on Wormley's creek, called Urbana." Whether he used these houses for merchandise or for public worship is not declared. But as he told Lord Cornbury on his trial in New York,—"but to give bond and security to preach no more in your excellency's government, if invited and desired by any people, we neither dare nor can do,"—we cannot suppose he was backward to preach whenever he had an opportunity in Virginia. Around where Norfolk stands there was a congregation of Presbyterians. After Makemie's death, the people enjoyed the labours of Mr. Macky. How long Mr. Macky served them is unknown.

In Maryland the places of Presbyterian preaching were Snow Hill, Rehoboth, or Pocomoketown, head of Monokin, Wicomico, and on Joseph Venable's land. The churches in these places have retained their light through many vicissitudes. They have witnessed in their seclusion the spread of the Presbyterian church; and have rejoiced in the wonders of grace. Of this part of Maryland, Spence in his letters says—"There is no body of land, of the same size, in the State, the soil of which was, and is, so poor." Yet on account of its position, and the laws of Maryland, it presented inducements to Emigrants, who desired freedom of conscience. Here they could find a residence convenient for commerce, and could worship God according to the conviction of judgment and not sin against the State. Here was the chosen spot for the first congregation of the Presbyterian Church, now so numerous and scattered over a wide country of inexhaustible richness. The Roman Catholic proprietor of the colony to insure freedom of religious worship for his own sect, the papists, obtained in the charter granted him by Charles the 1st, June 20th, 1632, a clause for entire religious freedom. In Maryland, "a man might live in peace, whether Jew, Mohammedan, or Pagan; whether Atheist, Deist, or Polytheist; provided he neither molested his neighbour, nor endangered the public morals." The severity of the Virginia laws were strongly in contrast with this lenity. Dissenters from the established Church of England found in Maryland a quiet abode till the Revolution in England in 1688.

The congregations that first worshipped in America according to the forms of the Presbyterian Church, on the Geneva or Scotch model, still have a name and a place among the people of God. He, that would visit these mother churches of the Presbyterian body in America, must go down to the narrow neck of land between the ocean and the Chesapeake. There he will find Snow Hill, in Worcester, formerly Somerset, and may walk among the monuments and burial mounds so tenderly referred to by Mr. Spence. Thence let him take an excursion to the head of Wicomico (or Salisbury), and to the head of Monokin (or Princess Anne), and he will be walking over ground consecrated by such men as Makemie, McNish, Hampton, Henry, Robinson, Davies, Finley, and Rodgers. Let him go to Rehoboth and he may find the spot, given, by the first preacher, for the "New Meeting House;" and then let him cross the Virginia line,—but, alas! he will not find Makemie's "dwelling house at Pocomoke,"—he may go to Onancock and Drummondstown, and walk around where Makemie lived and preached; and find in Accomack a congregation of Presbyterians rising, phœnix like, from the ashes of those who heard Makemie preach and pray. The simplicity and hospitality of the inhabitants of the Peninsula are as unchanged as the plains and streams on which they dwell; and the pious stranger shall be welcome now as in the days of the first preacher who succeeded in organizing Presbyterian churches in America.

Mr. Makemie came to America before any society, of which we have any knowledge, was formed in England to assist Evangelists in their preparation for their work in America, or in seeking their fields of labour, or during the years of their ministry. By what pecuniary means he entered the ministry, or crossed the ocean, we cannot say. Perhaps in reaching the field of his labours he might have been assisted by the persons that afterwards formed the London Union. It is probable that the people petitioning from Barbadoes, and Col. Stephens of Maryland, exerted themselves to remove all obstacles in the way of their proposed missionary. It is supposed that he passed the earlier years of his Evangelical labours in Barbadoes, and Somerset county Maryland, by whose united voice he had sought the new world. From the high regard with which his name is mentioned at Snow Hill, it is natural to conclude, that it was a place of his protracted labours, and perhaps also of his residence. Notwithstanding the rigorous laws of Virginia, as detailed in the preceding chapter, Makemie made that State his home, after his marriage. What support his congregations gave him is unknown. Judging from the arrangements he made with the society in London, when he introduced his co-labourers into Maryland, his congregations were not prepared to give a very liberal support. After his marriage his necessities were supplied by the fortune of his wife and the labours of his own hands. He is a singular instance of a man engaging in the work of an Evangelist and of a merchant, and prospering in both. Like Paul, he laboured, that he might preach the gospel, where, a competent support for a minister could not be obtained from the hearers, and God blessed him in his ministry and in his traffic. At his death there were congregations, gathered by his labours, and fostered by his pastoral care, sufficient to give employment to three ministers; and a sufficient amount of property acquired by marriage and by his enterprise to leave his family above want.

Uniformity of worship had been attempted in Virginia, and maintained by severe laws. The Puritans had been driven from the colony, and the Quakers oppressed and enfeebled. Scotch and Irish merchants, or factors for English merchants, allured by the advantages of trade, were scattered through the colony. There was a most appalling necessity for faithful ministers of the Gospel, whose orthodox doctrines should be commended by their consistent lives. Clergymen, that required the enactment of such laws, by a civil tribunal, as have been preserved in the statute book of Virginia, to restrain their dissipation, and prevent neglect of duty, could scarcely be expected to promote vital godliness. It is a matter of tradition that Makemie suffered often under the laws of Virginia. "He durst not deny preaching, and hoped he never should, while it was wanting, and desired." In defence of himself he appeared before the magistrates and before the Governor, and tradition says made a favourable impression. We have historical and legal evidence of his appearing before the magistrates in Maryland and the court in New York, but only strong conjectural evidence, besides tradition, of his being called before legal tribunals in Virginia.

The Act of Toleration, entitled—"An Act for exempting their Majesties Protestant subjects, dissenting from the Church of England, from penalties of certain laws"—passed 1st of William and Mary, chap. 18th, 1689, under some unpleasant restrictions, secured to protestant ministers and churches, permission to worship God according to their own consciences. The first public acknowledgment, in Virginia, of this law as a law of the State, or of England, that is now known, appears in 1699, ten years after its becoming the law of the British dominions. When it does appear, its position and accompaniments, are any thing but honorable to those to whom its provisions extended. All that dissented from the established forms of the Church of England, as they were in Virginia, were classed with the drunkard and swearer. Act 1st, 1699, entitled "an Act for the more effectuall suppressing of blasphemy, swearing, cursing, drunkenness and Sabbath breaking," —in its first section declares—"That if any person or persons brought upp in the Christian religion shall by writing, printing, teaching or advisedly speaking, deny the being of a God or the holy Trinity, or shall assert or maintain there are more gods than one or shall deny the Christian religion to be true, or the holy scriptures of Old and New Testament to be of divine authority, and be thereof lawfully convicted upon indictment or information in the General Court"—for the first offence, disqualification for office civil, ecclesiastical, or military; for the second offence, additional disabilities and " three years imprisonment without bail or mainprize." By the fourth section, profane swearing and drunkenness were punished by fines and lashes on "theire beare back well laid on." By the fifth section Sabbath breaking is provided for as follows—viz: " That if any person or persons of the age of twenty-one years or more doe neglect or refuse to resort to their parish church or chapell once in two months to heare devine service upon the Sabbath day, every person or persons soe neglecting or refuseing and being thereof lawfully convicted by confession or otherwise before one or more justice or justices of the peace where such offence shall be committed shall forfeit and pay for every such offence the sume of five shillings or fifty pounds of tobacco to be payed to the church warden of that parish, &c. —*Provided always*—that if any person or persons dissenting from the Church of England being every way qualified accord-

ing to an act of Parliament made in the first year of the reigne
of our sovereigne lord the King that now is, and the late Queen
Mary of blessed memory, entituled an act for exempting their
Majesties Protestant subjects dissenting from the Church of
England from penaltyes of certain laws, shall resort and meet
at any congregation or place of religious worship·permitted and
allowed by the said act of Parliament once in two months, that
then the said penaltyes and forfeitures imposed by the act for
neglecting or refuseing to resort to their parish church or
chappel as aforesaid shall not be taken to extend to such
person or persons, any thing in this act to the contrary notwithstanding."

On this Mr. Hening well observes—"Nothing could be more
intolerant than to impose the penalties by this act prescribed
for not repairing to church, and thus hold out the idea of
exemption by a compliance with the provisions of such a law.
as the statute of William and Mary, adopted by a mere
general reference, when not one person in a thousand could
possibly know its contents."

In this same year, 1699, an act was passed providing for a
thorough revisal of the laws. In the preamble of that act, the
province is styled "*his Majestie's ancient and great colony
and dominion;*" the origin probably of the phrase of the "*Ancient Dominion.*" This revisal, which was the fifth, was completed in 1705. In this revisal the 30th Act is for the sup-
pression of vice &c. In the clause about Sabbath breaking,
the time of absence from church was limited to "the space
of one month." The proviso for dissenters is in a parenthesis,
thus, (excepting as is excepted in an act of parliament passed
in the first year of King William and Queen Mary, intituled,
An act for exempting their Majestys' protestant subjects
dissenting from the Church of England, from the penalties
of certain laws"). The provisions of the Toleration Act are
no where given in the statute book. It was left for the dissenters to find them when their protection became necessary.
It is not probable that even this reference would have appeared
upon the statute book, had it not have been demanded by
the dissenters, "who knew law," and had plead the provisions
of the act of parliament for their defence. We know of no
other dissenters in the colony at this·time but the Quakers and
Makemie and his Presbyterian friends.

The Proviso made its appearance in April 1699. In the
October following, Mr. Makemie obtained his license according
to the requirements of the toleration act. "Accomack county,
s. c. These may certify to all to whom these presents may concern, That Mr. Francis Makemie, a dissenter and preacher in
the aforesaid county of Accomack, hath, at a court held in the

aforesaid county, October 5th 1699, performed and answered by taking the oaths, &c. enjoined by a certain act of parliament, made the 24th day of May Anno Domini 1689, in the first year of the reign of King William, and Queen Mary, entitled an Act for exempting their Majesties' protestant subjects, dissenting from the Church of England, from the penalties of sundry laws. And by his application to the Court, by petition, obtained order in October Court last, that his own house at Accomack town, and his dwelling house at Pocomoke, should be registered and recorded to be the first place of his constant and ordinary preaching. Which is attested, this 10th day of October A. D. 1699.

Per me JOHN WASHBURN, C. C. C. Accomack."

On the 15th of the same month (October) 1699, the following record appears, as given by Spence from an attested copy; viz. "Whereas Mr. Francis Makemie made application by petition to this Court, that being ready to fullfill what the law enjoynes to dissenters, that he might be qualified according to law, and prayed that his own dwelling house at Pocomoke, also his own house at Ononcock, next to Capt. Jonathan Liveley's, might be the places recorded for the Meeting, and having taken the oaths enjoyned by act of parliament instead of the oaths of allegeance and supremacy, and subscribed the Test, as likewise that he did in compliance with what the said law enjoynes, produce certificate from Barbadoes of his qualifications there, did declare in open court of the said county and owned the articles of religion mentioned in the statute made in the 13th year of Queen Elizabeth, except the 34th, 35th and 36th, and those words of the 20th article, viz.—the Church hath power to decide rights and ceremonies, and authority in controversies of faith,—which the Court have ordered to be registered and recorded, and that the clerk of Court give certificate thereof to the said Makemie, according as the law enjoynes."

These papers recognise Makemie as having been a preacher among dissenters,—that he had been previously qualified, or licensed, at Barbadoes to preach—and that now he was shielded by law in Virginia.

Beverly, in his History and Present State of Virginia, published in 1705 says, Book 4th, Part 1st, Chap. 7th, p. 27— "The people are generally of the Church of England, which is the religion established by law in the country, from which there are very few dissenters. Yet liberty of conscience is given to all other congregations pretending to Christianity, on condition they submit to all parrish duties." Free to exercise conscience, by paying an equal share to the support of the ministers of the established church, however much they disapproved of him personally or officially,—by receiving marriage from his hands and in the form of the state religion,—by paying all parish rates for building and repairing the public church, and purchasing and keeping in repair the glebe,—when they had done this, they might build their own meeting house and support their own minister. He goes on to say: "They have no more than five conventicles amongst them, namely, three small meetings of Quakers, and two of Presbyterians. 'Tis observed, that those counties where the Presbyterian meetings are, produce very mean tobacco, and for that reason can't get an orthodox minister to stay amongst them; but whenever they could the people very orderly went to church. As for the Quakers, 'tis observed by letting them alone they decrease daily." So it appears on account of the poorness of the tobacco the established clergy left some counties, although in 1696 their salary had been fixed at sixteen thousand lb. weight of that commodity.

If this statement be true we can the more easily understand why Makemie had not been more molested. We suppose he took his residence in Accomack soon after his marriage. There was no Episcopal minister to complain of him; and many of the inhabitants preferred to hear Makemie to passing silent Sabbaths, and many others were true Presbyterians. His increasing popularity awakened hostility. And the consequence of hostility was the acknowledgment of the Toleration Act, and the complete protection of Makemie. Beverly does not say which two counties held the Presbyterians. We know that Accomack was one. When he said there were but two conventicles for Presbyterians, he may have referred only to the public meeting houses, or he may have written loosely, as Makemie had some four places to preach in. He certainly did write loosely, because he omitted the congregation of French Huguenots which by Act 2d December, 1700, was recognised as a distinct parish, and exempted from "publick and county levies for the space of seven years." If he reckoned this congregation as one, then he wrote very carelessly in giving Makemie but one place.

Notwithstanding all obstacles Mr. Makemie was abundantly successful in his ministerial labors. His hearers and congregations multiplied; and the thoughts of all were turned to the mother country for a supply of ministers. He prepared for a voyage to England in the summer of 1703; and according to custom he, August 1st, executed a power of attorney to his wife and John Parker—"to do and transact all manner of business for him." This projected voyage did not take place. On the 30th May, 1704, he, according to the records of Accomack, executed a power of attorney to his wife, Andrew

Hamilton and James Kemps, reciting that he was about "to depart for Europe." This voyage was accomplished and occupied him about a year. A warm-hearted man would very naturally desire, after a protracted absence, to revisit his native land, renew the associations of his early life and recount his labours and the dealings of God with him in the colonies. Especially would he visit the surviving brethren of the Presbytery that sent him forth as Evangelist. That he did visit London and make arrangements for the supply of the congregations with Evangelical clergymen—and that he brought a number of ministers from his native province are matters of fact on record. From a letter addressed by the Presbytery of Philadelphia to Sir Edmund Harrison, a gentleman of influence with the dissenting ministers, bearing date May 1709, in the records of the Presbyterian Church, we learn—"The negotiation begun and encouraged by a friend, in the time when our worthy friend, Mr. Makemie (now deceased) was with you, for Evangelizing these colonies, was a business exceedingly acceptable to a multitude of people, and was likely to have been of great service, if continued, which makes us much grieved that so valuable a design was, so soon after its beginning, laid aside. Unto whom can we apply more fitly than unto our fathers." From a letter from the same Presbytery to the Presbytery of Dublin, bearing date Sept. 1710, we learn—"As to the state of the church in these parts, our interest truly is very weak, and we cannot relate this matter without sorrow of heart, since it is too much owing to the neglect of ministers at home. Our late Rev. brother Mr. Francis Makemie prevailed with the ministers of London to undertake the support of two itinerants for the space of two years, and after that time to send two more on the same conditions, allowing the former after that time to settle, which, if accomplished, had proved of more credible advantage to those parts, considering how far scattered most of the inhabitants be. But alas they drew back their hand, and we have reason to lament their deficiency. Had our friends at home been equally watchful and diligent as the Episcopal society at London, our interest in most foreign plantations might have carried the balance."

In the letter to Mr. Harrison, the Presbytery ask for £200 per annum,—"We doubt not but if the sum of about two hundred pounds per annum was raised for the encouragement of ministers in these parts, it would enable ministers and people to erect eight congregations, and ourselves put in better circumstances than hitherto we have been." In the letter to the Presbytery of Dublin, they say, what they request is—"you would raise one sixty pound to support an able well approved of young man from yourselves as an itinerant in these parts, among the dispersed children of God for a year, after which time we doubt not he may be settled comfortably." In their letter to Mr. Harrison they say—"it is well known what advantages the missionaries from England have of us, from the settled fund of their church, which not only liberally supports them here, but encourages so many insolences both against our persons and interests, which sorrowfully looking on, we cannot but lament and crave your remedy." To the Synod of Glasgow they say in their letter September, 1710—"May it please the pious and reverend Synod, in compassion to the desolate souls in America, perishing for want of vision, to send over one or more ministers, and support them for a longer or shorter time. We further represent, that according to the best of our judgment, forty pounds sterling, annually paid in Scotland, to be transmitted in goods, will be a competency for the support of each minister you send, provided that of your pious and christian benevolence you suitably fit them out." From these extracts we are led to conclude that the assistance yielded, by the ministers in London, and the Presbytery of Dublin, was rather occasional than systematic. Had it have been systematic the Presbytery say they might have had "the balance."

It the fall of 1705, after his return from England, we find Mr. Makemie, in the month of November, before the County Court of Somerset, with two ministerial brethren, John Hampton, and George McNish, whom the records style "his associates." Certificates were damanded for these gentlemen, according to law, for the unmolested exercise of their ministry. The religious aspect of Maryland had greatly changed since Makemie began to preach on the Eastern shore. Their consciences were unshackled. All men had liberty to worship God according to their consciences. In 1692 the Church of England became the Established Church of Maryland, and a tax of forty pounds of tabacco "per poll" was imposed on every "taxable" to meet the expense of building and repairing churches, and supporting ministers. In 1702, dissenters from the Church of England were declared entitled to the benefit of the Toleration Act; but their meeting houses were to be "unbarred—unbolted—and unlocked." It was necessary for these gentlemen to obtain a license, for the exercise of their office as ministers, in a State where conscience had once been free.

Opposition to the licenses of Messrs. Hampton and McNish, was raised by the vestry of the parish of Coventry; and the matter was referred to the Governor and Council. The Rev. Robert Keith, minister at Dividing Creek, was supposed to be the author of the opposition. He certainly united in it with all

his power. The following extracts from the records of the court
show the forms and spirit of the time. "At a court held for
Somerset County, at Dividing Creek, the 14th day of November, 1705, present Capt. John West, Major John Cornish, Mr.
Thos. Newbold, Capt. John Frankland, Capt. Chas. Ballard,
and Mr. Jos. Venables. "The petition of George McNish
humbly sheweth,—That your petitioner craveth that the usual
oaths according to law tendered to, and to be taken by dissenting Ministers and Preachers may be tendered to your petitioner,—George McNish." "The Rev. Robert Keith and Mr.
Alexander Adams,—exhibit as followeth,—That whereas, we
have good ground to believe, that Mr. Francis Makemy and
others his assistance are intended to address your worships on
account of a Tolleration granted to the dissenters, for preaching
and building meeting houses, and doing what else is incumbent
on them as such, and wee duly considering the import of the
matter; humbly desire that the whole as to the premises, be
remitted to his Excellency the Governor of this Province, and
the honourable Council of State thereof, By them to be
considered, ordered and determined as they shall think fitt:
And that nothing be done in the premises untill warrant or
order be obtained from them, as to whole premises, or any
part thereof. John Heath, Pro. Vestry." Upon considering
these two petitions, the Justices resolved—"Notwithstanding
the said McNish in decent manner, did require (he being a
dissenter from the Church of England) that he might be dignified as by law in this county to preach, offering to take the
oaths and subscribe the declaration,—to allow the said Vestry
petition to have its final result and determination by his said
Exncy and honble Council of State as prayed for."

On the 8th of January 1705, 6, the same justices or commissioners being present, "then did Mr. George McNish and
Mr. John Hampton their petition exhibit,"—having recounted
the provisions of the toleration act, and stated the fact that
they had previously offered themselves to the Court to take
the oaths required and perform whatever else was required by
law, they say—"we do humbly tender ourselves again to your
worships, as the proper court held by the Justices of the Peace
for this county empowered and required to administer such
oaths, and for receiving such subscriptions." The Court determined to wait the decision of his Excellency. This decision
was at length given, and bears March 13th 1705.

"Att a court held By her Majty's wor'll Justices of the
Peace for Somerset county, att Dividing Creek, the 12th day
of June, Anno Dom. 1706,—By his Exncy the Governor,
March the 13th 1705, ordered then that the worpfull Justices
of Somerset county, take the oaths of the Desenting ministers

according to the Act of Parliament of the first of King Wm. and Queen Mary, exempting her Majty's Protestant subjects from certain penaltys, &c.

"Signed per order W. BLADEN, Cl. Councell."

This decision of the Governor led the Court to enter the following record:—"This day appeared Mr. John Hampton and Mr. George McNish, exhibited an order from his Excellency the Governor and honorable Councill for their Qualification to preach in this county, in obedience thereunto this Court did administer the oaths appointed per Act of Parliament, to the said Hampton and McNish, who did comply therewith, and did likewise subscribe the Declaration, whereupon this Court did allow that the aforesaid Hampton and McNish should preach att the meeting house near Mr. Edgar's, the meeting house att the head of Monocan, the meeting house att Snowhill, and the meeting house on Mr. Joseph Venable's land, as per the Desenting preachers required."

As Mr. Joseph Venable sat on the bench, and one of the meeting houses stood "on Mr. Joseph Venable's land," it was well that the Court referred the petitions to the Governor, and waited patiently for his decision. Governor Seymour was greatly grieved at the conduct of the beneficed clergy, and proposed that the Governor and Council should have power to oversee and discipline the ministers of the established church, in the total want of a church judicatory in the province. This plan of the Governor was defeated on the pretence that it was an attempt covertly to introduce Presbyterian forms. The clergy never forgave him, and triumphing in his defeat and their security, grew worse and worse. Tradition says, that at Wicomico, the rector, while administering the Lord's Supper, upon tasting the bread, cried out to the church warden, "George—this bread is not fit for a dog." The condition of the clergy was such that a bishop of the Episcopal Church, now living, expressed amazement that God spared a church under such teachers to have any existence at all.

Some time after the return of Mr. Makemie from Europe, the Presbytery of Philadelphia was formed. The day of its formation will, probably, never be known, as the first leaf of their book of records is missing. It is not probable that it was formed till after the licensure or qualification of the ministers, Messrs. McNish and Hampton, who came over in 1705, and were qualified on the 12th of June 1706. It may however have been formed in the latter part of the year 1705. The records commence in the middle of a sentence. The business on hand, the trials of Mr. John Boyd; these were finished the next session of the Presbytery.—which was on the 27th of December. The year of this meeting is supposed to be 1706, as the next meeting took place in March 1707. It is not known that there is any matter of importance depending on the decision respecting either the year or the month on which the Presbytery was formed, farther, than it must have been formed previously to the close of the year 1706, and after the commencement of the year 1705.

The ministers that formed this Presbytery, or were united with it previously to December 27th, 1706, were Francis Makemie, George McNish, John Hampton, Samuel Davis, John Wilson, Nathaniel Taylor, and Jedediah Andrews. Makemie's residence was Ononcock, in Accomack county, Virginia. Messrs. Hampton, McNish, and Davis, preached on the Eastern Shore of Maryland. Mr. Taylor was settled on the Patuxent. Mr. Wilson resided in Newcastle. Mr. Andrews in Philadelphia. This last mentioned gentleman became the Stated Clerk of Presbytery and filled the office for many years. A Mr. John Macky is mentioned in the minutes of Presbytery, for 1712, as living on Elizabeth river. He never became a member of the Presbytery.

Mr. Makemie was Moderator of the Presbytery in December, 1706. During the sessions of Presbytery, in March, 1707, he, together with Mr. John Wilson, preached, according to appointment, on Hebrews, 1st chapter, 1st and 2d verses. Between these two meetings, Mr. Makemie, on his way to Boston, in Massachusetts, stopped in New York city; and suffered imprisonment for preaching a sermon. Being permitted to give bail, he returned home, attended the meeting of Presbytery in March, returned to New York and stood trial for the offence of preaching a sermon without leave of the Deputy Governor. At the next meeting which took place in Philadelphia, May 1708, Mr. Makemie was not present. But the record states that he had complied with the order made the year previous requiring him to—"write to Scotland to Mr. Alex. Coldin, minister of Oxam,—and to give an account of the state and circumstances of the dissenting Presbyterian interest among the people in, and about, Lewistown, and to signify the earnest desires of the people, for the said Mr. Coldin's coming over to be their minister; and that Mr. Makemie make report of his diligence herein against the next Presbytery." His absence from this Presbytery may have had connexion with his death. Before the next meeting Mr. Makemie had gone to the general assembly and church of the first born whose names are written on high.

The immediate cause of his death, and the manner, are equally unknown. His will bears date April 27th, 1708. It was proved, according to law, on the 4th of August, of the same year. Some parts of his will are of permanent interest.

Extracts shall be given from an attested copy by the Deputy Clerk of Accomack county.

1st. After giving to his wife and two daughters, each, forty volumes of English books, to be chosen by them from his whole liberary,—the will adds—"and the rest of my library of Books of all sorts, I give and bequeath unto Mr. Jedediah Andrews minister at Philadelphia, excepting my law books, and after his decease or removal from Philadelphia, I give and bequeath said Liberary to such minister or ministers as shall succeed him in that place and office, and to such only as shall be of the Presbyterian or Independent persuasion and none else. My will is, that as soon as said Books are remitted to Philadelphia, the number and names of said Liberary may be put upon record, to be preserved there, as a constant Liberary for the use of foresaid minister or ministers successively, forever. I give, will, and bequeath unto Mr. Andrew Hamilton and his heirs forever, all my law books to be found among my liberary Books, and thoes he already hath in possession." *Do you know law?* was the sneering inquiry put to him in New York on his trial.

2d. As a farther expression of kind feelings to Mr. Andrews—"I give and bequeath unto Mr. Jedediah Andrews, minister at Philadelphia, and his heirs forever, my black camlet cloak, and my new cane, bought and fixed at Boston;"—probably, when he fled from the attempt at a second arrest by the Deputy Governor of New York.

3d. In the further disposition of property, he empowers his Executrix—"to sell, dispose of and alien my house and lott at the new towne in Princess Anne county, on the Eastern Branch of Elizabeth River, as also my lott and house or frame of house in the new towne on Wormlye's creek, called Urbana, as also my lot Joyning to the new meeting House Lott, in Pocomoke town." The disposition of the meeting house lot has already been quoted.

4th. He provides residuary legatees. "And if my daughters aforesaid, die without issue of their natural Bodyes, their parts of all Estate reall and personall given by this will, I give and bequeath to my youngest sister Anne Makemie of the Kingdom of Ireland, and the two eldest sons of my brother John and Robert Makemie, both of the name of Francis Makemie, and their heirs forever."

5th. His disposition of his children. After naming his wife as Executrix, he proceeds—"committing to her and her only, the guardianship and the tutorship of my aforesaid children, whilst in minority, during her natural life, and in case of the death of my deare wife, Naomie Makemie, before this my will is proved and executed, or the arrival of my said daughters,

Elizabeth and Anne Makemie, at age, I do constitute, appoint and ordaine the Honorable Colonel Francis Jenkins of Somerset county, in Maryland, and Mary Jenkins, his Lady, and beloved Consort, Executors of this my last Will and Testament, and guardians to my said children during their minority, and till marriage, charging all persons concerned in the presence of Almighty and Omniscient God, to give and allow my said children a sober, virtuous Education, either here or else where, as in Britain, New England, or Philadelphia."

His daughter Elizabeth soon followed her father to the grave. The records of the court say that Mrs. Naomi Makemie applied for administration on the estate of her daughter Elizabeth, on the 6th of October, 1708.

His daughter Anne married a gentleman by the name of Holden. She lived to a great age, passing many years as a widow, and died possessed of a large estate. In her will, which bears date November 15th, 1787, she bequeathed one hundred pounds to the Pitt's Creek Congregation, the one that worshipped—"in the Meeting house near Mr. Edgar's,—to be disposed of by the Sessions for the support of a minister." This fund is still in existence. She made a donation of twenty pounds to the Rev. Jacob Ker. To the Rev. Samuel McMasters she gave—"forty six pounds; a mahogany desk, a bed and furniture, and a Negro woman called Keziah and her children."

Col. Jenkins who is named with such marked confidence in the will, died soon after Mr. Makemie, and left no children. He bequeathed a great estate to his wife.

Mr. John Henry, the successor of Mr. Makemie at Rehoboth, came, in year 1710, an ordained minister, from the Presbytery of Dublin, and was installed pastor the same year. At the meeting of the Presbytery, Sept. 20th, 1710, in which Mr. Henry was received, three other ministers were also united with the judicatory, James Anderson from the Presbytery of Irvine in Scotland, Joseph Morgan from New England, and Paulus Van Vleek from the Dutch Reformed. After their admission there is the following—"Memorandum; Upon the admission of these ministers above mentioned; three Elders more sat in Presbytery, namely, Mr. Peerce Bray, Mr. John Foord and Mr. Lenard Van Degrift." Mr. Henry was at the meeting of the Presbytery in 1716. His death is recorded on the minutes of Synod in 1717. Of him Mr. Spence says—"I remember to have seen, seventeen years ago, a manuscript strongly bound octavo volume, of from three to five hundred pages, entitled—Common Place. It was a mass of religious instructions prepared by Mr. Henry for his descendants. From my recollections of the book it enforced the prominent doctrines of the Confession of Faith, in their length and breadth, urged upon those who should inherit his name or blood, the faithful performance of the duties which result from them,—with his advice as to the best manner of performing those duties." He left two sons.

Rev. John Hampton came to America in 1705, was regularly invited to the congregation at Snow Hill in 1707, but was not installed till 1708. The services of his installation were performed by Rev. Mr. McNish alone; the other member of committee, Mr. Davis, having failed to attend on the occasion. After the death of Mr. Henry, Mr. Hampton was united in marriage with the widow. He was present at the Synod in Sept. 1720. His will was admitted to record Feb. 2d, 1721. His death was reported to Synod Sept. 1721, but the day of his decease is not mentioned.

Mrs. Mary Hampton, who had been connected in marriage, successively, with Colonel Jenkins, Rev. John Henry, and Rev. John Hampton, departed this life 1744. "Her maiden name"—says Mr. Spence—"was King. She was the daughter of an Irish Baronet. She was a distinguished woman, or as I have heard her called—a great woman. She is uniformly called on the public records—madam. She left two sons, the only descendants of herself, or Mr. Henry; they both attained manhood; were married, and their descendants may be found in Dorchester, Somerset, and Worcester Counties."

Rev. George McNish, the other "assistance" of Mr. Makemie, after declining calls from Monocan, Wicomoco—"the meeting house on Mr. Venable's land"—or Salisbury and Upper Marlborough, removed to Long Island in New York and became pastor of Jamaica in 1712. He resided in that place till his death in 1726. "By his exertions principally," says Mr. Webster, "the Presbytery of Long Island was formed consisting, besides himself, of the Rev. Samuel Pumry (or Pomroy) of Newtown, Rev. George Phillips of Setauket, and the Church in Southampton over which they ordained Rev. Samuel Gelston at their first meeting." Mr. McNish died in 1726.

Rev. Samuel Davis was a member of the Presbytery when the records commence, and was probably an original member. He was from Ireland. He preached in different places on the Eastern Shore and died in 1725.

Rev. John Wilson, another of the original members of Presbytery, was from Scotland. As early as 1704 was minister of New Castle on the Delaware. He died in 1712.

Rev. Nathaniel Taylor, another of the ministers that united to form the Presbytery, lived on the Patuxent. Dr. Balch of Georgetown gives a tradition that a colony of Scotch came to this country, about the year 1690, under the auspices of Colonel Ninian Beall, and settled on the Patuxent. From these was formed Upper Marlborough. Mr. Taylor came with them, or soon after them, to be their minister. His last attendance in Presbytery was in 1709. Dr. Hill thinks the congregation at Upper Marlborough was organized at a later period, by Rev. Mr. Conn. It was of Scotch material.

Rev. Jedediah Andrews was born in Hingham, Massachusetts, July 1674: was a graduate of Harvard in 1695; commenced preaching in Philadelphia 1698; was an original member of Presbytery and became its stated clerk; was Moderator of the first meeting of the Synod of Philadelphia in 1717; was Moderator of the Synod at the time the Rev. Robert Cross his copastor brought in the famous protest, by which the Presbytery of New Brunswick was excluded; remained with the majority when the minority withdrew; and lived to the advanced age of seventy-two years. Mr. Makemie expressed his great attachment to him, by the legacies of his will. Whether the church, of which Mr. Andrews was long pastor, was organized at time he began to preach in Philadelphia, or a few years afterwards, has been a matter of discussion. It is not necessary to decide the matter here. The churches of the Eastern Shore, at least some of them, are senior sisters. Mr. Andrews was preaching in Philadelphia at the time Mr. Makemie obtained his qualifications from the Court of Accomack. The church at Snow Hill was able to sustain a preacher when that of Philadelphia was not yet gathered. There can be no question of the talents and acquirements of Mr. Andrews. His long residence in Philadelphia, of itself speaks volumes for him. His education had been in New England, where Independency predominated. There were many elements of Presbytery in the churches of his fathers. The orthodoxy of New England was then entirely unquestioned, and of the strictest sort. The points of agreement between Makemie and Andrews were many; the subjects of difference few. Makemie had been the Evangelist of the Eastern Shore; Andrews the forming pastor in Philadelphia. Makemie had been accustomed to meet opposition, and, victorious or conquered, to hold unchanged his principles of faith and practice and forms of worship, he must gain the victory or be defeated. Andrews was a common friend chosen by warring elements, and was accustomed to consider how much could be yielded with a safe faith, and what could be done to harmonize professing christians who agree on great principles. Makemie fell in earlier life than Andrews; but Andrews might have wished to fall earlier than Makemie, could he have anticipated the cloud that would hang upon his age. Both orthodox in faith, Makemie was Presbyterian, by education, ex animo; Andrews probably by position and expediency. Andrews closed his ministry and his life in 1746.

Rev. Francis Makemie held a peculiar position. He was the first in a long and rapidly increasing series of ministers that resulted in the General Assembly of the Presbyterian Church in North America. He was first of a church, whose past history is full of events that have moulded rising generations. No civil State, or religious denomination, south of the Hudson, or perhaps in the Union, has done more for the advance of civil liberty, freedom of conscience and the public welfare. All these things give force to the inquiry—what was his creed? That he was Presbyterian in creed, and in church forms and church government, has never been doubted. The records of civil and ecclesiastical courts establish that fact. But how did he understand the Confession of Faith? Strictly or in latitude of meaning? In absence of direct testimony the appeal is to the circumstances of the case. During his trial in New York in 1707 he said—"As to our doctrines, my Lord, we have a Confession of Faith known to the Christian world, and I challenge the clergy of York to show us any false or pernicious doctrine therein." This Confession was the Scotch edition of the Westminster Confession, which was in use in Ireland. But how did he understand it? This question is answered by the following circumstances.

1st. The Presbyterian Church in Ireland was gathered by such men as John Livingston and Robert Blair,—men that acted a conspicuous part at the Kirk of Shotts in 1630. Seven hundred persons were hopefully converted at one meeting. And these two preachers were suspended by the prelates, for being there. The Irish Church took its form and fashion from Scotch materials, after the model of the Scotch Kirk, and its prototype in Geneva. What construction the Scotch put on their Confession then is not doubted.

2d. In 1643 the Solemn League and Covenant, was, with due forms, taken to some extent in England. It was pressed in Scotland, and those, that declined taking it, in that country, were considered enemies of civil and religious liberty. Experience proved the suspicion not to be groundless. Ireland by a particular clause was included in the league; and the Presbyterians of Ulster took the covenant joyfully. In 1644, it was offered to the congregations in Down, Antrim, Derry, Donegal, Tyrone, and Fermanaugh, by commissioners sent from Scotland for the purpose. It was received by the congregations with ceremony and great solemnity. It produced the same effects in Ireland as in Scotland. It drew the line between the friends and enemies of civil and religious liberty.

3d. The first Presbytery in Ireland was formed on the 10th

of June 1642, and consisted of five ministers. It was not slow to act. In 1654, when the Presbytery consisted of about twenty-four members, a resolution respecting ministers coming from abroad was passed, declaring—that they must come well recommended for learning, piety, and prudence. Another resolution declared,—that young men from Scotland, received on trials for the ministry, should be particularly tried, so that they might not be received on slight testimonials, or small qualifications. Another resolution declared,—that previously to ordination, the candidates, having gone through their trials should declare *their adherence to the Solemn League and Covenant.*

4th. In 1664, four ministers of the Presbytery of Lagan, the original Presbytery having been divided into five, were put in confinement, by Leslie, Bishop of Raphoe, for their adherence to Presbyterial doctrine and practice. Their confinement lasted six years. Their names were John Hart, Thomas Drummond, William Semple, and Adam White; one of these, Mr. Drummond, was Makemie's pastor.

5th. In 1681, Mr. Makemie was licensed by the Presbytery of Lagan, and soon after ordained to come to America in answer to two applications for ministerial help. About the same time four ministers of this Presbytery were put in confinement for holding a fast, according to the resolution of Presbytery, on account of the state of the country then suffering under great grievances from the monarch and the prelates.

6th. The trials and sufferings of the Scotch and Irish Church, were not on account of their doctrinal creed. They might have been as Calvinistic in their doctrines of belief as they pleased, if they had yielded to the king and the prelates, and admitted diocesan bishops. The difficulties with the Independents, in the time of Cromwell, would have been avoided by giving up their church sessions, or elders. Rather than submit to these things, they fled from Scotland to Ireland, and from Ireland to Scotland, going and returning, as the difficulties lessened in one, or hope brightened in the other. At last they turned to America, and emigrated in crowds. They brought their religion and their principles of liberty along with them, and ranked among the firmest advocates and sufferers, in the American Revolution.

It is not unfair to conclude that a man trained in these circumstances, understood the Confession in the sense of the Scotch Church. In action, there was, of necessity, some modification in Ireland, and more in America, arising from the sparseness of the population, and the feebleness of the congregations. It can scarcely be supposed that a church, which, during the fifty years of its existence suffered from two opposite reasons—that she conceded too little and too much—and amidst trouble and wounds was spreading her wings for a westward flight, should ordain a forerunner who was not supposed to be ex animo a Presbyterian. Makemie's trials proved his spirit. He suffered confinement like his pastor and his co-presbyters. In magnanimity and boldness he was akin with Livingston and Blair, and the host of Scotch ministers, who laid down their lives in the Grass Market in Edinborough, in defence of what Americans hold most dear. It is not to be supposed that Makemie thought less of Presbyterian forms in America than in Ireland, or would be more ready to give them up, when the difficulties were no greater, and the reasons for adherence no less; more especially, when the yielding of them on the one hand for Independency would not render him less obnoxious to the laws of the province, or on the other, for prelacy, add any thing to his usefulness.

The fruits of Makemie's labours are seen, in the places where he expended his strength. Snow Hill and Rehoboth are churches still. Accomack has its church. Elizabeth always feeble, has had some witnesses; and Norfolk now flourishes. Urbana never had a church, but on the opposite side of the Rappahannoc, Waddel passed some years of his most successful labours.

The landing place of the Pilgrims cannot be seen at Plymouth. Jamestown in Virginia has passed to a single church in ruins and a grave yard. But the religious principles of the Pilgrims have spread far and wide; and the political principles of Virginia have influenced the nation. The facts and principles that sustained Makemie in Somerset and Accomack have been felt through all the South and West. He stands first in the list of names that shine as a galaxy in the Ecclesiastical horizon; and as a defender of civil liberty and equal rights in America he had no superior.

CHAPTER III.

THE CONFINEMENT AND TRIAL OF REV. FRANCIS MAKEMIE FOR PREACHING A SERMON IN NEW YORK, 1707.

THE prosecution of the Rev. Francis Makemie, for preaching a sermon, in the incipient city of New York, is a singular fact in history. It embraces the principles and laws on which he was called before County Courts, Deputies and Councils in Virginia and Maryland, and also some peculiar to New York. A statement is here presented, that the public may have a better understanding of the arbitrary nature of all religious establishments, by contemplating the difficulties that embarrassed dissenters from the Church of England; and that a more just estimate may be formed of the man who stands first on the list of the ministers of the Presbyterian Church in the United States of America. The facts and arguments, with the exception of Lord Cornbury's statement, are taken from a pamphlet published at the time, and republished, in New York, in the year 1755. Mr. Makemie is supposed to be Author or Editor, in part; or that it was drawn up under his inspection.

In the month of January, 1707, the Rev. Francis Makemie, and Rev. John Hampton, on a tour to New England, tarried a few days in New York. Lord Cornbury, the Deputy Governor, hearing of these strangers, the one from Accomack, Virginia, and the other from Somerset, Maryland, entertained them at the castle. No preparation had then been made for either of the gentlemen to preach. There was then no regular Presbyterian congregation in the city. After dining with the Governor, Mr. Makemie was invited by some of the citizens to preach on the ensuing Sabbath. He consented. Application, without his approbation or knowledge, was made to the Governor, for permission for him to preach in the Dutch Church, and was refused. The Governor declared himself invested with power to decide who should be permitted to preach in the city or province.

On Sabbath, the 19th of the month, Mr. Makemie preached in the dwelling house of William Jackson on Pearl Street, in an open public manner; and baptized a child. Mr. Hampton, on the same day, preached, at Newtown on Long Island, to a regular congregation, whose house had been admitted to record, according to the requirements of the Act of Toleration. Mr. Makemie remained in New York, on Monday, went on Tuesday to Newtown, intending to preach there on Wednesday. Immediately on his arrival, Thomas Cardale, High Sheriff, and Stephen Luff, Under Sheriff of Queens County, arrested Messrs. Makemie and Hampton, on a warrant signed by Lord Cornbury, charging them with having—"taken it upon them to preach in a private house, without having obtained any license for so dong, which is directly contrary to the known laws of England:—and being likewise informed that they are gone into Long Island with intent there to spread their pernicious doctrine and principles to the great disturbance of the Church by law established, and of the Government of this province"— and directing the Sheriff to bring the bodies of "Makennan" and Hampton to fort Anne.

On account of the lateness of the hour, when the process was served, the prisoners were permitted, on their parole, to lodge that night at the house of two neighbours friendly to them; on the next day, Wednesday, they were carried round by Jamaica, seven or eight miles out of the way to New York, as if to make a show of them; and being detained there that night, they were on Thursday, about noon, taken to fort Anne, and, about three or four o'clock in the afternoon, brought before Lord Cornbury, in the Council chamber.

Lord Cornbury's statement ought first to be perused. It was obtained from the office in Albany by the Rev. R. Webster. It is as follows—

"To the Right Honorable Lords Commissioners for Trade and Commerce. On the 17th of January, 1705, 6 (6, 7) a man of this town, one Jackson, came to acquaint me that two ministers were come to town and desired to know when they might speak with me. I ordered my man to tell Jackson they should be welcome to come and dine with me. They came and I found one is named Francis Makenzie a Presbyterian preacher settled in Virginia; the other is John Hampton a young Presbyterian minister lately come to settle in Maryland. They pretended they were going to Boston and did not say one syllable about preaching here. They applied themselves to the Dutch minister and to the Elders of the French church for leave to preach in their churches; they were willing if they could get my consent. On the Monday following I was informed that M. had preached at the house of Jackson a shoemaker in this town, and that Hampton had preached on Long Island, and that Makenzie was gone there with intent to preach in all the towns, having spread a Report that they had a commission from the Queen to preach all along this continent. I was informed the same day that they had preached in several places in New Jersey, and had ordained some young men, after their manner, who had preached among the Dissenters there without it. When asked, they said they had no occasion to ask leave of any Governor, they had the Queen's authority for what they did. These reports with the information I had of their behaviour on Long Island induced me to send an order to the Sheriff of Queens county to bring them to this place. He did so on the 23d of January in the Evening. The Attorney General was with me. I asked M. how he came to preach in this Government without acquainting me with it. He told me he had qualified himself according to law in Virginia, and having done so would preach in any part of the Queen's dominions. He told me he understood the law as well as any man, and was satisfied he had not offended against any law; that the penal laws did not extend to, and were not in force in America.

I told him the Queen was graciously pleased to grant liberty of conscience to all her subjects, except Papists; that he might be a papist for all I knew, and that therefore it was necessary he should have satisfied the Government what he was before he ventured to preach. He told me he would qualify himself in any manner and would settle in this province. I told him whenever any of the people in either of the provinces under my Government had desired leave to call a minister of their own persuasion, they had never been denied; but that I should be very cautious how I allowed a man so prone to bid defiiance to government, as I found he was. He said he had done nothing he could not answer. So I ordered the High Sheriff of the city to take them into custody and I directed the Attorney General to proceed against them. He preferred an indictment against M. for preaching in the city without qualifying himself as the Act of Toleration directs. The Grand Jury found the Bill, but the petit jury acquitted him; so he is gone towards New England uttering many severe threats against me. As I hope I have done nothing in this matter but what I was obliged in duty to do, especially as I think it very plain by the Act of Toleration, that it was not intended to tolerate or allow strolling preachers, so I entreat your Lordships protection against this malicious man, who is well known in Virginia and Maryland to be a disturber of the peace and quiet of all the places he comes into. He is a Jack of all trades. He is a preacher, a doctor of physic, a merchant, an attorney, a counsellor at Law, and, which is worst of all, a disturber of Governments. I should have sent your Lordships, this account sooner but that I was willing to see the issue of the trial.

   " I am my Lords
    " Your Lordships most ob. Hum. Servt.
         " CORNBURY.
  "New York Oct. 14th, 1706," (7.)

" The brief narrative and genuine history of the several steps of sufferings by the confinement of Francis Makemie and John Hampton"—goes on to say, that when the ministers appeared before Lord Cornbury in the council chamber—His Lordship inquired "How dare you to take it upon you to preach in my government without my license?

Makemie replied—" We have liberty from an act of parliament made in the first year of the reign of King William and Queen Mary, which gave us liberty, with which law we have complied.

C.   "None shall preach in my government without my license.

M.   "If the law for liberty had directed us to any particular persons in authority for license, we would readily have observed the same; but we cannot find any directions in the act of parliament, therefore we would not take notice thereof.

C. "That law does not extend to the American plantations, but only to England.

M. "My Lord I humbly conceive that it is not a limited nor local act; and am well assured it extends to other plantations of the Queen's dominions, which is evident from certificates from courts of record of Virginia and Maryland, certifying we have complied with the law." These certificates were produced and read by Lord Cornbury, who was pleased to say they did not extend to New York.

C. "I know it is local and limited, for I was at the making thereof.

M. "Your Excellency might be at the making thereof, but we are assured there is no such *limiting clause* therein as is in local acts, and desire that the law may be produced to determine the point.

C. (Turning to the attorney, Mr. Bekely) "Is it not so, Mr. Attorney?

Attorney—"Yes, it is local, my Lord." And producing an argument he went on to say—"that all the penal laws were local and limited, and did not extend to the plantations; and the Act of Toleration being made to take off the edge of the penal laws, therefore the Act of Toleration does not extend to any plantations.

M. "I desire the law may be produced; for I am morally persuaded there is no limitation or restriction in the law to England, Wales and Berwick on Tweed; for it extends to sundry plantations of the Queen's dominions, as Barbadoes, Virginia, and Maryland, which is evident from certificates produced, which we could not have obtained if the act of parliament had not extended to the plantations. I presume New York is a part of her Majesty's dominions also; and sundry ministers on the east end of Long Island have complied with the law, and qualified themselves at court by complying with the directions of said law, and have no license from your Lordship.

C. "Yes, New York is of her Majesty's dominions; but the Act of Toleration does not extend to the plantations by its own intrinsic virtue, or any intention of the legislators, but only by her *Majesty's instructions signified unto me, and that is from her prerogative and clemency*, and the courts which have qualified these men are in error, and I will check them for it.

M. "If the law extends to the plantations any manner of way, whether by the Queen's prerogative clemency or otherwise, our certificates were demonstration that we had complied therewith.

C. "These certificates were only for Virginia and Maryland; they did not extend to New York.

M. "We presume, my Lord, our certificates do extend as far as the law extends; for we are directed by the act of parliament to qualify ourselves in the places where we live, which we have done; and the same law directs us to *take certificates of our qualification*, which we have also done; and these certificates are not to certify to such as behold us taking our qualifications, being performed in the face of the country at a public court; but our certificates must be to satisfy others abroad in the world, who saw it not, or heard any thing of it, otherwise it were needless. And that law which obliges us to take a certificate must allow said certificate to have a credit and a reputation in her Majesty's dominions; otherwise it is to no purpose.

C. "That act of parliament was made against *strolling preachers*, and you are such and shall not preach in my government.

M. "There is not one word my Lord, mentioned in any part of the law against *travelling* or *strolling* preachers, as your Excellency is pleased to call them; and we are to judge that to be the true end of the law which is specified in the preamble thereof, which is—'for the *satisfying scrupulous consciences, and uniting the subjects of England in interest and affection.*' And it is well known to all, my Lord, that Quakers, who have liberty by this law, have few or no fixed teachers, but are chiefly taught by such as travel, and it is known to all, that such are sent forth by the yearly meeting at London, and travel and teach over the plantations, and are not molested.

C. "I have troubled some of them, and will trouble them more.

M. "We hear, my Lord, one of them was prosecuted at Jamaica, but it was not for *travelling and teaching*, but *for particulars in teaching* for which he suffered.

C. "You shall not spread your pernicious doctrines here.

M. "As to our doctrines, my Lord, we have our Confession of Faith, which is known to the Christian world, and I challenge all the clergy of York to show us any false or pernicious doctrines therein; yea, with those exceptions specified in the law, we are able to make it appear that they are, in all doctrinal articles of faith, agreeable to the *established doctrines of the Church of England.*

C. "There is one thing wanting in your certificates, and that is signing the articles of the Church of England.

M. "That is the clerk's omission, my Lord, for which we are no way accountable, by not being full and more particular; but if we had not complied with the whole law, in all parts thereof, we should not have had certificates pursuant to said act of parliament. And your Lordship may be assured that we have done nothing in complying with said law but what we are still ready to perform, if your Lordship require it, and that ten times over. And as to the *articles of religion*, I have a copy in my pocket, and am ready at all times to sign, with those *exceptions specified by law.*

C. "You preached in a private house not certified according to act of parliament.

M. "There were endeavours used for my preaching in a more public place, and (though without my knowledge) your Lordship's permission was demanded for my preaching in the Dutch church, and being denied, we were under a necessity of assembling for public worship in a private house, which we did in as *public a manner* as possible *with open doors;* and we are directed to certify the same to the next Quarter Sessions, which cannot be done until the Quarter Sessions come in course, for the law binds no man to impossibilities; and if we do not certify to the next Quarter Sessions we shall be culpable, but not till then. For it is evident, my Lord, that this act of parliament was made and passed the Royal assent May 24th, and it being some time before the Quarter Sessions came in course, and all ministers in England continued to preach without one day's cessation or forbearance; and we hope the practice of England should be a precedent for America.

C. "None shall preach in my government without my license, as the Queen has signified to me by her royal instructions.

M. "Whatever direction the Queen's instructions may be to your Lordship, they can be no rule or law to us, nor any particular person who never saw, and perhaps never shall see them. *For promulgation is the life of the law.*

C. "You must give bond and security for your good behaviour, and also bond and security to preach no more in my government.

M. "As to our behaviour, though we have no way broke it, endeavouring always so to live, as to 'keep a conscience void of offence towards God and man,' yet if your Lordship requires it, we would give security for our behaviour; but to give bond and security to preach no more in your Excellency's government, if invited and desired by any people, we neither can nor dare do.

C. "Then you must go to goal.

M. "We are neither ashamed nor afraid of what we have done; and we have complied, and are ready still to comply, with the act of parliament, which we hope will protect us at last. And it will be unaccountable in England, to hear that

Jews, who openly blaspheme the name of the Lord Jesus Christ and disown the whole Christian religion,—the Quakers who disown the fundamental doctrines of the Church of England, and both the sacraments,—the Lutherans, and all others are tolerated in your Lordship's government, and only we, who have complied and are still ready to comply with the Act of Toleration, and are nearest to and likest to the Church of England of any dissenters, should be hindered, and that only in the government of New York and the Jerseys. This will appear strange indeed.

C. "You must blame the Queen for that.

M. "We do not, neither have we any reason to blame her Majesty, for she molests none, neither countenances nor encourages any who do; and has given frequent assurances, *and of late*, in her gracious speech to parliament, that she would inviolably maintain the toleration."

Here Lord Cornbury began writing precepts for discharging the prisoners from the custody of the sheriff of Queen's county, and for their commitment in New York. Mr. Hampton, who had hitherto remained silent, demanded a license to preach, according to Act of Toleration; Lord Cornbury absolutely denied it. Mr. Makemie then moved that the law be produced to determine the point whether it were local and limited or not. He said he doubted not the Attorney was able soon to produce the law; and further, he offered to pay the Attorney for a copy of that paragraph which contains the limiting clause.

C. "You, sir, know law?

M. "I do not, my Lord, pretend to know law; but I pretend to know this particular law, having had sundry disputes thereon." He here refers to his appearance before the courts of Maryland and Virginia. The mittimus being made out, the high sheriff of York city and county, Ebenezer Wilson, took them to his dwelling house, as the place of their confinement. On Friday the 26th, after sundry demands, by the prisoners, he gave them a copy of their commitment, viz.

"You are hereby required and commanded to take into your custody the bodies of Francis Makemie and John Hampton, and them safely keep, till further orders; and for so doing this shall be your warrant.

Given under my hand and seal this 23 day of January 1706, 7.

CORNBURY (seal)

To Ebenezer Wilson, Esq. High Sheriff of New York.

A true copy—Ebenezer Wilson."

This was made by the supreme authority, and not by the proper officers appointed for the commitment of offenders:—there is no mention of the Queen's authority or name:—there is no crime alleged:—and they were to be discharged by the Governor and not by "due course of law." Finding themselves imprisoned they sent the following petition by the hands of the High Sheriff, viz:

"To his Excellency, Edward Viscount Cornbury, Captain General and Governor in Chief of the Province of New York and New Jersey, and all the tracts of land depending thereon in America and Admiral of the same—the humble petition of Francis Makemie and John Hampton most humbly sheweth:

"That whereas your Excellency has been pleased to commit us to prison by a precept wherein there is no crime alleged we your Lordships most humble petitioners and prisoners, most humbly pray we may be permitted to know our crime. And your Excellencys most humble petitioners and prisoners further pray, as we are strangers on our journey to New England, above four hundred miles from our habitation, we may be allowed a speedy trial, according to law, which we humbly conceive to be the undoubted right and privilege of every English subject. And your Excellencys most humble petitioners and afflicted prisoners shall as in duty bound, always pray.

FRANCIS MAKEMIE.
JOHN HAMPTON."

To this petition, a verbal answer was returned, after some days,—"that Lord Cornbury did admire they should petition to know their crime, he having so often told them,—and that they might have a trial if they took the right way." What this "right way" was they could not ascertain though they made application both to the Sheriff and Attorney. They had no alternative, and therefore resolved to wait with patience till the arrival of the Chief Justice, Hon. Roger Mompesson, Esq., who resided in another province, and could not sign a Habeas Corpus, until he should come into the government of New York. In the meantime the Quarter Sessions of the city and county of New York came on, they petitioned Lord Cornbury, that in the custody of the Sheriff they might be permitted to apply for license, as the law directs—"which,"—say they—"we are again ready to do, we being resolved to reside in your Lordships government." This being rejected by Cornbury, they next addressed the Quarter Sessions, then sitting on the 5th of February, and requested, that, as their certificates from the courts in Virginia and Maryland were not admitted by Lord Cornbury as extending to his government,—they might be permitted in custody of the Sheriff to appear at their bar and be qualified again. Their petition was presented, handed about, but not read in open court. The Attorney General laid hold of it and was putting it in his pocket telling the court it was a libel on Lord Cornbury,—and that it was none of their business to administer the qualifications,—although the Act of Toleration declares expressly that it is the duty of Quarter Sessions so to do. The magistrates were probably not in possession of the law.

At the same time application was made according to the Toleration Act, for licensing the house of William Jackson, where Makemie had preached, as the place of public worship for those who chose to Assemble under the Toleration Act; this was also refused, after being under consideration two days, and the law being presented for their inspection; although, a short time before, a Quaker meeting house had been licensed on application of two men, upon the same act of Parliament.

By the Act of Toleration, when application was made to the Quarter Sessions, or other constituted authorities, the court was required to make register of the same; and an application, according to law, was a legal qualification in the eye of the law.

Chief Justice Mompesson arrived at New York some days before the March term; and to him, through their lawyer Mr. Reigniere, the prisoners presented their petition for a writ of Habeas Corpus. This petition was granted, after some days, and a writ of Habeas Corpus issued March 1706, 7. This writ demanding "the day and cause of their caption and detention," and neither having been expressed in the mittimus, the Governor made out a new mittimus dated "this 8th day of March A. D. 1706, (7)" in which their crimes are stated "for preaching in this province without qualifying themselves—and without my license first obtained"—and put it into the hands of the Sheriff on the same day he received the writ of Habeas Corpus, Saturday, March 8th, 1706, 7. On Monday afternoon the Sheriff told him he had another mittimus, wherein a supposed crime was specified—and also the clause—"till they shall be discharged by due course of law,"—and they must find securities. By this new mittimus, their imprisonment of six weeks and four days was admitted to be false imprisonment. The Sheriff, in presence of Mr. Reigniere their lawyer, and Dr. Wm. Johnstone and Wm. Jackson, refused to execute the writ of Habeas Corpus until the prisoners paid him twelve pieces of Eight for their commitment, and as many more for the return of the writ; and refused to give a receipt for the money when paid. They were then conducted to the Supreme Court; and on the new mittimus, gave bonds with two securities, Dr. Johnstone, Gentleman, and Mr. Jackson, Cordwainer, to appear the next day, and not depart without leave of the court.

In the return, made by the Sheriff, of the writ of Habeas Corpus, he gives the two mittimuses, of Lord Cornbury, in full. By the Second Mittimus, they were arrested not in the Queen's name, but by Cornbury's own authority; were accused of two crimes—of not qualifying according to law—and of preaching in New York without license from the Governor: whereas they had been qualified in Maryland and Virginia, and offered themselves to qualify in New York, both before Cornbury and the Quarter Sessions.

On Tuesday March 11th, the Supreme Court was in form, Messrs. Makemie and Hampton made their appearance; on the Attorney General's motion, they were required to appear the last day of the term. Mr. Reigniere, their attorney, moved that the writ of habeas corpus and all the proceedings of the Judges' Chamber might be made matter of record; the Attorney General opposed the record on the ground that the thing had not been done in open court. On the next day the Judge delivered to the Court a record of the proceedings in his chamber.

The grand jury were sworn the first day of the term, this matter was given them in charge, with little business beside, and after various meetings and consultations, the Attorney having dropped the name of John Hampton from the prosecution, they brought in their bill against Mr. Makemie on Friday afternoon, their vote being taken, one by one, as they came in from dinner. Some of the grand jury were justices of the peace, who at the Quarter Sessions had refused to have the petitions of the prisoners read, or to pay any attention to the applications for licensing a place of public worship. Four witnesses were examined, one of them Lord Cornbury's coachman, by name of Harris, and gave evidence that they heard no unsound doctrine, or any thing against the government; one of the evidences handed to the jury the act of assembly of New York for liberty of conscience for all, except Papists. The bill charges Mr. Makemie with having preached in New York, to an assembly of more than five persons, without having obtained permission, and without qualification; and also that he used other rites and ceremonies than those found in the book of common prayer. The date of the offence was put, in the bill, January 22d, whereas it took place on the 20th of that month. The bill being brought in the last day of the court, the trial was postponed till the next term, in June. Mr. Makemie on the bail, previously given, of £40 for himself, and £20 for Mr. Johnstone, gentleman, and £20 for Mr. Jackson, cordwainer, was permitted to return to Virginia. While the preparations for trial were going on, an order was given to Major Sandford, of East Jersey, to examine upon their oaths certain persons, to discover what discourse they had with some of their friends at the house of Mr. Jasper Crane of Newark; these persons were examined, but nothing found to suit the purpose, either of finding out a crime, or magnifying their faults.

In this stage of the business, we may suppose Lord Cornbury was willing, and expected, the matter should rest; Hampton was dropped from prosecution, having been punished by above six weeks confinement for offending the deputy;—and Makemie, the chief offender, was let out on bail, which he might forfeit, and thus be kept from New York, and the odium of a trial avoided. But Makemie was not the man to forfeit his bonds, or avoid a trial where the honour of the gospel was concerned. If Lord Cornbury had been excited against him, his spirit had been equally aroused to resist the persecution of the tyrannical deputy, and vindicate the right of Presbyterians in the incipient city of New York.

On his way home to Accomac, he attended the meeting of the Presbytery in Philadelphia, which commenced its sessions March 22, (Saturday) 1707. "Mr. Francis Makemie and Mr. John Wilson are appointed to preach upon Tuesday, upon the subjects appointed them at the last Presbytery, on Heb. i. 1st and 2d, by way of exercise and addition. March 25th, (Tuesday)—This day Mr. Francis Makemie and Mr. John Wilson delivered their discourses according to appointment." On Wednesday he was directed to write to Scotland for the purpose of obtaining Mr. Alexander Coldin as minister for the people about Lewistown. On the same day the following interesting overtures were passed; interesting in themselves, and particularly as the last important presbyterial act performed by Makemie; viz. "First—That every minister in their respective congregations, read and comment upon a chapter of the Bible every Lord's day, as discretion and circumstances of time, place, &c. will admit. Second over.—That it be recommended to every minister of the Presbytery to set on foot and encourage private Christian societies. Third over.— That every minister of the Presbytery supply neighbouring desolate places where a minister is wanting, and opportunity of doing good offers." The next meeting of Presbytery was after he had made his will. The supply of desolate places with the gospel was the object of his ministerial life.

Mr. Makemie returned from Accomac "with his man," to New York, in time to meet the Court on the first day of its sessions; the defendant's appearance was entered, and he was "ordered to plead to-morrow."

Wednesday June 4th 1707.

The defendant plead not guilty of any crime by preaching a sermon at York. Lord Cornbury being in the Jerseys, the Attorney moved that a copy of the Queen's instructions to the

Governor be received as evidence at the trial. Mr. Makemie objected—that there was time to get the original; or the Attorney might produce a certified copy. But finding that the trial would be put off another term unless the Attorney's copy were admitted, it was agreed that it should be received as if the original were present: Mr. Makemie observing—"he could not but wonder of what service these instructions, which were no law, could be to Mr. Attorney, seeing the presentment run upon statutes and act of parliament, and they expected to have a trial before a court who were judges of law and not of private instructions."

On Friday June 6th, 1707 the Petit jury was called: the defendant said he was under great disadvantage, being a stranger and not knowing either names or faces of the persons summoned as a jury; that he knew he had not the privilege of peremptory challenge;—but that he was informed that one of them—Mr. Elias Neace, in discourse with Mr. Anthony Young had prejudged the cause, by condemning him for preaching a sermon, and justifying Lord Cornbury's proceedings against him; and this being proved by the testimony of Mr. Young, Mr. Neace was set aside. Mr. Makemie farther said, "he was amazed to find that one so lately dragooned out of France for his religion, and delivered out of the galley, so soon prove a persecutor of the same religion for preaching a sermon in this city. The names of the jury are worthy of remembrance for the verdict they had the courage to render in face of the Governor and his attorney and the Justices of the Quarter Sessions: they were—John Shepherd, foreman, Thomas Ives, Joseph Wright, Thomas Wooden, Joseph Robinson, Bartholomew Larouex, Andrew Lauron, Humphrey Perkins, William Horswell, Thomas Carrell, Thomas Bayeux, and Charles Cromline.

Mr. Attorney produced a copy of the Queen's instructions signed by Lord Cornbury, which was allowed; these instructions were found to be the same as those given by King William to a former Governor; in the produced copy they were in two sentences; in the former instructions they were in two sentences but a great distance from each other; 1st. " *You are to permit a liberty of conscience to all persons except Papists, so that they be content with a quiet and peaceable enjoyment of it, not giving offence or scandal to the government. 2d. You are not to permit any minister coming from England to preach in your government, without a certificate, from the Right Reverend the Bishop of London; nor any other minister coming from any other part or place without first obtaining leave from the Governor.*"

The Attorney ordered four of Mr. Makemie's hearers to be called—Capt. John Theobalds, Mr. John Vanhorne, Mr. Wil-

liam Jackson, and Mr. Anthony Young; the defendant told the
Court the swearing of these witnesses was unnecessary—" I
own the matter of fact as to preaching, and more than these
gentlemen could declare on oath; for I have done nothing
therein, of which I am ashamed, or afraid; but will answer it
not only before this bar, but before the tribunal of God's final
judgement."

Attorney—"You own that you preached a sermon, and baptized a child at Mr. William Jackson's?"

Makemie—"I did."

A. "How many hearers had you?"

M. "I have other work to do, Mr. Attorney, than number
my auditory when I am about to preach to them."

A. "Were there above five hearing you?"

M. "Yes, and five to that."

A. "Did you use the rites and ceremonies enjoined by,
and prescribed in the Book of Common Prayer by the Church
of England?"

M. "No: I never did, nor ever will, till I am better satisfied in my conscience."

A. "Did you ask leave, or acquaint my Lord Cornbury
with your preaching at York, when you dined with him at the
fort?"

M. "I did not know of my preaching at York when I
dined with his Excellency; no, not for some days after. For
when we came to York we had not the least intention or design of preaching there, but stopped at York purely to pay our
respects to the Governor, which we did; but being afterwards
called and invited to preach, as I was a minister of the gospel
I durst not deny preaching, and I hope I never shall when it is
wanting and desired."

A. "Did you acquaint Lord Cornbury with the place of
your preaching?"

M. "As soon as I determined to preach leave was asked
but not by me; for it was the people's business and not mine,
to provide a place for me to preach in. And I would have
been admitted to preach in the Dutch Church, but they were
afraid of offending Lord Cornbury. And Anthony Young
went to the Governor to have his leave, or permission, for
my preaching in the Dutch Church, though all this was done
without so much as my knowledge. But my Lord opposing
and denying it, I was under the necessity of preaching where
I did, in a private house, though in a public manner with open
doors."

The Attorney then entered into a full statement of the
Statutes of Henry Eighth establishing the supremacy—from
thence he asserted the Queen's supremacy in Ecclesiastical

affairs and over Ecclesiastical persons,—that this supremacy had been delegated to the Governor and expressed in her majesty's instructions. He produced the Statutes of Elizabeth and Charles 2d for Uniformity—and concluded by saying "the matter of fact is plainly confessed—and I have proved it to be repugnant to the Queen's instructions and sundry acts of Parliament, and doubt not the jury will find for the Queen."

Mr. James Reigniere pleaded for the defendant—That the indictment charged three separate facts as crimes; first—that a pretended minister endeavouring to subvert the Queen's supremacy, did privately and unlawfully preach at Wm. Jackson's house, without license; Second,—that he did unlawfully use other rites and ceremonies than are in the book of Common Prayer;—and thirdly—that he was not qualified by law to preach—and had held an unlawful assembly. He denied that the defendant had preached privately: and also that he had preached unlawfully,—because he had violated no law forbidding the preaching to above five. He said the colony was governed 1st by the Common law of England: 2d, By express Statutes mentioning the Plantations: 3d, By laws of the colony: and that he had never read that preaching without license to above five is a crime; and it is not alleged to be against a Statute for the Provinces; it must then, to be a crime, be against a law of the colony;—let it be produced—where there is no law there can be no transgression. He argued that the Statutes of Elizabeth and James and Charles were either aimed at Popish recusants or restricted to England, Wales and Berwick on the Tweed. Besides there is no Established church in New York; and liberty of conscience is allowed by law of the Province—"That no person or persons who profess faith in God by Jesus Christ his only Son, shall at any time be any way molested, for any difference of opinion or matter of religious concernment, who do not under that pretence disturb the civil peace of the province."—"And all such persons may freely meet at convenient places within this province and there worship according to their respective persuasions." From this act the papists were excepted.

As to the third charge—he argued that as the penal statutes did not extend hither, there was no need of Toleration.—That the penal laws extend equally to all plantations alike, and if the penal laws extended to the plantations, then the crown would not tolerate the governments of Boston, Rhode Island, Connecticut, and others, which in their church affairs differ so much from the Church of England. But these are allowed the Liberty they always used in the church. "As therefore it does not appear by the common law of England, or any law of the province that his preaching is unlawful;—but on the contrary there is an express law of the province in favour of it, I humbly conceive that my client is not guilty of any offence against the law and I hope and expect the jury will acquit him."

Mr. William Nicholl next pleaded for defendant and said that as the attorney had brought history from the reign of Henry 8th he would bring some from the Bible, and would begin with the Acts of the Apostles, and show that preaching the gospel was never in itself, or by the common law, found to be a crime. The Apostle preached a new doctrine to the Athenians and was not condemned or imprisoned for it: it was no crime at Corinth; but when his preaching bore on the gains of the silversmiths at Ephesus, they made an uproar rushing into the theatre. It was no offence by the common law, but made so by the 5th of Richard 2d—2d of Henry 4th—2d of Henry 5th;—but all these Statutes were repealed by 1st of Edward 6th—and the acts of Elizabeth. The four acts against Conventicles are all local and in express words limited to England, Wales and Berwick on Tweed, "And this is further manifest from the constitutions of the plantations being, as it were, settled by national consent, for those whose thoughts in religious affairs could not square with the public establishment in church government, discipline, and ceremonies; as New England for Independents and Presbyterians; Rhode Island and New Jersey, and we may say New York for the several sorts of Dissenters in General; Pennsylvania for the Quakers, and Maryland for papists in particular. As to the Queen's instructions they are not, and cannot have the force of law. And it is already evidently proved that the Acts of the Assembly of New York allow of Liberty of Conscience with freedom of public worship to all but Papists." He said that this prosecution, (viz. on the authority of the Queen's prerogative and instructions) being the *first* in the plantations was made the *more remarkable*.

Mr. David Jamieson appeared next to plead for the defendant. He said he did not call in question the Queen's prerogative, but could not see that the Queen's instructions were a law to any body else but his Lordship, who is directed by them and accountable to the Queen if he does not obey them; they are private directions to himself, and can be no law to others; promulgation gives the finishing stroke to a law. He argued that the Statutes of Elizabeth and Charles against Conventicles were limited because in New York there was no established Religion for the whole province—On the East end of Long Island, there were, and always had been, Independent ministers, and the Dutch and the French have their own ministers. Part of enactments are in express words limited; and the 18th of Charles 2d for suppressing Conventicles, makes the third default banishment for seven years to the plantations (New England and Virginia excepted.) Mr. Makemie has not offended against the Act of Toleration; for Toleration is an exception from some restraint; and since the penal laws are not in force here neither is the Act of Toleration. There is no established church here—and we have liberty of conscience by act of Assembly made in the beginning of the reign of William and Mary, during the Government of Colonel Fletcher. This Province has not been more than about forty years in the possession of the crown of England, and is made up chiefly of foreigners and dissenters, and persecution would tend to disunite us all. And as this prosecution is the first of this nature known in the province, so it is hoped it may be the last.

Mr. Makemie then obtained permission to speak; and was expressing great astonishment that the Attorney should construe the Act of Toleration as applying to the province of New York, when he had produced an argument to prove that it was local, when Lord Cornbury was examining defendant for commitment.

Judge Mompesson.—"Gentlemen, do not trouble the Court with what passed between you before my Lord, or at any other time, but speak directly to the point."

M. "May it please your Honour, I hope to make it appear that it is to the point; and what was Mr. Attorney's argument then, is now mine. For whatever opinion I was of, while an absolute stranger to New York and its constitution, now, since I have informed myself thoroughly with its constitution, I am entirely of Mr. Attorney's opinion, and hope he will be of the same still. I allow of the Queen's supremacy, and in all the Attorney has said, I cannot learn one argument or word from all the quoted statutes, that preaching a sermon is the least contempt or overthrow of the supremacy; and I hope it is not unknown to any, that the oath of supremacy has been abolished by a law ever since the Revolution. And I cannot learn from any law yet produced, that Lord Cornbury has any power or directions to grant license to any dissenters, or that any of them are under any obligations to take license from his Lordship before they preach, or after." He then discussed the Queen's instructions to Lord Cornbury, at large, and with great force, to show that they applied only to members of the Church of England coming from England or other places. He also plead that the penal laws did not and could not extend to New York, where there is no law in favour of the Church of England, and no restriction on the liberty of dissenters. He concluded by saying—"And if Jews, who openly blaspheme the Lord Jesus—Quakers, and Lutherans, and all others, or most persuasions, are allowed even in this government, it is matter of wonder why we only should not be allowed of, but put to molestation, as we now are by present prosecution. Is it because we are Protestants? Is it because we are nearest alike the established church of England of any dissenters? Is it because we are the most considerable body of Protestants in the Queen's dominions? Is it because we have now, since the union, a national establishment in Great Britain as nearly related and annexed to the crown of England as the Church of England themselves? Sure, such a proceeding, when known, will and must be a prodigy in England."

Attorney—" It is impossible for any man to answer all that has been offered, where so much has been said; and by so many."

Makemie—"I verily believe it is impossible for the Attorney to answer what has been said; it is a great truth which he has uttered."

The Attorney then proceeded to argue that the penal laws, at least some of them were coextensive with the Queen's dominions. He said the kings and queens of England command their governors to grant licenses; and that it had been customary to take licenses from the governors.

Mr. Makemie replied at large; and concluded by saying,— "And whereas Mr. Attorney affirms that giving and taking license was very common and universal,—I am well assured there never was, neither is, to this day, any such practice in any plantations of America; and there are but few persons as yet in York government that have license;—for beside the two Dutch ministers who differ upon Long Island—and it is said these licenses are the cause of their difference—there is but one English non-conformist minister in all the government, who has taken a license;—and it is certain that Mr. Dubois, and sundry others of the Dutch churches have no license, neither will they submit to any such as are granted."

The Attorney then moved that the jury bring in a special verdict. The judges inclined that way too. The Attorney said, "The matter of fact is plainly confessed by the defendant, as you have heard, and you are to bring it in specially, for the jury are not judges of law."

Mr. Makemie—" May it please your honours—I am a stranger, who lives four hundred miles from this place, and it is known to the whole country what intolerable trouble I have been put to already, and we cannot consent to a special verdict, for that would only increase my trouble, multiply my charges, and give me further delay. Besides it is a known maxim in law—*that strangers are always to be favoured with expedition in justice.* This seems no way to admit of delay; and if this should be allowed of, no man's innocence would be able to protect him; for if I should be cleared I should suffer more attaint than if I were guilty of many penal laws in England. And as to the jury's judging of the law, and confessing the fact, I cannot see one point of law to be judged. It is true I have confessed preaching a sermon at the house of Mr. William Jackson,—but have not owned it to be a crime, or repugnant to any law, or inconsistent with any of the Queen's instructions; nor hath the attorney made any thing of this nature to appear,—for all those ancient statutes of Henry VIII. tend only to throw off the authority, supremacy, and jurisdiction of the Popes and See of Rome, and invest the kings and queens of England with that usurped authority, and to bring ecclesiastical persons under the civil jurisdiction of England, who in times of Popery were made accountable only to the See of Rome,—therefore they do not touch, neither are any way applicable to this case."

Attorney—" These gentlemen acknowledge, and say, that the ministers of the Church of England are to take license, and are obliged so to do; and if so the Dissenters should also—otherwise they must expect more favours and liberty than the ministers of the Church of England."

Makemie—" It is the constitution of the Church of England, that the ministers, notwithstanding their ordination, do not preach, or officiate as ministers until they procure a license from their Bishop; and they voluntarily bring themselves under oath of canonical obedience. But finally there is a great deal of reason why ministers of the Church of England submit to license; but not so with us. For it is only *bare liberty* which Dissenters have; but the *others* have not only *liberty*, but a *considerable maintenance* also, without which I never knew any of them value *liberty only*. And Dissenters having liberty only, without any maintenance from Government, are not at all under obligations, neither is it required of them to take license."

The Chief Justice then charged the jury—"Gentlemen; you have heard a great deal on both sides, and Mr. Attorney says, the fact is confessed by the defendant;—and I would have you to bring it in specially, for there are some points which I am not now prepared to answer; how far instructions may go, in having the force of law, especially when not published or made known;—and one objection made by Mr. Makemie—that is, the oath of supremacy of England is abolished; and how far it will go in this matter, I confess I am not prepared to answer. If you will take upon you to judge of law, you may; or bring in the fact specially. This is the first instance that I can learn that there has been a trial or prosecution of this nature in America."

The Jury asked for the Act of Assembly of New York; and

the defendant desired that the jury might have a copy of the Queen's instructions, which the Attorney opposed and denied. A constable was sworn to attend the jury, who withdrew and in a short time returned again; and being called, found the defendant *Not Guilty.*

The Court required the reasons for the verdict. The Chief Justice said, they might give reasons for their verdict, or not, as they chose. The foreman said the defendant had not transgressed any law. Another of the jury said, they believed in their consciences they had done the defendant justice. And so the verdict was confirmed.

Mr. Reigniere moved that the defendant be discharged; the Chief Justice referred it till to-morrow morning. Saturday, June 7th, 1707. "Ordered that the defendant be discharged, paying fees."

Mr. Makemie objected to paying such severe fees—but at length agreed to pay all just and legal fees to the Court and officers thereof, who acted indifferently as to this matter; but said it was unreasonable he should pay his prosecutors what they pleased.

It was affirmed that it was the practice; and no argument would be received. Makemie prayed that the bill might be taxed in open Court. This the Chief Justice declined; and it was referred to Robert Milward, Esq., one of the Assistant Judges, who was to give notice to Mr. Makemie or his attorney of the time and place. But no notice was given—and two new items added. The full amount was paid; and a receipt refused the defendant, though the money was paid in presence of two witnesses.

The amount of expenses paid by Mr. Makemie in consequence of this trial was 83*l.* 7*s.* 6*d.*; of this the Attorney General took 12*l.* 12*s.* 6*d.*; the Secretary 5*l.* 12*s.* 6*d.*; the High Sheriff, for commitment to his house, for Habeas Corpus, and returns and fees after trial, took 9*l.* 17*s.*; the Judges, under various pretexts, 4*l.* 6*s.* This is without a parallel in the history of the colony; that the High Sheriff and Attorney General should take fees from a defendant who was cleared by the jury.

Soon after his liberation, Mr. Makemie preached again in the church allowed to the French; his sermon was printed; great excitement followed; he was accused of being the author of a pamphlet which was spread abroad soon after his arrival in the province; and the Governor issued new process, and employed his officers, all day of a Sabbath, to find and arrest him again, and bring him to a confinement, and another trial. He escaped their hands, and fled out of the province; and thus gratified his persecutors by leaving York.

The following letter is the only one from the pen of Makemie known to be in existence. It was directed to Lord Cornbury; and bears date, Boston, July 28th, 1707:

"May it please your Lordship; I most humbly beg leave to represent to your Excellency my just astonishment at the information received from sundry hands, since my arrival in these colonies; and after so long and so expensive a confinement—so deliberate and fair a trial, before Judges of your Lordship's appointment, and by a jury chosen by your own Sheriff on purpose to try the matter—I have been legally cleared, and found guilty of no crime for preaching a sermon at New York; though my innocence should have protected me from unspeakable and intolerable expense, yet I am informed, may it please your Excellency, there are orders and directions given to sundry officers in the Jerseys for apprehending me, and a design of giving me fresh trouble at New York.

"If I were assured of the true cause of your Lordship's repeated resentments against me, I doubt not but my innocence would not only effectually justify me, but remove those unjust impressions imposed on your Lordship by some persons about you.

"As to my preaching—being found at the trial to be against no law, nor any ways inconsistent with her Majesty's instructions produced there; and considering the solemn obligations I am under both to God and the souls of men, to embrace all opportunities of exercising those ministerial gifts vouchsafed to me from heaven—to whom I do appeal—I have no other end, besides the glory of God and the eternal good of precious souls; I must assure myself your Lordship insists *not on this now as a crime*, especially in New York government, where all Protestants are upon an equal level of liberty, and where there exists no legal Establishment for any particular persuasion.

"I hear that I am charged with the *Jersey paper* called *Forget and Forgive*. Though the proving a negative be an hard task, and not an usual requisition or undertaking, yet why should there be any doubt about the thing itself; the matter it contains being altogether foreign from me, and no way concerning me; the time of its publication, being so soon spread abroad after my arrival, I am well assured none dare legally accuse me, while the real authors are smiling at your Lordship's mistake and imposition. Your informers deserve to be stigmatized with the severest marks of your Lordship's displeasure: and the authors will find a time to confront my sworn accusers of perjury; and besides that I never saw it until about the last of February.

"We have suffered greatly in our reputations, and particularly by being branded with the character of *Jesuits;* though my universal known reputation, both in Europe and America, makes me easy under such invidious imputations. I have been represented to your Lordship as being *factious*, both in the government of Virginia and Maryland. I have peaceably lived in Virginia; I have brought from Maryland a certificate of my past reputation, signed by some men of the best quality in the most contiguous county, ready to be produced at the trial, if there had been occasion for it. A copy of which I shall presume to enclose for your Lordship's perusal and satisfaction.

"I beg leave to represent to your Lordship my just concern at the sundry precepts for apprehending me, both in York and the Jerseys, as one of the greatest criminals; whereby I am prevented in performing my ministerial duties to many in your Lordship's government of my own persuasion, who desire it.

"I shall patiently expect your Lordship's commands and directions, in giving me an opportunity for vindicating myself in what is charged against me, and being always ready to comply with any qualifications enjoined and required by law.

"I beg leave of your Lordship, to subscribe myself,
Your Excellency's most humble and
Most obedient servant,
FRANCIS MAKEMIE."

CHAPTER IV.

THE SCOTCH IRISH.

THE congregations gathered by Makemie, in Maryland, flourished after his death; and the Presbytery, formed principally by his agency, increased greatly, and stretched first northward, and then southward, and at last westward, under the auspices of numerous Synods, and the General Assembly of the Presbyterian Church. For about thirty years after the death of Makemie, the number and influence of Presbyterians in Virginia were small. Not one flourishing congregation could be found, nor one active minister lived, in her borders. Then commenced a tide of emigration from his father land, the province of Ulster, Ireland, that spread over a beautiful section of Virginia, and filled up her wild borders with a peculiar race. The influence of that race of men on Virginia, in making her what she is, invests its history with an interest perpetually increasing, as the results of the meeting,—the collision,—and the intermingling of the Old English and Scotch Irish members of the British family, in the wilds of America, are manifested to the world. A sketch of the Old English stock is given in the first chapter. That race had a character peculiar and imposing. The Scotch Irish had a character equally as peculiar, and, though less imposing, more effective of religious eminence, and literary excellence, and not a whit behind in political aspirations, and self-denying labours in the cause of liberty.

A true estimate of Makemie, whose sufferings and labours and success, occupy the two preceding chapters, cannot be formed by considering him individually, or his actions in Virginia, and other provinces, apart from that race that gave him birth, and from the circumstances that moulded that race and made him what he was. Looking at him as he appears in Virginia, aside from his education, he appears to be the most singular man of his day; his course cannot be well understood. That he had principles of religion and morality of great energy and unchangeable power, is evident. And it is equally evident that they were not, what was anciently termed malignancy, or in more modern times, radicalism, or personal ambition, or enthusiasm, or bigotry, or jesuitical adherence to party. The current of his life flowed like a pure stream from an abiding equable fountain. To find that fountain we must cross the ocean, and search the records of his race in the province of Ulster, Ireland.

For a detailed account of the Scotch Irish,—their origin,—their principles of religion,—their church forms and government,—their awakenings—their sufferings—their abortive, yet almost romantic, effort at emigration to America, in the Eagle Wing,—their political opinions,—their expectations in emigrating to America,—their influence in Ireland,—and the formation of their religious and civil character,—the reader is referred to the Sketches of North Carolina, published the latter part of 1846, by Carter, New York. The recent appearance of that volume, and the fulness of detail in chapters 5th, 6th, 7th, 8th and 9th, render the attempt at further delineation unnecessary. One powerful, and proximate, cause of emigration, omitted in that volume, will be given in this,—The Siege of Londonderry and its consequences.

The two distinct families of the British Empire met in Virginia, in circumstances well calculated to stimulate to vehement exercise the principles of both, in civil and religious matters. Their mutual action and reaction improved both parties; and Virginia is, now, what neither, singly, could have made her. Both had fixed principles of civil and religious liberty; but their views of liberty in the State, and in the Church, were somewhat different both in theory and practice. The scions of the Old English stock, in the "ancient dominion," considered, the enjoyment of religious ordinances established, maintained, and defended, by the State, undisturbed and unawed by any foreign power, to be religious liberty, the liberty of the majority, the liberty of an independent State.

The Scotch Irishman, on the frontier, thought freedom of choice in regard to doctrines of belief,—forms of worship,—and ordinances of religion,—and the undisputed and undisturbed exercise of this choice, confirmed to every member of society, and defended by law, made religious liberty.

The civil liberty of the English scion was the liberty of Englishmen, of the national church, in England,—the liberty of King, Lords and Commons, with different grades in society, acting independently of all foreign powers. The Scotch Irishman thought freedom of person,—the right of possession of property in fee simple,—and an open road to civil honours, secured to the poorest and feeblest member of society, constituted civil liberty.

When these races came in collision, and their first meeting was a collision, there was exasperation and persecution; the strong arm of the law avenged the complaining Establishment on the sturdy defender of Calvinistic Presbytery. But when the soft hand of the seaboard grasped, in friendship, the toil hardened hand of the frontier, the "ancient dominion" gave refinement of manners, and received back religious freedom, on the only true and firm foundation, the Being, Attributes and Government of God, as revealed in the Gospel of his Son, our Lord Jesus Christ. And the blending powers gave being and life to the civil liberty of Virginia, the mother of Presidents and of States.

CHAPTER V.

SIEGE OF LONDONDERRY: ITS CONNEXION WITH THE VALLEY OF VIRGINIA.

THE Siege of Londonderry, a small, badly fortified city, on the West bank of the Foyle, in the province of Ulster, Ireland, forms an important chapter in the history of the Protestant succession in England. It is particularly interesting to multitudes in the United States, whose ancestors sustained the siege, shared in the joy of the victory, but not in the advantages, and finally became exiles, to the wilds of America, to enjoy a Protestantism too pure for England, or the nations of Europe. It is an unquestionable fact of history, though it may be slow in finding its place in volumes written by English hands for English eyes, that the shutting the gates of Derry, Friday, Dec. 7th, 1688, by the APPRENTICE BOYS, followed by the distressing siege of eight weary months, in which the Irish forces of James II, assisted by troops from France, heaped upon the inhabitants, and the soldiers gathered within the narrow walls, all that can be endured by mortal famished man,—ending, as the siege finally did, in the disgraceful departure of the popish forces,—turned the scale in favour of William of Nassau and secured to him the crown of England, and to the country at large the succession of Protestant Kings and Queens that have filled the throne to this day.

Had the gates of Derry remained open, or had the siege terminated in the early capitulation of the city, the forces from France and Ireland would have gone to Scotland to act in concert with the famous Claver'se in favour of James. Who can calculate the effects of that union of forces? Even supposing the hour of Claver'se had come, and he must fall in some indecisive victory, James might have defended his crown against his son in law, the Prince of Orange, if not to victory, at least to a prolonged and sanguinary contest. James had the rare fortune to turn all favourable circumstances and events against himself, and a singular inability to turn adversity to his favour. But the Scotch and Irish and French forces united under able leaders would have tasked both the courage and ability of William and his followers. Londonderry broke up all arrangements. Her siege consumed the money, the provisions, and the men that were to vindicate the rights of James. Claver'se waited, and in despair gained his last victory, and died an ignobly glorious death. Scotland was lost to James. Ireland, then the field of contest, was abandoned after the battle of the Boyne. James felt his crown was lost. But had Derry been possessed in time, the battle of the Boyne could not have been fought; the decisive battle would have been elsewhere. It is a matter of surprise, and scarcely to be accounted for, that a place so badly fortified as Derry could have held out so long. An experienced commander, exclaimed at a glance,—"It is impossible a military man should have attempted its defence: or that such an one should have failed in its reduction."

William of Orange landed in England on the 5th of November, 1688. That may be considered as the first act of hostility. James, in the distraction of his councils, summoned his forces from Ireland. He supposed that England or Scotland must be the battle ground. Lord Mountjoy who had possession of Derry, with a regiment of disciplined soldiers, left this little town, in the extreme north of Ireland, vacant, and hastened to the aid of James. The aged Earl of Antrim was ordered to occupy it with his regiment of Papists, loyal in principle, but less disciplined and incomparably less trustworthy than the forces of Mountjoy. The Papists of Ireland had never been reconciled to the Protestant emigration that occupied so large a portion of the province of Ulster. They were continually fomenting quarrels and making inroads. James I, the Charleses, as well as Cromwell had found it necessary to pacify Ireland with an armed force. James II. had no better experience of the friendship of the Papists for the English Church; or for himself till he made it evident he designed re-establishing the Roman Catholic forms and ceremonies. When the Prince of Orange took arms against James, the Papists in Ireland rallied in his defence. France sent money and an armed force to Ireland. In the course of the military movements that succeeded, Derry became the theatre of events great in their consequences to the king and the people, the Church and the State.

In the great emigration from England and Scotland promoted by James I. the northern part of the province was given to the citizens of London on condition they would fortify Londonderry and Coleraine. The country prospered in the hands of the Protestants who had resorted thither from London and other parts of the kingdom. With the increase of wealth, industry and population, there were no symptoms of increased friendship between the native Irish who were Papists and the immigrants who were Protestants. On the 3d of December, 1688, a letter was found in Cumber, county Down, informing Earl Mount Alexander, that on the succeeding Sabbath, the 9th of the month, the Irish throughout the Island, were to massacre the Protestants, men, women, and children; and that a Captain's commission would be the reward of him that killed the Earl, whom the writer as a personal friend urged to be on his guard. The Earl spread the alarm by sending copies of the letter through the country as far as Dublin. In the progress of the news it was found that other gentlemen had received similar warning. Expresses were sent to all the Protestant towns. The news reached Derry, on Thursday the 6th, while the place was yet vacant of any military force. The alarm here, as every where else, was great. Many circumstances concurred in producing belief in the rumoured conspiracy,—such as the massacre in 1641, which had not been general for want of power and concert,—the sermons and addresses of the priests at the mass houses,—the directions known to be given to the Irish every where to procure themselves good arms, —the busy preparation of skeins, or long knives by the blacksmiths throughout the kingdom,—and the repeated declarations amongst the Papists that some great event was about to take place advantageous to their cause. Every where the Protestants were aroused.

The messenger that brought the news to Derry, reported the forces of the Earl of Antrim to be near the city; that the advanced guard was within three or four miles when he passed. The city was filled with consternation at the double danger. The Rev. James Gordon, Presbyterian minister of Clondomet, near Derry, being in the town, and consulted by Alderman Tompkins, advised *to shut the gates and exclude the soldiery;* as the walls of the town were sufficient protection against forces unprovided with artillery. The aged and pious Bishop Hopkins, being also in town, was consulted by Alderman Norman, and gave his opinion against shutting the gates, as such a measure would irritate the soldiers of Antrim, and the inhabitants were not prepared for a siege. The terrified inhabitants assembled in groups; and here and there is heard a threat from the young men, the apprentices,—for Derry was extensively engaged in the manufacture of linen,—to shut the gates. The men in authority were engaged in discouraging any outbreak of passion; and were miserably hesitating between submission and resistance. Two companies of the advancing forces having reached the river, the commanding officers were ferried over the Foyle, and called for a conference with the city authorities, to adjust the manner of admission and the disposition of the forces. The Deputy Mayor, John Buchanan, was for giving them an immediate and honourable reception; Horace Kennedy, one of the Sheriffs, was for shutting the gates; the others were hesitating. The young men were assembled waiting the result and a signal from Kennedy. The discussion was prolonged. The soldiers, anxious to get to their expected quarters, without orders, began to cross the river and to approach the ferry gate. The young men took the alarm. Some ran to the guard, seized the keys, and hasting to the gates, shut them in the face of the soldiers. The other gates were speedily shut and secured. The names of the apprentices that led the way in this exploit, were Henry Campsie, William Crookshanks, Robert Sherrard, Daniel Sherrard, Alexander Irwin, James Stewart, Robert Morrison, Alexander Coningham, William Cairns, and Samuel Harvey. From the gates the young men hastened to the magazine, where their leader, Henry Campsie, is wounded by the guard, a reputed Papist. The sight of blood aggravated the populace. All the efforts of the Deputy Mayor, the Bishop, and the officers of Antrim, who were in the town, could not prevail on the people to open the gates. "The dull heads of the men of Londonderry"—says Makenzie—"could not comprehend how it could be a great crime to shut the gates against those whom they believed had been sent to cut their throats." Archbishop King observes—" No man could blame the youthful heroes for their decision on the occasion; they were startled even at the external appearance of the pack of ruffians now approaching the city, attended by crowds of ferocious women and armed boys; many of the captains and other officers of the regiment were well known there, having been confined in the goal for thefts and robberies."

The soldiers become impatient waiting at the gates, and clamour for admittance. The discussion is still going on between the officers and the leaders of the people. One James Morrison mounted the walls, and bid the soldiers "begone." As they refused to leave the gates, he turned around and cried out,—" bring about a great gun here." Immediately the soldiers fled, and re-crossed the river, to the main body. On Saturday the 8th, the Bishop left the place for his castle of Raphoe, and the greater part of the Papists departed from the city. Many of the Protestants in the surrounding country came within the walls for protection; and the inhabitants became more unanimous in the defence of the place.

The dreaded Sunday passed. There was no massacre. It will probably remain a mystery for ever to what extent a massacre was intended, whether for the whole Protestant population, or some neighbourhoods; and also whether the conspiracy failed from want of concert, or from the alarm that had aroused the whole country. But with the day, the fears of the Protestants of Derry did not pass. They kept the city closed and guarded. The forces of Antrim commenced the siege. News that the Prince of Denmark, the Duke of Ormond, and many of the nobility, had joined the Prince of Orange, encouraged the inhabitants of Derry to maintain their rights and defend their lives. The soldiers watched an opportunity to enter the town; and the inhabitants were on the alert to prevent surprise. The number of men in the city able to bear arms was small, not exceeding three hundred. About the same number might have been in the suburbs. The space included by the walls was small, of an oval form, its greatest diameter being about two thousand feet, the shortest about six hundred, situated on rising ground in the bend of the river on the west bank of the Foyle.

The Protestants and Papists, in the North of Ireland, passed the winter in military preparations and skirmishes, ranged as they now were, the one for King William, was proclaimed in January 1689, and the other for James, who had fled to France. The forces of James gradually got the better of the Protestants, and wrested from them one town after another, till few places besides Derry were left in their possession.

James, assisted by the troops and money of Lewis XIV. landed in Ireland the 12th of March 1689. After a short stay in Dublin, he marched with twelve thousand men, and a train of artillery, intending to overrun the province of Ulster, cross to Scotland, unite with Claverhouse, Viscount Dundee, and make a descent on England. By the 18th of the month he appeared before Derry. All other places submitted, except Inneskillen. The Protestant forces were dispersed, or gathered within the ramparts of these two places. The inhabitants of the country fled, in great numbers, at the approach of James; and when he commenced the regular siege and destructive bombardment of the city, there were crowded in the narrow space of the oblong walls of Derry, about twenty thousand people, men, women, and children, besides seven thousand three hundred soldiers armed for defence, but illy provided with artillery or ammunition. On the fate of Derry hung the fate of Ulster, and of Ireland. James is contending for his crown; the Protestants for religion and the blessings of a government of law; and neither is aware of the full importance of the struggle that is going on around the walls of that little city.

Colonel Lundy who commanded the forces within the city, in council with some of his officers, drew articles of capitulation, agreeably to a promise he had sent the king; and James waited, on horseback, through a whole drizzly day, without eating, to receive the articles, and make his repast within the walls. Many of the principal men were in favour of surrender; but the great body of the people were opposed, and under the guidance of Captain Adam Murray, a gallant Presbyterian gentleman, expressed their feelings so strongly, that Lundy first secreted himself, and then escaped from the city in disguise of a pedlar of matches. Major Henry Baker, and the Rev. George Walker, an Episcopal clergyman, from the county of Tyrone, advanced in years, a strenuous defender of the Protestant cause, who had taken refuge in Derry, were chosen governors. The armed forces were divided into eight regiments, with proper officers; Baker and Walker each retaining the command of one. James, wearied with the life in camp, returned to Dublin. By his inconsistent course he fixed the wavering Protestants in favour of his rival, and scarce made an attempt to gain the affections of those whom he subdued.

As Derry was the only remaining obstacle in Ireland, its reduction became an object of immediate importance. On the 18th of June, Count De Rosen entered the camp, with fifteen hundred men, to take the command and press the siege to a conclusion. The friends in Scotland were anxiously waiting the arrival of the French forces, and the supply of money. The siege therefore became more close, the assaults more frequent, the bombardment more severe. The besieged endured wounds, famine, pestilence, and all the miseries of a population crowded into a small area, and all exposed to the fire of the enemy. Their sufferings increased with the heat of summer. They were aggravated by the want of pure water. The wells were drawn low by the multitude, and the water became impure from the shaking of the foundations of the city, by the discharge of cannon from the walls, and from the camp of the enemy. The water from the clouds was tainted with brimstone from the showers of balls and shells that fell upon their roofs without intermission.

About the middle of June, Walker says in his journal—"Fever, dysentery and other diseases became very general, and a great mortality existed among the garrison and inhabitants of the city. In one day no less than fifteen commissioned officers died." The havoc among the besieged was immense. It is stated on good authority that upwards of twenty-seven thousand persons were shut in the city at the commencement of the siege. Of these, it is agreed, that about *one-third* perished; more than a thousand per month, or two hundred and fifty per week, or about thirty-five or six every day.

"On the 9th of July"—says Walker—"the allowance was a pound of tallow dignified by the name of French butter, to every soldier in the garrison. They mixed it with meal, ginger, pepper and anisseed, and made excellent pancakes."— "Charming meat"—says Captain Ash—"for during the preceding fortnight, horseflesh was eaten; and at this time the carcase of a dog was reckoned good meat. The famine became more severe and was aggravated by disease. Oatmeal, which before the siege, was sold for four pence the peck, could not be bought for less than six shillings. Butter sold for five pence the ounce. Other food was proportionably dear. Captain Ash mentions a poor famished man that dressed his dog to satisfy the cravings of his stomach. An equally hungry creditor enters and demands a debt, just as the feast was prepared. The debtor was unable to pay; the creditor was inexorable; and the dainty morsel was resigned to satisfy the claim.

On the 27th of July the market prices were, according to Walker's diary—Horseflesh one shilling and eight pence per pound; a quarter of a dog four shillings and six pence; a dog's head two shillings and six pence; a cat four shillings and six pence; a rat one shilling; a mouse six pence; a pound of tallow four shillings; a pound of salted hides one shilling; a quart of horse blood one shilling; a horse pudding six pence;

a quart of meal, when found, one shilling. A small fluke, a little fish, taken in the river could not be purchased for money, and could be got only in exchange for meal. "Mr. James Cunningham showed them"—says Walker—"where was a considerable quantity of starch, which they mixed with tallow, and fried as pancakes. This food proved a providential remedy for the dysentery which prevailed in the city, from excessive fatigue, mental anxiety, and unwholesome food."

On Sabbath, the last day of June, Governor Henry Baker died. His prudence, resolution, gentlemanly behaviour, patience and freedom from jealousy, rendered his loss to the garrison irreparable. Some days before his death, a council, in his sick room, united with him in appointing Col. Mitchelburn as his successor. There had been formerly a difference between these two men; this settlement of it proclaims at once the honourable standing of Mitchelburn, and the nobleness of Baker.

A graphic description of the actors and events of the eight months, appeared in a historical drama published soon after the siege. One scene characterizes the good humour of the heroic defenders of Derry amidst their severest sufferings. Mitchelburn is represented as giving a dinner to Governor Walker and four distinguished ladies. He thus addresses his guests at table,— "Gentlemen and Ladies—the first dish you see, in slices, is the liver of one of the enemy's horses that was killed the other day: it is very good meat, with pepper and salt, eaten cold. I have seven of these livers boiled, and after they are pickled they eat very well. This other is horse's blood fried with French butter, otherwise tallow, and thickened with oat meal. The third dish is what we call in French, ragout de chien,—in English, a ragout of the haunch of my dog; it does not eat so well boiled as roasted; but it eats best when baked. I have a horse's head in the oven, very well seasoned, but it will not be eatable till night."

On the day Governor Baker died, Mareschal de Rosen sent a declaration into Derry, that unless the place were surrendered that day, he would drive all the Protestants from Inneskillen to Charlemont, under the walls, and then make a general assault. On the next day he issued the following order—"As I have certain information that a considerable number of the wives and children of the rebels in Londonderry, have retired to Belfast and the neighbouring places, and as the hardness of their husbands and fathers deserves the severest chastisement, I write this letter to acquaint you, that you are instantly to make an exact search in Belfast and its neighbourhood, after such subjects as are rebellious to the King, whether men women boys or girls, without exception, and whether they are protected or unprotected, to arrest them and collect them together, that they may be conducted to this camp and driven under the walls of London-derry, where they shall be allowed to starve, in sight of the rebels within the town, unless they choose to open their ports to them." On the next day, the second of July, he drove about three thousand men, women and children, without respect to age or condition, sickness or health, to the walls of Derry, and there left them exposed, having first plundered them of food and clothing. On the next day he drove about a thousand more to join the naked starving company. Cries and lamentations resound from the walls, and from this wretched multitude. On the one side were the horrors of a siege, on the other naked-ness, and famine in the open air and upon the wet ground. Yet no voice from the common people proposed a surrender. The magistrates erected a gallows on a prominent part of the walls, and sent to De Rosen for a priest to come and confess the pri-soners, some of whom were officers of distinction, in preparation for death, as unless the multitude around the walls were sent away speedily, these prisoners should be hanged upon the gal-lows in sight of their friends in the camp. The distressed people around the walls exhorted the townsmen to hold out, and not be moved by their sufferings. The officers in De Rosen's camp exclaimed against the barbarity exercised upon the people under the walls and the ignominious death that awaited their friends, prisoners in the city. On the fourth of July, De Rosen gave permission for the unhappy people under the walls to re-turn to their homes, having kept some of them two, and others three days, without food. Hundreds were left dead under the walls, from the three days' famine and exposure; hundreds perished from hunger and fatigue before they reached their homes; and multitudes more were soon laid in their graves from the exposures of this dreadful pilgrimage, and the privations they suffered after their return to their homes plundered of every comfort, and many burned to the ground by the soldiery and the Rapparees. De Rosen plead as his excuse for this barbarity, the usages of the Continental commanders with whom he had served.

The women often took part in the battles that were waged almost daily around the ramparts. On the 4th of June this record was made—"the fair sex shared the glory of the defence of Londonderry on this occasion, for when the men, to whom they had, for the whole time, intrepidly carried ammunition, match, bread and drink, began to fall back, they rushed forward in a considerable number and beat back the grenadiers with stones as they attempted to climb up the trenches; and alto-gether they stemmed the torrent of war, till a reinforcement rushed from the city and repelled the assailants." The courage and endurance of the females never failed, in the sad offices of dressing the wounded and watching the sick, under the pressure of hunger and amidst scenes shocking to delicacy. They encouraged the men to maintain the siege and die honourably fighting rather than fall into the hands of the besieging papists.

About the middle of June the fleet, sent under the command of Major General Kirke, for the relief of the city, came in sight. The famished inhabitants rang the bells for joy. In consternation they saw it speedily depart. In a few days Kirke came in sight again, but did nothing effectual towards supplying the perishing inhabitants from the transports laden with provisions sent expressly for their relief. Messenger after messenger was sent from the town, and promise after promise of speedy assistance was sent back. The fleet again disappeared, and again returned to the sight of the famished inhabitants and mocked their hopes with the heavily laden transports. The General suffered in his reputation for these manœuvres, and made no satisfactory statement, further than his fears that his fleet could not encounter the fortifications, nor break the boom thrown across the harbour.

On the 16th of July, while the horrors of the siege were accumulating on Derry, Claver'se, the firm ally of James in Scotland, noted in the history of the sufferings of the Covenanters, impatient of waiting longer for the French and Irish forces detained at Derry, and irritated by the advance of the forces of King William into Scotland, gives battle at Killikrankie. Rushing on with his usual impetuosity he routed the opposing flanks, and pressing on to cut off their retreat through a narrow pass, he outrode his troops. Wheeling and raising his right hand above his head, to beckon his men, he received a fatal wound through the opening in his armour, and fell about the setting of the sun. His men gathered around him, carried him to his quarters, dressed his wound, and tried to cheer his spirits. The route of William's forces was complete. On the next day, having received a detail of the victory and dictated a letter to James, entreating a reinforcement, and stating that his wound was severe, but, he was told, not mortal, this scourge of the Covenanters passed to his last account. With him perished the fruits of his victory, and all the hopes of James in Scotland. The Siege of Derry must continue till the cause of James was ruined.

At last, when the last rations in Derry were dealt out to the famished inhabitants,—a half a pint of meal per man, when all were in dismay and certain expectation of death, their relief came. The ships were once more in sight. The starving inhabitants and unconquered soldiers gloated upon the distant fleet that tantalized their misery. But the fleet now came into the harbour. The Rev. James Gordon of Clondomat, near

Derry, who advised to the shutting of the gates, was compelled to leave his congregation by the barbarity of the besieging forces, and fled to Scotland. Hearing of the delay of Kirke, and the assigned reasons, he took a boat at Greenock, crossed over Loch Foyle, and got on board the fleet, and endeavoured by arguments and reproaches to stimulate the officers and men to afford the necessary relief. Kirke had a private interview with him, and for a time seemed doubtful whether to consider him a friend or a rash disorganizer. Gordon gave Kirke a plan of the harbour from his own knowledge, and finally persuaded him that the relief of the city was in his power. Kirke never mentioned this interview in any of his accounts of the siege. There is, however, no doubt of its having taken place.

About six o'clock in the afternoon of the Sabbath, July 28th, a moderate gale springing up, from the Northwest, the Dartmouth weighed anchor and stood towards Culmore. The fort immediately opened a brisk cannonade. Captain Leake fired neither great nor small shot, till he came on the wind of the castle; then he began to batter the walls, and sheltered the transports, casting anchor within musket shot of the fort. The Mountjoy passed the fort accompanied by the long boat of the Swallow prepared to cut the boom. She sailed on through a well directed fire from both sides of the river, and striking against the boom is repelled and runs aground. Her gallant commander is killed at the same moment by a musket ball. Favoured by the rising tide, and rebounding from a broadside discharged for the purpose, the Mountjoy soon floated again; and the boatswain's mate of the Swallow having cut the boom, the vessel once more in motion, by its weight breaks through that formidable barrier. The Phœnix followed by the Mountjoy, and towed all the way by the Swallow's boats, reached the quay about ten o'clock in the evening, to the inexpressible joy of the famished garrison, who had been watching with intense interest every turn and pause in their progress up the river. In two days the Siege of Derry was raised, and the cause of James was hopeless.

De Rosen despaired of bringing the city to a surrender and withdrew his army. The besiegers lost about nine thousand men around the walls of Derry, and about a hundred of the best officers perished. The joy of the besieged knew no bounds. Public thanksgivings to Almighty God were rendered by the people at large, and private rejoicings filled every house, that the hand of the destroyer was stayed. The news of the relief of Derry reached William at Hampton Court, on the 4th of August, by a messenger despatched by Kirke the morning after the vessels reached the quay; and to him it was the happy assurance that his crown was safe, and the war in fact decided. Scotland rejoiced in the happy termination of that siege, which had been the indirect means of the downfall of one who had hunted his fellow Protestants like a remorseless bloodhound. The whole land echoed the praises of the brave defenders of Derry: and William loaded some of the leading men with rich presents. But many of the greatest labourers shared the smallest permanent advantages.

Of the commanding officers in the Siege of Derry, such as colonels and field officers, the majority were of the Church of England. Of the captains and inferior officers the majority were Presbyterians; and of the soldiers and the inhabitants, there were fifteen Presbyterians to one Episcopalian. And yet, after this important siege, while the Episcopal Church was established in England, and the Presbyterians in Scotland, in Ireland,—where there was a mixture of Presbyterians and Episcopalians,—the Presbyterians, by whose bravery and sufferings the kingdom had been secured to the Prince of Orange, were compelled, after the Government was settled, to pay their tithes to the established church, and maintain their own ministers, and also to suffer other disabilities consequent on an Establishment. The soldiers in this siege were never paid the common wages of soldiers, for their sufferings from disease and famine, and their exposure to the worst forms of death. After two and thirty years of fruitless negotiations, there remained due to the eight regiments upwards of £74,000 sterling, not a farthing of which was ever paid.

The endurance of such multiplied sufferings by the people of Derry, in a place so small and rendered offensive by the putrid corpses of the multitudes that perished, for whom only the slightest burial could be obtained, and that slight burial torn up by dogs and the shot and shells from the enemy's camp, is marvellous; and that in the midst of their sufferings they should answer the summons to surrender, by the resolution—"*that no man on the pain of death should speak of surrendering the city,*" cannot be accounted for except that in their strong adherence to strong principles, the Almighty God held them up. That the feeble looking walls, which to human appearance might so easily have been battered down, remained unshaken; and the town which lay so fair to the shot of the enemy, should have escaped destruction, is wonderful. When De Rosen first beheld the place, he expressed his utter contempt, and declared "he would make his men bring it to him stone by stone"—and impiously swore, "by the belly of God," that he would demolish it and bury the defenders in its ruins. But the threatened walls stand yet.

After Ireland was subdued to the government of William, and the prospects of the Presbyterians not much improved even by the Toleration Act, reports full of hope from America reached the people of Ulster, and lured them once more to try the Atlantic. More than half a century had passed since the *Eagle Wing* had sailed and been driven back. Once more emigrants venture out, and the smiles of Providence are on their voyage. A part of the work for which they had been detained in Ireland was fully accomplished; and now they were sent to act an important part in the wilds of America. Ship load after ship load sailed for America from Ulster. And not a few from Derry sought the provinces in the new world. For half a century the emigration filled the frontiers of Pennsylvania and Virginia. One lady, whose ashes repose in the oldest burying ground in the Valley of the Shenandoah, that of the Opeckon church, and whose descendants in Virginia, Kentucky, Indiana, and Tennessee, are reckoned by scores and by hundreds, used to speak with tears of that memorable siege, and lament in bitterness "two fair brothers," whose death filled up in part the measure of sufferings at Derry. Devotedly pious herself, she is honoured by the fact, that a large proportion of her descendants have professed the religion of their mother, Mary Gamble Glass, the wife of Samuel Glass, and sister of the Gambles that settled in Augusta. And in Augusta those brothers reared families worthy of their ancestry; their names are not unknown in Virginia and the South. The names of the "*Apprentices*" are familiar names in the Valley of the Shenandoah.

The principles in exercise at Derry, were the principles to fit men for subduing a wilderness, and building a State, where there should be no king, no state religion.

Note.—For a more extended history of the Siege of Derry—consult Graham's History of the Siege—and Reed's History of the Presbyterian Church in Ireland.

CHAPTER VI.

PRESBYTERIAN COLONIES IN VIRGINIA.

FOR some years after the death of Makemie there was no congregation or colony of Presbyterians in Virginia. There were families of Scotch and Scotch Irish scattered through the province engaged in trade. Their influence in the colony was small. There were some families that had connected themselves with the Presbyterian church in the time of Makemie, but not in neighbourhoods sufficient to sustain a pastor. The colony of persecuted French Huguenots that had been invited to Virginia, and seated on the James River a little above Richmond, and protected in their worship, had voluntarily scattered and become intermingled with the English population in the neighbouring counties. The fairest opportunity was given to the Established Church to show her power and usefulness. Could she have possessed a sufficient number of pious men devoted to the work of the ministry, such as Blair attempted to provide by the College of William and Mary, she would now be the prominent and popular church, below the head of tide water in Virginia.

The majority of the numerous Presbyterian families, in Virginia, are descendants of emigrants from Presbyterian countries in Europe. Poverty and intolerance drove them from their mother country, and the necessity of providing a frontier line of brave people west of the Blue Mountains, compelled Virginia to relax her rigor and open her borders. There was never a large colony of Scotch in Virginia, though multitudes of Scotch families have been scattered through the land. The Presbyterians in Ulster province, Ireland, found their situation less agreeable than they had reason to expect, under William and Mary, and Anne, and George 1st, and George 2d. The Episcopal Church was favoured in England, the Presbyterian in Scotland; in Ireland the Presbyterians of Ulster were taxed to support the Established Church of England, which was not more numerous or loyal. From the time of the Eagle Wing to the siege of Derry, the emigration to America had been small. In the early part of the Eighteenth Century the emigration began, and like the mighty rivers in the new world, went on in a widening and deepening current, to pour into the vast forests of America, multitudes of hardy enterprising people. All the colonies from New York southward were enriched by ship loads of these people that came with little money, but with strong hands and stout hearts, and divine principles, to improve their own condition, and bless the province that gave them a home. A few congregations were formed in the New England States; one in New Hampshire at Londonderry in 1719;—another at Pelham, Massachusetts, and a small one in Boston about 1727. Pennsylvania offered the greatest attractions; and the banks of the Delaware gave the first rest to these pilgrims of "the green isle." The beautiful unoccupied regions in Pennsylvania, east of the mountains, were soon filled with thriving congregations. Holmes tells us, that in 1729—"there arrived in Pennsylvania from Europe, 6208 persons, for the purpose of settling in that colony." Of these more than five thousand were from Ireland. Mr. Samuel Blair writing about the congregation of New Londonderry, in Fagg's Manor, states—"The congregation has not been erected above fourteen or fifteen years from this time, (1740); the place is a new settlement, generally settled with people from Ireland, as all our congregations in Pennsylvania, except two or three, chiefly are made up of people from that kingdom." This congregation therefore must have been settled previously to the year 1726.

After the choice locations in Pennsylvania and Maryland were filled up, the emigrants crossed the Potomac, and stretched rapidly to the Catawba, along the frontiers in Virginia and North Carolina. Great efforts were made by the civil authorities, in Virginia, to induce these adventurous people to take their residence in the vast wilderness of the "Ancient Dominion." The protection of the frontiers was an object of legislation at an early period. In 1664, in order to prevent those murders, which the weakness of remote settlements invited from the savages, *it was ordered*—"that noe person shall hereafter seate above the plantations already seated, but with forceable hands well armed, at his first setting down." In the year 1679, the Legislature determined to build four houses for garrisons, on—"the heads of the ffower greate rivers,—att the head of Potomack river, Nicapico near Occoquon,—att the head of Rappahannock,—att the head of the Mattapony at or above the Indian townes,—att the head of James River, on the South side, above Capt. William Bird's;—and that every forty tithables within this colony be assessed and obleged to fitt out and sett forth one able and sufficient man and horse with furniture well and completely armed with a case of good pistols, carbine or short gunn, and a sword." This law was found inadequate, and was soon repealed, and the defence of the country committed to a company of Rangers. The same year encouragement was given to individuals to plant villages;—"Major Lawrence Smith will settle or seate, at or near the place on the Rappahannock River, where the ffort was built the yeare 1676, and have in readiness upon all occasions, at beate of drum, ffifty able men well armed, in defence of the inhabitants of Rappahannoc." The conditions was that he should "seate" two hundred men, besides the fifty soldiers, within the space of one mile along the bank of the river, and one fourth of a mile back from the river's edge, over whom he should exercise military authority. For these things he was to have about fourteen thousand acres of land lying along the river five and a half miles in length and four miles in breadth. An agreement was made by William Bird for a military colony, at the falls on James River, in consideration of a tract of land lying each side of the falls, about five miles in length and four in breadth. In 1701, large bodies of land, from ten to thirty thousand acres with exemption from taxes for twenty years, to companies settling on the frontiers,—on conditions, that there should be, in two years, on the land, one able bodied well armed man ready for defence, for every five hundred acres; and that these should live in a village of two hundred acres area, in the form of a square or parallelogram, laid off in lots near the centre of the tract; and that a fort should be built in the centre of the town. In 1705 it was enacted that every person, male or female, coming into the colony, for the purpose of making settlement, be entitled to fifty acres of land: families to have fifty acres for each member; no persons possessing less than five tithable servants or slaves, were permitted to take more than five hundred acres; and no persons whatever were to take up more than four thousand acres in one patent. These laws did not produce the effect designed. Villages did not spring up along the frontier as had been expected.

The settlements in the Valley of Virginia were not made in consequence of these laws, whose provisions were offensive. They were effected principally by the labours of three individuals to whom Governor Gooch made grants of extensive tracts of land, on condition that within a given time a certain number of permanent settlers should be located on the grants; Burden in Rockbridge County, Beverly in Augusta, and the Vanmeters on Opeckon in Frederick. Great efforts were made by these gentlemen to persuade emigrants from Europe and also from Pennsylvania and New Jersey, to take their residence in the Valley of the Shenandoah. Advertisements, describing in glowing terms the beauty and fertility of the valley, and offering a home to the poor emigrant on easy terms, were sent abroad in every direction, and attracted the attention of the hard working tenants in England, Ireland and Germany, to whom the offer of a farm in fee simple was the offer of wealth.

Joist Hite having obtained the grant of the Vanmeters, came in the year 1732, with sixteen families from Pennsylvania, and fixed his residence on the Opeckon, a few miles south of the present town of Winchester, on the Great Valley route, at a place now in possession of the Barton family. His three sons in law, Bowman Chrisman and Froman went a few miles further south. Peter Stephens took his residence where Stephensburg, Newtown, now is. The other families were scattered on Cedar Creek and Crooked Run. This was the first regular settlement west of the Blue Ridge in Virginia. From this time the emigration to the Valley of the Shenandoah, and to the region at the eastern base of the Blue Ridge, was rapid.

Michael Woods, from Ireland came in the year 1734 and settled at Henderson's quarter near Wood's Gap, in Albemarle. Three sons and three sons in law came with him and settled near. One of the sons in law, William Wallace, took his resi-

dence on Mechums river, in Albemarle, and his descendants occupy in part the possessions of their ancestor.   These were the
founders of Mountain Plain Congregation.

In the same year Richard Morgan led a company to the
neighbourhood of Shephendown on the Cohongoroton or Potomac, in Jefferson County.   Among the families that came with
him we find the names of Harper, Stroop, Forrester, Friend,
Swearingen, Forman, Lucas, Lemon, Mercer, Stockton, Buckles,
Taylor, and Wright.

About the year 1735 William Hoge removed from Pennsylvania and settled on the Opeckon, about three miles south of
Winchester.   Opeckon meeting house stands upon his track of
land.   The families of Glass, Vance, Allen, Colvin, White, and
others soon joined him and formed the Opeckon Congregation,
the oldest Congregation West of the Blue Ridge.

About this time a settlement was made on Cub Creek in
Charlotte County, and one on Buffalo Creek in Prince Edward,
by the influence of Mr. Caldwell; the former was then in Lu-
nenberg and the latter in Amelia.   This was followed in quick
succession by settlements at Concord and Hat Creek in Campbell County; and Rockfish, in Nelson County, then a part of
Albemarle.

About the year 1738 the Congregations of Tinkling Spring,
Stone Church and Mossy Creek, in Augusta County; all forming the Congregation of the Triple Forks of Shenandoah took
their beginning.

Soon after, the Congregation of Timber Ridge, Forks of
James in Rockbridge, and the Congregation of Back Creek in
Berkeley County, were commenced.

On the South Branch of Potomac, in Hardy County, settlements commenced about the year 1735; and soon after on the
Cacopon, in Hardy and Hampshire Counties.

Cedar Creek, in Frederick County was first occupied by the
sons in law of Joist Hite in 1732.   But about the time that
Opeckon was settled numerous families came to the creek, and
formed a Congregation.   Cedar Creek and Opeckon have always been united in their pastoral relations.

In about ten or twelve years from the settlement of Opeckon,
which was 1735, Presbyterian Congregations of Irish origin,
more or less direct, had been settled, at Falling Waters, in
Berkeley; Elk Branch and Bull Skin in Jefferson; Peeked
Mountain in Rockingham; North Mountain and the Pastures
in Augusta; New Providence in Rockbridge; and Roanoke in
Botetourt; all in the Valley of Virginia.   The Congregations
East of the Ridge were greatly enlarged; though the fertile
Valley allured the greater number of Emigrants.

"The people of Potomoke in Virginia" mentioned in the

minutes of the Synod of Philadelphia for the year 1719, must have had their residence somewhere East of the Blue Ridge. And though reported as having been "put in Church order," no other mention is made of them on the records of Synod, nor can any certain information be gathered respecting them. It is supposed they had their residence in Fauquier or Loudon.

The families that formed the greater part of the Settlements, moved in companies, and fixed their residences in neighbourhood, for the purpose of defence against the dangers of the wilderness, gratifying their social feelings, and enjoying the privileges of religious worship. The number of emigrants became so large, and their desire for the ordinances of religion was so strong, that the subject was brought before the Synod of Philadelphia in the year 1738. On Friday, May 26th—"Upon the supplication of John Caldwell, in behalf of himself and many families of our persuasion, who are about to settle in the back parts of Virginia, desiring that some members of the Synod may be appointed to wait on that Government to solicit their favour in behalf of our interest in that place:—overtured, That according to the purport of the supplication, the Synod appoint two of their number to go and wait upon the Governour and Council of Virginia, with suitable instructions in order to procure the favour and countenance of the Government of that province to the laying a foundation of our interest in the back parts thereof, where considerable numbers of families of our persuasion are settling, and that something be allowed out of our fund to bear the charges of said brethren, who shall be appointed, and that also provision be made for supplying the congregations of said brethren during their absence from them while prosecuting that affair: and that Messrs. Robert Cross, Anderson, Conn and Orme, prosecute said affair; and that Messrs. Thompson Dickinson and Pemberton prepare instructions for the said brethren, and write a letter in the name of the Synod to said Government, to be brought in and approved by the Synod——and it is further overtured that these brethren be allowed a discretionary power of using what money they have occasion for, to bear their expenses in a manner suitable to this design being accountable to the Synod for their conduct in this whole affair. Approved nemine contradicente."

On Tuesday 30th, the following letter was presented and approved—"To the Honourable William Gooch Esquire, Lieutenant Governor of the Province of Virginia, the humble address of the Presbyterian ministers convened in Synod, May 30th, 1738. May it please your Honour, we take leave to address you in behalf of a considerable number of our brethren who are meditating a settlement in the remote parts of your

Government, and are of the same persuasion as the Church of Scotland. We thought it our duty to acquaint your Honour with this design, and to ask your favour in allowing them the liberty of their consciences, and of worshipping God in a way agreeable to the principles of their Education. Your Honour is sensible that those of our profession in Europe have been remarkable for their inviolable attachment to the house of Hanover, and have upon all occasions manifested an unspotted fidelity to our gracious Sovereign, King George, and we doubt not but these our brethren will carry the same loyal principles to the most distant settlements, where their lot may be cast, which will ever influence them to the most dutiful submission to the Government which is placed over them. This we trust will recommend them to your Honours countenance and protection, and merit the free enjoyment of their civil and religious liberties. We pray for the divine blessing upon your persons and Government, and beg leave to subscribe ourselves your Honours most humble and obedient servants."

The next year, Monday the 28th of May,—"Mr. Anderson reports that in compliance with an order of Synod, last year, he had waited upon the Governor of Virginia, with the Synod's address, and received a favourable answer, the substance of which is contained in a letter from the Governor to the Moderator of the Synod, which is as follows:—Sir: By the hands of Mr. Anderson, I received an address signed by you, in the name of your brethren of the Synod of Philadelphia. And as I have been always inclined to favour the people who have lately removed from other provinces to settle on the western side of our great mountains: So you may be assured that no interruption shall be given to any minister of your profession, who shall come among them, so as they conform themselves to the rules prescribed by the Act of Toleration in England, by taking the oaths enjoined thereby, and registering the place of their meeting, and behave themselves peaceably towards the government. This you may please to communicate to the Synod as an answer to theirs.

Your most humble servant,

WILLIAM GOOCH.

"Mr. Anderson reports that his journey to Virginia cost fifteen pounds,—which the Synod allows out of the fund."

The John Caldwell named in this transaction was grandfather to the Hon. John Caldwell Calhoun of South Carolina. The colony he was the means of introducing laid the foundation of Cub Creek—in Charlotte,—Buffaloe, and Walker's Church in

Prince Edward,—and Hat Creek and Concord in Campbell. He himself settled at Cub Creek; the greater part of the families that formed that settlement, ultimately removed to West Virginia, now Kentucky.

Mr. Anderson visited the Presbyterian settlements that were then formed in Frederick Augusta and Nelson.

The reasons that actuated Governor Gooch to promise protection, in the exercise of their religious forms, in a State whose laws for uniformity were precise and enforced with rigour, were two: 1st, he wished a frontier line at a greater distance from Williamsburg; if possible, West of the great Mountains;—2d, he knew these people to be firm, enterprising, hardy, brave, good citizens and soldiers. To form a complete line of defence against the savage inroads, he welcomed these Presbyterian emigrants,—the Quakers,—and colonies from the different German States to the beautiful and luxuriant prairies of the Great Valley of the Shenandoah, on the head waters of the James, and along the Roanoke. At so great a distance from the older settlements, he anticipated no danger or trouble to the established church of the Colony, perhaps he never seriously considered the subject in the probable influence of the necessary collision of religious opinions.

Allured by the advantages offered in the colonies, multitudes of enterprising men were ready to leave their mother country. In that age of the world it was a hard necessity, that compelled men to abandon their birthplace, and traverse the ocean and seek a home in a distant wilderness. But the hope of independence cheered that necessity, and some prospect of more freedom in religion gladdened their hearts. The banks of the Delaware became the landing place of the voluntary exiles. After a short stay with their friends and countrymen in Pennsylvania, the families removed to the inviting Valley of Virginia, or the more distant banks of the Catawba in the Carolinas. When the most inviting regions in this southern direction were occupied, the succeeding immigrants crossed the Alleghanies, and soon filled West Pennsylvania, Kentucky and Tennessee.

The Scotch Irish Presbyterians, and the Germans, that first came to America, generally sought a home with the Quakers, in the land of Penn. About the same time families from each of these races of people were enticed, by the prospective comfort and wealth of Western Virginia, to build their cabins west of the Blue Ridge, in the "ancient Dominion." These have formed the mass of community, the middle class, the yeomanry, that body that ministers the strength and wealth and energy of the State, that drops some of its members to the lowest condition of society, and elevates others to the pinnacle, that moves on in the happy medium of wealth and poverty, the storehouse of enterprise, and the treasury of men in the day of emergency.

From necessity the families were located in neighbourhoods. And to this day, the Presbyterians, the Quakers, the Germans, both Lutheran and Reformed, have preserved their identity; though each from their proximity has exercised a silent influence over the others. In some parts of the Valley, large bodies of these different people, fully able to maintain their forms of religious worship, and their habits and manners and language, have found themselves in the vicinity of each other; and have maintained their own peculiarities, somewhat improved by their new situation. In other places the companies were small and became intermingled, and connected by marriage, and lost all their peculiarities, leaving nothing to designate their origin but their names.

In the southern part of the Valley of Virginia and in the Mesopotamia of North Carolina, and large districts of South Carolina, the Scotch Irish had the pre-eminence both in time and numbers. In other sections, the other races had the ascendency. All have exerted an influence in forming the society that enjoys the personal freedom and religious liberty, for which they laboured and endured, and by united efforts gained.

These sketches must of necessity be confined to the Presbyterian part of community, and treat of their location,—their progress,—their religious exercises,—the efforts for education and general literature,—their emigration westward, and their influence on society at large.

The political creed of the Presbyterian race has been given in the Sketches of North Carolina, chapter 9th, and need not be repeated here. Their religious creed is learned from the Confession of Faith, which gives in detail their doctrines of religion in regard to faith and practice, their principles of morals, their forms of worship, their church order and discipline. This Confession has been called the Scotch Confession, or more properly the Westminster Confession. In the interpretation of the doctrines of their Confession there was great unanimity. Understanding their creed according to the accustomed use of words, and the grammatical construction of sentences, they received and professed, as their common faith, those doctrines called the doctrines of the Reformation, in the sense in which they believed the Reformers themselves understood them, and wished others to understand them. To use a common phrase—their faith was Calvinistic. There were no professed Arminians or Antinomians amongst them. In their church government and forms of worship they were Presbyterians after the Scotch, or Geneva model.

But on the subject of "experience of religion" there soon sprung up a great division. Respecting man's fallen nature,—the extent and influence of depravity and original sin,—the necessity of the influences of the Holy Spirit, in conversion to God, and in devotional exercises,—the imputation of Adam's guilt and of Christ's righteousness,—justification by faith, and the absolute necessity of the new birth,—on all these, there was perhaps little diversity of opinion. But whether true spiritual exercises implied or admitted great excitement,—whether conversion was a rapid or very gradual work,—whether evidences of grace were decisive, or necessarily obscure,—whether true revivals were attended with great alarms, deep convictions, great distress and strong hopes and fears,—whether a collegiate course of education was a necessary preparation for the ministry of the gospel,—and whether personal experience of religion should form part of the examination of candidates for the ministry,—on all these subjects there were formed two parties, which debated, with due vehemence, the proper exercises of a Christian man, and of a Christian minister. The excitement of these discussions, about the time of the Presbyterian emigration to Virginia, distracted, and finally divided the Synod of Philadelphia, which embraced all the churches, of the Presbyterian faith, north of South Carolina.

The Presbyterian Church in Ireland, of which the Presbyterian Church in America is a scion, is the fruit of a great awakening, an account of which may be seen in the Sketches of North Carolina, chap. 6th, taken mostly from Reed's History of the Presbyterian Church in Ireland. Times of great excitement were not unfrequent in Ireland. The first great awakening in the Presbyterian churches of America commenced about the year 1732, in Freehold, New Jersey, under the preaching of Rev. John Tennent, son of William Tennent of the "Log College" on the Neshaminy. He died the same year, and his brother William succeeded as pastor. The good seed sown by the deceased pastor sprung up to eternal life under the watering of his brother, and the increase of the Spirit of God. The religious excitement in Freehold continued more than ten years, and was remarkably free from acts and doings that were objectionable.

The Rev. Jonathan Edwards gives an account of a great awakening under his ministry in Northampton about the year 1734, which spread into many of the neighbouring towns, ten in Massachusetts, and seventeen in Connecticut. He makes mention of the work of grace in New Jersey.

About the year 1739 the awakening became very extensive in New Jersey, under the preaching of the Tennents, Rowland, Dickenson and Frelinghuysen. The next year it was exten-

sively experienced in New Londonderry, under the preaching
of the Rev. Samuel Blair. It soon spread over a large part of
the Presbyterian population in Pennsylvania. The public mind
was highly excited on the subject of religion, and most deeply
agitated by earnest inquiries about the true exercises of Christian people. The awakening was general in most of the Congregations in New Jersey; and prevailed extensively in New
England. Edwards's works, Prince's Christian History, and
Gillie's Collections, which are taken very much from Prince's
History, give glowing accounts of the excitements and hopeful
conversions, that attended the preaching of the word. The
awakening extended to Virginia: and there it commenced without the ordinary means, preaching the word publicly. Under
the preaching of the word it became more extended; and the
effects are felt at this time all over Virginia and Kentucky and
Tennessee, North and South Carolina.

As the awakening in Virginia, that accompanied the preaching of the gospel, was more immediately connected with the
work of grace in Pennsylvania and Delaware, some extracts
will be given from an account, drawn up by the Rev. Samuel
Blair, of the work as it appeared in New Londonderry. There
it resulted in reformation of life and manners; and a creditable
profession of religion by a number in his Congregation; and
also in drawing the attention, of surrounding Congregations, to
personal religion. The man that had the greatest religious
influence on Virginia, Samuel Davies, was trained in the Congregation of Mr. Blair; and during this work of grace, he
entered Virginia with the spirit of that awakening. Extracts
from Mr. Blair's account will be read with interest by admirers
of Davies.

Extracts from Mr. Blair's Narrative.

"It was in the Spring Anno Domini 1740 when the God of
Salvation was pleased to visit us with the blessed effusions of
his Holy Spirit in an eminent manner. The very first open and
public appearance of this gracious visitation in these parts was
in the Congregation God has committed to my charge. The
Congregation has not been erected above fourteen or fifteen
years from this time: the place is a new settlement, generally
settled with people from Ireland, as all our Congregations in
Pennsylvania, except two or three are, chiefly, made up of
people from that kingdom. I am the first minister they have
ever had settled in the place. Having been regularly liberated
from my former charge in East Jersey, above an hundred miles
north eastward from hence; (the Rev. Presbytery of New Brunswick, of which I had the comfort of being a member, judging it
to be my duty, for sundry reasons, to remove from thence) at the

earnest invitation of the people here, I came to them in the beginning of Nov. 1739,—accepted a call from them that winter,—and was formally installed and settled amongst them as their minister, in April following. There were some hopefully pious people here at my first coming, which was a great encouragement and comfort to me." The state of the Congregations generally, and of the neighbouring Congregations, was mournful. Religious experience was confined to a few; such a thing as a general attention to personal religion was unknown, though attendance on public worship was reckoned essential to the well being of society; formality had taken the place of spirituality, and the mass of the people were satisfied with the rind without ever tasting the rich meat of gospel ordinances. A consequent dissoluteness of manners was creeping in as vital religion was dying out; outward observances were usurping the place of spiritual religion. "It was thought"—says Mr. Blair— "that if there was any need of a heart distressing sight of the soul's danger, and fear of divine wrath, it was only needful for the grosser sort of sinners; and for any others to be deeply exercised this way, (as there might sometimes be some rare instances observable) this was generally looked upon to be a great evil and temptation that had befallen some persons. The common name for such soul concerns were, *melancholy*, *trouble of mind, or despair*. These terms were in common, so far as I have been acquainted, indifferently used as synonymous; and *trouble of mind* was looked upon as a great evil, which all persons that made any sober profession and practice of religion ought carefully to avoid. There was scarcely any suspicion at all, in general, of any danger of depending upon self righteousness, and not upon the righteousness of Christ alone, for salvation. Papists and Quakers would be readily acknowledged guilty of this crime, but hardly any professed Presbyterians. The necessity of being first in Christ by a vital union, and in a justified state, before our religious services can be well pleasing and acceptable to God, was very little understood or thought of; but the common notion seemed to be, that if people were aiming to be in the way of duty as well as they could, as they imagined, there was no reason to be much afraid. According to these principles, and this ignorance of some of the most soul concerning truths of the gospel, people were very generally through the land careless at heart, and stupidly indifferent about the great concerns of eternity. There was very little appearance of any hearty engagedness in religion; and indeed, the wise for the most part, were in a great degree asleep with the foolish. 'Twas sad to see with what a careless behaviour the public ordinances were attended, and how people were given to unsuitable worldly discourse on the Lord's holy day. In public companies,

especially at weddings, a vain and frothy lightness was apparent
in the deportment of many professors; and in some places very
extravagant follies, as horse running, fiddling and dancing,
pretty much obtained."

" Thus,"—continues Mr. Blair—"religion lay as it were
dying, and ready to expire its last breath of life in this part of
the visible church.   I had some view and sense of the deplorable condition of the land in general; and accordingly the scope
of my preaching through that first winter after I came here
was mainly calculated for persons in a natural unregenerate
estate.   I endeavoured, as the Lord enabled me, to open up
and prove from his word, the truths, which I judged most necessary for such as were in that state, to know and believe, in
order to their conviction and conversion.   I endeavoured to deal
searchingly and solemnly with them, and, through the blessing
of God, I had knowledge of four or five brought under deep
convictions that winter."

Mr. Blair made a journey to East Jersey in March 1740.
A neighbouring minister, whose name he does not give—supposed to be either Mr. Craighead, afterwards famed in North
Carolina, or Mr. Gillespie,—" who appeared to be earnest for
the awakening and conversion of secure sinners," preached the
next Sabbath in his charge, from the words in Luke xiii. 7th.
Then said he to the dresser of his vineyard, behold, these
three years I come seeking fruit on this fig tree, and find none,
cut it down, why cumbereth it the ground—Under that sermon
great feeling was expressed,—" Some burst out with an audible
noise into bitter crying; a thing not known in these parts."
The news of this appearance of deep concern met Mr. Blair a
hundred miles from home, and rejoiced his heart.   Hastening
home he preached from Matthew vi. 33d, Seek ye first the
kingdom of God and his righteousness; and while he was
pressing the unconverted with reasons why they should seek
the kingdom and righteousness of God, he offered as one
reason—"that they had neglected too—too long—to do so
already"—many could not contain themselves but burst out
into the most bitter mourning.   Checking this outburst of
feeling he finished his discourse.

One young man came to converse with him on his soul's concerns, who had been a light merry youth.   He said he had
heard the sermon from Luke—cut it down—without concern.
On the next day—" he went to his labour which was grubbing,
in order to clear some new ground; the first grub he set about
was a pretty large one, with a high top, and when he had cut
the roots, as it fell down, those words came instantly to his
remembrance, and as a spear to his heart,—Cut it down, why
cumbereth it the ground—So thought he must I be cut down

by the justice of God, for the burning of hell, unless I get into another state than I am now in. He thus came into very great and abiding distress, which, to all appearance, has had a happy issue, his conversation being to this day as becomes the gospel of Christ."

Mr. Blair goes on to say—"I think there was scarcely a sermon, or lecture preached here through that whole summer, but there was manifest evidence of impressions on the hearers, and many times the impressions were very great and general; several would be overcome and fainting; others deeply sobbing hardly able to contain, others crying in a most dolorous manner, many others more silently weeping, and a solemn concern appearing in the countenances of many others. And sometimes the soul exercises of some, though comparatively but few, would so far affect their bodies as to occasion some strange, unusual bodily motions. I had opportunities of speaking particularly with a great many of those who afforded such outward tokens of inward soul concern in the time of public worship and hearing of the word; indeed many came to me of themselves in their distress, for private instruction and counsel; and I found, so far as I can remember, that, with far the greater part, their apparent concern in public was not just a transient qualm of conscience, or merely a floating commotion of the affections; but a rational fixed conviction of their dangerous perishing estate. They could generally offer, as a convictive evidence of their being in an unconverted miserable estate,— that they were utter strangers to those dispositions, exercises, and experiences of soul in religion, which they heard laid down from God's word as the inseparable characters of the truly regenerate people of God; even such as before had something of the form of religion; and I think the greater number were of this sort, and several had been pretty exact and punctual in the performance of outward duties. They saw that true practical religion was quite another thing, than they had conceived it to be, or had any true experience of.

"In this congregation, I believe there were very few that were not stirred up to some solemn thoughtfulness and concern more than usual about their souls. Those awakened were much given to reading in the Holy Scriptures and other good books. Excellent books, that had lain by much neglected, were then much perused, and lent from one to another, and it was a peculiar satisfaction to people to find how exactly the doctrines they heard daily preached, harmonize with the doctrines maintained and taught by great and godly men in other parts and former times."

"There was an earnest desire in people after opportunities for public worship and hearing of the word. I appointed in the spring to preach every Friday through the summer when I was at home; and those meetings were well attended, and at several of them the power of the Lord was remarkably with us. The main scope of my preaching, through that summer, was laying open the deplorable state of man by nature since the fall,—our ruined and exposed case by the breach of the first covenant,—and the awful condition of such as were not in Christ,—giving the marks and characters of such as were in that condition;—and moreover laying open the way of recovery in the new covenant, through a Mediator,—with the nature and necessity of faith in Christ, the Mediator. I laboured much on the last mentioned heads, that people might have right apprehensions of the gospel method of life and salvation. I treated much on the way of a sinner's closing with Christ by faith,—and obtaining a right peace to an awakened wounded conscience,—showing that persons were not to take peace to themselves on account of their repentings, sorrows, prayers, and reformations,—nor to make these things the ground of their adventuring themselves upon Christ, and his righteousness, and of their expectations of life in him;—and that neither were they to obtain or seek peace in extraordinary ways, by visions, dreams, or immediate inspirations;—but by an understanding view and believing persuasion of the way of life, as revealed in the gospel, through the suretyship, obedience, and sufferings of Jesus Christ,—with a view of the suitableness and sufficiency of that mediatory righteousness of Christ for the justification and life of law condemned sinners;—and thereupon freely accepting him for their Saviour, heartily consenting to, and being well pleased with, that way of salvation;—and venturing their all upon his mediation, from the warrant and encouragement afforded of God thereunto in his word, by his free offer, authoritative command, and sure promise to those that so believe. I endeavoured to show them the fruits and evidences of a true faith."

After some time, many professed faith in Christ, and expressed a hope that their sins were forgiven. The evidences they gave of true conversion, are stated by Mr. Blair. "It was very agreeable to hear their accounts, how that, when they were in the deepest perplexity and darkness, distress and difficulty, seeking God as poor condemned hell deserving sinners, the sense of the recovering grace, through a Redeemer, has been opened to their understandings, with a surprising beauty and glory, so that they were enabled to believe in Christ, with joy unspeakable and full of glory. It appeared that most generally the Holy Spirit improved for this purpose, and made use of some one particular passage or another of the holy Scripture, that came to their remembrance in their distress, some gospel offer or promise, or some declaration of God directly referring to the recovery and salvation of undone sinners, by the new covenant. But with some it was otherwise, they had not any one particular place of Scripture more than another, in their view at the time."

"Much of their exercise was in self-abasing, self-loathing, and admiring the astonishing condescension and grace of God towards such vile and despicable creatures, that had been so full of enmity and disaffection to him;—then they freely and sweetly, and with all their hearts, chose the ways of his commandments:—their inflamed desire was to live to him forever, according to his will and the glory of his name. There were others that had not had such remarkable relief and comfort, who yet I could not but think were savingly renewed, and brought truly to accept of, and rest upon, Jesus Christ, though not with such a degree of liveliness and liberty, strength and joy; and some of these continued for a considerable time after, for the most part under a very distressing suspicion and jealousy of their case."

"I was all along very cautious of expressing to people my judgment of the goodness of their state, excepting where I had pretty clear evidences from them, of their being savingly changed, and yet they continued in deep distress, casting off all their evidences;—sometimes, in such cases I have thought it needful to use greater freedom that way than ordinary;—but otherwise I judged that it could be of little use, and might readily be hurtful."

"There were some, who having very little knowledge or capacity, had a very obscure and improper way of representing their case. In relating how they had been exercised, they would chiefly speak of such things as were only the effects of their soul's exercises upon their bodies, from time to time; and some things that were just imaginary, which obliged me to be at much pains in my inquiries, before I could get just ideas of their case. I would ask them, what were the thoughts, the views, and apprehensions of their minds, and exercises of their affections at such times, when they felt, perhaps a quivering come over them, as they had been saying,—or a faintness,—or thought they saw their hearts full of some nauseous filthiness,—or when they felt a heavy weight and load at their hearts,—or felt the weight taken off and a pleasant warmness rising from their hearts,—as they would probably express themselves,—which might be the occasion or causes of these things they spoke of; and then when with some difficulty, I could get them to understand me, some of them would give a pretty rational account of solemn spiritual exercises. And upon a thorough careful examination this way, I could not but conceive good hopes of some such persons."

"But there were, moreover, several others, who seemed to think concerning themselves, that they were under some good work, of whom yet I could have no reasonable ground to think, that they were under any hopeful work of the Spirit of God. As near as I could judge of their case from all my acquaintance and conversations with them, it was much to this purpose:— they believed there was a good work going on, that people were convinced and brought into a converted state, and they desired to be converted too;—they saw others weeping and fainting, and heard people mourning and lamenting, and they thought, if they could be like those it would be very hopeful with them;— hence they endeavoured just to get themselves affected by sermons, and if they could come to weeping, or get their passions so raised as to incline them to vent themselves by cries, now they hoped they were got under convictions, and were in a very hopeful way;—and afterwards they would speak of their being in trouble, and aim at complaining of themselves, but seemed as if they knew not well how to do it, nor what to say against themselves, and thus they would be looking and expecting to get some texts of Scripture applied to them for their comfort;— and when any Scripture text, which they thought was suitable for that purpose, came to their minds, they were in hopes it was brought to them by the Spirit of God, that they might take comfort from it. I endeavoured to correct and guard against all such mistakes, so far as I discovered them in the course of my ministry; and to open up the nature of a true conviction by the Spirit of God, and of a saving conversion."

His account of those who appeared to be converts in this great awakening, given about four years after it seemed to come to a close, is interesting to us in forming our judgment of the work. After stating that those who had been slightly concerned, lost all their concern; and some, who appeared to have been deeply interested, gave up all attention to religion; and some, who were much concerned, appeared to have settled down on a false hope, he goes on to say—"There is a considerable number who afford all the evidence that can reasonably be expected and required, for our satisfaction in the case, of their having been the subjects of a thorough saving change. Their walk is habitually tender and conscientious; their carriage toward their neighbour just and kind, and they appear to have an agreeable peculiar love for one another, and for all in whom appears the image of God." "Indeed the liveliness of their affections in the ways of religion is much abated, in general, and they are in some measure humbly sensible of this, and grieved for it, and are carefully endeavouring to live unto God, much grieved with their imperfections, and the plagues they find in their own hearts; and frequently they meet with some delightful enlivening of soul: and particularly our sacramental solemnities for communicating in the Lord's Supper, have generally been very blessed seasons of enlivening and enlargement to the people of God." He also tells us that great harmony prevailed in his congregation, and few opposers to the work appeared amongst them, and few left his congregation to join with those ministers who opposed the work.

Mr. Blair closes his narrative of the awakening in his charge in the following manner—" This blessed shower of divine influence spread very much through this province that summer, and was likewise considerable in some places bordering upon it. The accounts of some ministers sometimes distinguished by their searching, awakening doctrine, and solemn, pathetic manner of address—and the news of the effects of their preaching upon their hearers, seemed in some measure to awaken people through the country to consider their careless and formal way of going on in religion, and very much excited their desires to hear those ministers. There were several vacant congregations without any settled pastors, which earnestly begged for their visits, and several ministers who did not appear heartily to put to their shoulders to help in carrying on the same work, yet then yielded to the pressing importunities of their people in inviting these brethren to preach in their pulpits, so that they were very much called abroad and employed in incessant labours, and the Lord wrought with them mightily; very great assemblies would ordinarily meet to hear them upon any day of the week, and oftentimes a surprising power, accompanying their preaching, was visible among the multitudes of their hearers. It was a very comfortable enlivening time to God's people, and great numbers of secure, careless professors, and many loose irreligious persons, through the land, were deeply convinced of their miserable perishing estate, and there is abundant reason to believe, and be satisfied, that many of them were in the issue, savingly converted to God. I myself had occasion to converse with a great many up and down, who have given a most agreeable account of very precious and clear experiences of the grace of God, several even in Baltimore, a county in the province of Maryland, who were brought up almost in a state of heathenism, almost without any knowledge of the true doctrines of Christianity, afford very satisfactory evidence of being brought to a saving acquaintance with Christ Jesus."

" Knowing I must not speak wickedly even for God, nor talk deceitfully for Him; upon the whole I must say it is beyond all reasonable contradiction, that God has carried on a

great and glorious work of his special grace among us."
This account is dated—New Londonderry, in Pennsylvania,
August 6th, 1744.

Mr. Blair mentions the itinerating practised by some heartily
engaged in the revival. This led to great complaints, and to
extravagances that increased the complaints against the itinerants and those who justified their course; and ultimately led
to doubts about the revival itself, and to disputes about the
exercises of religion characteristic of conversion. The account
given by Mr. Blair, respecting his congregation, will, in the
general, exhibit the state of things in many other congregations
in Pennsylvania, in Delaware, and also those in New Jersey,
and some parts of New York. And the same complaints
against itinerants, and extravagances came from different quarters. It would be grateful, if the limits of these sketches
would permit, to give at least a general view of the great excitement on religion, throughout the Philadelphia Synod, particularly its appearance in the different congregations. Much
practical wisdom could be gathered from the sayings and
doings of the actors in those interesting scenes.

A vehement dispute also arose about the proper qualifications
for a candidate for the gospel ministry. Ministers and churches
took sides, with some asperity of feeling. The line of separation was nearly the same as on the question about experience
of religion and the exercises of awakened sinners and converts.
Each party charged extreme views upon the other, and in a
measure drove each other into extremes, using unkind expressions and unjustifiable means, and defending unwarrantable
positions.

The discussion of these subjects became so warm that Ministers and Elders and Congregations were alienated, and the
Synod in 1741 was rent asunder, in circumstances of great excitement. This division continued about seventeen years. The
party that retained the name of the Synod of Philadelphia, was
familiarly called the "Old Side;" and the Synod of New York
formed by the other party, the "New Side." The feelings of
the two parties, at length became calm, the matters in dispute
were amicably adjusted, and the Synods united under the name
of the Synod of New York and Philadelphia.

There is no evidence that the parties disagreed on important
doctrines. Mr. John Davenport was guilty of most extravagant
conduct, perhaps the most objectionable known during the excitement. An opponent, the Rev. Mr. Fish, of Connecticut,
makes a statement respecting this singular man,—in the midst
of his irregularities "the good things about him was that
he was a fast friend of the doctrines of grace; fully declaring
the total depravity, the deplorable wretchedness and danger,

and utter inability of man by the fall. He preached with great earnestness the doctrines of man's dependence on the sovereign mercy of God; of regeneration; of justification by faith, &c. The things that were evidently and dreadfully wrong about him were, that he not only gave full liberty to noise and outcries but promoted them with all his power. When these things prevailed among the people, accompanied with bodily agitations, the good man pronounced them tokens of the presence of God. Those who passed from great distress to great joy, he declared, after asking them a few questions, to be converts. He was a great favourer of visions, trances, imaginations, and powerful impressions in others, and made such inward feelings the rule of his own conduct in many respects. The worst thing, however, was his bold and daring enterprise of going through the country to examine all the ministers in private, and then publicly declare his judgment of their spiritual state."

Novelty of doctrine does not appear to have been the sin of that generation of Presbyterians. Novelty of methods to promote revivals excited fears in the pious; and the breaking through acknowledged rules disturbed society. These errors brought a glorious awakening into disrepute, and gave opportunity to all, who were not friendly to spiritual religion, to oppose a genuine work of God. The extreme of one side was formality in religion; of the other, extravagant bodily exercises.

The emigrants to Virginia, though, in many cases, but a short time from their mother country, remained long enough in Pennsylvania and Delaware to become parties in the division; and in their choice of residence were in a measure governed by their religious associations and belief respecting this awakening. Neighbouring ministers in Virginia attached themselves to the different Synods, and their congregations sympathised with their pastors; and while the two Synods continued separate, were tossed with the violence of the storm that rent the congregations in Pennsylvania and New Jersey. In some cases, traces of this division can be seen to this day; in most cases, however, the difference of sentiment in their ancestors is known to their descendants only as a matter of history.

The Presbyterian congregations in Virginia reared their cabins on the frontiers under great excitement. They were strangers in a strange land; they were exposed to the murderous incursions of the savages incensed against the white man by a century of provocations; they were in search of a home in the wilderness, where every man's cabin might stand upon his own acres held in fee simple; they were, under a strong religious feeling, searching for the truth in principle, and in some good degree guiding their practice by their principles;

they expected the undisturbed exercise of their forms of religion according to the promise of the Governor of Virginia; they expected more freedom in political matters, than was enjoyed in Ireland, not having fully fashioned in their own minds what that freedom was, except no Peers of the realm, no Diocesan Bishops were to make part of their community; they expected equal enjoyment of civil rights, and the protection of the laws with advantages to all according to their merits, and promotion to the most worthy. And in less than half a century, this excitement, and these principles, in the wilderness, moulded a nature made firm by resistance to oppression, and hard to roughness by toil, in their father land, into a form and shape and temper such as Ireland and Scotland had never seen. The children realized, in their manhood, all their fathers panted for when they crossed the ocean, freedom in person,—freedom in property,—freedom in knowledge and religion. They possessed a land of rivers, plains, and mountains, which princes never traversed but in exile, were protected by equal laws and governed by rulers of their own choice.

Presbyterian ministers followed the steps of these colonies, first on short visits, then to become resident pastors of the infant congregations.

1st. James Gelston was sent from the Presbytery of Donegall in the year 1737, to visit the people on Opeckon. We do not hear of his making a second visit. The preaching place was near where Opeckon meeting house now stands.

2d. Mr. James Anderson was sent a special delegate from the Synod of Philadelphia in 1738, with a message to Governor Gooch. He visited the different colonies of Presbyterians in Virginia. He preached his first sermon in Augusta, supposed to be the first ever preached there, in the house of Mr. John Lewis near Staunton.

3d. A Mr. Dunlap, a probationer of the Presbytery of New York, spent about three months in the neighbourhood of Staunton, in the year 1739.

4th. Mr. John Thompson of the Presbytery of Donegall visited Virginia in the year 1739, and spent some time in the Opeckon neighbourhood,—in the neighbourhood of Staunton,— on Rockfish in Nelson,—on Cub Creek,—at Buffaloe,—and in Campbell county. "He took up voluntary collections for preachers of the gospel"—says the manuscript history of Lexington Presbytery—"and in doing justice to his memory it is proper to observe, that he was active in promoting the Presbyterian cause in Virginia." He was a man of great vigour and took an active part in the affairs of the church. Through his instrumentality Messrs. Black and Craig were sent by Presbytery, the one to the Triple Forks, and the other to Rockfish.

He lived for a short time at Buffaloe, to which place Mr. Sankey, his son in law, removed with his congregation, and continued their pastor for many years. He removed to North Carolina, and there died in the bounds of Centre congregation.

5th. Mr. John Craig visited Augusta, in 1739, as probationer, from Donegall Presbytery, and ultimately became pastor of the Triple Forks, or Tinkling Spring and Augusta.

6th. About the same time Mr. Black took his residence on Rockfish in Nelson.

7th. The next of whom we have any knowledge was Wm. Robinson. He visited the congregations in the Valley near Winchester and above Staunton—went to Carolina, and on his return visited Hanover. His visit forms a chapter in Virginia Church History.

8th. The next was Mr. John Roan, whose visit to Hanover excited great bitterness in members of the Established Church.

9th. Mr. John Blair visited the Valley and places east of the Ridge in 1745, and again in 1746; and during his last visit organized the congregations of North Mountain, New Providence, Timber Ridge, and Forks of James.

After this, visits were frequent; and the congregations made efforts for stated ministers. The Governor of Virginia assured the Synod that ministers and congregations should enjoy all the privileges of the Act of Toleration. But in time there was a difficulty about the construction of that law; and also whether the common sense of men, and the law itself were to be the interpreters, or the caprice of rulers and the majority, when the minority claimed privileges under the law, and the majority denied them. In another form it was the old question—whether the minority had any rights of conscience. The people in Hanover said they had rights under the law of God, and by the Toleration Act: Davies maintained their position with ultimate triumph.

CHAPTER VII.

RISE OF THE PRESBYTERIAN CHURCH IN HANOVER COUNTY, VIRGINIA; AND WILLIAM ROBINSON.

WHILE the settlements of the Scotch Irish were multiplying, in the Valley of the Shenandoah, and along the eastern base of the Blue Ridge, and on the waters of the Roanoke, forming a frontier line in defence of the "Ancient Dominion," and planting the germs of many Presbyterian congregations, which flourished in after days, events of singular interest began to show themselves in Hanover County, and in some neighbourhoods of the adjacent Counties, whose inhabitants were of true English descent, and in connection with the established church.

The history of the world shows, that there are times, when the public mind is readily turned to religion; and if, in such times, the gospel be presented in its purity and simplicity, the concerns of the soul become the all absorbing subject. One of these happy times of spiritual sunshine was enjoyed in Hanover in common with many other parts of the world, both in Europe and America. Reports of the religious exercises and excitements that prevailed in New Jersey, New England, and Pennsylvania, and some parts of Maryland, spread through Virginia. The coming in of the Presbyterian colonies gave interest to these reports, and reflecting men began to inquire respecting the nature of these things and their consequent importance. That some families, in Hanover and Louisa, were aroused to inquire for their salvation, by means not afforded in the parish churches, is a matter of undoubted history. The first human agency known to have had effect upon them, next after the reports concerning the revivals in the States to the North, was that of religious books, followed by discussions on the weighty truths contained. A few leaves of Boston's Fourfold State, in possession of a Scotch woman, fell into the hands of a gentleman, who in looking over them, felt a deep interest in the truth as there exhibited. The title of the book was on one of the leaves. He sent to England by the next ship, for the book. The perusal of that volume, in connection with the Bible, was blessed of God to bring him to a knowledge of himself,—of the way of life through Jesus Christ,—and, there is reason to believe, to a saving faith. Another gentleman got possession of Luther on the Galatians. Deeply affected with what he read, so different from what he had been hearing from the pulpit of the parish Church, he never ceased to read and pray till he found consolation in believing in Christ Jesus, the Lord his Righteousness.

Rev. Samuel Davies, in his letter to the Bishop of London, says—"About the year 1743, upon petition of the Presbyterians in the frontier counties of this colony, the Rev. Mr. Robinson, who now rests from his labours, and is happily advanced beyond the injudicious applauses and censure of mortals, was sent by order of Presbytery to officiate for some time among them. A little before this, about four or five persons, heads of families in Hanover, had dissented from the established church, not from any scruples about her ceremonial peculiarities, the usual cause of nonconformity, much less about her excellent articles of faith, but from a dislike to the doctrines generally delivered from the pulpit, as not savouring of experimental piety, nor suitably intermingled with the glorious peculiarities of the religion of Jesus. These families were wont to meet in a private house on Sundays to hear some good books read, particularly Luther's; whose writings I can assure your Lordship were the principal cause of their leaving the Church; which I hope is a presumption in their favour. After some time sundry others came to their society, and upon hearing these books, grew indifferent about going to church, and chose rather to frequent these societies for reading. At length the number became too great for a private house to contain them, and they agreed to build a meeting house, which they accordingly did. Thus far they had proceeded before they had heard a dissenting minister at all. They had not the least thought at this time of assuming the denomination of Presbyterian, as they were wholly ignorant of that church."

The Rev. James Hunt, of Montgomery county, Maryland, related to a gentleman, in Albemarle County, Virginia, who preserved the narrative, and published it in the 2d vol. of the Evangelical and Literary Magazine, edited by the Rev. John H. Rice, D.D.—"that in the County of Hanover four gentlemen, of whom his father was one, at the same time became convinced that the Gospel was not preached by the minister of the parish church, and that it was inconsistent with their duty to attend upon his ministrations. The consequence was they absented themselves on the same day. They having all been remarkably regular in their attendance; and if I recollect truly, having held some office in the parish, their absence was soon noticed, and a summons issued for them to appear before the proper officers to answer for their delinquency. As they had absented on the same day, it was their fortune to be called on the same day before the same officers. And here, for the first time, each found that three of his neighbours were delinquents as well as himself, and for the very same cause. Seeing no reason to change their opinions, or alter the course they had adopted, they determined to subject themselves to the payment of the fines imposed by law, and attended the church no more. They agreed to meet every Sabbath, alternately, at each others' houses, and spend the time with their families in prayer and reading the Scriptures, together with Luther's Commentary on the Galatians,—an old volume which by some means had fallen into their hands."

Mr. Samuel Morris, in his statement made to Rev. Samuel Davies, says—"In the year 1740 Mr. Whitefield had preached at Williamsburg, at the invitation of Mr. Blair, our Commissary. But we being sixty miles distant from Williamsburg, he left the colony before we had an opportunity of hearing him. But, in the year 1743, a young gentleman from Scotland had got a book of his sermons preached in Glasgow, taken from his mouth, in short hand, which after I had read with great benefit, I invited my neighbours to come and hear it; and the plainness and fervency of these discourses being attended with the power of the Lord, many were convinced of their undone situation, and constrained to seek deliverance with the greatest solicitude. A considerable number met to hear these sermons every Sabbath, and frequently on week days. The concern of some was so passionate and violent, that they could not avoid crying out, weeping bitterly, &c. And that, when such indications of religious concern were so strange and ridiculous that they could not be occasioned by example or sympathy, and the affectation of them would be so unprofitable an instance of hypocrisy, that none could be tempted to it."

Mr. Hunt's narrative says—"Curiosity prompted the desire to be amongst them,—one and another begged for admission, till their houses, on Sabbath, were crowded. And here a new scene opened upon their astonished view. Numbers were pricked to the heart,—the word became sharp and powerful,—'what shall we do,' was the general cry. What to do or say the principal leaders knew not. They themselves had been led by a small still voice, they hardly knew how, to an acquaintance with the truth; but now the Lord was speaking as on Mount Sinai, with a voice of thunder, and sinners, like that mountain itself, trembled to the centre. And it was not long before they had the happiness to see a goodly little number healed by the same word that had wounded them, and brought to rejoice understandingly in Christ."

Mr. Morris says—"My dwelling house was at length too small to contain the people, whereupon we determined to build a meeting house merely for *reading*. And having never been used to social prayer, none of us durst attempt it."

Mr. Hunt's narrative says—"And now their numbers became too large for any private house to contain them, another step is taken,—they build first one, and then another of what they called *reading houses*. Hence the number of attendants and the force of divine influence much increased."

Mr. Morris says—"By this single means"—that is reading—"several were awakened, and their conduct ever since is a proof of the continuance and happy issue of their impressions. When the report was spread abroad, I was invited to several places, to read these sermons, at a considerable distance, and by this means the concern was propagated." The phrase *Morris's Reading House* has come down to us, by tradition, as connected inseparably with the rise of Presbyterianism in

Hanover; it was applied first to the house erected on Mr. Morris's land, and then to another and another as they were erected to accommodate the people. The assemblies held regularly in these houses, together with the desertion of the parish churches rendered these gentlemen peculiarly obnoxious to the laws of the colony; and as the new opinions gained adherents in Hanover, it was urged that indulgence but encouraged the evil, and the strong arm of the law was invoked. "Our absenting ourselves from the church"—says Mr. Morris,—"contrary as was alleged to the laws of the land, was taken notice of, and we were called upon by the court to assign our reasons for it, and to declare what denomination we were of." Mr. Hunt says—"They were no longer considered as individual delinquents whose obstinacy might be sufficiently punished by the civil magistrate; but as a malignant cabal, that required the interposition of the executive. They were accordingly cited to appear before the Governor and Council. The exaction of frequent fines for non attendance at church they bore, with patience and fortitude, for the sake of a good conscience; but to be charged with a crime, of the nature and extent and penalty of which they had but indistinct conceptions, spread a gloom over their minds, and filled them with anxious forebodings more easily conceived than described. They were certainly and obviously a religious society, separate and distinct from the only one, the established church, which either the government or the people knew in the country, and yet they were without a name." Their acquaintance with the operation of the Toleration Act of William and Mary, passed 1688, and acknowledged on the Virginia statute book in 1699, must have been very slight; perhaps they knew neither of the Virginia act, or the Act of Toleration, as no circumstance in their lives had brought them to view. It is not probable they knew any thing of Governor Gooch's promise made in 1738, because none of the Scotch Irish had emigrated to Hanover, and these people were descended from members of the English church. If they knew of the unlimited toleration granted to the German colony on the Rappahannoc, in Madison county; or of the favour extended to the French Refugees, at the Manakin towns, on the James River above the falls; they looked upon these as peculiar cases, and precedents in a general way only, if at all, to people that had no church organization, or even a name. They were frequently called upon to appear before the magistrates of the county in explanation and defence, and to be fined. At last they were required to appear at Williamsburg, and to declare their creed and name before the Governor and Council, who assumed the entire control of matters pertaining to dissenters.

Mr. Morris says—in reference to the visit—"as we know but little of any denomination of dissenters, except Quakers, we were at a loss what name to assume. At length recollecting that Luther was a noted Reformer, and that his book had been of special service to us, we declared ourselves Lutherans." It does not appear that this plea exempted them from fines, for absence from church, while it shielded them from prosecution as disturbers of the public peace. Mr. Hunt, in his narrative, gives an interesting account of a visit made, by his father and some other gentlemen, to Williamsburg, to have an interview with the Governor and Council. He tells us that one of the company, travelling alone, was overtaken and detained, by a violent storm, at the house of a poor man on the road. He interested himself in looking over an old volume, which he found upon a shelf covered with dust. Upon perusing it he was amazed to find his own sentiments, as far as he had formed any on religious things, drawn out in appropriate language; and as far as he read, the whole summary met his approbation. Offering to purchase the book, the owner gave it to him. In Williamsburg, he examined the old book again, in company with his friends; they all agreed that it expressed their views on the doctrines of religion. When they appeared before the Governor they presented this old volume as their creed. Governor Gooch, himself of Scotch origin and education, upon looking at the volume, pronounced the men Presbyterians, as the book was the Confession of Faith of the Presbyterian Church of Scotland; and that they were not only tolerated but acknowledged as a part of the established church of the realm. Mr. Hunt thought, and used to tell the circumstance with great earnestness, that a violent thunder storm shaking the house and wrapping all in sheets of fire, had a softening influence on the minds of the Governor and Council, inclining them to deal gently with their fellow men. When the storm abated, the men were dismissed with a gentle caution from the Governor not to excite any disturbance in his majesty's colony, nor by any irregularities disturb the good order of society in their parish. And it is to be remarked that in all the varied forms in which these men were had before the civil authorities, they were never accused of any other crime than absenting themselves from the parish church, and meeting in private houses for public worship, except in one case, and then the accusation was found to be false.

The first minister, not of the Church of England, these people heard preach was *William Robinson*, of whom President Davies says—"That favoured man, Mr. Robinson, whose success, whenever I reflect upon it, astonishes me. Oh, he did much in a little time!—and who would not choose such an expeditious pilgrimage through the world!" Equal to Makemie in devotion to the cause, his superior, in all probability, in ardour and power over men's passions, he stands second in point of time on the list of those whom the Presbyterian Church in Virginia delights to honour, as an apostolic missionary, east of the Blue Ridge. Makemie's labours were on the sea shore; Robinson's at the head of tide-water; we see the fruits of the former in the still existing churches of Maryland and in the organization of the mother Presbytery of the General Assembly of the Presbyterian Church; and of the latter in the organization of those churches in Virginia, and the introduction of that master workman that gave character to the Presbytery of Hanover and the Synod of Virginia, and left an impress that a century of years has not done away. Some account of his life cannot be unacceptable.

Born near Carlyle, England, the son of a Quaker a physician of eminence and wealth, Robinson came to the years of maturity in expectation of an inheritance from his father and an aunt in London. On a visit to this aunt, he became entangled in the dissipation of the great metropolis, and contracted debts which his aunt refused to cancel, and which he had not the hardihood to present to his father. Resolved on emigrating to the colonies, in America, to improve his condition, he obtained from his aunt her reluctant consent, and a small sum of money to pay his passage. Taking his abode in New Jersey, he commenced teaching school as an honourable means of support and regaining his character. Thus far his career had been that of many other emigrants, who had hoped for that competence in America, which the condition of their birth, or their misguided actions had rendered hopeless in the land of their fathers. But here the similarity in a great measure ends. Though disgraced by his youthful irregularities, he was not degraded; ardent in his feelings and generous in his sentiments, he was not reckless; necessarily restrained from higher indulgences, he did not, like multitudes, compensate himself in those baser gratifications within his reach; far away from the inspection or control of relatives, he did not give himself up to the habits and appetites that have carried so many emigrants to an early and unhonoured grave.

Dr. Miller, in his Life of Rodgers, gives an interesting account of his conversion, during his residence in Hopewell, now Pennington, New Jersey. Riding late one night, while the moon and stars were shining with unusual lustre, he felt the first deep impression of heavenly things. Multitudes have said with the Psalmist,—"When I consider the heavens, the work of thy fingers, the moon and stars which thou hast ordained, what is man that thou art mindful of him, and the son of man that thou visitest him," While admiring the beauty of the heavens, Mr. Robinson said to himself—"How transcendently glorious must be the Author of all this beauty and grandeur!" With the suddenness of lightning the inquiry darted to his soul,—"but what do I know of this God?—have I ever sought his favour?—or made him my friend?" This impression, like a voice from heaven ringing in his ears, never left him till he found God reconciled to him in Christ Jesus. What he felt strongly, his ardent feelings forbid his concealing. Longing to make known the grace of that gospel in which he believed, he devoted himself to the service of God, in the Christian ministry. Being in the bounds of New Brunswick Presbytery he put himself under its care, April 1st, 1740, and on the 27th of the following May, at Neshaminy, he was licensed to preach the gospel. On the 4th of August 1741, he was ordained at New Brunswick. The next year he declined an invitation to be successor of the Rev. William Tennent at Neshaminy, and in November was sent as supply to the people of Nottingham, Maryland.

His race as a preacher was short but glorious: his vehement desires for the salvation of men consumed his body with the flames of love; and the monuments of his usefulness excited the astonishment of even Davies, a burning spirit in an exciting age.

He was sent, as Evangelist, by the Presbytery of New Castle, in the winter of 1742–3, in consequence of the earnest solicitations of the people, to visit the Presbyterian settlements in the Valley of the Shenandoah, and on the south side of James River, in Virginia; and the numerous settlements in North Carolina, on the Haw. On entering Virginia, he was seized near Winchester by the sheriff of Orange county, which then extended to the north branch of the Potomac, and was sent on his way to Williamsburg to answer to the Governor for preaching without license. Before he had proceeded far the sheriff released him to pursue his mission. He passed the winter in Carolina, and from the exposures to which his zeal subjected him, he contracted a disease from which he never recovered. On his return he preached with great success to the Presbyterian settlements in Charlotte, Prince Edward, Campbell and Albemarle. Here he was waited upon by a deputation that persuaded him to change his contemplated route to the head of the Shenandoah Valley, and turn back to the people of Hanover. He had proceeded as far as Rockfish Gap before he turned his course.

The messengers that waited on him were instructed to hear him preach, before they invited him to visit their county, and not to give him an invitation unless they thought his doctrines agreed with their views of religious truth. Mr. Hunt says—

"already"—that is, previous to Mr. Robinson's arrival—"difference of opinion had arisen which threatened the most serious evils. Some of their number, carrying some of the peculiar and distinguishing doctrines of the gospel to a licentious extreme, began to deny, not only the merit of good works, but their necessity—not only the efficacy of means, but their expediency, so that it was made a serious question among them, whether it was right to pray, as prayer could not, as it would be impious to desire it should, alter the divine purposes." When the delegates heard Mr. Robinson they were divided in opinion respecting his doctrines. "One," says Mr. Hunt, "thought that he was entirely evangelical: the other thought he dwelt too much on the necessity of works, and urged too strongly the use of means; and was afraid that thereby he at least clouded the doctrines of grace, and threw a veil over the glories of divine sovereignty in the salvation of man. But it was determined they should give him a cordial invitation in the name of the congregations." He at first declined; but their cordial and earnest invitation led him to think the call was from God, and after some deliberations in secret, he made arrangements for a visit to Hanover.

On the day appointed, Mr. Robinson, after a fatigueing journey, protracted through most of the night preceding, in order to prevent a disappointment, arrived, and found a large crowd assembled. Says Mr. Hunt—"their Reading House was soon filled to overflowing. But a venerable spreading oak embowered with the surrounding shades, gave him and the people shelter." Mr. Morris and friends proceeded immediately on Mr. Robinson's arrival to have an interview with him in private. In this they inquired of him his denomination, his doctrinal and practical views of religion, and his method of procedure. He produced his testimonials which were full and satisfactory as it regarded his ministerial standing; and gave them his creed and views of practical religion. "Being satisfied"—says Mr. Morris,—"about the soundness of his principles, and being informed that the method of his preaching was awakening, we were very eager to hear him." In none of the few particulars that are left us, of the proceedings of Mr. Robinson, does he show himself so worthy of his office as Evangelist, as in this interview. The knowledge of human nature, of the principles of the gospel, and the practical operations of grace in the heart, producing meekness and candour,—the giving an answer about his creed to those he came to instruct, and a reason of the hope that was in him to these people that did not know what they were themselves,—these things exhibited in this interview, show him to have been a man gifted from on high to be a teacher of babes and an instructor of wise

men. It is delightful to see in this *first preacher*, that frankness and candour about doctrines and practice and designs in
religion, that has so long characterized the ministry that have
followed him in succession. May it ever be their glory, that
no man that hears them often need ask,—and no stranger may
inquire but once—what are their doctrinal views.

On Sabbath, July 6th, 1743, the first sermon from a Presbyterian minister, was heard in Hanover county, Virginia. The
text was Luke xiii. 3,—"*I tell you, nay: but except ye repent
ye shall all likewise perish.*" What a subject for a warm-
hearted preacher to pour into the ears and hearts of an excited
people, assembled, for the first time, to hear an evangelical
minister proclaim the solemn truths of the gospel. "He continued"—says Mr. Morris—"with us preaching, four days successively. The congregation was large the first day, and vastly
increased the three ensuing. 'Tis hard for the liveliest imagination to form an image of the condition of the assembly on
these glorious days of the Son of Man. Such of us as had been
hungering for the word before, were lost in agreeable surprise
and astonishment, and some could not refrain from publicly
declaring their transports. We were overwhelmed with the
thoughts of the unexpected goodness of God in allowing us to
hear the gospel preached in a manner that surpassed our hopes.
Many, that came through curiosity, were pricked to their heart;
and but few of the numerous assembly on these four days appeared unaffected. They returned alarmed with apprehensions
of their dangerous condition, convinced of their former entire
ignorance of religion, and anxiously inquiring what they should
do to be saved. And there is reason to believe, there was as
much good done by these four sermons, as by all the sermons
preached in these parts before or since." This statement was
made in the year 1750; by "as much good," the writer probably means, as many souls hopefully converted. "Before Mr.
Robinson, left us,"—continues Mr. Morris—"he successfully
endeavoured to correct some of our mistakes; and to bring us
to carry on the worship of God more regularly at our meetings.
After this we met to read good sermons, and began and concluded with prayer and signing of psalms, which till then we
had omitted." What these mistakes were, has been stated, and
they were such as experienced men would expect to find in a
community where religious knowledge and experience were
novelties; mistakes, of which the proud are tenacious, and from
which the humble are speedily delivered by faithful teaching.

After spending four days in preaching publicly, and instructing and counselling privately, Mr. Robinson was constrained
to depart; his previous appointments called him on, and it was
rumoured that the officers of the law were preparing to arrest

him as an itinerant. The people, in part to remunerate him for fatiguing rides and incessant labours, but mostly, as an expression of gratitude, raised a considerable sum of money, and presented it to him. This, for various reasons, he refused. They pressed the matter: he, believing it to be injudicious to take any thing from them in the present condition of things, perseveringly refused.

"In this dilemma"—says Mr. Hunt—"the committee entrusted with it put it into the hands of the gentleman, with whom he was to lodge the last night of his stay in the county, with directions to convey it privately into his saddle bags, not doubting, but when, after his departure, he should find himself in possession of the money, he would appropriate it to his own use. This was accordingly done. And in the morning, Mr. Robinson having taken an affectionate leave of his kind friends, his saddle bags were handed to him, but he found them much more ponderous than when he came there. Searching for the cause, like Joseph's brethren of old, he found the money in the sack's mouth. Pleased with the benevolent artifice, he smiling said—'I see you are resolved I shall have your money; I will take it; but as I have told you before, I do not need it; I have enough, nor will I appropriate it to my own use; but there is a young man of my acquaintance of promising talents and piety, who is now studying with a view to the ministry, but his circumstances are embarrassing, he has not funds to support and carry him on without much difficulty; this money will relieve him from his pecuniary difficulties: I will take charge of it and appropriate it to his use; and as soon as he is licensed we will send him to visit you; it may be, that you may now, by your liberality, be educating a minister for yourselves. This money was appropriated by Mr. Robinson to the education of Samuel Davies. His promise was kept; he did not live to see the reality of his anticipation; he died in 1746, and Davies came to Virginia in 1747.

"This is the reason"—said a pious old lady to Dr. Rice—"that Mr. Davies came to Hanover; for he often used to say that he was inclined to settle in another place; but that he felt under obligations to the people of Hanover." On these facts the Editor of the Literary and Evangelical Magazine, the Rev. John H. Rice, D.D., remarked—"As far as we can learn this is the first money that ever was contributed, in Virginia, for the education of poor and pious youth for the ministry of the gospel. And really it turned out so well we wonder the people have not done much more in the same way."

Thus ends Mr. Robinson's personal labours in Virginia. One short visit to a number of congregations; to a few, two visits, in the same excursion; and he passes from the sight of these people forever. But his footsteps were impressed upon a rock. In Prince Edward, Charlotte, Campbell, and Hanover, the fruits of his labours have been visible for more than a century. He planted, others watered, God gave the increase. In Carolina, Mr. Davies says Mr. Robinson—"underwent great hardship without much success. But the case is now happily altered. A new congregation, I think upon the Pedee river, sent a petition lately to our Presbytery for a minister. Besides this I hear of several other places in North Carolina that are ripening fast for the gospel. O that God would send forth faithful labourers into his harvest." There is no tradition or record, in Carolina, of the visit of this man, yet we can scarcely believe that his fervent preaching, so effective elsewhere, was lost there. In the great day it will be seen where the seed was sown. Some one sowed seed there that has been as fruitful in its harvest, as the seed sown in Virginia by this favoured man."

Mr. Robinson's health declined, after this southern visit; but his bow abode in strength, and many arrows from the quiver of the Almighty were shot from his withering hands, into the hearts of the King's enemies. The accounts we have of him, from this visit, until his death, given by Mr. Davies, and Mr. Blair, who preached his funeral sermon, and Dr. Miller, in his Life of Rodgers, represent him as hasting with Apostolic speed, lighting up the horizon with his torch of fire, and expiring in midheaven. Mr. Davies says—"In Maryland also there has been a considerable revival (shall I call it?)—or first plantation of religion—in Baltimore county, where I am informed Mr. Whittlesey is likely to settle. In Kent county, and in Queen Anne's, a number of careless sinners have been awakened and hopefully brought to Christ. The work was begun and mostly carried on by the instrumentality of that favoured man Mr. Robinson, whose success, whenever I reflect upon it, astonishes me. Oh! he did much in a little time; and who would not choose such an expeditious pilgrimage through this world. There are in these places a considerable congregation, and they have made repeated efforts to obtain a settled minister. But the most glorious display of Divine grace, in Maryland, has been in and about Somerset county. It began, I think in 1745, by the ministry of Mr. Robinson, and was afterwards carried on by several ministers that preached transiently there. *I was there* about two months, when the work was at its height, and I never saw such a deep and spreading concern. The assemblies were numerous, though in the extremity of a cold winter, and unwearied in attending the word. And frequently there were very few among them that did not give some indications of distress or joy. Oh! these were the happiest days that ever my eyes saw. Since that, the harvest seems over there, though considerable gleanings, I hear, are still gathered. They have, of late, got Mr. Henry for their minister, a young man who I trust will be an "extensive blessing to that part of the colony. There was also a great stir about religion in Buckingham, a place on the sea shore, which has since spread and issued in a hopeful conversion in several instances. They also want a minister." These latter named places were the scenes of the labours of that Apostolic missionary, Francis Makemie. Buckingham, now called Berlin, the county seat of Worcester county, had for a time the labours of one of the Tennents.

Dr. Hill relates an interesting anecdote of Mr. Robinson while in Virginia. On the night before he was to preach in Hanover for the first time, Mr. Robinson rode late to reach a tavern within some eight or ten miles of the place of preaching.—"The tavern keeper was a shrewd, boisterous, profane man. When uttering some horrid oaths, Mr. Robinson ventured to reprove him for his profanity; and although it was done in a mild way, the innkeeper gave him a sarcastic look, and said—'Pray, Sir, who are you, to take such authority upon yourself?' 'I am a minister of the gospel,' says Mr. Robinson. 'Then you belie your looks very much,' was the reply. It is said Mr. Robinson had had the small pox very seriously, which had given him a very rough visage, and deprived of the sight of one of his eyes. It was with reference to his forbidding appearance, that the innkeeper seemed to question his ministerial character. 'But'—says Mr. Robinson—'if you wish certainly to know whether I am a minister or not, if you will accompany me, you may be convinced by hearing me preach.' 'I will,' says the innkeeper, 'if you will preach from a text which I shall give you.' 'Let me hear it,' says Mr. Robinson, 'and if there is nothing unsuitable in it, I will.' The waggish innkeeper gave him the passage from the Psalms— 'For I am fearfully and wonderfully made.' Mr. Robinson agreed that it should be one of his texts. The man was at Mr. Robinson's meeting, and that text was the theme of one of his sermons. Before it was finished, the wicked man was made to feel that he was the monster, and that he was fearfully and wonderfully made. It is said he became a very pious and useful member of the church; and it is thought Mr. Davies alludes to this instance when he says, 'I have been the joyful witness of the happy effects of those four sermons upon sundry thoughtless impenitents and sundry abandoned profligates, who have ever since given good evidence of a thorough conversion from sin to holiness.' Thus this good man cast the gospel net and caught of every sort, gathering whom his Lord called."

On the 19th of March 1746, he was dismissed from the Presbytery of New Brunswick to the Presbytery of New Castle, to become the pastor of the congregation of St. George's in Delaware. This church and congregation had been gathered in a revival under the preaching of Mr. Whitefield and Mr. Robinson; the latter was its first minister and about to be their permanent pastor. But in April following his course on earth was finished. His funeral sermon was preached on the 3d of August of the same year, by Mr. Samuel Blair. He was a martyr to the labours he voluntarily endured for the cause of Christ; having never had his health after his tour through Virginia and North Carolina. In pecuniary matters he was charitable almost to a fault. Feeling deeply for the misery of his race, he was unsparing of his property, or strength, or life, in the deliverance of men from the wrath to come.

He bequeathed his library to the Rev. Samuel Davies, his protege and fellow labourer.

CHAPTER VIII.

MINISTERS VISITING HANOVER AFTER MR. ROBINSON, AND PREVIOUS TO MR. SAMUEL DAVIES.

THE desire of the people of Hanover to hear the Gospel, as preached by Mr. Robinson, did not depart with that able Evangelist. His words continued to ring in their ears, and agitate their hearts. The efforts to compel a conformity to the established church, while its ministers preached in a manner so little accomodated to their necessities, only made these people long for freedom of conscience—and for a living ministry, whose doctrines, enforced by their godly lives, might be for their purification and life. The voice of all mankind demands that the priesthood shall be an example of the moral nature of their God.

The first minister that visited these people after Mr. Robinson, was Mr. John Blair, educated in the famous school of his brother Samuel Blair, at New Londonderry, in Faggs Manor, he was for a time a settled pastor in Cumberland County, Pennsylvania. He then succeeded his brother in Faggs Manor; and afterwards was Vice President of Nassau Hall, and Professor of Theology in that institution. He ended his days December 8th, 1771, at Wallkill, New York. An amiable man, he was well qualified for his various stations in life. Going from that extensive revival, that agitated, and refreshed, parts of Pennsylvania, New Jersey, New York and New England, to visit a people awakened by their own reflections, and reading religious books, and excited by the preaching of that ardent man, Mr. Robinson, his preaching was imposing and the effects encouraging. Mr. Morris, in the statement to Mr. Davies, says, "truly he came to us in the fulness of the Gospel of Christ. Former impressions were ripened and new ones made on many hearts. One night in particular, a whole housefull of people was quite overcome with the power of the word, particularly of one pungent sentence; and they would hardly sit or stand or keep their passions under any proper restraints. So general was the concern, during his stay with us, and so ignorant were we of the danger of apostasy, that we pleased ourselves with the thoughts of more being brought to Christ at that time, than now appear to have been, though there is still the greatest reason to hope that several bound themselves to the Lord in an everlasting covenant never to be forgotten."

The alarm caused in Hanover by the short visit of Mr. Robinson was greatly increased by the preaching of Mr. Blair, whose amiable deportment, genteel manners, and classical language, united with gravity of manners forbid the idea of attaching either vulgarity or disorder to the religion he professed and taught. No violence or insult was offered him during his short stay. His hearers, agitated beyond control, poured forth tears and sighs, and often broke out into loud crying. At the time it was impossible to tell how much this expression of feeling was from deep sympathy, and how much from the movings of the Holy Spirit.

Opposers were roused to anxious inquiry what they would do to arrest the propagation of these strange views and feelings on religious things. Absences from the parish church were more strictly observed, and the law was invoked to prevent apostasy from the ceremonies of the Church of England. Before his return to Pennsylvania, Mr. Blair visited the neighbourhoods in the Valley that favoured the Synod of New York, or the New Side, as it was called, North Mountain, which included Bethel and Hebron, the Pastures, New Providence, Timber Ridge, Forks of James or Monmouth, and Opeckon; and it is supposed also the Presbyterian neighbourhooods on Cub Creek and Buffaloe, and Hat Creek.

Some time after Mr. Blair's return to Pennsylvania, the Presbytery of Newcastle, the nearest Presbytery of the Synod of New York, sent Rev. John Roan to pay the people in Virginia a visit. A preacher of eminence, he had established a grammar school on the Neshaminy a few miles from Philadelphia. Rev. Dr. Rodgers was for some time a pupil of his. Mr. Roan remained in Virginia part of the winter of 1744 and 5, and preached with great effect not only in Hanover, but the neigh-

bouring counties. "He continued with us"—says Mr. Morris—
"longer than any of the former, and the happy effects of his
ministrations are still apparent. He was instrumental in beginning and promoting the religious concern in several places
where there was little appearance of it before. This together
with his speaking pretty freely about the degeneracy of the
clergy in this colony, gave a general alarm, and some measures
were concerted to suppress us." Mr. Roan had the warmth and
deep earnestness of Robinson and Blair, with less prudence and
caution; with the activity of Davies, he had less skill in managing an excited multitude. He spoke freely of the parish ministers, publicly and privately, inveighed against their delinquency
in morals, and their public ministrations; and turned the ridicule and scorn of his hearers against the teachers appointed and
supported by law. The parish clergy and their friends were
excited. Unable to refute the allegations, they appealed to the
strong arm of the law to protect their privileges, and restrain
both the speech and actions of their adversaries.

That there was cause for complaint against the parish ministers in Virginia, in 1744, is unquestionably true; and it is
equally true that Mr. Roan exposed their delinquency. How far
he indulged in the denunciatory spirit that prevailed in Pennsylvania and New Jersey, at that time, and was the ostensible
cause of dividing the Church, cannot now be determined. But
the excitement was great. And now commenced in earnest a
discussion about the rights of citizens in matters of religion,—
how far conscience was free,—and how far the law of the land,
that had slumbered, in Virginia, since the days of Makemie, had
become a dead letter.

The multitude crowded to hear Roan, some from curiosity,
and some from feeling. Opposition was expressed in reproaches, sneers, ridicule, and threats. The preacher's spirit took
fire, and his invectives were not measured. He saw evidence
of the power of God in melting the hearts of sinners to the
obedience of the gospel. Converts multiplied, and the violence
of opposition increased. Report after report went down to
Williamsburg that Roan was turning the world upside down.
Neighbourhood after neighbourhood was calling upon this fiery
preacher to declare to them the everlasting gospel. Opposers
were consulting how they might effectually silence him. Multitudes were responding a hearty amen to his earnest appeals.
In this state of things charges were made against him of blasphemous words and slanderous speeches. "A perfidious
wretch"—says Morris—"deposed he heard Mr. Roan utter
blasphemous expressions in his sermons."

Governor Gooch had promised protection to the Presbyterian colonies. He was not forgetful of that promise which had

filled the frontier counties with enterprising men that formed a
line of defence against the savages.   But reports reached him
from Hanover and James City, which were not frontier counties, and which contained no Presbyterian colony, such as
might have been found in Lunenburg, Charlotte, Prince Edward, Appomattox, Cumberland, Campbell, Nelson, Albemarle,
Rockbridge, Botetourt, Augusta, Frederick, Jefferson, and
Berkeley.   Charges of proselytism and blasphemy followed
these reports, and roused the mild and tolerant Gooch to inquire into the cause of this excitement and disturbance.   Report upon report, charge upon charge, exasperated his excited
spirit.   Witnesses were named, and express words were set
down.   The Governor took up the matter with vehemence, as
will appear from the following extracts from the records of
the General Court, preserved in the capitol in Richmond city.

The General Court, consisting of the Governor and Council,
commenced their regular sessions April 15th 1745.   " Present,
William Gooch Lieutenant Governor, John Robinson, John
Grymes, John Custis, Philip Lightfoot, Thomas Lee, Lewis
Burwell, William Fairfax."   The grand jury did not appear
till the fourth day, Thursday April 18th.   They were—" William Beverly, gent, foreman,—Benjamin Cocke, Richard Bland,
James Skelton, Richard Corbin, Mann Page, Francis Ness,
Daniel Hornby, George Douglass, Tarlton Fleming, Richard
Bernard, Ralph Wormley, William Nelson, Edmund Berkley,
Nathaniel Harrison, John Ravenscroft, James Littlepage, Nicholas Davies, Charles Ewell, Richard Ambler, Carter Burwell,
and John Harmer."   The Governor delivered them the following charge, which does not appear on the records of the Court,
but is copied from Burke, vol. 3d, p. 119 and onward, who
copied it from a Williamsburg paper—" Williamsburg, April
25th.   Thursday last being the fourth day of General Court,
his Honour the Governor was pleased to deliver the following
charge to the gentlemen of the grand jury; which they afterwards requested his Honour to permit to be published—

" *Gentlemen of the Grand Jury*, Without taking notice of
the ordinary matters and things, you are called to attend, and
sworn to make inquisition for, I must on this occasion turn to
your thoughts and recommend to your present service another
subject of importance, which I thank God has been unusual,
but, I hope, will be most effectual, I mean the information I
have received of certain false teachers that are lately crept into
this government; who, without order or license, or producing
any testimonial of their education or sect, professing themselves
ministers under the pretended influence of new light, extraordinary impulse, and such like satirical (Satanical, qu.?) and enthusiastical knowledge, lead the innocent and ignorant people into

all kinds of delusion; and in this frantic and prophane disguise, though such is their heterodoxy that they treat all other modes of worship with the utmost scorn and contempt, yet as if they had bound themselves on oath to do many things against the religion of the blessed Jesus, that pillar and stay of the truth and reformed church, to the great dishonor of Almighty God, and the discomfort of serious Christians, they endeavour to make their followers believe that salvation is not to be obtained (except, qu.?) in their communion.

"As this denunciation, if I am rightly advised, in words not decent to repeat, has been by one of them publicly affirmed, and shows what manner of spirit they all of them are of in a country hitherto remarkable for uniformity in worship, and where the saving truths of the gospel are constantly inculcated, I did promise myself, either that their preaching would be in vain, or that an insolence so criminal would not long be connived at.

"And therefore, gentlemen, since the workers of a deceitful work, blaspheming our sacraments, and reviling our excellent liturgy, are said to draw disciples after them, and we know not whereunto this separation may grow, but may easily foretel into what a distracted condition, by long forbearance, this colony will be reduced, we are called upon by the rights of society, and what, I am persuaded will be with you as prevailing an inducement, by the principles of Christianity, to put an immediate stop to the devices and intrigues of these associated scismatics, who having, no doubt, assumed to themselves the apostacy of our weak brethren, we may be assured that there is not any thing so absurd but what they will assert and accommodate to their favourite theme, railing against our religious establishment; for which in any other country, the British dominions only excepted, they would be very severely handled.

"However, not meaning to inflame your resentment, as we may without breach of charity pronounce, that 'tis not liberty of conscience, but freedom of speech, they so earnestly prosecute; and we are very sure that they have no manner of pretence to any shelter under the acts of toleration, because, admitting they have had regular ordination, they are by those acts obliged, nor can they be ignorant of it, not only to take the oaths, and with the test to subscribe, after a deliberate reading of them, some of the articles of our religion, before they presume to officiate. But that in this indulgent grant, though not expressed, a covenant is intended, whereby they engage to preserve the character of conscientious men, and not to use their liberty for a cloak of maliciousness,—to that I say, allowing their ordination, yet as they have not, by submitting to those essential points, qualified themselves to gather a congregation, or if they had, in speaking all manner of evil against us, have forfeited the privilege due to such compliance; insomuch, that they are entirely without excuse, and their religious professions are very justly suspected to be the result of jesuitical policy, which also is an iniquity to be punished by the judges.

"I must, as in duty bound to God and man, charge you in the most solemn manner, to make strict enquiry after those seducers, and if they, or any of them, are still in this government, by presentment or indictment to report them to the court, that we, who are in authority under the Defender of our faith, and the appointed guardians to our constitution and state, exercising our power in this respect for the protection of the people committed to our care, may show our zeal in the maintenance of the true religion; not as the manner of some is, by violent oppression, but in putting to silence by such method as our law directs, the calumnies and invectives of these bold accusers, and in dispelling as we are devoutly disposed, so dreadful and dangerous a combination.

"In short, gentlemen, we should deviate from the pious path we profess to tread in, and should be unjust to God, to our king, to our country, to ourselves and to our posterity, not to take cognizance of so great a wickedness, whereby the grace of our Lord Jesus Christ is turned into lasciviousness."

In this charge the Governor admits the existence of the Act of Toleration, and its applicability to the colony of Virginia. and urges that the preachers visiting in Hanover and the surrounding counties, were liable to the rigour of the law, because they had not taken license according to the provisions of the statute.

The next day the Grand Jury brought in various presentments, of which the following is the record on the files of the General Court: "April 19th, 1745. The Grand Jury appeared according to their adjournment, and were sent out of court, and after some time returned, and presented Daniel Allen and Randal Richardson, and John Evans for assault and battery,—true bill. They also made several presentments, not drawn into form, in the words following,—to wit,—We, the Grand Jury, on information of James Axford, do present John Roan for reflecting upon and vilifying the Established Religion, in divers sermons, which he preached at the house of Joshua Morris, in the parish and county of James City, on the 7th, 8th, and 9th of January last, before a numerous audience, in the words following, to wit,—'At church you pray to the Devil'—and 'That your good works damn you, and carry you to hell,'—'That all your ministers preach false doctrine, and that they, and all who follow them, are going to hell,'—and 'The church is the house *of the Devil,—that when your ministers receive their orders they swear that it is the spirit of God that moves them to it, but it is the spirit of the Devil, and no good can proceed out of their mouth.'*

"On the information of Benjamin Cocke, we present Thomas Watkins, the son of Edward Watkins, of the parish and county of Henrico, for reflecting on the Established Religion, on the 12th of this instant, by saying,—" your churches and chappels are no better than the synagogues of Satan.'"

"We present Joshua Morris, of the parish and county of James city, for permitting John Roan, the aforementioned preacher, and very many people, to assemble in an unlawful manner at his house, on the 7th, 8th, and 9th of January last past."

Mr. Roan returned to Pennsylvania, before the meeting of the court, at which this charge had been given. We have no record of his visiting the Presbyterian colonies along the frontiers. The probability is, however, that he did not neglect them. He never afterwards visited Virginia. He lies buried at Derry Meeting house, near Dixon's ford, on the Swatara, in Dauphin county, Pennsylvania.

Beneath this stone
Are deposited the remains
Of an able, faithful,
Courageous and successful minister of Jesus Christ
JOHN ROAN,
Pastor of the United Congregations of Paxton, Derry,
and Mountjoy,
From 1745, to October 3d, 1775,
Aged 59.

The Synod held its sessions in Philadelphia; and in their sessions on Monday, May 27th, 1745—"A letter from a gentleman in Virginia, with a printed charge given by the Governor of that colony, to the grand jury, was laid before the Synod; by which it appears that the government of that colony is highly provoked by the conduct of some of the new party who preached there, and therefore the Synod judge it necessary to send an address to that Governor, informing him of the distinction between this Synod and that separated party, that so their conduct may not be imputed to us, nor provoke that government to deny us the liberties and favours we have enjoyed under it. Therefore, the Synod appoints Messrs. Cross, Thomson, Alison, and Griffith, to be a committee to draw up said address against the next sederunt." The next morning—"the address to the Governor of Virginia was brought in and approved, and is as follows;—"To the Honourable William Gooch, Esq., Lieutenant Governor of the Colony of Virginia, &c.—The humble address, &c.—

"May it please your honour; The favourable acceptance which your Honour was pleased to give our former address, and the countenance and protection which those of our persuasion have met with in Virginia, fills us with gratitude, and we beg leave on this occasion in all sincerity to express the same. It very deeply affects us to find that any who go from these parts, and perhaps assume the name of Presbyterians, should be guilty of such practices, such uncharitable, unchristian expressions, as are taken notice of in your honour's charge to the grand jury. And in the meantime it gives us the greatest pleasure that we can assure your honour, these persons never belonged to our body, but are missionaries, sent out by some, who, by reason of their divisive and uncharitable doctrines, and practices, were in May, 1741, excluded from our synod, upon which they erected themselves into a separate society, and have industriously sent abroad persons whom we judge ill-qualified for the character they assume, to divide and trouble the churches. And therefore, we humbly pray, that while those who belong to us and produce proper testimonials, behave themselves suitably, they may still enjoy the favour of your honour's countenance, and protection. And praying for the divine blessing on your person and government, we beg leave to subscribe ourselves,

"Your honour's, &c,

ROBERT CATHCART, Moderator."

To this the Governor replied. The letter is preserved in the records of Synod of Philadelphia for 1746. "Gentlemen:— The address you were pleased to send me as a grateful acknowledgment for the favour which teachers of your persuasion met with in Virginia, was very acceptable to me, but altogether needless to a person in my station, because it is what by law they are entitled to."

"And in answer to your present address, intended to justify yourselves and members from being concerned in a late outrage committed against the purity of our worship, and the sound appointment of pastors for the services of the altar of the established church, which some men calling themselves ministers, were justly accused of in my charge to the grand jury, you must suffer me to say, that it very nearly affects me, because it seems to insinuate as if I was so uncharitable as to suspect men of your education and profession could be guilty of unchristian expressions, that can only tend to the increase of schism and irreligion, which I give you my word was far from my thoughts."

"As the wicked and destructive doctrines and practices of itinerant preachers ought to be opposed and suppressed by all

who have concern for religion, and just regard to public peace
and order in Church and State, so your missionaries producing
proper testimonials, complying with the laws, and performing
divine service in some certain place appropriated for that purpose, without disturbing the quiet and unity of our sacred and
civil establishments, may be sure of the protection of,

Reverend sirs, your most humble servant,

WILLIAM GOOCH.

Williamsburg, June 20th, 1845."

The principal interest of these two letters rests upon the admission, by the Synod of Philadelphia,—that their members had
no fellowship with the awakening in Virginia,—and the implied
assertion, that they had members of their body in Virginia who
had enjoyed the advantage of the Toleration Act of William
and Mary: and on the Governor's part—the admission that
dissenters from the Church of England were by law entitled to
protection in their worship,—and that they should have it, in
the colony, if not disturbers of the public peace.   Consequently
from Makemie's time there was no contention whether dissenters
could, or should be, tolerated in Virginia; but what kind of
toleration they should experience, or rather to what degree,
they should be tolerated.   The excitement that accompanied
this "great awakening," made it necessary to follow the letter
of the law, on the principles of sound interpretation.   The
rights of citizens and the laws of the land, were from this time
profoundly studied and better understood.

The people in Hanover, in their excitement and trouble,
looked to the Presbyteries of New Castle and New Brunswick,
which met under the title of—Conjunct Presbytery for counsel
and aid.   In the month of May 1745, the month next ensuing
the term of the indictment found against Mr. Roan, they sent
four delegates, of whom Mr. Morris says he was one, to meet
the brethren of the two Presbyteries that were then preparing
to form a Synod, which by the Union of the New York Presbytery was duly organized the next September, at Elizabethtown,
New Jersey.   Of this mission Mr. Morris says—"the Lord
favoured us with success.   The Synod drew up an address to
our Governor the Honourable Wm. Gooch, and sent it with
Messrs. Tennent and Finley, who were received by the Governor, with respect, and had liberty granted them of preaching
amongst us."   Mr. Morris speaks of the Synod as formed; he
is writing some time after the event; it would have been more
strictly correct, if he had said, the brethren that are *now*, or
were soon formed into—the Synod of New York.   The Synod
at its first meeting, at Elizabethtown, in September 1745, upon
considering the circumstances of the people in Virginia, "and
the wide door that is opened for the preaching of the gospel in

these parts, with a hopeful prospect of success, the Synod are unanimously of the opinion, that Mr. Robinson is the most suitable person to be sent among them, and accordingly they do earnestly recommend it to him to go down and help them as soon as his circumstances will permit him, and reside there for some months." No person more acceptable to the people could have been designated, or sent, to those, who looked, with joy, upon him as their spiritual father. But they saw his face no more; his radiant course was coming to its close. The next meeting of the Synod of New York, took place, in the city of New York, October, 1746. The death of Mr. Robinson is made a matter of record,—and,—"a supplication and call for a minister from Hanover, in Virginia, was brought into Synod and read; the Synod doth earnestly recommend the assisting of said people, to the Presbyteries of New Brunswick and New Castle. From these Presbyteries they received their supplies till the Presbytery of Hanover was formed."

Messrs. Gilbert, Tennent, and Samuel Finley, performed their missions, and were kindly received by the Governor, who gave them permission to preach in Hanover. "By this means," says Mr. Morris, "the dreadful cloud was scattered for a while, and our languid hopes revived. They continued with us about a week, and though the deluge of passions, in which we were at first overwhelmed, was by this time somewhat abated, yet much good was done by their ministry. The people of God were refreshed, and several careless sinners were awakened. Some that had trusted before in their moral conduct and religious duties, were convinced of the depravity of their nature, and the necessity of regeneration, though indeed there were but few ungenerate persons amongst us at that time, that could claim so regular a character, the most part indulging themselves in criminal liberties, and being remiss in the duties of religion, which, alas! is too commonly the case, still, in such parts of the colony, as the late revival did not extend to. After they left us we continued vacant for a considerable time, and kept our meetings for reading and prayer in several places, and the Lord favoured us with his presence.

Extracts from the Records of the General Court, held in Williamsburg, Oct. 19th, 1745.

"Present—The GOVERNOR,

JOHN ROBINSON,	LEWIS BURWELL,
JOHN GRYMES,	WILLIAM FAIRFAX,
JOHN CUSTIS,	JOHN BLAIR, and
PHILIP LIGHTFOOT,	WILLIAM NELSON, Esqrs., and
THOMPSON LEE,	WILLIAM DAWSON, *Clerk*.

" Our Lord the King,—against

| " John Roan, Thomas Watkins, son of Edward Watkins, James Hubbard, Joshua Morris, Charles Rice, Isaac Winston, Sen. and Samuel Morris, | Upon several informations exhibited against them for misdemeanours. |

" The said defendants by their attorneys respectively say that they are not guilty in manner and form as in the said information against them alleged and of this they severally put themselves upon the country—and the Attorney General of our Lord the King, likewise." The person first named in the preceding record, was the Rev. John Roan—the last mentioned, was Mr. Morris, the reader to the people, from whom the Reading House took its name, and from whose narrative frequent quotations have been made : the others were persons, at whose houses Mr. Roan had preached, or were implicated in the excitement. Mr. Roan's name does not appear after this date. Mr. Morris says, "Six witnesses were cited to prove the charge against Mr. Roan, but their depositions were in his favour; and the witness who accused him of blasphemy, when he heard of the arrival of Messrs. Tennent and Finley, fled, and has not returned since, so that the indictment was dropped."

Mr. Samuel Finley, one of the delegation, was pastor of Nottingham, Cecil county, Maryland. Born of pious parents in the county of Armagh, Ireland, in the year 1715, he was deeply impressed with a sense of religion when he was six years old. Emigrating to America, he landed in Philadelphia, September 28th, 1734. Having pursued his studies for the ministry, through many difficulties, he was licensed by New Brunswick Presbytery August 5th, 1740. Having preached with great acceptance, he was ordained as Evangelist, October 13th, 1742, and enjoyed much success in his labours at Deerfield, Greenwich and Cape May, New Jersey. In June 1744 he went to Nottingham, where was a large congregation of his countrymen and their descendants. He was installed pastor the same year he visited Virginia. He opened an Academy in Nottingham, and attracted scholars from a great distance, being justly famed as a scholar, and eminently qualified as a teacher. In this institution, Rev. Dr. McWhorter, Dr. Rush, Governor Henry of Maryland, Col. John Bayard, and a number of other eminently useful characters, received their education. Upon the death of President Davies in 1761, Mr. Finley was chosen his successor. In his early ministry he was much engaged in the great revival; and during his presidency, in the year 1762, there was a great attention to religion among the students, nearly one half being hopefully converted.

Mr. Finley was a man of small stature, round face, and

ruddy countenance. In the pulpit he was always solemn, and sometimes glowing with fervor. He possessed great knowledge of the human heart, and was remarkable for sweetness of temper, politeness and generosity. The University of Glasgow conferred on him the degree of Doctor of Divinity in 1763.

At the request of some people in New Milford, Connecticut, who had seceded from the Congregational church on account of the Arminian doctrine of the minister, he was sent by Presbytery to preach to them a short time. Lieutenant Governor Law, who belonged to the opposing party, taking advantage of the strict laws then in force in Connecticut, ordered him to be arrested, and carried from constable to constable, and from one town to another, to the borders of the State, and there dismissed.

Going to Philadelphia for medical advice, he closed his most useful and exemplary life, on the 17th of July 1776, in a joyful and triumphant manner. His biography would form a choice volume of Christian experience. He was an example of enjoyment in the profession of gospel truth, and in spiritual exercises.

The other minister appointed by the "Conjunct Presbytery," afterwards the Synod of New York, to visit Governor Gooch, was Gilbert Tennent, son of Rev. William Tennent, of "Log College" memory. Born in Ireland, Feb. 5th, 1703, the eldest of four brothers that became Presbyterian ministers, he was hopefully converted at the age of fourteen, under the ministry of his father. His education was completed at the "Log College." Licensed by New Castle Presbytery in the year 1725, he was the same year settled in New Brunswick. He was the chief instrument of the separation of the Synod in 1741, devoutly believing that a separation was necessary for the preservation and advancement of religion. He expressed his opinions of his opponents with great vehemence, in his famous "Nottingham Sermon." In 1743 he became pastor of the church in Philadelphia, which was gathered chiefly from "those who were denominated the converts and followers of Mr. Whitefield." A bold, ardent, practical, and unusually impressive preacher, his labours in the great revival were productive of visible and lasting good. In 1753 he was chosen with Samuel Davies, to represent the College of New Jersey before the churches in England. The journal of Mr. Davies has been preserved and makes a part of this volume. Nothing has yet appeared from the pen of Mr. Tennent, in the diary or journal form, respecting that successful visit. As Mr. Tennent had been a leading man in the division of the Synod, he was equally prominent in the reunion. In one he appeared a son of thunder, and in the other a son of consolation. He continued in

the ministry about forty years.   In a sermon preached before
the College, and published, by request, in 1757, he argues that
the pollution of Adam's race can be accounted for only by the
fact that Adam's sin was imputed to all his race.   He never
dissented from the orthodox construction of the Confession of
Faith.

"After these left us,"—says Mr. Morris—"we continued
vacant for a considerable time, and kept our meetings for reading and prayer in several places.   And the Lord favoured us
with his presence.   I was again prosecuted and repeatedly fined
in court for absenting myself from church and keeping up
unlawful meetings, as they were called.   The next that were
appointed to supply us were the Rev. William Tennent and
Samuel Blair.   They administered the Lord's supper amongst
us; and we have reason to remember it as the most glorious
day of the Son of Man.   The assembly was large, and the
novelty of the manner of administration did peculiarly engage
their attention.   It appeared as one of the days of heaven to
some of us; and we could hardly help wishing we could with
Joshua have delayed the revolution of the heavens to prolong it."

William Tennent, here mentioned, was the second son of
William Tennent of the "Log College."   In the course of his
preparation for the ministry he was taken ill and appeared to
die.   Saved from burial by the importunity of one who loved
him with peculiar tenderness, he revived.   All recollection of
his former acquirements was gone.   By degrees his mind was
restored to its proper action, and he finished his preparation for
the ministry.   More than six feet high, of a spare thin visage,
erect carriage, bright piercing eye, with a countenance grave
and solemn, he was always cheerful, and won youth to seek his
conversation.   He carried through life a lively recollection of
the scenes and things that occupied his mind during the days
he lay as one dead; they were a perpetual stimulus in his ministerial work.   He preached with indescribable power, in a
manner peculiar to himself, and seldom failed to interest and
impress his audience.   Of scrupulous integrity, independent
mind, and an uncommonly clear perception of human character,
he was a noted peace maker.   Living above the world, he finished his course March 8th, 1777, having been pastor of Freehold, New Jersey, forty-two years.

His associate, Samuel Blair, was famous in his day as an admirable preacher, a superior teacher, and a good writer.   Born
in Ireland, June 14th, 1712, he was early removed to Monmouth,
New Jersey; and completed his education at the "Log College"
of William Tennent.   He was licensed in 1733 by the Presbytery of Philadelphia, which then covered New Jersey.   The

next year he was ordained pastor at Shrewsberry, by the Presbytery of East Jersey, which had been set off from the Philadelphia Presbytery. Five years after, the Presbytery of New Brunswick was formed and he was a member. In the fall of 1739, by the advice of Presbytery, Mr. Blair removed to New Londonderry in Faggs Manor Chester county, Pennsylvania. The next year his congregation was visited with a powerful awakening, which spread to the neighbouring congregations, and ultimately reached Virginia under the preaching of Mr. Robinson, who found the soil prepared to his hand. Mr. Blair opened a school in which were educated some noted ministers of the Presbyterian Church—Alexander Cumming, settled in Boston,—John Rodgers, in New York,—John Blair Professor of Divinity at Nassau Hall,—Rev. James Finley, Hugh Henry, and Samuel Davies whose name is dear to Virginia and Nassau Hall. The attachment of Davies to Mr. Blair may be seen in his Journal. The feelings of tenderness and sentiments of respect expressed on a visit to the dwelling of the widow are worthy of the pupil and his teacher. Dr. Green tells us, in his History of the College of New Jersey, that Mr. Davies, on his return from Britain, in reply to an inquiry respecting the pulpit orators he had heard abroad, replied,—"that there was scarce one of them who exceeded, and most of them came far short of his old master, Mr. Blair, both as to the matter of their discourses, and the impression produced by their delivery. He died July 5th, 1751, at the early age of thirty-nine years and twenty-one days. His last sickness was brought on by a journey to Nassau Hall to attend a meeting of the Trustees. He lay a long time in Philadelphia; and feeling his end approaching, he sent for the elders of his church, and two members from each quarter of his congregation, and gave them his dying council. This was preserved and printed by his brother-in-law the Rev. Robert Smith of Pequa. Dr. Finley says,—"strict holiness was his choice."

These gentlemen, the Tennents and Finley and Blair, it is supposed visited the other Presbyterians in Virginia, as well as those in Hanover. Of this however we have no written document, or direct tradition further than—"Hat Creek in Campbell county was consecrated with the prayers of Gilbert Tennent."

"After Mr. Tennent and Blair were gone"—says Mr. Morris—"Mr. Whitefield came and preached four or five days, which was the happy means of giving us further encouragement, and of engaging others to the Lord, especially amongst the church people, who received the gospel more readily from him than from ministers of the Presbyterian denomination.

After his departure we were destitute of a minister, and followed our usual method of reading and prayer at our meetings, till the Rev. Mr. Davies, our present pastor, was sent us by the Presbytery to supply a few Sabbaths in the spring of 1747, when our discouragements from Government were renewed and multiplied."

The early Presbyterians in Virginia were enlightened by a galaxy of ministers, of which the church might glory in her best days. In the height of the religious excitement, they were called, in derision, by the clergy of the established church, and others who opposed,—dissenters,—enthusiasts,—fanatics,—new lights,—hypocrites,—while they themselves gloried in the names of Christians—and Presbyterians. Davies in writing to the Bishop of London acknowledged himself one of those designated by opposers—as "new lights;" but he shows that it was a misnomer. In Virginia the word "new light," in a little time, lost its opprobrium, and became among Presbyterians a technical phrase; but was never recognised as their proper name.

The labours of these men, Robinson, Roan, the Blairs, and the Tennents, laid the foundation on which Davies builded; and all united have had a controlling influence over Virginia Presbyterians in creed and practice, to this day. From the time of these men, the Virginia ministers and people have believed in awakenings,—in spiritual exercises in religion,—and the power of godliness in men's hearts and lives. From deep conviction they have been believers in the depravity of human nature,—the sovereignty of God,—original sin,—the divinity of Christ,—the influences of the Holy Spirit as a divine person,—and the absolute necessity of the new birth. Hoping for justification by the righteousness of Christ made theirs by faith, believing it would be safe to appear in it, in the judgment to come, ministers and people rejoiced in the unsearchable riches of Christ, through trials and difficulties that would make ordinary spirits tremble and quit the field. By the help of God they have left us a good report.

CHAPTER IX.

AT the death of Rev. James Blair, one of the greatest benefactors of Virginia, in the year 1743, the ecclesiastical and political condition of the colony had not ostensibly much changed, except by expansion. Looking back upon the progress of things, we now see the colony was even then on the eve of changes and revolutions that went on with rapidly increasing force and extending influence till consummated in complete political and religious liberty, the liberty of choice and of law.

The population had greatly increased, and was taking possession of the vallies beyond the Blue Ridge. The frontiers had been removed several days journey west of the head of tide water. Emigrations were flowing in, destined to have a greater influence on the State, than mere numbers, or wealth however increased. Virginia was esteemed loyal through all the changes and revolutions that shook the throne of England in the time of the Charleses, and the Jameses, and Cromwell, and the Prince of Orange. There was nothing to make her otherwise. She had a State religion with which the overwhelming majority were satisfied, and would probably have been forever had it been rightly administered. In her assembly she claimed and exercised all the independence a colony in her condition desired. Too weak to stand alone, she clung to the throne of England by which she had not felt herself oppressed. In the collisions with proprietors and the Board in London, the King had appeared the friend of the colony, which had not yet questioned his prerogative in Church and State. She had been indulged in her Legislature more than ever the Parliament of England had been, on account of her distance, and the apparent unimportance of the political bearing of her independent acts. And yet by her increasing area and population, by her habits of personal independence and increasing wealth, Virginia was rapidly preparing for the change from the most loyal to the most republican colony.

In her ecclesiastical concerns the elements of change were ready to be developed. The number of the clergy had increased with the increasing parishes, but had not improved in general character or influence. The Bishop of London said

of them, about this time,—in his letter to Dr. Doddridge—
"Of those who are sent from hence, a great part are the
Scotch or Irish, who can get no employment at home, and
enter into the service more out of necessity than choice.
Some others are willing to go abroad to retrieve either lost
fortune or lost character. For these reasons and others of
less weight I did apply to the King, as soon as I was Bishop
of London, to have two or three bishops appointed for the
plantations to reside there."

The support of the clergy was regulated somewhat differently, at this time, from the law and custom of 1688. At that
period, as stated in chapter first, a tax of sixteen pounds of
tobacco was levied on each of the titheables of the parish, for
the support of the minister. His support varied, consequently,
with the number of his titheable parishioners, as well as with
the quality of the tobacco cultivated. But in 1696, to remove
in part this inequality and secure a competent salary in all
parishes, it was enacted,—"that all and every parish minister,
or ministers, in all and every parish and parishes, in this dominion, incumbent in said parish or parishes, and therein officiating as minister, or ministers, shall have and receive for his
or their meantenance the sume of sixteen thousand pounds of
tobacco besides their perquisites." This law remained in force
till the Revolution. In the fluctuations of trade and the consequent changes in the price of tobacco, the operations of this
law were a source of great complaint to the clergy, and constant vexation to the whole country. The preamble of the law
sets forth, that this law was made for the advantage of religion
and its ministers; history declares it was the cause of sorrow
and endless disputes to both ministers and people, and embittered the revolutionary contest. Beverly tells us—"When
these salaries were granted, the Assembly valued tobacco at
ten shillings per hundred; but in all parishes where the sweet
scented grew, since the law for appointing agents to view the
tobacco was made, it has generally been sold for double that
value. The fee for a funeral sermon is forty shillings, or four
hundred pounds of tobacco; for a marriage, by license, twenty
shillings, or two hundred pounds of tobacco; and when the
bans are proclaimed only five shillings or fifty pounds of tobacco." There was also a dwelling house and glebe lands, &c.—
"in some parishes likewise, there are, by donation, stocks of
cattle and negroes, on the glebes, which are also allowed to the
minister, for his use and encouragement." The amount of
support given the clergy taken in connexion with their general
influence and their seeking from the Legislature greater emoluments, had an influence on the public mind preparatory to the
change which now began to appear.

In some particulars, the clergy of the established church have not received justice, at the hands of historians. Some of them were men of piety, whose death was triumphant. Many were men of classical education, who brought libraries of value from the mother country. Some of these, from necessity, and others from choice, opened classical schools, and taught thoroughly and extensively. The sons of the wealthy were instructed at these schools. To the parsons, whose morals were often distressingly loose, and whose religion was but a name, Eastern Virginia was for a long time indebted for her supply of educated men.

The citizens of Virginia were advancing in wealth and refinement; and in courtly manners, had no peers in the colonies, except in Boston, Massachusetts, Edenton and Newbern, North Carolina, and in parts of South Carolina. Williamsburg was the centre of taste and fashion and refinement. The sessions of the General Court, and the house of burgesses, collected the wealth and talent of Virginia, that vied in splendour with the representative of royalty. The entertainments of the Governor and Council in the capital were answered by entertainments in the country; and a season of revelry in the city was followed by a tour of visiting in the country. Young men seeking refinement of manners had specimens of the English gentlemen to copy. Wealth, dress, and address were every thing: and the two latter were often obtained at the expense of the former. A season unfavourable for tobacco brought dismay to those who were in the habit of anticipating their income. Sometimes, unhappily, the father left his son expensive habits, a worn out plantation, and a heavy debt; then degradation by poverty, premature death, or emigration to the western borders, were the alternatives. Too spirited to be degraded, and too proud to be mean, many families carried to new settlements, in the wilderness, easy manners, dear bought experience, and social refinement; and commencing life anew, ran a new course, less splendid and expensive, but not less amiable; less captivating, but not the less useful to the State. The farther the removal from Williamsburg, the less the dependence on the King: the more embosomed in the mountains, the more resolutely did the pioneers contend against authority that was not warranted by necessity and the plainest dictates of law. Above tide-water, the people simple in their habits, plain in manners, and accustomed to a roving and independent life, questioned every demand made upon their property, their persons, or their enjoyments. They were still loyal, because they had not been provoked by oppression. Their children were republicans; in England they would have been styled rebels.

The Rev. James Blair led the way for improvement in literature and science; and opened the path from obscurity to renown, for some of the greatest statesmen of their age. He did much that, in concurrence with other causes to be mentioned, brought about the Revolution in Virginia. He wished well to the colony, and laboured like a patriot, in all probability unconscious of the effects to be produced by his labours. He sought for mental improvement as a means to advance morals and religion. He accomplished what he designed, and unthinkingly perhaps, put in motion a mighty engine to shake the throne and set conscience free. He was the father of successful literary enterprise in Virginia, and all the South. Commonly called Commissary Blair, his glory is in being the founder of William and Mary College. Mr. Blair was born in Scotland, in the year 1665. Having a liberal Scotch education, he obtained a benefice in the Established Church of England, as set up in Scotland by the Stuarts. That form of government was never acceptable to the great body of the Scotch; and much less so were the ceremonies of worship. Mr. Blair, unwilling to perform the ministrations of his office amidst discontent and constant uneasiness, left Scotland, hoping to find in England an opportunity to labour in usefulness and peace. This was some time in the reign of Charles the Second. Compton, Bishop of London, made choice of him as a missionary to the Colonies, and prevailed on him to sail for Virginia in 1685. Mr. Blair's ministerial labours and general deportment in Virginia being highly acceptable to the planters and government officers, a favourable report of him reached the Bishop of London. When Sir Francis Nicholson was, in 1689, made Lieutenant-Governor of Virginia, the Bishop made Mr. Blair his Commissary. The Governor publicly entered upon his office June 3d, 1690. The next day, says Burke, the commission of Mr. Blair as Commissary was laid before the Council. The Commissary was the Bishop's deputy with limited powers. He might hold conventions of the clergy for the discipline of the Church, and might visit churches for that purpose; but could not ordain Priests or Deacons, or depose delinquent church officers, or confirm communicants. The office was more burdensome than profitable, and required peculiar talents for government. It gave Mr. Blair some advantage in his efforts to build a college, as he appeared as the representative of the Bishop of London. The salary was £100 from the quit rents.

The wants of the country deeply affected his mind before he became Commissary; and he had also contemplated the true remedy which was, in part, with the powers in England, and in part, with him in Virginia. To his part he addressed himself with all his strength. With the installation of the Governor and the proclamation of his own commission as Commissary, he brought forward his proposition for a College for Protestant Virginia. A subscription paper headed by the Governor and his Council soon amounted to 2500*l.* In the first assembly held by Nicholson, in 1691, the project of the College was highly approved and recommended to the patronage of their majesties; and Commissary Blair was appointed to present the address. Their majesties William and Mary highly approved the plan of the College; and sent over an ample charter by Governor Andress, bearing date February 14th, 1792. The Bishop of London was Chancellor, Mr. Blair President, with six professors, for Latin, Greek, Mathematics, Moral Philosophy, Divinity, and for the instruction of Indians. The name was William and Mary. The preamble of the charter says—" their trusty and well beloved subjects, constituting the General Assembly of the colony of Virginia, have had it in their minds, and have proposed to themselves, to found and establish a certain place of universal study, or perpetual college of Divinity, philosophy, languages, and other good arts and sciences—to the end that the church of Virginia may be furnished with a seminary of ministers of the gospel, and that the youth may be piously educated in good letters and manners, and that the Christian faith may be propagated among the Western Indians, to the glory of Almighty God." The corporation might hold property to the amount of 2000*l.* a year. Trustees were appointed, with full powers, to act till the College was completed; the whole then to pass into the hands of the President and Professors who were then to become a corporation. Their Majesties endowed the College with about 2000*l.* quit rents due them from the colony; with 20,000 acres of land; with the place of the Surveyor General of the colony, then vacant, worth about 50*l.* per annum; with the duty of a penny a pound on all tobacco exported to the sister colonies, worth about 200*l.* per annum; and the privilege of a Burgess in the Assembly. The Assembly of Virginia added the duty on skins and furs, worth about 100*l.* per annum; and from time to time made other liberal donations. The legislature determined that the College should not be located as first designed, at Townsends lands, but at Middle Plantations, near the church. This place was afterwards chosen as the capital, and named Williamsburg. The foundation of the College was immediately laid, in the form of a square; and two sides completed and occupied for purposes of instruction.

In erecting this College, Mr. Blair exhibited a patience and perseverance worthy of all praise. Colleges in colonies were not then popular either in England or the colonies themselves. In England many said,—" Let the colonists attend to the productions of the earth, and look to England for learning and learned men." When pressed on the subject of religion in the colony, one of the lords of trade imprecated a curse upon their souls—"let them make tobacco." In the colony those who thought they would lose by the application of the imports, as directed by their majesties, opposed the College. They said in the colony, that the planters, by means of the College and schools, would be drawn from their business, and the colony would become poor; and to the powers in England that the colonists would become too knowing to be obedient and submissive subjects. Mr. Blair urged that the English born in the colony were capable of everything, if provided with the means of a good education; that as Virginia lay between the colonies north and south, her College might be a common nursery; and that the native colonists would be put in a way of further improvement. He also insisted on the advantages arising to religion from such an institution, both in the colony, and also among the Indians on its borders. The christianising the Indians was a favourite project with the pious in England. Robert Boyle made a handsome donation to the College, to secure the education of young Indians, and their conversion to Christianity. He called the professorship, "Brafferton" from an estate in England purchased with the money, the income of which was to support the professor.

After sixteen years of labour, the College was in successful operation, with this drawback, that the scholars were mostly young beginners. Boys commencing their education, were sent to the professor of languages, and the College wore the aspect of an academy or high-school. More advanced scholars would not attend with these young beginners in a young institution. This difficulty arose from the want of proper schools, primary and classical, and could be remedied only by their multiplication. A greater drawback was from a fire, in 1705, during the short administration of Governor Nott. "Very little saved that was in it," says Beverly, "the fire breaking out about 10 o'clock at night, in a public time. The Governor, and all the gentlemen in town came up to the lamentable spectacle, many getting out of their beds. But the fire had got such power, before it was discovered, and was so fierce, that there were no hopes of putting a stop to it, and therefore no attempts made to that end."

The College, which was commenced in Henrico, in the early days of the colony, after receiving many endowments, was abandoned after the massacre by the Indians in 1622; and with it the high-school in Charles city, called the East India School, to be connected with the College, was given up. The act for a college, passed in 1662, existed on paper; and now the College of William and Mary, after the labours of sixteen years, was consumed. Mr. Blair was not discouraged. Under Governor Spottswood's administration, and by the favour of that gentleman, a new edifice was erected, and the College exercises resumed. Beverly says that Spottswood was a friend of the Indians. " There had been a donation of large sums of money, by the Hon. Robert Boyle, Esq., to this college, for the education of Indian children therein. In order to make use of this, they had formerly brought half a dozen of captive Indian children, slaves, and put them into the College. This method did not satisfy this Governor, as not answering the intent of the donor, so to work he goes among the tributary and other neighbouring Indians, and in a short time brought them to send their children to be educated; and brought new nations, some of which lived four hundred miles off, taking their children for hostages and education equally, at the same time setting up a school in the frontiers convenient to the Indians, that they might often see their children under the first managements, where they learnt to read, paying fifty pounds per annum out of his own pocket to the schoolmaster there; after which they were brought to the College, where they were taught till they grew big enough for their hunting and other exercises, at which time they returned home and smaller ones were taken in their stead." To the honour of the founders of the " University at Henrico" and of William and Mary College, the education of the Indian youth formed an important integral part of their plan, and was pursued with commendable spirit. But, as in the case of the school of Dr. Wheelock, and of Dartmouth College, comparatively little was effected by the benevolent effort. There was one difficulty never surmounted. The educated Indian must either abandon his nation, or live among barbarians. If he abandoned his country, the object of his education, influence over his nation for civilization, was lost. If he went to the barbarians, he must live single or take a savage for his wife, or do what was not thought of for a moment, marry a white woman. Modern efforts for the civilization of Indians are carried on in a different way marked out by experience, and embrace the education of females.

Besides performing the duties of Commissary and President of the College, Mr. Blair found time to write for the press. In 1722 there was published—" Our Saviour's Divine Sermon on the Mount, contained in the 5th, 6th and 7th chapters of St. Matthew's Gospel, Explained: And the practice of it recommended in divers Sermons and Discourses. In four volumes. By James Blair, Commissary of Virginia, President of William and Mary College, and Rector of Williamsburgh in that colony." A second edition corrected by the author, and published under the care of Dr. Waterland, was made in the year 1739. The Doctor prefixed a recommendatory notice.

He says that noblest of subjects, the Saviour's Sermon on the Mount, "is here explained with good judgment, so it appears likewise to be pressed with due force; in a clear, easy, yet masculine style, equally fitted to the capacities of common Christians, and the improved understanding of the knowing and judicious." He observes also—"how happy a talent the author had in deciding points of great moment in a very few plain words, but the result of deep consideration, and discovering great compass of thought. Dr. Doddridge, the Dissenter, author of the Family Expositor, in his Exposition, refers to Mr. Blair as a writer of authority—"Mr. Blair in his excellent discourses on this chapter has shown, what a beautiful correspondence there is between the characters described in these beatitudes, and the blessings connected with them." And again commenting on the doxology in the Lord's prayer, he says—"yet it is certainly very ancient; and as Bishop Hopkins, Mr. Blair, and other excellent writers have well observed, so admirably suits, and enforces every preceding petition, that I could not persuade myself to omit it."

Mr. Whitefield passed through Virginia in 1740, about three years before the death of Mr. Blair. In his journal for December 15th he says—"Paid my respects to Mr. Blair, Commissary of Virginia. His discourse was savory, such as tended to the use of edifying. He received me with joy, asked me to preach, and wished my stay were longer."

Mr. Blair's labours in Virginia was not to prevent his people leaning to dissent from the established church, for, except the few colonies of Presbyterians that were on the frontiers, and the German settlement on the Rappahannoc, and the Huguenots on the James, none of which caused any alarm, he knew nothing of dissent, in practice. His great labour was to supply Virginia with educated men, and the church with a proper ministry. As far as he succeeded he did the work of a true churchman and patriot.

Mr. Blair died, August 1st, 1743, aged eighty eight years. He had been a missionary fifty-eight years, and a minister of the gospel about sixty-two years; had acted as Commissary fifty-four years, and Presdent of the College fifty years. William and Mary is his enduring monument. The influence of that institution on the colony was gentle in its first operations; its advance regular, and yet quite imperceptible, at any one time. We cannot say we see its action till the time of the Revolution. There is no evidence that disloyalty was ever uttered from a Professor's chair. But there is evidence, that literature, and science, and religion, acting upon youthful minds, in this colony, remote from the fascinations of royalty, made republicans. The College was in its organization Episcopal, and probably will always remain so. It has had eminent men, of that denomination, at its head, both laymen and ministers; and is now under the supervision of a Diocesan. A detailed history of its origin, progress, troubles, and changes, with some notice of the eminent men that were its alumni would prove a volume of interest to the church to which, ecclesiastically, it belongs, and of value to the cause of literature and religion at large. Every man would like to know more of the mother college, at the South, especially after reading from one of the greatest politicians in America—"In the spring of 1760, went to William and Mary College, where I continued two years. It was my great good fortune, and what probably fixed the destinies of my life, that Dr. William Small of Scotland, was then Professor of Mathematics, a man profound in most of the useful branches of science, with a happy talent of communicative, correct, and gentlemanly, manners and an enlarged and liberal mind. He most happily for me, became soon attached to me, and made me his daily companion when not engaged in the school; and from his conversation I got my first views of the expansion of science, and of the system of things in which we are placed." This gentleman penned the Declaration of Independence and the Bill for Religious Liberty.

The influence of the African population on the colony was now fully seen. Politicians were sensible that slavery, as an element of society, gave rise to new habits, customs, laws, and usages; made the administration of law and justice peculiar; and gave a new turn to discussions about private rights. From being an instrument of wealth it had become a moulding power, leaving it a vexed question, which controlled society most, the African slave or his master. The number of slaves in Virginia in 1743 cannot be known. Governor Berkely tells us in 1671 there were 2000 slaves to a population of 38,000 whites. In 1790 by census there were 293,427 slaves and 454,881 whites. The increase of the slaves had been like multiplying 2000 by 146; the white, like multiplying 38,000 by 12, nearly. What was the relative number in 1743 is conjectural. But in that year the number of counties was thirty-six; and the House of Burgesses consisted of eighty members, two from each county, one from each of the towns of Norfolk, Williamsburg and Jamestown, and one from William and Mary College.

Philanthropists looked with deep interest on this new element in English society, and found in Virginia a phase of slavery diverse from all ancient or modern forms of servitude. Servants for life, scattered among the whites and outnumbered by them, the Africans in Virginia were under civilizing influences immeasurably superior to those in the West India islands.

While by their labour they conferred affluence and ease upon their masters; by thus being congregated in small numbers, and intermingled with the whites they were by degrees recovered from their native savageness, and led to some more becoming ideas of civilization and propriety. The meanest servant on a Virginia plantation, after a few years residence, knew more of the proprieties of life than the savage chiefs in Africa. Christian people looked upon this body of men with peculiar sympathy, and recognised a part of their Lord's vineyard unlike any found in Europe, and requiring the services of devoted ministers of the gospel. That such men were found, and that the spiritual welfare of this class of people was cared for in proportion to the white population, will appear in the history of religious denominations in the colony.

Two events of like nature, but differing in time and circumstance, had an influence on the religious aspect of the colony, and ultimately on its political condition. By permission of the Legislature a colony of Huguenots was planted in Virginia east of the Blue Ridge; and this in a few years was followed by a colony of Germans; each of which was permitted to have its own ministers and exercise its own forms of religion. The Huguenots, soon left their village at Manakin town, and intermingled with the English in the neighbouring counties. The Germans, in Madison county, have preserved their location and in some good degree their manners, but are fast loosing their language. They were followed by numerous colonies that made their home in the Valley of the Shenandoah. Their numbers and wealth prevailed to have some enactments of the Legislature recognising their existence and influence.

These colonies, on the frontiers, and the College near the eastern border of the province, grew together. Their influence, like the rivers on which they flourished, spread wider and deeper, and, at the time of Mr. Blair's death, began to assume the form of a head stream, meandering gently yet permanently through a rich and beautiful country of forests and intermingled habitations of men.

CHAPTER X.

REV. SAMUEL DAVIES, FROM HIS BIRTH TO HIS VOYAGE TO
ENGLAND.

THE month of April, 1747, in Hanover county, Virginia, was
one of those times in which, the current of human events, running on with increasing bitterness, takes an unexpected turn;
the waters of Mara are sweetened, and the night of clouds and
thick darkness has its morning of brightness and joy.

After Mr. Whitefield's visit, the Presbyterians were not only
without a minister, but grievously harassed by the pains and
penalties of the law. "Upon a Lord's day"—says Mr. Morris—"a proclamation was set up at our meeting-house, strictly
requiring all magistrates to suppress and prohibit, as far as
they lawfully could, all itinerant preachers,—which occasioned
us to forbear reading that day, till we had time to deliberate
and consult what was expedient to do. But how joyfully were
we surprised before the next Sabbath, when we unexpectedly
heard that Mr. Davies was come to preach so long amongst us,
and especially that he had qualified himself according to law,
and obtained the licensing of four meeting-houses among us,
which had never been done before."

No man had equal influence with Mr. Davies in gathering the
congregations and settling the ministers that composed the
Presbytery of Hanover, the first Presbytery south of the Potomac, in connexion with the Synods of New York and Philadelphia. His spirit and habits and tastes gave complexion to the
Presbytery, and the Synod that grew out of the Presbytery.
The incidents of his life will always be interesting to the Southern church, over which his influence is still exerted, and to the
generations to which he is still preaching by his posthumous
sermons.

Samuel Davies was born near Summit Ridge, about twelve
miles from Drawyer's Church, New Castle county, state of
Delaware, November 3d, 1723, of Welch extract, both by
father's and mother's side. His father was a farmer, of small
property, of moderate intellectual endowments, and of a blame-
less, religious life. His mother was possessed of superior
natural abilities, and was eminently and ardently pious. Of
her, Mr. Davies says, in a letter to Dr. Gibbons, of London,
that he was blessed with a mother whom he might account,
without filial vanity or partiality, one of the most eminent

saints he ever knew upon earth. "I cannot but mention to my friend an anecdote known to but few; that is, that I am a son of prayer, like my namesake, Samuel the prophet, and my mother called me Samuel, because, she said, I have asked him of the Lord. This early dedication to God has always been a strong inducement to me to devote myself to him as a personal act, and the most important blessings of my life I have looked upon as immediate answers to the prayers of a pious mother."

The father died the month next succeeding the son's acceptance of the presidency of the College of New Jersey, August 11th, 1759, aged 79 years. The mother survived the son some years, and was an inmate of the house of Dr. Rodgers of New York, the intimate friend of Mr. Davies, and his companion in their preparatory studies for the ministry, and their early exercise of the sacred office.

As there is some discrepancy in the dates given by the different notices that have been published respecting Mr. Davies, it is proper here to observe, that the dates given in this sketch, for his birth,—licensure,—ordination,—marriage,—settlement in Virginia,—his departure for England,—his return to Virginia,—his acceptance of the presidency,—his father's death, and other dates respecting his family, are copied from memoranda made by his own hand, in an interleaved quarto Bible, now in the possession of his descendants near Petersburg, Virginia.

Mr. Davies is represented as having been a sprightly docile child. As there was no school in the neighbourhood, his early instructions in the rudiments of education were from the lips of his mother. At about ten years of age he had the opportunity of attending an English school, some distance from home. According to his own opinion, while he made rapid progress in learning, during the two years of his attendance, he lost some of the deep impressions made by his mother's teaching, example and prayers. His habits of secret prayer were continued, and—"he was more ardent in his supplications for being introduced into the gospel ministry, than for any thing else." At the age of twelve years he received impressions of a religious nature that were abiding. In his fifteenth year, having a settled confidence of being justified by faith through grace, he made a public profession of religion by uniting with the Church. His heart was impressible, his conscience tender, his feelings lively; and in reviewing his own conduct, he became, at this early period, a severe and unsparing judge of himself, in all things pertaining to godliness.

His classical course was commenced under the tuition of an estimable and learned Welsh minister, a Mr. Morgan, a pupil of the Rev. Thomas Evans of the same nation. When Rev. Samuel Blair opened his famous school at Fagg's Manor, Chester county, Pennsylvania, young Davies was put under his tuition, and there completed his education. In that school strict attention was paid to the classics and the sciences. The acquisition of theological knowledge was sedulously encouraged from the commencement of the course. The standard of classical acquirement was high; and the acquaintance with the best writers on systematic theology was accurate. As evidence of the high standing of Mr. Blair's school, and its real efficiency, in making scholars, it may be observed, that from his students came—John Rodgers, the eminently prudent patriarch of the churches in New York city,—Alexander Cummins, nephew of Mr. Blair, for some time minister in New York, and afterwards in Boston,—Hugh Henry for a long time pastor of Monakin and Rehoboth, the ancient churches on the Eastern Shore of Maryland,—and Robert Smith, of Pequa, the father of Samuel Stanhope and John Blair Smith, whose names are indissolubly connected with the two Colleges, Hampden Sidney in Virginia, and Union in New York.

Mr. Davies was a student. Stimulated to close application, by his narrow means, and earnest desire for improvement, his slender frame became enfeebled, and, at the time his course of preparatory studies was completed, his health was very delicate. He was licensed by Newcastle Presbytery, July 30th, 1746.

Of the circumstances of his first marriage, nothing more is known than the following brief record taken from his Bible,—"Married to Sarah Kirkpatrick, October 23d, 1746."

On the 19th of February, 1747, he was ordained Evangelist, for the purpose of visiting the congregations in Virginia, especially those in Hanover county. He had been aided by these people in his preparatory studies by the agency of Rev. William Robinson; his few months of probation in the vacancies in Delaware and Pennsylvania had answered the high anticipations of his friends; and his prudence and piety were of that order called for in difficult posts in the Lord's vineyard. All these things designated him as the proper person to send to the interesting, yet perplexing field of Hanover county, Virginia. The civil suits instituted against Messrs. Roan, Morris, Watkins and others, in October, 1745, for holding religious worship, contrary to the law of the province, were still pending; and the agitation of the public mind by no means allayed. Davies was reluctant, doubting his own experience in church and political matters, and his bodily health; but in obedience to his presbytery, he set out for his destined field of labour.

Before visiting Hanover county, Mr. Davies passing down the Eastern Shore of Maryland and Virginia, and traversing the country once occupied by Makemie, repaired to Williamsburg, in Virginia. "I petitioned the General Court to grant me a license to officiate in and about Hanover, at four meeting-houses." The Governor, Mr. William Gooch favoured the application. The council hesitated. The tall, slim, well-formed youth, pale and wasted by disease, dignified and courteous in manner, won the Governor's favour. It were better he should lead the people in Hanover, according to law, than to subject them to fines and imprisonment for receiving instructions according to the law of their conscience, but contrary to the law of the land. The Governor remembered his promise that the Presbyterians acting according to the provisions of the law, should be protected, especially on the frontiers. The General Court was in session, the highest court in the province, composed of the Governor and council. The Governor presided. In state and parade, Virginia surpassed all the other provinces. Davies in after years may have appeared more grand, but he never appeared more interesting than when he modestly asked of the court, and finally obtained by the influence of the Govenor, permission to preach the gospel unmolested, to the vexed and harassed people of God, in Hanover. The license was issued in the following form :

"April 14th, 1747.

"Present—the GOVERNOR,

JOHN ROBINSON,	LEWIS BURWELL,
JOHN GRYMES,	WILLIAM FAIRFAX,
JOHN CUSTIS,	JOHN BLAIR, and
PHILIP LIGHTFOOT,	WILLIAM NELSON, Esqrs.
THOMAS LEE.	WILLIAM DAWSON, Clerk.

" On the petition of Samuel Davies, a Dissenting Minister, who, this day in Court, took the usual oaths to his Majesty's person and government, and subscribed the Test, and likewise publicly declared his assent thereunto, he is allowed to assemble and meet any congregations of Dissenters, at the several meeting-houses, on the lands of Samuel Morris, David Rice, and Stephen Leacy, in Hanover county, and on the lands of Thomas Watkins in Henrico county, without molestation, they behaving in a peaceable manner, and conforming themselves according to the directions of the acts of parliament in that behalf made."

In two days the trial of those indicted for worshipping contrary to law, while Mr. Roan was in the province, commenced. The granting Mr. Davies license to preach, and the licensing of houses, some of which were on the lands of the indicted, had no effect with the Council or Governor towards dismissing those arraigned for past offences of worshipping contrary to law and custom. In the opinion of the Court, justice required some victims to preserve the sanctity of the law; and the incensed church must be appeased by fines.

On the 17th of April, 1747, the Governor present, with same council as above, with the exception of Messrs. Burwell and Dawson, the case of Thomas Watkins the son of Edward Watkins, was called, and,—"continued to the next court at the motion and costs of the said Thomas."

On the 20th of the same month, same court present as at the signing the license, with the exception of Lightfoot, Lee, and Burwell, the case of Joshua Morris was taken up, and—"the Attorney General of our Lord the King saith he will not further prosecute of and upon the premises. Therefore it is ordered, that the indictment aforesaid be dismissed." The same record is made in the case of Charles Rice.

In the case of Isaac Winston, senior, the following record is made under the date of the 20th of the month. "This day came as well the Attorney General of our Lord the King, as the defendant by his attorney; and thereupon came a jury—to wit—Thomas Guille, James Roe, Benjamin Cocke, James Patton, Theophilus Field, Thomas Addison, John Woodson, George Waller, Peter Fontaine, Littleton Scarburgh, Major W. Harding, and Thomas Gray, who being elected, tried and sworn the truth to speak upon the issue joined, brought in a special verdict, in these words, to wit—We find that people did assemble at the house of the defendant, but not in a riotous manner, and that John Roan preached in said house, but not against the canons of the Church of England as set forth in the information;—and the cause is continued till the next court for the matters of law arising thereupon to be argued." This case was argued April, 1748.

On the same day, the case of Samuel Morris, labourer, was taken up and tried. The verdict rendered (the names of the jury omitted) was—"We find that Roan preached at defendant's house; and that he is clear of all charge against him, in the information. The case is continued till the next court for the matters of law arising thereupon to be argued." It was argued April, 1748.

On the 2d day of May, of the same year, and at the same sessions of the court, there is the following notice of Mr. Morris—"On motion of his Majesty's Attorney General, the King's writ of Certiorari is awarded to remove hither certain presentments of the Grand Jury made in the County Court of Hanover in November last, against Samuel Morris, Bricklayer, John Sims son of John Sims, and Roger Shackelford, Planters,—Thomas Green, Tailor, and William Allen, returnable here the sixth day of next court."

It may not be amiss to quote one more record of the General

Court, dated April 17th, 1747. "The Grand Jury appeared, &c.—They also presented Robert White Senr. Margaret White, and John White Junr. for impiously and blasphemously reviling our Holy Religion and the Common Prayer; for blasphemously asserting—the Cross in Baptism to be nothing but a whore's mark,—and for reviling the Bishops and Clergy of the Church of England." This suit was renewed in 1749, but dismissed in 1750. Unguarded and passionate expressions, in religious controversy, were avenged by the strong arm of the law, whose aid was invoked to sustain the privileged church; but no notice was taken of any harsh expressions used against dissenters, however unjust and severe.

From these scenes, in the court, Mr. Davies proceeded to Hanover, with an excited spirit; and was received with an outburst of joy. News had spread through the county that another preacher was expected by the people that worshipped in the Reading Houses; and a proclamation was attached to the door of the Reading House of Mr. Morris, warning all people against gathering to hear "itinerants," as the law would be enforced with rigour, on all delinquents. The Reading was omitted for a Sabbath—the alarm, in recollections of past sufferings, and of the suits still pending in the General and County courts, caused the people to pause and consult. The coming of Dr. Davies, with his license, was like a visit from the angel of mercy. His ardent sermons refreshed the congregations, and his legal protection turned the enmity of the opposers to their own mortification.

His account of his mission is short—"I preached frequently in Hanover, and some of the adjacent counties; and though the fervour of the late work was considerably abated, and my labours were not blessed with success equal to that of my brethren, yet I have reason to hope they were of service in several instances. The importunities they used with me to settle with them were invincible; and upon my departure, they sent a call for me to the Presbytery. After I returned from Virginia, I spent near a year under melancholy and consumptive languishments, expecting death."

Soon after his return from Virginia, his wife was taken from him, in a sudden and afflictive manner. The brief notice in his Bible is—"September 15th, 1747, separated by death, and bereaved of an abortive son." Grief for her loss oppressed his languishing frame, and thoughts of his own speedy dissolution mingled with his sighs for the departure of his beloved. His hectic assumed a more alarming cast, and his prospects of prolonged usefulness vanished. Dr. Gibbons relating the circumstances, as he received them from Mr. Davies, says—"finding himself upon the borders of the grave, and without any hopes of a recovery, he determined to spend the little remains of an almost exhausted life, as he apprehended it, in endeavouring to advance his Master's glory in the good of souls;—and as he told me,—he preached in the day, and had his hectic by night, and to such a degree as to be sometimes delirious, and to stand in need of persons to sit up with him."

Unwilling, in his weak state, to take charge of any congregation, he travelled from vacancy to vacancy, and from desolation to desolation, as much as his feeble strength would permit, and was every where made welcome. In the spring of 1748— "he began slowly to recover, though he then looked upon it only as the intermission of a disorder that would finally prove mortal. Many earnest applications were made for his pastoral services. The one from Hanover, "signed by about one hundred and fifty heads of families," came with renewed importunity, and aided by the voice of the living messenger despatched by the people to urge their call, moved his heart. He says— "but upon the arrival of a messenger from Hanover, I put my life in my hand and determined to accept their call, hoping I might live to prepare the way for some more useful successor, and willing to expire under the fatigues of duty rather than in voluntary negligence." It is scarcely possible for a missionary to have gone to Virginia in circumstances better calculated to make an impression in favour of the gospel which he preached. In his domestic afflictions and bodily weakness, Davies felt the sentence of death gone out and already in execution. His soul burned with the desire of usefulness, and his tongue uttered the earnest persuasions of a spirit that would reconcile man to God, and lay some trophies at the Redeemer's feet, before his lips should be locked up in the grave. He longed to carry with him to the heavens some gems for the eternal crown. The people of Hanover were ready for an elevated spirit to lead them on through common and uncommon difficulties, through trials incident to all men, and the trials peculiar to their situation from the laws of the province, complaints, ridicule, indictments, fines and heavy costs of court,—to virtue and honour and eternal life. Davies was the man for the situation; for what were all these difficulties to such a man expecting soon to be giving in to God the account of his stewardship?

In his second visit to Virginia he was accompanied by his fellow student and warm friend John Rodgers, whose biography has been so ably written by his associate in the ministry, Rev. Samuel Miller, D.D., of the Theological Seminary, Princeton, New Jersey.

These friends had pursued their studies for the ministry in times of the greatest religious excitement the country had ever known, a parallel to which is seldom found in any age or any part of the world. The great awakening in which the Presbyterian church in Ireland was gathered, more than a century previous, and the great excitement, commonly spoken of as "the great Revival of 1802," that spread over the Southern, and Western, and portions of the Middle States," with a power almost terrific, were of a similar nature, and like abiding consequences. Together, these form three links in the chain of God's remarkable gracious dealings with the Presbyterian portion of his church, especially that part found in America. The influence of the great Revival in Ireland was felt in every Presbyterian band of emigrants from the "Emerald Isle," that came in such numbers to the Middle, and Southern, and Western States, from Makemie's time to the American Revolution. That of 1740 and onwards, in New England, New Jersey, New York, Pennsylvania, Delaware, Maryland, and Virginia, laid broad and deep foundations for the spiritual church to arise in the wilderness. And that of 1802 lighted up the fires of the sanctuary in the South and West like a pioneer chain of forts, both a refuge and a temple for the adventurous emigrants. In all these there were, in places, many very exceptionable things. Extravagances in feeling and action arose in them all. Errors in doctrine crept in; many tares were sown with the wheat. But the seed was not all tares; neither did the tares possess the field. There were some wild vines; but many plants of Sorek struck deep roots, whose fruits have refreshed the world. We do not believe the good and the evil were inseparable, either in the nature or the circumstance of the case. But, could it be established that the good flowing from these great awakenings could not be separated from the evils that accompanied, a soul that loves the race of men, and reverences the Redeemer of the lost, might, in view of these awakenings, pray pour out thy Spirit, O Lord, O Lord review thy work—shake the earth, and let the desire of all nations come.

These young friends also received their education under the preaching and instruction of one who took a leading part in the excitements and agitations of that peculiar period; whose piety, and talents, and ministerial usefulness, and academical success, made the school at Fagg's Manor a rival of the Log College of the Tennents. Virginia can never forget Samuel Blair, or his school, while she holds the pupil, Davies, in becoming estimation.

At the earnest solicitation of Mr. Davies, Mr. Rodgers was appointed, by Presbytery, to accompany him, and engage, for a few months, in the work of Evangelist in Virginia. They commenced their journey in April, 1748, and proceeded directly to Hanover. On their way, as related by Dr. Miller, Mr. Rodgers was relieved from his distressing fear of thunder, by being exposed to the violence of a tempest of lightning and thunder in the thick woods, during a benighted ride. On reaching Hanover, they rested a Sabbath,—both preached,—and proceeded to Williamsburg, to obtain a license for Mr. Rodgers to preach in the province. Governor Gooch received the young ministers kindly, and favoured the application. When they appeared before the Council, Mr. Rodgers presented his testimonials from the Presbytery, and asked that they might be read, preparatory to his taking the oath, such as had been required of his friend Davies. Some of the Council objected to reading the papers, and demanded that the subject be made a matter of private consultation. The Governor requested the clerk to take the papers from the young gentlemen, and read them,—and repeated the demand; but the attorney and some of the Council objecting strenuously to the reading, before a consultation, Sir William, bowing to the young ministers, said,—"Gentlemen, you shall hear from us in a day or two." They immediately withdrew to their lodgings, shut themselves in their chamber, and poured out their hearts unto God. A separation seemed inevitable, or Virginia must be abandoned. Was it the will of God that the province should be left?—or that Davis should, solitarily, and as an exile, preach the riches of grace where a door, was by law, scarce opened to him alone, and by the providence of God, opened to a host of ministers?

On the afternoon of the next day, at the invitation of the Governor, they met him, at his residence, with three of the Council, who were friendly to the application. The Governor informed them, that unable to procure from the Council, a license for Mr. Rodgers, as he had desired, it was with the greatest difficulty he had prevented the recall of the license granted Mr. Davies the last year. The young men insisted that they had asked only for a *right*, and not a *privilege;*—that the Act of Toleration was explicit in making it a right to ask, and a duty to grant, license in such cases. The Governor admitted their construction of the law, and expressed his regret at the decision of the Council.

At the suggestion of the Governor, in a polite note sent to them that evening, the young ministers prepared a memorial in due form, and the next day presented it to the Council, while the Governor was prudentially absent. After the reading, the senior member of the Council filling the Governor's chair, exclaimed with warmth—"we have Mr. Rodgers out, and we are determined to keep him out;"—and dismissed the subject.

The excitement ran high; the suits commenced, years before, against certain gentlemen in Hanover, were in progress; at this session of the court, Isaac Winston, sen., and Samuel Morris were each fined twenty shillings with costs of prosecution. Some of the clergy of the Established Church were vehement in their opposition to these young men. One of the clergy of Hanover followed Messrs. Davies and Rodgers to Williamsburg, and complained that Mr. Rodgers had preached in the province without license, and demanded the rigorous enforcement of the law. From members of the Council he met encouragement: but from the Governor a rebuke—"I am surprised at you!—you profess to be a minister of Jesus Christ,—and you come and complain of a man,—and wish me to punish him for preaching the gospel! For shame, Sir! Go home, and mind your own duty. For such a piece of conduct, you deserve to have your gown stripped over your shoulders."

The Governor, and three members of the Council,—Mr. Blair, nephew of Commissary Blair the founder of William and Mary College—Rev. William Dawson, D. D., the successor of Rev. James Blair as Commissary and President of the College,—and another gentleman whose name is not given,—sympathised with the young dissenting ministers, (as they were termed,) treated them with great kindness, and endeavoured to procure a reconsideration of the case before the Council. After much consideration, however, farther efforts to obtain a license for Mr. Rodgers was abandoned, and he prepared to leave the province. "Almost all the intelligent men in the colony"—says Mr. Burke in his 3d vol. pages 121, 2—"and amongst the rest several who afterwards became distinguished as the champions of an unqualified freedom in every thing relating to the human mind,—and even the venerable name of Pendleton, appear in the class of persecutors; a proof that liberality and toleration are not instinctive qualities, the growth of an hour; but the result of wisdom and experience."

In the month of May 1748, Mr. Rodgers parting with his friend Davies, crossed the bay of Chesapeake, visited the scene of Makemie's labours, on the Eastern Shore of Maryland. There his preaching met with great acceptance. He passed on to Delaware, and the next year became pastor of the church at St. George's, gathered by the labours of Mr. Robinson, so favourably known in Virginia and Maryland. Mr. Davies went up to Hanover, and took his residence among a pious and inquiring people, whose pastor he continued about eleven years, laying the foundation of the Presbytery of Hanover, and moulding the spirit of the future Synod of Virginia. In the whole "Ancient Dominion" he had no fellow labourer with whom his heart might rejoice. West of the Blue Ridge, there were Miller and Craig, and on its eastern base at the head of Rockfish, Mr. Black;—but these were members of the Synod of Philadelphia, and for some years had no communication with Mr. Davies. Like David Brainerd, he laboured in solitude; Brainerd, with savages that had no sympathy for him, but in the neighbourhood of eminent Christian ministers; Davies, with kind and hospitable people that appreciated him, but no Christian brother near to counsel and to cheer. Brainerd finished his course as a minister, when Davies commenced his. Both laboured in weakness of body; both preached "as dying men to dying men." And the church will forever love to dwell upon their self-denial and success.

In writing to the Bishop of London, in whose diocese Virginia was reckoned, under date of January 10th, 1752, Mr. Davies reveals the state of mind with which he entered upon this solitary field of labour nearly four years previous. "I solemnly assure your Lordship that it was not the secret thirst of filthy lucre, nor the prospect of any other personal advantage, that induced me to settle here in Virginia. For sundry congregations in Pennsylvania, my native country, and in other northern colonies, most earnestly importuned me to settle among them; where I should have had, at least an equal temporal maintenance, incomparably more ease, leisure and peace, and the happiness of the frequent society of my brethren; and where I should never have made a great noise or bustle in the world, but concealed myself in the crowd of my superior brethren, and spent my life in some little service for God and his church, in some peaceful corner, which would have been most becoming so insignificant a creature, and more agreeable to my recluse natural temper. But all these strong inducements were overweighed by a sense of the necessity of the Dissenters, as they lay two or three hundred miles distant from the nearest ministers of their own denomination, and laboured under peculiar embarrassments for the want of a settled ministry."

In his letter to Dr. Bellamy he says: "The Honorable William Gooch always discovered a ready disposition to allow us all claimable privileges, and the greatest aversion to persecuting measures; but considering the shocking reports spread abroad concerning us, by officious malignants, it was no great wonder the Council discovered considerable reluctance to tolerate us. Had it not been for this, I persuade myself they would have shown themselves the guardians of our legal privileges, as well as generous patriots to their country, which is the character generally given of them." If in this case he thought more favourable of the Council, than circumstances justified, or Burke believed, his favourable opinions flowed from a charity that thinketh no evil. That the Governor was pleased with Davies is evident; and equally as evident that he was greatly incensed with some of the people in Hanover.

While Messrs. Davies and Rodgers were urging their applications for license for Mr. Rodgers, it has been observed that the trial of Isaac Winston, sen., took place, April 18th, 1748, before the Governor and Messrs. Robinson, Grymes, Lee, Fairfax, Blair, Nelson and Dawson, members of Council.—"The matters of law arising upon the special verdict being argued,—It is considered by the court, that the said Isaac make his fine with our Lord the King, by the payment of twenty shillings to his Majestys use, and that he pay the costs of prosecution."

The same verdict was rendered in the case of Samuel Morris. On the same day, the case of Thomas Watkins' son Edward, continued from the preceding year, was dismissed.

Mr. Morris in his narrative says: "Some who had invited him (that is Mr. Roan) to preach at their houses, were cited to appear before the General Court, and two of them were fined." Again he says: "While my cause was upon trial, I had reason to rejoice that the throne of grace is accessible in all places, and that helpless creatures can send up their desires in the midst of a crowd." Again he says: I was repeatedly fined in court for absenting myself from church, and for keeping up unlawful meetings as they were called."

From such tyrannical and exciting proceedings Mr. Davies went to Hanover and took his abode. His preaching during the summer of 1748 was blessed. The desire to hear the gospel from the lips of the young dissenter spread in every direction; people rode great distances to attend upon his ministry, and became desirous to obtain some portion of his services in their more immediate neighborhood for the benefit of their families and neighbours. To avoid all collisions with the public authorities resolutely bent on executing the laws in favour of the English church, petitions, from the different neighbourhoods, were laid before the General Court for an increased number of authorized houses of worship. The petitions were granted.

"November, 1st 1748.

"Present—of the council,—Robinson, Burwell, Fairfax, Blair, Nelson, and Lewis. On petition of divers of the inhabitants of the counties of Louisa, Goochland, and Carolina, Samuel Davies, a dissenting minister, who hath qualified himself according to the Act of Toleration, is allowed to assemble and meet any congregation of Protestant Dissenters, at the several meeting-houses to be erected on the land of Joseph Shelton, near Owen's Creek, in the county of Louisa,—on the land of Tucker Woodson, in the county of Goochland,—and on the land of John Sutton, at Needwood, in the county of Caroline, without molestation, they behaving in a peaceable manner. and conforming themselves according to the directions of the said Act of Parliament in that behalf made."

To avoid all difficulty, Mr. Davies requested the following

entry, of a fact which had been omitted, which was made,—viz., "On motion of Samuel Davies, a dissenting minister—it is ordered that the certificate of his reading, assenting to, and subscribing the articles of Religion according to the Act of Toleration be recorded."

This license added three places of preaching to the four previously occupied by Davies.   The seven were located,—three in Hanover, one in Henrico, one in Goochland, one in Louisa, and one in Caroline.   Of these, he says in his letter to the Bishop of London, "The nearest are twelve or fifteen miles apart, and many of the people have ten, fifteen, or twenty miles to the nearest, and thirty, forty, or sixty miles to the rest; nay, some of them have thirty or forty miles to the nearest."

Some time after the county court of New Kent gave license for his preaching, in St. Peter's parish, within their bounds,— but the excitement had become so high on the subject, that the General Court annulled the proceeding.

A copy of this petition from inhabitants of New Kent, is preserved among the writings of Mr. Davies.   It is itself a comment on the state of society.

" To the Worshipful Court of New Kent, the Petition of the Subscribers humbly showeth."

"Whereas we are Protestant Dissenters of the Presbyterian denomination, under the ministerial care of the Rev. Mr. Davies,—and therefore humbly claim the liberties, and immunities granted to such by the Act of Toleration, upon our taking the qualifications therein imposed, which we are willing to do ; and whereas our distance from the meeting-houses now licensed, renders our attendance on Public Worship, (*a word or two obliterated*) and sometimes impracticable, your petitioners, therefore, pray that a place on the land of William Clopton, in this county, may be recorded, according to the direction of the said Act, and licensed for our public religious use.

"And your petitioners as in duty bound shall pray &c. Blackmore Hughes—Roger Shackelford—Richard Muir—William Crumpton—Robert Brain—John Thompson—(*three or four names obliterated*) Charles Cuningham,—Simon Clement,— Abraham Lewis,—Thomas Francis,—Julius K. Burbidge."

At a court held for New Kent County, April 12th, 1750— "On the petition of divers of the inhabitants of the county of New Kent and Hanover, Samuel Davies a dissenting minister, who hath qualified himself according to the Act of Toleration is allowed to assemble and meet any congregation of Protestant Dissenters at a meeting-house to be erected on the land of Wm. Clopton in New Kent County without molestation, they behaving in a peaceful manner and conforming themselves according to the provisions of the said Act of Parliament in that behalf made.

Copy—Teste

JOHN DANDRIDGE, Clerk of County."

This license was revoked by the General Court.

In the case of Watkins, Morris, and others, the defence had been confined to the matters of fact in evidence—that they had assembled in a peaceable manner,—and had avoided all irritating epithets in their worship. And these facts were proved in face of the indictments. But the jury brought in a special verdict—guilty of the fact of assembling,—but not guilty of the irregularities charged in the bill. On the special verdict, they were fined, because they assembled contrary to the statutes, in houses not licensed by the Court. The Governor understood the law of the Province, and also the extent of his promise given to the emigrating Presbyterians; and was punctilious in the execution of both. It is not clear that the members of Council, or of the Bar, had the right interpretation of the Act of Toleration, in its effect upon their own laws.

In the discussion, which took place, upon the application for licensing the three additional places of worship, for Mr. Davies and his friends, the rights of Dissenters were fully canvassed. Mr. Davies and his friends contended, as Makemie had done, in his appearance before the Virginia Courts, and in his famous trial in New York, given in Chapter III. of these Sketches,—that in England, the Act of Toleration took off the edge of all the penal laws, under whatever name, made against Dissenters, upon their taking certain oaths;—that this Act of Toleration having been made a part of the Virginia code in 1699, also took of the edge of penal laws in Virginia, on like like conditions. This the Governor always admitted; and the Attorney General admitted in theory—but denied the application in England to be such as understood by Mr. Davies. Mr. Rodgers at the time of his application for licensure, in a private conference with the Governor, modestly expressed his opinion that, as a Dissenter in the eye of the Virginia law, he had a right to a license, on complying with the terms of the Act of Toleration. To this the Governor assented; but the Council dissented, and took it upon themselves to determine how many preachers the Dissenters in Hanover, and adjacent counties, ought to have, and refused Mr. Rodgers his license, and had some discussion about annulling that granted to Mr. Davies the previous year,—or declaring it to have been only temporary. At the time of the second application for places for Mr. Davies to preach in, the ground of discussion was changed; the question was, how many places of preaching should a Dissenting minister have? The Attorney General and others would have the Dissenters limited to a small number, some thought with the Bishop of London, that one place of preaching was all that a Dissenter in Mr. Davies' situation could ask for: and of consequence, that the number of Mr. Davies places of preaching should be lessened rather than increased.

Mr. Davies plead that he was not guilty of causing dissent in Hanover, that it sprung up, as all knew, without a preacher; —That the desire of people to attend on his preaching was not, while he observed the laws of the province, to be imputed to him as a crime:—That the ministers of the Established Church in Hanover and other counties had some two, and one three places of preaching, because their parishes were so extensive, and the population so sparse;—That the members of his church, with the families connected, were sufficient to form two respectable congregations, were they located in the vicinity of each other, and the places of worship;—that they were however greatly scattered, the mass being in Hanover, and the others in Henrico, Goochland, Louisa, Caroline, and New Kent, and at distances too great to attend at two places, except by riding thirty or forty miles;—That the intention of the Toleration Act was to enable the Dissenters from the Established Church to worship according to law, and under its provision;—that unless license was given for houses, in sufficient numbers, to accommodate the Dissenters, the intention of the Act of Toleration would not be followed out in its spirit;— and that the Dissenters would be compelled by the court to break the laws of the province which require the citizens to be in the regular habit of attending the parish church;—and that it could not be the design of the court, by withholding license, to compel the peaceable citizens to subject themselves to expensive and vexatious suits at law, or grieve their consciences.

The lawyers in attendance complimented Mr. Davies; the Governor and majority of the council sustained him. The young Dissenter gained laurels; and he rejoiced because it gave him opportunity to preach the gospel to his fellow men. The Attorney General, Peyton Randolph, could not be prevailed upon to put a favourable construction upon the law, and continued, for years, to throw obstacles in the way of the Presbyterians obtaining license for meeting-houses, especially when the petition came from neighbourhoods originally settled by others than colonies of Presbyterians. A great part of Mr. Davies' labour was in counties not originally Presbyterian; and his success was reckoned by the Attorney and others, as the progress of dissent to the detriment of the Established Church. Years after this petition, and after Mr. Davies had repeatedly appeared in Williamsburg, speaking of Randolph, he calls him "my old enemy,"—whose influence he dreaded in London, when on the mission for the College.

Mr. Davies entered the second time into the matrimonial state, being united in marriage October 4th, 1748, to Miss Jane Holt, of Hanover.   This lady, of whom he ever spoke with the greatest affection, bore him six children, and survived him many years.   His residence was about twelve miles from Richmond, in the neighbourhood of the meeting-house built near "Morris's Reading House."   This meeting-house is still standing; a plain, unpretending wooden building, capable of containing about five hundred people.   Over the pulpit are the letters S. D. In pleasant weather this building was quite too small for the multitudes that assembled.   The thick woods were then resorted to; and the opposers of the Dissenters were exasperated at the sight of crowds listening to the gospel in the deep shades of the forest.

The fact that so soon after his return to Virginia, there was need of three additional houses, is evidence of the great excitement attending the preaching of Mr. Davies.   Rev. Jonathan Edwards, under date of May 23d, 1749, says—"I heard lately a credible account of a remarkable work of conviction and conversion, among whites and negroes, at Hanover, Virginia, under the ministry of Mr. Davies, who is lately settled there, and has the character of a very ingenious and pious young man; whose support in his preparation for service, Mr. Robinson contributed much if not mostly to, and on his death-bed gave him his books."

In his lettter to Dr. Bellamy, Mr. Davies says, previously to 1751,—"there are about three hundred communicants in my congregation, of whom the greater number are, in the judgment of charity, real Christians, besides some, who through excessive scrupulousness, do not seek admission to the Lord's table.   There is also a number of Negroes.   Sometimes I see a hundred and more among my hearers.   I have baptized about forty of them within these three years, upon such profession of faith, as I then judged credible."

Mr. Davies was a very regular attendant upon the meetings of the Synod of New York, as the records show.   What was his habit with his Presbytery cannot be known, as the records of Newcastle Presbytery are not to be found.   In his attendance on Synod he always remembered the desolations of Virginia.   In May, 1749, the year after Mr. Davies settled in Hanover, the Synod met at Maiden Head.   Upon representation of the circumstances of Virginia—"Mr. Davenport is appointed, if he recover a good state of health, to go and supply Virginia."   At this meeting the first proposition for reconciliation and union with the Synod of Philadelphia was entertained.   The next year he Synod recommended to the Presbytery of New Brunswick—"to endeavor to prevail with Mr. John Todd upon his being licensed, to take a journey thither; and also to the Presbytery of New York, to urge the same upon Messrs. Syms and Greenman. Mr. Davenport is appointed to go into Virginia to assist in supplying the numerous vacant and destitute congregations there. The same is also recommended to Mr. Byram."

The Synod, at its meeting, in the month of September, of the same year,—"making inquiry how the several appointments for Virginia had been fulfilled, do find that Mr. Davenport has been there, and that Mr. Todd is licensed and preparing to go." Of this visit of Mr. Davenport, Mr. Davies says in his letter to Dr. Bellamy,—"I forgot to inform you in the proper place, that the Rev. Mr. Davenport was sent by the Synod to Hanover, last summer, and continued there about two months. And blest be God, did not labour in vain. Some were brought under concern, and many of the Lord's people much revived, who can never forget the instrument of it."

The established clergy of Virginia complained loudly of the proceedings of the General Court in the case of Mr. Davies, and in the year 1750, appealed to their Diocesan, the Bishop of London. Colonel Lee, the President of the Council, informed Mr. Davies of this, some time in the summer. Mr. Davies immediately began preparing a statement to lay before the Bishop. But in the month of August, after having proceeded some length, he postponed the work, and addressed the following letter:

To the Rev'd and Hon'ble Dr. William Dawson, Commissary of His Majesty's Council and President of the College of Wm. and Mary.

Rev'd and Honoured Sir:—As I am informed, you have written to England for Instructions with respect to the Dissenters in my Congregation, and particularly with respect to the meeting-house in New Kent; and as I suppose you have transmitted some account of them and that affair, in order to give light for an impartial determination, I request you to send me a copy of the representation you have made, or at least an account of the substance of it. As each party in such a case has a legal right to know the true state of it; and as I confidently presume your representation need not affect concealment as its defence and honour; I cannot look upon my request as a criminal curiosity to pry into inviolable secrets of Government; however Sir, if it should appear so to you, your refusal with the reasons of it will give it an easy and inoffensive check. I solemnly profess Sir, it does not proceed from a suspicion that you have knowingly and willfully given a partial and injurious representation of us. Your compliance Sir, or the reasons of your denial will lay peculiar obligations on,

Rev'd and Honoured Sir,

Your already obliged and most humble servant,

SAMUEL DAVIES.

Hanover, August 19th, 1750.

The desired answer, the representation, was never given to Mr. Davies by Dr. Dawson.

A statement of the situation of the Dissenters in Virginia, was sent by Mr. Davies to Dr. Doddridge, in England, a copy of which has not been preserved. Letters were sent to other dissenting ministers in England; and much sympathy was expressed for the suffering Christians in Virginia. No answer being received from Dr. Dawson, Mr. Davies completed the statement he had begun for the Bishop of London, and sent it to the care and discretion of his friends in England. A copy of this was preserved among Mr. Davies's papers; it covers a sheet of paper, and is drawn up in a historic form and in a style of great simplicity and frankness. The contents of it are all embraced in his second statement which will be given in full. Sometime in the year 1751, Mr. Davies received two letters from Dr. Doddridge, one of which has been preserved, but in a decayed state, and is as follows:

"Reverend and Dear Sir:—The former letter was written many months ago and it would be too long to tell you by what a series of providences it has been delayed. I must now tell you by the hand of a friend, as the hurry of my journey, and the great indisposition with which it has pleased God to afflict me, renders it difficult for me to write myself, that I have taken the affair of those prosecutions you mention and the refusal of your eighth license under the most serious consideration. On consulting with Dr. Avery as you desired, we both judged that as I had some acquaintance with the Bishop of London, it would be best I should write to his Lordship about it, and I really thought there was such a spirit of candour and piety in your letter as would plead your cause with him more powerfully than any thing that could proceed from any . . . . . I therefore sent a large extract from it, and received the . . . . Lordship which I here inclose, containing his answer to . . . . of the letter he received from and wrote to Virginia, on . . . . a copy of the licenses that were . . . I will not trouble . . . . my reply to his Lordship, the thing which I judge . . . . know with regard to it my dear friend is, ... Act of Toleration which to be sure you . . . . in exact agreement with it. That (I) know nothing of licensing . . . . . . the use of particular persons, nor persons to preach in such and such places; a minister licensed according to law has a right indifferently to preach in any licensed place whatsoever, and every licensed place is open to every qualified minister whom the proprietor or tenant will employ, and therefore I apprehend that three or four persons living one of them upon and the rest near the place for which you desire the eighth license ought to draw up a certificate to this purpose. We A, B, C, D, being Protestant Dissenters under the denomination of Presbyterians do hereby signify to his Majesty's justices of the peace (here you must determine the words for yourself) that we intend to make use of such a place situate in such a parish as a place of publick worship, and we do hereby demand that this our certificate be registered according to law. If upon this the court will not register the certificate, and give you a testimonial of that register for which you are to pay sixpence and which is what we call a license of the place, those whom I have consulted on this occasion apprehend that you will have just matter of complaint in our court . . . . . which we think you cannot have on the licenses that have . . . . us. As to your coming to these parts . . . . shall be extremely glad to see you, and shall think . . . . honoured with such a guest, but when I con . . . . . . inseparable from such a journey and voyage . . . . especially when I consider how much your . . . . . . of these new founded churches and true g . . . . . . had two or three brethren of lea . . . . you in the care of them and hope God will raise up some who may be disposed to bear a part of your burden. In these parts we want ministers extremely, and I never saw so great a number of destitute churches since I have appeared under a public character. I should gladly enlarge but my time will not permit, for this reason I must avoid saying any thing particularly of Mr. Schultz the Jewish missionary, of whom indeed I have heard nothing these two years but that the report we had concerning his death was false, and that he was a little while ago living at Venice. I have long been thoughtful about some scheme for forming a society for the propagation of the gospel among the Dissenters, and have made some efforts towards it this year; but it is judged most proper to defer the attempt for a while. However I believe something pretty considerable will be done towards encouraging the Mohawk school, in which Colonel Williams has been a great instrument. I would beg your prayers for me that it may please God to reestablish my health, and to give me opportunities of pursuing those various schemes of service as a tutor and writer as well as minister, on which I hope he knows my heart is set, and for the sake of which it is chiefly that I could wish to live. But it is a great joy . . . . . . that God will never want instruments to carry

on his . . . . : . he has in you raised up one of so great eminence doe . . . . . thanksgiving to many others as well as
myself. I . . . . possess the Archbishop of Canterbury
with whom . . , . . . almost two hours within these few days
with your character and the candour of your attempt . . . . .
service if the affair should ever come before the . . . . . . that
his Grace's designs are so pacifick and his disposition . . . . .
that neither you nor any of the Dissenters will suffer any
injustice that he can prevent; and indeed his Majesty is so
strenuous an asserter of the religious rights of all his subjects
that none either in civil or ecclesiastical stations must think of
recommending themselves to him by invading them. Join with
me in praying that it may please God to reestablish his health
and prolong his life, as I am sure you will in rejoicing in that
great revival that he seems lately to have received. May God
scatter down on you and all under your care the blessings of
his providence and grace, may all the agreeable hopes you have
received by those souls which God has graciously given you be
answered and exceeded, and be assured that to be recommended to their prayers will be esteemed a happiness by

Dear Sir,
Your affectionate brother
And humble servant,
P. DODDRIDGE."

Accompanying this letter were the following extracts: first,
from a letter from Virginia, bearing date July 27th, 1750, as
follows:—"Seven meeting-houses, situated in five counties,
have been licensed by the General Court for Mr. Samuel
Davies. In those counties there are eight ministers of the
established church. The justices of New Kent county lately
granted him a license to have a meeting-house in St. Peter's
parish. But their order has been superceded by the General
Court, it being judged that this affair is not within the jurisdiction of county courts. The instructions alluded to in the
answer of Peyton Randolph, Esq., Attorney General of Virginia, to the first question, is as follows:—'You are to permit a
liberty of conscience to all persons except Papists, so they be
contented with a quiet and peaceable enjoyment of the same,
not giving offence or scandal to the government. I most earnestly request the favour of your Lordship's opinion, whether,
in licensing so many meeting-houses for one teacher, they
have not granted him a greater indulgence than either the
King's instructions or the Act of Toleration intended. It is
not to be dissembled that several of the laity, as well as clergy,
are uneasy on account of the countenance and encouragement he has met with; and I cannot forbear expressing my own
concern to see schism spreading itself through a colony which

has been famous for uniformity of religion. I had almost forgot to mention his holding forth on working days to great numbers of poor people, who, generally, are his only followers. This, certainly, is inconsistent with the religion of labour, whereby they are obliged to maintain themselves and families, and their neglect of this duty, if not seasonably prevented, may, in process of time, be sensibly felt by the government."

The second extract that accompanied Dr. Doddridge's letter is a copy of the two licenses granted to Mr. Davies for preaching in the seven meeting-houses. A copy had been sent to the Bishop of London for his inspection, and this copy was sent back to Mr. Davies for his inspection.

The third extract accompanying Dr. Doddridge's letter is a part of the reply of the Bishop of London, sent to his correspondent in Virginia. The Bishop sent this extract to Dr. Doddridge, and he sent it to Mr. Davies. It bears date December 25th, 1750. "As to Davies' case, as far as I can judge, your Attorney General is quite in the right, for the Act of Toleration confines the preachers to a particular place, to be certified and entered, and so the practice here has been; and it was so far admitted to be the case that the Dissenters obtained a clause in the 10th of Queen Anne, to empower any dissenting minister to preach occasionally in any other county but that where he was licensed. I observe in one of the licenses, (a copy of which you sent me) Davies is permitted to assemble, &c., at several meeting-houses to be erected on the lands of Joseph Shelton, &c. Now, the Act of Toleration requires that the places of meeting shall be certified and registered, but how houses that are not in being can be certified and registered, I can't understand. The Act of Toleration was intended to permit the Dissenters to worship in their own way, and to exempt them from penalties, but it never was intended to permit them to set up itinerant preachers, to gather congregations where there was none before. They are, by the act of William and Mary, to qualify in the county where they live, and how Davies can be said to live in five different counties, they who granted the license must explain.

"In the act of William and Mary the Justices of the peace can admit of the teacher's qualifications, which is the reason I suppose of your Justices acting in the present case. If this power be lodged with the Governor, as your Attorney General takes it to be, I don't see how the Justices can interfere unless they suppose they can do whatever the Justices in England can do under the special authority of an act of parliament, which in many cases would be an absurd claim.

"Since I received yours I have been confined at home, and as the ships are soon going out, I have not time to advise upon this subject, and therefore what I have said must be taken only as my private opinion. But as this case concerns the church abroad very much, I will soon learn what the sense of our lawyers is here."

Besides these extracts, Dr. Doddridge sent Mr. Davies a copy of the letter from the Bishop of London, to him, inclosing the three preceding extracts. The Bishop's letter bears date

"London, 11 May, 1751.

"*Rev. Sir,*

"I am very much obliged to you for the open and candid manner in which you have communicated to me, the case of Mr. Davies, and an extract of his letter upon the subject. I wish all cases of this sort could be as fairly stated: it would exclude frivolous complaints, and bring the rest to be understood, which often times they are not. The best return I can make you, is to send you extracts, verbatim from the account I received from Virginia, and from the answer I returned. You have them enclosed.

" The question upon Mr. Davies's case, as far as it appears yet, relates to the meaning and construction of the act commonly called the Toleration Act. What I conceive the meaning to be, appears in the extract from my answer. If you consider the act, and the circumstance under which it was granted, you will not, I believe, see reason to think me mistaken. If you judge the liberty granted not sufficient, and that you, and every body, have a natural right to propagate their opinions in religion in such a manner as they approve themselves, that is quite another point, and in which Mr. Davies, who claims under the Act of Toleration, has no concern.

" If you suppose the Church of England to be (which I am persuaded you do not,) in the same state of corruption as the Romish church was at the time of the Reformation, there wants indeed no license, nor authority from the government to justify the methods of conversion which Mr. Davies is pursuing, and which the Methodists now do and long have pursued. But if the Act of Toleration was desired for no other view than to ease the consciences of those who could not conform—if it was granted with no other view, how must Mr. Davies's conduct be justified, who, under the colour of a toleration to his own conscience, is labouring to disturb the consciences of others, and the peace of a church acknowledged to be a true church of Christ? He came three hundred miles from home, not to serve people who had scruples, but to a county where the Church of England had been established from its first plantation, and where there were not above four or five dissenters within one hundred miles of it, not above six years ago. Mr. Davies says, in his letter to you, 'We claim no other liberties than those granted by the Act of Toleration.' So that the state of the question is admitted, on both sides, to be this: How far the Act of Toleration will justify Mr. Davies, in taking upon himself to be an itinerant preacher, and travelling over many counties, to make converts in a country, too, where till very lately, there was not a dissenter from the Church of England?

"You will observe in the extract from my letter, that I promised to take the opinion of lawyers upon the case; but I have not done it; which I tell you that you may not think I have an opinion and conceal it from you.

"Mr. Davies says, sundry of the people have been indicted and fined, and it is upon this information, I suppose, that you express yourself apprehensive that methods of severity, not to say of oppression, may be used. Of this I have heard nothing; but give me leave to set you right on one thing, and to tell you that my name neither is nor can be used for any such purpose. The Bishop of London, nor his commissaries, have no such power in the plantations, and I believe never desired to have it; so that if there be any ground for such complaint, the civil government only is concerned.

"There is another part of Mr. Davies's letter which gives me great concern. I mean the character he gives of the clergy and laity in Virginia. I dare say you have so much candor as to deduct something from the general character; knowing how hard it is not to suspect and charge corruption of principles, upon those who differ in principles from us. I have no such account of the clergy of Virginia as will justify this character; though there may be reason in some cases for very just complaints, and how can it be expected to be otherwise, considering the state of the Church of England abroad: the care of it as an Episcopal church, is supposed to be in the Bishop of London. How he comes to be charged with this care, I will not inquire now, but sure I am that the care is improperly lodged: for a bishop to live at one end of the world, and his church at another, must make the office very uncomfortable to the bishop, and, in a great measure, useless to the people. With respect to ordinances, it has a very ill effect; the people of the country are discouraged from bringing up their children for the ministry, because of the hazard and expense of sending them to England to take orders, where they often get the small pox, a distemper fatal to the natives of those countries. Of those who are sent from hence, a great part are of the Scotch or Irish, who can get no employment at home, and enter into the service more out of necessity than choice. Some others are willing to go abroad, to retrieve either lost fortunes, or lost character. For these reasons, and others of less weight, I did apply to the king, as soon as I was Bishop of London, to have two or three bishops appointed for the plantations, to reside there. I thought there could be no reasonable objection to it, not even by the dissenters, as the bishops proposed were to have no jurisdiction but over the clergy of their own church; and no more over them than should enable them to see the pastoral office duly performed; and as to New England, where the dissenters are so numerous, it never was proposed to settle a bishop in the country.

"You are probably no stranger to the manner in which the news of this proposal was received in New England. If you are, I will only say, that they used all their influence to obstruct the settling of bishops in the Episcopal church of England. Was this consistent even with a spirit of toleration? Would they think themselves tolerated, if they were debarred the right of settling ministers among themselves, and were obliged to send all their candidates to Geneva or Scotland for orders? At the same time that they exert this opposition, they set up a mission of their own for Virginia, a country positively Episcopal, by authority of their synod; and in their own country, where they have the power, they have persecuted and imprisoned several members of the church, for not paying towards supporting the dissenting preachers, though no such charge can, by any colour of law, be imposed upon them. This has been the case in New England. I am sorry to add, that some here, for whose characters and abilities I have due esteem, have not upon this occasion given signs of the temper and moderation that were expected from them.

"I do not willingly enter into these complaints even to you, who, I am confident, will make no ill use of them. I wish there was no occasion for them. In this wish, I am sure of your concurrence, from the love you bear to our common Christianity.

"I am, sir,

"Your most affectionate friend,

"Very humble servant,

"THOS. LONDON."

Mr. Davies having received these communications drew up at length a statement of the condition of the dissenters in Virginia, addressed to the Bishop of London, and sent it to his friends in England, to present to the Bishop, should they, upon perusal, think it advisable. It is as follows:

"*My Lord,*

"My little name would probably never have been made known to your lordship in this manner, were I not constrained by such reasons as I humbly presume will acquit me from the censure of a causeless instrusive application. Your lordship's general character and the high sentiments of your candour and impartiality your valuable writings have inspired me with, persuade me your lordship is a patient searcher after truth both in matters of speculation and fact; and therefore will patiently bear the following representation, though unavoidably tedious, especially when it is intended to reflect light upon *a case*, which in your lordship's own judgment, *concerns the church abroad very much*, and help to bring it to an impartial determination. And though my being unaccustomed to such addresses may render me awkward or deficient in some of the decent and precedented formalities with which I should approach a person of your lordship's dignity; yet I flatter myself my inward affectionate veneration will naturally discover itself in such genuine indications as will convince your lordship of its sincerity and ardour, and procure your indulgence to my involuntary imperfections.

" When his Honour the President of this Colony, the late Col. Lee, first informed me, that the case of the Protestant dissenters here had been laid before your lordship, I drew up a representation of it with all possible impartiality, in a letter intended for your lordship, dated August 13th, 1750. I had no suspicion that either the President or the Rev. Dr. Dawson had knowingly and wilfully misrepresented it; yet I had reason to conclude their representation was imperfect, as they were not thoroughly acquainted with the circumstances of the dissenters in these parts. This supposed imperfection I attempted to supply in that letter. But upon farther deliberation I concluded, it would answer no valuable end to send it; as I had then no opportunity of procuring the attestation of others, and I know a person's speaking in his own behalf is generally deemed a sufficient ground to suspect his veracity. Accordingly I kept it by me until about three months ago, when I sent it with some other papers upon the affair to a correspondent in London; leaving it wholly to his judgment, whether to present it to your lordship or not. I have not received any intelligence from him as yet, what he has thought proper to do; and therefore lest your lordship should not have received it, I shall as far as I can recollect lay the substance of it before you, together with such additional remarks as have been suggested to me by occurrences since that time.

" I informed my worthy friend Dr. Doddridge of the state of affairs here with respect to the dissenters, about a year and a half ago, and by his answer, I find he has laid a large extract of my letter before your lordship. I wrote it with all the unreserved freedom of friendship, as I did not expect it would have been presented to your lordship's eyes: yet I am glad you have seen it; as by comparing it with this, which it may

be presumed I write with more caution, your lordship may be
convinced I do not act in disguise, but make substantially the
same naked artless representation of truth to all parties.

"Dr. Doddridge has sent me a copy of your lordship's
letter to him, with the extracts of the letters from and to Virginia enclosed, as the fullest and easiest method of informing
me of your lordship's sentiments. This, my lord, will not, I
trust, weaken your ' confidence that he would make no ill use'
of your lordship's freedom with him, since the matter is of a
public nature, and the reason of his writing to your lordship
was, that he might inform me of your sentiments. And as I find
some misrepresentations in your lordship's letter, and the extracts enclosed, which I apprehend I can rectify; I hope, my
lord, you will not suspect I have so much arrogance as to encounter your lordship as a disputant, if I presume to make
some free and candid remarks upon them. My only design is to
do justice to a misrepresented cause, which is the inalienable
right of the meanest innocent; and as an impartial historical
representation will be sufficient for this purpose, 'tis needless to
tire your lordship with tedious argumentation.

"The frontier counties of this colony, about an hundred miles
west and south-west from Hanover, have been lately settled by
people that chiefly came from Ireland originally, and immediately from the Northern colonies, who were educated Presbyterians, and had been under the care of the ministers belonging
to the Synod of New York (of which I am a member) during
their residence there. Their settling in Virginia has been many
ways beneficial to it, which I am sure most of them would not
have done, had they expected any restraint in the inoffensive
exercise of their religion, according to their consciences. After
their removal, they continued to petition the Synod of New
York, and particularly the Presbytery of Newcastle, which was
nearest to them, for ministers to be sent among them. But as
the ministers of said Synod and Presbytery were few, and vastly
disproportioned to the many congregations under their care,
they could not provide these vacancies with settled pastors.
And what, my lord, could they do in this case? I appeal to
your lordship, whether this was not the only expedient in their
power, to appoint some of their members to travel, alternately,
into these destitute congregations, and officiate among them as
long as would comport with their circumstances? It was this,
my lord, that was the first occasion, as far as I can learn, of our
being stigmatized *itinerant preachers*. But whether there was
any just ground for it in these circumstances, I cheerfully submit to your lordship. The same method was taken for the same
reason (as I shall observe more particularly hereafter) to supply
the dissenters in and about Hanover, before my settlement

among them; and this raised the former clamour still higher. There are now in the frontier counties, at least five congregations of Presbyterians, who, though they have long used the most vigorous endeavours to obtain settled ministers among them, have not succeeded as yet, by reason of the scarcity of ministers, and the number of vacancies in other parts, particularly in Pennsylvania and the Jerseys : and we have no way to answer their importunate petitions, but by sending a minister now and then to officiate transiently among them. And as the people under my charge are so numerous, and so dispersed, that I cannot allow them at each meeting-house such a share of my ministrations as is correspondent to their necessity, the said Synod has twice or thrice in the space of three years sent a minister to assist me for a few Sabbaths. These, my lord, are the only itinerations that my brethren can be charged with in this colony, and whether they should not rather run the risk of this causeless charge, than suffer these vacancies, who eagerly look to them for the bread of life, to perish through a famine of the Word of the Lord, I cheerfully submit to your lordship.

"But as I am particularly accused of intrusive schismatical itinerations, I am more particularly concerned to vindicate myself; and for that purpose it will be sufficient to inform your lordship of the circumstances of the dissenters in and about Hanover, who are under my ministerial care.

"The dissenters here, my lord, are but sufficiently numerous to form two distinct organized congregations, or particular churches, and did they live contiguous, two meeting-houses would be sufficient for them, and neither they nor myself, would desire more. But they are so dispersed that they cannot convene for public worship, unless they have a considerable number of places licensed; and so few that they cannot form a particular organized church at each place. There are seven meeting-houses licensed in five different counties, as the letter from Virginia, I suppose from the Rev. Dr. Dawson informs your lordship. But the extremes of my congregation lie eighty or ninety miles apart; and the dissenters under my care are scattered through six or seven different counties. The greatest number of them, I suppose about one hundred families, at least, in Hanover, where there are three meeting-houses licensed: about twenty or thirty families in Henrico; and about ten or twelve in Caroline; about fifteen or twenty in Goochland, and about the same number in Louisa; in each of which counties there is but one meeting-house licensed: about fifteen or twenty families in Cumberland, where there is no place licensed; and about the same number contiguous to New Kent, where a license was granted by the court of that county, but afterwards superseded by the General Court. The counties here are large, generally forty or fifty miles in length, and about twenty or thirty miles in breadth; so that though they lived in one county, it might be impossible for them all to convene at one place; and much more when they are dispersed through so many. Though there are now seven places licensed, yet the nearest are twelve or fifteen miles apart; and many of the people have ten, fifteen, or twenty miles to the nearest, and thirty, forty, or sixty miles to the rest; nay, some of them have thirty or forty miles to the nearest. That this is an impartial representation of our circumstances, I dare appeal to all that know anything about them.

"Let me here remind your lordship that such is the scarcity of ministers in the Synod of New York, and so great the number of congregations under their care, that though a part of my congregation have, with my zealous concurrence, used repeated endeavours to obtain another minister amongst them to relieve me of the charge of them, yet they have not succeeded as yet. So that all the dissenters here depend entirely on me to officiate among them,' as there is no other minister of their own denomination within two hundred miles, except when one of my brethren from the northern colonies is appointed to pay them a transient visit, for two or three Sabbaths, once in a year or two: and as I observed they cannot attend on my ministry at one or two places by reason of their distance; nor constitute a complete particular church at each place of meeting, by reason of the smallness of their number.

"These things, my lord, being impartially considered, I dare submit it to your lordship,

"Whether my itinerating in this manner in such circumstances be illegal? And whether, though I cannot live in five different counties at once, as your lordship observes, I may not lawfully officiate in them, or in as many as the peculiar circumstances of my congregation, which though but one particular church, is dispersed through sundry counties, render necessary?

"Whether contiguity of residence is necessary to entitle dissenters to the liberties granted by the Act of Toleration? Whether when they cannot convene at one place, they may not, according to the true intent and meaning of that Act, obtain as many houses licensed as will render public worship accessible to them all? And whether if this liberty be denied them, they can be said to be tolerated at all? i. e. Whether *dissenters are permitted to worship in their own way,* (which your lordship observes was the intent of the Act) who are prohibited from worshipping in their own way, unless they travel thirty, forty or fifty miles every Sunday? Your lordship grants we would have no reason to think ourselves tolerated, were we obliged to send our candidates to Geneva or Scotland to be ordained; and is there any more reason to think so when great numbers are obliged to journey so far weekly for public worship?

"Whether, when there are a few dissenting families in one county and a few in another, and they are not able to form a distinct congregation or particular church at each place, and yet all of them conjunctly are able to form one, though they cannot meet statedly at one place; whether, I say, they may not legally obtain sundry meeting-houses licensed, in these different counties, where their minister may divide his time according to the proportion of the people, and yet be looked upon as one organized church? And whether the minister of such a dispersed church, who alternately officiates at these sundry meeting-houses should on this account be branded as an itinerant?

"Whether, when a number of dissenters, sufficient to constitute two distinct congregations, each of them able to maintain a minister, can obtain but one by reason of the scarcity of ministers, they may not legally share in the labours of that one, and have as many houses licensed for him to officiate in, as their distance renders necessary? And whether the minister of such an united congregation, though he divides his labours at seven different places, or more, if their conveniency requires it, be not as properly a *settled* minister as though he preached but at one place, to but one congregation? Or (which is a parallel case) whether the Rev. Mr. Barrett, one of the ministers in Hanover, who has three churches situated in two counties, and whose parish is perhaps sixty miles in circumference, be not as properly a settled parish minister, as a London minister whose parishioners do not live half a mile from his church?

"I beg leave, my lord, farther to illustrate the case by a relation of a matter of fact, and a very possible supposition.

"It very often happens in Virginia, that the parishes are twenty, thirty, forty, and sometimes fifty or sixty miles long, and proportionably broad; which is chiefly owing to this, that people are not so thick settled, as that the inhabitants in a small compass should be sufficient for a parish; and your lordship can easily conceive that the inhabitants of this infant colony are thinner than in England. The Legislature here has wisely made provision to remedy this inconveniency, by ordering sundry churches or chapels of ease to be erected in one parish, that one of them at least may be tolerably convenient to all the parishioners; and all these are under the care of one minister, who shares his labours at each place in proportion to the number of people there. In Hanover, a pretty populous county, there are two ministers, one of whom has two churches, and the other, as I observed has three; the nearest of which are twelve or fifteen miles apart: and in some of the frontier counties the number of churches in a parish is much greater. And yet the number of churches does not multiply the parish into an equal number of parishes; nor does the minister by officiating at so many places, incur the odious epithet of an itinerant preacher, a pluralist or nonresident. (Here again, my lord, I appeal to all the colony to attest this representation.) Now, I submit it to your lordship, whether there be not at least equal reason that a plurality of meeting-houses should be licensed for the use of the dissenters here, since they are more dispersed and fewer in number? The nearest of those licensed are twelve or fifteen miles apart; and as, if there were but one church in a parish, a great part of it would be incapable of attending on public worship; so if the number of my meeting-houses were lessened, a considerable part of the dissenters here would be thrown into a state of heathenism wholly destitute of the ministrations of the gospel, or obliged to attend statedly on the established church, which they conscientiously scruple. And indeed this will be the case with some of them if more be not licensed, unless they can go twenty, thirty, or forty miles every Sabbath. And here, my lord, it may be proper to observe, that in the Act of Toleration it is expressly provided— 'That all the laws made and provided for the frequenting divine service on the Lord's Day, shall be in force and executed against all persons that offend against the said laws, except such persons come to some congregation or assembly of religious worship, allowed or permitted by this Act.' So that the dissenters are obliged, even by that Act which was made designedly in their favour, to attend the established church unless they come to some dissenting congregation; and this obligation is corroborated, and the penalty increased by an act of our Assembly, which enjoins all adult persons to come to church at least once a month, 'excepting as is excepted in an act made in the first year of the reign of King William and Queen Mary,' &c. But how, my lord, is it possible for them to comply with this injunction, if they are restrained to so small a number of meeting-houses as that they cannot attend them? If the Act of Toleration imposes this restraint upon them, does it not necessitate them to violate itself? And if our magistrates refuse to license a sufficient number, and yet execute the penal laws upon them for the profanation of the Sabbath, or the neglect of public worship, does it not seem as though they obliged them to offend that they may enjoy the malignant pleasure of punishing them? The act of William and Mary, my lord, does not particularize the number of houses to be licensed for the use of one congregation; but only requires in general, that all such places shall be registered before public worship be celebrated in them; from which it may be reasonably presumed, the number is to be wholly regulated by the circumstances of the congregation. It is, however, evident that such a number was intended as that all the members of the congregation might conveniently attend. But to return. I submit it also to your lordship, whether there be not as little reason for representing me' as an itinerant preacher, on account of my preaching at so many places for the conveniency of one congregation, as that the minister of a large parish, where there are sundry churches or chapels of ease, should be so called for preaching at these sundry places, for the convenience of one parish? Besides the reason common to both, the distance of the people; there is one peculiarly in my favour, the small number of our ministers; on which account almost the half of the congregations that have put themselves under our synodical or presbyterial care, are destitute of settled pastors: which is far from being the case of late in the established church in Virginia. I shall subjoin one remark more: It is very common here, my lord, when a parish which has had sundry churches under the care of one minister, is increased, to divide it into two or more, each of which has a minister. And I submit it to your lordship, whether my congregation may not be so divided, when an opportunity occurs of obtaining another minister? And whether, till that time I may not, according to the precedent around me in the established church, take the care of all the dissenters at the places already licensed, and at that petitioned for, when I do it for no selfish views, but from the unhappy necessity imposed upon me by present circumstances, and am eager to resign a part of my charge as soon as another may be obtained to undertake it, which I hope will be ere long?

"I know but little, my lord, how it is in fact in England: but I will put a case. Suppose then there are fifteen families of dissenters at Clapham in Bedfordshire, fifteen at Wotten in Northamptonshire, fifteen at Kimbolton in Huntingtonshire, and fifteen in the North corner of Buckinghamshire; (if these places are not so pertinent as others that might be supposed, your lordship can easily substitute others, and your candour will overlook my blunder, as I have never seen England but in a map) and suppose, that these families not being able to form a distinct church in each shire and maintain a minister at each place, agree to unite into one organized church, and to place themselves under the care of one minister, who shall proportion his labours at sundry meeting-houses, one being erected in each shire for the conveniency of the families resident there: I humbly query, whether in this case such a congregation may not according to the act of William and Mary, claim a license for a meeting-house in each of these shires? Whether this could justly be suspected as an artifice 'to gather dissenting congregations where there were none before, to disturb the peace of the Church?' Whether the minister of such a dispersed congregation should be stigmatized an itinerant?—or (to adapt the illustration yet more fully to the case) suppose twice the above number in five contiguous shires or counties, capable of constituting two particular churches, and maintaining two ministers; and suppose the number of ministers so small, that they can obtain but one to settle among them, may they not, in these circumstances, unite in one church, and place themselves conjunctly under the care of one minister, sharing his labours among them at meeting-houses, in five counties, in proportion to their number at each place? And would not such a minister be justly looked upon as a settled minister? Or would he be limited to one county in this case, because the Act of Toleration requires him to qualify in the county where he lives. And this, my lord, suggests to me a remark in your lordship's letter to Virginia—'They [dissenting ministers] are by the 'Act of William and Mary to qualify in the county where they live, and how Davies can be said to live in five different counties, they who granted the license must explain.' You know, my lord, it is the judgment of our Attorney General, that county courts here have no authority in such matters; and your lordship has not declared your dissent from him. The council also has published an order, prohibiting county courts to administer qualifications to dissenting ministers, and appropriating that authority to the Governor or Commander in Chief. And how is it possible, my lord, we should qualify in the county where we live, since the Governor does not live there? It is hard, if after we are prohibited to qualify in county courts as we desire, the validity of our qualifications should be suspected, because we did not qualify there. As for myself I was required to qualify by his honour the Governor, in the general court, which consists of the Governor and Council, and as the epithet *General*, intimates, it is the supreme court of the whole province, and what is done therein is deemed as valid through the whole colony, as the acts of a county court in a particular county: and consequently I look upon myself, and so does the government, as legally qualified to officiate in any part of the colony where there are houses licensed.

"To all this, my lord, I may add, that though the Act of Toleration should not warrant my preaching in so many counties; yet, since, as your lordship observes, 'the dissenters obtained a clause in the 10th Queen Anne, to empower any dissenting preacher to preach occasionally in any other county but that where he was licensed;' and since the reason of the law is at least as strong here as in England, and consequently it extends hither, my conduct is sufficiently justified by it.

"All these things, my lord, furnish a sufficient answer to your lordship's question, 'How far the Act of Toleration will justify Mr. Davies in taking upon himself to be an itinerant preacher, and travelling over many counties to make converts, in a country too where, till very lately, there was not one dissenter from the Church of England?' And it appears to have been stated upon misinformation. When impartially stated, it would stand thus:

"How far the Act of Toleration will justify Mr. Davies, in sharing his labours at sundry places in different counties among the professed dissenters, who constitute but one particular church, though dispersed through so many counties and incapable of meeting at one place?—Or, thus:

"Whether legally qualified protestant dissenters, who are dispersed through sundry counties, and cannot meet at one place, and by reason of the scarcity of ministers cannot obtain but one among them, may not legally share in the labours of that one, and have so many houses licensed for him to officiate in as that all of them may alternately attend on public worship? And were the question considered in this view, I confidently presume, your lordship would determine it in my favour, and no longer look upon me as an itinerant preacher, intent on making converts to a party.

"But I find I have been represented to your lordship as an uninvited intruder into these parts: for your lordship in your letter to Dr. Doddridge writes thus, 'If the Act of Toleration was desired for no other view but to ease the consciences of those that could not conform; if it was granted with no other view, how must Mr. Davies's conduct be justified? who under the colour of a toleration to his own conscience, is labouring to disturb the consciences of others.—He came three hundred miles from home, not to serve people who had scruples, but to a country—where there were not above four or five dissenters within an hundred miles, not above six years ago.'

"To justify me from this charge, my lord, it might be sufficient to observe, that the meeting-houses here were legally licensed before I preached in them, and that the licenses were petitioned for by the people, as the last license for three of them expressly certifies, as your lordship may see: which is a sufficient evidence that I did not intrude into any of these places to gain proselytes where there were no dissenters before.

"But to give your lordship a just view of this matter, I shall present you with a brief narrative of the rise and increase of the dissenters in and about this county, and an account of the circumstances of my settling among them. And though I know, my lord, there may be some temptations to look upon all I say as a plausible artifice to vindicate myself or my party : yet I am not without hopes that one of your lordship's impartiality, who has found it possible by happy experience to be candid and disinterested even when self is concerned, will believe it possible for another also to be impartial for once in the relation of plain, public facts, obvious to all, though they concern him and his party ; especially when he is willing to venture the reputation of his veracity on the undeniable truth of his relation, and can bring the attestations of multitudes to confirm it.

"About the year 1743, upon the petition of the Presbyterians in the frontier counties of this colony, the Rev. Mr. Robinson, who now rests from his labours, and is happily advanced beyond the injudicious applauses and censures of mortals, was sent by order of Presbytery to officiate for some time among them. A little before this about four or five persons, heads of families, in Hanover, had dissented from the established church, not from any scruples about her ceremonial peculiarities, the usual cause of non-conformity, much less about her excellent Articles of Faith, but from a dislike of the doctrines generally delivered from the pulpit, as not savouring of experimental piety, nor suitably intermingled with the glorious peculiarities of the religion of Jesus. It does not concern me at present, my lord, to inquire or determine whether they had sufficient reason for their dislike. They concluded them sufficient ; and they had a legal as well as natural right to follow their own judgment. These families were wont to meet in a private house on Sundays to hear some good books read, particularly Luther's ; whose writings I can assure your lordship were the principal cause of their leaving the Church ; which I hope is a presumption in their favour. After some time sundry others came to their society, and upon hearing these books, grew indifferent about going to church, and chose rather to frequent these societies for reading. At length the number became too great for a private house to contain them, and they agreed to build a meeting-house, which they accordingly did.

"Thus far, my lord, they had proceeded before they had heard a dissenting minister at all. (Here again I appeal to all that know any thing of the matter to attest this account.) They had not the least thought at this time of assuming the denomination of Presbyterians, as they were wholly ignorant of that Church : but when they were called upon by the court to assign the reasons of their absenting themselves from church, and asked what denomination they professed themselves of, they declared themselves Lutherans, not in the usual sense of that denomination in Europe, but merely to intimate that they were of Luther's sentiments, particularly in the article of Justification.

"Hence, my lord, it appears that neither I nor my brethren were the first instruments of their separation from the Church of England: and so far we are vindicated from the charge of 'setting up itinerant preachers, to gather congregations where there was none before.' So far I am vindicated from the charge of 'coming three hundred miles from home to disturb the consciences of others—not to serve a people who had scruples, but to a country—where there were not above four or five dissenters at the time of my coming here.

"Hence also, my lord, results an inquiry, which I humbly submit to your lordship, whether the laws of England enjoin an immutability in sentiments on the members of the established church? And whether, if those that were formerly conformists, follow their own judgments, and dissent, they are cut off from the privileges granted by law to those that are dissenters by birth and education? If not, had not these people a legal right to separate from the established church, and to invite any legally qualified minister they thought fit to preach among them?—And this leads me back to my narrative again.

"While Mr. Robinson was preaching in the frontier counties, about an hundred miles from Hanover, the people here having received some information of his character and doctrines, sent him an invitation by one or two of their number to come and preach among them; which he complied with and preached four days successively to a mixed multitude; many being prompted to attend from curiosity. The acquaintance I had with him, and the universal testimony of multitudes that heard him, assure me, that he insisted entirely on the great catholic doctrines of the gospel, (as might be presumed from his first text, Luke xiii. 3,) and did not give the least hint of his sentiments concerning the disputed peculiarities of the Church of England, or use any sordid disguised artifices to gain converts to a party. 'Tis true many after this joined with those that had formerly dissented; but their sole reason at first was, the prospect of being entertained with more profitable doctrines among the dissenters than they were wont to hear in the parish churches, and not because Mr. Robinson had poisoned them with bigoted prejudices against the established church. And permit me, my lord, to declare, with the utmost religious solemnity, that I have been (as I hope your lordship will be in the regions of immortal bliss and perfect uniformity in religion) the joyful witness of the happy effect of these four sermons. Sundry thoughtless impenitents, and sundry abandoned profligates have ever since given good evidence of a thorough conversion, not from party to party, but from sin to holiness, by an universal devotedness to God, and the conscientious practice of all the social and personal virtues. And when I see this the glorious concomicant or consequent of their separation, I hope your lordship will indulge me to rejoice in such proselytes, as I am sure our divine Master and all his celestial ministers do; though without this, they are but wretched captures, rather to be lamented over, than boasted of. When Mr. Robinson left them, which he did after four days, they continued to meet together on Sundays to pray and hear a sermon out of some valuable book read by one of their number; as they had no prospect of obtaining a minister immediately of the same character and principles with Mr. Robinson. They were now increased to a tolerable congregation, and made unwearied application to the Presbytery of New Castle in Pennsylvania for a minister to be sent among them, at least to pay them a transient visit, and preach a few sermons, and baptize their children, till they should have opportunity to have one settled among them. The Presbytery complied with their petitions, as far as the small number of its members, and the circumstances of their own congregations, and of the vacancies under their Presbyterial care, would permit; and sent ministers among them at four different times in about four years, who stayed with them two or three Sabbaths at each time. They came at the repeated and most importunate petitions of the dissenters here, and did not obtrude their labours upon them uninvited. Sundry upon hearing them, who had not heard Mr. Robinson, joined with the dissenters; so that in the year 1747, when I was first ordered by the Presbytery to take a journey to Hanover, in compliance with the petition of the dissenters here, I found them sufficiently numerous to form one very large congregation, or two small ones; and they had built five meeting-houses, three in Hanover, one in Henrico, and one in Louisa county; which were few enough considering their distance. Upon my preaching among them, they used the most irresistible importunities with me to settle among them as their minister, and presented a call to me before the Presbytery, signed by about an hundred and fifty heads of families; which in April, 1748, I accepted, and was settled among them the May following. And though it would have been my choice to confine myself wholly to one meeting-house, especially as I was then in a very languishing state of health; yet considering that hardly the one half of the people could possibly convene at one place, and that they had no other minister of their own denomination within less than two hundred miles, I was prevailed upon to take the pastoral care of them all, and to divide my labours at the sundry meeting-houses.

"And now, my lord, I may leave yourself to judge, whether the imformations were just, upon which your lordship has represented me as not 'coming to serve a people that had scruples, but as disturbing the consciences of others, under the colour of a toleration to my own, and intruding into a country where there were not above four or five dissenters, &c." Your lordship must see if this account be true, (and thousands can attest it) that I had not the least instrumentality in the first gathering of a dissenting Church in these parts. Indeed I was then but a lad, and closely engaged in study. And I solemnly assure your lordship, that it was not the sacred thirst of filthy lucre, nor the prospect of any other personal advantage, that induced me to settle here: for sundry congregrations in Pennsylvania, my native country, and in the other northern colonies, most earnestly importuned me to settle among them, where I should have had at least an equal temporal maintenance, incomparably more ease, leisure, and peace, and the happiness of the frequent society of my brethren; never made a great noise or bustle in the world, but concealed myself in the crowd of my superior brethren, and spent my life in some little services for God and his Church in some peaceful retired corner; which would have been most becoming so insignificant a creature, and most agreeable to my recluse natural temper: but all these strong inducements were preponderated by a sense of the more urgent necessity of the dissenters here; as they lay two or three hundred miles distant from the nearest ministers of their own denomination, and laboured under peculiar embarrassments for want of a settled minister; which I will not mention, lest I should seem to fling injurious reflections on a government whose clemency I have reason to acknowledge with the most loyal gratitude.

"It is true, my lord, there have been some additions made to the dissenters here since my settlement, and some of them by occasion of my preaching. They had but five meeting-houses then, in three different counties, and now they have seven in five counties, and stand in need of one or two more. But here I must again submit it to your lordship, whether the laws of England forbid men to change their opinions, and act according to them when changed? And whether the Act of Toleration was intended to tolerate such only as were dissenters by birth and education? Whether professed dissenters are prohibited to have meeting-houses licensed convenient to them, where there are conformists adjacent, whose curiosity may at first prompt them to hear, and whose judgments may afterwards direct them to join with the dissenters? Or whether, to avoid the danger of gaining proselytes, the dissenters, in such circumstances, must be wholly deprived of the ministration of the gospel?

"For my farther vindication, my lord, I beg leave to declare, and I defy the world to confute me, that in all the sermons I have preached in Virginia, I have not wasted one minute in exclaiming or reasoning against the peculiarities of the established church; nor so much as assigned the reasons of my own non-conformity. I have not exhausted my zeal in railing against the established clergy, in exposing their imperfections, some of which lie naked to my view, or in depreciating their characters. No, my lord, I have matters of infinitely greater importance to exert my zeal and spend my time and strength upon;—To preach repentance towards God, and faith towards our Lord Jesus Christ—To alarm secure impenitents; to reform the profligate; to undeceive the hypocrite; to raise up the hands that hang down, and to strengthen the feeble knees;—These are the doctrines I preach, these are the ends I pursue; and these my artifices to gain proselytes: and if ever I divert from these to ceremonial trifles, let my tongue cleave to the roof of my mouth. Now, my lord, if people adhere to me on such accounts as these, I cannot discourage them without wickedly betraying the interests of religion, and renouncing my character as a minister of the gospel. If the members of the Church of England come from distant places to the meeting-houses licensed for the use of professed dissenters, and upon hearing, join with them, and declare themselves Presbyterians, and place themselves under my ministerial care, I dare say your lordship will not censure me for admitting them. And if these new proselytes live at such a distance that they cannot meet statedly at the places already licensed, have they not a legal right to have houses licensed convenient to them, since they are as properly professed dissenters, in favour of whom the Act of Toleration was enacted, as those that have been educated in non-conformity? There is no method, my lord, to prevent the increase of our number in this manner, but either the prohibiting of all conformists to attend occasionally on my ministry; which neither the laws of God nor of the land will warrant: or the Episcopal ministers preaching the same doctrines which I do; as I humbly conceive they oblige themselves by subscribing their own articles; and had this been done, I am verily persuaded there would not have been one dissenter in these parts: or my absolutely refusing to receive those into the community of the dissenters, against whom it may be objected that they once belonged to the Church of England; which your lordship sees is unreasonable. 'Tis the conversion and salvation of men I aim to promote; and genuine

Christianity, under whatever various forms it appears, never fails to charm my heart. The design of the gospel is to bring perishing sinners to heaven, and if they are but brought thither, its ministers have but little cause of anxiety and contention about the denomination they sustain in their way. Yet, my lord, I may consistently profess, that as I judge the government, discipline and modes of worship in the dissenting church more agreeable to the divine standard than those in the Episcopal, it cannot but afford me a little additional satisfaction to see those that agree with me in essentials, and are hopefully walking towards the same celestial City, agree with me in extra-essentials too; though this ingredient of satisfaction is often swallowed up in the sublimer pleasure that results from the other more noble consideration.—And here, my lord, that I may unbosom myself with all the candid simplicity of a gospel minister, I must frankly own, that abstracting the consideration of the disputed peculiarities of the established church, which have little or no influence in the present case, I am verily persuaded (heaven knows with what sorrowful reluctance I admit the evidence of it) those of the Church of England in Virginia do not generally enjoy as suitable means for their conversion and edification as they might among the dissenters. This is not because they are of that communion; for I know the gospel and all its ordinances may be administered in a very profitable manner in a consistency with the constitution of that church; and perhaps her ceremonies would be so far from obstructing the efficacy of the means of grace, that they would rather promote it, to them that have no scruples about their lawfulness and expediency; though it would be otherwise with a doubtful conscience: but because the doctrines generally delivered from the pulpit, and the manner of delivery, are such as have not so probable a tendency to do good, as those among the dissenters. I am sensible, my lord, 'how hard it is,' as your lordship observes, 'not to suspect and charge corruption of principles on those, who differ in principles from us.' But still I cannot help thinking that they who generally entertain their hearers with languid harangues on morality or insipid speculations, omitting or but slightly touching upon the glorious doctrines of the gospel, which will be everlastingly found the most effectual means to reform a degenerate world; such as the corruption of human nature in its present lapsed state; the nature and necessity of regeneration, and of divine influences to effect it; the nature of saving faith, evangelical repentance, &c.* I cannot, I say, help

* "I do not intend this, my lord, for a complete enumeration of evangelical doctrines, as I intimate by the &c., annexed.—For your lordship's farther satisfaction, I must refer you to Dr. Doddridge's Practical writings,

thinking that they who omit, pervert or but slightly hint at these and the like doctrines, are not likely to do much service to the souls of men: and as far as I can learn by personal observation or the credible information of others, this is too generally the case in Virginia. And on this account especially, I cannot dissuade persons from joining with the dissenters, who are desirous to do so; and I use no other methods to engage them but the inculcating of these and like doctrines.

"I beg leave, my lord, to subjoin one remark more to vindicate the number of my meeting-houses, and as a reason for the licensure of that in New Kent: that in a large and scattered congregation, it may be necessary the minister should officiate occasionally in particular corners of his congregation for the conveniency of a few families that lie at a great distance from the places where he statedly officiates for the conveniency of the generality. This, my lord, is frequently practised, in the parishes in the frontier counties, which are very large, though not equal to the bounds of my congregation. 'Tis no doubt unreasonable, that the minister should consult the conveniency of a few rather than of the majority; and therefore I preach more frequently at one of the meeting-houses in Hanover, where the dissenters are more numerous, than at all the other six. But, my lord, is it not fit I should so far consult the conveniency of a few families, who live in the extremities of the congregation, at a great distance from the place where I statedly officiate, as to preach occasionally among them four or five times a year? Though one or two of a family may be able to attend at the stated place of meeting, yet it is impossible that all should; and why may not a sermon be preached occasionally in their neighbourhood, where they may all attend? Again: though the heads of families may be capable of attending on public worship at a great distance themselves, yet it is an intolerable hardship that they should be obliged to carry their children thirty, forty, or fifty miles to be baptized. And is it not reasonable, my lord, I should preach among them occasionally, to relieve them from this difficulty once in three or four months? And may not houses be legally licensed for this purpose? The meeting-house in New Kent was designed for such occasional meetings: and when I have given an account of the affair, I doubt not but your lordship will justify the procedure of the County Court in granting a license for it. Some people in and about that county, particularly two gentlemen of

---

particularly his Rise and Progress of Religion, his Sermons on the Power and Grace of Christ, and on Regeneration; which I heartily approve as to matter and manner, and would imitate, as far as my inferior genius will admit.

good estates and excellent characters, who had been justices of the peace and officers in the militia, told me, that as they lived at a great distance from the nearest place where I statedly officiate, and therefore could not frequently attend there, they would count it a peculiar favour, if I would preach occasionally at some place convenient to them, though it were on week-days. I replied, that though I was wholly unable to perform ministerial duties fully to the people at the places already licensed, yet I should be willing to give them a sermon now and then, if they could obtain a license for a place. Whereupon they presented a petition to the County Court, signed by fifteen persons, heads of families, and professed Presbyterians, which (as your lordship has been informed) was granted; but afterwards superseded by the Council. Hence, my lord, you may see what was the occasion and design of this petition; and that it was not an artifice of mine as an itinerant, 'to gather a congregation where there was none before;' but wholly the act of the people, professed dissenters, for their own conveniency.

"I am surprised, my lord, to find any intimations in the letter from Virginia about the validity and legality of the licenses for seven meeting-houses granted by the General Court, especially if that letter came from the Commissary. These were granted by the supreme authority of this colony; and cannot be called in question by the Council without questioning the validity of their own authority, at least the legal exercise of it in this instance. And the Rev. Dr. Dawson himself (whom I mention with sincere veneration) sat as a judge in the General Court (for he is one of his majesty's Council here) when the licenses were granted, and did not vote against it. Whether I have since forfeited them by my public conduct, I dare appeal to himself; and whether there be any limitations of the number of meeting-houses for the conveniency of one congregation, in the Act of Toleration, or his majesty's private instructions to the Governor, I dare submit to any one that has seen them.

"What I observed above concerning my preaching occasionally on working days, and the reason of it, reminds me, my lord, of an unexpected charge against me in the letter from Virginia, expressed in terms contemptuous enough—'I had almost forgot to mention his *holding forth* on working days to great numbers of poor people, who generally are his only followers. This certainly is inconsistent with the religion of labour, whereby they are obliged to maintain themselves and families; and their neglect of this duty, if not seasonably prevented, may in process of time be sensibly felt by the Government.' Here, my lord, imaginary danger is traced from a very distant source; and I might justify myself by an *argumentum ad hominem:* my people do not spend half as many working days in attending on my holding.forth the Word of Life, as the members of the Church of England are obliged to keep holy according to their calendar. But I know recrimination, though with advantage, is but a spiteful and ineffectual method of vindication. I therefore observe, with greater pleasure, that as I can officiate but at some one of my meeting-houses on Sundays, and as not any one of the seven is tolerably convenient to the half of my people; many of them cannot have opportunity of hearing me on Sundays above once in a month or two; and I have no way to make up their loss in some measure but by preaching in the meeting-house contiguous to them, once or twice in two or three months on working days. And can this, my lord, have the least tendency to beggar themselves and families, or injure the Government, especially when such meetings are chiefly frequented (and that not oftener than once a fortnight or month) by heads of families and others, who can easily afford a few hours for this purpose, without the least detriment to their secular affairs? I can assure your lordship a great number of my hearers are so well furnished with slaves, that they are under no necessity of confining themselves to hard labour; and that they redeem more time from the fashionable riots and excessive diversions of the age than they devote to this purpose: and I wonder there is not an equal clamour raised about the modish ways of murdering time, which are more likely to be sensibly felt by the Government, and, which is worse, to ruin multitudes forever. *The Religion of Labour* is held sacred among us; as the temporal circumstances of my people demonstrate: which are as flourishing as before their adherence to me, except that some of them have been somewhat injured by the fines and concomitant expenses imposed upon them for worshipping God inoffensively in separate assemblies. But this hardship, my lord, I will not aggravate, as I very believe it was not the effect of an oppressive spirit in the Court, but of misinformation, and the malignant officiousness of some private persons.

"I am fully satisfied, my lord, were there a pious bishop resident in America, it would have a happy tendency to reform the church of England here, and maintain her purity: and therefore upon a report spread in Virginia, some time ago, that one was appointed, I expressed my satisfaction in it; and my poor prayers shall concur to promote it. I know this is also the sentiment of all my brethren in the Synod of New York, with whom I have conversed. I am, therefore, extremely surprised at the information your lordship has received concerning the reception of this proposal in New England, and 'that they used all their influence to obstruct it.' I never had the least intimation of it before, though some of the principal ministers there maintain a very unreserved correspondence with me; and I have also the other usual methods of receiving intelligences from a country so near. If it be true, I think with your lordship, that it is hardly consistent with a spirit of toleration, but it appears so unreasonable, and so opposite to the sentiments of all the dissenters whom I am acquainted with (and they are many, both of the clergy and laity) that the informers must be persons of undoubted veracity, before I could credit it. However, my lord, I am not concerned: the Synod of New York, to which I belong, I am confident, have used no means to oppose it: but would rather concur to promote it, were it in their power; and therefore, if your lordship deal with us *secundum legem talionis*, we expect favourable usage. The same things I would say concerning the prosecution and imprisonment of sundry members of the church in New England. I never heard so much as an uncertain rumour of it; and I am sure it is neither approved nor practised in the bounds of the Synod of New York. Were your lordship acquainted with the members of that Synod, you would own them as strenuous advocates for the civil and sacred rights of mankind, and as far from a bigoted intolerant spirit, as perhaps any in the world. And here, my lord, let me correct a small mistake (the effect of imperfect or false information, I suppose) in your lordship's letter to Dr. Doddridge; your lordship takes the persons in New England, who have been accessory to those prosecutions, to be members of the Synod, which sent me as a missionary to Virginia; whereas I am a member of another synod two or three hundred miles distant; and do not in the least act in concert with, or subjection to the ministers in New England.

"Your lordship huddles me promiscuously with the methodists, as though I were of their party. I am not ashamed to own that I look upon Mr. Whitefield as a zealous and successful minister of Christ; and as such to countenance him. I love him, and I love your lordship, (the profession, I hope, will not be offensive) because I hope you are both good men: and if my affection to him proves me one of his party, I hope your lordship will conclude me one of your own too: yet I am far from approving sundry steps in Mr. Whitefield's first public conduct; and I am glad to find by some of his late writings that he does not approve of them himself. The eruptions of his first zeal were, in many instances, irregular; his regulating his conduct so much by impulses, &c., was enthusiastic, and his freedoms in publishing his experience to the world, in his journals, were, in my opinion, very imprudent. As to the rest of the methodists, I know but little of them; and, therefore, must suspend my judgment concerning them.

"Our loyalty to the Government is so well attested and universally known, that I presume none have ventured to surmise the contrary to your lordship; and this renders it needless for me to offer anything to demonstrate it.

"Thus, my lord, in the simplicity of my heart, I have laid before your lordship an impartial view of the state of affairs relating to the dissenters here, as it appears to me; and made some remarks on your lordship's letter to Dr. Doddridge, and the letters from and to Virginia. I please myself with the persuasion that I have not indulged the contradictious, angry humour of a contentious disputant; nor the malignant partiality of a bigot: and it will afford me peculiar satisfaction, if it should be equally evident to your lordship. All the apologies I could make could not atone for my tediousness, were it impertinent or avoidable; but as one that has not naturally a concise method of communicating his thoughts, could not fully represent the matter in fewer words, I promise myself your lordship's forbearance.

"I am persuaded, my lord, were you convinced the representation I have given is just, your lordship would turn advocate for the dissenters here, that the matter might be determined in their favour, I am therefore anxious to take some method to convince your lordship it is so; and I can think of no better method than to give those that may look upon themselves concerned to refute me, an opportunity to make the experiment, by publishing this letter to the world. This I should undoubtedly have done, and sent your lordship a printed copy, had I not been scrupulous of making so free with your private letters without your consent. If your lordship approve of this expedient, I shall, upon the first information of it, send it to the press.

"May the great Shepherd and Bishop of souls shed the richest blessings of his providence and grace upon you; and long continue your lordship to be consumed in pious services for the Church of God!—whatever reception this letter meets with, this shall be the ardent wish and perpetual prayer of,

"My Lord,
"Your Lordship's
"Most dutiful servant,
SAMUEL DAVIES.

"Hanover, in Virginia, Jan. 10, 1752.

"POSTSCRIPT.

"I am heartily sorry, my lord, that the character I gave of the clergy and laity in Virginia, in my letter to Dr. Doddridge, has given your lordship great concern. I have no doubt of its sincerity, though I am uncertain whether it was occasioned by a suspicion of calumniating partiality in me, or of truth in my account, or both.   There was no part of your lordship's letter that afflicted me so deeply as this; yet, I thought to have passed it over in silence, and accordingly made no remarks upon it in the preceding letter; because, as I have not been so happy since as to see reason to retract my former account, I could not relieve your lordship from your pious anxiety; and as it is a tender point, and the information comes with a poor grace from me, I thought the mentioning the many unwelcome evidences of its justice, which force themselves upon me all around, would but increase your lordship's concern, and confirm the suspicion of my partiality, which you intimate in your letter to the Dr., though with tenderness.   But considering that I write to one that will not officiously spread the account, to the disgrace of religion; and who may be able to administer remedies to so deplorable a case, if seasonably informed of it; and that your lordship's correspondents here may be under as strong a temptation to extenuate such matters, as I may be supposed to be to aggravate them; and consequently a medium between the two may appear to your lordship to be most just: considering also that it seems necessary for my own vindication, though I do not desire to build my reputation on the infamy of others: I have determined to give your lordship the following brief account, which I am willing should pass under the severest scrutiny.

"I am sensible, my lord, 'how hard it is not to suspect and charge corruption of principles upon those who differ in principles from us;' and how natural it is to a party spirit (and alas! parties are generally animated with such a spirit) to magnify the practical irregularities of other denominations. Sensible of this, and how inconsistent such a temper is with the generous religion of Jesus, I have conscientiously kept a peculiar guard upon my spirit in this respect: and yet (with shame I confess it) I have not been entirely a stranger to its malignant workings; though I am conscious that my prevailing and habitual disposition is candid and generous: otherwise I should be self-condemned in pretending to be a minister or even follower of the Lamb of God.   At present, my lord, I feel myself calm and impartial; and could I make my letter the transcript of my heart, your lordship would believe me.   I solemnly profess I am conscious of no indulged party spirit; however, I am so sensible of my own weakness, that I may implicitly suspect I may be imperceptibly tinctured with it; and therefore your lordship may, at the venture, 'deduct some things from the general character.'   I shall say but little of the differences in speculation betwixt me and the clergy and others

here: both because such errors may not be so pernicious as
vicious practices and the neglect of religious and moral duties;
and because these are more disputable, and I may be more
liable to mistakes about them.   But, my lord, I cannot indulge
an implicit suspicion of my partiality so far as to rush into universal skepticism about plain, public, indisputible facts, obvious
to my senses.   I can see, I can hear, with certainty.   I cannot be so infatuated with prejudice as to be incapable of distinguishing between a religious and profane life, between a relish for divine things, and a contemptuous neglect of them, between blasphemy and prayer, drunkenness and sobriety, &c.
And I shall chiefly take notice of such obvious facts, about
which there is no dispute between the church of England and
the dissenters.   I would also have it noticed, my lord, that I
would not have this account looked on as a history of the
state of religion in Virginia in general; but only in those counties (and they are not very few) where I have had opportunity
of personal observations: and these, if I may believe general
fame, are not more degenerate than the rest.

"I confess, my lord, with pleasure, that there are sundry of
the laity in the sphere of my acquaintance in the Church of
England, who are persons of good morals and have a veneration
for religion; and some of them, I doubt not, are sincere Christians, whom I cordially love: and that with more ardent affection than those of my own denomination, who appear destitute
of real religion; and alas! there are many such, I fear.   These
pious conformists can witness, that I have not been officious in
endeavouring to proselyte them to my party; and that, when
conversant with them, I rather choose to dwell on those infinitely more important and delightful subjects in which we agree,
than those little angry peculiarities in which we differ.   I also
cheerfully own (nor is the concession forcibly extorted from me)
that sundry of the established clergy are gentlemen of learning,
parts and morality, and I hope honestly aiming at the salvation
of men; though I cannot but disagree with them in some doctrines, and humbly conceive their public discourses generally
are not well adapted to promote their pious end.   But, my
lord, notwithstanding these concessions, religion may be in a
very languishing situation and vice triumphant in this colony.
There may be a few names even in Sardis, who have not defiled
their garments; and yet the majority have at best but a name
to live, while they are dead.   I must therefore now lay before
your lordship the disagreeable part of the character; and if I
expatiate more largely upon it than the former, it is not because
I take a malignant pleasure in so doing, but because my present
design urges me on to the unwelcome task.

"If I am prejudiced in favour of any church, my lord, it is

of that established in Scotland; of which I am a member
in the same sense that the Established Church in Virginia
is the Church of England: and therefore, should I give your
lordship an account of the state of religion there, you would not
suspect it of excessive severity. Now, my lord, suppose I had
resided four years in Scotland, preached frequently, and obtained
a pretty extensive acquaintance in five different counties, gone
sometimes as a hearer to the established kirk, and been occasionally at courts and the like public conventions; spent a week
at sundry times in the metropolis, and a day or two in some of
the principal towns; lodged in private families frequently in
various parts of the country; and (which I may mention as of
some weight in conjunction with the other opportunities of personal observation) received frequent and well attested informations from multitudes from various parts, and of different
denominations; your lordship would grant that I had sufficient
opportunities to make some observations on the state of religion, and could not suspect that my partiality would render
me so implicitly confident that religion was in a flourishing
state, as that I should take no notice of obvious public facts,
that obtruded themselves upon my senses; or so pervert my
judgment as to conclude all was well in spite of the most
glaring evidence.—Suppose then, my lord, that by all the dis-
coveries I can make in these circumstances, I find the generality grossly ignorant of the nature of living Christianity and
many of the most important doctrines of the gospel: if I find
a general unconcernedness about their eternal states discovered
in their discourse and practice, and no religious solemnity, no
relish for divine things, no proper anxieties about their spiritual state intimated by those genuine indications which nature
gives of such dispositions: if concern about such things, and a
life of strict holiness even in a member of the established
church, be generally ridiculed as a fanatical singularity: if the
Sabbath is prostituted by many to trifling amusements or guilty
pleasures; and if worldly discourse be the usual entertainment
without the sanctuary before and after divine service: if by far
the greatest number of families call not upon God, nor maintain
his worship in their houses: if in parishes where there are
many hundreds of adults, there be not above fifty or sixty communicants; and sundry of these too, persons of abandoned
characters: if multitudes, multitudes toss the most sacred and
tremendous things on their daring tongues by profane oaths
and shocking imprecations; and beastify themselves with excessive drinking, as though it were a venial sin: if I get me to
the great men, and find that these also generally have burst
the bonds, and broken the yoke; that they discard serious
religion as the badge of the vulgar, and abandon themselves

to lawless pleasures, to gaming, cock-fighting, horse-racing, and all the fashionable methods of killing time, as the most important and serious business of life: if public worship be frequently neglected, or attended on with trifling levity; and yet the most build their hopes of heaven on these insipid formalities, regardless of the manner of their devotion: in a word, if the trifles of time and sense engross all the thoughts and activity of the generality; and the infinite concerns of eternity be neglected, or attended on as matters by the by:—if, my lord, I should find this to be the state of affairs in Scotland, could my prejudice in favour of that church so far bias me, as that I could not see religion to be in a most deplorable situation in her? Or would my character of Virginia in my letter to Dr. Doddridge be too satirical in such a case?

"This, my lord, is the just character of the generality of the laity here; my senses tell me so; and I cannot doubt of it more than of my own existence. I do not mean that all the parts of this character are generally complicated in one person; but that one part of it is the character of some, and another of others, and that the whole promiscuously is the character of the generality of the laity here: and were I as much prejudiced in favour of the church established in Virginia as I may be supposed to be of that established in Scotland, I could not conscientiously give a better account of it.

"Further; suppose, my lord, on observing religion in so melancholy a situation in Scotland, I have opportunity of observing also what measures are taken by the established clergy there for its revival, and to promote a general reformation, and find to my sorrowful surprise, that the generality of them, as far as can be discovered by their common conduct and public ministrations, are stupidly serene and unconcerned, as though their hearers were crowding promiscuously to heaven, and there were little or no danger;—that they address themselves to perishing multitudes in *cold blood*, and do not represent their miserable condition in all its horrors; do not alarm them with solemn, pathetic and affectionate warnings, and expostulate with them with all the authority, tenderness and pungency of the ambassadors of Christ to a dying world, nor commend themselves to every man's conscience in the sight of God; that their common conversation has little or no savour of living religion, and is not calculated to excite thoughtfulness in the minds of the unthinking creatures they converse with;—that instead of intense application to study, or teaching their parishioners from house to house, they waste their time in idle visits, trifling conversation, slothful ease, or at best, excessive activity about their temporal affairs;—that sundry of them associate with the profane, and those that are infamous for the neglect of religion, not like their professed Master, to reform them, but without intermingling any thing serious in their discourse, or giving a solemn check to their guilty liberties; nay, that some of them are companions with drunkards, and partakers in their sottish extravagances;—that they are more zealous and laborious in their attempts to regain those that have joined with other denominations, or to secure the rest from the contagion by calumniating the dissenters, than to convert men from sin to holiness; if, my lord, I should find this to be the general character of the clergy in Scotland, how could I avoid the unwelcome conclusion, that such are not likely to be the successful instruments of a general reformation? And who that has not sacrificed to bigotry all his regard to the immortal weal of mankind, would not rejoice in this case to see a reformation carried on in Scotland by a minister of the Church of England? For my part, I solemnly profess I would; for though by this means sundry would fall off from the established church, yet there would be a greater probability of their escaping eternal destruction, and being made members of the church triumphant in the regions of bliss; which would be infinitely more than a reparation of that little breach of a party.

"What I now suppose, my lord, in Scotland, is evident matter of fact in Virginia, unless my eyes and my ears deceive me, and I see phantoms instead of men. The plain truth is, a general reformation *must* be promoted in this colony by some means or other, or multitudes are eternally undone: and I see alas! but little ground to hope for it from the generality of the clergy here, till they be happily changed themselves; this is not owing to their being of the Church of England, as I observed before: for were they in the Presbyterian Church, or any other, I should have no more hopes of their success; but it is owing to their manner of preaching and behaviour. This thought, my lord, is so far from being agreeable to me that it at times racks me with agonies of compassion and zeal intermingled: and could I entertain that unlimited charity which lulls so many of my neighbours into a serene stupidity, it would secure me from many a melancholy hour, and make my life below a kind of anticipation of heaven. I can boast of no high attainments, my lord; I am as mean and insignificant a creature as your lordship can well conceive me to be: but I dare profess I cannot be an unconcerned spectator of the ruin of my dear fellow mortals: I *dare avow* my heart at times is set upon nothing more than to snatch the brands out of the burning, before they catch fire and burn unquenchably. And hence, my lord, it is, I consume my strength and life in such great fatigues in this jangling ungrateful colony.

"Hence, my lord, you may collect my sentiments concerning an absurdity your lordship mentions in your letter to Dr. Doddridge, that I should attempt to make converts in a church which I acknowledge in the meantime to be a church of Christ. I freely grant the Church of England to be a church of Christ: but when I see multitudes ready to perish, and no suitable means used for their recovery, can it comfort me to think they perish in a church of Christ? The articles and constitution of the established church are substantially good, and her ceremonies are little or no hinderance, as I observed before, to the edification of those that do not scruple them; but her members in this colony are *in fact* generally corrupted; and I think, were I one of her ministers, I should rather ten thousand times see men pious dissenters, than graceless conformists. It is true, had I no other objection against conformity but the present degeneracy of the members of the church, it would be my duty to endeavour to promote a reformation in her communion: but as I cannot conscientiously conform on some other accounts, the only practicable method for me to attempt the reformation of her members is that which I now pursue.

"I shall only add, my lord, that I humbly conceive the informations or personal knowledge upon which your lordship has characterized a great part of the clergy in Virginia, may afford you equal concern with my character of them. I dare avow a more noble spirit than to catch at it with a malignant satisfaction as a confirmation of mine: and therefore I humbly request, nay, demand as a piece of justice, that your lordship would not look on my remark on it as the language of such a disposition. I only remind you of it for my own defence, and it shall never be officiously propagated by me. If, as your lordship observes, 'of those that come from England,' (and the most of them come from thence), '*a great* part are of the Scotch or Irish, who can get no employment at home, and enter into the service more out of necessity than choice;' if 'others go abroad to retrieve either lost fortunes or lost characters;' how can it be expected, my lord, that persons who enter into holy orders, or come to Virginia from such sordid views as these, should deserve a better character than I gave of them to the Dr. or than I have now given your lordship? But I forbear—your lordship will forgive the inaccuracies of this postscript, as I have written it in unavoidable haste."

This letter, an evidence of the honesty and simplicity of Davies' heart, rather than his worldly wisdom, was never submitted to the Bishop's inspection.

In September 1751 the Synod of New York met at Newark, New Jersey. From the minutes of the meeting is the following extract—"A motion being made to the Synod by Mr. Davies of the necessity of sending to England an account relating to the dissenting interest in Virginia, the Synod does order that a representation of the circumstances of the Presbyterian congregations in that colony be made and signed, in the name of the Synod, by Messrs. Burr and Pemberton, to Dr. Doddridge and Dr. Avery; and also a certificate of Mr. Davies' character."

Of the correspondence between Mr. Davies and Dr. Benjamin Avery there remain but two letters, one from each writer. That from Mr. Davies bears date May 21st, 1752.

"*Rev. Dear and Worthy Sir:*—I have been so happy as to receive yours of February 22d, about a fortnight ago by Mr. Holt. I also received last December the letter you mentioned from the Rev. Dr. Doddridge, informing me of the sentiments of the Lord Bishop of London on my affairs, and giving his advice and yours how to proceed. Upon receiving the Doctor's letter and the extracts enclosed from the Bishop of London, I was surprised to find what unjust representations had been made of my conduct, and the circumstances of the dissenters here to his lordship; and concluded that till they were rectified we could not expect the negotiations of our friends in England in our behalf should succeed. I therefore wrote at large to his lordship giving him an account of our circumstances here; which letter I sent to Mr. Mauduit, to be communicated by him to you and Dr. Doddridge (the melancholy news of whose decease had not then reached me) and after correction to be sent, if you judged it proper, to the bishop. At the same time I wrote to you soliciting your interest in behalf of the dissenters here, which I find by yours, your generous temper rendered needless; but whether any of them are come safe to hand I know not.

"Since I received yours I have been uneasy lest my letter to his lordship should be put into his hands without your approbation; as my sentiments therein expressed, concerning the mission of bishops to North America, were different from yours in your letter to me. When I expressed my satisfaction in the proposal, I spoke in the simplicity of my heart and according to my judgment, which I have had no reason to alter since, but only your dissent; in which I put implicit confidence as you have better opportunities to discover the consequences of such missions than I. That the settlement of bishops in the dissenting colonies would be injurious to them I easily see; but I find by the Bishop of London's letter to Dr. Doddridge, that this was not proposed. And I was not able to discern what injury the settlement of a bishop in Virginia or Maryland, where the Church of England is established, would be to the few dissenters in them; and I was not without hopes it might tend to purge out the corrupt leaven from the established church, and restrain the clergy from their extravagances, who now behave as they please, and promise themselves impunity as there is none to censure or depose them on this side the Atlantic.

However, dear sir, if you think me mistaken, you may take
what measure you think proper to prevent any ill consequences
that may be occasioned by the unreserved declaration of my
opinion in my letter to his lordship. And as I shall hereafter
impose upon you the trouble of receiving and reviewing the
papers I may find occasion to transmit to England on the
affairs of the dissenters in Virginia, I not only allow, but
request you, sir, to correct or suppress them as your superior
judgment may direct you. As I judge the matter is of great
importance to the interest of religion in this colony, I would
not willingly incur guilt by omitting any means in my power
to reflect light upon it; but for want of judgment and a more
thorough acquaintance with the state of affairs in England, I
may sometimes fail in the right choice or prudent use of means
for that purpose; and therefore to prevent any ill consequences,
I must call in the assistance of your judgment and that of the
committee.

"I waited on the Governor and Council about a month ago,
in company with one of my brethren, the Rev. Mr. John Todd
who applied to their Honours to be qualified to officiate in and
about Hanover county, as my assistant; and with much difficulty our petition was granted. But they refused to license
any more meeting-houses, where either of us might officiate
occasionally, in such places as are inconvenient to the meeting-
houses already licensed. I have strong expectation Mr. Todd
will settle in Hanover to relieve me of a part of my charge,
which I hope will prove a happy providence to this colony, and
particularly to the dissenters, as he is a pious, prudent youth,
and a very popular preacher; and his settlement will tend in a
great measure to remove the odium that has been unjustly
flung upon me as an itinerant, because of my officiating at so
many places.

"I am fully satisfied, sir, that as you intimate the Act of
Uniformity and other penal laws against non-conformity are
not in force in the colonies; and consequently that the dissenters have no right nor indeed any need to plead the Act of
Toleration as an exemption from those penal laws. But sir,
our Legislature here has passed an act of the same kind with
those laws, though the penalty is less, requiring all adult
persons to attend on the established church. As this act was
passed since the Revolution, it was necessary that Protestant
dissenters should be exempted from its obligations and tolerated to worship God in separate assemblies; (though indeed,
at the time of its enaction, viz., the 4th of Queen Ann, there
was not a dissenting congregation, except a few Quakers, in
the colony) and for this purpose, our Legislature thought fit
to take in the act of Parliament made for that end in England,

rather than pass a new one peculiar to this colony. This, sir, you may see in my remonstrance to the Governor and Council which I find has been laid before you. Now it is with a view to exempt ourselves from the obligations of the above law made by our Legislature, that we plead the Act of Toleration, and we plead it not as *an English law*, for we are convinced it does not extend hither by virtue of its primitive enaction, but as *received into the body of the Virginia laws* by our Legislature. And though for some time, some pretended to scruple, and others denied that the Act of Toleration is in force here even in this sense; yet now I think it is generally granted, and all the question is about the intent and meaning of this Act; particularly whether a dissenting congregation, that is very much dispersed, and cannot meet at one place, may claim a right by virtue of said act, to have a plurality of places licensed for the convenience for the sundry parts of the congregation? And whether it allows a dissenting minister to divide his labours among two congregations at sundry meeting-houses when by reason of the scarcity of ministers each congregation cannot be furnished with one? I hope, sir, all occasion for the latter will be removed by Mr. Todd's settlement, but the former will still continue, as the dissenters, Mr. Todd's congregation and mine, cannot be accommodated without a plurality of meeting-houses. Seven have been licensed, four of which will be under his care, and three continued under mine, and in these we purpose to officiate stately. But there is a number of dissenters in four or five places who cannot obtain ministers of their own, nor attend on our ministry at the places licensed already, by reason of distance; and they are very desirous to have houses licensed among them, where any qualified dissenting minister whom they shall invite, may officiate occasionally, and the only question, sir, which we would have determined in England, is, whether the Act of Toleration entitles them to have houses licensed among them for that purpose.

"We doubt not of your zeal, dear sir, to manage the affair; and we cheerfully leave it to you and the gentlemen of the committee to determine the most proper time to prosecute it. But this, sir, I would inform you of, that we are not asking a favour of the Government, but entering a legal claim. If it be determined by competent authority, that the Act of Toleration does not allow the dissenters to have meeting-houses licensed, where they may occasionally meet for public worship, we shall quietly resign our claim, till some favourable juncture happens, when we may petition for the enlargement of our liberties. But if we may legally make this claim; if dissenters enjoy this privilege in England; and if the rulers there judge that the Act of

Toleration entitles them to it, then we humbly conceive that the pushing the matter to a determination could be attended with no ill consequences ; as we only pressed for an explication of the Act of Toleration, with reference to Virginia, according to its true intent and meaning in England, whether the determination of such a point belongs to the lawyers, to judges, or to his majesty and council, you, sir, can determine : though an authoritative order from the latter would be most regarded by our rulers ; and all the order we desire is this, that wherever ten or fifteen families of Protestant dissenters, who cannot attend at the meeting-house already licensed, apply for licenses at the General Court, they shall be granted them. It has been confidently affirmed to me by some of the Council that the dissenters in England have no such privilege. In this, sir, I request your information ; for if this be the case we must resign our claim.

"I send you inclosed a copy of a certificate given to the clerk of the General Court last April, to be presented to the Court. He showed it to the Governor and some of the Council, in my presence, before they sat in court, and their answer was—'That it would be in vain to present it in court, for they would grant no more licenses till they had received answer from England, whither they had written for instructions.' Another certificate was presented to a county court, and rejected, and a third would have been presented to the General Court had I not discouraged the persons concerned, by informing them it would be in vain. The certificate is drawn up in the form prescribed by Dr. Doddridge in his letter to me ; and it was his judgment that in case it should be refused, we should have just ground of complaint in the courts of England. I therefore send you a copy of it, that you may make what use of it you think expedient. The persons concerned in all these certificates live thirteen, twenty, thirty, forty miles from the nearest of the places already licensed, and therefore unless they can obtain places licensed contiguous to them, they will be generally deprived of public worship altogether.

"I also send you a narrative of the state of religion among the dissenters here in Virginia, printed in Boston ; and if it engage your fervent prayers, intermingled with thanksgivings for us, my end is obtained. I also present you with a collection of poems, which, though beneath your notice in all other respects, will, I hope, be acceptable as a token of impotent gratitude.

"I have had some thoughts of laying our affairs before the General Assembly of the Church of Scotland, and soliciting their interest in our behalf. My motives are partly that their concurrence may enforce your attempts in our favour; and especially to convince the world that I am a Presbyterian minister, which some here have pretended to scruple; and I can think of no better expedient for this end than to prevail on the General Assembly to espouse my cause. But in this, and in all other affairs of the like nature, I am wholly at your direction and control; and as I shall request my friends in Scotland to act in concert with you, it will be still in your power to follow your own judgment.

"Though I apply to you as a petitioner for a favour, yet, when I assure you that I affectionately love you, and remember you when I bow my knees to the God and Father of our Lord Jesus Christ, you will not, I hope, suspect it as an artifice to bribe your friendship. Though my warmest gratitude is due for your generous and pious zeal for the interests of dissenters, yet I have a disinterested esteem for you on account of your personal worth, which universal fame has not permitted me to be unacquainted with. I request your prayers, dear sir, for me, that I may be faithful and successful in that part of the Lord's vineyard which his providence has assigned me; and for my people, that their light may so shine before men, &c.

"The news of Dr. Doddridge's death gave an incurable wound to my spirit; and Zion through all her divisions has felt the blow. I should be glad to know what posthumous writings of his are put to the press, and particularly, whether he lived to finish his Family Expositor, which is very acceptable in Virginia, and of great service already to sundry families.

"I expect, dear sir, you will write to me as frequently as you can, for my mind is uneasy till the matter be determined; till then, I hope, I shall exercise that patience, and show that quiet submission, which you in the name of the committee have so kindly recommended to me. I request you to return my most grateful acknowledgments to them, and assure yourself that I am, reverend and worthy sir, your obliged and most humble servant,

Samuel Davies.

"Hanover, May 21st, 1752.

"I write in a hurry, and therefore you will exercise your candour, sir, towards my blunders and inaccuracies."

Letter from Dr. Avery to Mr. Davies.

" Rev. and Dear Sir—Yours of the 21st of May came safe though directed in a way which for many years I have not been used to; having not preached these thirty years past. Mr. Mauduit received yours of an earlier date designed for the Bishop of London, which he communicated to me, and we agreed that it was by no means advisable to send it to his lordship. I shall not enter into any debate with you concerning the scheme proposed for erecting a Bishoprick in North

America. The less is said on that head, either on your or on our side of the water, I believe the better. But one thing in yours addressed to his lordship greatly surprised me. You represent your friends in North America, particularly in New York, Virginia and Massachusetts, as far as your correspondence reaches, if not as desiring, yet as very willing to acquiesce, in having such an ecclesiastical superior officer sent over to America with power to ordain, confirm, &c. Now all my accounts from Connecticut, the Jerseys, and the Massachusetts, directly and strongly contradict this. They uniformly speak of it as a measure quite inconsistent with their peace and tranquillity. From both the ministry and laity in all those colonies, I have received thanks for my having done the little I did do, or indeed could do to prevent such an appointment taking place; and I have had the most importunate, repeated solicitations to prevent so sore a calamity as that seemed likely to prove to the colonies. These I have had from many quarters; and some of them expressed in strong and irritating terms. Yours to his lordship is the first letter I have seen from those parts expressing a desire, or so much as an indifference and coolness on that head.

"This must be my excuse for not forwarding your letter to his lordship, though on several other accounts on which I cannot enlarge, I should not have thought it proper to be put into his hands; some relating to himself, and some to yourself; but I will add one that would have been an objection to me had I approved of every sentiment in the letter; I well knew the length would have caused his lordship to have treated your letter with a contempt and disregard it did not deserve. For in cases which these great men, whether in church or state, have most at heart, I have repeatedly seen that they cannot bear long and minute representations.

"The next subject of your letter is an inquiry, whether you are not entitled according to the Act of Toleration to license as many meeting-houses as you see fit. Now if the Act of Toleration be, in so many words, adopted, or wrought into your constitution and made a proper law of your colony, and is to be interpreted as the Act of Toleration is understood here, nothing can be more plain than that you may certify, record, or register as many houses for religious worship, as the dissenters in the colony think they want, or choose to have. If I was disposed to certify or register twenty houses in the parish in which I live as designed for religious worship, and demand it in the same form in which you tell me you have done, on paying sixpence either at the Quarter Sessions or in the Session . . . . . . Court, the officers of those courts would not dare refuse it; if they did, we know where to apply . . . . . .

bench would immediately grant a mandamus, and oblige the clerk of the peace, or the proper officer in the Ecclesiastical Court to do as we desired. Where you are to apply for redress according to the laws of your colony, we cannot say. Perhaps you have no Justices of the Peace or General Quarter Sessions, but every thing is adjudged among you by your Governor and Council. From them indeed you have an appeal to the King and Council; but redress this way cannot readily and speedily be procured. Such appeals must be attended with very great expense.

"Though I well knew the Attorney General's and other eminent lawyers' opinion on this question before, I have taken Sir D. Ryder's opinion on this head for your use, and herewith send it over to you, hoping that when his excellency your worthy Governor and the Council shall see, peruse, and consider it, they will no longer refuse your friends' request.

"When you certify places as designed for religious worship, you are not obliged to say who is to officiate in that place, your unnecessarily saying that has furnished the gentlemen who refuse and oppose you, with an handle. But the design of this proviso was not either to prevent the multiplying our places for worship, or to oblige us to ascertain and specify the persons who are intended to officiate in those places. In the proviso there is not a word relating to the qualifications, much less to the names of the persons to be employed therein. There are indeed other clauses of that Act relating to the qualifications of ministers [*a couple of lines wanting*] mentioned in the Act.

"I cannot advise you to have any recourse to the General Assembly of Scotland. I do not see how an application to them will or can stand you in any stead.

"I thank you for the historical account you sent me of the state of religion in the colony, and for the ingenious poems which accompanied your obliging letter. I have perused both the one and the other with pleasure, and my most fervent prayers shall not be wanting that the cause of religion, virtue, truth, liberty, and the most extensive charity may daily gain ground in Virginia and all your neighbouring colonies.

"Dr. Doddridge's death is a great wound to the dissenting interest, and indeed to the interest of religion. Our consolation must be, that the Lord reigns, who can carry on and perfect his work even without instruments, or by the means of such who seem to be much less fitted and qualified for such service than those which He has thought fit to remove.

"May your health be confirmed and re-established, your valuable life prolonged, your usefulness be long continued and daily increasing, and your faithful endeavours to serve God and promote the welfare of your fellow creatures with respect to their most important interests, be attended with the most desirable success. In which wishes the gentlemen of the committee concur.

> "With, Rev'd and dear Sir,
> "Your sincere friend
> and humble servant,
> "Benj. Avery."

"P. S. You may be pleased when you show the Attorney General's opinion to his Excellency to let him know that you received it from me whom I flatter myself he will recollect, as he has seen me often both in London and at Bath; and pray present him with my most respectful compliments."

The opinion of Sir Dudley Rider is not to be found: but its meaning is not to be mistaken. It evidently decided two things,—that by the English interpretation of the Act of Toleration the dissenters might ask for the licensure of as many houses as they thought necessary without fear of refusal,—and that this interpretation properly extended to Virginia. We see from the letter of the bishop of London, that his lordship entertained a different opinion. The Governor and Council of Virginia claimed the right, as supreme executive and judiciary of the colony, to determine the number of houses of religious worship to be allowed dissenters, and also their location. From this decision of the Governor and Council there was no redress but by an appeal to the King and Council, which was both troublesome and expensive. Here the matter rested till Mr. Davies visited England. After his return from England he received two letters from the committee of the dissenters, which will be given in their chronological order. They show the interest taken in the cause of the dissenters in Virginia, by the dissenters in England; and that all hope of redress from civil authority lay in an appeal to the King.

Amid all his labours, in seven preaching places, besides his journies to attend upon the judicatories of the church, Mr. Davies found time and strength and disposition to make frequent missionary excursions to the sections of country now included in the counties of Cumberland, Powhatan, Prince Edward, Charlotte, Campbell, Nottoway and Amelia. One of his excursions is referred to in the following account by Rev'd Archibald Alexander, D. D., of Princeton, who from his residence of many years in Prince Edward and Charlotte during the latter part of the eighteenth and the beginning of the nineteenth century, had full opportunity of becoming acquainted with the early history of the congregations. It is taken from a brief memoir of Major James Morton, which appeared in the Watchman and Observer for February 18th,

1847.—"When Mr. Davies took long tours of preaching, which he usually did in the course of the year, he was commonly accompanied by a pious young man, not merely as a companion, but as a pioneer to ride on before, and find a place of lodging; for many people were unwilling to receive a "*New-light*" preacher into their houses, in those days. In this service young John Morton (father of Major Morton) was sometimes employed, for having been converted under Mr. Davies's ministry he was delighted to have the opportunity of enjoying his company and pious conversation. The writer has often heard old Mrs. Morton, of Little Roanoke Bridge, called *the mother in Israel*, relate the circumstance of Mr. Davies's first visit to that place. Young John Morton, who was a relative, came, one day to know, whether Mr. Davies, the New-light preacher, could be lodged there that night. Her husband, called, by way of distinction, Little Joe Morton, not being at the house, she could not answer. But when he was sent for, from the field, and the question was proposed to him, after a few moments consideration, he answered in the affirmative; and Mr. Morton went back to the inn, and brought Mr. Davies to the house. And with him Christ and salvation came to that house. Both of the heads of the family, under the influence of the gospel, as heard from Mr. Davies, became truly and eminently pious. And their conversion was the foundation of the *Briery Congregation*, of which Little Joe Morton was the first elder, and before they had a regular minister, was more like a pastor than a ruling elder; for every Sabbath he would convene the people, and read to them an evangelical sermon; and regularly catechise the children out of the Shorter Catechism. The writer never saw this excellent man; but he can truly say he never knew any layman to leave behind him a sweeter savour of piety. None was ever heard to speak of him after his decease, otherwise than with respect bordering on veneration. And all the children of this pious pair became members of the Presbyterian Church; and if all their children and grandchildren were collected together, who are members of the church, they would form a large congregation; and among them would be found several preachers of the gospel."

In these circuits for preaching, it was the habit of Mr. Davies either to preach at the places where he lodged, or to give a lecture to the family and servants, at evening worship. These services were pre-eminently blessed; many neighbourhoods have traditions of their usefulness. Every visit enlarged his circuit and increased the number of places that asked for Presbyterian preaching.

In the year 1752 the Synod of New York met at Newark, on the 29th of September, the day after the Commencement of

New Jersey College, located in that place.   On the second day
of the sessions, in the afternoon—"Mr. Davies is come to the
Synod; his not coming in the beginning of this session occasioned by mistaking the time of meeting."   The Rev. Jonathan
Edwards, on a visit to his son-in-law, Mr. Burr, the President,
being present at the meeting of Synod, was enrolled a corresponding member.   Mr. Edwards preached before the Synod
from James ii. 19—"Thou believest there is one God; thou
doest well; the devils also believe and tremble."   "The Synod
agreed to desire the Rev. Mr. Edwards to publish his sermon
preached before them."   The sermon was printed under the title,
"True Grace distinguished from the Experience of Devils."

"Upon a representation of the destitute circumstances of
Virginia, the Synod appoint Mr. Greenman and Mr. Robert
Henry, to go there sometime betwixt this and the next synod."
Mr. Edwards, under date of November 24th, 1752, writes to a
gentleman in Scotland,—"When I was lately in New Jersey,
in the time of the Synod there, I was informed of some small
movings and revivals in some places, on Long Island, and in
New Jersey.   I then had the comfort of a short interview with
Mr. Davies of Virginia, and was much pleased with him and his
conversation.   He appears to be a man of very solid understanding, discreet in his behaviour, and polished and gentlemanly in his manners, as well as fervent and zealous in religion.   He gave an account of the probability of the settlement
of Mr. Todd, a young man of good learning and of a pious
disposition, in a part of Virginia near to him.   Mr. Davies
represented before the Synod the great necessities of the people, in the back parts of Virginia, where multitudes were remarkably awakened and reformed several years ago, and ever
since have been thirsting after the ordinances of God.   The
people are chiefly from Ireland of Scotch extraction.   The
Synod appointed two men to go down and preach among these
people; viz. Mr. Henry, a Scotchman, who has lately taken a
degree at New Jersey College, and Mr. Greenman, the young
man who was educated at the charge of Mr. David Brainerd."
This opinion of Edwards was formed of Davies in an assemblage
of great men, assembled on a great occasion, the Commencement of their College, and the meeting of their Synod.

Mr. Todd, referred to in the above extracts, was finally settled in Virginia.   He was installed Nov. 12th, 1762.   The
sermon preached by Mr. Davies, on the occasion, was publish-
lished.   From the dedication, the following fine extracts show
the disposition and ministerial course of the two men.   It is
addressed "To the Rev. Clergy of the Established Church of
Virginia."

"In the following sermon, and appendix, gentlemen, you

may be informed of our sentiments concerning the nature and
design and various duties of the ministerial office. The following sermon will also inform you, gentlemen, what is the substance of the doctrines we generally preach; whether they are
the rigid peculiarities of Presbyterianism, or the generous
truths of catholic Christianity; whether they are the raw innovations of ' *New Lights,*' or the good old doctrines of the
Church of England, of the Reformation, and to say all in a
word, of the Bible. If you would know, revered sirs, what
has been that strange charm that has enchanted people in these
parts to leave the stated communion of the established church,
and to profess themselves dissenters; we can solemnly assure
you, and our hearers of every denomination are our witnesses,
that it has not been any public or private artifice of ours to
expose the liturgy and clergy of the Church of England; but
the plain, peaceable preaching of such doctrines as are mentioned in the following sermon, in weakness, and in fear, and
in much trembling. And if we may believe the united testimony of our adherents, it was an eager thirst after these doctrines, rather than a dissatisfaction with the peculiar modes of
worship in that church, which first induced them to dissent."

In the same dedication, he gives an extract from a letter he
had previously sent to the Commissary, Dr. Dawson—"for
whose memory"—he says—"I have a sincere veneration,
written at his motion, to give him, and the other gentlemen of
the Council, to whom he promised to communicate it, an impartial account of the dissenters here; and what he was pleased to
request, I may, I hope, inoffensively present to you. I am
not fond, sir, of disseminating sedition and schism; I have no
ambition to Presbyterianize the colony. But I may declare
without suspicion of ostentation, or wilful falsification, that I
have a sincere zeal, however languid and impotent, to propagate the catholic religion of Jesus in its life and power; though
I feel but little anxiety about the denomination its genuine
members assume. The profession of Christianity is universal
in this colony; but alas, sir, if the religion of the Bible be the
test of men's characters, and the standard of their final doom,
multitudes, multitudes, are in a perishing condition. Their
ignorance, their negligence, their wrong notions of vital Christianity, their habitual neglect of its known duties, their vicious
practice proclaim it aloud; and he that can persuade himself
of the contrary, in spite of evidence, is possessed of a charity
under no rational or scriptural regulations. For my part, sir,
should I believe that religion is in a flourishing state in this
colony, I must renounce the Bible, disbelieve my eyes, and my
ears, and rush into universal scepticism. Could I indulge the
pleasing dream, my life below the skies would be an anticipation

of heaven. I do not conclude religion is in so lamentable a state
because I see the generality pray by form, receive the sacrament kneeling,—or in word, because they conform to the debated peculiarities of the established church;—no sir, I freely
grant that these things are not the test of men's characters;
these may be so far from hindering, that for what I know, they
may promote living religion, in such as have no scruples about
them;—but the unwelcome evidences that force the conclusion upon me, are, the general neglect, and stupid unconcernedness about religion, the habitual omission of its duties, and
the vicious practices that glare upon me around, and which are
utterly inconsistent with true religion in any denomination.
I pretend to no superior sanctity above the established clergy,
who are piously aiming at the great end of their office,—and I
allow myself the pleasure of hoping there are such in Virginia.
I pretend to no Apostolic powers and privileges, immediate
revelations and impulses, but renounce the claim as presumptuous and enthusiastical. I am as mean and insignificant a
creature as you can well conceive me to be. But I dare profess, sir, that even a heart so insensible as mine, is at times
dissolved into compassion and racked with agonies of zeal, when
so dismal a scene opens around me; I dare profess, I cannot
stand an unconcerned inactive spectator of the ruin of my fellow
sinners, but would very gladly spend and be spent for them,
though the more abundantly I love them, the less I should be
loved. I am bold to avow so much pious humanity, as that I
would exert myself to the utmost, in my little sphere, for their
recovery; and since I am disabled by some conscientious scruples, to attempt it in the communion of the established church, I
humbly conceive, I am warranted to attempt it in a separate
communion. This, sir, is my only design, and, as I told you in
conversation, I think it would be no great stretch of charity to
suppose, that even a dissenter may be more distressed to see
multitudes rushing on, in a thoughtless career to ruin, than to
see them conform to the Church of England; *and more zealous
to convert them from sin to holiness, than from party to party.*"
He thus concludes his dedication to the established clergy,
in the following manner. "This account of my conduct and
designs, gentlemen, I have seen no reason to retract, and my
procedure since it was written, which was about a year ago
(1752) has not been inconsistent with it. And till my practice
be proven inconsistent with it, these unreserved declarations of
my designs must be deemed sincere, and worthy to be credited:
unless mortals can produce authentic credentials to warrant
their assuming the prerogative of Omniscience, and judging the
secrets of men. My sole design is to give you an impartial
account of the doctrines with which we entertain our hearers:

that you may judge how far we deserve to be censured and opposed as '*innovators, disturbers of the peace of the church, sowers of heresies and sedition.*' And if the following sermon answer this end, the design of its publication with respect to you, is fully obtained. But if I should be so unhappy as to be disappointed in this, I must support myself by reflecting upon the inoffensiveness and integrity of my intentions; and as Chrysostome observes, in the quotation from him in the title page—it is a sufficient relief under all his labours, and more than equivalent for them all, when one can be conscious to himself, that he regulates his doctrine to the approbation of the Deity. And to translate my first motto from Clemens of Alexandria, he is in reality a presbyter of the Church, and a true minister of the will of God, who teaches the doctrines of the Lord Jesus, and practices accordingly; and though he be not honoured with the first seat upon earth, he shall be enthroned in heaven. To that state of perfect uniformity in sentiment, and everlasting friendship, may you be conducted, when you have served your generation according to the will of God! And then may divine grace afford some humble place, among the myriads of glorified immortals, to the unworthy mortal who is, and therefore desires to be esteemed—Reverend sirs, your affectionate brother, hearty well wisher, and humble servant,

SAMUEL DAVIES."

"Hanover, January 9th, 1753.

About a month before the installation of Mr. Todd, Mr. Davies preached before the Presbytery of New Castle, October 11th, 1752, from these words,—"For Zion's sake I will not hold my peace, and for Jerusalem's sake I will not rest, until the righteousness thereof go forth as brightness, and the salvation thereof as a lamp that burneth." By the desire of Presbytery and the congregation it was published, being printed at the office of B. Franklin and D. Hall, in Market street, Philadelphia, 1753,—with a preface by Rev. Samuel Finley. This sermon is given nearly complete in the 9th vol. of the Literary and Evangelical Magazine, by J. H. Rice, D.D. The design of the sermon is, "I. Mention some measures which the ministers of the gospel should pursue for the advancement of religion in the world. II. Offer some important considerations to engage us to use such measures with unwearied diligence and zeal." A sermon that would well have a place in his printed volumes.

Another extract from Dwight's Life of Edwards, found on page 498, will throw some light on the history of these times. In writing to the Rev. John Erskine of Scotland, he expresses himself thus—"What you write of the appointment of a gentleman, to the office of Lieutenant Governor of Virginia, who is a friend to religion, is an event that the friends of religion in America have great reason to rejoice in, by reason of the late revival of religion in that province, and the opposition that has been made against it, and the great endeavours to crush it, by many of the chief men of the province. Mr. Davies, in a letter I lately received from him, dated March 2d, 1752, mentions the same thing. His words are—'We have a new Governor, who is a candid condescending gentleman. And as he has been educated in the Church of Scotland, he has a respect for the Presbyterians; which I hope is a happy omen.'

"I was, in the latter part of last summer, applied to, with much earnestness and importunity, by some of the people in Virginia, to come and settle among them, in the work of the ministry, who subscribed handsomely for my encouragement and support, and sent a messenger to me with their request and subscriptions; but I was installed at Stockbridge, before the messenger came." He does not say what his feelings were about the call, or Virginia as a place of labour. Under a previous date, July 5th, 1750, Mr. Edwards says,—"As to my subscribing to the substance of the Westminster Confession, there would be no difficulty; and as to the Presbyterian government, I have long been perfectly out of conceit of our unsettled, independent, confused way of church government in this land; and the Presbyterian way has ever appeared to me most agreeable to the word of God, and the reason and nature of things."

Mr. Robert Henry, appointed by the Synod of 1752, to visit Virginia, was installed pastor of Cub Creek, in Charlotte, and Briery in Prince Edward. Mr. Todd performed the services. Mr. Todd took part of the congregations for whom Mr. Davies obtained licensed houses on his first visit and settlement. Mr. Henry took his position on the south-western frontier, and was not installed till June 4th, 1755, after Mr. Davies' visit to England.

Besides these personal labours to promote the extension of gospel truth in Virginia,—his multiplied preachings in his seven houses for public worship,—his numerous and fatiguing missionary excursions to the frontiers east of the Blue Ridge,—his particular attention to the coloured people,—his efforts to supply the vacancies around him with ministers from the northern Presbyteries,—Mr. Davies began early to rear up preachers of the gospel in Virginia. He did not desire to complete their education under his own eye, as appears from his communications with Mr. Pattillo on that subject. He looked to New Jersey College, then the favourite institution of the Synod of New York, as the proper place for the students to complete their studies. Mr. Davies was instrumental in bringing forward and aiding in different stages of their education, Mr. John

Wright, a graduate of New Jersey College, in 1752; Mr. Pattillo, so favourably known in Carolina history; Mr. John Martin, the first licentiate of Hanover Presbytery; Mr. William Richardson, ordained in 1758, and intimately connected with North and South Carolina history; James Waddel, whose name fills a chapter in Virginia history; and Mr. James Hunt, a son of one of his elders, and a graduate of Princeton in 1759. Mr. Davies promoted classical schools, though his multiplied labours prevented his being the head of one in Virginia.

Mr. Davies endeavoured faithfully to perform the duties to which he was called, by the providence of God, in Hanover county, and on the frontiers of Virginia. His post was one of arduous labours. He was brought into intimate relations with all grades of society, from the African slave on the plantations, to the Governor and Council; and in all he was equal to his position. "He seems"—as one said of him, on seeing him pass through a courtyard—"as an embassador of some mighty king;" and as such sustained his Master's cause with dignity and success. By his apostolical labours he had been improved in strength of body, activity of mind, and ardour of piety. He had become accustomed to take large views of things, and to act on great principles, with confidence, in great emergencies. He had learned to govern himself, and by convincing and persuading to govern others. God gave him great success in his ministry; every thing to which he put his hand appeared to prosper; and as was said of the patriarch—"whatsoever they did there"—among the dissenters in Virginia—"he was the doer of it." The eyes of the church, in America and England, had been turned upon the dissenters in Virginia, struggling for the rights of Christians and of freemen; and suddenly and unexpectedly, Davies found them turned upon himself, and heard the voice of his brethren calling him to new labours and self-denial, in another sphere.

CHAPTER XI.

THE MISSION OF MESSRS. DAVIES AND TENNENT TO GREAT BRITAIN.

THE Synod of New York met at Newark, New Jersey, September, 1751. On the first day of the session—"a petition was sent into the Synod, by the Trustees of the College of New Jersey, desiring that the Rev. Mr. Ebenezer Pemberton might be appointed to make a voyage to Europe, to solicit benefactions for said College; and likewise requesting that some members of· the Synod might be appointed to go immediately to New York, to treat with Mr. Pemberton's congregation upon said affair. The Synod taking the matter into consideration, do appoint Messrs. Aaron Burr, Richard Treat, William Tennent, and Samuel Davies, to be a committee to go immediately to New York and treat with Mr. Pemberton's congregation upon said affair." On the evening of the next day the committee returned and reported,—"that their attempts were to no purpose in the affair of their mission." Mr. Jonathan Edwards, in a letter to Mr. Erskine, Scotland, July 7th, 1752, says,—"There was a design of Mr. Pemberton's going to England and Scotland. He was desired by the Trustees, and it was his settled purpose to have gone last year; but his people and his colleague Mr. Cummings, hindered it. His intention of going occasioned great uneasiness among his people, and created some dissatisfaction towards him, in the minds of some of them. Since that, President Burr has been desired to go, by the unanimous voice of the Trustees. Nevertheless, I believe there is little probability of his consenting to it; partly on account of his having lately entered into a married state."

In 1752, an application was made to the Synod by the Trustees, that a collection be taken up, in all the congregations, for the use of the College. The Synod agreed, and directed the collection to be made previously to the ensuing May. Many of the contributions, made in obedience to the recommendation of Synod, were generous; but the sum obtained was far from being sufficient to sustain a college. The Legislature had been applied to for patronage, repeatedly, and had as often refused all pecuniary aid. A mission to Great Britain was again talked of; and the eyes of the Trustees were now turned to Messrs. Davies and Tennent, as their messengers to the motherland.

On the 4th of October, 1753, the Synod of New York, holding its meeting in Philadelphia—"application was made to the Synod in behalf of the Trustees of the College of New Jersey, requesting the Synod to appoint two of their members, viz: Gilbert Tennent and Samuel Davies, to take a voyage to Europe on the important affairs of the said College: to which the Synod unanimously consent."

At this time, the College of New Jersey existed only on paper, and in the hearts of the Synod of New York, and a few pious people. There were no permanent funds, library, philosophical apparatus, faculty, building, or "local habitation." It had a noble President, and had been sending out graduates.

Of the fifty young men who had received the degree of A. B., twenty-six had entered the ministry, of whom five went to Virginia, and one as a pioneer in North Carolina. Davies felt its importance. The instruction of youth in the classics and sciences, as well as theological and other professional studies, had, in all the country south of New England, with the exception of the College of William and Mary, in Virginia, been left to the enterprise and benevolence of individuals. Those who took the lead in the education of youth were clergymen, some from the spirit of their station, some from necessity, and some from both causes combined, as teaching in some of its forms is the minister's appropriate employment.

Rev. William Tennent, sen., who opened the famous school Neshaminy, commonly known as the "Log College," died in 1746. Rev. Samuel Blair, his pupil, towards the close of Tennent's life, opened a similar school at New Londonderry, from which came Davies and Rodgers, and many other preachers. Rev. Samuel Finley, afterwards President of Nassau Hall, opened a similar school at Nottingham, which, after the death of Mr. Blair, was the place of instruction patronised by Newcastle Presbytery; and the fame of Finley spread far and wide. In the meantime, Rev. Jonathan Dickinson, of Elizabethtown, New Jersey, was engaged in giving instruction, in the liberal studies, and became equally famous as a teacher and preacher. Sometime before his death, the members of the Synod of New York were impressed with the conviction of a permanent collegiate institution; and applied to the Legislature for a charter for a a college, of which Mr. Dickenson was expected to be the President. The charter was obtained October 22d, 1746, but not being satisfactory was never acted upon. Mr. Dickenson went on with his course of instruction, preparing young men for the bachelor's degree, till his death, October 17th, 1747. Governor Belcher, a man admired for the suavity of his manners, and venerated for his piety, obtained a new charter in September, 1748. About two months afterward, the first commencement of the College was held at New Brunswick; and six young gentlemen received their first degree. After the death of Mr. Dickenson, the students had been under the care of Rev. Aaron Burr of Newark, who, on this first commencement day was, by the unanimous vote of the Trustees, chosen President.

Some of the members of Synod were not pleased with the second charter; and though named in it as trustees, did not at first give the College their cordial support. The Rev. Jonathan Edwards, in a letter to Mr. Erskine of Scotland, May 20th, 1749, says,—"I have heard nothing new that is very remarkable, concerning the College in New Jersey. It is in its infancy. There has been considerable difficulty about settling their charter. Governor Belcher, who gave the charter, is willing to encourage and promote the College to his utmost; but differs in his opinion concerning the constitution, which will tend most to its prosperity, from some of the principal ministers that have been concerned in founding the society. He insists upon it that the Governor, for the time being, and four of his Majesty's Council for the province should always be of the Corporation of Trustees; and that the Governor should always be the President of the Corporation. The ministers are all very willing that the present Governor, who is a religious man, should be in this standing: but their difficulty is with respect to future governors, who, they suppose, are as likely to be men of no religion and Deists, as otherwise. However, so the matter is settled, to the great uneasiness of Mr. Gilbert Tennent in particular, who, it is feared, will have no further concern with the College on this account. Mr. Burr, the President of the College, is a man of religious and singular learning, and I hope the College will flourish under his care."

Rev. Mr. Gilbert Tennent had not been active for the College as had been expected. By this appointment for the mission to Europe, this honest hearted man was compelled either to set himself in opposition to brethren whose judgment he respected, and whose esteem was dear, or embrace the College as the child of his affections, and the object of his labours. He chose the latter. Mr. Davies from his position was the most interesting minister in the Presbyterian Church. His name, at home, and abroad was associated with thrilling incidents and reminiscences. Many in England desired to see the young champion of toleration in Virginia. The friends of Mr. Tennent wished to secure the services of that able man; and desired his being sent on the mission as a relief from the pressure of some severe domestic bereavements.

While the Synod of New York was thus occupied in laying the foundation of the present flourishing College, Nassau Hall, the Synod of Philadelphia was not idle. In the year 1739, Rev. John Thompson, a leading man of the old-side, proposed to the Presbytery of Donegal the erecting a school to be under the care of Synod. The Synod, in May, of the same year, unanimously approved the design,—"And in order to the accomplishing it did nominate Messrs. Pemberton, Dickenson, Cross and Anderson, two of which if they can be prevailed upon, to be sent home to Europe to prosecute this affair with proper directions. And in order to this, it is appointed that the commission of the Synod, with correspondents from every Presbytery, meet in Philadelphia, the third Wednesday of August next. And if it be found necessary that Mr. Pemberton should go to Boston pursuant to this design, it is ordered that the Presbytery of New

York supply his pulpit during his absence." This commission of Synod met in August, and after much prayerful consideration, resolved to call the Synod to meet the last Wednesday in September, in Philadelphia,—"And that Messrs. Andrews, Cross and Treat do prepare what addresses, letters, credentials, or other instruments may be proper against the meeting of Synod." On the minutes of Synod for the next year is the following record—"The war breaking out between England and Spain, the calling of the Synod was omitted and the whole affair laid aside." Dr. Coleman of Boston had assured the Synod of the co-operation of the Boston clergy in erecting the school. Here the matter rested for some years.

In the year 1743, after the disowning of the New Brunswick Presbytery, and the actual, though not formal divisions of synod, the members of the Philadelphia Synod, called the "Old-side," resumed the business of the school, by a committee from the Presbyteries of Philadelphia, New Castle and Donegal. This committee resolved that the school be opened. The next year the synod approved the designs, and took the school under its care. The first article of the plan was—"that there be a school kept open where all persons who please may send their children, and have them instructed gratis in languages, philosophy and divinity." The support of the school was to be derived from yearly contributions by the congregations under the care of the Synod. Rev. Francis Alison, the finest scholar in the two Synods, was appointed master, with the privilege of choosing his own usher. "The Synod agree to allow Mr. Alison twenty pounds per annum, and the usher fifteen pounds." In the year 1746, May 30th, the synod, in reply to a letter from President Clapp, of Yale College, say—"Some years ago our Synod found the interests of Christ's kingdom likely to suffer, in these parts, for want of a college for the education of young men. Mr. William Tennent set up a school among us, where some were educated, and afterwards admitted to the ministry, without sufficient qualifications, as was judged by many of the synod. And what made the matter look worse, those that were educated in this private way denied the usefulness of some parts of learning that we thought very necessary. It was therefore agreed to try to erect a college, and apply to our friends in Britain, and Ireland, and New England. But when we were thus projecting our plans, the war with Spain was proclaimed, which put a stop to our proceedings then. The Synod then came to a public agreement to take all private schools where young men were educated for the ministry, so far under their care as to appoint a committee of our Synod to examine all such as had not obtained degrees in the European or New England colleges, and give them certificates if they were found qualified, which were to serve our Presbyteries instead of a college diploma, till better provision could be made. Mr. Gilbert Tennent cried out that this was to prevent his father's school for training gracious men for the ministry; and he and some of his adherents protested against it, and counteracted this our public agreement, admitting men to the ministry which we judged unfit for that office. While these debates subsisted, Mr. Whitefield came into the country, whom they drew into their party to encourage divisions. And by his interest Mr. Gilbert Tennent grew hardy enough to tell our Synod he would oppose their design of getting assistance to erect a college wherever we should make application, and would maintain young men at his father's school in opposition to us. This, with his and his adherents' divisive practices, obliged the Synod to exclude him, and others of his stamp, from their communion. Upon this the Synod erected a school in the year 1744. It was agreed that the said school should be opened under the inspection of the Synod, where the languages, philosophy and divinity should be taught gratis, to all that should comply with the regulations of the school, being persons of good character and behaviour. Several ministers and gentlemen have helped us to books to begin a library; and we hope that in time we may obtain assistance from England, Ireland, and elsewhere, to enable us to found a college. We have not obtained a charter as yet, but have reason to hope we may procure one, if there be occasion. We excluded from synodical communion the four Tennents, Blair, Craighead, Treat, and Mr. Wales. These, especially the Tennents, Blair and Treat, being the ringleaders of our divisions, and the destroyers of good learning and gospel order among us; and they with a few others that joined with them, erected themselves into a separate body, and licensed and ordained men for the work of the ministry, that were generally ignorant and warm in the division scheme, and they have troubled Virginia and the New English government." In the year 1749 the plan of the school was modified, Mr. Alison's salary was increased, and he was permitted to receive tuition from all, except those the trustees should judge unable to bear the expense. Mr. Alison removed to Philadelphia in the year 1752, to take charge of the academy in that city. When that institution was erected into a college he was put at its head. These circumstances checked the efforts of the Synod for erecting a college. This school flourished under the care of Mr. Alexander McDowell, to whom, in 1754, Mr. Matthew Wilson was added as assistant. In 1755 a donation of books was received from Dublin, with which the Synod resolved to commence a public library, under the care of their own body.

This statement of a few facts respecting the action of the

two Synods, and their friends, for their favourite schools, will throw light upon the position of Messrs. Tennent and Davies as delegates to Europe for the advancement of the interests of New Jersey College; the journal of Mr. Davies will be read to greater advantage;—and the perplexities of Mr. Tennent better understood. Mr. Tennent was at times almost overwhelmed, by meeting copies of his Nottingham sermon in England, and by the private letters sent from America calculated to prejudice the pious people in England against him and his cause. Before his mission to England, Mr. Tennent had become an advocate of the union of the two Synods, to whose division he had contributed no small share. On his return to Philadelphia, his zeal and energy contributed not a little to the harmony of the Church and the union of the Synods under the name of Synod of New York and Philadelphia. "He that confesseth and forsaketh shall find mercy." The Church has long since spread her mantle of love and sweet remembrance, over his memory; and a reference to his imprudent zeal will do him no harm, while it may be a warning to others against indulgence in passionate denunciation, and hasty judgment of character and Christian standing.

The summer of 1753 was passed by Messrs. Tennent and Davies in preparations for their voyage. Davies parted with his family and congregation for the long absence, with great reluctance. Mr. Tennent, on account of his bereavements in his family, had less to bind him to Philadelphia. On the 3d of September, Mr. Davies says—"I took leave of some thousands, yesterday, in public; and to-day I parted with some of my select friends, and my dear spouse, my honoured parents, and three helpless children, and left them in a flood of tears."

The departure of the delegation was delayed. On Saturday, November 17th, they went on board a vessel bound to London. Mr. Davies kept a journal. That relates to his labours, trials, and success. It was written in two small volumes; one of which was obtained from his family by Dr. Rice, and is preserved in the library of the Union Theological Seminary in Prince Edward, Virginia; the other was found by Dr. Cuyler, in Philadelphia, and by him deposited in the library of Nassau Hall. These two manuscripts are nearly entire, as they came from Mr. Davies' pen. "Of almost all the men mentioned by him"—says Dr. Rice, in his Magazine, vol. 2d, pp. 334, 5— "we have biographical sketches, made by their acquaintances, since their death; and it is wonderful to observe how the hints of Davies coincide with the fuller accounts of others. He must have possessed great powers of observation, and a wonderful faculty of looking into human character."

Messrs. Davies and Tennent parted in Edinburgh: Mr. Ten-

nent, to visit Glasgow and Ireland; Mr. Davies, the principal
towns in England,—as he says—"solitary and sad." They
met again in London, Oct. 1754. In November Mr. Tennent
sailed directly for Philadelphia. Mr. Davies took passage for
York in Virginia, the same month, but on account of unfavourable weather did not leave the coast for about six weeks. The
voyage was long and unpleasant. He landed in York, Feb. 13th
1755: the next day waited on the Governor in Williamsburg,
and on the morning of the 15th reached home—"and found all
well."

The success of the mission to Great Britain surpassed expectation. A large amount of money was secured; all doubts as to
the permanency of the College put to flight; public sympathy
was excited for the suffering dissenters in Virginia; contributions
were secured for the education of pious young men at Nassau
Hall; and a greater interest awakened for the welfare of the
Indians in the provinces. For immediate effect, or permanent
usefulness, no delegation from the colonies to the mother country
ever equalled that of Messrs. Tennent and Davies for Nassau
Hall.

———

CHAPTER XII.

JOURNAL OF REV. SAMUEL DAVIES, FROM JULY 2, 1753, TO
FEBRUARY 13, 1755.

July 2d, 1753.—Gratitude to the God of my mercies constrains me to own myself
the favourite child of Divine Providence; as it has generally disposed of me in a
manner different from, and sometimes contrary to my expectation, my purpose and
desire. Such an unexpected and undesired event was my separation from my
brethren and settlement in Virginia; and yet I have since looked upon it as a providential dispensation for the recovery of my health, to harden me against opposition, to increase my popularity, to make me acquainted with the world, as well as
with books, to supply the most necessitous congregation, and upon the whole, to
enlarge the sphere of my usefulness more extensively than so insignificant a creature
had reason to expect. And now as Divine Providence contrary to my expectation,
seems to call me to a very important embassy for the church and for the public;
and as it will tend much to my future satisfaction, to have the reasons of my procedure by me for a review in the hour of perplexity; I think it expedient to state
the affair in writing and to keep a diary of all the remarkable occurrences I may
meet with in my voyage, which I intend to begin about **** hence, unless Providence lay something in my way that may acquit me from the obligation which I seem
to lie under to undertake it. And it is my prayer to the God of my life, and the
guide of my youth, that He, who condescends to manage even my mean affairs,
would clear up my path of duty before me, and make it as agreeable as obvious,
whether it lead me to the ends of the earth, or confine me to the exercise of my
ministry at home. The College of New Jersey erected about eight years ago with
the most ample privileges, is of the greatest importance to the interests of religion
and learning in three colonies,—New York, the Jerseys, and Pennsylvania,—and
to the dissenters in Maryland, Virginia, and both Carolinas. There is now about

£3000 in the college fund; but this will hardly be sufficient for the erection of proper buildings; and if it should all be laid out for that end, there will be nothing left for maintenance of the professors and tutors, to furnish a college library, and to support pious youths for the ministry, who are unable to support themselves at learning.

Upon application made to Great Britain, there has been encouragement given to expect some assistance, especially if some proper persons were sent over to represent the affair, and to solicit and receive contributions. The Trustees first endeavoured to employ Mr. Pemberton in the service, who was well qualified, and had no family at the time, and was willing to undertake the embassy; but his congregation most unreasonably refused, though Mr. Cumming, his colleague, was still to continue with them, and another minister would have been appointed to officiate in his stead. After this disappointment (near two years ago) some of the Trustees importuned me to undertake the affair; but considering my youth and other defects I could hardly think them in earnest. However, I mentioned the personal, domestic and congregational difficulties in my way, and urged them with as much earnestness as was necessary to resist their importunity. Last fall, they renewed their application and I my refusal; and I never expected to hear more of it. But last winter the Board of Trustees unanimously voted me to undertake the voyage. When I was informed of it by a letter from worthy President Burr, it struck me into a consternation and perplexity unknown before. All the tender passions of the husband, the minister, the father and the son, (all which relations centre upon me) formed an insurrection in my breast against the proposal, and with these I have struggled ever since. My conjugal anxieties were increased by the languishing state of my tenderer and better part, which my absence for so long a time might perhaps increase. I was also afraid lest my dear congregation, whose hearts are so excessively set upon me, should suffer by my absence. The dangers of the seas likewise appeared terrible; and above all, my just conciousness of my want of qualifications for so important an embassy, sunk my spirits; and yet my remonstrances on this head would not be regarded by others. After all the deliberation and consultation in my power, I determined to take no notice of the many difficulties in my way which were superable, but to insist only on these two things as the conditions of my compliance; the one for the support of my family, and the other for the relief of my congregation; viz. that a proper person should be sent to supply my pulpit during my absence: and that he should be maintained at the expense of the College, that my salary might run on for the support of my family. These proposals I sent to the Trustees in a letter per post; but not trusting to the loitering and uncertain medium of correspondence, I despatched a messenger off to bring me an immediate answer. Upon his return, I found the Trustees had readily consented to my proposals; and therefore expected my compliance with their vote.

I was also informed of this important incident, that Mr. G. Tennent, by the death of his wife and mother, had no domestic incumbrance to prevent his going: and that the Trustees had applied to him for that purpose, and he had consented to the undertaking in conjunction with me. The expectation of so accomplished a partner in the embassy did, in a great measure, remove the despondencies arising from my want of qualifications, and in the mean time confirmed the sense I had of this, as I looked upon it as a very intelligent hint from divine Providence, of my unfitness for the embassy alone. On this and sundry other accounts I was very much animated to the undertaking by the prospect of so worthy and agreeable a companion. But then upon hearing that Mr. Tennent was appointed, and that he had consented, I had a new set of scruples about the necessity of my going: for it was at first proposed that I should go alone; which supposed that *one* alone might perform the embassy; and if I, or indeed any member of the Synod could do it alone, then undoubtedly Mr. Tennent can. But these scruples were removed by such considerations as these, suggested by the Trustees. That the going of two would give an air of importance to the embassy, and additional weight to our negotiations. That by this means, the affair which requires expedition, would be transacted much more speedily. That this would render the voyage more agreeable to both: and that my refusal might furnish Mr. Tennent and his congregation with occasion to refuse too. To these I may add, what has most weight with me, that the dissenters in Virginia lie under such intolerable restraints, that it is necessary to seek a redress; that now is the only proper season for it, and that none can manage this affair as well as myself, who am concerned in it, and so well acquainted with it.

Another consideration that had a great deal of weight with me, was this, that my congregation, my parents and even my tender hearted weeping spouse, did either consent to the undertaking, when it was laid before them, or discovered a kind of submissive reluctance. This disposition could not but extort my approbation, even when it shocked me as an omen of my going ; and it endeared the agreeable companion of my life so much more to me that so long an absence from her will if possible, be still more painful. The various opportunities I may have of personal improvement, and that in things in which a pedant and a recluse is most deficient ; the various friendships that may be contracted which may tend much to the honour and security of dissenters here, who stand so much in need of *patrónage*, are also considerable excitements.

I observe a strange concurrence of events happens to engage me in the embassy, and at once to hint my insufficiency for it alone and clear the way for Mr. Tennent's going too. Had providence removed his wife and mother a little earlier, before the Trustees had pitched upon me, they would undoubtedly have applied to him only ; as I am convinced nothing but necessity could have caused them to make application to me, at so great a distance, and so unfit (alas ! I feel myself so) for the business. Had his wife and mother died sometime after, it would have been too late for him to go ; and I must have gone alone. If I had only written per post, and not sent a messenger with my answer immediately, they would have looked upon my delay as a denial, and consequently employed Mr. Tennent alone. These and sundry other circumstances, I think I may without a tincture of enthusiasm, look upon as providential dispensations, adjusting matters so as to order my going, yet not alone, which I am fully convinced, would be injurious to the affair.

Then I consider that there is so much need to make some attempts for the security and enlargement of the privileges of the dissenters in Virginia, and that if I were obliged to undertake a voyage for that end alone, at the expense of the congregation, it would be very burdensome to them and me ; I cannot but conclude that it is with a view to this that Providence has directed the Trustees to make application to me ; for considering my known want of qualifications, and the little acquaintance the most of the Trustees have with me, their vote appears to me utterly unaccountable, without supposing such a providential direction. This is the more remarkable ; as this seems, on many accounts, the most proper crisis to do something in behalf of the dissenters here ; as Mr. Tennent's influence in conjunction with mine, will probably be of great service in the affair ; and as it will not carry so selfish and irritating an aspect to be managed, by the by, as if it were made the sole business. I am also encouraged from the reflection that my congregation will not probably suffer in my absence ; as Mr. Wright, I expect, is well accomplished for the place ; and my cautious and prudent Rev. Mr. Todd, will be so near at hand to assist in cases of difficulty. The Commissioners for Indian affairs, will be glad of this opportunity for the propagation of the religion of Jesus among the poor savages ; and it is likely we shall succeed in raising contributions for that end. And oh ! how transporting the thought, that these barbarians may be cultivated by divine grace, in the use of the proper means, and polished into genuine disciples of the blessed Jesus. For this alone, it would be worth one's while to spend and be spent. On these accounts I do generally conclude it will be my duty to undertake the embassy, unless Providence evidently acquit me of the obligation, by laying some insuperable obstruction in my way.

As to the temper of my mind, under this conviction of duty, I have found frequent reasons of resignation to the Divine pleasure, and a willingness to follow the calls of duty to the ends of the earth. At other times I have been eager for the undertaking, and afraid of a disappointment. At others I have been extremely intimidated, and shrunk away from the prospect ; the dangers of sailing, and the difficulty of the mission, the pain of a separation, and the anxieties of so long an absence from my people, my parents, my children, and especially my dearest creature, have sunk my spirits into the depth of despondency, so that my thoughts, night and day, were hardly ever fixed upon anything else. My principal difficulty, at present, arises from the languishing state of my dear wife, which I am afraid has some tendency towards a consumptive illness. I think I could break through the strongest complicated ties of the paternal and filial relation, and cast my helpless family upon the care of Providence : but the thought that my wife should pine away in my absence, without the satisfaction my company would afford her, or that by the anxieties of separation, her constitution should be injured, this thought seems utterly insupportable, and alarms all my tender and anxious passions. That which at present appears duty to me is this, that I should go upon the mission with this liberty reserved, that if I hear of my wife being dangerously ill, I may immediately return. O ! thou God of our life, with all the importunity so languid a soul is capable of exerting, I implore thy gracious protection for her, that she may be supported in my absence, and that we may enjoy a happy interview again. My temporal affairs are much embarrassed, and if I should be removed into the eternal world in this voyage, I know not how my poor helpless family could possibly subsist; and none but such as have felt the anxieties of the father, the son, and the husband, in such a circumstance, can conjecture what I feel at times under this timorous apprehension. But I would check it as arguing a diffidence in Divine Providence, and not well-grounded, for I am mortal at home, as well as abroad. My present anxieties are collected into one point, viz., my wife's indisposition. She was so languishing, and attended with such threatening symptoms of a growing consumption, the day before yesterday, that I have been in the utmost perplexity ever since, till to-day that I have set down to state the affair, and come to the conclusion before mentioned, to go with this liberty reserved, that I may return immediately, in case my wife's disorder is become dangerous.

July 11.—Through the indulgence of Divine Providence, my tenderer half, *animae dimidium meae*, has been considerably better for some days; and my Billy and Johnny, that have been disordered, are recovered; which encourages me to undertake the voyage. But alas! my conscience is this day burdened with guilt, and I cannot apply to the pacifying blood of Christ, which alone can purge the conscience from dead works, to serve the living God.

July 13.—Mr. Wright arrived here by order of Presbytery—to know whether I intended to undertake the voyage. I was exceeding glad to see my former friend and pupil invested with the sacred character, and advanced to the honour of an ambassador for Jesus; but it cast me into considerable perplexity to find that it was his opinion there was no necessity for my going to Europe in behalf of the College, since Mr. Tennent was going; and that he was very unwilling to stay here any time to supply my pulpit, and absolutely refused to stay all the time of my absence, as it would deprive vacant congregations of his labours, and him of an opportunity to look out for a settlement, for a considerable time. I was at length freed from my perplexities, and determined to go, by considering,—That the Trustees are the best judges of the necessity of my going with Mr. Tennent, and they are very eager for it, otherwise they would not continue their application to me; for my voyage, all things considered, will probably *cost the college* more than Mr. Tennent's,—That Mr. Wright's judgment may be something perverted by his reluctance to stay here so long,—That the affairs of the dissenters in Virginia would alone be sufficient reason for my going; and possibly I might be obliged to go soon, upon this account alone, if I should not take this opportunity,—And that Mr. Todd, who, I am sure, will be uneasy in the absence of his friend, and who knows the state of affairs here, is fully convinced that it is my duty to go. On these accounts I resume my former *conclusion*, that it will be my duty to undertake the embassy, though I am PERPLEXED to know how my congregation can be supplied in my absence, unless Mr. Wright determines to stay here, at least till next spring.

September 3d, 1753.—This morning I felt the painful rupture of the tender relative ties which bind my heart to Hanover. I took my leave of some thousands yesterday, in public: and to-day I parted with some of my select friends, and my dear, dear spouse, my honoured parent, and three helpless children, and left them in a flood of tears. To thee, O Lord, I then solemnly committed them, and now I renew the dedication, I know not if ever I shall see them again; but my life and theirs are in the hands of divine Providence, and therefore shall be preserved as long as is fit. My tender passions were melted into a flood of tears at parting; but now through the goodness of God, they are subsided into a calm, though at times I am twinged with a sudden pang of anxiety. Rode in company with my kind friends Mr. Morris, Mr. Brame, and Mr. Todd, who is to go along with me to the Synod.

I have been uneasy for some time, to find that sundry in my congregation were not pleased with Mr. Wright's preaching. But now, to my unspeakable satisfaction, I find they are generally engaged to him in a tolerable degree; and I hope his ministrations will be of more service than mine, during the time of his continuance here; though he has met with such occasional shots as may occur in conversation, which may deserve to be recollected. Mr. Finley told me he had lately almost imbibed a notion which he formerly rejected, viz.—That compassion proceeds from a selfish principle. Because both persons in the extremity of misery—and that know nothing of misery—are incapable of it.

Saturday.—As the committee is to meet at Mr. Finley's next Wednesday, I intend to stay here till then. To-day, the hurries of my journey being over, my thoughts can find leisure to make frequent excursions to Hanover, and tenderly hover around my dear wife and family. Ah! what pangs of anxiety I frequently feel! May the Lord bless all that are dear to me, and favour me with a happy return to them!

Sunday.—Preached at Mr. Finley's on Deuteronomy x. 13, a sermon which I preached in Hanover with great satisfaction and prospect of success; but alas! I have lost the spirit with which it was first delivered; and indeed I can but very rarely retain the spirit of preaching in the hurries of a journey. The materials of the sermon were very solemn, and nothing appears to me a more unnatural incongruity, than to speak the most solemn truths with a trifling spirit. Indeed, the incongruity appeared to me so great, that I was obliged to omit sundry things, though written before me in my notes, for want of a heart to express them with suitable tenderness and fervour. There appeared some small solemnity among the hearers; but oh! how far short of what I have seen in this place, in the days of the right hand of the Most High. Conversed with my ingenuous and dear friend, Mr. Finley, in the evening; and communicated to him my sentiments upon the great influence which the body has to deprave the soul, which I apprehend is much greater than is generally supposed: which appears from the frequent use of the metaphor *flesh* in the Scriptures to denote moral depravity; which supposes that the flesh, literally taken, has a special causality in it; otherwise there would be no ground for the metaphor, but it would be as proper to denote sin by the term spirit or soul, from the different inclinations of the soul according to the different states of the body, and as the variety of bodily habits may be the occasion of a variety of sinful inclinations, so the habit of the body may be constantly such, amid all its changes, that it may perpetually influence the mind to sin in general.

Monday, September 10, 1753.—Continued at Mr. Finley's—"Stung with the thoughts of home; the thoughts of home rush on my heart"—and I can find no relief from them but either in thoughtless levity, or in devotion. Read some part of the appeal in favour of the Candid Disquisitions; and never was more pleased with the candour, impartiality, and moderation of an author. How becoming, how graceful, how advantageous is such a spirit to the cause of truth and its advocates! May I deeply imbibe it! Alas, I have been perplexed this day with the vigorous insurrection of sin in my heart; but my resistance and humiliation has not been proportioned. Oh! wretched man that I am.

Tuesday.—Mr. Roan and Mr. Smith met in committee, and Mr. Finley and I in conjunction with them revised and corrected a draft, drawn up by Mr. Blair, of a warning or testimony of the Presbytery of New Castle against several errors and evil practices of Mr. John Cuthbertson, a Scotch bigot, ordained by one Mr. McMullen, who was deposed by the General Assembly of Scotland, and subscribed the deposition with his own hand; and one Mr. Nairn, who was one of the seceders, and afterwards excommunicated by them. The errors on which the Presbytery animadvert, are these—That God has made over Christ and all his benefits to all that hear the gospel, by a deed of gift (as he affects to speak) so that every sinner that hears the gospel offer, ought to put in a claim of right to him as his Saviour in particular—That saving-faith consists in a persuasion that Christ is *mine* and that he died for *me* in *particular*—That Redemption is universal as to purchase—That civil government, both heathen and Christian, is derived from Christ as Mediator.

Wednesday.—Continued revising the testimony against Mr. Cuthbertson. Preached a sermon on Rev. i. 7, and acted the orator; but alas! I had not the spirit of preaching. Enjoyed pleasing conversation with my dear brethren; but ah! I am still stung with the thoughts of home. My dear wife frequently enters my mind, and raises a passionate commotion there.

Thursday.—In the forenoon assisted in the review of the testimony against Mr. Cuthbertson. Rode in the afternoon to Mrs. Blair's, in company with Mr. Smith, and enjoyed much satisfaction in the free mutual communication of our Christian and ministerial exercises. How happy am I in having so many valuable friends in various parts! The sight of Mrs. Blair and my old walks about her house in the happy days of my education, raised a variety of tender and solemn thoughts in my mind. When I passed by the meeting-house where I so often heard the great Mr. Blair, I could not help crying, "Oh! how dreadful is this place! this is no other than the house of God, and this is the gate of heaven."

Friday.—Rode from Mrs. Blair's to Chester. And as I was generally alone, my spirits were very low, and my mind anxious about my dear family, my congregation and my approaching voyage. "Lord I am oppressed, undertake for me."

Saturday.—Rode into Philadelphia, was kindly received by Mr. Tennent, and my friends there. I visited Captain Grant, and was surprised with the clause in a letter from Mr. De Berdt of London to him, "That the principles inculcated in the College of New Jersey are generally looked upon as antiquated and unfashionable by the dissenters in England." A dismal omen to our embassy, and I fear to the interests of religion.

Sunday.—Heard Mr. Tennent preach an excellent sermon on—"Deliver us from evil," or as he justly rendered it "from the evil one" πονηρου; in which he exposed the wiles and devices of Satan in a very judicious manner. I preached two sermons, one in the afternoon and one by candlelight on Rev. i. 7. In the first, I was cold hearted and abashed with the fear of man; but in the last I had some freedom and boldness. I esteem the least degree of liberty and solemnity in preaching the gospel a very great blessing in the hurries of a journey. In conversation was much pleased with the pious simplicity of my spiritual father, Mr. Tennent.

Monday, September 17.—Went with Mr. Tennent to wait on the Governor and Secretary; but they were not at home. Waited on three Lutheran ministers, and Mr. Stanter, a Calvinist; and was not a little pleased with their candor and simplicity. How pleasing is it to see the religion of Jesus appear undisguised in foreigners! I am so charmed with it, that I forget all national and religious differences; and my very heart is intimately united with them.

Tuesday.—Rode solitary and sad from Philadelphia to Trenton. Spent the evening with Mr. Cowel, an agreeable gentleman, of the Synod of Philadelphia; but my spirits were so exhausted that I was incapable of lively conversation, and was ashamed of my blundering method of talking.

Wednesday.—Rode on, and came to Mr. Spencer's, at Elizabeth Town, where I was most kindly received, and my spirits cheered by his facetious conversation.

Thursday.—Came to Newark, and was received with much affection by the worthy President. Was honoured with a visit and free conversation with his excellency the Governor. Was uneasy to find that the Trustees seem to expect that I should furnish myself with clothes in this embassy. With what pleasure would I do it were it in my power, but alas! it is not; and therefore, notwithstanding all the pliableness of my nature, I *must* insist upon their providing for me in *this* respect, as one condition of my undertaking the voyage.

Friday.—Waited on his Excellency, in company with the President and his lady. Was kindly received, and the Governor insisted that I should preach for Mr. Spencer next Sunday come se'en night, that he might have an opportunity of hearing me. O! that I may be enabled to shake off the fear of man, and preach with the simplicity and boldness of an ambassador for Christ. Conversed with Mr. Ross, who informed me of the spread of Arminianism among the ministers in New England.

Saturday.—Was employed in drawing up a petition from the Synod of New York to the General Assembly of the Church of Scotland in behalf of the College. Conversed with Mr. Hoit, a pious youth at college. Was much depressed in spirit at the prospect of the voyage, and the thoughts of home. May the God of my life support me.

Sunday.—Heard the President preach a valedictory sermon to the candidates for a degree, who are to leave the College this week. His subject was, "And now my son, the Lord be with thee, and prosper thee." And I was amazed to see how readily good sense and accurate language flowed from him extempore. The sermon was very affecting to me, and might have been so to the students. Preached twice in the afternoon, and in the last sermon my heart was very solemn and tender; and there appeared some signs of concern among the hearers. In the evening I had a little dispute with the President about *the truth* of one proposition, which I principally laboured to prove, "That persons in this age may be said virtually to have crucified Christ, because they have the same temper with the Jews, and because their conduct towards Christ, is as like to that of the Jews as their circumstances will allow."

Monday, September 24, 1753.—My drooping spirits were exhilarated by free conversation with the President. Spent the most of the day in finishing the petition from the Synod of New York to the General Assembly. Attended in the evening on a meeting for Psalmody, and was much charmed with the power of harmony. Amid the variety of new objects that draw my attention, my thoughts often take a sudden flight to Hanover, and hover round my Chara, and my other friends there. O may indulgent heaven preserve and bless them.

Tuesday.—Was confined with a sore leg which was a little hurt by a fall out of my own door, a day or two before I left home; and though then but a slight wound, and I took little notice of it for two or three weeks, it has been so inflamed and irritated by travelling, preaching, &c., that I think it is now dangerous; and sometimes look upon it as a providential obstruction in my way of undertaking the voyage.

Wednesday.—This day I delivered a thesis, (*personales distinctiones sunt æternæ,*) and vindicated it in a public dispute against three opponents; and afterwards was honoured with the degree of Master of Arts. Dined with the Governor and Trustees. Heard Mr. Todd preach an honest sermon in the evening.

Thursday.—Received eighty pounds proc. from the treasurer, to bear the expenses of the voyage. Went to New York in company with Mr. Hoit, a promising young man, and I had agreeable conversation with him upon original sin, the influence of the flesh upon the spirit to incline it to sin. Arrived at New York in the evening; and lodged at my good friend Mr. Hazard's. Was sorry to find the Presbyterian congregation there in such confusion.

Friday.—Was confined to the house by my sore leg, and took physic, &c. I had some dangerous and gloomy apprehensions of the consequences. Mr. Pemberton, Mr. Cumming, and Mr. Van Horn paid me a visit. In the evening took the advice of the Honourable William Smith, Esq., upon the affair of the dissenters in Virginia. His opinion was that the reversing the order of the County Court for a meeting-house, by the General Court, would be a sufficient ground of complaint in England.

Saturday.—Waited on Mr. Cumming; sailed to Elizabeth Town with Mr. Woodruff. Was pleased with the company of my Br. Mr. Spencer and Mr. James Brown.

Sunday.—Preached in Elizabeth Town according to his Excellency's order, on Jer. xxxi. 18, but had very little freedom or solemnity.

Monday.—Took my leave of his Excellency. Rode with Mr. S. and Mr. B. to Mr. Richards', a pious minister under the deepest melancholy and temptation, harassed with perpetual suggestions to cut his own throat. I gave him my best advice, and gave an account of my own melancholy some years ago. Lodged at Mr. Brainard's, the good missionary among the Indians, and was pleased with his account of the progress of religion among them, though now they are scattered by reason of their land being fraudulently taken from them.

Tuesday.—Took a view of the Indian town; and was pleased at the affection of the poor savages to their minister, and his condescension to them. Rode on towards Philadelphia, and spent the time in pleasing conversation, principally on the affairs of the Indians, with Messrs. Spencer, Brainard and Brown.

Wednesday.—Came into Philadelphia—Mr. Treat opened the Synod with a sermon in these words: "Who was faithful to him that called him, even as Moses also was faithful in all his house." Saw my dear friend Mr. Rodgers and many of my brethren.

Thursday.—Attended on the Synod.

Friday.—Did the same. Heard Mr. Bostwick in the evening preach an excellent sermon on Acts ii. 11. He has, I think, the best style extempore of any man I ever heard.

Saturday.—Was informed that Mr. G. T. had taken some offence at my conduct as too forward and assuming; but it was soon removed by a free conversation. Attended on the Synod and used my utmost endeavours to obtain some supplies for my poor people, beside Mr. Wright; and succeeded so far that Messrs. Brainard, Rodgers, Henry, Bay, Blair and J. Finley were appointed to go there four or six weeks each. I hope this will turn to the benefit of my dear congregation. O that God may go with his messengers thither! The commissioners from New York made application to the Synod for the redress of their grievances; and a committee was appointed to go there for that purpose—of which Mr. Rodgers and I (much against my will) are to be members. Heard Mr. Bostwick in the evening on "Godliness is profitable for all things, &c.," and was not a little charmed with both his matter and language.

Sunday.—Had the happiness of sitting as a hearer for one Sabbath, a privilege I have often desired and needed, but could seldom enjoy. Mr. Horton preached in the morning an honest judicious sermon on "Christ the wisdom of God and the power of God." Mr. Bay in the afternoon on "Behold the Lamb of God, that taketh away the sins of the world." He was much daunted and confused. Mr. Bostwick in the evening on "When Christ who is your life shall appear, then shall ye also appear with him in glory." My pleasure under his sermon was renewed and even increased.

Monday, October 8th.—Preached a sermon in the morning from Isaiah lxvi. 1, 2.—and through the great mercy of God my heart was passionately affected with the subject; and what tended not a little to increase my affection was my observing the venerable Mr. Tennent weeping beside me in the pulpit. Spiritual poverty and humility appeared very amiable and charming to me.—Humility is not that gloomy sullen mortifying thing which it is generally accounted; but a most sweet and pleasing grace. O it is no small ingredient of the happiness of a penitent, and a most congruous ornament to a mean degenerate creature. Visited the academy in company with sundry of my brethren, and entertained with a view of what was remarkable in it. Heard some of the little boys declaim; and though I was pleased with their distinct and accurate pronunciation, I thought in delivering some of the orations, especially those of Brutus and Anthony, they were extremely languid, and discovered nothing of the fire and pathos of a Roman soul. Indeed this is one defect of oratory; a defect few seem sensible of, or labour to correct. Rode in the evening as far as Chester on my way to the Presbytery. Sat up late, and wrote letters to my Hanover friends, particularly to my dear spouse, full of anxieties. How strongly does she attract my heart!

Tuesday.—Rode to the Presbytery at Fagg's Manor, solitary and pensive. Was refreshed in the company of my dear brethren. Lodged at Mrs. Blair's, where every thing suggested to me the image of the incomparable Mr. Blair, once my minister and tutor, but now in superior regions.

Wednesday.—Mr. Hog, who has been discouraged by the Presbytery hitherto, lest his genius should not be fit for the ministry, was licensed, having given more satisfaction as to his abilities than was formerly expected.—Voted that Mr. John Brown should be ordained to-morrow, and that I should preside. Alas! I am confounded at the prospect of such a solemnity, as I have no time for proper preparations, and my thoughts are scattered amid so much hurry.

Thursday.—Spent two or three hours in study, and went and preached a sermon on Acts xx. 28, with a good deal of inaccuracy and confusion; though with some tender sense of the subject. Mr. Brown was ordained; and I have hardly ever thought myself in so solemn a posture, as when invoking the God of heaven with my hand upon the head of the candidate. May the Lord be his support under the burden of that office which he has assumed, I doubt not with very honest and generous intentions. Parted with my favourite friend, Mr. Todd, not without tears.

Friday.—Continued attending on the Presbytery. Messrs. Harris and McAden were examined with a view to trial, and acquitted themselves to universal satisfaction. The complaints of the many vacant congregations are so affecting, that the growing number of promising candidates is a most pleasing sight. Rode in the evening in company with Mr. Charles Tennent and Mr. Rodgers to Whiteclay Creek.

Saturday.—Was much disordered with a lax and a wind cholic, and could do little worth mentioning. In the evening had a fit of the fever and ague. When I am not relieved by a humble dependence on divine Providence, I am shocked at the thought of being taken ill abroad.

Sunday.—Was very much pained with the cholic, and in that condition preached two sermons, in Mr. Tennent's meeting-house, to a people I formerly lived among, on Deut. xxix. 10—13. I had a little freedom considering with how much pain I spoke ; and that last night I had very little sleep, but was in a kind of delirium. Rode in the evening to my dear brother's, Mr. Rodgers, but found that even the pleasures of friendship cannot always support a sinking spirit.

Monday, October 15.—Stayed at Mr. Rodgers's much indisposed.

Tuesday.—Was somewhat easier.

Wednesday.—Preached a sermon on Isaiah lxvi. 1, 2—but alas! I had but little freedom or tender affection. My soul was rejoiced to see my old friends, and observe the continuance of their respect for me.

Thursday.—Stayed in St. George's. Read in Mathew Mahew's Sermon on the Death of the Christian, &c.—through divine goodness I am much recovered; though still out of order with a cold. O that my soul might prosper.

Friday.—Mr. Rodgers and I intended to begin our journey to New York to attend on the committee; but Mrs. Rodgers was unexpectedly taken ill, and this morning delivered of a daughter, about a month before the expected time. I found a disposition to bless the Lord on her account. How great is his goodness! My own indisposition, and Mr. Rodgers not going along with me, will prevent my going to New York. Rode in the evening to New Castle, and spent some time with Mr. Bedford; but alas, felt little disposition to religious conversation. I am confounded when I think how I trifle away my time.

Saturday.—Rode to Philadelphia in solitude—my thoughts were trifling, or distressed me with anxieties about my dear friends in Hanover; and in company with a parcel of gentlemen, I perceived myself too much a coward in the good cause of God. Lodged at Mr. Hazzard's.

Sunday.—Preached in Philadelphia, first on Jer. xxxi. 18, 19, 20, then on verse 3d, ("I will be their God, and they shall be my people") and in the last sermon had a little freedom and solemnity. Was refreshed with an information from my dear and valuable friend Captain Grant, of a person that was awakened by my sermon on Isaiah lxvi. 1, 2. O! it is unspeakable mercy, that such a creature is not wholly thrown by as useless. Had much satisfaction in a free and affectionate conference with Captain Grant, upon experimental religion, &c. Lodged at his house.

Monday, October 22.—Visited Mrs. Johnston in sickness, and had some free conversation with her about her state. I was secretly afraid of her piety, and yet I could find no sufficient evidence to disprove it. Mrs. Rodgers unbosomed herself to me, and gave me an account of some affecting, overwhelming views of the wisdom of God in the work of redemption, which she had lately had, it was really astonishing. How good is God to his poor children even in this melancholy world! in some happy hours they rejoice with joy unspeakable and full of glory. Dined at

Mr. Macky's with Captain Bowen. Spent an hour at Mr. Bradford's. Saw my translation of Cleanthus' Hymn to the Creator, published in the Virginia Gazette.

Thursday, November 8.—I have been so extremely hurried for about fifteen days, that I have not had leisure nor composure to keep a regular diary. I must therefore content myself with a general review. Mr. Tennent treats me with the utmost condescension, and the unbounded freedom of friendship; and my anxieties at the prospect of the voyage are much mitigated by the pleasure of his conversation. I have been treated with uncommon kindness during my stay in Philadelphia by many, and have contracted sundry new friendships, from which I hope to receive happiness hereafter, and especially to enjoy the benefit of many prayers. I have preached about twenty sermons in Philadelphia; and though my being so long delayed was extremely disagreeable as well as unexpected to me; yet, if Providence intended my stay for the good of but one soul, I desire to be content. In sundry sermons the Lord departed from me, and I know not when I have preached so often with so much languor. But in my six last sermons, I had more freedom, and my popularity increased, so that the assemblies were very large.—Last Sabbath evening in particular, I was solemnized in preaching on that dreadful text, Hebrews vi. 7, and though I was afraid it would shock many of the audience, that they would not hear me again; to my pleasing surprise, I found them much more eager to attend afterwards than before. At the final judgment it will be known what was the effect. Mr. Kinersly and Mr. Jones, gentlemen of very good sense, and of the Anabaptist persuasion attended upon my ministry constantly, and showed me much respect. There are a number of Antinomians in town, who have been long finding fault with Mr. Tennent. They generally attended and approved, except one sermon: and I cannot but think it somewhat remarkable, that though my sermons were studied three hundred miles distant, and long ago, yet they are generally as well adapted to oppose the Antinomian notions, as if they were designed for that end. To-day I left the city, conducted by Messrs. Hazzard, Spafford, Hall, Beaty, Chambers, Bedford, Chief, Man, seven or eight of my friends, and came to Chester. Alas! I find the insurrection of sin violent in my heart; and my anxieties about home are sometimes extremely severe, especially when I forebode a long absence. I find my heart at once so exceeding sinful, and insensible of its own depravity, that I am really shocked at myself; and the prospect of death, or the dangers of the sea, in my present temper, strikes me with a shuddering horror. It is sin, alas! that intimidates me: and this removed, I could face death in its most tremendous forms, with a calmness and intrepidity. To be miserable and to be a *sinner* is the same thing, and I feel that I can never be happy till I am more holy.

Friday, November 9.—Was unexpectedly detained in Chester by bad weather. Spent the day in pensive sadness, "stung with the thought of home" and distressed with my own corruptions—"Behold I am vile." Enjoyed Mr. Rothwell's company.

> Sin haunts my steps, where'er I fly,
> In every place is ever nigh.
> As streams from mountain springs attend
> The travellers still as they descend;
> So sin the source of all my woe,
> Still bubbles up where'er I go.
> Sin spreads a dark, tremendous cloud
> Of horrors o'er my solitude:
> Presents a thousand forms of death
> To shock my soul from duty's path;
> Wraps present time in dreadful gloom,
> And damps my hope of time to come;
> Intimidates my soul ashore,
> And makes old ocean louder roar:
> Gives darker horrors to the storm,
> And danger a more shocking form.
> Companion dire by land or sea!
> No bliss, no calm, till freed from thee,
> And change of place is change of misery.

Saturday, November 10.—Rode from Chester to my dear friend Mr. Rodgers, thoughtless alas, of the exceeding depravity of my heart. Fell into company with Mr. Ross, an Episcopal minister, who asked me what objections I had against being episcopally ordained, and when I mentioned some of my objections in the most calm manner, fell into an unreasonable passion.

Sunday, November 11.—Heard Mr. Rodgers preach a very good sermon on this text, "Herein is love, not that we loved God, &c.," and my mind was deeply impressed with such thoughts as these, "We have heard a great deal of the extreme sufferings of one Jesus; and what effect has the pathetic representation upon the hearers? Why, the generality hear it with dispassionate negligence and stupidity, though a few here and there drop a tear at the relation. Thus it is when the agonies of the Redeemer are represented; but were we informed that a dear friend or relative was seized by a company of ruffians and put to the most extreme torture; what horror would strike us! what tender passions rise in every heart! Why then are we no more affected with the sufferings of this Jesus? Who is he? is he some worthless being that we are no way concerned with? Or is [he] a criminal that deserved all the agonies he suffered? If this were the case our stupidity would not be strange. But how strange must it appear, when we are told that this Jesus is the man that is God's fellow! the Saviour of sinners! crucified for our sins!—Received the Lord's supper with some degree of dispassionate solemnity and calmness of mind, and counted it my happiness to have an opportunity of joining in so solemn an ordinance with my dear Mr. Rodgers. Preached in the evening on John vi. 37, in an unstudied, confused manner; yet some seemed encouraged by it to go to the Redeemer.

Monday, November 12.—Went to see my relations in the tract; and when I passed by the places where I had formerly lived, or walked, it gave a solemn turn to my mind. Ah! how much have I sinned wherever I have been! and what solemn transactions have been between God and my soul in these my old walks! Visited two graveyards in my way, to solemnize my mind among the mansions of the dead. O! how solemn eternity appeared! how frail and dying the race of mortals! and how near my own dissolution! Returned to Mr. Rodgers', and unbosomed ourselves to each other with all the freedom of Christian friendship.

Tuesday, November 13.—Went to Mr. Stuart's, at Reedy Island, in company with my dear Mr. Rodgers, to wait for the ship coming down. Had a free conversation with him about my religious exercises. My worthy friend, Mrs. Dushane, desired me to write an epitaph for the tombstone of her sister, lately deceased, and I had neither leisure nor composure. I wrote three, leaving it to the friends of the deceased to make their choice.

> Does beauty spread her charms? does wealth o'erflow?
> Does health bloom fresh, or youthful vigour glow?
> Are all earth's blessings in profusion pour'd?
> And all their sweets with no affliction soured?
> Ah! trust not these to guard from early death,
> All these adorned the precious dust beneath.

Or,

> Ye that in beauty or in youth confide,
> Come view this monument to blast your pride;
> The charms of beauty, youth in flowing bloom,
> Wither'd at morn, lie mould'ring in this tomb,
> And you may meet the same surprising doom.

Or,

> This monument proclaims this solemn truth,
> Beauty is fading, frail the bloom of youth;
> Life short, a dream, an empty show,
> And all is fleeting vanity below.
> Careless spectator! learn from hence to die;
> Prepare, prepare for immortality.

Wednesday, November 14.—Continued waiting for the ship, and the delay made me uneasy; as I have been now about ten weeks from home, and yet my embassy is as much undone as when I left home. I find the enterprise to which Providence seems to call me more and more difficult; for my anxieties about my dear family, and about my life as necessary to their comfortable subsistence, are hard to be borne. May the God of heaven support me and them! Communicated to Mr. Rodgers some new thoughts of mine about the Divine government, as adapted to the nature of man, and about the Divine Providence towards men and angels; with which he was pleased.

Thursday, November 15.—The ship is not yet come down, and the wind is contrary, which affords me some uneasiness; though blessed be God, I feel myself habitually resigned to his Providence. O! that I might, with cheerful fortitude, endure the painful rupture of the tenderest bonds of affection for his sake, and encounter danger and death undaunted in his cause!

Friday, November 16.—Mr. G. Tennent is come down here to wait for the ship; and my spirit was revived with his facetious, and in the meantime spiritual conversation.

Saturday, November 17.—On board the London.—12 o'clock, A. M., the ship came down, and we went on board; and as I went along endeavoured to commit myself to God, and to implore his blessing and protection in this voyage. Perhaps I may never set foot on shore more, till I land in the eternal world; solemn thought! Father, into thy hands I commit my spirit. I now seem to enter upon a new state of existence, when I leave my native land, and enter upon the dangerous element of water. May I live to God while tossing upon it! may the sickness of the sea, which I expect, be sanctified to me! and may our conversation and preaching be useful to the company!

Sunday, November 18—5 o'clock, A. M.—The wind blew up fair and we set sail. The novely of my situation and the noise on deck hindered my sleeping, so that I am heavy and indisposed. I bid farewell to my native shore with a kind of pleasing horror; pleased that Providence has given us an opportunity of sailing after so long a delay, and shocked with the thought that I may never see my dear friends, and particularly my other self, any more. I cannot but be deeply sensible of the kindness of heaven in ordering my father and friend, Mr. Tennent, to be my companion in the embassy, not only for the right management of it, but for my social comfort. O that I may retain a consciousness of integrity in the cause of God, and universal devotedness to him! It is this, I find, can best support me amidst the dangers of sea and land.

> When the storm thickens, and the ocean rolls,
> When nature trembles to the frighted poles,
> The pious mind nor doubts nor fears assail,
> Tempest are zephyrs, or a gentle gale.

Wrote some letters, particularly one of friendship to Mr. Rodgers. I never parted with any one in a more solemn and affectionate manner than I did yesterday with him. We retired, and each of us prayed in the tenderest and most pathetic manner, giving thanks to God, for that peculiar friendship which has subsisted between us, and committing each other to the care of heaven for the future. The hurries of preparation for the ocean deprived Mr. Tennent of an opportunity of praying, and speaking to the company; and I was incapable of it by reason of sea sickness. About 3 o'clock, P. M., the pilot left us, and we entered the vast Atlantic.

Monday, November 19.—We are now out of sight of land—*Cœlum undique et undique pontus*. It would be particularly pleasing to me to survey the wonders of the majestic ocean; but have been confined to bed most of the day, and am so much out of my element that I am neither fit for conversation nor curious observation. However, I feel calm within, and resigned to the divine will—O Lord, bless my dear family.

Tuesday.—Continued in the same condition as yesterday.—Fair weather.—In the evening was very low spirited, and had most solemn thoughts of my own state and the eternal world. Alas! how shocking a companion is a sense of guilt.

Wednesday, Nov. 21.—The wind is contrary, and the waves run high. My sea sickness continues; and I am a very heavy companion to Mr. Tennent, which is particularly afflictive to me; but through the goodness of God he is cheerful and courageous.

Monday, Nov. 26.—I have been so extremely sick and low spirited, and the sea so boisterous, that I have been unable to keep a diary for these four days; but now through the great goodness of God, I am somewhat recovered, and the violence of the winds and waves is somewhat abated. Though my bodily disorder has not been very painful, it has utterly indisposed my whole frame, and in all my life I never felt such a degree of lowness of spirits, proceeding not from any gloomy imaginations, but entirely from the disorder of animal nature. I affected solitude, had no relish for conversation, no tender passions, no lively anxieties about any thing, but seemed dead to all things in the compass of thought. I had no appetite, and the little I eat I vomited up immediately; and the smell of the ship, whenever I entered into the cabin was nauseous beyond expression. Now and then I forced a little cheerfulness, but it was wholly unnatural. The perpetual motion of the ship, which vastly exceeds all the ideas I could form of it upon land, kept me in a constant confusion, and I could neither walk nor stand nor sit with safety, nor lie in bed composed. Last Friday the wind blew hard, and the sea run very high, and frequently dashed over the ship; but on Saturday the violence was greatly increased. We sailed about eight or nine knots an hour, over watery valleys and mountains, that seemed insurmountable. This vast ship so deeply laden is tossed about like a little cork, and the passengers reeled like drunken men. This morning we had no wind, though the waves swelled high; but about ten o'clock it blew fresh and fair. My spirits are more lively, and my appetite is something better, though I am still universally disordered. There is one thing I have reason to bless God for, in a particular manner, viz. that though the ocean was extremely turbulent, and dangers threatened on every hand, and though my spirits were sunk to such an unusual degree of dejection, yet I was hardly at all terrified with danger, but calm and resigned. Yesterday Mr. Tennent sung and prayed, and made a pertinent, plain address to the sailors, and they seemed attentive. Yesterday and to-day we prayed together alternately in our room; and felt some tenderness and importunity in so doing. O that we may in this inactive season be laying up proper furniture for active life upon shore! It is a most majestic survey, to see how the waves rise in ridges of mountains, pursue each other, and dash in angry conflict; and it is most amazing how we can possibly live upon so turbulent an element. To form and rule such an ocean is a work becoming a God.

Tuesday, November 27.—Since yesterday, in the afternoon, I have had a tolerable flow of spirits, and been pretty well, except a lingering fever. The time begins to pass away agreeably in conversation with dear Mr. Tennent, and the captain, who is a very pleasant companion. The wind not very hard, and we have a little respite from the intolerable perturbations of the angry deep. Prayer in our rooms together, in the morning and afternoon, with some freedom.

Wednesday, November 28.—Was more refreshed with sleep last night, than since I have been on board, and find myself to-day more free from fever than yesterday. Blessed be the God of my mercies. It is almost quite calm, and the little wind that blows is not fair. We are now and have been— [Here a leaf is entirely lost, and the corner of another so torn as to render it impracticable to decypher it.]

Friday, November 30.—To-day so much distressed with a sense of guilt that I have no turn for reading or religious conversation, nor am I anything but a burden to myself. This evening the wind is fair; but we have had some dangerous squalls. We now sail about . . . . knots an hour. Read an account of the shipwreck and the amazing deliverance of Joseph Baily and company; and was more sensible of the goodness of God in our preservation.

Saturday, December 1.—I am in better health than since I have been on board. Slept comfortably last night. We have sailed before a fair wind for about thirty-six hours and have made good way. Read a sermon of Mr. Taylor's to young men against the errors that some Antinomians maintain, and Mr. Dickinson's able defence of his sermon in answer to Mr. Beach.

Sunday, December 2.—This day has passed by very unprofitably, as we had no opportunity of carrying on any thing like public worship, till about seven o'clock in the evening, when I sung a psalm, gave an exhortation to the company and prayed. Had some sense of divine things, and a desire to affect the hearers, but no freedom of speech in proportion. Read a chapter in the Greek Testament, and Mr. Dickinson's second vindication of sovereign grace. To-day I have been much discouraged with a view of my unqualifiedness for the important business I am going upon. Had sundry intervals of tender thoughts about my dear family. O that my painful absence from them may be of service to the public! this would be more than a sufficient compensation. To-day the wind is squally, but drives us on our course seven or eight knots an hour. Last night was very turbulent, and I could sleep but very little, which made me indisposed to-day.

Monday, December 3.—Was out of order. The wind turbulent, and the sea run high. Alas! how unprofitably my life glides by in this state of inactivity.

Tuesday, December 4.—Had very little rest last night by reason of the violent tossing of the ship. I laboured under a sense of guilt, which made me very fearful of the dangers of the sea. God pity me of little faith. Read Mr. Dickinson's Vindication of Sovereign Grace, &c. Since I noticed it last, Mr. Tennent and I have prayed each of us twice in our room, and one of us alternately in the cabin in the evening. The tossing of the vessel is utterly inconceivable to one that never felt it.

Wednesday, December 5.—The wind favourable; and my habit of body better than usual. It undoubtedly rains more upon sea than land; for there has not been one day (that I remember) since we left the capes, but we have had some rain. I am very pensive about my dear family and congregation.—May the God of heaven bless them!

Thursday, December 6.—Last night I was so pained with the toothache, that I was but about an hour in bed, and then had no sleep; and all this day I have been in perpetnal pain. But in the evening I sweat my head; and through mercy found immediate relief. It has pleased the Lord to afflict me many ways in this voyage. May it be a preparative for usefulness, when I enter upon the stage of activity on the British coast! and may I be purged in the furnace of affliction! It is very squally and the sea runs mountain high. It is astonishing we are not swallowed up in this boisterous deep.

Friday, December 7.—The wind is contrary and the seas run very high. We are obliged to lie by, and make no progress in our way.

Saturday, December 8.—Was indisposed and low spirited, unfit for reading or society, and affected a sullen retirement. Alas! how my days pass by in a state of inactivity! Unless I gain more life upon my arrival, I shall be but a cypher, or an incumbrance to Mr. Tennent in our embassy. May I be enabled to show my resignation to the Divine will in my present state, by cheerful passive obedience, and may it be a preparative for active obedience when my circumstances admit of it! Read Mr. Prince's excellent sermon upon the agency of God in drought and rains, which suggested to me a variety of new thoughts, theological and philosophical. It is the best discourse upon such a subject that I ever saw. Read some in Harris's Collection of Voyages. About ten o'clock at night my spirits were somewhat exhilarated in conversation with my worthy companion. Found more freedom than usual in intercession for my dear absent friends, particularly for Mr. Rodgers, and my Chara, whom I promised particularly to remember on Saturday evenings. How my heart longs and pines after my dearest creature, and the little pledges of our mutual love! Oh! when shall I see them again! It is much warmer on sea than land; for we have not needed fire above two or three days since we have been on board. There is a great plenty of birds to be seen all over this ocean.

Sunday, December 8.—Have made but little or no proficiency in knowledge, or holiness, or any valuable acquisition, this day, by reason of indisposition and lowness of spirits. Alas! of how little importance or usefulness am I in the world! My soul is mortified to reflect upon my own insignificancy.—Read some of my old notes, particularly on Psalms xx. 11, and Luke xiii. 3, and was both pleased and surprised to find that ever any sentiment of importance has proceeded from a mind now so barren.—Read a sermon of Mr. Kenedy's, of Belfast, on the conclusion of the last peace, on the words of Hezekiah, "Good is the will of the Lord, since peace and truth shall be in my days." It is our unhappiness, on board, that we cannot get opportunity of preaching to the crew twice on Sunday. However, in the evening, Mr. Tennent preached on John iii. 5, and the discourse was judicious, plain, pungent and searching, and well adapted to do good. O that the power of God may attend it to the consciences of the company! I would bless the Lord that while I am useless, he enables my dear partner to do some thing for him. At night Mr. Tennent prudently gave the conversation a religious turn, and I endeavoured to keep it up. But alas! how ungrateful are such subjects! with what dexterity will men avoid them, or divert the discourse from them! Rainy weather.—Wind S. E., and a high sea for the most part of the day. My dear Chara has often recurred to my thoughts, and frequently I imagine myself talking with her. It is a mercy that God has made any of my fellow creatures of importance to my happiness; but my absence from them affords me additional uneasiness. Thus the sweets of life have their stings.

Monday, December 9.—I spent the day chiefly in reviewing and improving my notes; but the violent motion of the ship, and my indisposition, rendered me incapable of doing anything to purpose. In the evening the seas run very high, and broke over the deck with prodigious violence. While we were at evening worship, we shipped a sea which was like to wash the carpenter overboard. It is really an instance of the vigilant care of Providence that we are not swallowed up in these turbulent waters.

Tuesday, December 10.—Was employed as yesterday. The wind moderate, but not from a favourable quarter. Read in Harris's Collection of Voyages, concerning the Dutch settlement in the East Indies, which are very large and flourishing.

Wednesday, December 11.—I have nothing new or remarkable to take notice of with regard to myself. The wind fresh and fair N.W.

Thursday, December 12.—My mind has been in a very uneasy, timorous situation all the day, especially in the evening. Every shock the ship received from the dashing waves gave an equal shock to my spirit. Guilt made me afraid of sinking in these boisterous waters. How timorous a thing is guilt! It trembles at imaginary dangers and fears, where no fear is. We have sailed seven, eight, nine, or ten knots an hour for about forty hours past, and it is expected we are about one hundred leagues from the British coast.

Friday, December 13.—Much disordered and low spirited. I am quite dispirited, when I reflect upon my own insignificancy, and am afraid I shall be of little or no service in our embassy. Wind fresh and fair, and we have sailed about three hundred and fifty miles these last forty-eight hours. Sounded at 4 o'clock, P. M., and found ground at ninety fathoms, sounded at 12 o'clock at night, and found bottom at seventy fathoms. Read in Harris's Collection of Voyages the shocking account of the barbarities of the Dutch, exercised upon the English, at Amboyna, in the East Indies ; *quid non mortalia pectora cogis auri sacra fames ?*

Saturday, December 14.—Much indisposed in body, but peaceful in mind. Sounded frequently, and found ground from sixty-five to forty-five fathoms. It continues cloudy, and we can make no observation ; so that we know not where we are, though the captain conjectures we are in the British channel. There is great danger of running aground, or upon rocks, but the Lord reigneth, and we are in his hands.

Sunday, December 15.—We find to-day that we have run up the channel, and gone past the Scilly, and as far as the Start point, before we knew where we were. Thus Providence has been our pilot, and we have run our course as directly, and free from danger, as if we could have made observations of the latitude, which we have not been able to do for sundry days. Saw sundry ships, spoke with one of them, a Danish vessel, which told us where we were, viz., about twenty miles S.W. of the Start. Was much indisposed, desponding and inactive in the forenoon ; but in the evening was somewhat revived in discoursing to the ship's company from Luke xiii. 3. I had more freedom of solemnity than I expected, and the company seemed seriously attentive. I am often afraid I have done, and shall do no service to these precious immortals on board ; and I am yet uncertain what will be the event. I have this evening made a feeble but sincere attempt, and I leave it in the hands of God ; not expecting ever to speak to them more. Weather moderate, though cloudy, and the wind fair.

Monday, December 16.—Found in the morning we had passed by the Isle of Wight, in the night, we soon saw land at Beachy Head ; went on towards the Downs, &c.

Tuesday, December 17.—We entered the Downs in the morning, where lay about thirty-three ships. Heard that one Captain Davies, from Philadelphia, was cast away about six weeks ago, a little before us in the channel. We came up with Captain Mesnard, who sailed from Philadelphia eight days before us. I looked upon it as a favourable providence, that we did not take our passage with him, as it would have been longer. This is the more remarkable, as his ship was famed for sailing fast, which ours was not. Sundry boats came to us, and I was shocked to hear the infernal language of the boatmen. Alas, the whole world lieth in wickedness. Was entertained in taking a view of the coast, as we sailed along. Saw Dover Castle and town, and a seat of the Duke of Dorset. It is a pretty large town ; and so is Dale, which we saw a little after, where there is a castle, and at Walmer. Passed by Margate, a considerable town ; but did not come near enough to take a particular view of it. How pleasing does the land appear after so long a confinement upon the ocean ! especially as the landscape is beautifully variegated with towns, churches, windmills, forests, green cornfields, &c. We passed the N. Foreland, and cast anchor to lie all night ; and the winds being contrary, the days very short, and the darkness hindering us, it is expected that it will take us some time going from hence to London, a distance of about seventy miles by water, and —— by land, which is very disagreeable. But I am heartily sick of the sea.

It is just four weeks and four days since I left the American shore ; and though I have hardly ever had a more melancholy time, yet I have great reason to take notice of the goodness of Providence to me in my voyage, both as to its shortness, safety, plenty, and indeed the moderateness of the weather, considering the season. Alas, that I find myself so little disposed to make grateful returns. I am really shocked at myself as a monster of ingratitude. Though I am now above three thousand miles from home, and have been near four months absent, my thoughts are often wafted thither upon eager wings, and hover round the dear objects of my love. Whether I shall be again conducted over this spacious ocean, and see my friends, is wholly unknown to me ; but I forbear—for I can hardly bear the anxiety of separation, and the thought of never enjoying another interview with them, especially my other dearer half. We are about twenty souls aboard ; passengers Mr. Tennent, Mr. Matt. Clarkson, Miss Shirley, John Crosby, and a little girl in the cabin, and two in the steerage. This morning the pilot came on board, one Grovenor, who was captain of a little privateer in the late war, and behaved very gallantly. At night when all were gone to bed, enjoyed an hour of most pleasant and friendly conversation with dear Mr. Tennent, upon the arduous duties of the ministerial office. I relate things just as they occur to a careless mind, without any order ; and though my principal design is to make religious remarks, yet, for my future amusement or improvement, I shall take notice of the curiosities of nature and art. The English oysters differ from those in America. They are almost round, flat, and not clustered. There is a species of fish here called the Whiting, which is very delicate. The banks along the shore from Beachy Head to this place are chalk.

Wednesday, December 18.—Lay at anchor, the wind and tide being against us. Would willingly have gone to London by land, but Mr. Tennent did not choose it. Nothing remarkable occurred to-day.

Thursday, December 20.—We weighed anchor and endeavoured to pass through the Narrows, setting up a beacon and two buoys to push the ship along; but the wind and tide being against us, we were obliged to cast anchor again, and lie by. The Church of * * * * * is opposite to us, it has no steeple. Read the memoirs of the "Fortunate Country," a romance that has a better tendency than most that are in vogue. I think it an evidence of the chimerical taste of the present age, that it runs mad after these romantic pieces. Read a part of Roxana, the history of an abandoned prostitute, pretendedly penitent. Was shocked at the wickedness of some of the ship's crew: and sorry our endeavours had so little effect upon them.

Friday, December 21.—In the morning weighed anchor, and passed through the Narrows with safety. The passage is but a few yards wide; and though it be somewhat of an obstruction to the English trade, as it is attended with danger, to pass, &c., yet this is more than compensated by its good natural fortification against foreign invasion. There is such a number of vessels in sight that we seem to form a kind of town upon sea, and live in good neighbourhood. About 11 the tide failed us, and we were obliged to cast anchor, having passed by a land bank called the Spaniard, where there is a buoy. We now lie off Shippy Island; the land appears high and hilly. By calculating our expenses hither we find that they have amounted to more than £125, which will be very burdensome to the College unless our application in Great Britain be successful. In the evening the tide favouring though the wind was contrary, we weighed anchor, and sailed by the Nore, where there is a vessel instead of a lighthouse, with lights fixed to her masts, as it appeared to me at a distance. The Nore is about —— miles above the mouth of the river Thames. At 11 o'clock we cast anchor.

Saturday, December 22.—We weighed anchor about 7 o'clock in the morning and sailed up within about four miles of Gravesend, and the tide failing we were obliged to cast anchor. We now see land on each side of the river, and the landscape is beautifully variegated with green fields, forest, houses, &c. We passed by the little town of Lee. Read in "the Spirit of Laws," an ingenious performance, with many new and valuable sentiments. In the evening my heart spontaneously dictated the following lines:

> While objects various, strange and new,
> In numerous prospects rush to view,
> The thoughts of friends, the thoughts of home,
> Engross my heart and still find room.
> Chara with what strange, magic art,
> Dost thou so distant, charm my heart?
>
> Not seas can quench, nor distance cool,
> The flame of love that fires my soul;
> Nor works of nature or of art
> Can raze thine image from my heart.
> I shrink to view those days to come,
> While cruel absence is my doom.
> Indulgent Heaven! contract those days,
> And give my anxious bosom ease.

Sunday, December 23.—We weighed anchor in the morning, and passed by Gravesend, a little town that has an agreeable appearance; opposite to which is a fort, I think called Tilberry. We also passed by Northfleet and Greys, two small villages. Saw a gibbet and the remains of a malefactor hanging on it. A shocking sight! Pirates that commit great crimes on sea are executed near this place that seamen may see them. The churches on both sides of the river are very numerous. They seem old gothic structures with square-steeples without spires. The custom house officers came on board, and the hurries and impieties on board rendered the sanctification of this holy day extremely difficult. The Lord help me? Spoke with a ship from Virginia, Capt. Whiting; prepared a short letter for my dear, and overtook the ship below Gravesend. As we returned the boatmen had occasion to go ashore at Gravesend, where an odd affair happened, fit to be mentioned among the adventures of a knight errant. We staid in an ordinary a few minutes; but as I had but a penny about me, I could call for nothing. When we went down to take boat again, behold the boat was gone, and the boatman called and hallooed for her a good while, but had no answer. I was obliged to return to the ordinary where I sat pensive and confounded with an *empty* pocket; and was afraid the ship would go away and leave me, and that I should be obliged to go to London by land, without any thing to bear my expenses. After I had sat till about 7 o'clock the boatman with joy pictured in his countenance, came and told me the acceptable news that he had found the boat. Some fellow had occasion for her and took her to a vessel at some distance, and as it was very dark it was a wonder she was found. The poor boatman anxious for his boat had cried out, "well I would give sixpence to know where my boat is." Another immediately held him to his word and lent him his boat to go and look for her. As we were going up to the ship, it was so dark, that we could not see her, and went about a mile above her. The old boatman and his son fell a scolding about the place where the boat lay, and to decide the difference we called at two or three sloops that lay at anchor; but after bawling sufficiently we could find nobody; and we were obliged to grope on till we got safely to the ship. And the relation of our adventure afforded no small entertainment to the company. While I was at Gravesend there came in the room a company of sailors belonging to the East India ships, who cursed and blasphemed in the most infernal manner that ever I heard in my life. My spirit was quite oppressed to hear them. Alas! to what a shocking degree of impiety may human nature arrive! We have passed five or six East India ships in the river; they are very large and magnificent, immensely rich and well armed. Mr. T. had no opportunity of speaking to the ship's company, by reason of their hurry. Indeed there is nothing that has the appearance of a Sabbath among sailors. Mr. T. naturally remarked upon it, "that where no good is to be done the door is not opened."

Monday, December 24.—We set sail in the morning and passed by Greenhive, a little village near which Lord Concannon has a seat; we also passed by a seat that formerly belonged to Lord Baltimore. Through Divine goodness, I find my body recovered to usual health; and I believe the fresh provisions, we yesterday received from shore, were conducive to it. Passed by Woolwich, a town on the left hand, beautifully varied with sundry kinds of buildings. Here is the king's dockyard; fifteen or twenty men of war lay at it. Here also is an office of ordnance, where cannon, &c., for the king's ships are cast; we saw a vast quantity lying on the wharf. Passed by Blackwall, a town on the right hand; where lay two men-of-war, and a great number of East India ships in repair. We counted no less than twelve wind-mills, which seemed to animate the air, when they were all in motion. Passed by Greenwich on the left hand, and took particular notice of the hospital there, which is one of the most stately edifices I believe in the world. It consists of two vast buildings fronting one another, and the governor's house above, seems to join them. Here lay four of the king's yachts, one of which is the most beautiful vessel that art can form, and in it his Majesty sails for Hanover. Hamstead House is in sight, upon a hill above Greenwich. We saw the steeple of St. Paul's below Blackwall. We cast anchor at Deptford, along side of a man-of-war. At Deptford there is another of the king's dock-yards. From hence sundry of the passengers went to London; but Mr. T. and I determined to stay till to-morrow. In the evening we heard that Mr. Dennys De Berdt had been very inquisitive about us, and probably provided a lodging for us.

Tuesday, December 25.—We sailed up the river, and were not a little struck with the prodigious number of ships in view. Their masts look like vast forests. About 10 o'clock Mr. Neave, one of the owners of the ship came on board and asked us to dine at Mr. Neates, his partner, where we were kindly received. We came up by the tower, in sight of London bridge and landed. As it was Christmas day the bells in all the churches were ringing, and formed a concert of the most manly, strong and noble music to my ear, that I ever heard. The steeple of St. Dunstan's is of such curious architecture, that when the bells ring it shakes like a tree shaken with the wind, though it consists of stone. After dinner our friends Capt. M'Pherson and Captain M'Cullock conducted us to Mr. De Berdt's, who is a most amiable pious gentleman and entertained us very kindly till we could provide a lodging. Mr. Tennent was extremely low spirited and silent, which afforded me no small concern; and I was afraid of conversing freely, while he was silent, lest I should seem to arrogate the preference.

Wednesday, December 26.—Were visited by Mr. Hall, a venerable old gentleman, author of some of the Lime street Sermons, who seems to be of a true puritanic pirit and full of religion. Were visited by Mr. Gibbons, my dear correspondent, who informed us of the general apostasy of the dissenters from the principles of the Reformation. He told me that Dr. Doddridge's motto under his picture was, *Dum vivimus vivamus:* that Dr. Young had erected two schools, over the door of one of which he had written, *Doctrinæ filia virtus;* and of the other, *Filia matre pulchior*. Were visited by good Mr. Crutenden, who sent me over ten pound sterling worth of books to be distributed among the poor in Virginia. Mr. Whitefield having sent us an invitation last night to make his house our home during our stay here; we were perplexed what to do lest we should blast the success of our mission among the dissenters, who are generally disaffected to him. We at length concluded with the advice of our friends and his, that a public intercourse with him would be imprudent in our present situation; and visited him privately this evening; and the kind reception he gave us revived dear Mr. Tennent. He spoke in the most encouraging manner as to the success of our mission, and in all his conversation discovered so much zeal and candour, that I could not but admire the man as the wonder of the age. When we returned, Mr. Tennent's heart was all on fire, and after we had gone to bed, he suggested that we should watch and pray; and we rose and prayed together till about 3 o'clock in the morning.

Thursday, December 27.—Spent the time cheerfully in private. Conversed with Mr. Loyd, a serious man, and dear Mr. Gibbons, who spent the evening with us revising Mr. Pearsal's Meditations for a second edition.

Friday, December 28.—Went up the monument, a vast pillar, in memory of the dreadful fire in 1666. It has a Latin inscription signifying the beginning, and progress of the conflagration. Another as far as I remember in these words:—*Furor papisticus, qui horrenda, patravit, nondum restinguitur*. And another to the same import in English. I went up to the top along winding stairs, in the form of a screw. From thence I could take a view of this vast overgrown city, and the people in the streets seemed degenerated into pigmies. Went to the Virginia coffee-house to inquire for letters, &c., but alas! none were arrived. We took up our lodgings at Mr. Thomas Cox's in Winchester street, a sober religious family;—blessed be God.

Saturday.—Continued retired, preparing for a public appearance.

Sunday, December 30.—Preached in the morning for Mr. Winter, assistant to Mr. Hall, on Isaiah lxvi. 1, 2, but alas! I was dull and senseless. Dined with Mr. Salvage, a most valuable christian, in company with a pious youth, one Mr. Elliston, who is at learning for the ministry, and was for some time under Dr. Doddridge's care. In the afternoon I preached for one Mr. Dews who was indisposed, in a Baptist congregation, with some freedom, on Jer. xxxi. 18, 20. It is grievous to see how small the congregations are in this vast city. Spent the evening at one Mr. Edwards's, a Turkey merchant, who treated us very kindly. He is a member of the committee for the management of the civil affairs of the dissenters. I find Mr. Stennet, a Baptist minister, has most influence in court of any dissenting minister. Mr. Tennent preached in the afternoon at Mr. Hall's, and in the morning went to hear Mr. Chandler. I find it is the custom here for the clerk to choose the psalm.

Monday, Dec. 31.—Went according to his lordship's appointment to wait upon the Marquis of Lothian; but as we did not know the distance we did not come soon enough, and the Marquis was gone out. We went through St. James' Park, which is a beautiful place. Passed through the King's palace, where we saw the footguards in waiting. Went to see the new bridge of Westminster, which is the most noble piece of workmanship of the kind, I suppose in the world. It consists of Portland stone neatly hewn. Went into Westminster Hall, a spacious old building, where courts are held. Though the roof is so long, it is supported without one pillar. The walls of London are generally demolished, but here and there they remain; and above the gates are buildings of gothic structure. There is such a vast number of beggars here, that one cannot walk in the street without being pained with their importunity; for he cannot supply them all, and there are so many impostors among them that it is hard to distinguish real objects of charity. Dined at one Mr. Lloyd's, a solid, humorous, religious old gentleman in Southwark, who seems a hearty friend to our mission. There are so many parties here that it is very perplexing to us how to behave so as to avoid offence, and not injure the business of our embassy. The Independents and Baptists are more generally Calvinists, than the Presbyterians; though I fear some of them are tainted with Antinomianism.

Tuesday, Jan. 1, 1754.—Went to hear Mr. Chandler in Salters' Hall, and was pleasingly entertained with a sermon on the parable of the unjust steward. Mr. C. is undoubtedly a most ingenious, accurate gentleman; but I did not discern so much of experimental religion in this discourse as I could wish. Went afterwards to the Amsterdam coffee-house, where the Congregational and Baptist ministers meet on Tuesdays. Was introduced into the conversation of venerable Mr. Price, Dr. Watts' colleague; and then went at Mr. Gibbon's invitation to dine at Mr. Shuttlewood's in Trinity House, where the corporation meets that has the care of lighthouses, &c. for the direction of sailors. Was entertained with sundry curiosities, viz. two Indian canoes, one of the bark of a tree—two very large globes—the pictures of sundry who have been benefactors of the society. Went in the evening to hear Mr. Whitefield in the Tabernacle, a large spacious building. The assembly was very numerous, though not equal to what is common. He preached on the parable of the barren fig tree, and though the discourse was incoherent, yet it seemed to me better calculated to do good to mankind than all the accurate, languid discourses I have heard. After sermon enjoyed his pleasing conversation at his house.

Wednesday, Jan. 2.—Waited on the Marquis of Lothian, at his house, and were very kindly received. The unaffected grandeur of the nobleman, and the simplicity and humility of the Christian, cast a mutual lustre on each other. He gave all the encouragement in his power with regard to our embassy. This was the first time I ever appeared before a nobleman, and I have reason to be thankful that I was not at all dashed with the fear of man. My Lord Leven came and dined with us, and we laid before their lordships the state of the College. Lord Leven told us that he had delayed an application in favour of some foreigner till the ensuing Assembly, and was afraid that if he should be appointed to be his Majesty's commissioner for the ensuing year, that affair would interfere with ours. But upon the whole their lordships gave us encouragement by intimating that they were sensible of the importance of the design, and had it at heart. We continued with their lordships till about five o'clock, then took coach and went to Mr. Godwin's, a serious and reserved gentleman in conversation, but very fluent as I am told in the pulpit. We laid before him our design, and he seemed sensible of its importance.

Thursday, January 3.—Breakfasted with Mr. Chandler, a Presbyterian minister of uncommon sagacity and readiness. He has been formerly suspected of Arminianism and Socinianism; but now he appears to be a moderate Calvinist. He promised his influence in favour of our design. We afterwards waited upon Dr. Guise, and informed him of our business; but he seemed to discourage us, on account of the many annual expenses lying upon the dissenters in this city; for the relief of the poor; for the support of ministers in the country, the education of youth, &c. Spent the evening very agreeably with Mr. Gibbons, in company with Mr. Crutenden and Mr. De Berdt. I laid before them our business; and they candidly gave me their best advice. We find it a disadvantage that we have so few letters to the Presbyterians here, who are the most numerous and rich. For the sake of expedition, we have agreed to go separate at times, and therefore Mr. Tennent went this evening to good Mr. Hall's. I have been so pained with the toothache, that I had but little sleep these three nights, and I write this about three o'clock in the morning. As we enjoyed the happiness on board to pray together in our room twice a day, Mr. Tennent and I determined to observe the same method in our lodgings, beside the stated devotion of the family.

Friday, January 4.—Being much indisposed with the toothache, I was obliged to stay at home. Wrote a letter to my dearest with uncommon solicitude. O when will these days of cruel absence be over! Mr. Tennent went and introduced the affairs of our mission to Mr. Spilsbury, Mr. Stennet, and Mr. Bradbury; and had some encouragement from them all.

Saturday, January 5.—Mr. Tennent being indisposed and fatigued, I visited Mr. Bowles, the famous print seller, in the morning. He is a gentleman of good sense, but of uncommon humour; and I verily thought, by the reception he gave the affair of our mission, that he would be no friend to it; but before we parted he surprised me with a present of a map of London, and a promise of five guineas to the college. Dined at Mr. Jasper Mauduit's, the hearty friend of the dissenters in Virginia, one of the committee that have the management of the secular affairs of the dissenters in court. He promised me something farther, if possible, should be done on their behalf, before my return. We communicated the affair of the college, and Mr. Tennent happening to mention repeatedly the Calvinists as the principal persons concerned in it, it was like to engage us in an unseasonable dispute with Mr. Mauduit's brother, upon the Calvinistic principles. We found they were both of latitudinarian, anti-Calvinistic principles, and would not countenance the college, unless it were upon a catholic plan. We showed them the charter and they were satisfied. One of them informed us that the king has given a considerable sum for the support of English schoolmasters among the German Protestants in Pennsylvania, and if we could make it appear that our college might be useful for the education of such, we might probably have a share of it for that purpose. We were also informed that the society here for Propagating Christian Knowledge, would probably give something out of their fund, in case a number of Indian youth might be educated in our college. Both these proposals would have a happy tendency, could they be carried into execution. But we are afraid the Philadelphia Academy will interfere with the former. In the evening wrote a letter of thanks to the Marquis of Lothian, and another to Lord Leven, enclosing a copy of our instructions which his lordship had desired.

Sunday, January 6.—Heard Mr. Newman, a Presbyterian in or near Charter House Square, on Psalm cxvi. 16, "O Lord truly I am thy servant; I am thy servant," and though I am informed he is an Arminian, I was much pleased with his sermon. It was full of manly, rational and ingenious sentiments; and more in Mr. Howe's strain than any sermon I ever heard. He is a minister of the congregation of which good Dr. Wright was pastor. Preached in the evening in Mr. Gibbon's meeting-house, on Luke ii. 34, 35, and had some freedom and solemnity. Conversed a little with the great grandson of Oliver Cromwell; and I remember a few days ago, I drank tea with his great granddaughter, one Mrs. Field. Drank tea with two granddaughters of the famous Sir Henry Ashurt, the friend of the ejected ministers. Mr. Tennent preached for Mr. Chandler, and was kindly treated. I am so hurried that I have no time to write my journal, but about twelve o'clock at night. Therefore I am obliged to be very short.

Monday, January 7.—Went to visit Mr. Oswald and Mr. Buckland, booksellers; but the former was not at home. In the evening visited Mr. Winter, a Congregational minister; but his dry orthodoxy, and severe reflections upon those that deviated from rigid Calvinism, were disagreeable to me. Heard good Mr. Whitefield in the evening on "Who hath delivered us from the power of darkness, and hath translated us into the kingdom of his dear Son."—In the morning Mr. Tennent and I waited on Mr. Newman, and communicated our business. He is a grave gentleman, and treated us kindly. He intimated that the Academy which the Presbyterians are about to erect, would probably interfere with our concern, and gave us ground of discouragement.

Tuesday, January 8.—Dined at Mr. Eleazer Edwards's, a Turkey merchant in Devonshire Square, of the Baptist persuasion. There we enjoyed Mr. Stennet's company, and his sons. He is a judicious, prudent, and candid gentleman, and has more influence in court than any dissenting minister in London. Mr. Tennent, having visited Mr. Partridge, the agent of Pennsylvania, was advised to apply to some of the court, particularly to the Lord Chancellor, Lord Halifax, and Mr. Pelham; and he seemed inclined to do it. But to me it appeared very doubtful; I was afraid that in case the college should be discountenanced by them, they would find some flaw in the charter, and so overset it, and that a refusal at court, would have a bad influence on those that might otherwise contribute towards it. We consulted Mr. Stennet, and he was fully of my mind. He gave us an account of the affair of the glebe in New England, in which the Episcopal party was cast after a trial of some hours in the privy council. He also related a conference he had with the Duke of Newcastle, and the Archbishop of York, about the mission of bishops into America, which was very entertaining; but I have no time to relate such things. In the evening we visited Mr. Ward, the bookseller; who appeared a zealous friend to the college. At night finished a letter to my dearest, with such tender affection, as I could hardly bear.

Wednesday, January 9.—Waited on Mr. Penn, the proprietor of Pennsylvania. He treated us kindly, but gave us no encouragement as to our mission, on account of the Academy in Philadelphia, which he apprehended himself under peculiar obligations to promote. Went thence to Kensington to see Mr. Ziegenhagen, his Majesty's German chaplain, a good old Lutheran minister. He has much of the solemnity of the Christian, and a tender concern for the church of Christ in general. Dined at an inn; but when we called for the reckoning, we found the generous old gentleman had prevented us, and sent word that he would pay for all our expenses there. Called at Mr. Pitiuis's, at the Savoy, a Lutheran minister, but he was not at home.

Thursday, January 10.—Visited Dr. Jenning's, and were kindly received. He appears a sociable, affectionate, and pious man. He keeps an academy of about twenty students. He seemed to favour our design; but was apprehensive that the privileges granted in our charter, were so ample, that he feared, if it were known in court, they would be curtailed; especially, since the government here would not allow the colleges in New England the power of conferring any degree above A. M., though it was granted them, by a law of their own province. Spent the evening agreeably at one Mr. Gibson's, in company with Mr. and Mrs. De Berdt.

Friday, January 11.—Visited Dr. Earle, an old Presbyterian minister, of a good character, but of a stern, incomplaisant behaviour. He received us dryly, and would not so much as read or hear our recommendations; but afterwards cordially promised that he would inquire of Mr. Stennet and Mr. Chandler, about the affairs of our mission, and that if they approved of it, he would concur with them in proper measures to promote it. Visited Mr. May, a Presbyterian minister, but he plead that he had no influence, his congregation was much in debt, &c., &c.; and absolutely refused to concur. Went to the New England coffee-house; conversed with Mr. Partridge, the agent for Pennsylvania. Spent the evening at Mr. Ward's, where I had a short interview with one Mr. Thompson, a young minister. I forgot to mention that in the morning we waited on —— Belchier, Esq., member of Parliament, and gave him a letter from Governor Belcher. He treated us kindly, and promised us assistance.

Saturday, January 12.—Went to visit Mr. Streatfield, but he was not at home. Spent an hour in agreeable conversation with Mr. Gibbons, and another with Dr. Guise. Dined at Dr. Belchier's, but was low-spirited, and so unsociable that I was ashamed of myself. There is such a number of ministers here, that it is rare for a stranger to be invited to preach; and we have little prospect of usefulness that way as yet. The Presbyterians particularly, being generally Armenians or Socinians, seem shy of us.

Sunday, January 13.—Heard Mr. Lawson in the morning, on Job i. 12, and he seemed to aim honestly at experimental religion, and delivered himself extempore with fluency, though not with a great deal of accuracy. In the afternoon preached for Mr. Gibbons on these words, " I will be your God and ye shall be my people." I had a good deal of readiness and vivacity, though alas! but little tender solemnity. Spent the evening in pleasing conversation with dear Mr. Gibbons, who was much affected and pleased with my sermon, and proposed to me to publish it with a collection of his, which he intended for the press. He showed me an incomparable elegy of a minister upon his daughter who died in her 11th year, which was commonly ascribed to Mr. Howe, and indeed is worthy of him. He told me that Dr. Trapp composed an epitaph for himself, in which were the two lines addressed to his people,

> " If in my life I tried in vain to save,
> Hear me, at last, O hear me from the grave."

He read me a few letters of one Mr. Thomas, whose life he has published; which were as excellent as any thing I ever heard of the kind. Mr. Tennent preached for Mr. Gibbons, A. M., and for Mr. Stennet, P. M. I find a good number of the people are displeased with his using notes.

Monday, January 14.—Visited Mr. Lawson, the minister of the Scotch Church, and had a very friendly reception. Spent an hour with Mr. Whitefield. He thinks we have not taken the best method to keep in with all parties, but should " come out boldly" as he expressed it; which would secure the affections of the pious people from whom we might expect the most generous contributions. Dined and spent the evening very agreeably with Mr. Cruttenden, who is a most hearty friend.

Tuesday, January 15.—Heard Dr. Guise in Pinners Hall preach a judicious experimental discourse on these words,—" And the peace of God shall keep your hearts through Jesus Christ." It was well adapted to comfort the people of God; but the languor of his delivery, and his promiscuous undistinguishing manner of address, seem to take away its energy and pungency. Dined at Mr. Jones's, a pious, judicious Christian, and spent the evening there with Mr. Whitefield, Mr. Gibbons, &c. Mr. Tennent's heart was opened for free religious conversation, and we spent a few hours very profitably. In sundry places here, we hear of Mr. Hudson, a good minister that was lately here from Carolina, and preached with uncommon acceptance.

Wednesday, January 16.—Mr. Tennent went to visit Mr. Oswald, and visited Mr. Pike, in Horten square, an Independent minister. He appears * * * * in principle, and a great friend to experimental religion, and promised to promote the college. He has a penetrating, philosophical genius, and is properly a man of books. He made me a present of his *Philosophia Sacra*, and his sermon on " charity and zeal united." Spent about two hours in learned and religious conversation with him. I found his method of examining any doctrine is, to read over the whole Bible in the original, and having extracted all the texts that refer to it, to form a judgment upon the whole. I next visited Dr. Lardner, the celebrated author of " The Credibility of the Gospel History,"—and I was really surprised at the sight of him, as he differed so much from the idea which I had formed of so great a man. He is a little, pert, old gent, full of sprightly conversation; but so deaf that he seems to hear nothing at all. I was obliged to tell him my mind and answer his questions in writing; and he keeps a pen and paper always on the table for that purpose. He treated me very kindly, and constrained me to dine with him. I next visited Dr. Grosvenor, a venerable, humble, and affectionate old gent, who, under the infirmity of old age, has declined the exercise of his ministry for two or three years. I have hardly seen a man that discovered so much tenderness and humility in his very aspect. He offered me Baxter's or Williams's works; but I told him I would receive them only for the use of the College, and in that view they would be very acceptable. He then insisted that I would accept two pieces of his, for my own private use, viz: The Mourner, and an Essay on Health. Spent the evening in writing to my dear brother Mr. Todd.

Thursday, January 17.—It being rainy, we stayed at home preparing a petition in behalf of the College.

Friday, January 18.—We submitted our petition to Mr. Chandler's correction. He advised us to represent in it the use of the College " to keep a sense of religion among the German Protestant emigrants, settled in the British plantations, to instruct their children in the principles of our common Christianity, and to instruct them in the knowledge of the English language, that they may be incorporated with the rest of His Majesty's subjects." Mr. T. approved of the addition; but I could not help scrupling it, because the College is not immediately intended to teach the English language. However, I submitted.

Saturday, January 19.—Visited Dr. Avery. He is an amiable gentleman, very affable, of a soft, ready address; and seems qualified by Divine Providence designedly to act for the dissenters in court. He said he thought it his duty, as he is now on the confines of another world, to withdraw from the public management of their affairs; that they might learn to manage without him before he goes off the stage. He seemed diffident about our success in our mission, on account of the prodigous expenses lying upon the dissenters on various accounts. Went to St. Dunstan's coffee-house, where we had some friendly conversation with Mr. Smith, a young clergyman of the established church, the author of the poem upon visiting the Philadelphia Academy. He did not appear so great an enemy to our design as we expected. At 2 o'clock we were sent for by a company of lords and gentlemen, who have the disposal of the money lately given by the King for the support of schools among the Germans in Pennsylvania. Mr. Chandler, who is the company's secretary, introduced our affair, and our petition was read. There was no time to consider it, and it was deferred till their next meeting. For my part, I have no hope of success. Spent part of the night in great perplexity, not knowing what to preach on to-morrow.

Sunday, January 20.—Preached for Mr. Price, a Presbyterian minister, on Hebrews, xii. 14, an inaccurate, blundering discourse; and alas! I had no sense of my subject. Heard Mr. Tennent, P. M., preach an honest and plain sermon; and while I was pleased with its simplicity, I was uneasy lest its bluntness might be offensive. Dined at Captain Gibson's, with Mr. Price, &c. Went in the evening, and heard Mr. Price preach at Salter's Hall, to a large auditory, (a thing rarely seen here) on " My yoke is easy," &c. He is by far the best orator I have heard in London; and excepting a few Arminian sentiments, his sermon was truly excellent. He is an affable, affectionate gentleman, and is the likest man to Mr. Pemberton, both in conversation and in the pulpit, that I have seen. Returned home melancholy and low-spirited, from a review of my poor day's work, and sought relief in conversation with dear Mr. Tennent. I am afraid I shall do little good in this city. The congregations are so small that it is enough to damp one's zeal in preaching to them.

Monday, January 21.—Spent most of the day in revising and transcribing a petition in behalf of the College, and we resolved to soften the terms in the clause about the German Protestants. Spent the evening at Mr. Gibbons', where Mr. Llwellen and Mr. Stennet, jr., were met for improving conversation, and I find it is their method to meet every Monday night.

Tuesday, January 22.—We went to Mr. Chandler's, with a design to submit our petition to his correction. We found Mr. Slaughter and Mr. Smith there, when we introduced the conversation about the Germans, and observed that our College would be a happy expedient to unite the Calvinists among them with the English Presbyterians. Mr. Smith replied that a union would not be desirable; for a separation would keep up a balance of power. Mr. Tennent answered, that an union in a good thing is always desirable. Upon which Mr. Chandler says, " I have seen a very extraordinary sermon against union," and he immediately reached Mr. Tennent his Nottingham Sermon. It threw us both into confusion, and gave such a damp to my spirits, as brought me in mind of my mortifications in the General Court in Virginia. Mr. Tennent went about to vindicate himself, and when I had recovered from my consternation, I put in a word. But all had no effect. We found that sermon and the examination of Mr. Tennent's answer to the protest, had been put into Mr. Chandler's hands; and he had formed his judgment so precipitately from a partial view of the case, that he told us " he would do nothing for us." Mr. Smith alleged that the College was a party design, that though the charter was catholic, yet so many of the trustees were Presbyterians, that they would manage matters with arbitrary partiality,—that the trustees in New York city complained that there were not more trustees of other denominations. We went away perplexed, and heard an excellent sermon in Pinner's Hall by Mr. Rawlins on a subject very seasonable to us, " He will regard the prayer of the destitute." Went to the Amsterdam coffee-house, where the ministers meet, and afterwards dined at Mr. Ward's. Returned home, and prayed together for direction, and consulted what measures we should take to remove Mr. Chandler's prejudices. The Lord direct us in this difficult affair ! I am shocked to think of the inveterate malignity of the Synod of Philadelphia who have sent their accusations after Mr. Tennent so far.

Wednesday, January 23.—Waited on Mr. Chandler to remove his prejudices. His turning against us seems to have so threatening an aspect upon our mission, that it kept me awake part of last night, and mingled with my anxious dreams. Mr. Tennent made honest, humble concessions with regard to the Nottingham Sermon, as—" that it was written in the heat of his spirit, when he apprehended a remarkable work of God was opposed by a set of ministers—that some of the sentiments were not agreeable to his present opinion—that he had painted sundry things in too strong colours—and he plead,—that it was now thirteen years ago—and that since he had used all his influence to promote union between the Synods; of which he produced his Irenicum as a witness—that if the sermon was faulty, it was but the fault of one man, and should not be charged upon the whole body." We showed him the minutes of our Synod, to give him a view of the state of the debates. As he disapproves of all subscriptions of tests of orthodoxy, he disapproved of our adopting act. I exerted all my powers of pathetic address, to give him a moving representation of the melancholy case of the churches under our care—of the dreadful consequence of a disappointment in our mission—of the hardships we had exposed ourselves to, in prosecuting it, &c. Upon the whole he seemed something softened, and promised that he would not use his influence to blast our design, but would himself contribute towards it. He invited me to preach for him next Sunday come se'en night, which I did not expect. Waited upon Dr. Lawrence, a Presbyterian minister, who treated us with great freedom and friendship. He advised us to prepare petitions, one for the Presbyterians and one for the Independents; for the animosities among some of them were so strong, that the very sight of the names of one party would hinder the other from subscribing; and the Independents would cry it was a Presbyterian project, when they saw the petition recommended by Presbyterians, and vice versa. Dined with good old Mr. Pierce, Dr. Watts' former colleague, in company with Mr. Savage, his assistant. He is an humble, affectionate gentleman, and seemed to have our mission at heart; but apprehended we should have little success here at present, because the collections for their own funds are just at hand. We requested him to recommend our petition; but he declined it at the time. From the present view of things, I think if we can but clear our expenses, we shall be well off. Went in the evening to Mr. Bradbury's. He is still sprightly and gay, and sings a tune now and then; though so very aged. He subscribed a recommendation of the petition, and seemed particularly concerned for its success.

Thursday, January 24.—Went to Dr. Guyse, Dr. Lardner, Dr. Benson, and Mr. Price, to get our petition recommended; and they all complied. Dr. Guyse is a steady, deliberate gentleman, and now appears more in our interest than upon our first application. Dr. Benson talked in a sneering manner of the account of the conversions in Northampton, New England, published here by Dr. Watts and Dr. Guyse. He is a gentleman of great abilities, but counted a Socinian. Mr. Prior is a sociable, sprightly, generous gentleman, of latitudinarian principles, but a hearty friend to every laudable institution. He uninvited subscribed ten guineas to the College. We waited also on Mr. Hall, but he declined subscribing then, to make way for his seniors. He is an Israelite, and bitterly laments the declension of the times. In the evening I wrote to Mr. Wright, &c. But alas! I am so hurried that I have no time for correspondence.

Friday, January 25.—Went with much hesitation to Mr. Chandler's and he to our agreeable surprise, recommended our petition. This will have a happy effect, not only as his name will have influence with many, but as it will bind him to secresy with regard to the calumnies spread about Mr. Tennent, for he cannot with a good face give injurious representations of a design which himself has recommended. We went next to Mr. Stennet's, and he also subscribed. But Mr. Newman, a Presbyterian minister, chose to have more time to consider. Dr. Lawrence, one of the few Calvinistic Presbyterians, did also cheerfully subscribe; and so did Mr. Rawlins, a good old independent minister, whom we waited upon in the evening. Dined with Mr. Bradbury, who has been in the ministry about fifty-seven years. He read us some letters which passed between Mr. Whitefield and him in 1741; occasioned by Mr. Whitefield's reproving him in a letter for singing a song in a tavern, in a large company, in praise of old English beef. The old gentleman sung it to us, and we found it was partly composed by himself, in the high flying days of Queen Anne.

He is a man of a singular turn, which would be offensive to the greatest number of serious people. But for my part, I would say—

> I knew 'twas his peculiar whim,
> Nor took it ill as come from him.

Saturday, January 26.—Spent the morning in writing letters; and went to Newington to dine with Mr. Bowles, who treated us kindly, and gave me five guineas for the College.

Sunday, January 27.—Preached for Mr. Price, A. M. in Berry street; when I entered the pulpit, it filled me with reverence to reflect that I stood in the place where Mr. Clarkson, Dr. Owen, Dr. Watts, &c., had once officiated. My subject was Jer. xxxi. 18, 19, 20. I was favoured with some freedom. Blessed be God, I have not been disturbed with the fear of man, since I have been in this city. Dined with good old Mr. Price, who treated me with all the tender affection of a father. Preached, P. M. in the Scotch church in Founders' hall, where Mr. Lawson is minister, on Rev. i. 7. I was encouraged to see a crowded auditory, of persons from various congregations; and though I had not much solemnity, was enabled to speak gracefully and oratorically. Drank tea at Mr. Mauduit's; who is a very candid serious man, though a friend and occasional hearer of Dr. Benson. He gave me some enconragement that something would be done in favour of the poor dissenters in Virginia. Heard Mr. Furnace in the evening on the case of Felix, an ingenious discourse.

Monday, January 28.—Waited on good Mr. Pike, and he readily subscribed our petition; but had it much at heart that only pious youth, should be admitted to learning for the ministry; a method that has been pursued here for some years, by the King's head society. He told us, that he believed all that would be given by his friends, must be appropriated for this purpose; and that they would give upon no other footing. The venerable Dr. Grosvenor also signed our petition. Dined at Dr. Lawrence's, an open hearted candid gentlemen; and went thence to Mr. Rawlin's, a judicious, experimental divine, who also signed, and promised that what could be got among his friends, he would take the trouble to collect himself. He married a good fortune, but a bad wife; and now, since her death, he has a considerable estate, and keeps his coach. Mr. Lawson not only subscribed, but gave us four guineas. Visited Mr. King, a talkative minister, who amid all his pretended friendship discouraged us.

Tuesday, January 29.—Went in the morning to Dr. Jennings, a courteous, sensible gentleman, who keeps an academy. He signed the petition, and invited me to preach for him. Went thence to Salter's Hall, and heard Dr. Earle, the oldest minister in London, on these words:—" An inheritance among them that are sanctified through faith in me." He preached extempore, with much accuracy and judgment, and what he said had a tendency to do good. I waited on him and Mr. Barker, a celebrated minister, in the vestry room, and though the old gentleman treated me, as he does every body else, with his natural sternness, he and Mr. Barker readily signed the petition. Went from thence to Hamlin's coffee-house, where the Presbyterian ministers meet on Tuesdays, and there Dr. Allen and Dr. Benson subscribed. Dr. Benson did it with this sneer, " That he was no friend to subscriptions," meaning tests of orthodoxy. He asked me whether an Arminian, an Arian, or a Socinian, would be admitted into our College. The reason of his inquiry was, that the charter says " that all persons of *all denominations* shall be admitted to equal advantages of education ;" and he apprehended that an Arminian was not said to be of any particular denomination. Mr. Tennent went among the honest Independents at the Austrian coffee-house, and got sundry names. Dined at Mr. Holmes's, a courteous gentleman of Mr. Newman's congregation, in company with dear Mr. Gibbons, a great grandson of Oliver Cromwell. I was much pained with a wind cholic. In the evening went to the Amsterdam coffee-house, where the Independent ministers met for friendly conversation, and to consult about the affairs of the churches; for they have no other associations, as the Presbyterians have no other Presbyteries. Indeed, there seems to be no government exercised jointly among either of them. The English Presbyterians have no elders nor judicatories of any kind; nor seem to me to agree but in very few particulars with the church of Scotland. I find the Calvinistic Presbyterians, as well as the Baptists, choose to frequent the Independent coffee-house, rather than associate with their Presbyterian brethren of Arminian or Socinian sentiment, at Hamlin's. Mr. Halford and Mr. Towle subscribed to our petition; and the rest present, particularly Dr. Guyse, appeared heartily in our interest.

Wednesday, January 30.—We waited upon Dr. Gill, the celebrated Baptist minister. He is a serious, grave little man, and looks young and hearty, though, I suppose, near sixty. He signed our petition, though he modestly pleaded that his name would be of little service, and that the Baptists in general were, unhappily, ignorant of the importance of learning. Went thence to Mr. Price, and got his subscription. At 12 o'clock, waited on the committee, of which Dr. Avery is chairman. We laid before them our credentials, and requested them to recommend our petition; but they apprehended it would be improper. They cordially gave us their best advice. They had no time to consider the case of the oppressed dissenters in Virginia; but promised it should be done at their next meeting. There were fourteen present. Spent the evening in writing letters; at night waited on Mr. Savage, who is famed for his liberality to all pious undertakings. I found the good man was cooled towards us, because we associated with the rich and great, and persons of all denominations promiscuously;—and did not keep a more public intercourse with Mr. Whitefield, and employ some house to preach in frequently. He seemed also insensible of the necessity of learning in a minister; and was doubtful whether he would give any thing towards our College.

Thursday, January 31.—Visited Mr. Richardson, an Independent minister, and Mr. Walker, tutor of the oriental languages in Dr. Marriot's academy, who readily signed our petition. Mr. Tennent went to Mr. Denham, but had no admission. Dined at Mr. Hall's, and was cheered and edified with his facetious and yet heavenly conversation.

Friday, February 1.—Took a walk to Westminster, to get the names of the Scotch ministers to our petition; but could find none at home but Mr. Crookshank and Mr. Patrick, who readily signed. The former was indisposed, and I had not much conversation with him; but he appears an affectionate humble man. Mr. Patrick appears a serious man, and deeply lamented the declension of religion in London, among the dissenters; and said that the revivals of religion which they had were chiefly in the Church of England, by means of Mr. Whitefield. In my return I took a walk through St. James's Park, and find it contains a vast quantity of land.

Saturday, February 2.—Went to Westminster, and got Mr. Kippies and Mr. Oswald to sign the petition. Mr. Kippies was a pupil of Dr. Doddridge's, and is a very modest and affectionate youth. He succeeds the late Dr. Hughs. Mr. Oswald seems to be a devout humble man. He is acquainted with Mr. Erskine, Mr. McLaurin, and sundry good ministers in Scotland, his native country. Dined at good Dr. Guise's, in company with his son, who is also a minister, and a sociable, pleasant companion. Went thence to Mr. Burroughs, an Arminian Baptist, with whom the late Dr. Foster was colleague for some time. Spent the evening with Mr. Edward Calamy, the fourth of the name. He is a sensible, pleasant gentleman, but has imbibed the modish divinity. He has declined the exercise of his ministry for about three years, by reason of indisposition.

Sunday, February 3.—Preached A. M. for Mr. Crookshank on Luke xiii. 24, with considerable freedom, and the assembly appeared attentive, and some of them affected. Preached P. M. in the old Jewry for Mr. Chandler, on Luke ii. 24, to a very brilliant assembly, but a blunder I made in mentioning text, threw me into confusion, which I did not recover through the whole discourse; and I felt more of the fear of man than since I have been in this city. Drunk tea with Mr. Chandler at one Mr. Adair's; but was so mortified with a review of my sermon, that I had no heart for conversation; and I returned home exceedingly dejected. I was afraid that my poor management would bring disgrace upon religion, and the affairs of our mission. In short, I have not had so melancholy an evening for a long time. The Lord help me!

Monday, February 4.—Visited Mr. Denham, a Presbyterian minister; but he was so affected with the gout that he could not give me an audience; but put me off till next Monday. Went thence to Mr. Prior's, and spent an hour with him in free conversation. He is an amiable, candid and generous gentleman. He gave me ten guineas for the College; and he is a learned and ingenious man. I think that the Trustees should compliment him with the degree of A. M. as a reward to his merit and generosity. He made me a present of three discourses of his, one of which I heard him deliver at Salter's Hall; and I presented him with one of mine, preached before the Presbytery. Dined with Mr. Muir, a Scotch minister, settled in an Independent congregation; a very affectionate man, and he seems to have a serious sense of religion. Went to Mr. Mitchel's, who is also a Scotch minister of an Independent congregation, but not so sociable as the former to me. They both signed the petition. Spent a social hour very pleasantly with Dr. Jennings, who, though a great student, and a universal scholar, has nothing of the stiff pedant in his behaviour. Spent a few minutes with good Mr. Hitchin, who is famous for a zealous, experimental preacher, and hearty friend of Mr. Whitefield. He cheerfully signed the petition, and promised his influence. Spent the evening most agreeably at Mr. Towle's, an ingenious young minister of the Independent persuasion. We interchanged our thoughts on sundry subjects, and particularly I communicated to him my thoughts on the Divine government as adapted to the nature of man, the beauty of rectoral justice, and various methods which God has wisely taken to display it, &c. He advised me to digest my thoughts upon these subjects, and publish them because they were new. I find to my surprise, that my poems and sermon before the Presbytery are very acceptable to sundry here; and I have been pressed by some to let them pass an edition here; but I am afraid of every thing that might be looked upon as ostentation in my present circumstances. Mr. Towle proposed to keep a correspondence with me for the future; a proposal very acceptable to me.

Tuesday, February 5.—Heard Mr. Rawlins at Pinners' Hall, on his former text, " He will regard the prayer of the destitute, &c.;" and though his delivery is heavy, I have heard very few preach so solid, judicious, and experimental a discourse. Went among the Independent ministers at the Amsterdam coffee-house, and obtained three names more to our petition, viz.—Dr. Milner, Mr. Thompson, and Mr. Hayward. Dined at one Mr. Charles Buckstone's, with Mr. Gibbons, who treated me very kindly, and gave me five guineas for the College, without solicitation. We have now got sixty names to our petition, which I think quite sufficient; but Mr. Tennent thinks we should get the recommendation of the principal ministers, round about the city, as well as in it. But this, I am afraid, will take up so much time, that we cannot finish our applications for private contributions before we are obliged to set out for Scotland. I think it is a remarkable smile of Providence, that we have so much success in getting the ministers of the city to recommend our petition, as it will have weight, not only here, but with the General Assembly. Spent part of the evening at Mr. Mauduit's, who had sent for me, to advise me to draw up a more particular account of the College; and the sum necessary to carry it to maturity, that people might regulate their donations accordingly.

Wednesday, February 6.—Went to Mr. Stennet's, who went with us to introduce us to the Duke of Argyle, to deliver Governor Belcher's letter. We found eight or ten gentlemen and noblemen waiting in his grace's levee. His Grace took us into his library; a spacious, elegant room, about forty feet long and twenty broad, furnished all round with books, philosophical instruments, curiosities, &c. His Grace told us, after reading the letter, that as the college related to the plantations, we ought first to apply to the lords of trade and plantations, and if they approved of it, he would willingly countenance it, both here and in Scotland. He advised us to apply to Lord Halifax, or Lord Duplin; and Mr. Stennet accordingly went to the latter, (while we staid at a coffee-house), and showed him our instructions from the Trustees, and the petition we had drawn up. Mr. Stennet told him he applied to his lordship in confidence; and his lordship assured him he would do nothing to injure us. He thereupon told him we had our charter only from a Governor; and asked him whether he thought it would be deemed valid in court. His lordship replied that he doubted it; but he would soon satisfy himself, by inquiring into the extent of the Governor's commission. And in case it appeared valid, he would advise us to lay the matter before the Archbishop of Canterbury, and he himself would go with Mr. Stennet to Mr. Pelham, in our favour: and so introduce the matter in court. For my part, I am afraid of all applications in that quarter, lest we lose our charter, and stir up an opposition; and it is against my mind that the matter has been carried so far. Dined at Mr. Stennet's, who gave us five guineas for the College. Went home anxious about the fate of an application to the lords of trade and to the court.

Saturday, February 9.—My hours are so interrupted, that I cannot every day keep an account of my proceedings. Providence has smiled upon our undertaking so far, that we have about eighty guineas promised, twenty of which are from the Rev. Mr. Rawlin, who has a large estate without children, and a heart proportionably generous.

Sunday, February 10.—Preached in a vacant Baptist congregation, which formerly had one Mr. Bently for their minister. They have generally, as I am informed, imbibed some Antinomian notions, particularly that no offers of grace should be made to the unconverted, because they are dead in sin, and incapable to receive them. I preached before and afternoon on Isaiah xlv. 22, with some freedom; but as my sermon was full of exhortations to sinners to look to Christ, I suppose it did not well suit the taste of the people. Dined with good Mr. Savage, who used a very inoffensive freedom in making remarks upon my sermon, which he seemed to think was not sufficiently evangelical.—Preached in the evening at Shakspeare Walk, to a very crowded auditory, on Zech. vii. 12, 13, and had unusual freedom, though my body was much exhausted, and my voice broke by a bad cough, with which I have been afflicted ever since I left home. My subject was terrible, and I was afraid it might be offensive; but the uncommon security of this place requires an alarm. The people seemed eagerly attentive; and there appeared a greater prospect of success than I have had in this city. This lecture is attended alternately by the ministers of the town; and is intended to support a charity school of thirty children. I addressed myself to the little creatures and they seemed very attentive.

Monday, February 11.—Visited Mr. Mill and delivered Mr. Donald's letter. He and his partner, Mr. Oswald, advised us to apply to the lords of trade to encourage our embassy. But I am afraid of the consequence. Went to Mr. Denham, a Presbyterian minister, and had a long and difficult dispute with him, about the importance and necessity of our College,—the validity of the charter without the Royal approbation, &c., which he managed with great dexterity. It was my happiness to have my thoughts ready, and I made such a defence as silenced him. His name is of great importance, and I was solicitous to obtain it to our petition; but had lost all hope of it, when, to my agreeable surprise, he subscribed. Visited Dr. Jennings, who took me to his academy, and showed all his philosophical curiosities, two orreries,—an experiment to show that all the colours of the rainbow blended form a white,—a mushroom petrified,—two or three Testaments in MS. before the art of printing, which were very elegantly written,—sundry stones in the shape of a coiled snake,—shells, minerals, Æolus's harp, a plica pilonica, &c. He has a most curious and philosophical turn, and is very sociable and communicative. He promised five guineas at least towards the College.—Spent the evening agreeably with Mr. Savage, Dr. Watts's successor, and sub-tutor with Dr. Jennings.

Tuesday, Feb. 12.—Went to Salter's Hall, and heard the great Mr. Barker, on these words, "Not as though I had already attained," &c. His sermon was very accurate and judicious, and in the Calvinistic strain. I find, that though real religion, and the principles of the Reformation are better retained among the Independents, and though there be a considerable number of learned and judicious ministers among them, yet the greatest number of learned and polite men are among the Presbyterians; and sundry of them deserve the character, who Arminianize and Socinianize very much. Went to the Presbyterian coffee-house, as it is called, and got Mr. Furneaux's name to the petition. Dined with my serious friend, Mr. Manduit, who promised five guineas to the College. Had a long conversation with Samuel Dicker, Esq., a notorious deist.

Wednesday, Feb. 13.—Waited on Mr. Towle, who gave us five guineas; but it rained so much that we staid at home P. M., and I wrote a few letters to my friends at Hanover. That dear place contains all that is dearest to me in the world, my congregation, my friends, my parents, my children, and especially my dearest Chara. Alas! my heart breaks at the thought.—Heard Mr. Whitefield in the evening.

Thursday, Feb. 14.—Waited on Mr. Stennet to hear Lord Duplin's opinion of the validity of our charter; but he was indisposed, and had not waited on his lordship. Visited Mr. Brine, a Baptist minister, who is reputed a speculative Antinomian, though a good man. Dined with Mr. Anderson, of the South Sea House, a friendly, polite gentleman, and a secretary of the correspondents here with the Society for propagating Christian knowledge in Scotland. I find his uncle was the grandfather of the Andersons in Hanover. Visited Dr. Avery, who treated me with the most unreserved candour. Spent the evening with Mr. Thomson, jr., an ingenious young Baptist minister, who though educated a strict Calvinist, has imbibed the modern latitudinarian principles. I had an amicable dispute with him about the lawfulness and expediency of subscribing tests of orthodoxy beside the Scripture.

Friday, Feb. 15.—Visited the venerable, stern Dr. Earley, and he gave me five guineas for the College. Went then to Mr. Spilsbury's, Presbyterian minister at Salter's Hall. He seemed reluctant to assist, and put me off. Dined with Mr. Bowles, jr., and had a very agreeable conversation with the old gentleman, though my spirits were very low, and I had no list for action. He made some candid remarks upon my sermons, and told me that he heard Mr. Chandler and his people were not well pleased with my sermon there, but thought it too rigidly orthodox. Spent the evening most agreeably with my friend Mr. Cruttenden, who is a very considerable poet, as I find by some poems of his he put into my hands to correct.

Saturday, February 16.—We have reason to observe the goodness of God in the success we meet with in the business of our mission, having already got near £200, which I really thought at first would be as much as we could get in all. Our obtaining the attestation of so many ministers to our petition (in all sixty-seven) appears the best expedient we could have fallen upon; and as they are of the three denominations of dissenters, it gives us access to people of all these denominations.—We have concluded to print five hundred copies of our petition, to put into the hands of our friends, to dispose among such as might contribute to the design, that the way may be prepared for our making personal application to them. This morning I waited on Dr. Lardner, Mr. Pike, and Mr. Guyse, who gave me about seven guineas between them towards the College.—Had some conversation with Mr. Guyse, who is a free sociable gentleman, though very low spirited to day. I hardly think there has been one in London these many years, who has contracted so extensive acquaintance with the ministers of this city, as I have, in less than two months. I am sometimes low spirited and bashful, especially in company with my seniors, that I cannot behave so as to recommend myself. However, I hope to settle such correspondence as may be for my future advantage. Dined at Mr. Wright's, son-in-law to Mr. Mauduit, and spent the afternoon at home, preparing for to-morrow when I am to preach for Dr. Jennings. I find the hurries of our business, the variety of company and objects, and the want of time for thoughtfulness and retirement have dissipated my thoughts, and deadened my devotion. I am extremely uneasy in my situation. I long to be at home in my study, and with my dear family; for the character of a recluse student suits me much better than that of a man of business. But it is the providence of God that called me to this instance of selfdenial, and I must submit, nay I would cheerfully acquiesce in it. Though I take but too superficial notice of it, yet alas! I feel sin still strong in me. *Cœlum, non animum mutant, qui trans mare currunt.* When I seriously think how depraved I am, I hardly know what conclusion to draw about myself. God pity me, the vilest of his creatures.

Sunday, February 17.—Heard Dr. Jennings, A. M. on Rom. viii. 7, 8, and he spoke in the language of the convictive preachers of the last age, to my great satisfaction. Dined with one Mr. Eads, a very serious good man. Preached P. M. on Ps. xcvii. 1, with usual freedom and clearness to the great satisfaction of the good Doctor. Spent the evening with him; and he is so free and communicative of knowledge, that his company is very entertaining and instructive. I meet with none in London like him in this respect. He read me a dissertation of his upon the tree of life. A late writer supposes that the word rendered tree, though singular, has a plural signification, and meant all the trees of the garden, except that of knowledge. So the Greek ξυλον, and the English *wood* has a plural signification. The author supposes that all the trees in Eden might be called a *wood* of life, because they were sufficient for the support of life without the other productions of the earth, which are raised by labour. The Doctor supposes that there were other trees of pleasure and innocent luxury, but not absolutely necessary for Adam's subsistence, and that the tree of life was a particular species of tree, the fruit of which was the necessary support of life, as bread is now, &c.

Saturday, February 22.—This week I have been so hurried, that I could not keep a daily journal. Last week we dispersed our petitions among the ministers to give away among their people. We have been diligent in making private applications; but met with many disappointments, partly from gentlemen being from home, or indisposed, or unwilling to contribute; and partly by the prejudices raised in the minds of some by Mr. Tennent's Nottingham sermon, which is dispersed through the town from hand to hand very officiously. Mr. Tennent was so damped with it yesterday, that his spirits were quite sunk and he gave up the hope of success, and wished himself in Philadelphia again. But this morning we had reason to observe the remarkable interposition of Providence, in raising us up after a dejection. Mr. Tennent waited on Wm. Belchier, Esq., a churchman, that seems to have no sense of religion; and from whom we expected little or nothing; but he surprised us by subscribing £50. Blessed be the God of heaven, who has the hearts of all men in his hands, and rules them as he pleases. I went to Hackney, about three miles off; had an interview with Mr. Hunt, one of the ministers there, a serious, sociable man. Waited on Samuel Lesingham, Esq., a gentleman in great respect among the dissenters; and Stamp Brooksbank, and —— Sheafe, Esqrs., the latter of which gave me a very cold reception. Hackney is a very agreeable place, where there are sundry magnificent seats and gardens. This week I have waited on —— Lamb, Esq., Mr. Benjamin Bond, sen., Mr. —— Hollis, Sir Joshua Van-Neck, and spent last Wednesday night very agreeably with Mr. Stennet, jun., an affectionate Baptist minister. Dined yesterday with Mr. Robert Keen, in the Minories, a pious affectionate young gentleman, in company with good Mr. Cruttenden. We have been solicited to preach a charity sermon next Wednesday for the dissenting school in Bartholomew Close; and as Mr. Tennent refused, and cast it upon me, I was obliged to consent; though when I consider my hurry, want of preparation, the number of ministers that may attend, &c., the prospect strikes me with horror. May God prepare me! Dined last Thursday at Mr. Brine's, a Baptist minister and a warm advocate for the doctrines of Calvinism, with something of Antinomian tincture.

Sunday, February 24.—Preached the morning lecture at Mr. Godwin's meeting-house, in Little St. Helen's, at 7 o'clock, the earliest that ever I preached in my life. There was a considerable assembly considering it was so early. My subject was, "Yield yourselves unto God," and as I had but one hour's time for the whole of public worship, I could handle it but superficially. Took a coach and went to Mr. Oswald's meeting-house, where I preached both fore and afternoon. My subject A. M., was John iii. 6, and P. M., John iii. 3. I spoke with some freedom. But alas! the spirit of awful solemnity, so commanding and impressing to an audience, which has frequently animated my sermons, seems now to be departed from me; and when I speak on solemn subjects, with an air of unconcernedness, or mere natural vivacity, I feel guilty, and seem to myself to make a very ridiculous appearance. Such preaching, alas! has but little weight with an auditory. The congregation in the afternoon was very full, which encouraged me.

[*Here some is wanting.*]

Monday, February 25.—Went to Hackney, but were disappointed of waiting on several we intended. Went thence to Newington, and visited Mrs. Abney, daughter of the late Sir Thomas Abney, a courteous humble lady. The steward showed me Dr. Watt's study, and some of his manuscripts. I find he wrote but little of his sermons. As his books were taken away, there was nothing pleased me so much as the pictures of sundry great men, ranged in the order the Dr. has left them. There were two vacancies, in one of which is written, with the Dr's own hand,

Est locus pluribus umbris.—Hor.

and in the other,

Quis me doctorum propria dignabitur umbra.

This is the place the Doctor tenderly describes in his elegy upon Gunston. I saw the turret, and the venerable oaks and elms, &c.

Tuesday, February 26.—Staid at home in the morning, preparing to preach a charity sermon to-morrow, the prospect of which is very terrifying to me. Went, P. M., to the House of Lords, with the Rev. Mr. Thompson, and was introduced by a Mr. George Baskerville, a lawyer, whose company I enjoyed on the way, and in the evening. He is the most facetious mortal I ever conversed with; and sometimes he gives such a loose to his wit that one would think he had no respect to any thing sacred; and yet he gave five guineas to the College, and talked at times very pertinently on divine subjects. The House of Lords is but an ordinary old building: but the assembly is the most brilliant and august that one can conceive. It was opened by a prayer read by the youngest bishop; at which all but members were ordered to go out; but Mr. Thompson and I were conveniently concealed behind a curtain, and were not excluded. The bishops made an odd appearance to me in their dress of black and white! The judges were to give their opinions and the reasons, seriatim, on a case relating to the insurance of a privateer, whose company mutinied. Five of them spoke, each near an hour, and I was charmed with their clear reasoning; and one of them had a handsome address.

Wednesday, February 27.—Preached a charity sermon at Mr. King's meeting-house, on "I will be their God, and they shall be my people." There was a large auditory, and a considerable number of ministers, viz. Dr. Guyse, Mr. King, Mr. Gibbons, Mr. Guyse, Mr. Hickman, Mr. Brine, &c. I have hardly ever preached with greater disadvantage; partly by reason of a fright, occasioned by searching my pockets sometime before I could find my notes; and partly from my great hurry; for I found after I had consented to preach, that the committee that have the management of the secular affairs of the dissenters, were to meet on the same day; and Mr. Mauduit wrote to me to get Mr. Tennent to preach for me, (which he would by no means do) or conclude exactly at 12 o'clock. These things cast me into a perturbation of mind, and yet I had as much freedom and tenderness as I have had in the city; for which I desire to be humbly thankful. The ministers thanked me heartily for my sermon, and seemed well pleased with it. Immediately after sermon I took coach and went to Pinner's Hall, to wait on the Committee. They had been consulting the Virginia laws, and reading the papers I had sent them; and they told me they were all heartily engaged in my interest, but after the best deliberation, they were apprehensive that the Act of Toleration was not so adopted as to become a proper law of Virginia, but only one paragraph was received, which exempts dissenters from penalty for absenting themselves from the established church. This surprised me; as I still think my reasons for my former opinions are unanswerable. They at least advised me to get a petition drawn up to the King and Council, and subscribed by the dissenters in the frontier counties, which they apprehended would be of more weight than one from Hanover, because they were educated dissenters, and were a good barrier against the French and Indians. They appointed some, of their members to assist me in drawing up a petition; and I intend to wait on them as soon as possible for that end. May the Providence of God smile on the attempt.

[*Some wanting.*]

Monday, March 4.—Had but little heart for business. Visited Mr. Waugh, the bookseller, and his father-in-law, Mr. Field. Spent the evening at Mr. Mauduit's in conversation upon the case of the dissenters in Virginia. I find Peyton Randolph, Esq., my old adversary, is now in London; and will no doubt oppose whatever is done in favour of the dissenters in Hanover.

Tuesday, March 5.—We determined to publish a larger account of the rise and present state of the College; as we find some are not fully satisfied with the short account given in our petition. This has cost us some pains, and the more so, as Mr. Tennent's style and mine are so different. Went to the Amsterdam coffee-house, to see the ministers, and spread our petitions, about 1 o'clock.

Wednesday, March 6.—Heard Mr. Halford preach a charity sermon in Mr. Chandler's meeting-house for the fund to support the widows and children of dissenting ministers. His text was, " Whatsoever thy hand findeth to do," &c. His matter was tolerably good, but delivered in a most wretched manner. I met him at the door, as he was coming into the meeting-house, and asked him how he did? He answered, " I am in fear and much trembling," and when I told him, that I hoped the Lord would be with him,—the good man burst into tears. This gave me occasion to reflect upon my own presumption, who preached there with much less diffidence. Visited Mr. Jackson, who was educated a churchman, but is now a dissenter; who has had the reading of all our papers relating to our mission, and would do nothing implicitly. He said he was afraid our College would fall into Episcopal hands; and that he was not well affected to Governor Belcher's character, for accepting of the place of Governor of New England, and espousing the interests of the court, when he was sent over as agent to oppose them. But to my agreeable surprise he gave me ten guineas for the College. Waited in the evening on Mr. Blackwell, whom, through mistake, I took to be a dissenter, but found to be a churchman, and one of the contributors to the Society for Propagating Christianity in foreign parts. He made as wide a mistake, and took me to be a Moravian, till I undeceived him. He appeared a very candid gentleman, and took the affair under consideration. I have been more than usually anxious this day about my dear wife. Oh! that I knew how she is! I find that neither time nor distance can erase her image from my heart. This day the Honourable Henry Pelham, Esq., prime minister, died; which has struck the town into a consternation. He has left a general good character behind him; and the court is puzzled to know whom to choose in his place.

[*Some wanting.*]

Saturday, March 16.—Last Sunday, I preached A. M.; for Mr. Gibbons, on these words, " So then is neither he that planteth any thing, &c.," and as I was deeply sensible of the withdrawing of Divine influences, and the inefficaciousness of the means of grace without them, my tender passions were frequently moved throughout the sermon, and in the conclusion burst out into a flood of tears. Sundry of the hearers were tenderly affected, particularly Mr. Cromwell, great grandson of the famous Oliver; who gave Mr. Gibbons three guineas for the College, after sermon, thanked me for my discourse with tears in his eyes. He afterwards conducted me to Dr. Stennet's, and talked freely and warmly of experimental religion. —Dined at Mr. Samuel Stennet's, in company with his brother, who is also a minister.—Preached P. M., for Dr. Stennet, and my spirits were so exhausted with my forenoon discourse that I had not much tender solemnity. Spent the evening with Mr. Stennet, jr., who seems a pious ingenious youth. We have determined to publish a larger account of the college for the satisfaction of such as have a historical curiosity, or desire to be informed of it as a matter in which they are concerned as contributors; and we have been busy this week in preparing and spreading it through the town. Spent the evening very agreeably with Mr. Cruttenden, who read me an ingenious dissertation of his in favour of Dr. Watts's version of the Psalms, and upon my request made me a present of it. Spent another evening with that heavenly man, Mr. Hall, whose conversation is an agreeable mixture of piety and wit. Had an interview with Mr. Wm. Hervey, brother to the celebrated author of the Meditations. He is a modest, humble gentleman, and though of the Church of England, has a zealous regard for the exploded doctrines of Calvinism and experimental religion. Heard Mr. Read last Tuesday, at Salter's Hall, on these words, " Enter not into judgment with thy servant," &c. But there was such a legal spirit diffused through the sermon, that I thought it rather calculated to promote the security, than the conversion of sinners. I could not help thinking of a pun I have heard of a minister, who preached a sermon upon these words, " Salt is good, but if the salt have lost its savour," &c. and when he was desired to publish it, he said " He believed he would, and dedicate it to the preachers at Salters' Hall; for they wanted seasoning."—Yesterday I drew up a petition for the dissenters in Virginia, and carried it to Dr. Avery to correct. The death of Mr. Pelham,—the prospect of sending a bishop over to America,—the confusion between the Governor and Assembly in Virginia,—and Mr. Randolph, my old adversary being now in London, are all great obstructions at present to the relief of my oppressed people. And the committee, on these accounts, think this a very improper time to make any application in their favour. As Dr. Stennet has a great deal of influence in court, I gave him, last night, a particular account of the rise and progress of the dissenting interest in Virginia, and the restraints and embarrassments the people laboured under from the government. He was very much moved with the account, and promised me his utmost influence in their favour.—He had been yesterday waiting upon the Duke of Newcastle, to condole the death of his brother, and told me that it was the most tragical scene he ever saw. Dined at Mr. Wm. Stead's in company with Mr. Cornthwaite, his minister, a Seventh-day Baptist Socinian. Had an interview a few days ago with Mr. Grant, minister in Northamptonshire. He has no learning, but is a very solid, judicious, and pious man, and I am told popular and successful in his ministry.

Sunday, March 17.—Preached A. M., for Mr. Lawson at Founder's hall, upon Luke xiii. 24, and the hearers were attentive, though neither they nor myself, very solemn. Preached P.M. at Unicorn Yard, for Mr. Thomson, on Psalm xcvii. 1, and acted the orator with a tolerable grace. Preached an evening lecture on Jeremiah xxxi. 18–20, for Mr. Mitchell, at Mr. Hitkin's meeting-house, and the sight of the auditory, the most crowded I have seen in London, cast me into an agreeable ferment, and constrained me to pray in the pulpit for Divine assistance; and I hope I was answered, for I had more than usual freedom and solemnity.

[*Some wanting.*]

Tuesday, March 19.—Went to the Amsterdam coffee-house among the Baptist and Independent ministers, where I enjoy most satisfaction. Received the thanks of the governors of the charity school, in Bartholomew's Close, for my sermon there, which were presented to me in a very respectful manner by Dr. Guyse, as their deputy. Though it be hard to repress the workings of vanity, even in a creature so unworthy as I am, under so much applause, yet I think my heart rises in sincere gratitude to God for advancing me from a mean family, and utter obscurity, into some importance in the world, and giving me so many advantages of public usefulness. Indeed I hardly think there is a greater instance of this in the present age. Alas! that I do not better improve my opportunities. Went to Hamlin's coffee-house among the Presbyterians, where they are generally very shy and unsociable to me. They have universally, as far as I can learn, rejected all tests of orthodoxy, and require their candidates, at their ordination, to declare only their belief of the Scriptures. Mr. Prior, with the appearance of great uneasiness, told me that he had heard we would admit none into the ministry without subscribing to the Westminister Confession; and that this report would hinder all our success among the friends of liberty. I replied that we allowed the candidate to mention his objections against any article in the Confession, and the judicature judged whether the articles objected against were essential to Christianity; and if they judged they were not, they would admit the candidate, notwithstanding his objections. He seemed to think that we were such rigid Calvinists that we would not admit an Arminian into communion, &c. I proposed to converse with him another time for his satisfaction. Alas! for the laxness that prevails here among the Presbyterians. *Quantum O mutati!* Spent yesterday evening with Mr. Mauduit, who had been waiting upon the House of Commons to obtain a repeal of a clause in a bill, that might be injurious to the dissenters, though levelled against the Jacobites; and he succeeded; the members of Parliament, especially now before the election, being very unwilling to disoblige the dissenters. The court is all in confusion about choosing one to fill up Mr. Pelham's place; and the king is much perplexed. He says he hoped to spend his old days in peace, but all his peace is buried in Mr. Pelham's grave. As I have received no letters, as yet, from Hanover, I am extremely anxious about my dearest creature, my family, and congregation. Did they know my uneasiness, they would write to me, I am sure.

Sunday, March 24.—Preached for two gentlemen of very different sentiments, Dr. Guyse and Dr. Benson; at the former's meeting-house, A. M., on Matthew xxii. 37, 38, and Romans viii. 7; at the latter's, on Psalm xcvii. 1. Dr. Benson's people make a very polite appearance; but I could see little signs of solemnity among them; and alas! I neither had nor thought it proper to indulge a passionate solemnity. Last Thursday evening, I preached a lecture at Depthford, on Isaiah lxvi. 1, 2, to a number of poor, honest people. Lodged at Mr. Salway's there.

Called in my return at Deckam, and visited Dr. Milner, who keeps a boarding school of about twenty boys. He is a gentleman of good powers and extensive learning, especially of the classic kind. I find he is the author of the large grammars of the Latin and Greek, which were so serviceable to me, when at learning. Preached yesterday P. M., for Dr. Stennet, in a small congregation of Seven-day Baptists, who seem very serious people.

[*Some wanting.*]

April 7, 1754.—We have had most surprising success in our mission; which, notwithstanding the languor of my nature, I cannot review without passionate emotions. From the best information of our friends, and our own observation upon our arrival here, we could not raise our hopes above £300; but we have already got about £1200. Our friends in America cannot hear the news with the same surprise, as they do not know the difficulties we have had to encounter; but to me it appears the most signal interposition of Providence I ever saw. Preached last Sunday A. M., for Dr. Benson, and P. M., for Mr. Gibbons, and yesterday for do. I have sent a petition to Virginia, at the direction of the committee, to be subscribed by the dissenters there, and transmitted to be presented to the King in council.

Sunday, April 14.—The same objects occur, and the same business engages my attention, with little variety. Last Sunday, I went to Hackney, and heard my good friend, Mr. Hunt, on these words, " Ye are brought nigh by the blood of Christ." With pleasure received the sacrament, administered in a form I have not yet seen. Preached in the afternoon in the pulpit where Dr. Bates and Mr. Henry once stood, and found some freedom, (1 John iii. 2.) Lodged at my kind friend's, Mr. Bowles, and offered a few extempore thoughts to the family at his request. Isaiah, xlv. 22. Waited upon Lord Leven, Judge Foster, Sir Joseph Hankley, &c. The business of our mission goes on with surprising success. Spent the evening with Dr. Benson, and had a friendly dispute with him about subscribing articles of faith. Had an interview with Mr. Prior, and endeavoured to satisfy him about the catholicism of our College. Received a letter from my dear brother Mr. Todd, which informed me of the welfare of my spouse and family. The very sight of it threw me into a passionate ferment, that did not soon subside. O how kind is God to me and mine! To-day I preached for Mr. Towle, A. M., Genesis xix. " Escape" &c., and P. M., for Mr. Kippis, Matthew xxv. ult. Had an interview with Mr. Walker, a minister lately come from New England, who is no friend to Mr. Tennent, but has been representing his character in an injurious light.

Sunday, April 21.—Preached at Peckham, (a village about three miles from London), for Dr. Milner, on Psalm xcvii. 1, and 1 John, xxiii. But I had not much freedom or solemnity, though I found some of the people were pleased with the discourses. Lodged at Dr. Milner's; but as he was not at home, I spent the time in conversation with his son, a Doctor of Physic, an ingenious philosophical youth.

Sunday, April 28.—Preached for Dr. Allen, at Dr. Earle's meeting-house, on 2 Cor. iii. 18, with much oratorical freedom; but alas! not with much Christian solemnity and affection. My address caught the attention of the auditory; but I am afraid the truth had not a proportionable impression on their hearts. The old, good, stern Dr. Earle was one of my hearers, and cordially expressed his approbation. Went immediately to assist Mr. Oswald at his sacrament, and served two tables, and communicated myself according to the mode of the Church of Scotland. Preached P. M. on John xii. 32, 33, with some freedom. But amid my incessant hurries, I had but little concern about my own immortal state. My nature is quite fatigued and exhausted with the labours of my mission in this vast city; and I am afraid my constitution will be broken with them. I was last week pleasingly entertained with an artificial aviary, &c.

Newcastle-upon-Tyne, May 7, 1754.—The General Assembly in Scotland drawing near, and the hurries and confusions of the election of members of Parliament for London rendering the additional applications we might otherwise have made inexpedient at the time, we set out for Edinburgh in a post-chaise, last Friday. This method of travelling is very expeditious, as we have change of horses at every twenty or fifteen miles. We have been under the special guardianship of Providence, both by sea and land, ever since we left home; but never more remarkably than in this journey. We were twice in the most imminent danger of death; last Saturday, near Caxton, by one of the horses becoming unruly, and his running and kicking, breaking the shafts, harnessing, &c., all to pieces; and yesterday, by the hostler suddenly pulling back the top of the chaise while we were in it, which caught Mr. Tennent's head and pulled him back with such violence that he was very much strained, and the blood gushed out of his nose. Providence, no doubt, has some important design in these alarming trials. May they prove seasonable mortifications before extensive success, which might otherwise exalt us above measure! 'Tis an honour to be employed in public service; and I have cause of grateful joy rather than complaints. But I never engaged in such a series of wasting fatigues and dangers as our present mission is attended with. And what painful anxieties about by wife, family, congregation, and the success of our applications, have disturbed my breast, this heart only knows, which has felt them. I have often walked the tedious crowded streets of London from morning to evening, till my nature has been quite exhausted, and I have been hardly able to move a limb. It was but seldom that I could relax myself in conversation with a friend, by reason of incessant hurries: and when I have had an opportunity, my spirits have been so spent, that I was but a dull companion. My hurries have also denied me the pleasure of a curious traveller, in taking a careful view of the numerous curiosities of nature and art in London. But all these disadvantages have been more than balanced by the success we have had, having collected about £1700, notwithstanding the ungenerous opposition made against us by the pretended friends of liberty and catholicism, which is matter of the utmost astonishment to our friends as well as ourselves. 'Tis but little that so useless a creature can do for God, during the short day of life; but to be instrumental in laying a foundation of extensive benefit to mankind, not only in the present but in future generations, is a most animating prospect: and if my usefulness should thus survive me, I shall live to future ages in the most valuable respects.

We passed through a great many villages on our way to Newcastle, but none very remarkable. This town is considerably large, and has six dissenting ministers in it, viz., Messrs. Ogilvie, Athrin, Arthur, Murray, Rogerson, and Lothian. The two last are colleagues, and have imbibed the Arminian and Socinian sentiments. Mr. Lothian is a very smart, ingenious young gentleman, and I am told a very popular preacher. The other four, especially Mr. Ogilvie, appear very affectionate, serious and good men. They were all unanimous to promote the business of our mission, and treated us with uncommon respect. We are going to the General Assembly with great discouragement, as we expect a powerful opposition; but the Lord our God is in the heavens: he doth whatsoever he pleaseth.—Dined last week at my affectionate father's, Mr. Price, with Mr. Thomas Morgan, of Langhore, Carmaethanshire, in South Wales: a very agreeable young minister, who preaches generally to about two thousand poor people. We agreed to correspond with each other.

Thursday, May 9.—Arrived safe in Edinburgh. Passed by Preston Pans, where Col. Gardiner was killed. Saw his seat, and the field of battle, which struck me with a melancholy horror. Passed through Berwick upon Tweed, a considerable town. Scotland makes a better appearance on the way that we travelled than I expected: though there are a great many of the poorest huts that ever I saw. My mind is perplexed about the success of our mission here, and all appears gloomy before me. My spirits are generally low, though I feel a kind of stupid serenity of mind.

Friday, May 10.—Visited the Rev. Mr. Webster, who received us with great candour and friendship, and gave us his best advice about our design. We find it is likely to be difficult to succeed with the General Assembly, not only by reason of the opposition that may be occasioned by Mr. Cross's malignant letter, but also on account of the three general collections that have been successively made of late, and the application expected this year from Holland. We waited on Dr. Cumming, who had received one of Mr. Cross's letters, and showed him our credentials, &c., to remove or anticipate his objections; and from his professed benevolence to the design, after reading them, we had reason to hope we had succeeded. Visited Mr. Robertson, Professor of the Oriental Languages, who showed us uncommon friendship, and seemed to know the heart of a stranger. He introduced us to Mr. Hamilton, the Professor of Divinity, a simple, candid gentleman, who was friendly to our design. Took a view of the Royal Infirmary, Harriot's Hospital, &c., which are stately buildings.

Thursday, May 16.—We have visited Professor Hamilton, a very modest, pious man, Principal Goudie, Mr. George Wishart, the favourite preacher of the polite in this city, Mr. James Watson, an affectionate minister, Mr. Johnston, minister in the Castle, Mr. Lindsay of Leith, and some ministers whom we have occasionally seen. They all treat us with great respect. Last Monday dined with the Lord Provost, and his lordship gave us a very friendly reception, and promised us all the services in his power. Last Sunday heard Mr. Kinlough in the forenoon, who gave us an excellent lecture and sermon; and Dr. Cumming in the afternoon, on the Preface to the Lord's Prayer, who preached pretty much in the strain of our fashionable moderns. Supped with our excellent friend Mr. Webster. Heard Mr. Clog open the Synod of Lothian and Tweedale on Tuesday on these words, "Lord, I am thy servant," &c. His sermon was simple and honest. Waited on the Synod, and was surprised and grieved to see so much altercation about the place of Clerk to the Synod, which is here a lucrative post. In the heat of the debate, one Mr. Hume, a young minister, flung out some intolerably severe reflections on the Presbytery of Dunkeith, on account of their prosecuting one Mr. Logan, a candidate, for false doctrine. He said that the Presbytery of Dunkeith had been upon the side of inhumanity and persecution in their treatment of as worthy a youth as ever honoured the cloth, and he was glad to find them now upon the side of humanity, though in the meantime of injustice. The Presbytery immediately entered a prosecution against him, and it raised a prodigious ferment in the Synod. But at length the parties withdrew with a committee, and at length Mr. Hume gave them satisfaction, and submitted to an open rebuke from the Moderator. Alas! there appears but little of the spirit of serious Christianity among the young clergy. The Patronage Act is like to be ruinous to the Church of Scotland; for of nine hundred and eighty parishes in it, about seven hundred are in the gift of the king, *i.e.* of the prime minister, and therefore they are used as engines of ministerial power, tempting the clergy to cringe to the court, and introduce mercenaries into the churches. Yesterday preached an evening sermon for Mr. Webster on Jeremiah xxxi. 18, 19, 20. Sundry ministers were present. We have taken a view of the Castle here, which is amazingly fortified by nature and art, and has the command of the whole city, and could soon lay it in ruins. We have been busied yesterday and to-day in writing an answer to Mr. Cross's letter; which we find is like to have a bad effect. There is one Mr. Logan here, who shows us great respect. He has been a preacher for many years, and preaches sometimes still; but has never accepted of a congregation, and therefore has not been ordained. He seems to be an excellent, holy, humble man.

Sunday, May 19.—Preached in the Tolbooth church to a very crowded auditory, on Jeremiah xxxi. 33. I had but little tender sense of the subject; and yet, to my surprise, I found afterwards that many were greatly pleased and edified; only some did not like my using notes. Preached P. M. for Mr. Wishart in the Trone church on Rev. i. 7, with a little more freedom to a very gay and crowded auditory, and afterwards supped with him, who treated me very kindly. Yesterday went to Lord Drummore's country seat to wait upon him. I was pleased with his motto on the side of his house, as well suited to a rural seat.

——————————— Seize
The plough, and greatly independent live.

Above which was written,

Deo, Patriæ, Amicis.

Last night received a packet from Hanover, the very sight of which raised my passions to such a ferment, that they are not yet subsided. Alas! I find my dearest has been very ill; but is happily recovered. I am afraid my friends conceal the worst from me, lest it should make me uneasy. What painful anxieties I feel about her! Last Friday visited Mr. Gilbert Elliot, a lawyer, who is also a member of the Assembly, and has received a letter to our prejudice from his brother in Philadelphia. He promised us that he would review it, and if there were any objections that required an answer, he would inform us of them. Waited also on the Rev. Mr. Kay, who was very friendly, though he had seen Mr. Cross's letter.

Thursday, May 23.—The General Assembly met. The Lord Commissioner went in state from his house to the church, attended by a great number of the nobility, and the streets were lined with ranks of soldiers. The crowd was very great, both within the church and without. The sermon was preached by Mr. Webster on Psal. cxxxvii. 5, 6, and a very masterly, oratorical discourse it was; delivered with a manly boldness and fluency. Professor Hamilton was chosen Moderator, *nem. con.*, and then the King's commission to the Lord Commissioner was read, which was in Latin: and also the King's letter to the General Assembly. Then the Commissioner made a speech, which the Moderator answered in a very handsome manner. Then followed a long debate about the time when they should determine a debate between Mr. Edmunstone and the Rev. Mr. Hindman about the Clerkship. The Earl of Marchmont made a very animated speech upon the occasion.— Mr. Tennent being confined by a sprained foot, I waited yesterday on the Earl of Marchmont; and in the evening we both waited on the Lord Commissioner, where we also found the Earl of Findlater. They read our credentials, &c. and treated us kindly. Saw our dear friends, Messrs. McLaurin, Gillies, John Erskine, &c., whose conversation has been very refreshing to us.

Saturday, May 25.—Attended upon the General Assemby, when the debate about the Clerkship was determined in favour of Mr. Edmunstone. Sundry long speeches were made upon the occasion by Dr. Cumming, Mr. Tremble, Mr. Trail, Mr. Mc Clagen, Prof. Murryson, Prof. Lumsden, Lord Drummóre, the Earl of Breadalbine, the Earl of Marchmont, Mr. Webster, Mr. Gordon, &c., and most of them spoke with surprising readiness, pertinency, and argument. Yesterday we waited on the Committee for Bills, where the petition from the Trustees was read, and it was agreed that it should be transmitted to the General Assembly, with the opinion of the Committee in its favour, which is a happy omen. To-day it was determined that the matter should be heard on Monday next. We find Mr. Cross's letter put into sundry hands, and sundry are prejudiced against Mr. Tennent, on account of his Nottingham Sermon, which is industriously spread here.

Sunday, May 26.—Preached A. M. in the Cannon-Gate Church, for Mr. Watson, when a great number of ministers were present. My subject was 1 John, iii. 2, and blessed be God, I was not dashed, but had considerable freedom and solemnity. In the afternoon, heard Mr. Ballantine, who surprised me with a torrent of strong sense, poured out extempore, without interruption, from beginning to end. I think Scotland may boast a greater number of good speakers, than any country I have been in, and I believe their accustoming themselves to speak extempore, has been of great service to them in it. Drank tea at the Rev. Mr. Blair's, in company with Mr. Shaw, Professor of Divinity in St. Andrews, &c., who conversed with apparent friendship about the design of our mission, and proposed that a part of the collection should be applied to the support of poor pious youth for the ministry, which motion he promised to make in the Assembly. Supped with the Rev. Mr. Gardine, who intimated that he expected the Assembly would be divided in their sentiments about our petition, according as they were friends or adversaries to Mr. Whitefield, which gave us very alarming apprehensions, because his friends are the minority.

Monday, May 27.—Last night was so full of anxieties about the success of our application, that I could not sleep. To-day the petition from the Trustees and the Synod of New York, and our credentials, were read, and Mr. Lumisden, Professor of Divinity at Aberdeen, got up to speak. As I knew not whether he was a friend or foe, my heart palpitated when I saw him rise; but I soon found he was a hearty friend. He made an ingenious speech upon the importance of a learned ministry— the necessity of the College of New Jersey for that end—the duty of the General Assembly to promote such Institutions in general, and especially among the Presbyterians in those Colonies, " who (says he) are part of ourselves, having adopted the same standard of doctrine, worship, and government with this church." Mr. McLagan got up next, and spoke to the same purpose, and upon a motion being made that the petitions should be agreed to, there was not one objection through the whole house, but it passed without a vote. This was a matter of pleasing surprise, and I could not forbear darting up my grateful praises to Heaven, for so remarkable an interposition of Providence. A great number of the nobility and gentry were present, (the Duke of Argyle, the Earl of Breadalbine, Lord Drummore, the Marquis of Lothian, Sir George Preston, Mr. Dundas, &c. &c.), and we knew there were sundry among the laity and clergy, that were not friendly to our application, but they did not mutter a word. The collection for the German emigrants in Pennsylvania, I am informed, met with opposition, and perhaps this was the first petition of the kind, that ever passed *nem. con.*, though I hardly think there was ever a greater appearance of opposition. The approbation of the General Assembly will be attended with many happy consequences, particularly it will recommend our College to the world, and wipe off the odium from the Synod of New York, as a parcel of schismatics. It must, no doubt, be mortifying to Mr. Cross, to find we have succeeded, notwithstanding his ungenerous, clandestine efforts against us. Dined with the Marquis of Lothian, at Lord Ross's, who treated me with all the kindness and freedom of a friend. Lady Ross appears a sincere, good woman. Went with the Marquis in his coach to the Committee appointed to draw up an act and recommendation for a national collection; but they left it to a sub-committee, consisting of Dr. Cumming, Mr. Webster, Professor Shaw, Mr. McLagan, and Bailie Ingram. Received a packet from Virginia, in which was a most tender, ingenious letter from my dearest, which I could not but read over and over, with the most passionate emotions. How good is God to me in preserving her life, so important to my happiness, notwithstanding of threatening sickness. There is one circumstance with regard to our application to the General Assembly which seems remarkably providential, viz: that Mr. Yair, minister of Camfire, who intended to present a petition for the Salsburgers, and which would have interfered with ours, did not arrive till last Saturday, when ours had been presented.

Thursday, May 30.—Waited on the Society for Propagating Christian Knowledge, of which the Marquis of Lothian is President, and, at their request, gave them our best advice about the best method of conducting the mission among the Indians. They also drew up a letter recommending the College of New Jersey to be annexed to the General Assembly. Dined with his grace, the Lord Commissioner, where we had the most splendid entertainment I have seen.

Sunday, June 2.—Preached A. M. for Mr. Gardine, in Lady Easter's, on Luke xiii. 24, and P. M. at South Leith for Mr. Walker, on Hebrews vi. 7, 8. I had some freedom at Leith, but much afraid lest so shocking a subject should give offence; and yet I could not get my mind kept from it. Lodged with Mr. Walker, who is a most humble judicious man, and I am told one of the best preachers in Scotland. He is shortly to be removed to the High Church in Edinburgh.

Monday, June 10.—Preached yesterday A. M. for Mr. Kinlock in the High Church before the Lord Provost and the magistrates, on 2 Cor. iv. 18. But my head was confused and my heart languid. Preached P. M. for Mr. Glen, in the Little Kirk on Psalm xcvii. 1, with much more vivacity; though without a tender solemnity. Last Friday spent a few hours with Lady Francis Gardiner, who gave me an account of many of her trials and deliverances. She seems to mind nothing but religion, and hardly rises out of her bed, excepting to go to public worship. Last Saturday, dined with Dr. Cumming; and had sundry hours of free conversation with him. Informed him of the opposition of the dissenters in Virginia, and solicited his interest with the Duke of Argyle; which he freely promised me. Spent an evening with Mr. Ramsay and lady Hume, who are a pattern of humility and piety in high life. Mr. Robertson, professor of the Oriental languages, is a pious learned man, and I am often conversant with him. Last Thursday preached in the College Church on Isaiah lxvi. 1, 2, with freedom and solemnity. I find I begin to grow popular here, especially among the religious. I spent an evening at Mr. M'Lagan's in a society of agreeable young gentlemen, who meet for singing hymns and instructive conversation.

Saturday, January 15th, 1754.—I left Edinburgh the day before yesterday in company with my excellent friend Wm. Ramsay, Esq. Passed through Lithgow, a considerable town on the way to Glasgow, where there is a stately old palace, now going to ruin. Called at the Rev. Mr. John Adair's of Falkirk, who insisted so earnestly upon my staying till Monday, and preaching for him, that I could not refuse. He is a most judicious pious minister, and a friend to the liberty of mankind in opposition to the exorbitant claims of church power which the high-flying clergy have run into. His wife, a great-grand-daughter of the famous Mr. David Dickson, is a gentlewoman of uncommon sense and piety. In short, I have hardly been so happy in conversation since I left home. I met with more Christian friendship in Edinburgh than any where in Great Britain. There is too general a decay of experimental and practical religion; and yet there is a considerable number of pious people in the city. I preached twice again in the college-kirk, and I have had repeated information, that my languid ministrations have been remarkably blessed to many. I have been at Culross visiting Mr. Erskine. He really exceeds the high character I had heard of him for a hard student, a growing genius, and uncommon zeal for the public good. In short, he promises much service to the Church of Scotland.—I find a great number of the clergy and laity have of late carried church-power to an extravagant height, deny to individuals the right of judging for themselves, and insist upon absolute universal obedience to all the determinations of the General Assembly. I heard sundry speeches in the House on this head, which really surprised me. The nobility and gentry who are lay-elders, are generally high-flyers: and have encroached upon the rights of the people, especially as to the choice of their own ministers. Violent settlements are enjoined by the authority of the General Assembly, and there is no prospect of a redress.—There is a piece published under the title of the Ecclesiastical Characteristics, ascribed to one Mr. Weatherspoon, a young minister. It is a burlesque upon the high-flyers under the ironical name of *moderate men:* and I think the humour is nothing inferior to Dean Swift. Mr. Tho. Walker has also written well on the subject. Sundry overtures were brought into the General Assembly: particularly—for examining into the qualifications of ruling elders—for re-examining ministers, licensed or ordained by other churches, before they are admitted into this—altering the form of deposition according to the nature of the case, and making a distinction between deposition from the office of the ministry, and deposition from the exercise of it in this church as an establishment. I found by sundry speeches on the last overture, that even Dr. Owen or Dr. Doddridge would have been deposed, had they lived in the Church of Scotland.

Mr. Tennent set out for Glasgow, and thence to Ireland on the 1st inst., to attend on the General Synod there; and I am left solitary and sad to take a tour through the principal towns in England. I am generally so extremely low-spirited, and full of anxieties, that I can hardly live. This disables me from pursuing my mission with proper vigour and alacrity. My dear wife and family dwell upon my heart night and day; and I am uneasy about my congregation lest they should not be well supplied in my absence.

Monday, June 15.—Was conducted by Mr. Adams on my way to Glasgow; and I have rarely parted with a friend with so much reluctance. Yesterday preached for him to his congregation, which is very numerous (about three thousand) A. M. on Jer. xxxi. 18—20; P. M. on Heb. vi. 8; in the evening on Josh. xxiv.—"Choose ye this day whom ye will serve." In the two last sermons, I was helped to address myself solemnly and convictively to impenitents; but I could see no appearances of any promising impressions. Mr. Young, assistant to Mr. Adams, is a man of great seriousness and extensive reading. Passed through Kirkuntilloch, a small town where Mr. Erskine was formerly settled; but Mr. Stoddard, the present minister, being abroad, I had not the happiness of an interview with him. Passed by Kilsythe, where good Mr. Mobe was minister, and the very sight of a place, where the power and grace of God was so illustriously displayed, solemnized my mind.

Friday, July 5.—Lodged in Glasgow at Mr. Archibald Ingram's, one of the magistrates of the city, where I was treated with uncommon hospitality. I staid in Glasgow about ten days, and I never was in a place where I received so many evidences of public respect. I spent Sunday evening in company with the Lord Provost and the other magistrates, who met on purpose to put honour upon me. They conferred upon me the usual ceremony, the freedom of the city, and conferred the same honour upon Mr. Tennent and Mr. Burr. In Glasgow there is a considerable number of serious people; and they are very happy in their ministers. Mr. McLaurin is a most affectionate, public-spirited gentleman, of a most facetious turn in conversation, and an uncommon genius, though his modesty denies the world the advantage of it. He has a surprising dexterity of introducing into prayer all the remarkable occurrences of conversation. Mr. Gillies is a most lively image of Christian simplicity, and is uncommonly zealous and laborious in his ministry. Mr. John Hamilton is a man of clear judgment, and a graceful address. I heard him preach an excellent sermon on the love of God in sending his Son to be a propitiation. Mr. Cross is a rational, argumentative preacher, without much pathos or solemnity. Mr. James Stirling is a serious, judicious man, more fit for the closet or the pulpit, than for conversation. Mr. Craff, whom I had not opportunity of seeing, is the favourite of the polite. Professor Leehman is a very modest, bashful gentleman, but very accurate and judicious, and his candour is acknowledged by all, though suspected by some of verging towards Arminianism. I spent near a day in his company; and he showed me all the curiosities of the College. The library-room is large, but not well filled. The most striking curiosity that I saw was a collection of pictures lately imported from France. One was the picture of the dead body of Christ taken off the cross and carrying to the sepulchre. The prints of the nails in his hands and feet, the stab of the spear in his side, the effusion of the blood, &c. were so lively, that they unavoidably excited a sort of popish devotion in me. I preached six times whilst in Glasgow; thrice for Mr. Gillies on Jer. xxxi. 18—20, Jer. xxx. 32—"I will be their God," &c.; and on Luke ii.—"Behold this child," &c.; once for Mr. Hamilton on Isaiah lxvi. 2. Mr. Hill holds his sacrament in the Baronry church; there were two sermons within and without on Saturday and Monday; and a great many sermons in the tent on Sunday, one of which I preached on Rev. i. 7, on which text I had also preached on Saturday. There were twenty-three tables, two of which I served. The assembly at the tent was also very numerous. There appeared a general attention; but no great affection or solemnity. I had an opportunity once more of communicating; but alas! I felt but little of the fervour of devotion; and in all my ministrations in Glasgow, I perceived more of the man than the Christian, and I could not see the same assurances of success as in Edinburgh. One thing is remarkably commendable in this city, viz. the conduct of the magistrates in general, who very punctually attend on public worship, not only on Sundays, but week-days. While in Glasgow, I was very much indisposed with a lingering fever, and so languid and low spirited that I was hardly fit for any of the purposes of active life. Sometimes I was afraid I should never see my native country, nor enjoy the company of my earthly all. I found, to my agreeable surprise that Governor Dinwiddie had kindly recommended me to his friends, particularly to the Provost, his brother, and Mr. M'Culloch, his brother-in-law. I spent a night with the former, and he and his family showed me the most friendly respect. I was also a night with Mr. M'Culloch, at Cambuslang, the obscure village so famous for the late extraordinary revival of religion. He is a humble, holy minister of Christ, not famed for popularity; which is a strong presumption that the late religious commotion there was not the effect of oratory, but of Divine power. His wife is an uncommonly judicious, pious woman; and his only son, a youth about fourteen, is very affectionate, and parted with me with tears. I preached there on " Neither is he that planteth anything," &c., and I endeavoured to adapt my discourse to the circumstances of the people. I had not much sensible freedom, and I could not see any uncommon signs of approbation or success among the people; only they heard with gravity and attention. The next day they sent a messenger to Glasgow, with a letter to me, signed by near thirty in the congregation, thanking me for my sermon, and requesting a copy of it to be published, or at least for their own use. The last part of the proposal, I consented to. The repeated solicitations I have met with in America, in London, Edinburgh, Glasgow, &c., to publish some of my sermons, have made me think seriously of finishing and publishing a collection of them, if Providence ever grant me a return. Perhaps they may be of service in places far remote from the sphere of my usual labours. There are six churches in Glasgow. The New Church is a fine building, but not yet finished. The High Church is an ancient structure, very large, and contains three distinct congregations under one roof. I had a long conversation with Mr. M'Culloch upon the affairs of the dissenters in Virginia; particularly their oppressions from the government. I have reason to believe that Governor Dinwiddie would favour them, were it not so opposite to his interest. Mr. M'Culloch consulted me about a donation of £200 for propagating the gospel among the Indians, &c. Having stayed in Glasgow about ten days, I returned through Edinburgh; saw sundry of my dear friends, and preached on Sunday for Mr. Webster, A. M., and for Mr. Geo. Lindsay of Leith, P. M.; in the first discourse I was fervent and solemn, in the second languid and exhausted. In Edinburgh, there are sixteen ministers; and I think all the churches but two are collegiate. In Leith there are two churches and three ministers. I had the honour of the Earl of Leven and his family for my hearers last Sunday.

Monday, July 1.—Parted with my friends in Edinburgh, and as many of them, particularly Mr. Hogg and family, are very dear to me, I have scarcely felt such strong emotions of friendship since I left home. Rode to Haddington, about twelve miles, in company with one Mr. Dixon, a serious, devout man, from Edinburgh, who assisted my judgment about the propriety and lawfulness of joining in the sacrament with Mr. Gillespie, who was deposed by the General Assembly. His excellent friend, Professor Robertson, conducted me about six miles. He is one of the best linguists, especially in the oriental languages, in Great Britain, has an insatiable thirst for knowledge, and has travelled far to gratify it. His soul is formed for friendship. Lodged in Haddington, at Provost Dixon's, who treated me with hospitality. Had an interview with the Rev. Mr. Stedman, one of the ministers of the town; who, I find, is one of the high-flyers; but he promised me his friendship in the business of our mission.

Tuesday, July 2.—Passed through a well-improved country, beautifully variegated with hills and valleys, and the sea frequently in sight, and arrived in Berwick in the evening.

Wednesday, July 3.—Waited on Mr. Somerville, and Mr. Turner, ministers in Berwick; and proposed the business of my mission. The former has given up his charge, partly on account of his indisposition, and partly on account of the divisions in his congregation, occasioned by one that was formerly his assistant. The latter has but a small part of his former congregation, the rest having chosen his assistant, Mr. Monteith, for their minister, and rejected him because he would not receive him for his co-pastor. These reasons discouraged him from soliciting collections for me. I applied to Mr. Monteith, who gave me some ground to hope he would raise a public collection. I went to visit Mr. Thompson, minister of Spittal, about a mile from Berwick, but could not see him. However, I waited on Mr. Shatton, the principal man in his congregation, and secured his interest, and wrote to Mr. Thompson, begging he would endeavour to have a congregational collection. Berwick had two large congregations of dissenters, formerly; but they are sadly weakened by their divisions. The place is surrounded with high walls and mounts, and has sundry garrisons. The ruins of the old castle are very majestic. The bridge is near as long as that of London, and contains fifteen arches.

Thursday, July 4.—Set out for Alnwick. Rode about ten miles on the sea-shore, which is a very good road when it is not high water. Saw Holy-Island about three miles off, where is a castle, that makes a considerable appearance at a distance. Alnwick is a pretty large town, with sundry very good houses, a majestic old castle, of great dimensions, surrounded with a wall. There are two dissenting ministers in it; Mr. Sayr and Mr. Waugh. The latter was not at home; and I had no other way of communicating my mission to him but by leaving a letter for him, against his return. I waited on Mr. Sayr, who appears a judicious old gentleman. He proposed to make a public collection. Wrote to Mr. Buckham, minister of Branton, requesting the same favour.

Friday, July 5.—As I passed through Morpeth, I called upon Mr. Atchinson, the dissenting minister, who seemed willing to make a collection in his place. When I came to Newcastle in the evening, I found a comedy called the Careless Husband was to be acted, and as I apprehended I should not be known, and consequently give no offence, I went to gratify my curiosity. But the entertainment was short of my expectation.

Saturday, July 6.—Waited on Mr. Rogerson, Mr. Lothian, Mr. Atkin, &c. I found they had affected nothing in favour of our mission; but they promised to concur with me now. My indisposition of body, the dissipation of mind occasioned by constant company, the fatigues and anxieties that attend the prosecution of my mission, and my solicitude about my dear family, and American friends, have so weakened my body and depressed my spirits, that I am hardly able to walk the streets, or keep up my part in conversation. I am often so mopish and absent in mind, that I am heartily ashamed of myself, as making a very ridiculous figure. What would I now give to spend an hour in my study, or in the endearments of society, with my Chara, my earthly all! Were I more strongly actuated with the impulses of a public spirit, my labour would be more tolerable; but, alas, that languishes in the present depression of my mind. I am plagued, amid this languor, with the vigorous insurrections of sin. I hardly know a truth attested by such long uninterrupted experience as this, that no change of climate, no public character, no exercises, no company, and in a word, nothing that ever I have tried, can extirpate the principle or suppress the workings of sin in this depraved heart. Spent the evening with Michael Munzies, Esq., a very pious gentleman, who was once a lawyer.

Sunday, July 7.—Preached A.M. for Mr. Ogilvie, who was out of town; on Isaiah lxvi. 2, and had some sense of the subject. In the afternoon for Mr. Rogerson, on Psalm xcvii. 1, to a very gay congregation, with some freedom; but my apprehensions that the peculiarities of the gospel would be disagreeable to their taste, laid me under a painful restraint; lest their being offended should prejudice my mission. Indeed, I am puzzled to know what is duty in this case. Spent the evening at Mr. Louthian's, who is a very friendly ingenious man; but has unhappily imbibed the sentiments of Dr. Foster, and Mr. Taylor of Norwich. I had a long dispute with him, upon original sin. I found that the principal reason of our difference was, that those secret tendencies and workings of the heart; and that languor in religion, which I looked upon to be sinful, he thought entirely innocent, and apprehended that man by complaining of these, complained that they were men and not angels; and murmured that they were placed so low in the scale of being; and he was of Mr. Pope's mind—

> "In pride, in reasoning pride, our error lies;
> All quit their sphere, and rush into the skies.
> Aspiring to be gods, if angels fell;
> Aspiring to be angels, men rebel."

Friday, July 12.—I have been busy in waiting upon sundry persons to solicit their benefactions; and I have got about thirty guineas in the English congregation. The ministers of the Scotch congregations, which are five in number, are very friendly, but their people are poor. They intend to collect what they can, and transmit it after me to London. Yesterday, the Right Honourable Lord Ravensworth coming to town, hearing of the design of my mission, sent for me; and I had a long conversation with his lordship about it. He found fault with our not first applying to the government, &c., &c.; and I was afraid from his forming so many cavils that he would oppose. But as I took my leave of his lordship, he complimented me with five guineas.

Saturday, July 13.—Went in company with Mr. Munzies to wait on James Bowes, Esq., member of Parliament for the county of Durham. He is a gentleman of a vast estate; and he took an ambitious pleasure, like Hezekiah, to show me all his glory; and indeed, I never have seen so fine a country-seat in any part of Great Britain. Here a wilderness exhibits all the rude beauties of uncultivated nature. There stately rows of trees disposed by art, appear in regular uniformity. Here artificial mounts rise, and valleys descend. There verdant walks and pastures open far to the view. Here rises a pile of buildings in the antique form; and then an obelisk lifts its head on high. He showed me his plate, a part of which is gilt with gold, and the value of the whole is computed to be £17,000 sterling. But alas! he gave me but five guineas. He is of an ancient family, famous in the days of William the Conqueror. He advised me to wait upon the Bishop of Durham, which afforded me a great deal of anxiety, lest I should take a wrong step.

Sunday, July 14.—Preached A. M. for Mr. Atkin, on Jeremiah xxxi. 18, 20, and P. M. for Mr. Louthian, on 2 Corinthians, iv. 18, and in the evening for Mr. Ogilvie, on Romans vi. 13 ; the last to a very crowded auditory, and with great freedom, and appearance of success. Received a packet from Hanover, which raised all my friendly passions into a ferment. I had a very soft, ingenious letter from my Chara ; and her generous self-denial in not desiring me to hasten home till I have finished my mission, gave me an agreeable surprise, and made me reflect with shame upon my own impatience. I find my favourite friend Mr. Rodgers (who still dwells on my heart) has been universally acceptable, and hopefully successful in Hanover. And that my honest brother Mr. Wright, is extensively serviceable in and about Cumberland. May God take to him his great power, and reign !

Wednesday, July 15.—Rode to Durham, and took a view of the stately Cathedral there. The art of painting in glass, which is lost among the moderns, discovers its beauties on the windows in sundry pieces of Scripture history. I am still puzzled whether to wait upon the Bishop or not.

Tuesday, July 16.—Determined to wait on the Bishop, and his lordship gave me a condescending reception. He particularly inquired whether the Church of England had any share in the management of our College—complained of the intolerant principles of the dissenters in New England—asked me if I had waited upon the Archbishop of Canterbury, or obtained the approbation of the Society for Propagating the Gospel in Foreign Parts ; and told me that till I had done so, he could not in a public character do anything in favour of the design. But he gave me five guineas as a private person ; which afforded me no small satisfaction, as it may open the door for further benefactions in the Established Church. It is matter of pleasing wonder to me, that notwithstanding the present languor of my spirits, and my natural bashfulness, I can with freedom and composure converse with these great men. Rode to Darlington, a fine little town ; and came in the evening to Northallerton, which deserves the same character. As the way is tedious without company, and my time precious, I read as I ride, and while I am waiting ; which is both instructive and amusing. I have read, since I left Berwick, an excellent piece of history, entitled a Short Critical Review of the Life of O. Cromwell. Among other things new to me, I find that Cromwell had some thoughts of restoring the king, until he found him treacherous—that he had the offer of the title of king himself, but thought it impolite to accept of it. I am now reading Dr. Watts's excellent piece on the Happiness of Separate Spirits, &c. Wrote a letter to my Chara.

Wednesday, July 17.—As I heard there is a great number of rich people that resort to the medicinal waters of Scarborough this season of the year, I determined to go thither, in hopes of some benefactions. Arrived there in the evening, having ridden about fifty miles, through a great number of little villages, Helmsay, Pickering, Brutton, &c. Supped with a disagreeable company of young rakes, and was very low spirited.

Thursday, July 18.—Waited on the dissenting minister, Mr. Whittaker, a serious old gentleman. I found his congregation was very inconsiderable ; and that they were but few strangers come to town as yet ; and therefore that my journey here will be lost. Scarborough is a fine little town, situated on the sea shore, where they bathe, and drink the medicinal waters, which I found purgative. An old castle now in ruins stands upon an eminence, something like that in Edinburgh, and is of vast dimensions.

Friday, July 19.—Rode to Hull, in company with a friendly gentleman, Mr. Ellis, minister of Cove, one of Dr. Doddridge's pupils ; who like many others of them, has imbibed the modern sentiments in divinity. The word Orthodox is a subject of ridicule with many here. The dissenting ministers here take greater liberties than I should choose. They make no scruple of gaming, attending on horse races, mingling in promiscuous companies on the bowling-green, &c. The town of Beverly, through which we passed, is pretty large, and looks new and flourishing. It has a stately ancient minster or cathedral (for I know not the difference) of a very delicate structure.

Sunday, July 21.—I have waited on Messrs. Wildboar, Withers, Cunningham and Dawson, ministers in Hull ; and solicited them to raise a public collection in their congregations ; but they seemed to hesitate about the propriety of it, which afforded me no small discouragement ; for I can neither take time, nor do I think it worth while to make private applications. I begin to fear that my expenses and fatigues in travelling to the principal country towns will hardly be compensated ; and therefore think it will be best for me to return directly to London. But I am quite uncertain which will be most expedient. Preached A. M. in the Presbyterian meeting-house for Mr. Withers, and P. M. in the Independent meeting-house for Mr. Wildboar, with some freedom, especially at the former. But alas ! the solemn affectionate addresses which once I was capable of, I seem now to have lost; and I am sometimes afraid of returning to my own people, lest I should not recover it. The Presbyterian congregation here is upon the decline; and I am told, an unhappy difference subsists between the pastor and assistant. Here, as well as elsewhere, the Presbyterians have gone off from the good old doctrines of the Reformation. Hull, (or as it is properly called, Kingston-upon-Hull) is a large populous town, surrounded with a wall and three trenches. The buildings are generally good and new. The harbour very commodious. The river Humber, into which the Hull empties itself, is about two-and-a-quarter miles over; about twenty miles from the sea. There is an old castle where the invalids of the army are placed as a garrison, with sundry pieces of cannon. Had a long conversation with Mr. Cunningham, Mr. Wildboar's assistant, a candid friendly youth, educated in London under Dr. Marryat. He appears a hearty friend to experimental religion. How do I long for retirement in my study, and the company of my Chara !

Monday, July 22.—I went to visit sundry gentlemen of the established church; but they were generally from home; only Alderman Purratt gave me two guineas.

Tuesday, July 23.—Received a letter from my father and friend, Mr. Tennent, informing me that the Synod of Ulster and the Presbytery of Antrim had agreed to make a collection through all their bounds, and that he was advised to make private applications in Dublin, which he hardly hoped to finish this month. How solitary shall I be till the happy hour of our meeting ! After repeated importunities, the ministers in Hull seem determined to make public collections ; only Mr. Withers complains that he is not able to be active in the affair, and Mr. Dawson, his assistant, seems very cautious, and apprehensive of imposture ; and upon the whole, I have no raised expectations. Mr. Cunningham is more and more dear to me, as I converse with him. Had an interview with Mr. Harris, minister of Beverly ; but I could not determine whether he purposed to make a collection in his congregation.

Thursday, July 25.—Having arrived in York last night, I took a view of the city this morning, in company with the Rev. Mr. Root. The city is large, about four miles in circumference, surrounded with a wall, along which there is an agreeable walk. The Cathedral is very magnificent, and the paintings in the glass are curious. There are twenty-three parishes. The houses in general have but a mean appearance, and are not so close as in most other cities. The gaol is the most stately building for the purpose that I have ever seen. Mr. Root, a bold, mercurial gentleman, promised to make a collection among his people. But here I may make a remark which may be applied to all such cases. That as I know the natural negligence of mankind in the absence of the solicitor of such charities, I have but little hope that any thing considerable will be transmitted after me to London.

Friday, July 26.—On waiting on Mr. Whitaker and Mr. Thomas Walker, ministers in Leeds, (where I arrived last night) I find they have had collections in their congregations very lately, and are now about another ; and consequently nothing can now be done for my mission ; but they promise to make a collection four months hence. Mr. Walker is a solid, judicious man, though gone off from the old divinity. He has the character of a very popular preacher.

Saturday, July 27.—Went to Wakefield, and proposed the affair of my mission to Mr. Ouldrid, minister there, who, upon consulting Messrs. Mills, his principal hearers, gave me encouragement that they would do something ; though they had lately expended a great sum in building a meeting-house. Had an interview with Col. Beverly, from Virginia, and my old pupil, Thomas Smith. Returned to Leeds in the evening.

Sunday, July 28.—Though I have had a more lively flow of spirits since I have been in Leeds than for some time ; yet being engaged to preach for Mr. Whitaker in the morning, I was so much confused in the prayer before sermon, that I was obliged to break off abruptly, lest I should speak nonsense, or run into repetitions. I hardly remember that my understanding was ever so suddenly clouded ; and I was really afraid lest the Lord was about to take it away from me. In the sermon I a little recovered my senses, and spoke with unexpected freedom. Preached, P. M. for Mr. Walker, and hardly ever found my mind emerge so suddenly out of darkness and confusion ; or my body and mind better disposed to act the orator. The dissenting ministers here have so generally imbibed Arminian or Socinian sentiments, that it is hard to unite prudence and faithfulness in conversation with them. They are many of them gentleman of good sense, learning, candour, and regular in their morals, entertaining and instructive companions, and friends to the liberty of mankind. But what shall I say ? They deny the proper divinity and satisfaction of Jesus Christ, on which my hopes are founded. They ascribe a dignity and goodness to human nature in its present state, contrary to my daily sensations : and they are not so dependent upon divine influences as I find I must be. Are they or I mistaken? Is the mistake in such circumstances essential? It is with the utmost reluctance I would admit the conclusion: and yet I cannot avoid it. The denial of the divinity of Christ introduces an essential innovation into the Christian system; and yet the greatest number of the dissenting ministers under the Presbyterian name in England, as far as I have observed, have fallen into that error; and the people love to have it so; and what will be the end of these things? It is a strong presumption with me against these new doctrines, that I have observed wherever they prevail, there practical serious religion, and generally the dissenting interest too, declines, and people become careless about it. Some of them go off to the Church of England, and others fall into deism. And it is matter of complaint that the deists generally, if not universally, are of the Whig-party, and join sation with the gentlemen of the new scheme, I am generally upon the reserve about my own principles, lest it should prejudice them against the business of my mission. But when I reflect upon it, I seem to despise myself as a coward. My the Low-Churchmen. Alas! how are the principles of liberty abused! In conver-conscience indeed does not generally accuse me of guilt in this respect; but a sense of honour or pride, or I know not what to call it, makes me look mean and sneaking to myself.

Tuesday, July 30.—Communicated my business to Messrs. Haines and Wadsworth, ministers of Sheffield, about thirty miles from Leeds. They are gone off into the new scheme; and I apprehended their suspecting me to be of the old-fashioned faith, rendered them more indifferent about my business. They complained that their people were poor—that they were just about raising a collection for a neighbouring minister. However, they faintly promised they would try to do something among their people about Christmas. Sheffield is a large town, rich in cutlery ware manufactured in it.

Wednesday, July 31.—Waited on Mr. Pye, who was yesterday out of town. He is minister of the congregation that separated from that where Messrs. Haines and Wadsworth now officiate, about forty years ago, on account of their innovations. Mr. Pye appears a serious man, and deeply concerned about experimental religion: and I believe will show himself a hearty friend to our mission. Rode to Chesterfield, a little town about twelve miles off; but Mr. Haywood, minister there, not being at home, I could only leave my printed papers for him, and write to him.

Thursday, August 1.—Rode about twenty-seven miles over the Peak of Derbyshire, and came to Derby, which is a very agreeable town, with sundry very good houses in it. Mr. Rogerson, the Presbyterian minister, gave me encouragement that he would collect something among his people. I was delighted with an inscription upon a monument on the side of the church, erected by a tender husband for his wife, who died in her sixtieth year:

> " She was—but words are wanting to say what:
> Think what a WIFE should be, and she was that."

The longest epitaph would not have been so striking and significant to me: and it brought my Chara to my mind. Though I hurry on as fast as I can, yet I find it takes a long time to negotiate my business at so many places. I often think of Bristol with anxiety, where, I am afraid, I shall be long detained. And I am often calculating with pensive melancholy, as I ride along, how long it will be before my return home: for there my earthly happiness lies. I am so diffident of mankind, that I am afraid these transient applications will turn to little account. I suspect they will be forgotten when I turn my back. And this renders my itinerations more discouraging.

Friday, August 2.—Breakfasted with Mr. Rogerson, at one Mr. Crompton's, who belongs to his congregation. He seemed diffident of the recommendations, because they were in print; and would do nothing till he received the recommendation of Mr. Lawrence, &c. from London. Rode to Nottingham, about sixteen miles. It is a large town, and the buildings are generally good, and some of them magnificent, though I have seen none equal to some in Derby. It is situated on the river Trent, which is navigable for small vessels. The Arian and Arminian controversy has lamentably divided the dissenters here. Mr. Ross and his people retain the old-fashioned faith; and Dr. Eaton and his people have imbibed the newfangled notions. They both received my mission favourably; and I hope will do something in favour of it. Dr. Eaton is a very grave and contemplative man, of a refined magisterial behaviour. I find there are some serious people here who warmly espouse the doctrines of grace. I spent this evening agreeably in a small company of them, and I met with one Mr. Wells, a pious youth of the Academy at Plasterers' Hall, who is very friendly, and kindly attends me wherever I go. Here are the ruins of an old castle, with many subterranean edifices; and in the midst, the Duke of New Castle has a stately palace. The castle was demolished by Oliver Cromwell; and I was surprised to observe from what a great distance he flung his bombs.

Saturday, August 3.—Visited Mr. Harross, Dr. Eaton's assistant, and engaged him to make a representation of the affairs of my mission to-morrow, in order to a public collection. Had an interview also with Mr. Radford, a good old minister who has for some time declined the exercise of his ministry; and with Mr. Williams, who has a large estate lately fallen to him, and therefore he preaches only occasionally.

Sunday, August 4.—Preached A. M. for Mr. Ross with some degree of freedom; and P. M. for Dr. Eaton to a very crowded congregation, with the usual restraint proceeding from a fear of prejudicing them against my mission by a solemn Calvinistic sermon. After sermon they collected £21 15s., which much surpassed my expectation. Spent the evening agreeably in a religious society of a number of serious men; who were much pleased and edified by my sermon!

Monday, August 5.—Went in company with Mr. Ross and his deacons to make private application to his people; and collected about thirty guineas in three or four hours. Spent an hour with Mr. Radford who has an uncommon sense of religion upon his spirit, and a peculiar dexterity in giving the conversation a religious turn.

Tuesday, August 6.—Dined with John Dean, Esq., whose history is very extraordinary. He met with a most amazing deliverance at sea about forty years ago, of which he has published an account, and which he now annually commemorates by a sermon. He was about fifteen years in the service of Peter the Great of Muscovy, and at last banished by him because he would not join in a war against the English. He was for many years his Majesty's Consul at Ostend. Has been at most of the courts in Europe, and by conversation with various nations has learned five or six languages. He is now near eighty, and has from nothing raised such a fortune, that he has a very handsome living, and has retired from business about fifteen years. The history of his deliverance at sea is, I think, by far the most extraordinary that I have ever seen. Spent the evening in a religious society.

Wednesday, August 7.—Preached for Mr. Ross to a numerous auditory on Jeremiah xxxi. 18—20; but not with proper solemnity. I was honoured with the presence of three or four ministers. I afterwards found some of the rigid Calvinists were not pleased with my sermon; because not explicit upon original sin. And I doubt not but another party were displeased upon quite a different account. How impossible is it to please men! My success in Nottingham has far exceeded my most sanguine expectations. I have received above £60, which is more than has ever been collected there on such an occasion.

Thursday, August 8.—Breakfasted with Mrs. Hallows, a lady belonging to Dr. Eaton's congregation. She has studied Dr. Clark, and is a dexterous disputant in the Trinitarian controversy. I have seldom been so closely attacked upon the proper Divinity of the Son of God; and it cast me afterwards into a pensive melancholy study upon the point. Rode to Loughborough, thirteen miles, and waited on Mr. Statham, the dissenting minister; but his congregation is so small that he could do little for my mission; though very friendly and sociable. Lodged in Leicester, a large town (eleven miles), but the minister, Mr. Worthington, not being at home, I could only leave my papers for him.

Friday, August 9.—Rode to Northampton (thirty-two miles) through Harborough. The town looked desolate and melancholy to me, when I thought upon the removal of the excellent Dr. Doddridge into a better world. The dear remembrance of him engaged my tender thoughts as I rode along, and threw me into pensive melancholy. How much has my mission suffered by his death! I think I never felt such friendly sensations towards an entire stranger. Waited on Mr. Gilbert, his successor, but found him in company; so that I had no time for conversation.

Saturday, August 10.—In conversing with Mr. Gilbert, I found there is but little prospect of success in this town; the people being lately put to very great expense about their own affairs. Visited the Rev. Mr. Hervey at Weston Favel, and spent most of the day in endearing conversation with him. I have observed that when I have contracted personal acquaintance with great authors, they have seldom answered the idea I had formed of them from their writings. But Mr. Hervey greatly exceeded it. The spirit of devotion animates his conversation; and the greatest modesty and delicacy of imagination adorns it. The Scriptures are his favourite topic, and he charms one with his remarks upon their beauties. He also frequently throws out some pertinent quotation from the Latin and Greek classics, of which he is an excellent master. Blessed be God that there is such a man on this guilty globe.

Sunday, August 11.—Preached A. M. in Dr. Doddridge's pulpit; and the sight of his monument with a very significant inscription, struck my mind with uncommon energy. My subject was " I will be your God," &c., and I had some freedom, but little solemnity. The congregation is decreased since the Doctor's death; as they can find none to supply his place fully. And some of the people have left the society, pretending that Mr. Gilbert does not preach the doctrines of grace. But I hope it is but a pretence; for I heard him P. M. preach an ingenious experimental discourse on " Look unto me and be ye saved," &c. He also administered the sacrament and spoke very judiciously and pertinently on the occasion. And I was not a little pleased to find him a weeping petitioner to heaven in prayer. Drunk tea with Mrs. Doddridge, for whom I found a greater friendship than I could decently express. A great number of the people jointly requested me to give them a sermon in the evening; with which I complied, and preached on Isaiah lxvi. 2, with considerable freedom. Many gave me the warmest expression of their satisfaction, and seemed quite revived. Spent the evening after sermon in conversation with Mr. Gilbert (who is naturally grave and reserved) and his assistant, Mr. Warburton.

Monday, August 12.—Went in company with Mr. Warburton and Mr. Wilkinson to make private applications among the people, and received about £16, of which Mrs. Doddridge procured me three guineas. Dined with her, and found her conversation animated with good sense and piety. She remembered me as a correspondent of the dear deceased (as she calls the Doctor), and treated me with uncommon friendship. I was surprised that she could talk of him with so much composure, notwithstanding her flowing affections. She told me she never had a more comfortable season, than when returning from Lisbon, on the boisterous ocean, after the Doctor's death.

Tuesday, August 13.—Finished my application in which I was much obliged to Mr. Warburton for his company. Spent an hour with dear Mrs. Doddridge, and at her requst, parted with prayer, in which I found my heart much enlarged. She made a remark that has often occurred to me since, " that she rejoiced that the dear deceased was called to the tribunal of his Master with a heart full of such generous schemes for the good of mankind, which he had zeal to project, though not life to execute." May this be my happy case! There are such charms in a public spirit, that I cannot but wish I could imbibe more of it. And in this view, I rejoice in the fatigues and anxieties of my present mission : though I am quite unmanned, when the thoughts of my Chara rush upon my heart : and the prospect of so long an absence is hardly supportable. Rode through Newport, a considerable town, and came to Holbourn in the evening, on my way to London. Thither I find the attraction of friendship strongly draws me.

Wednesday, August 14.—Called at St. Albans, a large town, and a prodigious thoroughfare. Mr. Hirons, the minister, was not at home ; and therefore I could do nothing there to promote my mission. The country has a delightful appearance to a traveller in their company; and particularly Dr. Avery. The turnpike roads are good, and almost surrounded with fine houses, especially between St. Albans and London. The fields are covered with all sorts of grain, and white ready for harvest. It is indeed the land of plenty. But oh! it is a sinful land. I am shocked with the blasphemy and profaneness of the inhabitants; especially the vulgar, who are not under the restraint even of good manners. Arrived in London in the evening, and was revived at the sight of my friends.

Wednesday, August 21.—Set out for Yarmouth, and came twenty-nine miles to Chelmsford. The people in London think we have received enough ; and there is little prospect of further benefactions there. Visited sundry of my friends, and had great pleasure in their company; particularly Dr. Avery, Mr. Ward, Mr. Forfeit, Mr. Thomson, Mr. Samuel Stennet, Mr. Savage, Mr. De Berdt, &c. Preached last Sunday for Mr. Hall, on Hebrews, xii. 14, and saw their mode of public baptism. Mr. Hall made a long discourse, like a sermon, on the nature, design, subjects, mode, &c., of the ordinance ; prayed, and without laying any particular obligations on the parent, took the child in his arms, and baptised it, and then concluded with prayer. Waited on Sir Joseph Hankey, knight and alderman, and received £5 5s. Last Tuesday heard Mr. Bradbury, at Pinner's Hall.

Thursday, August 22.—Visited Mr. Hukford, an old minister, and Mr. Phillips, his assistant; who seemed favourable to the business of my mission, and promised to do something against my return that way. Proceeded to Colchester (twenty-one miles) and visited Mr. Cornel, who appears a warm friend to experimental religion, though I am told, he is, or at least has been, of a very peevish, unministerial temper. He was once assistant with Mr. Hall, in London. He promised to solicit benefactions for the College. Colchester is a pretty large town, I am told of considerable trade. The old wall is almost demolished. Here is also a church or two in ruins, destroyed by Oliver Cromwell, because the place stood out very obstinately against him. Here is an Independent, a Presbyterian, and a Baptist congregation. But the Presbyterian is vacant, and the Baptist is supplied only by a layman; and therefore, I thought it not worth my while to apply to them.

Tuesday, August 27.—From last Friday till this morning, I have been in Ipswich, a very considerable town; and I have hardly spent so many days so happily, and with such a flow of spirits in England. Here lives good Mr. Notcult, whose pious sermons I have seen in America. He is in his eighty-third year; and brought me in mind of old Simeon. He breathes a spirit of devotion, and is waiting for a dismission from earth, with patient and yet eager expectation. His people love their old prophet, and cheerfully afford him a maintenance, though he has been laid aside from public labour above a year. Mr. Gordon is assistant, and now invited to be pastor. He kindly invited me to lodge at his house: and I was greatly edified with his free and pious conversation. He has experimental religion much at heart, and preaches it honestly, and with some success to his people. He is remarkably punctual in private devotion; and upon the whole seems to walk with God. I contracted a friendship with him, which I trust will be immortal; and which I shall endeavour to cultivate by correspondence, when I return to my native country. O how delightful is the conversation of such a minister after I have seen so many of a contrary character. Preached for him last Sunday, A. M., on Jeremiah xxxi. 33, and in the evening, on Isaiah lxvi. 1, 2, with some freedom; and the good people seemed to eagerly drink in the doctrine, and were much pleased. This gave me hope that they would be generous to the College; and I was not disappointed: for on Monday, Mr. Gordon and his clerk went among the people, and collected £23 9s., which is very considerable for people in their circumstances. It is their practice, on Monday evening, to repeat the sermon of the preceding day: with which I complied at their request. There is also a Presbyterian congregation in Ipswich, of which Mr. Thomas Scott is minister. He is suspected of Arminian and Arian principles; but if the suspicion be true, I am sure he differs greatly from the generality of the fraternity with whom I have conversed. His soul seems formed for friendship; and he loves and speaks well of many Calvinists and Trinitarians. He is a gentleman of extensive learning, a fine genius, and a good poet. He is engaged in a practical paraphrase on the Book of Job, with notes; and I think he has executed his scheme to excellent purpose. He also showed me sundry other poetical pieces of his, with which he intends to oblige the world. I preached for him last Sunday, P. M., on Psalm xcvii. 1, and he was heartily pleased with my sermon. I can confide in him that he will exert himself in soliciting his benefactions from his people; though he did not think it so proper now as hereafter; and his people are few and ungenerous; and therefore he could give me no great encouragement. He is brother to Dr. Scott of London, who was once his father's assistant in Norwich, and having imbibed the Socinian sentiments, opposed his own father; and occasioned a division in the congregation. At length he commenced M. D., and laid aside the ministry. Rode through Woodbridge, Wickam-market, Saxmundam, &c., and came to Yoxford. As I was riding along, I formed a resolution to draw up a history on my return, of my present mission, the state of the dissenters in England, of the Church of Scotland, &c., as far as I had opportunity of making observations; and present the MS. to the College of New Jersey; as it may be entertaining and instructive to the students, and perpetuate the remembrance of the remarkable providences we have met with in favour of the Institution. But alas! such are my hurries and the fickleness of my mind, that the most of my schemes of this kind are unexecuted.

Monday, Sept. 2.—Arrived in Yarmouth last Wednesday, where I have continued ever since; and lodged at the Rev. Mr. Frost's, who has treated me with such uncommon kindness as I shall never forget. He is an universal scholar, particularly he understands the languages. He has a public spirit, and a very devout and good heart. In prayer he has an uncommon dexterity in descending to particulars; and is almost as doctrinal and historical as a preacher, and as flourishing as a poet. Preached for him yesterday A. M. and in the evening, with considerable freedom and much to his satisfaction. The people also seemed attentive, and some of them affected. The congregation here is but small and poor; and the friends of my mission hardly hoped for more than twelve guineas at the public collection, but to our agreeable surprise, I received about £24. This I ascribe to the blessing of God upon my sermons, and Mr. Frost's warm recommendation. And I think it an evidence of the remarkable interposition of Providence in favour of the College, that wherever I have stayed to make a collection it has doubled what was ever raised before on the like occasion. I waited on the Presbyterian minister, Mr. Milner; but he refused to propose the matter to his congregation, under pretence that he had engaged to use all his influence to promote a Presbyterian Academy in Lancashire. I strongly suspect that the Institution has been misrepresented to him, perhaps by Dr. Benson, as a Calvinistic scheme, or as in the hands

of bigots.—Yarmouth is one of the finest towns I have seen in sight of the sea, on
the river Yare, with a most spacious, commodious key. The buildings are generally good, and some of them of flint; one in particular, of great antiquity, is of
polished flint.

Saturday, September 13.—I have been in Norwich about ten days: and lodged at
Mr. Pauls', an excellent young gentleman, who has passed through a great many
spiritual trials, and had a series of remarkable experiences. He was once warmly
engaged with the Methodists; but since Mr. Wheatley's brutal abominations have
come to light, he has left him. This unhappy man had preached a long time here
with great warmth and earnestness: endured with the most lamb-like patience the
most cruel treatment from the mob, which even endangered his life, and been
instrumental to awaken multitudes to a serious sense of religion. But has at last
been found guilty of repeated criminal commerce with sundry women, though his
own wife was then alive. With a loud voice does this event cry to all the professors of religion, " Be not high-minded but fear." O that none that seek thy face
O Lord, may be ashamed on my account! My excellent friend, Mr. Frost, attended
me to Norwich; and used all his influence to prepare the way for me among the
people. Mr. John Scott is also remarkably friendly. But Mr. Taylor and his
assistant Mr. Bourne, being abroad, and Mr. Wood having retired into the country
for his health, I found it difficult to introduce the affair of my mission; especially
as Mr. Tozer, Mr. Wood's colleague, is not on a good footing with his people, and
is about to remove from them to Exeter; and therefore did not think it prudent to
be active in the business. Preached for him the weekly lecture last Friday, on
Isaiah lxvi. 2, and also last Sunday, P. M. on Isaiah xlv. 22, with considerable
freedom. After which I gave an account of the business of my mission. And I
find both the sermon and the account were very acceptable to the hearers. A public
collection was proposed to be made next Sunday, but Mr. Scott and some others
concluded to make private applications to the principal people; which he and Mr.
Lincoln did yesterday, and received about £47. Yesterday the famous Mr. Taylor
came home, and I waited on him in the evening. He is a very sociable, friendly
gentleman, and talks very freely and warmly about Christianity; and seems zealous
for its propagation through the world. He gave me the strongest expressions of
friendship to my design; but said that as his congregation was just now at the
expense of above £3000 in building a pompous new meeting-house, he could not
urge it upon them. Last Monday, on my way to Halesworth, to see Mr. Wood, I
passed through Burles, a fine little town; dined with Mr. Lincoln, a young dissenting minister there, who seems a cordial Calvinist. Spent two nights and a day
with Mr. Wood, and my soul was charmed with the excellent spirit of the man.
He is a judicious, solemn, prudent minister, and I think England can boast of but
few like him. He is as warmly engaged in the affair of our mission as Mr. Tennent
or myself: and notwithstanding his indisposition, has laboured to promote collections in the congregations around. He is generally loved and revered by those of
different sentiments, as well as of his own. He was the favourite friend of the late
Dr. Doddridge, and seems to possess much of his spirit. His soul is pregnant with
noble projects for the good of his whole species, as far as his influence extends.
His expressions in prayer are remarkably striking and solemn. I intended to have
left Norwich to-day, but I find it is so generally desired by my benefactors, that I
should stay another Sabbath, that I could not but consent. Norwich is accounted
the third city in England; about one and a half miles in length and one in breadth,
the houses very close and crowded with inhabitants. It contains about thirty-one
parishes, a fine cathedral with a spire of prodigious height, four dissenting congregations, besides the Quakers. The old Bridewell wall of polished flint is a remarkable curiosity. The principal manufacture is wearing stuffs. Last Saturday visited
Mr. Steam, a serious, illiterate Baptist preacher, who conversed very freely upon
experimental religion, and promised his influence for me with his small congregation.

Sunday, September 15.—How frail is life! how uncertain! How thin the parti-
tion betwixt time and eternity! how quick the transition from the one to the other!
of how great importance is it to be always prepared! These reflections are occasioned by my unexpected sudden approach to the eternal world last night, I think
the nearest ever I made. My life hung in a doubtful scale: and one grain would have
turned it. I spent the evening at Mr. Lincoln's, in company with him, his son and
daughter, Mr. Scott and Mr. Paul. At supper I was well, but my appetite was
faint. After supper I was well while I smoked a pipe: but when I began a second,
I found my spirits flag, and I could not keep up my part in conversation. Then I
began to sicken, and made a motion to go home. We walked out of the parlour;
and as I was just taking leave of the family, I instantly fell down dead on the floor,
and continued, they told me, without any appearance of life for near two minutes

Then I began to struggle, and draw my breath with great force and difficulty, so as to agitate my breast and my whole frame. In about two minutes I suddenly came to myself, and was greatly surprised to find myself fallen on the floor, and my friends about me in such a fright, rubbing my hands and temples, for I had lost all consciousness, and did not in the least perceive my violent fall. They immediately sent for a surgeon, but before he came I began to recover. I was able to walk home, with one supporting me, and though I was greatly enfeebled and exhausted, and my heart heaved and struggled to throw off the blood, I had a little refreshing sleep. This morning I found myself very weak, and a pain at my heart, occasioned, I suppose, by the difficulty of the circulation of blood. I preached, A. M. for Mr. Bowrn, assistant to Mr. Taylor, but had very little vivacity or solemnity. Preached P. M. for Mr. Tozer, with unexpected life and freedom, and to the great satisfaction of the people, and was surprised to find they collected near £20 at the doors.

In the evening I was so exhausted that I could hardly live; but at supper I most remarkably found myself refreshed by my food.

Monday, Sept. 16.—Continued weak, and pained at my heart; and as the doctor as well as myself apprehended it was an apoplectic fit, occasioned by the stagnation of the blood, I had blood drawn this morning; and I was obliged to defer my journey. When I first returned to my senses after the fit, I was quite serene and peaceful in mind. But when I began to reflect upon my circumstances, as being among strangers in a strange land, having a dear helpless family so far from me, whose subsistence depends upon my life, and being so poorly prepared for the enjoyments and employments of heaven, it gave me no small alarm; though I had much more firmness and intrepidity of mind than I could have expected. Nothing in this world affected me so much, as to foresee the effects which the news of my sudden death would have upon my dear Chara. Lord, prepare us both for the parting stroke. I can't but reflect upon it as a remarkable providence, that when I was seized with the fit, I was at a friend's house, and among friends—that I should fall with so much violence, and yet not be hurt. Had I been riding, my fall might have killed me. Had I been alone or among strangers, I would have had none to take proper care of me. But all circumstances were happily ordered by Divine Providence.

Tuesday, Sept. 17.—After taking an affectionate leave of my Norwich friends, I set out for Wattesfield, (about thirty miles) and lodged with the Rev. Mr. Harmer, a friendly, sociable, and ingenious gentleman. His congregation have formed a fund for occasional expenses; and instead of a public collection, he intends to apply to the deacons to give a share of that to the College. Wattesfield is a little country village, but the dissenting congregation is pretty numerous, and afford their minister a handsome living.

Wednesday, Sept. 18.—Came to Bury St. Edmund's, where there are two dissenting congregations, but they are few. Mr. Savile is an ancient minister of great integrity and humility, and a lover of all good men. He is a warm friend to experimental religion, and rejoices in the conversion of sinners by whatever means it be accomplished. He has a particular friendship for the despised Methodists, because one of them, Mr. Skelton, with whom I had some agreeable conversation, was the instrument of making religious impressions upon his daughters.—Mr. Follet is an ingenious, modest young gentleman, a pupil of Dr. Doddridge, not so thoroughly Calvinistic as Mr. Savile.

Thursday, September 19.—Preached Mr. Savile's Lecture P. M. with some freedom and great popularity. And I hope the people here will make a handsome collection, though I can't stay to receive it. Bury is a town of great antiquity, but its ancient grandeur is declined. The ruins of an old abbey, demolished at the Reformation, are very stately; particularly the gate, which is still entire. The walls of the abbey were about two and a half miles in circumference. Here I received the melancholy news of the death of that excellent man, my particular friend Mr. McLaurin of Glasgow. That city has lost one of its brightest ornaments, the Church of Scotland one of its most excellent ministers, and the College of New Jersey one of its best friends. But heaven has received a new inhabitant from this sinful world. May I be prepared to follow. *Sic mihi contingat vivere, sicque mori!*

Friday, September 20.—Came to Sudbury and found Mr. Hextal the minister, and Mr. Gainsborough one of his people, very friendly to me and my mission. Lodged with the latter. Mr. Hextal is one of Dr. Doddridge's pupils, and is possessed of an excellent spirit. He has not fallen into the theological innovations; but goes on in the good old way. Here I was refreshed with an interview with my kind friend, the Rev. Mr. Hunt of Hackney.

Monday, September 23.—Preached yesterday twice for Mr. Hextal on Jeremiah xxxi. 33, and Isaiah xlv. 22. But alas! with more affected than real earnestness and solemnity. I gave an account publicly of the business of my mission, and they collected about £18. I find my lowness of spirits returned, which makes me affect solitude, and so impatient of constant company, that I am quite unsociable. I also feel the effects of my late fit, and am sometimes apprehensive of its return. But alas! sin is still strong in me, and makes frequent vigorous insurrections, which I cannot suppress. God be merciful to me a sinner. Last night was much pleased with Mr. Gainsborough's prayer in his family. Mr. Hextal, Mr. Gainsborough and Mr. Fenn went this morning among the principal people to solicit them to enlarge their benefactions; and they succeeded so well, that with what they received yesterday, they made up about £43; besides £5 5s. from one Mrs. Rowe of Long Melford. Rode in the evening to Braintree, in company with Mr. Davidson. Lodged at Samuel Ruggle's, Esq. a gentleman of vast estate and very serious disposition. He generously subscribed £30 to the College. I find the people here are so importunate, that I must stay and preach next Sunday. There are few congregations of dissenters in England so numerous as this, which consists of about twelve hundred; and they seem in general to be a very serious people.

Wednesday, September 25.—Preached for Mr. Davidson on Isaiah xlv. 22, and the Lord made the discourse acceptable to his people.

Thursday, September 26.—Went to Coggeshal, the place where the excellent Dr. Owen was once minister, and communicated my business to the Rev. Mr. Petto, a very friendly man; who promised to lay it before his people. But from what he knows of their dispositions, he could give me little or no encouragement. Went thence to Colchester, and spent the evening with Mr. Cornell, in agreeable conversation. He had communicated the affair to his people, but they were not disposed to favour it.

Friday, September 27.—Went to Witham, and waited on the Rev. Mr. Burnet; but his people were not willing to assist. All the comfort I can take in this short tour, is the reflection that I have taken all the means in my power to promote my important mission.

Saturday, September 28.—I was at leisure in the forenoon; and revived the remembrance of the many delightful hours I have spent in my study at home in reading and contemplation. How do I languish and pine for retirement; and what painful anxieties about my Chara distress my mind. At the request of friendly ministers and others in various parts of Great Britain, I have determined to give my Sermon on Isa. lxii. 1, a second edition. May God attend it into the world. The reading of it was very reviving to Mr. Davidson; who is eminently possessed of the ministerial zeal which it recommends. The more I conversed with him, the more my heart is united to him. I find Mr. Erskine has published the imperfect notes of my Sermon on 1 John ii. 2, which he has corrected, in general, to my taste. His Preface in favour of the College has already had happy effects in Braintree, and excited sundry to double their intended benefactions.

Sunday, September 29.—Preached twice for Mr. Davidson with some freedom; and afterwards joined in the Lord's Supper, with some little devotion. Gave a public account of my mission extempore; and though the collection had been made, I received six pounds more. Was entertained with Mr. Ruggles's devout manner of spending the evening in his family, examining his children, reading a sermon, singing and prayer.

Monday, September 30.—As I was parting with Mr. Ruggles, he was pleased to add £20 to the £30 he had promised, and told me he did not know but he might do yet more. Such a remarkable benefaction could not fail of raising in me a flow of gratitude to God, whose favouring providence has attended me in so uncommon a manner in this mission. Mr. Davidson conducted me about eight miles towards Chelmsford. His soul is formed for friendship, and I could not part with him, without some tender emotions. He is very happy in his people, who seem to be generally possessed with a very serious spirit, and are about 1200 in number. When I came to Chelmsford, I found the ministers there, Mr. Hukford and Mr. Philips, had raised £6 in their little congregation, in my absence. They importuned me to stay and preach, but my hurries would not permit. This day has given me another occasion to record a providential deliverance. As I was riding at a gallop, my horse fell down, and tumbled almost quite over, and I very narrowly escaped his rolling over me. The people that saw me fall were much alarmed, and apprehended my life in the greatest danger. But blessed be God, I did not receive the least injury. Alas! I am afraid that the frequency of such deliverances will render them so familiar, that I shall not take a proper notice of them, and contract a kind of insensibility in danger.

Tuesday, October 1.—I arrived in London, and found by a letter from Mr. Tennent, that he has almost finished his applications in the West, and that he intends to come to London as soon as possible, to prepare for embarking for America.—

The prospect of so speedy a return gave me no small pleasure. But the prospect of a winter passage was very shocking, especially as I had such a melancholy time in my last voyage, and in the present diffident state of my mind, I am not a little intimidated at the dangers of the seas. Received a reviving packet from my dear Mr. Rodgers, Captain Grant, Mr. Allen, &c., which informed me of a happy situation of affairs at home, excepting that the dissenters are still denied the licensure of more meeting-houses.

October 20.—My father and friend arrived in town about fifteen days ago; and his presence and conversation was very reviving to me. He has had very remarkable success and received above £500 in his tour. We are determined to embark for Philadelphia as soon as possible, with Captain Hargrave. We shall have but very poor accommodations; and I am afraid bad company. On settling our accounts, we are surprised to find our expenses run so high; as we have not been extravagant. Since I have been in London, I have moved in the same circle, and nothing new has occurred; but that I find by conversation with Dr. Stennet, there is a prospect of obtaining licences in the Bishop of London's Court, for meeting-houses in Virginia. Since I have been in town I have preached for Mr. Gibbons, Mr. Hunt, at Dr. Marryatt's meeting-house, Dr. Gifford, and to-day for Mr. Townsend at Newington, and for Dr. Guyse.

Sunday, October 27.—Preached for Mr. Hayward A. M., on Hebrews vi. 7, 8, with more solemnity and freedom than, alas! has been usual with me of late; and I thought I perceived a general concern among my hearers, who were numerous by accessions from other congregations. I observe a set of hearers that generally attend me whenever I preach, particularly the young students in the Academy. Preached P. M. for Mr. Crookshank on Isaiah lxvi. 1, 2. In the evening heard Mr. Bulkley at the Old Jewry, where the celebrated Dr. Foster was wont to hold his lecture. His discourse was finely composed, and delivered with a tolerable address; but alas! how anti-evangelical! Yesterday we waited on Messrs. John and Charles Westley. Notwithstanding all their wild notions they appear very benevolent, devout and zealous men, that are labouring with all their might to awaken the secure world to a sense of religion; and they are honoured with success. But I am afraid their encouraging so many illiterate men to preach the gospel, will have bad consequences. I heard one of them last Tuesday night, but he explained nothing at all. His sermon was a mere huddle of pathetic confusion, and I was uneasy, as it might bring a reproach upon experimental religion. The despised Methodists, with all their foibles, seem to me to have more of the spirit of religion than any set of people in this island. Mr. Locke's epitaph written by himself, *Hic situs est Johannes Locke. Si qualis fueri trogas? Mediocritate sua contentum se vixisse respondet. Literis eousque tantum profecit, ut veritati unici literet: hoc ex scriptis illius disce, quæ quod de eo reliquum est, majore fide tibi exhibibunt, quam epitaphii suspecta elogia. Virtutes, siquas habuit, minoris sane quam quas sibi laudi, tibi in exemplum proponeret; vitia unà sepeliantur. Morum examplar si quæras, in evangelio habes: vitiorum utinam nusquam: mortalitatis certi (quod prosit) hic et ubique.*

Monday, November 18.—We came yesterday to Gravesend, in the Charming Anne, Capt. Baker; having taken leave of my friends, and left London last Friday. My father and friend, Mr. Tennent, sailed with Capt. Hargrave, for Philadelphia, last Wednesday. The impossibility of getting the Trustees together, and of my travelling home by land from Philadelphia, determined me, with Mr. Tennent's consent, to deny myself the pleasure of his company, and sail directly for Virginia, that I may the sooner see my earthly all at home. And now, when I am about to encounter the terrors of a winter passage over the tumultuous ocean, I would solemnly commend myself to the God of my life, and the Ruler of sea and land: and though I am but a very insignificant creature, yet as I am of no small importance to my helpless family, I wish and pray that if it please God, I may be favoured with a safe passage. Since October 27, I have preached for Mr. Hall, Mr. Winter, Dr. Stennet, Mr. Lawson, Dr. Gifford, &c. I cannot but observe that I found unexpected freedom and solemnity in preaching a neglected old sermon, that I thought not worthy of hearing, from Heb. xi. 1. I have met with so many solicitations, both in conversation and by letters, to publish some of my sermons, that I continue my purpose of finishing some of them for that purpose. Now, when I have parted with London forever, I cannot but think with affection upon the many friends I have left behind me, who are entitled to my warmest gratitude. I have preached in many of the pulpits of the three denominations; and from the warm approbation of a number, I cannot but hope, I have been of some service in that way; though, alas! nothing to what might be expected or wished. The petition from Virginia being returned, I waited with it on Dr. Avery, Mr. Mauduit, &c., and communicated it also to Dr. Stennet, and begged he would act in concert with the committee; which he cheerfully promised. And indeed I expect more from his influence and zeal, than from the committee, that seem very slow and dilatory in their motions. As the majority of them are of the new scheme, they cannot look upon the dissenting interest in Virginia, as a religious interest, because founded on principles which they disapprove; and therefore they can only espouse it, as the cause of liberty : but a zeal for it in this view, is not so vigorous a principle as the other. The courtiers are so regardless of religion, abstracted from politics, that it will be difficult to carry such a point with them, especially as the whole weight of the government of Virginia will lie on the other side. However, I am in hopes, the alternative of taking out licenses in the bishop's court, or of presenting the petition, will succeed; and I have begged the committee and Dr. Stennet to take one or the other method, as they think most expedient.

Friday, Nov. 22.—Came down the river as far as the North Forland, having been detained by contrary winds. We are near thirty-two souls on board; but alas! I am at a loss for an agreeable companion. Human nature appears among the sailors in a very mortifying light. They are so habituated to blasphemy, that oaths and imprecations flow spontaneous from them : and I am in pain and perplexity what measures I shall take for their reformation. Considering what sort of men cross the seas, it is a miracle of Divine patience, and an evidence this is not the state of retributions, that so many of them are safely conducted through the dangers of the ocean. Alas! I have my own share of sins, and it shocks me to think how unholy I still am.

Thursday, Nov. 29.—We came to the Downs last Sunday, and were detained there waiting for a fair wind, till this afternoon, when we set sail. Through the great goodness of God, I have not as yet felt any thing of sea sickness, as I expected : and I now hope I shall escape it. I spend my time, as well as I can, in reading, and transcribing my own sermons for the press. I have read the Bishop of London's Sermons on the Evidences of Christianity, Dr. Wright on Hardness of Heart, &c. I have peace of mind; but alas! I feel great languor in devotion, and but little zeal to promote the advantage of those with whom I converse.

Saturday, Nov. 30.—The wind being contrary, we were obliged to put into Plymouth, a very good harbour; where there are about twenty-six men of war, a garrison, and one or two old castles.

Sunday, Dec. 1.—I purposed to preach to the company, but the hurries of getting fresh water, and clearing out to sea again, upon the wind becoming fair, prevented me. Alas! I live a very unprofitable life; and long to be restored to my sphere of usefulness among my own dear people.

Monday, Dec. 2.—Having set sail yesterday in the afternoon, we got out into the Channel; but it soon grew calm, and we were tossed up and down all night with prodigious swells, which are more disagreeable when there is no wind. This morning the wind shifted and blew violently; and finding we could not get out to sea, we put back for Plymouth, and got there in the evening, after a day and night useless labour. I found the return of sea-sickness, which quite depressed my spirits, and threw my whole frame into disorder. We have now been about three weeks on board, but have made but little way. This delay is a severe trial of my patience. When shall I see my home? Shall it ever be?—Though our return to Plymouth last night was disagreeable at first, yet afterwards I could not but look upon it as a happy providence; for the wind blew with such prodigious violence, that had we been in the Channel we should have been in no small danger.

Wednesday, Dec. 4.—Went to Plymouth in hopes to have got a contribution for the College, and waited on Mr. Baron and Mr. Moor, dissenting ministers there; but they told me the dissenting interest there was so low, that I could expect nothing.

Sunday, Dec. 8.—The winds still continue against us, so that we cannot get out of the harbour of Plymouth. This delay is the more disagreeable, as the ship's company, to which I am confined, are a parcel of the most profligate, audacious sinners, that I have ever been among. My ears are grated with the most shocking imprecations and blasphemies, that one would think they could not proceed but from the mouths of infernal spirits. Alas! to what a pitch of wickedness may human nature arrive! This day I had an opportunity of speaking to them from Heb. xii. 14, and I endeavoured honestly to discharge my conscience; and found no small pleasure and tranquillity after I had unburdened my heart. What effect it may have, must be discovered by their future conduct. Alas! I languish and fret to be delayed so long from my dearest creature at home. How lively and agreeable her image rises in my mind. May God give me patience and fortitude under the disappointment.

Wednesday, Dec. 11.—We are still delayed in the harbour of Plymouth; but we have still growing reason for thankfulness that we got safe in here; for the weather has been very uncertain and boisterous, and we have just heard that a ship was lost last Sunday night, on the rocks called the Monades, in the Channel, while trying to put into Falmouth, and all the company perished; and had we been in the Channel, we would probably have shared the same fate. May I be fortified to meet all the events before me!

Saturday, Dec. 14.—We are still detained at Plymouth; and last night both the ship and our lives were in the greatest danger. About six o'clock in the evening it blew a mere hurricane, which continued till about twelve o'clock. The wind blew so strong that one could hardly stand upon deck. It drove a large Dutch ship from her anchors, and she ran against a large rock on shore. She fired a gun as a signal of distress; and having got assistance, she got off. We found she was driving down against our vessel; and being much larger, she would probably have sunk her, or broke her to pieces. As we were trying to get out of the way, our anchors got loose, and we drove at the mercy of the wind and waves. The Dutch vessel struck against us once or twice; and afterwards we run upon a large Antigua ship; and were obliged to lie by her side for some time. Another ship was very near us on the other side; and we were in danger of being dashed to pieces between them. At last, with great difficulty, we anchored in a place where we lay safe till morning; but had not the wind abated, we should, in all probability, have dashed against some of the ships, or the rocks, which might have been fatal to us. This morning we endeavoured to get in a safer place, but we ran aground, and were obliged to stick till high water; and we could not anchor well till the evening, though the men had been hard at work all day, and most of last night; and after all, a large ship came this evening within a yard of us. I endeavoured to commend myself into the hands of God, in the extremity of danger; but when death, especially in such circumstances, appeared near, it filled me with solemn horror. And when I afterwards reflected upon my diffidence, it depressed my spirits not a little, to find that I am not fortified against all the events of this mortal state. Alas! it would not be thus with me had I lived nearer to God, and under more realizing impressions of the eternal world. O! that I may take the warning; and may my present impressions be lasting and efficacious, and not prove a transient fit of extorted devotion! I am sorry to find that my discourse last Sunday to the ship's company had no effect upon sundry of them. When they vent their passions, or are in a hurry, or alarmed with danger, they cannot speak without oaths and curses; which is so shocking that I can hardly venture upon deck, lest I should hear them. Alas! how depraved, how diabolically wicked is human nature.

Friday, December 20.—We have been on board five weeks, (a longer time than our whole voyage from Philadelphia) and this morning, the wind blowing from the east, we set sail. I find myself already much disordered with sea-sickness; and I am like to have a melancholy passage.

Saturday, December 28.—For this week past, we have had the usual vicissitudes of sailors, sometimes foul and sometimes fair. We had one night of very boisterous weather, and we could not enjoy a moment's rest in any posture. Last Sunday I hoped to have spoken once more to the ship's company; but I was so disordered with sea sickness that I was not able. Alas! I lead a most useless life. When I am able, I read in Bishop Burnet's History of his own Life and Times; in which is a more full account of the strange intrigues of courts than can be met with in most of histories. He is always fond of searching into the springs and causes of actions; and no doubt he discovers the true ones; but sometimes this temper betrays him into censorious conjectures about the hearts of others, of which he was no judge. The spirit of moderation and piety that breathes through his writings is quite charming. The reign of King Charles II. appears a scene of luxury and debauchery, changes in the ministry, imaginary plots, and prostitution to the French interest. The short reign of King Henry II. was a continued struggle of Popery and arbitrary power against liberty and the Protestant religion. But the steps taken were so hasty and precipitant, that nothing but an enthusiastic bigotry could have directed to them or expected success from them. The reign of William and Mary would have been one illustrious day, had it not been so unhappily clouded with factions between the whigs and tories; and the latter lay as a dead weight upon all the generous projects of that hero for the public good. Queen Anne's reign was nothing but a contest for victory between the whigs and tories; and in the last four years of her reign the latter unhappily got the superiority, and concluded the disadvantageous peace at Utrecht, when the French lay so much at mercy, that honourable terms might have easily been obtained.

Thursday, January 9, 1755.—For above a fortnight, we have had but very little fair wind; some days have been very squally, and others quite calm, with very high swells; which is extremely disagreeable. Two days ago we had no wind, and the seas run very high; and the ship got between two large swells, and not obeying her helm, went almost round, and we were in the greatest danger of sinking. The captain, as pale as death, cried out to get the boats loose, that in them we might commit ourselves to the ocean, and endeavour to get to a ship in sight; but it pleased God that the vessel righted, and we were safe beyond all expectation. May this providential deliverance have proper impressions upon me! The two last Sundays I have entertained the ship's company with two discourses, one on the love of God, and the other on striving to enter in at the straight gate. I continue much disordered, and so languid and inactive that I am good for nothing. When I am able, I spend my time in reading the Universal History, volumes five and six, but I am not a little mortified to find my memory so slippery.

Sunday, January 12.—Was so much out of order, that I was not able to entertain the company with a sermon; and alas, my spirits were so low, and the prospect of success so discouraging, that I had no heart to attempt it.

Saturday, January 18.—This last week has been the most painful and melancholy that I have seen for many years. I have had the tooth-ache in the most violent degree; so that I had no rest night nor day; indeed it was sometimes so violent that it made me almost quite delirious. I have had little or no sleep in bed for these five or six nights; but to-day I have a little ease; and oh! how sweet is it, after so much pain.

Sunday, January 26.—We have had some days of the most calm weather that I have seen at sea; but last Friday night, a violent storm blew up from the N. W.; which lasted about thirty hours. It is impossible for the most lively imagination, without the help of sight, to form an idea of the aspect of the ocean at such a time; and it is most astonishing the little vessel we float in, is not dashed to pieces by the furious conflicts of the waves, which toss her about like a cork, and give her such shocks that she trembles in every joint. It is a very good subject for a poem; but, alas! all my poetical powers are dormant.

> Inconstant, boisterous element; the type
> Of human life. Now gentle calms compose
> The wide-extended surface; to the eye
> Opens a level plain, a sea of glass,
> Smooth as the standing pool, or purling stream,
> Or only rising gradual, and flow
> In vast majestic swells, not wild, abrupt
> A watery precipice; such as these eyes
> Now see collecting all their terrors round,
> On every side. Above, the clouds, replete
> With winds and angry fire tremendous, lower.
> The lightning flashes a malignant glare
> Through the thick gloom, and helps but to descry
> The horrors of the dark, and danger's frown.
> Now the fierce flash spreads out in sheets of flame,
> Round heaven's wide canopy—meantime the winds
> Collect their forces, and discharge their rage
> On the fermenting deep; 'till watery hills,
> And mountains rise, and roll along, beyond
> The ken of sight; or by quick-shifting winds,
> Driven adverse, dash in furious conflict; then
> The mountains break in a tumultuous roar,
> The angry foam flies up to heaven in showers,
> And burns and sparkles in the briny waves.
> Sure 'tis the war of elements; the shock
> Of nature in convulsions; 'tis the ' wreck
> Of worlds!' What horrid images can show
> The dreadful scene! What loud tremendous sounds,
> What wild, tumultuous verse can represent
> The blended roar of thunder, winds and waves
> In tumult—Now how naturally distress
> Casts up to heaven the wild imploring eye,
> And eager cries for help. Now, now we sink!
> Strange! we survive the shock! Now fiercer still,
> The waves assault our bark, convulse each joint,
> And spread a tremor through each rib of oak.
> Now we shall rise no more. Strange! we emerge,
> Tossed like a cork, we float from wave to wave.

From the huge, watery precipice we plunge
The yawning gulph below : while the howling winds,
And roaring waves, and midnight's hidden glooms,
Surround us—O thou Ruler of the seas,
Send forth thy mighty mandate, " Peace, be still."
And calm their rage.—But can even mercy hear
Such daring rebels, who, in one vile breath,
Blend prayers and curses ? But, alas ! my heart,
Look home; thou art not innocent; my guilt
May hurl these furious hurricanes in air,
And arm each billow of the sea against me.
But have not I, a suppliant at thy throne,
Indulgent Father, have not I bewailed
My guilt in deep repentance ? has not faith
Applied the Saviour's blood !—

I have reason to observe, with pleasure, that my mind, for some days, has been more engaged than usual in calm, and I hope, complacential surveys of divine things, especially of the method of salvation through Christ. I am fully convinced that is the only religion for sinners; and as such I would cordially embrace it. Were it not for this, what insupportable terrors would danger and death wear !

Friday, January 31.—The weather has been very uncertain, and the winds contrary. The greatest part of this day has been a dead calm; but such a violent sea has run as I have never seen; and as the ship had no wind to direct her course, she was tossed about in the most terrible manner, and it seemed next to a miracle to me, that she was not dashed to pieces or overset. It is six weeks to day since we sailed from Plymouth; and no less than eleven weeks since I came on board. What with sea sickness, what with the wickedness of the company, and the anxieties of absence from my other self, it has been a melancholy time to me. Now when I am out of business, my heart is always at home; and so long a delay by contrary winds has been no small trial to my patience. What tender images of domestic happiness rise before me, whenever I recollect the favourite idea of my Chara! I have now seen a good deal of the world; and I am more and more convinced that she is the person fitted to make me happy. I have had death frequently before me in this passage; and it is still uncertain whether ever I shall see my home, though we suppose we are now near soundings. With this solemn prospect I have been frequently shocked; though at times I seemed supported with more of the calmness and fortitude of a Christian, than a person so unholy could expect. I am quite discouraged in my attempt to reform the ship's company, particularly the C——, who has many amiable qualities blended with his vices. I have spoken to him repeatedly in the most solemn manner I could; but after all, they forget themselves so far that they swear and imprecate in my hearing. Alas ! the more I know of human nature, the more I am convinced of its utter depravity.

Sunday, February 2.—It is a remarkable mercy that I am now alive, and capable to take memorials of any thing that happens in the regions of mortality. About six o'clock the night before last, a violent storm blew up from the north-east, which continued near thirty-six hours; and I never was more apprehensive of danger. The waves beat with such violence against the ship that one could hardly expect but she would have been dashed to pieces or overset; and the captain and the most veteran sailors were full of alarming apprehensions. Alas ! how helpless are we on this boisterous element—all our dependence upon one feeble bottom: and no other way of safety or deliverance. I think there is no phenomenon in nature so terrible, as a storm at sea; especially in the night. It requires no small fortitude, to stand upon the deck and take a view of it.

What horrors crowd around ! Destruction frowns
In all its frightful shapes. The lowering clouds
Spread out their solid glooms, and not a star
Emits a ray of charming light. The winds
Discharge their whole artillery, rear vast piles
Of waves on waves, and watery pyramids,
Capped with white foam. Our feeble barque,
Our sole defence, denies us hope; the waves
In deluge break o'er her, dash her sides,
And threaten to o'erwhelm her. Hark ! the roar
Of breaking precipices, and the howl
Of furious winds, that from the bottom turn
The wild fermenting ocean : while the night
Spreads her thick glooms o'er all the dreadful scene.

Friday, February 7.—Our dangers and our deliverances have again been renewed. After a very calm morning last Wednesday, when the sea was as smooth as ever I saw it, it blew up a violent storm from the south which lasted till this morning, about forty-eight hours. Its terrors exceeded all the appearances in nature that I had ever seen; and those that had been long accustomed to the sea, agreed they had hardly ever seen a more dangerous storm. We were obliged to lie-to, as the sea-phrase is, near two nights and two days, and drove at the mercy of the winds and waves. I was in a careless, guilty frame when the storm came on: and I never felt so deeply the terrors of being seized by danger or death in such a frame. The sight of death frowning upon me on every side, threw my mind into a ferment like that of the ocean round me. Sometimes indeed I had some intervals of serenity and resignation: but generally my views were gloomy, my fears outrageous, and my heart faint. I endeavoured to commend myself to God, and to resign my dear family to his care: but alas! I could not do it with cheerfulness. I never appeared to myself so helpless in all my life: confined to a little vessel, in the midst of mountainous seas, at a dreadful distance from land, and no possible prospect of escaping death, if any accident should befall the ship. I could do nothing but lie in bed, hearing the howl of winds and roar of waves without, and tossed from side to side by the motion of the vessel, which sometimes rolled so violently that she lay almost on her beam-ends, and I was afraid she would not recover. The waves broke over her so as to wash the men from one side of the deck to the other, and dashed in through the dead-lights into the cabin. I often fell upon my face praying in a kind of agony, sometimes for myself, sometimes for the unhappy ship's company, and sometimes for my dear destitute family, whom the nearest prospect of death could not cross from my heart. To increase our calamity, we knew not where we were. By our log-book we should have been on shore two days ago, but we saw little signs of land. It had been cloudy for four or five days, so that we had no observations to discover our latitude. However, we perceived we had gone too far to the southward upon the coast of Carolina, and were much afraid lest we should run ashore on the dangerous sands near Cape Hatteras. But hitherto God has preserved us; and if my life can be endeared to me or my friends by remarkable deliverances, it will be of more importance than ever. To-day has been cloudy and squally, and in the evening a dead calm, a sure presage of a storm; and now it begins to blow again. May God pity us, and deliver us from this dangerous element, the territory of Death.

Wednesday, February 12.—Blessed be God, we had the welcome sight of land this morning; and suppose we are on the coast of North Carolina, about twenty leagues south of Cape Henry. The wind is contrary, and if a storm should rise, we might be driven out to sea again.

Since my last remarks, we have had strong gales, and violent storms of snow, with very intense cold. It has been so cloudy, that we have had no good observation for nine days; and our reckoning of longitude being out, we knew not where we were. We have been expecting land, and sounding for ground, these fourteen days; but were still disappointed till this morning. If the longitude, which has been so long sought for in vain could be certainly discovered, it would be vastly to the advantage of navigation. Though my mind has been in such a confusion, during the passage, that I have not been able to make any useful remarks to any advantage; yet the various phenomena of the ocean have suggested to me such hints as might be well improved by a spiritual meditant. And I shall take short memorandums of them, that if I should happen to be disposed for it hereafter I may improve upon them. The majestic appearance of this vast collection of waters, may suggest to us—the majesty—and power of God, the author—and his uncontroulable government who rules so outrageous an element as he pleases, and stills it with one almighty mandate "Peace, be still," and the terror of the conflagration which shall dry it up. The alternate storms and calms are a picture of the mutability of human life in this world—of the various frames of a Christian. As storms and hurricanes purify the sea and keep it from corrupting; so afflictions are necessary to purge and sanctify the people of God, and shall work together for their good—and so God brings good out of evil. It is calm in some parts of the ocean while it is tempestuous in others—so particular persons—and countries, are alternately happy and miserable. The sea in the ferment of a storm gives us an image—of a mind agitated with furious lusts and passions—and a riotous mob. The ship is our only safety—so is Christ to the soul, amid the ruins of sin. After a storm and a gloomy night, how welcome and cheering is the return of a calm, and the morning light! So is the return of peace, and the light of God's countenance to a soul in darkness and distress. The want of an observation to discover the latitude, in cloudy weather, leaves the mariner perplexed about his course. Thus perplexed is the Christian, when God withdraws the light of his countenance, or when the meaning of the Scripture is uncertain. It is a great disadvantage to navigation, and occasions the loss of many ships, that the longitude is not discovered. Thus would it have been with the moral world, if it had not been favoured with the light of revelation; and thus is the heathen part of mankind at a loss about the way to heaven.

After a long and dangerous voyage, how eager are the seamen looking out for land, and how rejoiced at the sight of it. Thus eager are some Christians, and thus eager should they all be, to see Immanuel's land, and arrive there.

It is a striking evidence of the degeneracy of human nature, that those who traverse this region of wonders, who see so many dangers and deliverances, are generally thoughtless, vicious, and impenitent.

Arrived in York, February 13, 1755. The next day called in Williamsburg, waited on the Governor, and rode to Mr. Holt's that night. Came home next morning, February 15, and found all well.—What shall I render to the Lord for all His goodness?

————————Expression fails,
Come, more expressive silence, muse His praise?

CHAPTER XIII.

REV. SAMUEL DAVIES—FROM HIS MISSION TO EUROPE TO HIS DEATH.

DURING the absence of Mr. Davies from Virginia, hostilities had commenced on the frontiers. In May 1754, blood had been shed by forces under the command of Colonel Washington, who unawares fell upon a party of French and Indians, near the Great Meadows, as they were advancing to surprise Fort Necessity. England and France, both desiring the control of North America, were entering the fierce contest that decided the fate of that great continent. Hostilities commenced at the confluence of the Alleghany and Monongahela rivers. Some Virginians were fortifying the place, now Pittsburgh. A large French force drove them from the position. Washington met the force advancing upon him near the Great Meadows; and in July was compelled, by a superior force of French and Indians, to capitulate on honourable terms. Preparations were made to carry on with great vigour, the war thus begun. English and French forces were collected; and efforts were made to enlist the numerous warlike tribes of Indians, in the contest. The French were the more successful in arraying these barbarous allies under their flag; and without pity turned the fury of Indian warfare upon the English frontiers.

According to ancient charters, Virginia extended from the Atlantic to the Pacific shores, and covered some of the posts the French were most anxious to maintain, both for the safety of their colonies and the ultimate possession of the great Valley of the Mississippi, if not the whole continent. The Virginia frontiers were east of the grand Alleghany, scattered along the Valley of the Shenandoah, and the head streams of the Potomac, the James and Roanoke. On these, the Indians, from Ohio, claiming the beautiful valleys and streams as the residence of their fathers abandoned at the approach of the English, but not given up, began their incursions with midnight attacks, the tomahawk and scalping knife, merciless slaughter, and dreary captivity. The whole country was filled with alarm. Consternation seized the frontiers. The more remote, and the more timid families, retired and formed neighbourhoods with blockhouses of sufficient capacity to afford shelter to all, and strength to resist an attack, from a savage enemy. Some of the more brave fortified their log houses and maintained their post.

Mr. Davies, on his return to his family, partook of the alarm, though his dwelling was far east of the Blue Ridge. He felt the necessity of vigorous action by the colonists, and of the special protection of Divine Providence. The Provincial Legislature had appointed the 5th of March as a day for fasting and prayer to Almighty God. Mr. Davies preached on that day, in Hanover, from the words, "The Most High ruleth the kingdom of men and giveth it to whomsoever he will," (Dan. iv. 25,) a truly Christian, patriotic sermon, calculated to excite among his hearers proper sentiments of devotion, and love of country. On the 10th of July, 1755, the army under General Braddock suffered a signal defeat. The savages in the interest of France broke in, like a torrent of fire, upon the terror stricken frontiers. The soldiers escaping from the massacre, that followed the battle, carried the news of the disaster; deserting their companions, many of them never rallied, but sought their homes and a shelter east of the mountains, and were arrested at the head of tide water as deserters spreading terror by their flight, and their frightful narrations of savage barbarities. On the 20th of the month Mr. Davies preached in Hanover, on the words of Isaiah chap. xxii. verses 12, 13 and 14 : "And in that day did the Lord God of Hosts call to weeping and to mourning, and to baldness, and to girding with sackcloth; and behold joy and gladness, slaying oxen and killing sheep, eating flesh and drinking wine: let us eat and drink for to-morrow we die." This text had been chosen, and a few pages of manuscript had been written in view of the distress of the country, under an uncommon drought, and the calamity of a French and Indian war. When the appalling news of Braddock's defeat reached Hanover, Mr. Davies completed, and delivered to his people, a sermon worthy the occasion and of himself. On the first report of the defeat and the approach of the cruel enemy not only the more exposed families forsook their dwellings, but apprehending an immediate assault from the advancing foe, many proposed to abandon all the frontiers and return to the thickly settled portions of the province or to other provinces. After lamenting the sins that had brought these accumulated sufferings upon the country, Mr. Davies proceeds:—"Let me earnestly recommend it to you to furnish yourselves with arms, and put yourselves into a posture of defence. What is that religion good for that leaves men cowards on the appearance of danger. And permit me to say, that I am particularly solicitous that you, my brethren of the dissenters, should act with honour and spirit in this juncture, as it becomes loyal subjects, lovers of your country, and courageous Christians. That is a mean, sordid, cowardly soul, that would abandon his country, and shift for his own little self, when there is any probability of defending it. To give the greater weight to what I say, I may take the liberty to tell you I have as little personal interest, as little to lose, in this colony as most of you. If I consulted either my safety, or my temporal interest, I should soon remove my family to Great Britain or the northern colonies, where I have received very inviting offers. Nature has not formed me for a military life, nor furnished me with any degree of fortitude and courage; and yet I must declare, that after the most calm and impartial deliberation, I am determined not to leave my country while there is any prospect of defending it. Certainly he does not deserve a place in any country, who is ready to run from it upon every appearance of danger. The event of the war is yet uncertain; but let us determine that if the cause should require it, we will courageously leave house and home and take the field." After much pathetic address on personal religion, he thus closed: —"It is certain many will be great sufferers by the drought, and many lives will be lost, in our various expeditions. Our poor brethren in Augusta, and other frontier counties, are slaughtered and scalped. In short it is certain, be the final issue what it will, that our country will suffer a great deal; therefore be humble. Be diligent in prayer for our army, and for the unhappy families on our frontiers. And may the Lord of Hosts be with us, and the God of Jacob be our refuge."

This spirit of Davies was, in general, the spirit of the dissenters, who formed the line of frontiers in Virginia. The more isolated and exposed retreated; the stronger neighbourhoods girded themselves for the war. The congregations on the Cowpasture river, in Augusta, were broken up by savage inroads, part of the families retreated to the Valley of the Shenandoah, and part with their pastor, Mr. Craighead, ultimately took their abode in Mecklenburg county, North Carolina.

On the 17th of August, Mr. Davies delivered a thrilling sermon to the first volunteer company raised in Virginia after Braddock's defeat—"to march over trackless mountains, the haunts of wild beasts or fierce savages, into a hideous wilderness, to succour their helpless fellow-subjects, and guard their country." It was commanded by Captain Overton. The text chosen for the occasion was 2d Samuel, x. 12: "Be of good courage, and let us play the men for our people, and for the cities of our God; and the Lord do that which seemeth him good." Fervent piety and ardent patriotism are commingled throughout the discourse. Connected with this sermon is this remarkable sentence—"I may point out to the public that heroic youth, Col. Washington, whom I cannot but hope Providence has hitherto preserved in so signal a manner, for some important service."

In the midst of these agitating scenes, the activity of Mr. Davies, in his ministerial duties, was not at all abated. He seemed never to forget that he was a minister of the gospel. On the 4th of June, 1755, Mr. Robert Henry, of whom mention has been made, was installed pastor of Cub-creek, in Charlotte, and Briery, in Prince Edward. Cub-creek was settled by a colony led by Mr. Caldwell, and Briery was the fruit of Mr. Davies' visit, improved by Mr. Henry. On the last Sabbath of July, Mr. John Wright was installed pastor of the church in Cumberland county. He had been a pupil and protege of Mr. Davies. The church in Cumberland was gathered from the labours of Mr. Robinson, followed up by the missionaries that followed him, and also from the visits Mr. Davies was able to make from time to time. In December of the same year the Presbytery of Hanover was formed; Mr. Davies presided as Moderator, but, on account of indisposition, was excused from preaching. The Presbytery consisted of six ministers, three of whom, Messrs. Todd, Henry and Wright, had been introduced into their charges by the influence of Mr. Davies, and occupied part of the ground over which he used to ride. By this increase of ministers the specious objections to licensing more houses for dissenters—viz. the number of houses for a minister—was removed, though all difficulty was not removed.

Under date of March 1755, Mr. Davies writes to a member of the Society in London for Promoting Religious Knowledge among the Poor.

"*Dear Sir:*—Divine Providence has safely conducted me through the numerous dangers of sea and land, and replaced me in my former sphere of usefulness and happiness. The confluence of so many mercies at one time, the tender guardianship of heaven over my dear family and friends, the review of my remarkable success in the important business of my mission, and promising situation of religion amongst my people, threw me into a ferment of grateful passions, which are not yet subsided, though I have been at home about six weeks. I doubt not, as a friend, you will congratulate me, and, as a Christian, assist me in returns of gratitude and praise to my Divine Benefactor.

"As there is a propriety in transmitting to you an account of the distribution and reception of the noble charity of that generous Society to which you belong, I must confine myself to that, and refer you to my correspondents for other articles of intelligence. Though there are very few of the white people in this colony in abject poverty, yet there are many in such low circumstances, that they cannot spare money to purchase good books, and many more so stupidly ignorant and insensible of their want of instruction, as to esteem it an unnecessary charge, and so excuse themselves from it as a needless expense. On one or other of these accounts, there are few houses in Virginia well furnished in this important respect. Multitudes are without any assistance of this kind, and even Bibles are not always to be found among them. To some of these I have distributed—The Compassionate Address, Dr. Doddridge's Rise and Progress, Mr. Baxter's Call, &c., with the best advice I could give them, and hope I shall be able to send you an agreeable account of the happy effects of the distribution.

"But the poor neglected negroes, who are so far from having money to purchase books, that they themselves are the property of others; who were originally African savages, and never heard of Jesus or his gospel, till they arrived at the land of their slavery in America, whom their masters generally neglect, and whose souls none care for, as though immortality were not a privilege common to them with their masters,—these poor unhappy Africans are objects of my compassion, and I think the most proper objects of the Society's charity. The inhabitants of Virginia are computed to be about 300,000 men, the one-half of which are supposed to be negroes. The number of those who attend my ministry at particular times is uncertain, but generally about three hundred, who give a stated attendance; and never have I been so struck with the appearance of an assembly, as when I have glanced my eye to that part of the meeting-house where they usually sit, adorned, for so it has appeared to me, with so many black countenances eagerly attentive to every word they hear, and frequently bathed in tears. A considerable number, (about an hundred) have been baptized, after a proper time for instruction, and having given credible evidence, not only of their acquaintance with the important doctrines of the Christian religion, but also a deep sense of them upon their minds, attested by a life of strict piety and holiness. As they are not sufficiently polished to dissemble with a good grace, they express the sentiments of their souls so much in the language of simple nature, and with such genuine indications of sincerity, that it is impossible to suspect their professions, especially when attended with a truly Christian life and exemplary conduct.

"My worthy friend, Mr. Todd, minister of the next congregation, has near the same number under his instruction, who, he tells me, discover the same serious turn of mind. In short, sir, there are multitudes of them in different places, who are willing and eagerly desirous to be instructed, and embrace every opportunity of acquainting themselves with the doctrines of the gospel, and though they have generally very little help to learn to read, yet to my agreeable surprise, many of them, by dint of application, in their leisure hours, have made such a progress, that they can intelligibly read a plain author, and especially their Bibles; and pity it is that any of them should be without them. Some of them have the misfortune to have irreligious masters, and hardly any of them so happy as to be furnished with these assistances for their improvement. Before I had the pleasure of being admitted a member of your Society, they were wont to come to me with such moving accounts of their necessities in this respect, that I could not help supplying them with books to the utmost of my small abilities; and when I distributed those amongst them, which my friends, with you, sent over, I had reason to think that I never did an action in all my life that met with so much gratitude from the receivers. I have already distributed all the books that I brought over, which were proper for them. Yet still on Saturday evenings, the only time they can spare, my house is crowded with numbers of them, whose very countenances still carry the air of importunate petitioners for the same favours with those who came before them. But alas, my stock is exhausted, and I must send them away grieved and disappointed. Permit me, sir, to be an advocate with you, and by your means, with your generous friends, in their behalf. The books I principally want for them are Watts' Psalms and Hymns, and Bibles. The two first they cannot be supplied with any other way than by a collection, as they are not among the books your Society give away. I am the rather importunate for a good number of these, as I cannot but observe that the negroes, above all the human species I ever knew, have an ear for music, and a kind of ecstatic delight in Psalmody; and there are no books they learn so soon, or take so much pleasure in, as those used in that heavenly part of divine worship. Some gentlemen in London were pleased to make me a private present of these books for their use, and from the reception they met with, and their eagerness for more, I can easily foresee how acceptable and useful a large number would be among them. Indeed nothing would be a greater inducement to their industry to learn to read, than the hope of such a present, which they would consider both a help and a reward for their diligence.

"I hardly know of any modern institution which bears so favourable an aspect on the declining interests of religion as your Society. They deserve the pleasure of hearing the happy effects of their generosity at the distance of four thousand miles, in these ends of the earth, and it is no small happiness to me that the strictest veracity allows me to transmit so agreeable an account. Thus may the inhabitants of Great Britain receive blessings in answer to prayers put up for them in America, where I am sure they have many affectionate intercessors, amongst whom be pleased to number

Your sincere and much obliged friend,

S. DAVIES."

The preceding letter was preserved by Gillies; and from him we learn that the correspondent of Mr. Davies was so delighted with the communication that he sent a copy to a friend with the following sentiment—" My soul triumphs in the thought of an African church formed and raised in the deserts of America, nor can I wonder that my worthy friend esteems his congregation *adorned* with these outcasts of the earth, as they appear to others, now flying as a cloud, and flocking into Christ as doves to their windows. The thought of such an auditory in the attitude he represents them, diligently attentive to every word they hear, and often bathed in tears, gives me a pleasure I cannot easily describe. O how I love their black faces! The members of our Society have generously given up the distributions which fell to their share to this important service."

The members of the Society were so interested in this—"first attempt of this nature that has ever been made with any considerable success"—that collections were made to procure Watts' Psalms and Hymns, with other religious books, for distribution by Mr. Davies, in some measure according to his wants; and plans were proposed and sent to Mr. Davies in Hanover, the object of which was the obtaining, if practicable, some three or four young Africans who still retained their native language, were pious, and of good abilities, to be educated at the College in New Jersey, for the benefit of which large donations had been received in England, that they might become missionaries to Africa. The books reached America in due time; of their reception and disposition, Mr. Davies shall give an account in a letter preserved by Gillies, under date of March 2d, 1756. "*Dear Sir:*—Your last letter, with the large donation of books that attended it, gave me the most agreeable surprise that ever I met with in my whole life. I

speak the very truth, sir, I did not think myself worthy in any
measure to be the instrument of so much good, nor had I the
least expectation, that a letter from my hand would ever be
honoured with such extensive success. As an honour conferred upon me; as an evidence that the spirit of Christian
charity is far from being extinct in your great metropolis, even
in this infidel and debauched age; as a present advantage, and
in the meantime a favourable omen with regard to futurity, to
the neglected heathen slaves in this Christian country; as an
acceptable offering to God; and as fruit that will abound to the
account of the benefactors; in all these, and sundry other
views, I rejoice in it, I feel that even a heart so insensible as
mine, is not proof against the sensations of pious gratitude
upon such an occasion. It has more than once cast me into
the posture of adoration and praise before the throne of grace,
that I am not left unassisted in the delightful work. I dare
say, some scores, both black and white, bond and free, concur
with me in the most ardent returns of gratitude to the author
of every good gift, for a charity of such extensive usefulness.
And to you, dear sir, who have been so active in promoting it,
and to my other friends who have concurred in the same way,
to the Society which gave so favourable a reception to my
representation, and to all the contributors, whether within or
without the Society, I return the most humble and affectionate
thanks from myself, and from their many beneficiaries, who
cannot write, nor make their acknowledgments themselves; and
if the prayers of these poor strangers to the throne of grace,
who have lately learned to bow and weep, and cry there, have
any efficacy, your pious generosity will be rewarded an hundred fold, both in this and the future world. I count myself
happy, sir, that I can retaliate you, and the other benefactors
of this scheme, in that way, in which only you desire it, and
that is by giving you an account of the distribution and acceptance of the books among those for whom they were intended; and this I shall do, with the utmost alacrity and
cheerfulness to the best of my knowledge.

"My hurries of various kinds are so incessant, and my correspondence so extensive, that I have no leisure to take copies
of my letters, and my memory can retain but a very general
idea of them; therefore, if in comparing them, you find some
mistaken references, defects or repetitions, you need not be
surprised; but as far as I can recollect, I gave you a pretty
full account in a former letter of the numerous African slaves
in the colony, and now I only design to add a few particulars
which are new, or did not then occur to my mind. When the
books arrived, I gave public notice of it, after sermon, at the
next opportunity, and desired such negroes as could read, and

such white people as would make a good use of them, and were so poor that they could not buy such books, to come to me, at my house, and I should distribute them amongst them. On this occasion I also enlarged upon a new topic of conviction, both to the slaves themselves and their masters. Since persons at so great a distance, who had no connection with them, were so generously concerned to Christianize the poor negroes, and had been at so much pains and expense for that end, then how much more concerned, how much more zealous, and industrious should their masters be, to whom the care of their souls as well as of their bodies is committed, and who enjoy the advantage of their laborious service! and how much more ought the poor negroes to be concerned for themselves? and how much more aggravated would be their guilt and ruin, if they persisted in obstinate infidelity and wickedness, after so much pains had been taken with them for their conversion? This I found afterwards proved a very popular topic of conviction, and made some impressions upon the minds of not a few.

"For some time after this, the poor slaves, whenever they could get an hour's leisure from their masters, would hurry away to my house, and receive the charity with all the genuine indications of passionate gratitude which unpolished nature could give, and which affectation and grimace would mimic in vain. The books were all very acceptable, but none more so than the Psalms and Hymns, which enable them to gratify their peculiar taste for psalmody. Sundry of them have lodged all night in my kitchen, and sometimes when I waked about two or three o'clock in the morning, a torrent of sacred harmony poured into my chamber, and carried my mind away to heaven. In this seraphic exercise, some of them spend almost the whole night. I wish, sir, you and their other benefactors could hear any of these sacred concerts. I am persuaded it would surprise and please you more than an Oratorio, or a St. Cecilia's day. The good effects of this pious charity are already apparent. It convinces the heathen, that, however vicious and careless, about the religion they profess, the generality of the white people are, yet there are some who really look upon it as a matter of the utmost importance, and universal concern, and are actuated with a disinterested zeal to promote it. It has excited some of their masters to emulation, and they are ashamed, that strangers on the other side of the Atlantic, should be at pains to teach their domestics Christianity, and they should be quite negligent themselves. It furnishes the most proper helps for such of the negroes as can read, and are piously disposed, and some of them are evidently improving in knowledge. It has excited others to learn to read; for as I give books to none but such as can read, and are piously

disposed, they consider them as a reward for their industry;
and I am told that in almost every house in my congregation, and in sundry other places, they spend every leisure
hour in trying to learn, since they expect books as soon as they
are capable to use them. Some of them, I doubt not, are excited to it by a sincere desire to know the will of God, and
what they shall do to be saved: others I am afraid are actuated
by the meaner principle of curiosity, ambition and vanity.
However, be the principle what it will, I cannot but rejoice in
the effect, as it renders them more capable of instruction in the
great concerns of religion. This charity may also be of great
service in a political point of view; for now, when the French
and Indians are invading our country, perpetrating the most
horrid barbarities and depredations upon our frontiers, we
have not been without alarming apprehensions of insurrections
and massacre from the numerous slaves among ourselves, whom
they might seduce to their interest by the delusive promises of
liberty; and while they do not feel the restraints of conscience
and Christianity, our apprehensions are but too well grounded.
I have done my utmost, without hinting my design to them, to
prevent so dismal a calamity; and for this purpose I have endeavoured to convince them, that there are many of the English, as well as myself, who are really solicitous for their
welfare, which has given me no small popularity amongst them;
and especially to bring them under the restraints of the pacific
religion of Jesus, which has so friendly an influence on society,
and teaches a proper conduct for every station in life. Now I
can distribute these books amongst them as tokens of disinterested benevolence, as helps to understand Christianity, and
in the meantime to detect the impostures, superstitions, and
cruelties of Popery. For this latter purpose the *Protestant's
Resolution* is extremely well calculated.

"To all this I may add, as I have the honour of distributing
the books, it gives me a very handsome opportunity of speaking
seriously and with particular application to many, who might
not otherwise come in my way. There are thousands of negroes
in this colony who still continue in the grossest ignorance, and
most stupid carelessness about religion, and as rank pagans as
when they left the wilds of Africa. And there are not a few
of this unhappy character, even in the bounds of my congregation, which by the by is about sixty miles in circumference.
But I think, sir, my ministry of late has been most successful
among them. Two Sundays ago I had the pleasure of seeing
forty of their black faces around the table of the Lord, who all
made credible profession of Christianity, and sundry of them
with unusual evidence of sincerity. Last Sunday I baptised
seven or eight adults, who had been catechumens for some time.

Indeed, many of them seem determined to press into the kingdom of God, and I am persuaded will find an abundant entrance when many of the children of the kingdom shall be shut out.

"One of the catechumens, baptised last Sunday, I conversed with the evening before. He addressed me to this purpose, in broken English—'I am a poor slave, brought into a strange country, where I never expect to enjoy my liberty. While I lived in my own country, I knew nothing of that Jesus, which I have heard you speak so much about. I lived quite careless what will become of me when I die, but I now see that such a life will never do; and I come to you sir, that you may tell me some good things concerning Jesus Christ, and my duty to God; for I am resolved not to live any more as I have done.'—Such a simple address is very striking oratory to me, and would my time allow, I could give you many such specimens. There is one happy circumstance which I think very remarkable, and that is, that notwithstanding the odium Protestant dissenters lie under in this colony, where they were not known till very lately, and notwithstanding the usual disaffection which those bear to vital religion who have none themselves, yet the negroes in these parts are fully allowed to attend upon my ministry, and sometimes upon my private instructions, even by such masters as have no religion at all, or are bigots. Indeed, it is the object of my zeal, not to make them dissenters, but good Christians and good servants. But when I consider, how often the most candid and generous endeavours are misconstrued by bigotry, much more by impiety, I cannot but wonder my attempts meet with so little opposition, and escape suspicion, and I cannot but look upon it as a very promising presage.

"I have distributed sundry of the books among the poorer sort of white people, with this charge, that they would not keep them by them, as a private property, (except the Bibles, for which they would have a constant use in their families) but circulate them about among such of their neighbours as would seriously peruse them, that they might be as extensively serviceable as possible. Some of them have since discovered to me what solemn impressions they received in reading them. I sent a few of each sort to my friend and brother, Mr. Wright, minister in Cumberland, about ninety miles hence, where there is a great number of negroes, and not a few of them thoughtful, and inquisitive about Christianity, and sundry of them hopeful converts. He has been faithful in the distributing, and informs me they meet with a very agreeable and promising reception. He is very laborious in his endeavours to instruct the negroes, and has set up two or three schools among them, where they attend on Sundays, before and after sermon, for they have no other leisure time.

"It affords me no small pleasure, that you have some more

books in reserve for me. I know I have had vastly more than my proportion, as a member of the Society, and I cannot have the face to solicit farther benefactions. Nay, it pains me to think, that by directing the channel towards this new world, some places nearer home may have been drained, or left un-watered. But alas, dear sir, when I reflect upon the almost universal neglect of the many thousands of poor slaves in this wide-extended country, that they generally continue heathens in a Christian country, that but few of their masters will furnish them with such means of instruction, and that they are absolutely incapable of furnishing themselves; when I reflect upon the burden of guilt under which my country groans on this account; when the impressions of these things are fresh upon my mind, I am quite insatiable, and can never say it is enough. Alas, what are four or five hundred books among so many thousand negroes, that attend upon my ministry, at the sundry places where I alternately officiate; and sundry of them who are well disposed I am obliged to send away without a book, for they were all distributed in a few days after their arrival, and I took care not to give one of each sort to every particular person, but ordered them to borrow and lend among themselves. I earnestly desire to have something to distribute among them, that would at once help them to read and teach them the rudiments of Christianity. I have had thoughts of attempting such a thing myself, if I knew how to discharge the expense of the press; though I have no peculiar qualification for it; but this, that I might perhaps adapt myself better to their mode of thinking and speaking, than those that have no acquaintance with them. Dr. Watts's sets of *Catechisms* are the best I know extant, for the last of these purposes; and therefore when my next nomination comes, I beg you would send me a considerable proportion of them. Thus, sir, I have given you an account of the use I have made of this generous charity, and the happy effects that are likely to follow from it; and I have only this request to add, that the friends of religion with you, would help it forward, not only in this way, but also with their importunate prayers. This assistance is greatly needed, and earnestly desired, by their, as well as, sir,

"Your most obliged, and most affectionate humble servant,

SAMUEL DAVIES."

In these labours for the spiritual welfare of the negroes, so feelingly described by Mr. Davies, his young co-labourers, Todd, Wright and Henry participated, and with corresponding success. There was no obstacle thrown in the way of their instructing the slaves; masters that were themselves opposed to "dissenters, yet freely allowed the negroes to attend" their ministry; and also to receive private instruction on religion. The influence of their labours was great upon the negroes, and the effect abiding. In the year 1819, Dr. Rice thus writes in the Magazine, page 203—"There is now a considerable congregation of their descendants at Polegreen, a church in Hanover, at present under the pastoral care of the Rev. John D. Blair. But many of the members of Davies' church belonged to the estate of Col. Byrd. These were sold, and several of them taken to the county of Charlotte. The writer has seen some of the survivors who could read well, and knew perfectly the Assembly's Catechism." He might have added that he had been for a time their minister, and possessed their confidence and affections. "At this day there are not fewer than one hundred negro communicants in a congregation called Cub-creek, in the county just mentioned. Of these a very large proportion can read, and are instructed in religious doctrines and duties beyond many professors among white people. And they afford an experiment of sixty or seventy years standing of the effect of this sort of discipline among slaves." This was one of Mr. Henry's preaching places; he was successful in his preaching to the negroes, beyond any of his cotemporaries.

Dr. Rice, in the Evangelical Magazine, vol. 2, p. 118, tells an anecdote of Mr. Davies, on the authority of Captain John Morton, grandfather of Mrs. Rice. The time of the occurrence mentioned must have been previous to the mission to Europe. After stating the fact that Mr. Davies made frequent visits to Williamsburg, to meet the Governor and Council, he says— "On one occasion, by special permission, he spoke for himself. Captain John Morton accompanied him. The circumstances of the case were often detailed by the Captain with great satisfaction." What the point to be argued was—whether the propriety of licensing a particular house, when so many had already been licensed for one permanent minister; or the construction to be put upon the Act of Toleration, that of the Attorney General Ryder, or of the Attorney General Randolph—is not stated. It would seem the permissions accorded proceeded rather from an inclination in the King's officers to amuse themselves with the poor dissenters, than from any other motive. The Attorney General was Peyton Randolph. He took his position, and delivered a speech of great legal learning. When Davies rose to reply there was a general titter through the court. His very first remark, however, discovered so intimate an acquaintance with the law on the subject, that marks of surprise were manifest on every countenance. In a short time the lawyers present began to whisper—the Attorney General has met his match to-day, at any rate. The general sentiment among the members of the bar, as expressed in the hearing of Captain Morton, was—"there is a most excellent lawyer spoiled." In volume 1 of the Magazine, p. 272, there is another reference to this tradition. A gentleman of high standing in Virginia became deeply impressed with a sense of religion, and was aroused to seek the salvation of his soul. He inquired of a bookseller for some religious books. Davies' printed Sermons were offered to him ; and at first refused. But recollecting to have heard his father recount the circumstances of a Mr. Davies coming in contact with the Attorney General at Williamsburg, while he was a student of law at that place, and remembering that his father esteemed him a most extraordinary man, he purchased the volumes. The reading was specially blessed to him, and he was led to rejoice in the hope of the gospel. He ever afterwards spoke of the sermons as his father had spoken of their author—as "most extraordinary."

Of Mr. Davies' labours as pastor, Dr. Rice, in the second volume of the Literary and Evangelical Magazine, p. 202, says— "We have learned from aged people, who sat under his ministry, that his powers of persuasion seemed sufficient for the accomplishment of any purpose which a minister of the gospel would undertake. Many, for instance, who had grown up in ignorance of religion, who were married and settled in life, and had children around them, were prevailed on to learn the elements of religious knowledge. A mother might often be seen rocking her infant in a cradle, sewing some garment for her husband, and learning her catechism at the same time. A girl employed in spinning would place her book of questions at the head of the wheel, and catching a glance at it as she ran up her yarn on the spindle, would thus prepare for public catechising ; and boys, who were accustomed to follow the plough, were often to be seen, while their horses were feeding at mid-day, reclining under an old oak in the yard, learning the weekly task. Young and old were willing to be taught by their preacher ; and when assembled for catechetical instruction, the elders of the church and heads of families were always examined first. This course of instruction was not brief, and quickly finished, as is the case now. Households generally were furnished with a few standard works, of good old times; and were expected to study them carefully. The writer has scarcely ever visited a family, the heads or fathers of which belonged to Mr. Davies' congregation, in which he did not find books or remnant of books, such as Watson's Body of Divinity, Boston's Fourfold State, Luther on the Galatians, Flavel's Works, Baxter's Call to the Unconverted, and Saint's Everlasting Rest, Alleine's Alarm, and others of similar character. And these were studied with a care and attention which greatly promoted the improvement of the public. In fact, Davies' churches were schools in which people were taught better things than the ancient sages ever communicated to their disciples. The effect of this discipline remains to this day."

The French and Indian war wasted the spirits and resources of the colonies. In the Spring of 1758, the work of raising recruits by voluntary enrolment went on heavily, and Mr. Davies was called once more to rouse the citizens of Hanover to becoming action. The influence of his war sermons appears to have been irresistible: and an examination of them might be advantageous to those who may be called to address soldiers. It will be seen that the prominent truths of the Gospel are held forth clearly; and man's dependence on God's providence and Christ's intercession forcibly inculcated as the very ground of hope for success. Dr. John H. Rice tells us, Magazine vol. 2d, pp. 359, 360—"We have conversed with aged friends, who remember well those times, and the despondency and consternation that pervaded the colony. They were themselves at the meetings of the people, when Davies preached these sermons; and they represent in lively terms the dejection and gloom depicted on every countenance, when every murmur of the western breeze seemed to be associated with the war-whoop of the savage, and the wail of the victims of French and Indian cruelty. And they say, that as the preacher poured forth the strains of his eloquence, his own spirit was transfused into his hearers: the cheek that was blanched with fear reddened, and the drooping eye kindled with martial fire, and at the conclusion, every voice was ready to say—'Let us march against the enemy—let us conquer or die.' Particularly we have been told, by eyewitnesses, that the effect of the following passage was most powerful." It was delivered on the 8th of May, 1758, at a general muster in Hanover county, for the purpose of raising a company for Captain Meredith; and is a part of Sermon sixty-third, in the printed volumes. About the middle of the sermon he exclaimed—"May I not reasonably insist upon it, that the company be made up this very day before we leave this place. Methinks your king, your country, nay your own interest command me: and therefore I insist upon it. Oh! for the all pervading force of Demosthenes' oratory—but I recall my wish that I may correct it,—Oh! for the influence of the Lord of armies, the God of battles, the Author of true courage, and every heroic virtue, to fire you into patriots and true soldiers this moment! ye young and hardy men, whose very faces seem to speak that God and nature formed you for soldiers, who are free from the incumbrance of families depending upon you for subsistence, and who are perhaps but of little service to society while at home, may I not speak for you, and declare at your mouth,—here we are all ready to abandon our ease, and rush into the glorious dangers of the field, in defence of our country? ye that love your country, enlist; for honour will follow you in life or death in such a cause. You that love your religion, enlist; for your religion is in danger. Can Protestant Christianity expect quarters from heathen savages and French Papists. Sure in such an alliance the powers of hell make a third party. Ye that love your friends and relations, enlist; lest ye see them enslaved and butchered before your eyes.'

"After the close of the discourse we have been informed that a company was made up for Captain Meredith, in a few minutes,—and that more offered their names than the captain was authorized to command. Davies repaired from the muster ground to the tavern to order his horse; and the whole regiment followed him, and pressed round him to catch every word that dropped from his lips. On observing their desire, he stood in the tavern porch, and again addressed them until he was exhausted with speaking."

It is not a matter of surprise that Mr. Davies found himself quite unmolested, at this time, in performing his ministerial services wherever duty and convenience invited him. The Attorney General could scarcely venture to throw impediments in the path of the best recruiting officer in the province.

While Messrs. Davies and Tennent were in England, they had frequent opportunities for advice and consultation on the best method of removing the grievances of the dissenters in Virginia. It was the opinion of the leading dissenters that the General Court in Virginia had no right to limit the number of houses for public worship to be allowed dissenters,—neither had the Court a right to specify the persons to preach in particular houses;—that all licensed ministers might preach in all licensed houses as far as the law was concerned;—that any number of families might demand the registering of their house,—and of course the people of New Kent were oppressed by the revoking of their license. This was Dr. Doddridge's opinion, sent to Mr. Davies in Virginia, shortly before his death, as is gathered from his letter, large fragments of which remain.

But as the General Court persisted in their course, the committee of the Deputation of Protestant Dissenters, resolved in February 1755, to bring the subject before the King in Council, not by petition for liberty of worship, but by appeal from the prosecution of the authorities in Virginia, in the way expressed in the two following papers, which were sent over to Mr. Davies, in reply to the petition referred to in his journal.

"*Rev. Sir:*—The committee of the Deputation of Protestant Dissenters have received your petition to the King in Council about licensing houses for religious worship; and after the most mature consideration and advice thereon, they find it will not be prudent to present it at present. And their advice to you is—that when any house or place for religious worship is wanted, that you apply first to the County Court for a license thereof,—if refused there, then apply for license to the Governor and Council,—if refused there, then apply to the Governor alone for a license,—and if he refuses, then use such house or place for religious worship, as if it had been licensed,—and if prosecuted for so doing acquaint the Committee therewith, and they will then send you further directions how to act.

"Signed by order of said committee, by

Your most humble servant,

NATHL. SHEFFIELD,

Secretary to the said Committee.

"Ironmonger's Lane, 5th February, 1755."

"*Rev. Sir:*—As a secret instruction to you which is not to be divulged until necessity requires it, I am by order of the said Committee to inform you that if any persons are prosecuted in your courts in Virginia for using such unlicensed houses or places for religious worship, after such application for license as in the other letter is directed—that then such person or persons so prosecuted should appeal to the King in Council here, and the Committee will take care to prosecute such appeal. Keep this advice in your own breast until a proper time of appeal comes.

"Signed by order of the said Committee, by

Your most humble servant,

NATHL. SHEFFIELD,

Secretary to the said Committee."

No appeal ever went to England. The difficulty thrown in the way of dissenters was greatly lessened during Braddock's war. Still the labour and expense of a journey to Williamsburg were required to obtain license; and delays were thrown in the way. Some ventured, as Mr. Wright in Cumberland, to use a house for worship during the ravages of the Indian wars, without license, and were unmolested. After the established clergy became involved in contentions with the Legislature about the payment of their stipend of sixteen thousand pounds of tobacco, whether it should be paid in kind, or at an estimated value set by the Legislature, less attention was paid to dissenters. While this contest waxed hotter and hotter, dissenters of different names multiplied; and the rigour of the courts relaxed. This unadvised proceeding of the clergy did more for the dissenters than all their appeals to natural or constitutional law had been able to accomplish.

We come now to an event in the life of Mr. Davies which
filled the people of Hanover with distress,—his removal to
Princeton College, New Jersey. Of this Mr. Davies says, in
his farewell sermon—"both my first settlement here and my
final removal were altogether unexpected." On the death of
the President of Nassau Hall, Mr. Burr, Rev. Jonathan Edwards was called to preside over that important institution.
His presidency was limited to a few weeks; having been inaugurated, February 16th, 1758, he ended his days on the 22d
of the following March. Rev. James Lockwood of Wethers-
field, Connecticut, was, April 19th, chosen his successor. The
want of unanimity in the election, with other circumstances,
prevented his acceptance. The next election, August 16th,
was in favour of Mr. Davies of Virginia; and was by him immediately submitted to a called meeting of Presbytery. On
the 13th of September, the Presbytery met in Hanover, and
unanimously decided against his removal from Virginia. Mr.
Davies used his influence to secure the election of his friend,
Samuel Finley. The Trustees, looking over the whole subject,
turned unanimously upon the man who had plead their cause
to such advantage in England and Scotland, and stood up so
nobly and successfully for the gospel in Virginia; and not discouraged by the refusal of Presbytery, laid the subject before
the Synod of New York and Philadelphia, at its meeting, in
May, 1759. On Thursday 17th, "An application to the Synod,
from the Board of Trustees of the College of New Jersey, for
the liberation of Mr. Davies from his pastoral charge, that he
may accept the Presidency of the said College, to which they
had elected him, was brought in and read. A supplication
was also brought in from Mr. Davies' congregation, earnestly
requesting his continuance with them. The Synod having
seriously considered the congregation's supplication, and fully
heard all the reasonings for and against Mr. Davies' liberation, after solemn prayer to God for direction, do, upon the
whole, judge that the arguments in favour of said liberation
do preponderate, and agree that Mr. Davies' pastoral relation
to his congregation be dissolved in order to his removal to the
College, and do accordingly hereby dissolve it."

The sentiments and feelings of Mr. Davies, on the subject of
his removal from Virginia, are best expressed in his own language, in Sermon 82d, which he delivered, Sabbath, July 1st,
1759, in Hanover, on the words,—"*Finally, brethren, farewell.
Be perfect; be of good comfort, be of one mind; live in
peace; and the God of love and peace shall be with you,*"
2 Cor. xiii. 11. In the introduction, he says,—"A few
weeks before I made my first visit to Hanover, I had no more
thoughts of it as my pastoral charge, than of the remotest

corner of the world; but was preparing to settle in ease near my native place, till the more urgent necessity and importunity of the people here, constrained me to alter my resolution. It is known to no mortal but myself with what reluctance, fear, and trembling I accepted your call. The rawness and inexperience of my youth, and the formidable opposition then made both by Church and State, when a dissenter was stared at with horror, as a shocking and portentous phenomenon, were no small discouragements in my way. For some years I durst hardly venture to appear but in the pulpit or my study; lest, by a promiscuous conversation with the world at large, I should injure the cause of religion, by some instance of unguarded conduct. In short, my self-diffidence rose so high, that I often thought I had done a great exploit, when I had done no harm to this important interest, which I had a sincere desire, though little ability, to promote. When, after many an anxious conflict, I accepted your call, I fully expected I was settled among you for life; and whatever advantageous offers have been made to me on either side of the Atlantic, have not had the force of temptations. It was in my heart to live and die with you; and such of you as best know my circumstances, and how little I shall carry from Virginia after eleven years labour in it, must be convinced in your own conscience, and can assure others, that worldly interest was not the reason of my attachment. To satisfy you of the reason of my present removal I will give you a brief impartial account of the whole affair.

"The College of New Jersey, though an infant institution, is of the utmost importance to the interests of religion and learning, in several extensive and populous colonies. From it both Church and State expect to be supplied with persons properly qualified for public stations; and it has already been very useful to both in this respect. Before the irreparable breach made in it, by the death of that excellent man, President Burr, its members were increased to near a hundred; and there was no small prospect of considerable additions every year. But, alas! President Burr, its father, is no more. Upon his removal, the Trustees made choice of the Rev. Mr. Edwards to succeed him, the profoundest reasoner, and the greatest divine, in my opinion, that America ever produced. His advancement to the place gave the public sanguine expectations of the future fame and prosperity of the College. But alas! how short is human foresight! how uncertain and blind are the highest expectations of mortals! He was seated in the President's chair but a few days, when he was taken sick and died, and left a bereaved society to lament the loss, and pine away under it. An earthquake spread a tremor through a great part of our solid continent on that melancholy day in which he died (March 22d,

1758); but how much more did Nassau Hall tremble when this pillar fell! Some of the Trustees, to my great surprise, had some thoughts of me upon the first vacancy that happened. But knowing the difficulty of my removal, and being very unwilling to leave my congregation, they made an attempt, upon President Edward's death, to furnish the College with another; and therefore, chose the Rev. Mr. Lockwood, a gentleman of a worthy character in New England. But being disappointed as to him, they elected me on the 16th of last August, and were at the trouble and expense of sending two messengers to solicit the affair with me and the Presbytery. I can honestly say, never did anything cast me into such anxious perplexities. Never did I feel myself so much in need of Divine directions, and so destitute of it. My difficulty was not to find out my own inclination which was pre-engaged to Hanover, but the path of duty; and the fear of mistaking it, in so important a turn of my life, kept me uneasy night and day. I submitted the matter to the Presbytery, and gave them an honest representation of it, as far as it was known to me. As I was at an entire loss in my own mind to discover my duty, I could not, upon the authority of my own judgment, approve or regret their decision; but I cheerfully acquiesced in it, and sent it, with my own negative answer, to the Board of Trustees, and expected never to hear any more about it. But the Trustees, to my still greater surprise, made a second application, requesting I would act as Vice-President during the winter, till the Synod should sit, when the judgment of the Presbytery might be referred to that higher judicature. After making all the inquiries in my power what was my duty in so perplexing a case, I thought I had certainly found out the will of God, and returned an absolute refusal in the strongest terms; transferring all my interest at the Board to another gentleman, (Dr. Finley) whom I looked upon as incomparably better qualified for the place, and of whose election I then had considerable hopes. Upon this I was as much settled in Hanover, in my own mind as ever; and, as many of you may remember, publicly congratulated you upon the pleasing prospect. But how was I surprised, and struck into a consternation, to receive a third application in more importunate terms than ever! This again unsettled my mind, and renewed my perplexities; though I was encouraged to hope, that when I had so sincerely committed my way unto the Lord, he would direct my path, and order things so, as that the result should discover my duty. This third application, as I informed the Trustees in my answer, constrained me only to admit a *mere possibility* of its being my duty to comply, but my mind was still almost established in the contrary persuasion. It constrained me only to lay myself open to conviction, and no longer shut up the avenues of light; and, therefore, I came to this conclusion—To mention, at large, all my difficulties and objections,—to insist that my first election should be null, because my electors were not then apprised of my objections,—and to leave it to the Trustees, after hearing all that could be said against it, whether to re-elect me at their next meeting. But even this was not all; I farther insisted, that in case they should re-elect me, it should be referred to the Synod of New York and Philadelphia, whether I should accept the place.

"The result of the affair, when left upon this footing, has been, that I was re-chosen at the Board of Trustees by a much greater majority than at first; and that the Synod, consisting of an unusual number of ministers from various parts, after hearing at large what could be said upon both sides, not only consented to my acceptance of the proposal, but even dissolved my pastoral relation to my dear charge, and ordered my removal by an almost unanimous vote. This has brought the tedious, anxious affair to a final issue."

Mr. Davies immediately repaired to Princeton, and on Thursday the 26th of July, entered upon the duties of his office; and on Tuesday, 26th of September, was inaugurated as President of the College.

The greater part of the printed sermons of Mr. Davies were written under the pressure of his pastoral duties and evangelical labours in Virginia, which were incessant and excessive. They are the preparations he made for his continually recurring calls for pulpit labours. Many of them bear the date of their first delivery. His frequent and continued absences from home forbade extensive reading, or a very free use of a library; but were favourable to meditation and reflection, and lively mental action, as he journeyed through the silent forests. His constant collision with men of talent and influence, and the perpetual excitement on religion, formed and improved his mental habits, excited his warm and devotional feelings, and gave him a facility in his pulpit preparations he might never have attained in the full enjoyment of literary and theological treasures, in a congregation that permitted a sedentary life. The few hours he could spend in study, or with his pen, he was prepared to use to the greatest advantage on some angelic theme that had been the subject of his solitary meditations; or some point in morals or theology forced upon his attention by the necessities or passions of his fellow men. The spiritual wants of his flock dictated his sermons; and his ardent desires to do his hearers good, together with his simplicity of soul and fear of God, gave wonderful point to his arguments and illustrations. His power of sympathy was wonderful; he seemed at once to enter into the true condition of the people with whom he min-

gled, and to be able in his discourse to make them enter into
his feelings about them, and partake of his emotions.   He
wrote his sermons with care, and carried them to the pulpit,
and often read them, and often preached without reading, or
omitted some of his preparations, or added to them, as circumstances and his own feelings prompted.   In this way, his short
time for preparation was amply sufficient, as the same sermon
might be used repeatedly on one of his wide circuits; and the
severe exercise on horseback promoted his bodily vigour, and
enabled him to apply his mind with all its force, under strong
excitement.   He makes no parade of learning, but every where
in his sermons it is evident that large stores were at his command; that he felt strongly, and thought clearly, and reasoned
forcibly from great principles and important facts.   At the
twang of his silver bow the heart was pierced through and
through; and with an angel's tenderness he was pouring in the
balm of Gilead to the wounded spirit.   And in all this the man
was not seen; his message only was heard.   Men saw, and felt,
and were excited, and convinced, and driven on to act, as by
the moving of their own souls.   They praised no set words of
argument, admired no figures, lauded no flights of oratory, but
felt themselves swept along to believe as he believed, and feel
as he felt.   When removed from the presence of the man, then
they knew his charms must have been fascinating, and his
power unresisted.

Sometimes as we read his Sermons, we begin to think, he is
dealing too much in words; but, when we read again, and catch
something of his spirit, his ardent heart seems pausing for a
moment on truth rich in thought and feeling,—and then he
hurries us along to take another view, to hear another statement, and to contemplate a kindred truth.   Sometimes we
think he is going to make a parade of learning, and theological
lore, and philological treasures; but suddenly, he leads us off,
under the conviction of truth, and with excited feelings, to the
discussion of some subject in morals or religion in which we are
ourselves deeply interested.   Sometimes we wish there had
been more argumentative discussion on some of the great and
disputed doctrines of the Gospel; but, on second consideration,
we do not see what could have been gained in a sermon addressed to a mixed audience, by more of the appearance of logic.
He has stated the truth, he has illustrated it, and applied it,
and made his hearers believe with him.   Like a skilful pleader
before a jury, he mingles principles, and facts, and feelings,
with some apparent disorder, but resistless effect.   He seems
to have known for what he preached, and to whom he preached.
There is a most wonderful congruity between the circumstances of the man, of the people, and the manner of his

preaching; and humanly speaking here was the secret of his success. Always in earnest, he was always timely; nothing kept him back from declaring the truth he judged fitting the condition of things; and nothing could make him utter what he judged ill appropriate. That noble sense of propriety he always carried with him, was a special gift of God, cherished by education and guided by the Holy Ghost, on whom he fully relied for help and for all his success. In his devotion to his work and simplicity and timeliness of his address, he is worthy of all admiration. His care in preparing his sermons may be known by the declaration—"every sermon, I think worthy of the name, cost me four days hard study in the preparation."

Always earnest in his preaching, frequently excited, he was never boisterous. His subject excited him, his congregation excited him, his sense of responsibility impressed him, and his fervent spirit found vent in impassioned words. In his journal he tells us—that some sermons he had prepared and delivered under great excitement in America he could not deliver in England, without omitting parts, because he was not in proper frame to express such sentiments. He could not feign the orator. His outward man was excited in unison with his aroused spirit; yet he never seemed to make a gesture; he only uttered his sentiments with becoming motions of his body, and tones and modulations of his voice. He often preached to excited multitudes, but never forgot he was God's minister.

Virginia mourned his departure; and Nassau Hall rejoiced in his accession. The wonderful sympathy of the man is seen in the readiness with which he accommodated himself to his entirely new field of labour. He comprehended his situation. The change from the labours of an Evangelist in Virginia to the Presidency of a College, was complete, and perhaps too sudden for his physical strength. The historians of Nassau Hall all agree in awarding high praise to Mr. Davies for the wisdom of his plans, the energy of his efforts, and the success that attended his labours to advance the interests of the College. His whole heart and soul were in the work; he felt that all eyes were turned upon—that the friends of the College in Europe and America were kindly, yet anxiously observing his proceedings. He rose early and studied late; and to the last, appeared as in Virginia, to do the things, and preach the sermons befitting the occasion which called him forth. *This year thou shalt die*, (Jeremiah xxviii. 16,) was the subject of his new-year sermon, January 1st, 1761, at Nassau Hall. On the 4th of February he appeared before his Saviour in Paradise. His sickness was of short duration. On Saturday he was bled for a violent cold, and transcribed for the press his sermon on the death of George II.; on Sabbath he preached twice in the College hall; on Monday morning at the breakfast table he was seized with chills, followed by an inflammatory fever, which greatly affected his brain. In his moments of the right exercise of reason he was composed, and referred to his condition affectionately and solemnly. During the wanderings of his mind, his imagination and inventive powers were busy in the contrivance of some plan of benevolent action, or the effecting of some good for his fellow men. During the ten days of his sickness, both in the wanderings of a diseased brain and in the clearer exercises of reason, he exhibited a truly Christian interest about the great work to which he had been called.

The father of Mr. Davies died August 11th, 1759, aged seventy-nine years, having lived with him in Hanover for years. His mother survived him. When the corpse of her son was laid in the coffin, she stood over it, gazed at it intently for some minutes,—and exclaimed—"There is the son of my prayers and my hopes,—my only son,—my only earthly supporter. But there is the will of God,—and I am satisfied."

Dr. Rodgers of New York, the early friend and companion of the son, like the beloved disciple, took the mother to his own home, from that hour, and ministered to her wants till the day of her death.

The family record, written in his own hand, in his Bible, preserved by his descendants, says he was born November 3, 1723. Accordingly, he was thirty-seven years and three months old on the day of his death. He died early, having lived fast and done much.

Makemie stands as the father of the Presbyterian Church in America; Davies as the apostle of Virginia. To no one man, in a religious point of view, does the State owe as much; no one can claim a more affectionate remembrance by Christian people. His residence in the State is an era in its history. To Virginia we look for the record and fruits of his labours. The Virginia Synod claims him as her spiritual father; and the Virginia creed in politics acknowledges his principles of religious freedom and civil liberty. His influence on politics was indirect, but not the less sure. The sole supremacy of Christ in the Church,—the authority of the Word of God,—the equality of the ministers of religion,—and individual rights of conscience,—principles for which he plead before the General Court, and in the defence of which he encountered such men as Pendleton, Wythe, Randolph, and the whole host of the aristocracy, are now a part and parcel of the religious and political creed of an overwhelming majority of the citizens of the "Ancient Dominion." He demonstrated the capability of the Church of Christ to sustain itself, not only without the fostering aid of the State, but under its oppressive laws. He showed the patriotism of true religion;—and in defending the principles of Presbytery, he maintained what Virginia now believes to be the inalienable rights of man. The time of Mr. Davies' labours in Virginia embraced that interesting part of Patrick Henry's life, from his eleventh to his twenty-second year. This great orator, in his youth, could not have been unacquainted with the dissenting ministers of his native county; and it is scarcely possible he was unaffected by his ministrations. Two of his sisters, Lucy Henry, who married Valentine Wood, and died in Havanna,—and Jane Henry, who married Colonel Samuel Meredith, and lived and died at New Glasgow, Amherst county, were known to be pious people, and members of the Presbyterian Church;—and we have the authority of an elder in the church, now living, a grandson of Lucy Wood, that they were members of Mr. Davies' congregations. The first popular pleading of Mr. Henry was in Hanover, against the authorized construction of those very laws under which Mr. Davies and the dissenters had groaned, and from which they had obtained but partial relief. The oratory of these great men was much of the same kind. Both reasoned from great principles and facts, and addressed human nature with an overflowing heart, on subjects to which the souls of men are ever alive,— their individual rights and personal interests. What Dr. Finley said of one may be said of both—"the unavoidable consciousness of native power made him bold and enterprising. Yet the court proved that his boldness arose not from a partial, groundless self-conceit, but from true self-knowledge. Upon fair and candid trial, faithful and just to himself, he judged what he could do; and what he could, when called to it, he attempted, and what he attempted he accomplished." The same bold eloquence that roused the militia of Hanover in Braddock's war, was heard again in Hanover and Williamsburg, calling to arms in the revolutionary contest. Mr. Henry, through life, held to the religion of the Bible. In another chapter the influence of Presbytery on the civil constitution of Virginia will be traced at large, and the indirect influence of Mr. Davies and his co-labourers fully seen.

Mr. Davies' own pen shall close this sketch of his life, with the beautiful and characteristic sentiments in his correspondence with Dr. Gibbons as preserved by Dr. Finley. "I desire seriously to devote to God and my dear country, all the labours of my head, my heart, my hand, and pen: and if he pleases to bless any of them, I hope I shall be thankful, and wonder at his condescending grace. O my dear brother! could we spend and be spent, all our lives, in painful, disinterested, indefatigable service for God and the world, how serene and bright would it render the swift approaching eve of life! I am labouring to do a little to save my country, and, which is of much more consequence, to save souls from death, from that tremendous kind of death, which a soul can die. I have had but little success of late; but blessed be God, it surpasses my expectation, and much more my desert. Some of my brethren labour to better purpose. The pleasure of the Lord prospers in their hands.

"Blessed be my Master's name, this disorder"—a violent sickness from which he was just recovering—"found me employed in his service. It seized me in the pulpit, like a soldier wounded in the field. This has been a busy summer with me. In about two months I rode about five hundred miles, and preached about forty sermons. This affords me some pleasure in the review. But alas! the mixture of sin, and of many nameless imperfections that run through, and corrupt all my services, give me shame, sorrow, and mortification. My fever made unusual ravages upon my understanding, and rendered me frequently delirious, and always stupid. But when I had any little sense of these things, I generally felt pretty calm and serene; and death, that mighty terror, was disarmed. Indeed, the thought of leaving my dear family destitute, and my flock shepherdless, made me often start back, and cling to life; but in other respects, death appeared a kind of indifferency to me. Formerly I have wished to live longer, that I might be better prepared for heaven; but this consideration had very very little weight with me, and that for a very unusual reason, which was this:—after long trial I found this world a place so unfriendly to the growth of every thing divine and heavenly, that I was afraid if I should live any longer, I should be no better fitted for heaven than I am. Indeed, I have hardly any hopes of ever making any great attainment in holiness while in this world, though I should be doomed to stay in it as long as Methuselah. I see other Christians indeed around me make some progress, though they go on with but a snail-like motion. But when I consider that I set out about twelve years old, and what sanguine hopes I then had of my future progress, and yet that I have been almost at a stand ever since, I am quite discouraged. O, my good Master, if I may dare call thee so, I am afraid I shall never serve thee much better on this side the regions of perfection. The thought grieves me; it breaks my heart, but I can hardly hope better. But if I have the least spark of true piety in my breast, I shall not always labour under this complaint. No, my Lord, I shall yet serve thee; serve thee through an immortal duration; with the activity, the fervour, the perfection of the *rapt seraph that adores and burns.* I very much suspect this desponding view of the matter is wrong, and I do not mention it with approbation, but only relate it as an unusual reason for my willingness to die, which I never felt before, and which I could not suppress.

"I am rising up, my brother, with a desire to recommend Him better to my fellow sinners, than I have done. But alas! I hardly hope to accomplish it. He has done a great deal more by me already, than I ever expected, and infinitely more than I deserved. But he never intended me for great things. He has beings both of my own, and of superior orders that can perform him more worthy service. O! if I might but untie the latchet of his shoes, or draw water for the service of his sanctuary, it is enough for me. I am not an angel, nor would I murmur because I am not.

"In my sickness, I found the unspeakable importance of a Mediator, in a religion for sinners. O! I could have given you the word of a dying man for it, that Jesus, that Jesus whom you preach, is indeed a necessary and an all sufficient Saviour. Indeed he is the only support for a departing soul. *None but Christ, none but Christ.* Had I as many good works as Abraham or Paul, I would not have dared build my hopes on such a quicksand, but only on this firm eternal Rock."

CHAPTER XIV.

THREE AUXILIARIES TO THE CAUSE OF LIBERTY OF CONSCIENCE.

WHAT was not granted to petition and argument and English construction of colonial law, was yielded to the force of circumstances. The French and Indian war, commonly known as Braddock's war, which, after many provocations and preliminary atrocities, broke out in its fury in 1755, by the strange agency of fire and sword, the tomahawk and scalping knife, plead the cause of freedom of conscience with a success hitherto unknown. Rev. Francis Makemie had appeared before the civil authorities in Virginia, Maryland and New York with some success; Rev. Samuel Davies and his coadjutors had laid the cause before the Governor and Council of Virginia, repeatedly, and had gained something for freedom of conscience; but houses for public worship could not be occupied without permission from the civil authorities, and each application for a house of worship was heard on its own merits. The opinion of the Attorney General of England had been obtained in favour of the dissenters in Virginia, but that had no effect upon the action of the General Court of the colony, who maintained their own construction of their own laws, one of which they claimed the Act of Toleration to be.   Mr. Davies had visited England, and the dissenters sympathising with him and his people and the dissenters in the colony, and in the provinces generally, held frequent councils, and their committee armed him with their best devices after his return, to aid him in the arduous struggle for religious liberty.   But what had not been gained by English interpretation of law, by appeals to the law of nature, or by equal administration of law, was wrought out by sterner agencies.   The chains, that were not loosed, were broken.

On his return from England, Davies found the whole frontier of Virginia in distress; the alarm pervaded the whole colony. There was an apprehension that the plans of the French officers, in making inquiries for the routes from the Ohio to the Potomac, were to be followed by an armed force of French and savages, excited by the success that met them at the Great Meadows.   The invasion, which was the true policy of France, was looked upon by the colonists as certain; and consternation seized many stout hearts.   The frontiers of Virginia were generally inhabited by dissenters from the Established Church, and pincipally of the Presbyterian creed and forms of worship; and these frontiers were all exposed to Indian depredations.   Some of the most powerful sermons and addresses delivered by Davies were poured forth to arm the frontiers in their defence; and their success was equal to their merit and intention.   The shock of savage war was felt only by the dissenters' families, their cabins were burned, their wives and children fled or were murdered.   The rest of the colony only sent forth soldiers in common with the frontiers; and the Virginia soldiers were always terrible to the savages.

During the confusion of this savage warfare, the Presbyterians, east of the Blue Ridge, chose houses for worship and occupied them without license or molestation.   The Rev. Mr. Wright, the Presbyterian minister in Cumberland county, which was then a frontier, under date of August 18, 1755, says— "People generally begin to believe the Divine government, and that our judgments are inflicted for our sins.   They now hear sermons with solemnity and attention; they acknowledge their wickedness and ignorance, and believe that the New-light clergy and adherents are right.   Thus you see, dear sir, that amidst all our troubles God is gracious, and brings real good out of our real evils; adored be his great name.   I have seen, last Lord's day, above a hundred weeping and trembling under the word. *I now preach any where, being so distant from the metropolis, and the time being so dangerous and shocking.*"   West of the

Blue Ridge, the inhabitants were generally dissenters, coming into the province such, there was always less difficulty in obtaining license for houses of worship, than in those counties east of the Ridge, where no dissenters, or but few, had settled, and those that appeared were converts from the established church. The terrible scourge of war, which fell heaviest on the dissenters, brought with it some ease in matters pertaining to conscience; people were permitted to worship where they pleased when the expectation of invasion oppressed the whole body politic.

The next powerful auxiliary in the cause of liberty of conscience was the course pursued by the established clergy in regard to their salaries. Their stipends had been fixed and collected by law, and were levied and paid in tobacco. At first a certain number of pounds was levied on each poll. By act 11th, 1696, it was ordered that each parish minister "shall have and receive, for his or their maintenance, the sume of sixteen thousand pounds of tobacco besides their lawful perquisites, and that it shall and may be lawfull for the vestry &c., to levy the same in their respective parishes." By the same law it was also ordered that parishes too weak to pay the salary might be united at discretion of the governor, under one minister, in numbers sufficient to sustain a minister. On account of the neglect of parishes, accidental or designed, in formally inducting the ministers into their parishes, there arose difficulties about the glebes, and the salaries of the ministers. In 1748, in consequence of a suit brought by the Rev. Mr. Kay of Richmond county, concerning the glebe of Lunenburg parish, which was decided in his favour by the General Court, the Legislature in session at the time of the decision of the court, to prevent similar suits, by act 34th ordered that the glebe lands should contain two hundred acres of " a good and convenient tract of land"—with " proper dwelling and out-houses : that the salary should be 16,000 pounds of tobacco," and each, with an allowance of four per cent." for shrinkage;—" and every minister received into any parish as aforesaid, shall be entitled to all the spiritual and temporal benefits of his parish, and may maintain an action of trespass, against any person or persons whatsoever, who shall disturb him in the possession and enjoyment thereof." By Act 51 of same year, section 30—" And for preventing all mistakes and controversies concerning the allowance to be made, upon the payment of public, county, or parish levies, be it enacted that the levies aforesaid shall all be laid in nett tobacco."

In the year 1755 the clergy of the Establishment petitioned for an increase of their salary, stating—according to Dr. Hawks, quoting from Bland's letter, p. 117—" that the salary appointed by law for the clergy is so scanty that it is with difficulty they support themselves and families, and can by no

means make any provision for their widows and children, who
are generally left to the charity of their friends—that the small
encouragement given to clergymen is a reason why so few come
into this colony from the two Universities; and *that so many
who are a disgrace to the ministry find opportunities to fill the
parishes;* and that the raising the salary would prove of great
service to the colony." This petition was not granted; the
time was unfavourable, whatever might have been the disposition of the legislature;—the troubles with the French and
Indians were increasing, and ended, in the summer, in a furious
war,—and the staple of Virginia that year failed. Whether
the petition of the clergy was reasonable, depends upon circumstances connected with the rate of living at that time. Their
stipends were a glebe of two hundred acres with the proper
buildings, and sixteen thousand pounds of tobacco, which at
two pence per pound would amount to £133 6s. 8d., together
with marriage and funeral fees. This might or might not have
been a sufficient support, according to the style of living adopted by the clergy. If they followed, or were expected to follow,
the more wealthy planters in their rate of expenditures, it was
certainly too small; if they followed the middling class of people, it was generally enough, with proper economy. If, however, it was really too small, they asked for an increase of
salary at an unfortunate time. For on account of a severe and
protracted drought, which spread its influence over the whole
country, and was peculiarly oppressive in Virginia, the Legislature in October of this year 1755, passed Act 5th—*to enable
the inhabitants of this colony to discharge their Tobacco debts
in money for the present year.* The preamble is—" Whereas
by reason of the great drought a very small quantity of tobacco
is made, so that the inhabitants of this colony are not able to
pay their public, county and parish levies, and the officers' fees,
and other tobacco debts, in tobacco this present year according
to the directions of the laws now in force; for remedy whereof,
and to prevent sheriffs and other collectors of the public dues,
from taking advantage of the necessities of the people, and ex-
acting exorbitant prices for tobacco due or payable to them
from the poor and needy—the enactment is—'that it shall be
lawful to and for any person or persons, from whom any tobacco is due by judgment, for rent, by bond, or upon contract,
or for public county and parish levies, or for any secretaries,
clerks, sheriffs, surveyors, or other officers' fees, or by any
other ways or means whatsoever, to pay and satisfy the same
either in tobacco, according to the directions of the act of Assembly, intituled, An Act for amending the staple of tobacco,
and preventing frauds in his Majesty's customs,—or in money,
at the rate of sixteen shillings and eight pence, for every hun-

dred pounds of nett tobacco, and so in proportion for a greater or lesser quantity, at the option of the payer.'" This act was to continue in force ten months. By this law the tobacco was rated at its usual value, when there was a fair crop, two pence per pound. And as this was the rate when the debts were contracted, the legislature determined there was no injustice to the creditors in paying them the estimated value of their debts. There was no complaint heard against this law during its continuance.

In September of the year 1758, the Legislature re-enacted the law of 1755. The preamble states—"It being evident, from the prodigious diminution of our staple commodity, occasioned by the unseasonableness of the weather in most parts of the colony, that there will not be tobacco made to answer the common demands of the country ; and it being certainly expedient, at all such times, to prevent, as much as possible, the distresses that must inevitably attend such a scarcity—be it therefore enacted," &c. The crop failed ; and the price of tobacco was greatly raised, getting as high as fifty shillings a hundred. The beneficial clergy complained loudly of this law, that by it they were compelled to receive their salary at the rate of two pence per pound for tobacco, when it was worth sixpence or more, and thus instead of about £400, the real worth of their salary, they received less than £134 ; and added that the action of the law was unjust, as the depreciation of tobacco had never been made up to them,—and their salaries were small. The commissary, the Rev. John Camm, of Williamsburg, assailed the law, which in a pamphlet written with great severity, he styled "The Two-penny Act." Colonels Richard Bland, and Loudon Carter replied with equal severity. The excitement spread through the colony. A portion of the clergy met in convention at the College of William and Mary, and instructed their Commissary, Mr. Camm, to make a representation on the subject to the Bishop of London, or the Lords of Trade. "It is probable," says Dr. Hawks, p. 118—"that this complaint was made to their diocesan, as there is extant a letter from that prelate to the Board of Trade, in which he inveighs against this law, as being subversive of the rights of the clergy." Mr. Camm replied to the Colonels under the title—"The Colonels Dismounted ;" and the Colonels rejoined, and carried the people generally with them. The excitement against the clergy became so great, that the printers in Virginia declined publishing for them ; and Mr. Camm resorted to Maryland for publication. The king in council, however, denounced the act of 1755 and 1758 as an usurpation, and declared it null and void.

"This was," says Dr. Hawks—"an unfortunate contest for

the church and the clergy. In every conflict of the kind, the merits of the questions, originally involved in the dispute, are apt to be lost sight of; and in the ardour of controversy, it is not unusual for men to transfer their condemnation from opinions to those who avow them; and such there is reason to believe was the course pursued in this instance. While among the clergy there were some who were above just suspicions or reproach, it must be owned that, as a body, they were any thing but invulnerable; and the opportunity for censure, afforded by their conduct was too inviting to be overlooked by their antago-nists. The leading laymen looked around, and saw almost every parish supplied with an incumbent of some sort, while the state of religion was in their view, far from flourishing; they did not hesitate to impute this condition of things to the clergy them-selves—and the people at large were ready enough to lend a willing ear to the charge. It was not that there was any par-tiality for the dissenters, for the general sentiment was against them; but there was growing up in men's minds a gradual alienation from the church, because it was identified with those who were suspected of being more anxious to enrich themselves than to benefit the souls of others; and men began to admit the suspicions that the establishment was proving a burden, instead of a blessing. Doubtless, injustice was done, in the process, to many a worthy man, who was made to suffer by the indiscrimi-nate censure which visited this order, while he probably would have been as prompt as any one in removing those who had subjected both the church and himself to undeserved reproach. This unfortunate dispute is recorded because it was one of the links in a chain of causes which was operating silently, but surely, for the prostration of the church; every thing which pro-voked hostility and awakened prejudice, of course prepared men's minds for the final blow struck in the stormy times of that Revolution, to which the country was even then approaching with unexpected but certain step."

The preceding view of the contest of the clergy with the Legislature and the public at large, is undoubtedly correct, and is more impressive as coming from the pen of an able defender of the Episcopal Church. After the admission made by him, it would seem ungenerous, here, to cite any instances of de-linquency in the clergy, which aided in increasing the excite-ment produced by this contest. The clergy continued the con-test; and after the king in council had pronounced the law null and void, they commenced suits in the civil courts, to re-cover damages for the withholding their sixteen thousand weight of tobacco or its proper value in money. One suit only was brought to an issue, that instituted by the Rev. James Maury of the county of Hanover. Of this, says Mr. Wirt, in his Life of Patrick Henry, p. 40, "The record of this suit is now before me. The declaration is founded on the act of 1748, which gives the tobacco ; the defendants pleaded specially the act of 1758, which authorizes the commutation into money at sixteen shillings and eightpence; to this plea the plaintiff demurred; assigning for causes of demurrer, first, that the act of 1758 not having received the royal assent, had not the force of a law ; and secondly, that the king in council, had declared the act null and void. The case stood for argument on the demurrer to the November term, 1763, and was argued by Mr. Lyons for the plaintiff, and Mr. John Lewis for the defendents; when the Court, very much to the credit of their candour and firmness, breasted the popular current by sustaining the demurrer." On the first day of the following December, Patrick Henry appeared to argue the cause before a jury on the question of damages, Mr. Lewis having abandoned the cause as desperate. This is the famous case, in which Patrick Henry made his first appearance before a court, and won laurels as a pleader. The scene is well described by Mr. Wirt. Mr. Henry boldly maintained, that the people had only consulted their own safety by the law of 1758, and the king's veto was only an instance of royal misrule ; and that notwithstanding the dissent of the king in council, the act ought to be considered as the law of the land. The jury seemed willing to admit his position, yet according to law returned a verdict of *one penny damages*. The court overruled the motion for a new trial.

No other case was brought to trial; they were all throughout the colony ultimately dismissed by the clergy, who took their revenge by an angry pamphlet from the pen of Mr. Camm. Mr. Maury did not think it advisable to prosecute an appeal, judging it to be entirely useless, in the excited state of the public mind. The tradition respecting this man is, that he was a clergyman worthy of his office, irreproachable in his morals, a believer in the gospel, whose faith triumphed in the last hour; his last expressions were those of praise. There were some advantages in having this cause tried at the suit of Mr. Maury; and there were some serious disadvantages in bringing the suit in Hanover, the home of Davies, and the strong hold of the dissenters east of the Blue Ridge.

The Legislature maintained the legality of their enactment in 1755, and 1758, and to prevent, as far as possible, any decision of the lower courts in favour of the clergy in their contest against the application of this act to their salaries, it was resolved on the 7th of April, 1767—"that the committee of correspondence be directed to write to the agent, to defend the parish collectors from all appeals from judgments here

given, in suits brought by the clergy for recovering their salaries, payable on or before the last day of May, 1759; and that
this house will engage to defray the expense thereof." The
influence of the established clergy was now gone; and the
people and the Legislature of the colony waited only for a
fitting opportunity to break down their legal power: and such
an opportunity, in a few years, occurred. The clergy were not
sensible of their danger, at this time, when their rescue might
possibly have been achieved; when their infatuation left them,
their ruin was unavoidable.

The third auxiliary was found in the efforts and influences of
the denomination of Christians called Baptists. There was a
Baptist church, gathered in Isle of Wight county, by a minister
from England, as early as the year 1714. But the denomination did not spread much in Virginia for many years. About
the year 1743, a few Baptist families settled on the Opeckon
in Berkeley county, and formed a church, which spread both
in the Valley and east of the Blue Ridge, particularly by the
labours of David Thomas, till by the year 1770, we are told by
Semple, in his History of the Baptists in Virginia, p. 295, the
regular Baptists had churches scattered through all the Northern Neck above Fredericksburg. And between the years 1770
and 1780, by the labours of Mr. Lunsford, a young preacher of
extraordinary powers, their churches were extended to the Bay
Shore.

The Separate Baptists, as they were termed under circumstances, which with the name have passed away, made their
first appearance about the year 1754, when Shubael Stearns set
out from New England on a mission to the southward, and
took his abode on the Calapon in Hampshire county. Remaining here a short time, he and his companions removed to North
Carolina and settled on Sandy Creek in Guilford county.
Here the denomination greatly increased; and from this spot
shot out its branches over North and South Carolina and Virginia. The most noted agent in extending the denomination in
Virginia was Samuel Harris, of Pittsylvania. He was hopefully converted, in very interesting circumstances about the
year 1758, and immediately commenced preaching through the
counties bordering on North Carolina. About the year 1766,
he went through the counties on the north side of James River;
and on the 20th of November, 1767, assisted in forming the
church of Upper Spottsylvania, consisting of twenty-five members, the first Separate Baptist church between James and Rap-
pahanoc Rivers. By the time the Revolutionary war commenced,
members of the Separate Baptist denomination were found from
the Blue Ridge to the Bay Shore, both north and south of
James River.

While the contest between the established clergy and Legislature about the salaries of the clergy, was alienating the public mind from the established church herself, the zealous Baptist preachers were calling the attention of men to the great interests of religion, and preaching, according to their ability, the gospel, without money and without price. Generally without education, but under strong convictions of the necessity of conversions to God, they appealed to the hearts of men on subjects always interesting, but at that time almost novel to the mass of their hearers, reared as they were in the bounds of a parish. Repentance, conversion to God, justification by faith in the imputed righteousness of Christ sounded strangely in the ears of many who were not altogether strangers to the forms of religion. These were the doctrines urged upon the hearts of their hearers by the Baptist ministers, with all the energy of excited spirits inflamed by their contemplations of divine truth, and their thoughts and visions of the spiritual world. Multitudes became believers under their fervent exhortations.

For a time, says Mr. Semple, pp. 14, 15—"the Baptists of North Carolina and Virginia were viewed by men in power as beneath their notice; none, said they, but the weak and wicked join them; let them alone, they will soon fall out among themselves, and come to nothing. In some places this maxim was adhered to, and persecution in a legal shape was never seen. But in many others, alarmed by the rapid increase of the Baptists, the men in power strained every penal law in the Virginia code to obtain ways and means to put down these disturbers of the peace, as they were now called. It seems by no means certain that any law in force in Virginia authorized the imprisonment of any person for preaching. The law for the preservation of peace, however, was so interpreted as to answer this purpose; accordingly, whenever the preachers were apprehended, it was done by a peace-warrant. The first instance of actual imprisonment, we believe, that ever took place in Virginia, was in the county of Spottsylvania. On the 4th of Jan. 1768, John Waller, Lewis Craig, James Childs, &c., were seized by the sheriff, and bailed before three magistrates, who stood in the meeting-house yard, and who bound them in the penalty of one thousand pounds, to appear at court two days after. At court they were arraigned as disturbers of the peace; and at their trial they were vehemently accused by a certain lawyer, who said to the court—May it please your worships, these men are great disturbers of the peace, they cannot meet a man upon the road but they must ram a text of Scripture down his throat. Mr. Waller made his own and his brethren's defence so ingeniously that they were somewhat puzzled to know how to dispose

of them. They offered to release them if they would promise
to preach no more in the county for a year and a day. This
they refused; and therefore were sent into close jail. As they
were moving on from the court-house to the prison, through the
streets of Fredericksburg, they sung the hymn—'Broad is the
road that leads to death.'   After four weeks, Lewis Craig was
released from prison—Waller and the others continued in jail
forty-three days, and were then discharged without any conditions. While in prison they constantly preached through the
grates. The mob without used every exertion to prevent the
people from hearing, but to little purpose. Many heard,
indeed, upon whom the word was in power and demonstration."

The confinement of these men drew from the Deputy
Governor, John Blair, under date of July 16th, 1768, a letter
that does honour to his head and heart, directed to the King's
attorney in Spottsylvania.

"*Sir*,—I lately received a letter signed by a good number of
worthy gentlemen, who are not here, complaining of the Baptists; the particulars of their misbehaviour are not told, any
further than their running into private houses, and making dis-
sensions. Mr. Craig and Benjamin Waller are now with me
and deny the charge; they tell me they are willing to take the
oaths as others have; I told them I had consulted the Attorney
General, who is of opinion that the General Court only have a
right to grant licenses, and therefore I referred them to the
Court; but on their application to the Attorney General, they
brought me his letter, advising me to write to you—that their
petition was a matter of right, and that you may not molest
these conscientious people so long as they behave themselves in
a manner becoming pious Christians, and in obedience to the
laws, till the court when they intend to apply for license, and
when the gentlemen, who complain, may make their objections
and be heard. The Act of Toleration (it being found by experience, that persecuting dissenters increases their numbers) has
given them a right to apply, in a proper manner for licensed
houses, for the worship of God, according to their consciences;
and I persuade myself the gentlemen will quietly overlook their
meetings till the court. I am told, they administer the sacrament of the Lord's Supper, near the manner we do, and differ
in nothing from our church but in that of Baptism, and their
renewing the ancient discipline, by which they have reformed
some sinners, and brought them to be truly penitent. Nay, if
a man of theirs is idle, and neglects to labour and provide for
his family as he ought, he incurs their censures, which have had
good effects. If this be their behaviour, it were to be wished

we had some of it among us; but at least, I hope, all may remain quiet till the court.

I am, with great respect to the Gentlemen, Sir,

Your humble servant,

JOHN BLAIR.

"Williamsburg, July 16th, 1768."

"When this letter came to the attorney"—says Semple—"he would have nothing to say in the affair."

Patrick Henry, who had a few years before brought himself into notice by his famous plea against the parsons, in Hanover, hearing of the situation of these Baptist ministers confined in Spottsylvania jail, rode some fifty miles to volunteer his services on the day of their second trial. He entered the courthouse, almost entirely unknown, while the indictment was reading by the clerk. The king's attorney having made some remarks in defence of the prosecution, Mr. Henry taking the paper containing the indictment, said—"May it please your worships, I think I heard read by the prosecutor, as I entered the house, the paper I now hold in my hand. If I have rightly understood, the king's attorney has framed an indictment for the purpose of arraigning, and punishing by imprisonment, these three inoffensive persons before the bar of this Court for a crime of great magnitude,—as disturbers of the peace. May it please the Court, what did I hear read? Did I hear it distinctly,—or was it a mistake of my own? Did I hear an expression, as of a crime, that these men, whom your worships are about to try for misdemeanor, are charged with,—with—what?"—Then in a low, solemn, heavy tone he continued—"preaching the gospel of the Son of God?" Pausing amid profound silence, he waved the paper three times round his head, then raising his eyes and hands to heaven, with peculiar and impressive energy, he exclaimed—"Great God!" A burst of feeling from the audience followed this exclamation. Mr. Henry resumed—"May it please your worships, in a day like this,—when truth is about to burst her fetters,—when mankind are about to be aroused to claim their natural and inalienable rights—when the yoke of oppression that has reached the wilderness of America, and the unnatural alliance of ecclesiastical and civil power, are about to be dissevered,—at such a period, when liberty,—liberty of conscience,—is about to wake from her slumberings, and inquire into the reason of such charges as I find exhibited here to-day in this indictment,"—here he paused, and alternately cast his piercing eyes upon the Court and upon the prisoners, and resumed,—"If I am not deceived, according to the contents of the paper I now hold in my hand, these men are accused of preaching the gospel of the Son of God!—Great God!" A deeper impression was visible as he paused, and slowly waved the paper round his head. "May it please your worships, there are periods in the history of man, when corruption and depravity have so long debased the human character, that man sinks under the weight of the oppressor's hand,—becomes his servile, his abject slave; he licks the hand that smites him;- he bows in passive obedience to the mandates of the despot; and in this state of servility he receives his fetters of perpetual bondage. But may it please your worships, such a day has passed away. From that period when our fathers left the land of their nativity for these American wilds,—from the moment they placed their feet upon the American continent, from that moment despotism was crushed, the fetters of darkness were broken, and heaven decreed that man should be free,—free to worship God according to the Bible. Were it not for this, in vain were all their sufferings and bloodshed to subjugate this new world, if we their offspring must still be oppressed and persecuted. But, may it please your worships, permit me to inquire once more, for what are these men about to be tried? This paper says, for preaching the gospel of the Saviour to Adam's fallen race." For the third time he slowly waved the indictment around his head, and lifting his eyes to heaven in a solemn dignified manner, and again looking at the Court, he exclaimed with the full power of his strong voice—"*What laws have they violated?*" The scene now became painful,— the audience were excited,—the attorney was agitated,—the bench and bar were moved; and the presiding magistrate exclaimed, "Sheriff, discharge those men."

Spottsylvania in a few years wiped away this stain, when the gentlemen assembled in Fredericksburg, in opposition to Dunmore, on the 29th of April, 1775, pledged themselves "to preserve their liberty at the hazard of their lives and fortunes," —and appealed to "God to save the liberties of America."

In different counties the persecution of the Baptists continued. Its weight fell mostly upon those who were called Separate Baptists, who did not, for various reasons, obtain license for their houses of worship, as the regular Baptists generally did. Semple, pp. 294 and 5. At the meeting of the southern district at Hall's meeting-house in Halifax, the second Saturday of May, 1774,—"Letters were received from preachers confined in prison, particularly from David Tinsley, then in Chesterfield jail. The hearts of their brethren were affected at their sufferings, in consequence of which, it was agreed to raise contributions for their aid. Agreed to set apart the second and third Saturday in June, as public fast days, in behalf of our poor blind persecutors, and for the releasement of our brethren." These fast days aroused all the sympathies of their brethren, and of multitudes who had no special attachment to either the persons or doctrines of the Baptists.

In this state of things, it is not wonderful, if the Baptists showed themselves opposed to all laws that favoured one denomination of religion to the detriment of all, or any others; or if they sought opportunities to gain in religion, what all classes were now seeking to gain in the State, freedom from oppression.

By the agencies that have been glanced at, freedom of conscience began to have a place in men's ideas, and to become a subject of public discussion: and when, the next year, the subject of religious freedom began to be agitated, in the Legislature, as a thing to have an existence and a home in Virginia, it is supposed by Mr. Jefferson, that two thirds of the people of Virginia were dissenters from the Established Church.

CHAPTER XV.

PROGRESS OF FREEDOM OF CONSCIENCE, DURING THE TIMES OF THE REVOLUTION, AND THE AID GIVEN BY MR. JEFFERSON AND MR. MADISON.

DURING the American Revolution, all classes of community were agitated, and all interests were discussed in private meetings and public assemblies. From causes already stated, a large portion of the inhabitants of the colony of Virginia had become dissenters from the Established Church. The continuators of Burke's History say, page 180—"The dissenters constituted at least two thirds of the people"—at the time of the Declaration of Independence. In the class of dissenters he probably ranked Presbyterians, Baptists, Germans, Quakers, and those by education favourable to the Episcopal church, but, disinclined to the Establishment on account of the proceedings of the clergy. Should his statement be thought to be extravagant it will yet be conceded by all, that, the number opposed to the Church of England, as established in America, was very large.

The attention of the General Assembly was favourably turned to the condition of religious congregations—and the subject of toleration necessarily became a subject of legislative action. That something must be done to relieve those, disagreeing with the forms and creed of the Church of England, was beyond discussion or doubt. But what should be done? what could be done that should satisfy all parties? Toleration became of course a subject of discussion, in private circles, and the halls of government. What did toleration mean? Was it to be extended to religious denominations in its classical and restricted sense; or, as some demanded, in its unlimited meaning? In the years immediately preceding the war of the Revolution, the majority of the legislature were for toleration in its restricted sense—an Established Church with freedom from legal disabilities to dissenters. This was some advance upon the ideas of toleration in the times of Davies; but very far from the demands of those who were called dissenters, two branches of whom contended that the true meaning of toleration was an equality of privileges and protection to all denominations, by the civil powers. The attempts to prevent the spread of dissent, which fell so heavily on the Baptists from the year 1768 and onwards, but convinced the more thoughtful Episcopalians that some degree of restricted toleration must be granted to the citizens of Virginia, or society must be shaken to its foundations. To appease the agitated community a bill was proposed granting privileges to dissenters. The records of Hanover Presbytery say, that at a meeting of the Presbytery at Rockfish meeting-house, in Nelson county, October 15th, 1773—"Presbytery took the bill of toleration into consideration, and judge it expedient that some two persons do attend the Assembly as Commissioners of the Presbytery to transact that affair in their name and behalf. The Presbytery do therefore appoint the Rev. John Todd and Captain John Morton, a ruling elder, to attend the Assembly on that business, and wish they may not fail in business of that importance. The Presbytery do trust the matter entirely to them, to act as their prudence may direct and the nature of the case may require. And they do also order that a paper now before them may be transmitted to Captain Morton as what contains their thoughts on this subject, that from it those gentlemen may take such hints, or make such use as they find expedient."—The members of Presbytery present, were Rev. Messrs. Craig, Brown, Rice, Leake and Irvin; with elders Alexander Read, Andrew Hays and Nicholas Hays. Nothing was done, in Assembly that year, to remedy the disabilities of dissenters. No laws of any kind were passed in 1774 owing to the disagreement between the Governor and the Assembly. The Presbytery of Hanover, meeting at the house of Robert Caldwell, on Cub-creek, Charlotte county, October 14, 1774—present the Rev. Messrs. Rice, Leake, Irvin and Wallace; with elders Thomas Montgomery, Robert Mitchell and Robert Caldwell—feeling apprehensive of legislative action on the subject of religious privileges, "agree to meet on the second Wednesday of November next, at the house of Colonel William Cabel, of Amherst, to remonstrate against a bill entitled—"*A bill for extending the benefit of the Act of Toleration to his Majesty's subjects dissenting from the Church of England in the colony of Virginia.*" Provisions that might have satisfied the Presbyterians in 1755, when Davies plead so earnestly for them, were rejected in 1775 when the spirit of the Revolution was abroad. At Timber Ridge, April 13, 1775, the Presbytery took into consideration the petitions and remonstrances drawn up at Colonel Cabel's, the preceding November. But all that had passed on this agitating subject was of no immediate avail, as the Assembly were in session but a few days, and adjourned from Williamsburg to meet, as a Convention, in Richmond on the 17th of July.

The first step of the Convention was to raise an armed force, to resist Governor Dunmore. On the 17th page of the Journal of the Convention, under date of August 16th, 1775, it is recorded—"An address from the Baptists in this colony, was presented to the Convention and read, setting forth—that however distinguished from their countrymen, by appellations and sentiments of a religious nature, they nevertheless consider themselves as members of the same community, in respect to matters of a civil nature, and embarked in the same common cause; that, alarmed at the oppression which hangs over America, they had considered what part it would be proper for them to take in the unhappy contest, and had determined that in some cases it was lawful to go to war, and that they ought to make a military resistance against *Great Britain*, in her unjust invasion, tyrannical oppression, and repeated hostilities; that their brethren were left at discretion to enlist, without incurring the censure of their religious community; and under these circumstances many of them had enlisted as soldiers, and many more were ready to do so, who had an earnest desire their ministers should preach to them during the campaign; that they had therefore appointed four of their brethren to make application to this Convention for the liberty of preaching to the troops at convenient times, without molestation or abuse, and praying the same may be granted to them. Resolved that it be an instruction to the commanding officers of the regiments or troops to be raised, that they permit dissenting clergymen to celebrate divine worship, and to preach to the soldiers, or exhort, from time to time, as the various operations of the military service may permit, for the ease of such scrupulous consciences as may not choose to attend divine service as celebrated by the chaplain." Mr. Semple, in his history tells us, page 62, that— "Jeremiah Walker and John Williams being appointed by this association, went and preached to the soldiers, when encamped in the lower parts of Virginia: they not meeting with much encouragement, declined it after a short time." He also informs us that—" It was resolved to circulate petitions to the Virginia Convention, or General Assembly, throughout the State, in order to obtain signatures. The prayer of these was, that the church establishment should be abolished, and religion left to stand upon its own merits; and that all religious societies should be protected in the peaceable enjoyment of their own religious principles, and modes of worship. They appointed Jeremiah Walker, John Williams, and George Roberts, to wait on the Legislature with these petitions."

This movement was honourable to the suffering Baptists; they were willing to fight for their country, and only asked for the privilege of their own ministers in the army; and the action of the Legislature shows how far the principle of religious toleration had advanced. When all men were called to defend their common country, against an alarming danger, as in the French and Indian war, then the law-makers discovered that those who fought their battles ought to be indulged with freedom of conscience. Granted in one position, and one set of circumstances, there was no stopping till it was granted to all men and in all cases.

The Convention that assembled at Williamsburg, May 6th, 1776, having declared on the 15th, that there was no alternative left—" *but abject submission to the will of those overbearing tyrants, or a total separation from the crown and government of Great Britain*"—instructed the delegates representing the colony in general Congress to propose to that body—"*to declare the United Colonies free and independent States.*" They then, on the 12th of June, adopted a Bill of Rights, and on the 29th of the same month adopted, with amendments, a constitution, drawn up by Colonel George Mason, with a preamble by Mr. Jefferson, the spirit of which is in accordance with the national Declaration of Independence proclaimed in the following July. The last clause of the Bill of Rights is in these words—" That religion, or the duty we owe to our Creator, and the manner of discharging it, can be directed only by reason and conviction, not by force or violence, and therefore all men are equally entitled to the free exercise of religion according to the dictates of conscience; and that it is the mutual duty of all to practise Christian forbearance, love and charity towards each other." These declarations breathe the spirit of civil and religious liberty, and spoke the true feelings of the majority of the citizens of Virginia. Civil liberty had been discussed, with intensity of interest, for a long period, by the whole community; and its limits and boundaries were comparatively early settled to public satisfaction. Religious liberty had, by degrees, claimed the public attention, and for a little time, excited deep interest; but its proper meaning was not well understood. While abroad the contest was for the defence of civil liberty against the power of the mother country; at home it was raging for an ill-defined liberty of conscience, and the disseverance of religion from the civil power. That something ought to be done for dissenters was evident; but what should actually be done was the matter of contention. The true principle,—the free exercise of religion according to the dictates of conscience,—was well expressed in the Bill of Rights, but appears, after all, not to have been well understood by many of the delegates to the Assembly. Many seemed to think that an established religion, with toleration, was freedom enough. The first General Assembly at the Capitol in Williamsburg, under its new constitution, convened October 7th, 1776, and early in its session entered upon the subject of religious freedom.

The Presbytery of Hanover sent up the following

MEMORIAL I.

To the Honourable the General Assembly of Virginia.

The Memorial of the Presbytery of Hanover humbly represents,—That your memorialists are governed by the same sentiments which have inspired the United States of America; and are determined that nothing in our power and influence shall be wanting to give success to their common cause. We would also represent, that dissenters from the church of England, in this country, have ever been desirous to conduct themselves as peaceable members of the civil government, for which reason they have hitherto submitted to several ecclesiastical burdens, and restrictions, that are inconsistent with equal liberty. But now when the many and grievous oppressions of our mother country, have laid this continent under the necessity of casting off the yoke of tyranny, and of forming independent governments upon equitable and liberal foundations, we flatter ourselves that we shall be freed from all the incumbrances which a spirit of domination, prejudice, or bigotry, hath interwoven with most other political systems. This we are the more strongly encouraged to expect, by the Declaration of Rights, so universally applauded for that dignity, firmness and precision with which it delineates and asserts the privileges of society, and the prerogatives of human nature; and which we embrace as the *magna charta* of our commonwealth, that can never be violated without endangering the grand superstructure, it was destined to sustain. Therefore we rely upon this *Declaration*, as well as the justice of our honourable Legislature, to secure us the *free exercise of religion according to the dictates of our consciences:* and we should fall short in our duty to ourselves, and the many and numerous congregations under our care, were we, upon this occasion, to neglect laying before you a state of the religious grievances under which we have hitherto laboured; that they no longer may be continued in our present form of government.

It is well known, that in the frontier counties, which are justly supposed to contain a fifth part of the inhabitants of Virginia, the dissenters have borne the heavy burdens of purchasing glebes, building churches, and supporting the established clergy, where there are very few Episcopalians, either to assist in bearing the expense, or to reap the advantage; and that throughout the other parts of the country, there are also many thousands of zealous friends and defenders of our State, who, besides the invidious, and disadvantageous restrictions to which they have been subjected, annually pay large taxes to support an establishment, from which their consciences and principles oblige them to dissent: all which are confessedly so many violations of their natural rights; and in their consequences, a restraint upon freedom of inquiry, and private judgment.

In this enlightened age, and in a land where all, of every denomination are united in the most strenuous efforts to be free, we hope and expect that our representatives will cheerfully concur in removing every species of religious, as well as civil bondage. Certain it is, that every argument for civil liberty, gains additional strength when applied to liberty in the concerns of religion; and there is no argument in favour of establishing the Christian religion, but what may be pleaded, with equal propriety, for establishing the tenets of Mahomed by those who believe the

Alcoran: or if this be not true, it is at least impossible for the magistrate to adjudge the right of preference among the various sects that profess the Christian faith, without erecting a chair of infallibility, which would lead us back to the church of Rome.

We beg leave farther to represent, that religious establishments are highly injurious to the temporal interests of any community. Without insisting upon the ambition, and the arbitrary practices of those who are favoured by government; or the intriguing seditious spirit, which is commonly excited by this, as well as every other kind of oppression; such establishments greatly retard population, and consequently the progress of arts, sciences, and manufactories: witness the rapid growth and improvements of the northern provinces, compared with this. No one can deny that the more early settlement, and the many superior advantages of our country, would have invited multitudes of artificers, mechanics, and other useful members of society, to fix their habitation among us, who have either remained in their place of nativity, or preferred worse civil governments, and a more barren soil, where they might enjoy the rights of conscience more fully than they had a prospect of doing it, in this. From which we infer, that Virginia might have now been the capital of America, and a match for the British arms, without depending on others for the necessaries of war, had it not been prevented by her religious establishment.

Neither can it be made to appear that the gospel needs any such civil aid. We rather conceive that when our blessed Saviour declares his *kingdom is not of this world*, he renounces all dependence upon state power, and as his *weapons are spiritual*, and were only designed to have influence on the judgment, and heart of man, we are persuaded that if mankind were left in the quiet possession of their unalienable rights and privileges, Christianity, as in the days of the Apostles; would continue to prevail and flourish in the greatest purity, by its own native excellence, and under the all disposing providence of God.

We would humbly represent, that the only proper objects of civil government, are the happiness and protection of men in the present state of existence; the security of the life, liberty, and property of the citizens; and to restrain the vicious and encourage the virtuous by wholesome laws, equally extending to every individual. But that *the duty which we owe our Creator, and the manner of discharging it, can only be directed by reason and conviction;* and is nowhere cognizable but at the tribunal of the universal Judge.

Therefore we *ask no ecclesiastical establishments for ourselves;* neither can we approve of them when granted to others. This indeed would be giving exclusive or separate emoluments or privileges to one set (or sect) of men, without any special public services to the common reproach and injury of every other denomination. And for the reasons recited we are induced earnestly to entreat, that all laws now in force in this commonwealth, which countenance religious domination, may be speedily repealed—that all, of every religious sect, may be protected in the full exercise of their several modes of worship; and exempted from all taxes for the support of any church whatsoever, further than what may be agreeable to their own private choice, or voluntary obligation. This being done, all partial and invidious distinctions will be abolished, to the great honour and interest of the State; and every one be left to stand or fall according to merit, which can never be the case, so long as any one denomination is established in preference to others.

That the great Sovereign of the Universe may inspire you with unanimity, wisdom and resolution; and bring you to a just determination on all the important concerns before you, is the fervent prayer of your memorialists.

Signed by order of the Presbytery.

JOHN TODD, *Moderator.*
CALEB WALLACE, *P. Clerk.*

Mr. Jefferson was a leading member of the House of Delegates, and appeared as the champion of religious as well as civil freedom; a champion that never lost a cause in which the freedom of the people was concerned. What course of argument had led him to this true principle, he has not given us; and it is of no consequence to the present investigation. It is a well ascertained fact, that he knew well the power of the religious principle. He shall give his own statement, Vol. I.

Works, pp. 5, 6. Describing the influence of the news of the Boston Port Bill, upon himself, Mr. Henry, R. H. Lee, Francis Lightfoot Lee and some others,—in June, 1774,—he says—"We were under conviction of the necessity of arousing our people from the lethargy into which they had fallen, as to passing events; and thought that the appointment of a day of general fasting and prayer would be most likely to call up and alarm their attention. No example of such a solemnity had existed since the days of our distresses in the war of '55, since which a new generation had grown up. With the help therefore, of Rushworth, whom we rummaged over for the revolutionary precedents and forms of the Puritans of that day, preserved by him, we cooked up a resolution, somewhat modernizing their phrases, for appointing the 1st day of June, on which the Port Bill was to commence, for a day of fasting, humiliation and prayer, to implore Heaven to avert from us the evils of civil war, to inspire us with firmness in support of our rights, and to turn the hearts of the king and parliament to moderation and justice. To give greater emphasis to our proposition, we agreed to wait the next morning on Mr. Nicholas, whose grave and religious character was more in unison with the tone of our resolutions and solicit him to move it. We accordingly went to him in the morning. He moved it the same day; the 1st of June was proposed; and it passed without opposition. The Governor dissolved us. We returned home, and in our several counties invited the clergy to meet the assemblies of the people on the 1st of June, to perform the ceremonies of the day, and to address to them discourses suited to the occasion. The people met generally, with anxiety and alarm in their countenances, and the effect of the day, through the whole colony, was like a shock of electricity, arousing every man and placing him erect and solidly on his centre."

Well acquainted with the power of the religious principle in men, in a political point of view, Mr. Jefferson was the advocate of the most unrestrained, personal, religious freedom. He gives the following account of his proceedings, in October, 1776, at the first meeting of the Legislature of Virginia under its new constitution ; after the memorial from Hanover Presbytery, with petitions and memorials from other bodies had been presented; Works, vol. I. pp. 31, 32,—"By the time of the Revolution, a majority of the inhabitants had become dissenters from the Established Church, but were still obliged to pay contributions to support the pastors of the minority. This unrighteous compulsion, to maintain teachers of what they deemed religious error, was grievously felt during the regal government, and without hope of relief. But the first republican legislature, which met in '76, was crowded with petitions to abolish this spiritual tyranny. These brought on the severest contests in which I have ever been engaged. Our great opponents were Mr. Pendleton and Robert Carter Nicholas; honest men, but zealous churchmen. ' The petitions were referred to the committee of the whole House on the state of the country; and, after desperate contests in that committee, almost daily from the 11th of October to the 5th of December, we prevailed so far only, as to repeal the laws which rendered criminal the maintenance of any religious opinions, the forbearance of repairing to church, or the exercise of any mode of worship; and further, to exempt dissenters from contributions to the support of the Established Church; and to suspend only until the next session, levies on the members of that church for the salaries of their own incumbents. For although the majority of our citizens were dissenters, as has been observed, a majority of the Legislature were churchmen. Among these, however, were some reasonable and liberal men, who enabled us, on some points, to obtain feeble majorities. But our opponents carried, in the general resolutions of the committee of November 19, a declaration that religious assemblies ought to be regulated, and that provision ought to be made for continuing the succession of the clergy, and superintending their conduct."

MEMORIAL II.

To the Honourable the General Assembly of Virginia.

The memorial of the Presbytery of Hanover, humbly represents,—That your memorialists and the religious denomination with which we are connected, are most sincerely attached to the common interests of the American States, and are determined that our most fervent prayers and strenuous endeavours shall ever be united with our fellow subjects to repel the assaults of tyranny and to maintain our common rights. In our former memorial we have expressed our hearty approbation of the Declaration of Rights, which has been made and adopted as the basis of the laws and government of this State; and now we take the opportunity of testifying that nothing has inspired us with greater confidence in our Legislature, than the late act of Assembly declaring that equal liberty, as well religious as civil, shall be universally extended to the good people of this country; and that all the oppressive acts of parliament respecting religion which have been formerly enacted in the mother country, shall henceforth be of no validity or force in this commonwealth. As also exempting dissenters from all levies, taxes, and impositions, whatsoever, towards supporting the church of England as it now is or hereafter may be established. We would, therefore have given our honourable Legislature no further trouble on this subject, but we are sorry to find that there yet remains a variety of opinions touching the propriety of a general assessment, or whether every religious society shall be left to voluntary contributions for the maintenance of the ministers of the gospel who are of different persuasions. As this matter is deferred by our Legislature to the discussion and final determination of a future Assembly, when the opinions of the country, in general, shall be better known; we think it our indispensable duty again to repeat a part of the prayer of our former memorial, " That dissenters of every denomination may be exempted from all taxes for the support of any church whatsoever, further than what may be agreeable to the private choice or voluntary obligation of every individual; while the civil magistrates no otherwise interfere, than to protect them all in the full and free exercise of their several modes of worship." We then represented as the principal reason upon which this request is founded, that the only proper objects of civil governments are, the happiness and protection of men in the present state of existence, the security of the life, liberty, and property of the citizens, and to restrain the vicious and encourage the virtuous by wholesome laws equally extending to every individual : and that the duty which we owe our Creator, and the manner of discharging it, can only be directed by reason and conviction, and is no where cognizable but at the tribunal of the universal Judge.

To illustrate and confirm these assertions, we beg leave to observe, that to judge for ourselves, and to engage in the exercise of religion agreeable to the dictates of our own consciences is an unalienable right, which upon the principles that the gospel was first propagated, and the reformation from Popery carried on, can never be transferred to another. Neither does the church of Chrrst stand in need of a *general assessment* for its support ; and most certain we are that it would be no advantage, but an injury to the society to which we belong : and as every good Christian believes that Christ has ordained a complete system of laws for the government of his kingdom, so we are persuaded that, by his providence, he will support it to its final consummation. In the fixed belief of this principle, that the kingdom of Christ, and the concerns of religion, are beyond the limits of civil control, we should act a dishonest, inconsistent part, were we to receive any emoluments from human establishments for the support of the gospel.

These things being considered, we hope we shall be excused for remonstrating against a general assessment for any religious purpose. As the maxims have long been approved, that every servant is to obey his master ; and that, the hireling is accountable for his conduct to him from whom he receives his wages ; in like manner, if the Legislature has any rightful authority over the ministers of the gospel in the exercise of their sacred office, and it is their duty to levy a maintenance for them as such ; then it will follow that they may revive the old establishment in its former extent ; or ordain a new one for any sect they think proper ; they are invested with a power not only to determine, but it is incumbent on them to declare, who shall preach, what they shall preach ; to whom, when, at what places they shall preach ; or to impose any regulations and restrictions upon religious societies that they may judge expedient. These consequences are so plain as not to be denied ; and they are so entirely subversive of religious liberty, that if they should take place in Virginia, we should be reduced to the melancholy necessity of saying with the Apostles in like cases " Judge ye whether it is best to obey God or man ;" and also of acting as they acted.

Therefore, as it is contrary to our principles and interest ; and, as we think, subversive of religious liberty, we do again most earnestly entreat that our Legislature would never extend any assessment for religious purposes to us, or to the congregations under our care. And your memorialists, as in duty bound, shall ever pray for, and demean themselves as peaceable subjects, of, civil government.

Signed by order of the Presbytery,

RICHARD SANKEY, *Moderator*.

Timber Ridge, ⎱
   April 25, 1777. ⎰

The Rev. Messrs. Samuel Stanhope Smith and David Rice were the committee of Presbytery that drafted the memorial.

The preparation of the bill for establishing religious freedom is thus given by Mr. Jefferson—Works, vol. I. pp. 34, 35, 36— " Early, therefore in the session of '76, to which I returned, I moved and presented a bill for the revision of the laws ; which was passed on the 24th of October, and on the 5th of November, Mr. Pendleton, Mr. Wythe, George Mason, Thomas L. Lee and myself were appointed a committee to execute the work. We agreed to meet in Fredericksburg to settle the plan of operation, and to distribute the work. We met there accordingly, on the 13th of January, 1777. The first question was, whether we should propose to abolish the whole existing system of laws, and prepare a new and complete Institute, or preserve the general system, and only modify it to the present state of things. Mr. Pendleton, contrary to his usual disposition in favour of ancient things, was for the former proposition, in which he was joined by Mr. Lee. * * * This last was the opinion of Mr. Wythe, Mr. Mason and myself. When we proceeded to the distribution of the work, Mr. Mason excused himself, as, being no lawyer, he felt himself unqualified for the work, and he resigned soon after. Mr. Lee excused himself on the same ground, and died indeed in a short time. The other two gentlemen, therefore, and myself divided the work among us. * * * * * * We were employed in this work from that time to February, 1779, when we met at Williamsburg, that is to say, Mr. Pendleton, Mr. Wythe and myself; and meeting day by day, we examined critically our several parts, sentence by sentence, scrutinizing and amending, until we had agreed on the whole. We then returned home, had fair copies made of our several parts, which were reported to the General Assembly, June 18th, 1779, by Mr. Wythe and myself, Mr. Pendleton's residence being distant, and he having authorized us by letter to declare his approbation. We had in this work, brought so much of the common law as it was thought necessary to alter, all the British statutes from *Magna Charta* to the present day, and all the laws of Virginia, from the establishment of our Legislature, in the 4th of Jae 1st to the present time, which we thought should be retained, within the compass of one hundred and twenty-six bills, making a printed folio of ninety pages only. Some bills were taken out, occasionally, from time to time and passed; but the main body of the work was not entered upon by the Legislature, until, after the general peace, in 1785, when by the unwearied exertions of Mr. Madison, in opposition to the endless quibbles, chicaneries, perversions, vexations and delays of lawyers and demi-lawyers, most of the bills were passed by the Legislature, with little alteration."

"The bill for establishing religious freedom, the principles of which had, to a certain degree, been enacted before, I had drawn in all the latitude of reason and right. It still met with opposition; but, with some mutilations in the preamble, it was finally passed." The passage of the bill spoken of took place in December 1785, more than six years after it had been first reported to the House. Says Mr. Jefferson, p. 143, vol. 1st, "I proposed the demolition of church establishment, and the freedom of religion. It could only be done by degrees; to wit, the act of 1776, c. 2d, exempted dissenters from contributions to the Church, and left the Church clergy to be supported by voluntary contributions of their own sect; was continued from year to year, and made perpetual in 1779. I prepared the act for religious freedom in 1777, as part of the revisal, which was not reported to the Assembly till 1779, and that particular law not passed till 1785, and then by the efforts of Mr. Madison."

In the interval, between the bringing in the bill in 1777 and the passage in 1785, the contest for religious liberty was going on in the Legislature, and was debated throughout the State. Various efforts were made by men of talents and influence to preserve a modification of the Establishment, with toleration to dissenters. Some feared that public worship could not be kept up in the State, if the Church and State were dissevered; others were unwilling to break down the time-honoured forms and ceremonies of the State religion, believing them useful if not necessary, and clinging to them with the fondness of early associations.

During the session of Assembly in the summer of 1777, when public expectation was all alive anticipating the changes that would be proposed and probably made, by the committee of revision, the Presbytery of Hanover met at Concord in Bedford county, June 19th—present, Rev. Messrs. Rice, Irvin, Wallace and Graham; with Archibald Campbell, John Irvin, and Hugh Wair, elders. "The Presbytery considering it as probable that our General Assembly may come to a final determination concerning church establishments, at their next session, which may make it of importance for this Presbytery further to concern themselves in the case before our next stated meeting, we therefore appoint the Rev. Messrs. Sankey, Todd, Rice, Wallace, and Smith, or any of them, a committee to meet at Hampden Sidney on the 26th of September, or sooner if any two of them shall judge it necessary, to do and act in behalf of this Presbytery, in that case." Nothing definitive, however, was done by the Assembly, on the vexed question, this year. The payment of the salaries of the Episcopal clergy was farther postponed, first from the session in the spring to the session in the fall; and then " until the end of the next session of Assembly." In May 1778, the suspension was continued, "until the end of the next session of Assembly." In October the suspension was continued until the " end of the next session of Assembly." In May 1779, it was again " suspended until the end of the next session of Assembly."

The Baptists, at their General Association, held at Anderson's meeting-house, in Buckingham county, in May, 1778, appointed a committee—"to inquire whether any grievances existed in the civil laws that were oppressive to the Baptists. In their report they represented the marriage law as being partial and oppressive. Upon which it was agreed to present to the next General Assembly a memorial, praying for a law affording equal privileges to all ordained ministers, of every denomination."—Semple, 64.

At their meeting, at Dupuy's meeting-house, in Powhatan county, the second Saturday in October of the same year, (1778)—"a committee of seven members was appointed to take into consideration the civil grievances of the Baptists, and make report. They reported on Monday :—

"1st. That should a general assessment take place, it would be injurious to the dissenters in general.

"2d. That the clergy of the former established church suppose themselves to have exclusive right of officiating in marriages, which has subjected dissenters to great inconveniences.

"3d. They therefore recommend that two persons be appointed to wait on the next General Assembly, and lay the grievances before them." And for this purpose "Jeremiah Walker and Elijah Craig, (and in case of the failure of either) John Williams, were appointed to attend the General Assembly."

In May, 1779, a bill—"establishing religious freedom"—and providing for a general assessment; putting all denominations on an equality; was proposed, and passed two readings in the House of Delegates. At this stage its progress was arrested, that the sense of the people might be ascertained.

At the meeting of the Legislature, in October, 1779, the sense of the public being known—an act was passed in the following terms—"Be it enacted by the General Assembly—That so much of the act entitled—An act for the support of the clergy, and for the regular collecting and paying the parish levies,—and of all and every other act or acts providing salaries for the ministers, and authorizing the vestries to levy the same, shall be, and the same is hereby repealed."—Hening, 10th vol. p. 197.

The established church was by this act shorn of the greater part of her support; the clergy still retained the glebes, and claimed the privilege of marriage ceremonies, with their fees; and the vestries still had the right of laying taxes for the support of the poor.

At a meeting of the Baptist Association, at Nottoway meeting-house, in Amelia county, second Saturday of October, 1779, Mr. Walker, of the committee to wait on the Assembly, having seen Mr. Jefferson's bill on religious freedom, made report to his brethren, on which the following record was made—"On consideration of the bill establishing freedom, agreed—That the said bill, in our opinion, puts religious freedom upon its proper basis: prescribes the just limits of the power of the State with regard to religion; and properly guards against partiality towards any religious denomination; we, therefore, heartily approve of the same, and wish it to pass into a law."

"Ordered—that this our approbation of the said bill be

transmitted to the public printers, to be inserted in the Gazettes."

"It seems that many of the Baptist preachers, presuming upon a future sanction, had gone on to marry such people as applied for marriage. It was determined that a memorial should be sent from this association, requesting that all such marriages should be sanctioned by a law for that purpose. For a set of preachers, to proceed to solemnize the rites of matrimony, without any law to authorize them, might at first view appear incorrect, and indeed censurable; but we are informed that they were advised to this measure by Patrick Henry, as being the most certain method of obtaining the law."

In October, 1780, the Legislature passed an Act declaring what shall be a lawful marriage. From this act, found in Hening, vol. 10, pp. 361, 362, the following extracts are sufficient for the present purpose:

"For encouraging marriages and for removing doubts concerning the validity of marriages celebrated by ministers, other than the Church of England, be it enacted by the General Assembly—That it shall and may be lawful for any minister of any society or congregation of Christians, and for the society of Christians called Quakers and Menonists, to celebrate the rites of matrimony, and to join together as man and wife, those who may apply to them, agreeable to the rules and usage of the respective societies to which the parties to be married respectively belong, and such marriage, as well as those heretofore celebrated by dissenting ministers, shall be, and they are hereby declared good and valid in law."—By the second clause, Quakers and Menonists were excused from getting license for marriage, or from publication of bans, which were obligatory on all others. By the third clause, the fee for marriage ceremony was "twenty-five pounds of tobacco and no more, to be paid in current money at the rate which shall be settled by the grand jury at the term of the General Court next preceding such marriage." By the fourth clause, certificates of marriage were to be returned to the clerk of the county, on penalty of five hundred pounds. By the fifth clause it was enacted— "That the courts of the different counties shall, and are hereby authorized on recommendation from the elders of the several religious sects, to grant license to dissenting ministers of the gospel, not exceeding the number of four of each sect in any one county, to join together in holy matrimony, any persons within their county only; which license shall be signed by the judge or elder magistrate under his hand and seal." This act, clogged as it was, to be in force from the first of January 1781, was an advance in religious liberty. The solemn vows to live as husband and wife might be uttered, in words, and with forms,

agreeable to the tastes and consciences of the parties concerned. The Presbyterian settlements, in the Valley of the Shenandoah, were greatly relieved, by the provisions of the law,
from acts that were becoming habits, and doings that were
rapidly becoming customs, under the report of which their
civility and delicacy were suffering, in the estimation of others
unacquainted with their necessities. There being but few
ministers of the Church of England in the Valley,—and their
demands for riding any distance to perform the marriage ceremony exorbitant, and their often refusing to leave their homes
at all, wedding parties often rode in company to the minister's
house for the ceremony; these rides became occasions for dissipation of that kind, and exhibition of manners of that sort, as
fastened upon the people of the Valley imputations not justified
by the real facts in the case. What was done, by necessity
of law, was neither vulgar or immodest in those suffering the
compulsion.

In the month of April 1780, the Presbytery of Hanover met
in the Tinkling Spring congregation, in Augusta county;—
present Rev. Messrs. Todd, Brown, Waddel, Rice, Irvin,
Smith and Crawford. On the 28th of the month, being at
Mr. Waddel's—"A memorial to the Assembly of Virginia,
from this Presbytery,—to abstain from interfering in the
government of the church—was prepared, and being read in
Presbytery, is appointed and directed to be transmitted to the
House."

"The Presbytery do request Colonel McDowell and Captain
Johnson to present their memorial to the Assembly, and to
second it by their influence; and Mr. Waddel and Mr. Graham
are appointed to inform these gentlemen of the request of
Presbytery."

At a meeting of the Presbytery of Hanover, held at Bethel,
Augusta county, May 19th, 1784;—present Rev. Messrs.
Graham, Scott, Wilson, Houston, Smith, Montgomery, Irvin,
Brown, Carrick and Rankin;—with—Samuel McCutchin,
Robert McNutt, and Samuel Craig, elders;—"On motion made
by Mr. Smith that a committee be appointed to prepare a memorial to the Assembly at their present session upon certain
infringements of religious liberty, which exist in this State,—
the Presbytery agreed to appoint him and Mr. Waddel to that
business, and that they make their report to-morrow. May
20th, Mr. Smith from the committee appointed yesterday produced a draught of a memorial, which Presbytery approved of;
and appointed Messrs. Smith and Waddel to have it presented
to the Assembly, and to preserve a copy for the inspection of
Presbytery at our next stated meeting.

MEMORIAL OF THE PRESBYTERY OF HANOVER IN MAY, 1784.

To the Honourable Speaker, and House of Delegates of Virginia.

Gentlemen,

The united clergy of the Presbyterian Church in Virginia, assembled in Presbytery, request your attention to the following representation. In the late arduous struggle for every thing dear to us, a desire of perfect liberty, and political equality animated every class of citizens. An entire and everlasting freedom from every species of ecclesiastical domination, a full and permanent security of the unalienable rights of conscience, and private judgment, and an equal share of the protection and favour of government to all denominations of Christians, were particular objects of our expectation, and irrefragable claim. The happy Revolution effected by the virtuous exertions of our countrymen of various opinions in religion, was a favourable opportunity of obtaining these desirable objects without faction, contention, or complaint. All ranks of men, almost, felt the claims of justice, when the rod of oppression had scourged them into sensibility, and the powerful band of common danger had cordially united them together against civil encroachments. The members, therefore, of every religious society had a right to expect, and most of them did expect, that former invidious and exclusive distinctions, preferences, and emoluments conferred by the State on any one sect above others, would have been wholly removed. They justly supposed that any partiality of this kind, any particular and illicit connexion or commerce between the State, and one description of Christians more than another, on account of peculiar opinions in religion, or any thing else, would be unworthy of the representatives of a people perfectly free, and an infringement of that religious liberty, which enhances the value of other privileges in a state of society.

We, therefore, and the numerous body of citizens in our communion, as well as in many others, are justly dissatisfied and uneasy, that our expectations from the Legislature have not been answered in these important respects. We regret that the prejudices of education, the influence of partial custom, and habits of thinking confirmed by these, have too much confounded the distinction between matters purely religious, and the objects of human legislation, and have occasioned jealousy and dissatisfaction by injurious inequalities, respecting things which are connected with religious opinion, towards different sects of Christians. That this uneasiness may not appear to be entertained without ground, we would wish to state the following unquestionable facts for the consideration of the House of Delegates.

The security of our religious rights upon equal and impartial ground, *instead of being made a fundamental part of our constitution, as it ought to have been*, is left to the precarious fate of common law. A matter of general and essential concern to the people, is committed to the hazard of the prevailing opinion of a majority of the Assembly at its different sessions. In consequence of this, the Episcopal church was virtually regarded as the constitutional church, the church of the State, at the Revolution; and was left by the framers of our present government, in that station of unjust pre-eminence which she had formerly acquired under the smiles of royal favour. And even when the late oppressive establishment of that church was at length acknowledged an unreasonable hardship by the Assembly in 1776, a superiority and distinction in name was still retained, and it was expressly styled the *established church* as before; which title was continued as late as the year 1778, and never formally disclaimed: our common danger at that time not permitting that opposition to the injustice of such distinction which it required and deserved.

But "a seat on the right hand of temporal glory as the established mother church" was not the only inequality then countenanced, and still subsisting, of which we now have reason to regret and complain. Substantial advantages were also confirmed and secured to her, by a partial and inequitable decree of government. We hoped the time past would have sufficed for the enjoyment of these emoluments, which that church long possessed without control by the abridgment of the equal privileges of others, and the aid of their property wrested from them by the hand of usurpation; but we were deceived. An estate computed to be worth several hundred thousand pounds in churches, glebes, &c., derived from the pockets of all religious societies, was exclusively and unjustly appropriated to the benefit of *one*, without compensation or restitution to the rest, who in many places, were a large majority of the inhabitants.

Nor is this the whole of the injustice we have felt in matters connected with religious opinion. The episcopal church is actually incorporated, and known in law as a body, so that it can receive and possess property for ecclesiastical purposes, without trouble or risk in securing it, while other Christian communities are obliged to trust to the precarious fidelity of trustees chosen for the purpose. The episcopal clergy are considered as having a right, *ex officio*, to celebrate marriages throughout the State, while unnecessary hardships and restrictions are imposed upon other clergymen in the law relating to that subject passed in 1780, which confines their exercise of that function to those counties, where they receive a special license from the court by recommendation, for recording which they are charged with certain fees by the clerk; and which exposes them to a heavy fine for delay in returning certificates of marriages to the office.

The vestries of the different parishes, a remnant of hierarchical domination, have a right by law to levy money from the people of all denominations for certain purposes; and yet these vestrymen are exclusively required by law to be members of the episcopal church, and to subscribe a conformity to its doctrines and discipline as *professed and practised in England.* Such preferences, distinctions and advantages granted by the Legislature exclusively to one sect of Christians, are regarded by a great number of your constituents as glaringly unjust and dangerous. Their continuance so long in a republic, without animadversion or correction by the assembly, affords just ground for alarm and complaint to a people, who feel themselves, by the favour of Providence, happily free; who are conscious of having deserved as well from the State as those who are most favoured; who have an undoubted right to think themselves as orthodox in opinion upon every subject as others, and whose privileges are as dear to them. Such partiality to any system of religious opinion whatever, is inconsistent with the intention and proper object of well directed government, and obliges men of reflection to consider the Legislature which indulges it, as a party in religious differences, instead of the common guardian and equal protector of every class of citizens in their religious as well as civil rights. We have hitherto restrained our complaints from reaching our representatives, that we might not be thought to take advantages from times of confusion, or critical situations of government in an unsettled state of convulsion and war, to obtain what is our clear and incontestable right.

But as the happy restoration of peace affords leisure for reflection, we wish to state our sense of the objects of this memorial to your honourable house upon the present occasion; that it may serve to remind you of what might be unnoticed in a multitude of business, and remain as a remonstrance against future encroachments from any quarter. That uncommon liberality of sentiment, which seems daily to gain ground in this enlightened period, encourages us to hope from your wisdom and integrity, gentlemen, a redress of every grievance and remedy of every abuse. Our invaluable privileges have been purchased by the common blood and treasure of our countrymen of different names and opinions, and therefore ought to be secured in full and perfect equality to them all. We are willing to allow a full share of credit to our fellow citizens, however distinguished in name from us, for their spirited exertions in our arduous struggle for liberty; we would not wish to charge any of them, either ministers or people, with open disaffection to the common cause of America, or with crafty dissimulation or indecision, till the issue of the war was certain, so as to oppose their obtaining equal privileges in religion; but we will resolutely engage against any monopoly of the honours or rewards of government by any one sect of Christians more than the rest; for we shun not a comparison with any of our brethren, for our efforts in the cause of our country, and assisting to establish her liberties, and therefore esteem it unreasonable that any of them should reap superior advantages for, at most, but equal merit. We expect from the representatives of a free people, that all partiality and prejudice on any account whatever will be laid aside, and that the happiness of the citizens at large will be secured upon the broad basis of perfect political equality. This will engage confidence in government, and unsuspicious affection towards our fellow citizens. We hope that the Legislature will adopt some measures to remove present inequality, and resist any attempt, either at their present session or hereafter, to continue those which we now complain of. Thus by preserving a proper regard to every religious denomination as the common protectors of piety and virtue, you will remove every real ground of contention, and allay every jealous commotion on the score of religion. The citizens of Virginia will feel themselves free, unsuspicious, and happy in this respect. Strangers will be encouraged to share our freedom and felicity; and when civil and religious liberty go hand in hand, our late posterity will bless the wisdom and virtue of their fathers. We have the satisfaction to assure you that we are steady well wishers to the State, and your humble servants.

THE PRESBYTERY OF HANOVER.

The subject of a general assessment was brought before the Legislature, in its two sessions, in the year 1784, by petitions from several counties, which prayèd—that, "as all persons enjoyed the benefit of religion, all might be required to contribute to the expense of supporting some form of worship or other." From the inhabitants of Mecklenburg, Lunenburg and Amelia, the petition said—"that they conceive the stability of our government, and the preservation of peace and happiness among the individuals of it, depend in a great measure, on the influence of religion, without which no government, however wisely formed, can long exist; that they consider its rapid declension, within a few years, as proceeding from the inattention of the Legislature, which has an undoubted right to compel every individual who partakes of those blessings, which are originally derived from it, to contribute to the support of it, and praying *that an Act may pass for a general assessment for that purpose, and for securing to the Protestant Episcopal Church the property vested in it.*"

That from the Protestant Episcopal Church, says Dr. Hawks, pp. 156, 157—set forth that—"their Church laboured under many inconveniences and restraints by the operation of sundry laws in force, which direct modes of worship, and enjoin the observance of certain days, and otherwise produce embarrassment and difficulty; and praying that all acts which direct modes of faith and worship and enjoin the observance of certain days may be repealed; that the present vestry laws may be repealed or amended; that the churches, glebe lands, donations, and all other property heretofore belonging to the established church may be forever secured to them by law; that an act may pass to incorporate the Protestant Episcopal Church in Virginia to enable them to regulate all the spiritual concerns of that Church; and in general, that the Legislature will aid and pratronize the Christian religion."

The Presbytery of Hanover met at Timber Ridge, October 27th, 1784—"Mr. Smith agreeable to an order of last Presbytery, produced a copy of the memorial presented to the last sessions of the General Assembly, complaining of certain imfringements on our religious liberty. The Presbytery approves of the memorial and ordered it to be recorded in the Presbytery book. Messrs. Graham and Smith were appointed a committee to prepare a memorial to be presented at the present session of the General Assembly of the State, and to produce it to-morrow for the inspection of the Presbytery." On the next day a memorial was presented—"complaining of, and praying a redress of certain grievances." The Presbytery approved it and ordered it to be sent to the Assembly then in session.

MEMORIAL IV.

The Presbytery of Hanover, to the Assembly, in October, 1784.

To the Honourable Speaker and House of Delegates of Virginia,
Gentlemen,

The united clergy of the Presbyterian church of Virginia assembled in Presbytery, beg leave again to address your honourable house, upon a few important subjects, in which we find ourselves interested as citizens of this State.

The freedom we possess is so rich a blessing, and the purchase of it has been so
high, that we would ever wish to cherish a spirit of vigilant attention to it, in
every circumstance of possible danger. We are anxious to retain a full share of
all the privileges which our happy revolution affords, and cannot but feel alarmed
at the continued existence of any infringement upon them, or even any indirect
attempt tending to this. Impressed with this idea as men, whose rights are sacred
and dear to them, ought to be, we are obliged to express our sensibility upon the
present occasion, and we naturally direct our appeal to you, gentlemen, as the public guardians of your country's happiness and liberty, who are influenced we hope
by that wisdom and justice which your high station requires. Conscious of the
rectitude of our intentions and the strength of our claims, we wish to speak our
sentiments freely upon these occasions, but at the same time with all that respectful regard, which becomes us, when addressing the representatives of a great and
virtuous people. It is with pain that we find ourselves obliged to renew our complaints upon the subjects stated in our memorial last spring. We deeply regret
that such obvious grievances should exist unredressed in a Republic, whose end
ought to be the happiness of all the citizens. We presumed that immediate redress would have succeeded a clear and just representation of them ; as we expect,
that it is always the desire of our representatives to remove real grounds of uneasiness, and allay jealous commotions amongst the people. But as the objects of the
memorial, though very important in their nature, and more so in their probable
consequences, have not yet been obtained, we request that the house of delegates
would be pleased to recollect what we had the honour to state to them in that
paper at their last sessions ; to resume the subject in their present deliberation ;
and to give it that weight which its importance deserves. The uneasiness which
we feel from the continuance of the grievances just referred to, is increased under
the prospect of an addition to them by certain exceptionable measures said to be
proposed to the Legislature.—We have understood that a comprehensive incorporating act, has been and is at present in agitation, whereby ministers of the
gospel as such, of certain descriptions, shall have legal advantages which are not
proposed to be extended to the people at large of any denomination. A proposition has been made by some gentlemen in the house of delegates we are told, to
extend the grace to us, amongst others, in our professional capacity. If this be so,
we are bound to acknowledge with gratitude our obligations to such gentlemen for
their inclination to favour us with the sanction of public authority in the discharge
of our duty. But as the scheme of incorporating clergymen, *independent of the religious communities to which they belong*, is inconsistent with our ideas of propriety,
we request the liberty of declining any such solitary honour should it be again proposed. To form clergmen into a distinct order in the community, and especially
where it would be possible for them to have the principal direction of a considerable public estate by such incorporation, has a tendency to render them independent, at length, of the churches whose ministers they are; and this has been too
often found by experience to produce ignorance, immorality, and neglect of the
duties of their station.

Besides, if clergymen were to be erected by the State into a distinct political
body, detached from the rest of the citizens, with the express design of " enabling
them to direct spiritual matters," which we all possess without such formality, it
would naturally tend to introduce that antiquated and absurd system, in which
government is owned, in effect, to be the fountain head of spiritual influences to
the church. It would establish an immediate, a peculiar, and for that very reason,
in our opinion, illicit connexion between government, and such as were thus distinguished. The Legislature in that case would be the head of a religious party,
and its dependent members would be entitled to all decent reciprocity, to a becoming paternal and fostering care. This we suppose, would be giving a preference,
and creating a distinction between citizens equally good, on account of something
entirely foreign from civil merit, which would be a source of endless jealousies,
and inadmissible in a republic or any other well-directed government.—The prin-

ciple too, which this system aims to establish, is both false and dangerous to religion, and we take this opportunity to remonstrate and protest against it. The real ministers of true religion, derive their authority to act in the duties of their profession from a higher source than any Legislature on earth, however respectable. Their office relates to the care of the soul, and preparing it for a future state of existence, and their administrations are, or ought to be, of a spiritual nature suited to this momentous concern. And it is plain from the very nature of the case, that they should neither expect, nor receive from government any permission or direction in this respect. We hope therefore that the House of Delegates shares so large a portion of that philosophic and liberal discernment, which prevails in America at present, as to see this matter in its proper light—and that they will understand too well the nature of their duty, as the equal and common guardians of the chartered rights of all the citizens, to permit a connexion of this kind we have just now mentioned, to subsist between them and the spiritual instructors of any religious denomination in the State.—The interference of government in religion, cannot be indifferent to us, and as it will probably come under consideration at the present session of the Assembly, we request the attention of the honourable House, to our sentiments upon this head.

We conceive that human legislation, ought to have human affairs alone for its concern. Legislators in free States possess delegated authority, for the good of the community at large in its political or civil capacity.

The existence, preservation and happiness of society should be their only object; and to this their public cares should be confined. Whatever is not materially connected with this, lies not within their province as statesmen. The thoughts, the intentions, the faith, and the consciences of men, with their modes of worship, lie beyond their reach, and are ever to be referred to a higher and more penetrating tribunal. These internal and spiritual matters cannot be measured by human rules, nor be amenable to human laws. It is the duty of every man, for himself, to take care of his immortal interests in a future state, where we are to account for our conduct as individuals; and it is by no means the business of a Legislature to attend to this, for THERE governments and states as collective bodies shall no more be known.

Religion, therefore, as a spiritual system, and its ministers in a professional capacity, ought not to be under the direction of the State.

Neither is it necessary to their existence that they should be publicly supported by a legal provision for the purpose, as tried experience hath often shown; although it is absolutely necessary to the existence and welfare of every political combination of men in society, to have the support of religion and its solemn institutions, as affecting the conduct of rational beings more than human laws can possibly do. On this account it is wise policy in legislators to seek its alliance and solicit its aid in a civil view, because of its happy influence upon the morality of its citizens, and its tendency to preserve the veneration of an oath, or an appeal to heaven, which is the cement of the social union. It is upon this principle alone, in our opinion, that a legislative body has a right to interfere in religion at all, and of consequence we suppose that this interference ought only to extend to the preserving of the public worship of the Deity, and the supporting of institutions for inculcating the great fundamental principles of all religion, without which society could not easily exist. Should it be thought necessary at present for the Assembly to exert this right of supporting religion in general by an assessment on all the people, we would wish it to be done on the most *liberal plan*. A general assessment of the kind we have heard proposed is an object of such consequence that it excites much anxious speculation amongst your constituents.

We therefore earnestly pray that nothing may be done in the case, inconsistent with the proper objects of human legislation or the Declaration of Rights as published at the Revolution. We hope that the assessment will not be proposed under the idea of supporting religion as a spiritual system, relating to the care of the soul and preparing it for its future destiny. We hope that no attempt will be made to point out articles of faith, that are not essential to the preservation of society; or to settle modes of worship; or to interfere in the internal government of religious communities; *or to render the ministers of religion independent of the will of the people whom they serve.* We expect from our representatives, that careful attention to the political equality of all the citizens, which a Republic ought ever to cherish; and that no scheme of an assessment will be encouraged which will violate the happy privilege we now enjoy of thinking for ourselves in all cases where conscience is concerned.

We request the candid indulgence of the honourable house to the present address; and their most favourable construction of the motives which induce us to obtrude ourselves into public notice. We are urged by a sense of duty. We feel ourselves impressed with the importance of the present crisis. We have expressed ourselves in the plain language of freemen, upon the interesting subjects which called for animadversion; and we hope to stand excused with you, gentlemen, for the manner in which it is executed, as well as for the part we take in the public interests of the community. In the present important moment, we conceived it criminal to be silent; and have therefore attempted to discharge a duty which we owe to our religion as Christians; to ourselves as freemen; and to our posterity, who ought to receive from us a precious birthright of perfect freedom and political equality.

That you may enjoy the direction of Heaven in your present deliberations, and possess in a high degree the spirit of your exalted station, is the prayer of your sincere well wishers,

THE PRESBYTERY OF HANOVER.

There was a strong impression that some kind of assessment would be demanded by a majority of the citizens of the State. And it appears that, for a time, there was a leaning that way, in some, at least, of the members of Presbytery: for at the same session of Presbytery in which the foregoing memorial was prepared, the following—"plan was also introduced, agreeably to which alone Presbytery are willing to admit a general assessment for the support of religion by law; the leading principles of which are as follows:—1st. Religion as a spiritual system is not to be considered as an object of human legislation, but may in a civil view, as preserving the existence and promoting the happiness of society. 2d. That public worship and public periodical instruction to the people, be maintained in this view by a general assessment for this purpose. 3d. That every man, as a good citizen, be obliged to declare himself attached to some religious community, publicly known to profess the belief of one God, his righteous providence, our accountableness to him, and a future state of rewards and punishments. 4th. That every citizen should have liberty annually to direct his assessed proportion to such community as he chooses. 5th. That twelve titheables, or more, to the amount of one hundred and fifty families, as near as local circumstances will admit, shall be incorporated, and exclusively direct the application of the money contributed for their support. Messrs. Todd, Graham, Smith and Montgomery are appointed to present the memorial, and attend the assembly with the plan of an assessment."

At the first meeting of the General Committee of the Baptist Church, which assembled October 9th, 1784, says Mr. Semple, p. 70—"The law for the solemnization of marriage, and the vestry law, were considered political grievances. They also resolved to oppose the law for a general assessment, and that for the incorporation of religious societies, which were now in agitation. A memorial to the General Assembly, praying for a repeal of the vestry law, and an alteration in the marriage law, was drawn and committed to the hands of the Rev. Reuben Ford, to be presented to the next Assembly"—which was to meet on the eighteenth of the month.

The session of the General Assembly of the State, which was commenced on the 18th of October, 1784, in the city of Richmond, was one of great interest. Men of the finest talents and most extended information were members. The true relations of Church and State was inquired into with patience, vigour, conscience, keenness and judgment, in the exercise of great talents and eloquence. On the 17th of November, Mr. Matthews reported, from the committee of the whole house, on the state of the commonwealth, the following resolution, viz.

" *Resolved*, That it is the opinion of this committee, *that acts ought to pass for the incorporation of all societies of the Christian religion which may apply for the same.*"

The ayes and noes being called for on this resolution, there were, ayes sixty-two, noes twenty-three. Patrick Henry, the great champion of popular rights, gave his whole influence in favour of this bill, under the strong conviction that religion should have protection from the State in some form.

The members of the Protestant Episcopal Church having applied for incorporation, and therefore being within the provisions of the resolution, leave was given the same day to bring in a bill for the incorporation of the clergy of that church. The committee to bring in the bill were—Carter M. Harrison, chairman—Patrick Henry, Thomas Smith, William Anderson, and Mr. Tazewell. These reported a bill which was passed into a law. Hening, vol. 11th, p. 532. " Whereas the clergy of the Protestant Episcopal Church, by their petition presented, have requested, that their church may be incorporated,—Be it enacted by the General Assembly—That every minister of the Protestant Episcopal Church, now holding a parish within this commonwealth, either by appointment from a vestry or induction from a governor, and all the vestrymen in the different parishes now instituted, or which hereafter may be instituted within this commonwealth, that is to say,—The minister and vestrymen of each parish respectively, or in case of a vacancy, the vestry of each parish, and their successors for ever, are hereby made a body corporate and politic, by the name of,— 'The Minister and Vestry of the Protestant Episcopal Church,'—in the parish where they respectively reside," &c. By this law each vestry could hold property not exceeding in income 800*l.* yearly; could sue, and be sued; and perform all necessary acts of a vestry and a corporation; and hold the glebe lands and the churches. A convention of the church was to be called, and the government of the church to be vested in the convention, both as to its forms and doctrines.

The Assembly at this session (October, 1784,) remodeled the marriage act of 1780, Hening, vol. 11th, p. 503, and enacted—

"that it shall and may be lawful for any ordained minister of the gospel, in regular communion with any society of Christians, and every such minister is hereby authorized to celebrate the rites of matrimony according to the forms of the church to which he belongs;"—thus doing away all privilege, and precedence, of one denomination over another, in performing the marriage ceremony.

During the same session (October, 1784,) the committee, to whom had been committed various petitions, praying—that as all persons enjoyed the benefits of religion, all might be required to contribute to the expense of supporting some form of worship or other,—brought in a bill entitled—" *A bill establishing a provision for teachers of the Christian religion.*" The preamble was in the following words,—"Whereas the general diffusion of Christian knowledge hath a natural tendency to correct the morals of men, restrain their vices and preserve the peace of society; which cannot be effected without a competent provision for learned teachers, who may be thereby enabled to devote their time and attention to the duty of instructing such citizens as, from their circumstances and want of education cannot otherwise attain such knowledge; and it is judged such provision may be made by the legislature, without counteracting the liberal principle heretofore adopted and intended to be preserved, by abolishing all distinctions of preeminence amongst the different societies or communities of Christians." This act passed to its third reading, and had the approbation and influence of Patrick Henry. Its provisions were without partiality to sect or people. All persons subject to taxes were, at the time of giving in their titheables, to declare to what denomination of Christians they would give their support, and to which they would appropriate the sums assessed on them. If they made no specification, the sums assessed were to be applied to the encouragement of seminaries of learning in the counties where such sums might arise. On its third reading, its progress was arrested, and the engrossed bill was sent out for the examination of the public, that expressions of opinion might be given, indicating the will of community, and the course to be pursued by the Legislature. The subject matter of the bill was widely and most earnestly discussed, and the opinion of the dissenters, and a large portion of community that were not properly called dissenters, conveyed to the Legislature in unequivocal language.

The Presbytery of Hanover met at Bethel in Augusta county, May 19th, 1785; present Rev. Messrs. John Todd, John Brown, William Graham, Archibald Scott, Edward Crawford, John B. Smith, William Ervin, Moses Hoge, Samuel

Houston, Samuel Carrick, and Samuel Shannon;—with elders James Henry, William McKee, John Tate, James Hogshead, William Yool, and Andrew Setlington. "A petition was presented to the Presbytery from the session of Augusta congregation, requesting an explication of the word '*liberal*' as used in the Presbytery's memorial of last fall; and also the motives and end of the Presbytery in sending it to the Assembly. Messrs. Hoge and Carrick are appointed a committee to prepare an answer to the above petition and report to Presbytery."

'On motion, the opinion of Presbytery was taken,—whether they do approve of any kind of an assessment by the General Assembly for the support of religion. *Presbytery are unanimously against such a measure.*"

The question from Augusta congregation referred to that part of the memorial of the preceding fall which says—"Should it be thought necessary at present for the Assembly to exact this right of supporting religion in general by an assessment on all the people, we would wish it to be done on the most liberal plan." Did this mean that they approved of an assessment,—or that they acquiesced,—or merely submitted; that they wished a large assessment,—or one that favoured all equally, without any distinction of sect? Whatever may have been the private opinions of any of the members in 1784 and previous, or the influence of that popular champion, Patrick Henry, over their judgments when first contemplating a subject of which he was the advocate,—now when the whole subject was thrown before the people, and the principles to govern the connexion of Church and State to be settled by a popular vote, the Presbytery in full session declared themselves unanimously against all assessments by the Legislature for the support of religion.

"On motion, the opinion of the Presbytery, and likewise of several members of different congregations present was taken, whether a General Convention of the Presbyterian body was expedient in our present circumstances. It was unanimously agreed to; and an invitation was accordingly signed by the ministers and several private members of the Presbyterian Church to the whole body to send representatives to a Convention proposed to be held at Bethel, on the 10th day of next August."

The Convention met on the appointed day; and prepared, and sent forth a memorial, drawn principally by Rev. William Graham, rector of Liberty Hall, Lexington. This paper expresses the true feeling of the Presbyterian Church, after much private and public discussion.

MEMORIAL V.

To the Honourable the General Assembly of the Commonwealth of Virginia,

The Ministers and Lay Representatives of the Presbyterian Church in Virginia, assembled in Convention, beg leave to address you.

As citizens of the State, not so by accident but choice, and having willingly conformed to the system of civil policy adopted for our government, and defended it with the foremost at the risk of every thing dear to us, we feel ourselves deeply interested in all the measures of the Legislature.

When the late happy Revolution secured to us an exemption from British control, we hoped that the gloom of injustice and usurpation would have been forever dispelled by the cheering rays of liberty and independence. This inspired our hearts with resolution in the most distressful scenes of adversity and nerved our arm in the day of battle. But our hopes have since been overcast with apprehension when we found how slowly and unwillingly, ancient distinctions among the citizens on account of religious opinions were removed by the Legislature. For although the glaring partiality of obliging all denominations to support the one which had been the favourite of government, was pretty early withdrawn, yet an evident predilection in favour of that church, still subsisted in the acts of the Assembly. Peculiar distinctions and the honour of an important name, were still continued; and these are considered as equally partial and injurious with the ancient emoluments. Our apprehensions on account of the continuance of these, which could have no other effect than to produce jealous animosities, and unnecessary contentions among different parties, were increased when we found that they were tenaciously adhered to by government notwithstanding the remonstrances of several Christian societies. To increase the evil a manifest disposition has been shown by the State, to consider itself as possessed of supremacy in *spirituals*, as well as *temporals;* and our fears have been realized in certain proceedings of the General Assembly at their last sessions. The engrossed bill for establishing a provision for the teachers of the Christian religion and the act for incorporating the Protestant Episcopal Church, so far as it secures to that church, the churches, glebes, &c. procured at the expense of the whole community, are not only evidences of this, but of an impolitic partiality which we are sorry to have observed so long.

We therefore in the name of the Presbyterian Church in Virginia, beg leave to exercise our privilege as freemen in remonstrating against the former absolutely, and against the latter under the restrictions above expressed.

We oppose the Bill,

Because it is a departure from the proper line of legislation ;

Because it is unnecessary, and inadequate to its professed end—impolitic, in many respects—and a direct violation of the Declaration of Rights.

The end of civil government is security to the temporal liberty and property of mankind, and to protect them in the free exercise of religion. Legislators are invested with powers from their constituents, for this purpose only ; and their duty extends no farther. Religion is altogether personal, and the right of exercising it unalienable; and it is not, cannot, and ought not to be, resigned to the will of the society at large; and much less to the Legislature, which derives its authority wholly from the consent of the people, and is limited by the original intention of civil associations.

We never resigned to the control of government, our right of determining for ourselves, in this important article ; and acting agreeably to the convictions of reason and conscience, in discharging our duty to our Creator. And therefore, it would be an unwarrantable stretch of prerogative, in the Legislature, to make laws concerning it, except for protection. And it would be a fatal symptom of abject slavery in us, were we to submit to the usurpation.

The Bill is also an unnecessary, and inadequate expedient for the end proposed. We are fully persuaded of the happy influence of Christianity upon the morals of men ; but we have never known it, in the history of its progress, so effectual for this purpose, as when left to its native excellence and evidence to recommend it, under the all directing providence of God, and free from the intrusive hand of the civil magistrate. Its Divine Author did not think it necessary to render it dependent on earthly governments. And experience has shown, that this dependence, where it has been effected, has been an injury rather than an aid. It has introduced corruption among the teachers and professors of it, wherever it has been tried, for hundreds of years, and has been destructive of genuine morality, in proportion to the zeal of the powers of this world, in arming it with the sanction of legal terrors, or inviting to its profession by honours and rewards.

It is urged, indeed, by the abettors of this bill, that it would be the means of cherishing religion and morality among the citizens. But it appears from fact, that these can be promoted only by the internal conviction of the mind, and its voluntary choice, which such establishments cannot effect.

We farther remonstrate against the bill as an impolitic measure :

It disgusts so large a proportion of citizens, that it would weaken the influence of government in other respects, and diffuse a spirit of opposition to the rightful exercise of constitutional authority, if enacted into a law :

It partially supposes the Quakers and Menomists to be more faithful in conducting the religious interests of their societies, than the other sects—which we apprehend to be contrary to fact :

It unjustly subjects men who may be good citizens, but who have not embraced our common faith, to the hardship of supporting a system, they have not as yet believed the truth of; and deprives them of their property, for what they do not suppose to be of importance to them :

It establishes a precedent for farther encroachments, by making the Legislature judges of religious truth. If the Assembly have a right to determine the preference between Christianity, and the other systems of religion that prevail in the world, they may also, at a convenient time, give a preference to some favoured sect among Christians :

It discourages the population of our country by alarming those who may have been oppressed by religious establishments in other countries, with fears of the same in this: and by exciting our own citizens to emigrate to other lands of greater freedom :

It revives the principle which our ancestors contested to blood, of attempting to reduce all religions to one standard by the force of civil authority :

And it naturally opens a door for contention among citizens of different creeds, and different opinions respecting the extent of the powers of government.

The bill is also a direct violation of the Declaration of Rights, which ought to be the standard of all laws. The sixteenth article is clearly infringed upon by it, and any explication which may have been given of it by the friends of this measure in the Legislature, so as to justify a departure from its literal construction, might also be used to deprive us of other fundamental principles of our government.

For these reasons, and others that might be produced, we conceive it our duty to remonstrate and protest against the said bill; and earnestly urge that it may not be enacted into a law.

We also wish to engage your attention a little farther, while we request a revision of the act for incorporating the Protestant Episcopal Church : and state our reasons for this request. We do not desire to oppose the incorporation of that church for the better management of its *temporalities;* neither do we wish to lessen the attachment of any of the members of the Legislature, in a private capacity, to the interests of that church. We rather wish to cultivate a spirit of forbearance and charity towards the members of it, as the servants of one common Master who differ in some particulars from each other. But we cannot consent that they shall receive particular notice or favour from government as a Christian Society; nor peculiar distinctions or emoluments.

We find by the act, that the convenience of the Episcopal Church hath been consulted by it, in the management of their interests as a religious society, at the expense of other denominations. Under the former establishment, there were perhaps few men who did not, at length, perceive the hardships and injustice of a compulsory law, obliging the citizens of this State by birthright free, to contribute to the support of a religion, from which their reason and conscience obliged them to dissent. Who then would not have supposed that the same sense of justice, which induced the Legislature to dissolve the grievous establishment, would also have induced them to leave to common use, the property in churches, glebes, &c., which had been acquired by common purchase.

To do otherwise was, as we conceive, to suppose that long prescription could sanction injustice; and that to persist in error, is to alter the essential difference between right and wrong. As Christians also, the subjects of Jesus Christ, who are wholly opposed to the exercise of spiritual powers by civil rulers, we conceive ourselves obliged to remonstrate against that part of the incorporating act, which authorises and directs the regulation of spiritual concerns. This is such an invasion of Divine prerogative, that it is highly exceptionable on that account, as well as on account of the danger to which it exposes our religious liberties. Jesus Christ hath given sufficient authority to his church, for every lawful purpose : and it is forsaking his authority and direction, for that of fallible men, to expect or to grant the sanction of civil law to authorise the regulation of any Christian society. It is also dangerous to our liberties, because it creates an invidious distinction on account of religious opinions, and exalts to a superior pitch of grandeur, as the church of the State, a society which ought to be contented with receiving the same protection from government, which the other societies enjoy, without aspiring to superior notice or regard. The Legislature assumes to itself by that law, the authoritative direction of this church in spirituals; and can be considered in no other light than its head, peculiarly interested in its welfare; a matter which cannot be indifferent to us—though this authority has only as yet been extended to those who have requested it or acquiesced in it. This church is now considered as the only regular church in the view of the law: and it is thereby raised to a state of unjust pre-eminence over others. And how far it may increase in dignity and influence in the State, by these means, at a future day, and especially when aided by the emoluments which it possesses, and the advantages of funding a very large sum or money without account, time alone can discover. But we esteem it our duty to oppose the act thus early, before the matter be entangled in precedents more intricate and dangerous. Upon the whole, therefore, we hope that the exceptionable parts of this act will be repealed by your honourable House; and that all preferences, distinctions, and advantages, contrary to the fourth article of the Declaration of Rights will be forever abolished.

We regret that full equality in all things, and ample protection and security to religious liberty were not incontestibly fixed in the constitution of the government. But we earnestly request that the defect may be remedied, as far as it is possible for the Legislature to do it, by the adopting the bill in the revised laws for establishing religious freedom. (Chap. 82 of the Report.)

That Heaven may illuminate your minds with all that wisdom which is necessary for the important purposes of your deliberation, is our earnest wish. And we beg leave to assure you, that however warmly we may engage in preserving our religion free from the shackles of human authority, and opposing claims of spiritual domination in civil powers, we are zealously disposed to support the government of our country, and to maintain a due submission to the lawful exercise of its authority.   Signed by order of the Convention.

                                                    JOHN TODD, *Chairman.*

Attest, DANIEL McCALLA, Clerk.
   Bethel, Augusta County,
      13th August, 1785.

On Saturday, August 18th, 1785, the General Committee of the Baptist Church met at Dupuy's meeting-house in Powhatan. Mr. Ford made report,—"That according to the directions given him, he presented a memorial and petition to the Honourable General Assembly: that they met with a favourable reception; that certain amendments were made to the marriage law, which he thought satisfactory. To this report the General Committee concurred." Upon considering the engrossed bill for a general assessment, which had been sent out for the consideration of the public, and for the expression of opinion, the General Committee resolved,—"That it be recommended to those counties which have not prepared petitions, to be presented to the General Assembly, against the engrossed bill for a general assessment for the support of the teachers of the Christian religion, to proceed thereon as soon as possible:—that it is believed to be repugnant to the spirit of the gospel, for the Legislature thus to proceed in matters of religion:—that no human laws ought to be established for that purpose; but that every person ought to be left entirely free in respect to matters of religion:—that the holy Author of our religion needs no such compulsive measures for the promotion of His cause :—that the gospel wants not the feeble arm of man for its support:—that it has made, and will again, through Divine power, make its way against all opposition:—and that should the Legislature assume the right of taxing the people for the support of the gospel, it will be destructive to religious liberty. Therefore, this Convention agrees unanimously, that it will be expedient to appoint a delegate to wait on the General Assembly, with a remonstrance and petition against such assessment. Accordingly the Rev. Reuben Ford was appointed."

The Legislature met on Monday, October 17th, 1785, and received, from all parts of the State, memorials and petitions expressing decided opposition to the bill for a general assessment. The bill and the memorials were considered in committee of the whole house. Mr. Madison brought forward Mr. Jefferson's bill, prepared in 1779, and advocated it. Of him Mr. Jefferson, who was not present to advocate his bill, thus writes, vol. 1st, p. 33—"He came into the house, in 1776, a new member and young; which circumstance concurring with his extreme modesty, prevented his venturing himself in debate, before his removal to the Council of State, in November, '77. From thence he went to Congress, then consisting of few members. Trained in these successive schools, he acquired a habit of self-possession, which placed at ready command the rich resources of his luminous and discriminating mind, and of his extensive information, and rendered him the first of every Assembly afterwards of which he became a member. Never wandering from his subject into vain declamation, but pursuing it closely, in language pure, classical and copious, soothing always the feelings of his adversaries by civilities and softness of expression, he rose to the eminent station which he held in the great National Convention of 1787; and in that of Virginia which followed, he sustained the new Constitution in all its parts, bearing off the palm against the logic of George Mason, and the fervid declamation of Mr. Henry. With these consummate powers were united a pure and spotless virtue which no calumny has ever attempted to sully. Of the powers and polish of his pen, and of the wisdom of his administration, in the highest offices of the nation, I need say nothing. They have spoken, and will forever speak for themselves."

The Rev. John B. Smith, President of Hampden Sidney College, one of the committee of Hanover Presbytery, had permission to be heard before the committee of the whole house, and spoke on three successive days against the general assessment bill. In him were combined the powers of logic and declamation. Self-possessed, he was fervid in debate. Mr. Henry's argument and declamation in favour of a general assessment, joined to his personal character, had, for a time, drawn Mr. Smith, and that acute reasoner, William Graham, to favour the bill. But further reflection on the ultimate bearing of the bill, led them to take the opposition to the Governor. Deservedly influential and popular, Smith knew, when he appeared before the committee of the whole, that he represented the whole Presbyterian population in the State; and that he spoke, on the subject, the opinions and decisions of the numerous Baptists. He plead the principles of natural law, and the purity of morals and religion involving the welfare of the State. Madison knew that he spoke the opinions of all the dissenters, and of many that were not dissenters from the religion of the State, and he plead the principles of natural law and of political rights, that men's thoughts were free in religion as in politics.

The bill for a general assessment was lost in the committee of the whole; and Mr. Jefferson's bill was reported to the house. And on the 17th of December, 1785, an engrossed bill, entitled,—"An act for establishing religious freedom," passed the house. Mr. Henry says,—"in the preamble to this act, some variations have been made from the original bill, as reported by the revisors, which renders the style less elegant, though the sense is not affected."

"AN ACT FOR ESTABLISHING RELIGIOUS FREEDOM.

" Whereas, Almighty God hath created the mind free;—that all attempts to influence it by temporal punishments or burthens, or by civil incorporations, tend only to beget habits of hypocrisy and meanness, and are a departure from the plan of the holy Author of our religion, who, being Lord both of body and mind, yet chose not to propagate it by coercions on either, as was in his almighty power to do;—that the impious presumptions of legislators and rulers, civil and ecclesiastical, who being themselves but fallible and uninspired men, have assumed dominion over the faith of others, setting up their own opinions and modes of thinking as the only true and infallible, and as such endeavouring to impose them on others, hath established and maintained false religions over the greater part of the world, and through all time;—that to compel a man to furnish contributions of money for the propagation of opinions which he disbelieves, is sinful and tyrannical; that even the forcing him to support this or that teacher of his own religious persuasion, is depriving him of the comfortable liberty of giving his contributions to the particular pastor whose morals he would make his pattern, and whose powers he feels most persuasive to righteousness, and is withdrawing, from the ministry, those temporary rewards, which, proceeding from an approbation of their personal conduct, are an additional incitement to earnest and unremitting labours for the instruction of mankind;—that our civil rights have no dependence on our religious opinions, any more than our opinions in physics and geometry;—that therefore the proscribing any citizen as unworthy the public confidence, by laying upon him an incapacity of being called to offices of trust or emolument, unless he profess or renounce this or that religious opinion, is depriving him injuriously of those privileges and advantages to which, in common with his fellow-citizens, he has a natural right;—that it tends only to corrupt the principles of that religion it is meant to encourage, by bribing with a monopoly of worldly honours and emoluments those who will externally profess and conform to it;—that though indeed those are criminal who do not withstand such temptations, yet neither are those innocent who lay the bait in their way;—that to suffer the civil magistrate to intrude his powers into the field of opinion, and to restrain the profession or propagation of principles, on supposition of their ill tendency, is a dangerous fallacy, which at once destroys all religious liberty, because he being, of course, judge of that tendency, will make his opinions the rule of judgment, and approve or condemn the sentiments of others only as they shall square with or differ from his own;—that it is time enough for the rightful purposes of civil government, for its officers to interfere when principles break out into overt acts against peace and good order;—and finally, that truth is great, and will prevail, if left to herself; that she is the proper and sufficient antagonist to error, and has nothing to fear from the conflict, unless by human interposition disarmed of her natural weapons, free argument and debate, error ceasing to be dangerous when it is permitted freely to contradict them.

"2d. *Be it enacted by the General Assembly,* That no man shall be compelled to frequent or support any religious worship, place, or ministry whatsoever, nor shall be enforced, restrained, molested, or burthened in his body or goods, nor shall otherwise suffer on account of his religious opinions or belief; but that all men shall be free to profess, and by argument to maintain, their opinion in matters of religion, and that the same shall in no wise diminish, enlarge, or affect their civil capacities.

"3d. And though we well know that this Assembly, elected by the people for the ordinary purposes of legislation only, have no power to restrain the acts of succeeding Assemblies, constituted with powers equal to our own; and that, therefore, to declare this act to be irrevocable, would be of no effect in law; yet we are free to declare, and do declare, that the rights hereby asserted are of the natural rights of mankind, and that if any act shall be hereafter passed to repeal the present, or to narrow its operation, such act will be an infringement of natural right."

The yeas and nays upon this bill were as follow:—*Ayes*, Joseph Fry, Wilson Cary Nicholas, Joseph Eggleston, Samuel William Anderson, Hickerson Barksdale, John Clark of Campbell, Samuel Hawes, Anthony New, John Daniel, Henry Southall, French Strother, Henry Fry, William Gatewood, Meriwither Smith, Charles Simmes, David Stuart, William Pickett, Thomas Helm, Christopher Greenup, James Garrard, George Thompson, Alexander White, Charles Thruston, Thomas Smith, George Clendennin, John Lucas, Jeremiah Pate, Ralph Humphreys, Isaac Vanmeter, George Jackson, Nathaniel Wilkinson, John Mayo, Jun., John Rentfro, William Norval, John Roberts, William Dudley, Thomas Moore, Carter Braxton, Benjamin Semple, Francis Peyton, Christopher Robertson, Samuel Garland, Benjamin Logan, David Scott, William Pettijohn, Robert Sayres, Daniel Trigg, William Hartwell Mason, Griffin Stith, David Bradford, James Madison, Charles Porter, William Harrison, Benjamin Lankford, John Clarke of Prince Edward, Richard Bibb, Cuthbert Bullet, Daniel Carrol Brent, Williamson Ball, Andrew Moore, John Hopkins, Gawin Hamilton, Isaac Zoane, John Tayloe, John Whittaker Willis, Andrew Kincannon, and James Innes.—67.

Noes, Thomas Claiborne, Miles King, Warlick Westwood, John Page, Garland Anderson, Elias Wills, William Thornton, Francis Corbin, Willis Riddick, Daniel Sanford, John Gordon, Edward Bland, Anthony Walke, George Lee Turberville, William Garrard, John Francis Mercer, Carter Basset Harrison, Richard Cary, Jr., William Cary, and Richard Lee.—20.

After an experiment of more than half a century, the bill for religious freedom holds its place among the fundamental laws of the Virginia statute book. Religion and morals have not suffered. Four colleges, two theological seminaries, and the University, have been added to the public institutions for instruction. Authorised ministers of the gospel have increased about ten-fold; and professors of the religion of the gospel in the same proportion. Churches, academies, and schoolhouses are multiplying throughout the extended State. All parties agree that "the mind is free;" that even prisoners, slaves, and convicts enjoy freedom of conscience.

CHAPTER XVI.

JAMES WADDELL, D. D., AND THE CHURCHES IN THE NORTHERN
NECK.

COULD we catch a view of the fleeting things of life, as they
were passing in Pennsylvania, at the time the preaching of
Davies was causing unusual excitement in Virginia, and could
we visit Nottingham, the residence of Dr. Finley, and look into
the school of the worthy pastor, then gaining its eminence
as "a log college," we should see the germs of some eminent men, and might trace the characteristics of their future
life. In one amiable, ambitious boy, the confident of his
school-mates, would be found the physician and philanthro-
pist, Benjamin Rush; in another bold and open-hearted lad,
Governor Martin of North Carolina, of Revolutionary memory;
in another persevering youth, Ebenezer Hazard, noted for his
collections of documents of interest to coming generations; and
in the cheerful faces around would be observed the amiable
Judge Rush and the warm-hearted physician William Tennent,
and also the Rev. William M. Tennent, of Abington. In that
young man, tall, spiritual, with musical voice, his left arm
thrown back under his coat, sometimes reciting as a scholar,
and sometimes acting as tutor to the younger boys, we should
recognise James Waddell, who fills a page in Virginia literature, immortalizing William Wirt, the author of "The Blind
Preacher;" and who, occupying a large space in the history of
Hanover Presbytery, cannot be passed over in any history of
the United States,—one of the *men* of his own generation,
and a man for all generations.

He was born in the province of Ulster, Ireland, July, 1739.
His parents, who were of Scotch origin, and of the Presbyterian faith, emigrated to America in the autumn of 1739, and
settled in Pennsylvania. Here he remained under the care of
pious parents till he was about fourteen years of age, enjoying
with his sister Sally, and two brothers William and Robert,
the affectionate instructions of a pious mother, whose prayers
often thrilled his heart and left their recollection forever. The
particular circumstance, in addition to his natural talents, that
turned the attention of his parents to seek a liberal education
for him, in preference to his brothers, and hedged him into a
professional life for usefulness, and a livelihood, was a painful
occurrence. When a small boy, he went hunting with his

brothers. A hare was chased into a hollow tree. In the excitement of cutting him out, as his brother was bringing a blow
with the axe, James thrust his hand under its edge, and in a
twinkling it was severed almost in twain. Hastily gathering
up the fingers and part of the hand, and pressing them to the
stump, he ran to his parents. The mutilated hand was band-
aged and the wound healed; but the fingers and the lower part
of the hand never afterwards increased in size, and were capable of very little action. The situation of their son in consequence of this event, induced the parents to seek for him a
liberal education, for which his powers of mind were admirably
adapted.

His progress at the "log college" of Dr. Finley, at Nottingham, was rapid; and his acquirements unusually correct. His
Greek studies were carried on under the Rev. Mr. Campbell, a
Scotchman, and a noted Greek scholar. On account of his proficiency, and to assist him in his education, he was promoted to be
tutor in the school; and afterwards served in the same capacity
in the school of Rev. Robert Smith, of Pequa, the father of
Messrs. Samuel Stanhope, and John Blair Smith, of happy
memory in the Virginia churches. Through life he was considered a model of correctness in Latin prosody; and there is
still in existence a system of rules, in his hand-writing, used by
him while at Nottingham, remarkable for simplicity and ease of
adaptation in acquiring a correct knowledge of Latin measure.
His high standing among his fellow students was undiminished
through life. And to be held in high estimation by such men
is evidence of the excellence of the attainments, the native
worth, and winning manners of Waddell.

While a member of Dr. Finley's school, he became hopefully
pious. He always dated his religious impressions to the instructions of his mother; in very early life, he often longed to see
Christ on earth, that he might ask him, who healed withered
limbs, to heal his hand; and thought with what eagerness he would
run to him were he to be found; and while yet a youth, he asked
Him who, unseen, is ever present with the penitent, and he gave
him of the water of life. As soon as his mind became settled
on the great question of his salvation, through Christ and his
cross, he devoted himself to the work to which his mother's faith
had previously dedicated him, the ministry of the gospel. In
reference to this period of his life, he has been heard to say—
that a sweet and almost overpowering sense of his acceptance
with God, was granted to him, such as in after life was seldom
renewed. His obligations to the Saviour were acknowledged.
His choice was made; and a constraint was on him to preach
the gospel. When we consider the consequences of his preaching,
and the providence that shut him up to a course of education,

by which he came into the ministry, we cannot but believe he was called of God.

When about nineteen years of age, allured by favourable representations, he set out for South Carolina, with the intention of teaching school, for a time, by way of enabling him to complete his theological studies. On his way through Virginia, he called on the Rev. Samuel Davies, in Hanover county, and felt the attractive influence of that good man. The interest was mutual. The appearance of Waddell, and his statements, won the heart of Davies. A tall, graceful young man, hedged in by a painful providence, and seeking a maintenance and an education, and the ministry, with an unblemished character, and tender heart, could not have an interview with Davies, without feeling himself beloved; and to feel himself beloved by a man whom all admired, was to be a captive. Davies looked at the desolations around him with compassion, and looked on Waddell as he had done on Pattillo and Richardson and Wright. The consequence was, Waddell took part in the classical school of the Rev. John Todd, of Louisa, the early associate of Mr. Davies, and commenced the studies preparatory for the sacred ministry in Virginia, which thenceforth became his home.

He offered himself to Hanover Presbytery as a candidate for the gospel ministry, during its meeting, at the Stone Church, Augusta county, in April, 1760. On the 25th of September of the same year, at Buffalo, the pastoral charge of Mr. Sankey, the following record was made—" Mr. James Waddell having at our last offered himself on trial as a candidate for the gospel ministry, he was desired to prepare a discourse to be delivered this Presbytery, which he has done accordingly, and has been examined on sundry extempore questions in divinity, his Christian experience and motives to the ministry; with all which the Presbytery are well pleased, and sustain them as parts of trial, and appoint him an exigesis on that question *An Christus qua Mediator sit adorandus*, and a sermon on the same subject, the text to be chosen by himself, to be delivered at our next Presbytery, which for that purpose is to meet at the Byrd in Goochland the 4th Wednesday of December." This meeting appointed for December did not take place. But in the records of the meeting of the Presbytery held at Tinkling Spring, in Augusta, April 2, 1761, it is stated that the following representation was made and approved. " Louisa, January 21, 1761.—As the Presbytery for Mr. Waddell's further trials was prevented from convening by the inclemency of the weather; that he might not longer be confined to studies remote from, but might prosecute those that have a more immediate reference to, the work of the ministry, and that the Church might not suffer by the disappointment, Messrs. Todd and Pattillo proceeded to hear his exigesis, and a sermon from Philippians ii. 9, 10, and approved of them as very satisfactory. They also examined into his knowledge of the Latin, Greek and Hebrew languages, together with the sciences of rhetoric, logic, ontology, moral and natural philosophy, and astronomy; in all of which he gave very pleasing and satisfactory evidence of his knowledge, intending to report the same to the next Presbytery; and presuming on their concurrence, appoint him popular trials, to be delivered with their permission at our next,—viz. a lecture on Isaiah lxi. 1, 2, 3, and a sermon on John v. 10."

The Presbytery, having approved the proceedings of Messrs. Todd and Pattillo,—"further examined Mr. Waddell on sundry branches of learning, heard his popular sermon and lecture, and examined him in divinity, do express their satisfaction with the several trials he has passed through; and on his subscribing the Confession of Faith, as the confession of his faith, and conformity to the Directory, and on promising subjection to the Presbytery in the Lord,—the Presbytery do license and appoint him to preach the gospel as a candidate for the holy ministry, and heartily recommend him to the acceptance of the churches." He then signed the following declaration. "I believe the doctrines contained in the Confession of Faith to be agreeable to the Word of God, contained in the Old and New Testament, and subscribe them accordingly, as the confession of my faith.— JAMES WADDELL." This confession, or declaration, was written at the top of a page in the records of the Presbytery, and beneath are the autographs of the members of Presbytery written in the order of seignority, and as they became members of Presbytery. In the latter part of his life the subject of this sketch dropped an *l* from his name. His descendants generally have preserved the *ll* and give the accent to the last syllable. "Mr. Waddell is to supply in all our vacancies in Virginia, and those in North Carolina that depend on this Presbytery, at his discretion, till the fall Presbytery."

The numerous vacancies of the Presbytery visited by Mr. Waddell, expressed their approbation of his services by inviting him to be their pastor. The extent of the desolations, and the exhibition of ministerial talent by the young candidate, may be judged by the record at the fall meeting of Presbytery, October 7th, 1761,—"The following calls were put into Presbytery for Mr. Waddell, viz:—one from Upper Falling and Peaks of Otter,—one from Nutbush and Grassy Creek,—one from Brown's meeting-house and Jenning's Gap,—one from Hallifax,—none of which he thought fit to take under consideration." On the next day a call was put in from Bedford, which he took under consideration till the next meeting of

Presbytery. He was directed to spend half the time intervening the next Presbytery, in Bedford, and half among the vacancies that had put in calls for his services.

At the spring meeting of the Presbytery, April 8th, 1762,
at the Byrd meeting-house in Goochland county—"Mr. Waddell is appointed to supply in Bedford, Hanover, and the
Northern Neck, and other vacancies at discretion." At the
same meeting a committee was appointed, consisting of Rev.
Messrs. Sankey, Todd, Henry, Pattillo, and Hunt, to meet at
Harris's Creek, in Prince Edward, on the third Wednesday
of June, to attend to a case of discipline—"and to receive Mr.
Waddell's trials for ordination, viz :—*Num Electio sit condi-
tionalis*,—and a sermon on Romans x. 4; and the Presbytery empower said committee to receive Mr. Caldwell as a member of Presbytery, if he offers himself with proper credentials,
and to appoint him where to preach. The said committee, if
they sustain Mr. Waddell's trials, are to proceed to his ordination, at which Mr. Todd is to preside."

On the appointed day, June 16th, 1762, three of the committee met, viz :—Rev. Messrs. Sankey, Henry and Pattillo,—
with elders, William Campbell, David Caldwell, and William
Smith. "Mr. Waddell opened the committee with a sermon
on Romans x. 4, according to appointment. Mr. Sankey
chosen moderator; Mr. Pattillo, clerk. Thursday 17th, committee met according to adjournment p. p. s. q. s. The committee having considered Mr. Waddell's sermon and thesis,
with his defence of the same, sustained them as satisfactory
trials for ordination, to which they accordingly proceeded, by
fasting, prayer, and imposition of hands, at which Mr. Pattillo presided, by a sermon on 2 Cor. v. 20 ;—and he is now
present as member of this judicature."

The time of Mr. Waddell's visiting the Northern Neck, and
some of the circumstances are given in Colonel Gordon's
journal. In the month of August after his licensure we are told
the congregation expressed a desire to hear him; and in the
succeeding October Mr. Todd visited the people and gave them
reason to hope that Mr. Waddell would visit them about
Christmas. This expectation was not realized; and in April,
1762, Mr. Criswell attended Presbytery, and obtained the
order of Presbytery for Mr. Waddell to visit them. The
journal, April 18th, 1762, says—"May the Lord be praised, I
at last have had the comfort of going with my wife and family
to meeting where Mr. Waddell performed to admiration." On
the last Sabbath of May (the 30th day) the congregation made
out a call, which, on Monday June 7th, after the communion
administered by Mr. Todd, was handed to Mr. Waddell by
Colonel Gordon. He declined the call, but promised to visit

the people again.   On the 17th of the month he was ordained
in Prince Edward as has been related; and on the 7th of
October at a meeting of the Presbytery at Providence, Louisa,
—"Mr. Waddell accepts of a call from Lancaster and Northumberland counties, in which the Presbytery heartily concur."
The inclinations of Mr. Waddell, strongly in favour of a congregation in the neighbourhood of York, Pennsylvania, which
offered him inducements to become their pastor, were yielded
to the solicitations of the congregations, the elders, and the
advice of brethren in the ministry, in Virginia; and of the
numerous and promising fields of labour presented to him, in
Virginia, he made choice of the lower part of the Great
Northern Neck.

That portion of Virginia contained between the two rivers
Potomac and Rappahannoc, comprising the grant made to
Lord Fairfax, has been known as the Northern Neck; but
commonly the appellation has been confined to that district
that lies below tide water.   Of this long narrow strip of
country, embracing the extremes of soil, and abounding in
harbours and the luxuries of the ocean, Mr. Waddell chose the
lower part, embraced principally in the two counties of Lancaster and Northumberland, and lying along the mouths of
the two rivers and the intervening shore of the Great Chesapeake.   This part of Virginia will hold a place in history
should some natural or moral desolation sweep the race of
man entirely from its soil.   It is the birth place of some of
the worthies of the Revolution; and will rejoice in the names
of Washington, and Monroe, and Lee, and Fitzhugh, and Ball
and Carter.   In a religious point of view, too, it is remarkable.
The established church was set up here in its vigour, and with
every advantage to be found in the colony; and with a succession of worthy ministers it must have flourished, under
those divine influences promised by the great Head of the
church.   But in no part of the State was the faultiness of
the clergy more lamentable or more visible; and no where
was the vindication of the purity of the gospel of Christ
more loudly demanded, by God's glory and the lost condition
of man.   And God honoured his truth in the face of the
abuses of his ordinances, and the mockers at spiritual
religion.   Before the people in Hanover assembled to hear
Samuel Morris read gospel truth, and paid fines for seeking salvation out of the pale of the established church, a
layman had assembled the people of the Northern Neck
for religious instruction, and had witnessed the hopeful conversion of sinners to a life of godliness.   "There resided,"
says Dr. Miller in his life of Rodgers, "in the great Northern
Neck, between the Rappahannoc and Potomac rivers, a certain

John Organ, a pious schoolmaster from Scotland. Soon after his establishment in that country, finding that there was no place of public worship in his immediate neighbourhood, and that a large portion of the people wholly disregarded the ordinances of religion, and were sunk in carelessness and profligacy, his spirit was stirred within him to attempt something for the spiritual advantage of his neighbours. Accordingly, he collected in private houses such of them as were tolerably decent and sober, and had any sense of religion, and read to them the Scriptures and other pious writings, accompanied with prayer and singing. For several years nothing more was attempted; especially as the frowns of the government were soon directed towards this little flock, and the laws against dissenters rigorously enforced against them. In a short time, however, after the formation of the Synod of Philadelphia, the people of Organ's neighbourhood made an application to that body for supplies. This request was granted; and the Rev. Mr. Anderson, who had before resided in New York, but was then settled in Pennsylvania, was sent by the Synod to preach among them, to organize a church, and to intercede with the government on their behalf. Mr. Anderson succeeded in attaining all these objects. He preached to great acceptance, and with much impression; and formed a church which has continued to the present day." Mr. Anderson mentioned by Dr. Miller, was James Anderson, from the Presbytery of Irvine in Scotland, who entered the Rappahannoc river, Virginia, April 1710; was the next year settled in New Castle; and in 1718 in New York; and in 1726 removed to Donegal. He was admitted member of the Philadelphia Presbytery September 20th, 1710. " At the desire also of Mr. James Anderson, he was admitted, upon producing sufficient testimonials of his abilities and qualifications for the ministerial work, and that he was duly licensed and ordained thereunto." Too little is known of this minister, whose visit to the Governor of Virginia in 1738 was eminently successful in procuring protection for the colonies of Presbyterians, as has been recorded in another chapter. Whether Mr. Anderson made two visits to the Governor is not clear; though it is evident from the records of the Presbytery that two communications were sent to the Governor, one in 1738, by Mr. Anderson, and the other in 1723, the messenger not named.

The location of the church gathered by Mr. Organ cannot be fully ascertained; and there is no evidence that they ever had a church building. All the notices we can find in the records concerning the Potomac settlements are the following: at the third meeting of Synod, held September 12th, 1719—" The Synod having received a letter from the people of Potomake, in Virginia, requesting the Synod's care and diligence to provide them an able gospel minister to settle among them, it was appointed that the Rev. Mr. Daniel McGill should go and preach to that people in order to settlement upon mutual agreement, and that a letter be writ to said people by Masters Conn and Cross, and by them be brought into the Synod for approbation." This letter was brought in and approved and sent,— and the next year, we find the following record, viz.— "Mr. McGill reported to the Synod, that according to last year's appointment, he went to Potomake, in Virginia, and after some months continuance there, put the people into church order. The said congregation of Potomake in Virginia have sent a letter to the Synod, manifesting their hearty approbation of Mr. McGill's whole conduct among them, and desiring his settling with them as their minister. The affair of Potomake deferred till afterwards"—and though taken up and committed to the committee of bills and overtures, nothing further was done, during the meeting of Synod. We hear nothing further from Virginia till Thursday, 27th September, 1722, at a meeting of the Synod in Philadelphia—"A representation being made by some of our members of the earnest desire of some Protestant dissenting families in Virginia, together with a comfortable prospect of the increase of our interest there, the Synod have appointed that Mr. Hugh Conn, Mr. John Orme, and Mr. William Stewart, do each of them severally visit said people, and preach four Sabbaths to them, between this and the next Synod."

At the next Synod, September 19th, 1723, "a letter from the people of Virginia being read, the consideration of it was deferred till to-morrow;"—the next day the same preacher was appointed to visit them,—"and it is recommended to Mr. Jonathan Dickinson to preach to said people before next Synod, some Sabbath days. Ordered that Mr. Jones and Mr. Andrews write a letter to the people of Virginia; and that a letter be writ to the Governor of Virginia by Messrs. Dickinson and Cross, and that the said letter to the people of Virginia, and also this, be brought into Synod for approbation." The next day—"a letter to the Governor of Virginia was read and approved."

The next year, September 16th, 1724, at the meeting of the Synod, it appears that "Mr. Orme fulfilled the appointment of Synod with respect to his preaching in Virginia; Mr. Conn did not and gave his reasons, which were sustained; Mr. Stewart did not, the reasons not known, he being absent. A letter from the people being read and considered, the Synod *have referred that whole affair to the Presbytery of New Castle*, and orders a letter to be writ to that people." From this time till the year 1738, when Mr. Anderson was sent with a letter to the Governor of Virginia, of which a full account is given elsewhere, there is on the records of the Synod but one notice of Virginia matters; and as the records of the Presbytery of Newcastle, to whom the affairs of Virginia were referred, are lost, no further facts, or direct information will or probably can be obtained about the localities of the people referred to, as "the people of Virginia"—or "the people of Potomake, Virginia."

From the death of Mr. Makemie in 1707, the Presbyterian cause in Virginia declined. In 1718, the Synod declare, there was no Presbyterian minister in the colony. "In a short time after the formation of the Synod of Philadelphia,"—says Dr. Miller—"the people of Organ's neighbourhood made application to that body for supplies." Where that neighbourhood was situated nothing more is known than that it was in the region between the Potomac and Rappahannoc rivers, known as the Northern Neck; and as this region was not settled at that time west of the Blue Ridge, the neighbourhood must have been between the Blue Ridge and the Bay Shore. God had been mindful of his covenant, and blessed the truth of the gospel to the awakening and hopeful conversion of many under the labours of Organ; but it is not known that the people in the Northern Neck ever had a church building or a pastor till the time of Mr. Waddell.

"The people of Potomake," mentioned in the records of 1719, if not the same people as those of Organ's neighbourhood, lived in the same general bounds, and were located somewhere between the Blue Ridge and the Bay Shore. The suggestion that they were Scotch Irish Presbyterians, located some where in the Valley of Virginia, is inadmissible, because there were no white inhabitants of the Valley any where along the Potomac or Shenandoah previous to about the year 1733; and no Presbyterian congregation before 1736 or 1737.

Respecting—"the Protestant dissenting families of Virginia"—mentioned in the year 1722, and in 1724 referred to the Newcastle Presbytery, we have no farther knowledge, and know not where to look for them, but in the Northern Neck, in Accomac, the residence and burial place of Makemie, or on Elizabeth River near Norfolk, or on York River, in each of which places there were Presbyterians.

What favour the dissenters met with from the civil authorities in Virginia, is evident from the following record of the Synod, the only one referring to Virginia previous to 1738:—Saturday, September 22d, 1733—"Upon an overture of the Committee to the Synod concerning a representation of Mr. Hugh Stevenson, respecting harsh and injurious usage he met with from some gentlemen in Virginia, the Synod ordered Mr. Stevenson to lay a representation thereof before them, which he accordingly did in writing. And after hearing the same and reasoning upon it, it was agreed that a letter be writ by the Synod, and sent to the General Assembly of the Church of Scotland, together with a copy of Mr. Stevenson's representation, in order to use our interest with that venerable Assembly for our being assisted with money from the Societies for the Propagation of Religion, or elsewhere, to enable us to maintain some itinerant ministers in Virginia, or elsewhere, as also to procure their assistance to obtain the favourable notice of the government in England, so as to lay a restraint upon some gentlemen in said neighbouring province, as may discourage them from hampering such itinerant ministers by illegal prosecutions; and if it may be, to procure some assistance from his Majesty for our encouragement by way of *regium donum.*" Two copies of this letter were sent. Mr. Stevenson was a minister in good standing, and probably was sent into Virginia by the Presbytery of Newcastle, to whom the request from Virginia had been committed. This record shows that the spirit of the province was unchanged between the time of Makemie and that of Davies; freedom of conscience was unknown. How far this despotism in religion affected the morals of the Northern Neck, will be séen in the treatment of Mr. Waddell, while his successful labours for spiritual religion excited the attention of the community as Davies' had done in Hanover.

Owing to the loss of the records of Newcastle Presbytery, we can find no certain dates of the actings and doings of the dissenters in the Northern Neck until 1755. The following letter from the Appendix to Gillies' Collections, shows there were Presbyterians of active piety, under unfavorable circumstances, maintaining the cause of spiritual religion, and carrying the gospel to the cabins of the slaves. The letter bears date September 5th, 1755—" *Dear Sir:* You take notice in your letter of my poor and weak endeavours for the instruction of the negroes; I did, indeed, (as far as I could) lay open their condition to some acquaintances; and from a very good friend in Glasgow, have received books which enable me to do them more service. The condition of this part of the country is very melancholy. There is little inquiry made after good books among our great folks; plays, races, cock-fighting, &c., are more acceptable. No wonder that their slaves are neglected. But when I saw them working on the Sabbath, or fishing, or heard they were doing so; or that they could not speak a word without swearing, and were ignorant almost as brutes of the evil consequences of such things, these considerations and the advice of a Christian friend, induced me to do something; but they are very thoughtless, and some whom I have earnestly dealt with seem still unconcerned; yet there are two or three, or more, that seem to break off their wickedness, and serve God. In my advices to them, I do not go out of the sphere of a private Christian. I hear them repeat the Mother's Catechism and read in the New Testament. There are some who come to me at present on the Sabbath once in a fortnight, when we have no sermon. Some persons have objected against their learning, as if it made them worse, but that effect has not followed on any that have been with me, so far as I know; on the contrary, they come to serve from conscience, whereas it was before from dread. I was speaking to them, not to learn when they should be working. No,—they said, for that would be theft, to steal time from our masters. Some make very good progress. Some can read in the New Testament. Several, before I came, could read, but had no books, which I have helped them to, from those I got from Glasgow. And they read to the rest. But alas! there is little seriousness amongst us here in this country. When I go amongst Mr. Davies' people, religion seems to flourish; it is like the suburbs of heaven. The poor negroes seem very thankful to any that instruct them, Mr. Todd informed me he preached a sermon to them, and they thanked him, and seem desirous of further knowledge. It is very agreeable to see the gentlemen in those parts at their morning and evening prayers, with their slaves devoutly joining with them. From about the date of this letter for a series of years, the cause of religion flourished more in the Northern Neck than any other part of the State. And this prosperity was connected with two individuals, Colonel James Gordon and Rev. James Waddell, assisted by a company of gentlemen of the old school of manners and habits of intercourse.

Colonel James Gordon of Lancaster county, Virginia, may be considered as the nucleus of the congregations, in Lancaster and Northumberland, to which Mr. Waddell devoted the most active part of his ministerial life. A Scotch Irishman, he emigrated from Newry, County Down, Ireland, and took his abode, in early life, in Lancaster. His brother John resided on the opposite side of the river Rappahannoc in Middlesex county, at Urbanna, the county seat, and a port of entry. These brothers were enterprising and successful merchants, and became wealthy and influential; and have numerous descendants in Virginia and scattered over the South and West. The Gordons of Albemarle are the descendants of John. The time of their emigration cannot now be stated exactly, but from circumstances we are led to the conclusion that it must have been previous to, or about the time that Mr. Anderson visited the

Governor, at the request of Mr. Caldwell and the appointment of Synod, in the year 1738, to secure for the colonies, about to emigrate to Virginia, their religious privileges. The brothers were closely connected through life; James, however, was the most active in religious matters, and in this view calls for more particular attention. A man of enterprise, of popular manners, habits of hospitality, of extensive landed and personal property, by education and principle a Presbyterian, he stood firm in his religious opinions and practice, and received the reward of his faith and devotion. A man of system, he was in the habit of keeping a journal, in which he made daily entries in a brief manner, of his domestic concerns, his mercantile affairs, his farming operations, and events of interest in the neighbourhood, or the country at large. He registered the names of all visiters at his house, whether to dine, or lodge, or remain a longer time; and is equally particular in noticing all his absences from home, either on business, or friendly visits. Of this journal, there remains only a fragment, which appears to be the middle part of a large volume. There is not one long sentence in the journal, except in the copies of two or three letters which found their way into the volume; yet the brief dry notices, of a man of business and careful observation, crowded together, as the events took place, day after day for five years, give a graphic sketch of Virginia life in the Northern Neck, in its fairest form. Without the least ostentation, in this journal kept only for his own eye, to direct his business and correct his memory, he shows himself the hospitable Christian gentleman, and makes us feel the power and necessity of the gospel. All the knowledge we have of Mr. Waddell's labours in the Northern Neck, and of the gathering of the congregations in Lancaster and Northumberland is, with one exception, derived from this journal, and from the records of Hanover Presbytery. Mr. Gordon's name does not appear on the records of Presbytery, yet from the interest he took in the religious welfare of his family and neighbours, it is more than probable he was active in the applications made for supplies from Hanover Presbytery. Were the records of Newcastle in existence, we might find some notices of a previous date.

The first application from the Northern Neck was, April 27th, 1757, in Hanover—"An importunate application being made to Mr. Davies from some people in and about Richmond county, to come and preach to them, the Presbytery appoint him to preach there the last Sabbath in June." In July, 1757, a request came—"from Lancaster and Northumberland. The Presbytery appoint Mr. Davies three Sabbaths in the Northern Neck and one at Petersburg, between this and the Spring meeting." In January, 1758, Mr. Pattillo was directed to spend "the third and fourth Sabbaths in April in the Northern Neck." At the meeting of Presbytery, April 26th, 1758, Mr. Pattillo excused himself for not fulfilling his appointments in the Northern Neck, and was appointed to preach—"the third Sabbath of June in Lancaster; the Friday before in Richmond; the fourth in Northumberland; the first of July in Westmoreland, and the second at discretion." In September, 1758—"Presbytery appoint a sacrament in the Northern Neck, the last of March next. Petitions for supplies were presented from Essex, Lancaster, Northumberland, and Westmoreland." Mr. Davies was appointed one Sabbath in the Northern Neck this Fall, and another in the Spring at the sacrament there: Mr. Todd was appointed—"to assist at the sacrament in Lancaster, before next Presbytery." This appointment was fulfilled. Application for supplies were continued from meeting to meeting till Mr. Waddell accepted a call from the congregation and became their resident minister. The first date is Friday, December 22d, 1758. The entries are about the arrival of ships, and the price of tobacco, which was then three pence per pound, and it was supposed would soon be four pence. On Monday, Christmas day, his wife and daughter attended Wicomico church, in Westmoreland county.

"1759, January 8th, Monday—Went with Mr. Criswell to Northumberland Court. Mr. Leland and Mines behaved like blackguards in respect to Mr. Criswell, who went to get scholars, and engaged several, though the parsons did all they could against him, which seemed to make the people more fond of sending their children. I think such ministers should be stripped of their gowns. Tuesday 9th.—Went to Colonel Conway's, where Mr. Criswell and myself dined, and were very agreeably entertained. The old gentleman, I believe, has now fully dropped opposing the meeting-house, which is mostly occasioned by a letter he lately received from Mr. Ben. Waller, who informs him that dissenters have power to build houses and enjoy their religion by Act of Toleration, and complains much of the Church of England's last petitioning the king about a law that was lately passed in this colony, that set their salaries at $\frac{16}{8}$ per cwt.,—which they call the Two-penny Act, which is like to make a great noise in this country. Thursday, 11th.—Mr. Criswell began keeping school at Ball's; had but five scholars.

"Monday 15th.—Tobacco has got to 30 shillings per cwt.; it seems it will run very high this year. I'm at a loss what to think of it."—On the 13th of February, he says tobacco was 40 shillings per cwt. We notice these prices because the course pursued by the clergy respecting their salaries, which were estimated by pounds of tobacco, and the acts of the Legislature on the subject, had a most important bearing on the established church, and contributed not a little to her downfall.

In February and March he speaks of a meeting-house in progress—but does not speak of its location. It was probably the one built in Lancaster not far from his residence.

"Wednesday, March 21st, 1759.—Sowing oats in the young peach orchard. Went to Colonel Selden's, where I had the pleasure of meeting dear Mr. Davies, Mr. Shackelford, and Colonel Thornton our Adjutant. Thursday 22d.—Went from Colonel Selden's to general muster. Mr. Davies staid there till we had done the exercise; and then came home with me with Colonel Thornton, Colonel Selden, and Major Flood. Friday 23d.—Went to meeting; a large company; where Mr. Davies gave us an excellent sermon, and where we met Captains Morris, Craighead, De Graftemead, and Smith. They all came here in the evening; likewise Mr. Todd, (Rev.) Mr. Blackwell, Colonel Taylor, and Mrs. Boyd; a full house.

"Saturday 24th.—Went with the above to meeting. Mr. Todd preached to a large company. Sabbath, 25th. A comfortable day to me. The Lord's Supper was administered; forty-four communicants besides the Hanover gentlemen. Mr. Davies and Todd at Colonel Selden's. Monday 26th.—Mr. Davies preached in Northumberland, and Mr. Todd at our meeting-house. We had a fine sermon. Monday, April 9th.—Went to Northumberland Court. Tobacco at 40 shillings and rising. Gave Mr. Minzie Mr. Davies' letter, that seemed to give him much uneasiness, and I am persuaded he will not enter into a dispute with Mr. Davies if he can avoid it. Thursday 26th.—Robert Hening came home this morning and brought a letter from Mr. Minzie to Mr. Davies, which in my opinion is very stupid and foolish.

"May 7th, 1759.—Got to Richmond Court about six o'clock. Many people at court. Tobacco seems to fall very fast, so that the merchants wanted to sell as well as the planters; that I don't believe there was one hogshead sold; 40 shillings was demanded, but I did not hear that 30 shillings was offered. Friday 18th.—Went to court-house. Court set but a short time. Minis's play was read in the ordinary by Mr. Packer, that received it from Mr. Rinehard, who said he found it in the court-yard. Minis and Leland at the head of the mob; pretty fellows to be teachers of the people.

"June 9th, 1759, Saturday—This day my daughter Anne was married to Mr. Richard Chichester, about 11 o'clock forenoon (he then names all the company.) The parson, Mr. Cam, went off first about 4 o'clock, and most all went off at night, and before it."—On the next day they all went to the Episcopal church. It seems some of the family generally attended the

Episcopal church, though the Colonel did not often. This Mr. Cam took an active part in the contest between the clergy and the Legislature about the value of tobacco, in which the clergy were paid. " Friday 22d, Mr. Chichester set off to-day to visit Mr. Davies, in Hanover, before he left the colony. I wrote to him. His going away gives us here and in Hanover county, the greatest uneasiness. But I trust God will direct us in the way to heaven. Sunday 24th—At home, Mr. Criswell read us a fine sermon—had all the people in that we could.

"July 1st, Sunday—We went to the meeting-house, but very doubtful of Mr. Martin's coming ; but about 12 o'clock we had the pleasure to see him. He gave us two excellent sermons. Monday 2d—Went to meeting. This season there was a large company,—all seem so much pleased with Mr. Martin. Tuesday 3d—Went to meeting, very near as many as yesterday. Last night Mr. Martin lay here. We had a very large company also this night ;—he lectured last night. Monday 9th— Went to Northumberland Court,—my wife, Molly and Betty, and Lib Chichester went with me as far as Mr. Conway's. The paper was read about Minzie and Leland publicly, which occasioned a large company some mirth—Minzie sat till it was read—but then went out from the company much displeased. It appears these ministers will repent their farce that has pleased them so much. Thursday 19th—Mr. Downman came here,— has got fifteen thousand seven hundred pounds of tobacco subscribed towards a meeting-house in Northumberland. Tuesday 24th—Yesterday received a long letter from Mr. Maine, a mate of Captain Young's ship, who appears to be a pious Christian.

" August 25th, Sunday—At home with my wife and family, where I have much more comfort than going to church, hearing the ministers ridicule the dissenters.

" September 21st, Friday—Went with my family to meeting, where we had an excellent sermon, preached by the Rev. Mr. Todd. ('I will love thee, O Lord'.) Mr. Henry is not come over the Bay,—which is not disagreeable to me, as he is not qualified in the colony. Saturday 22d—Went to meeting with our company, where there was a greater number of people. The text was John iii. 14, 'Peace be to thee, our friends salute thee.' Sunday 23d—The comfortable sacrament of the Lord's supper was this day administered at our meeting-house, by Mr. Todd; fifty-three communicants : none from Hanover. Religion seems to increase amongst us, for which we have cause to adore the great God for such blessings. Monday 24th—Went to preaching to-day,—when we all parted. Mr. Todd to Captain De Graftemead's to-night—texts—Friday, Psalm xviii. 1 ; Saturday, John iii. 14 ; Sunday, Jeremiah l. 4, 5 ; Monday, Genesis xxxii. 26.

"Thursday, October 3, 1759.—Received a letter from Mr. Joseph Taylor, of White Haven, giving me an account of my dear mother and the rest of my relations at Newry. Sunday 7th.—Went with my wife to White Chapel Church, where we heard Mr. Cam preach a very indifferent discourse—nothing scarcely but external modes,—much against Presbyterians—so that I was much disappointed by going to church, for it was mis-spending the Lord's day. How I lament the want of a good minister for our church, that we may all see the things that be-long to our peace before it be too late. Sunday 28.—Major Campbell called here this morning on his way from James' River, and brought the agreeable news of the surrender of Quebec and Montreal,—but with the great loss of our great and brave Gene-ral Wolfe who was killed in the engagement.

"Saturday, December 8, 1759.—Mr. Hunt and Mr. Kil-patrick came,—that much revived us. Mr. K. gave us a sermon at night. Sunday 9.—Rained hard but we went to meeting, where we met a great many people, considering the weather,— had a good discourse from 16th verse, fifth chapter, Song of Solomon.

"Tuesday, February 19, 1760.—Went with my wife to the school, and treated the boys with pancakes and cider—got them play in the afternoon. Thursday 28.—Went to Colonel Con-way's, but could not agree with him for his tobacco. As I cannot be of his way of thinking in regard to religion he seems to take opportunity to hurt my interest. But I endeavour to trust in God that I may not fear what man can do unto me. Monday, May 26.—(After sacramental service by Mr. Todd, in Northum-berland) went to meeting to-day,—a pretty large company of the common people and negroes,—but very few gentlemen. The gentlemen that were inclined to come are afraid of being laughed at; Mr. Minzie endeavours to make it such a scandalous thing.

"Friday, October 10, 1760.—Mr. Criswell wrote from school the agreeable news of the arrival of the Rev. Mr. Davies in the colony,—he has gone to Hanover; Mr. Hunt came to Colonel Selden's last night, so that I hope we shall have the comfort of hearing him preach a Sunday in our meeting-house. Saturday 11.—Mr. Hunt, Mr. Maring and Mr. Criswell came before din-ner, but with disagreeable news that Mr. Davies will not return this way. Sunday 12.—Went to meeting,—heard a fine dis-course well delivered, I think, by Mr. Hunt. I think we must have him for our minister if we can, as I believe he will give general satisfaction. Sunday 19.—Went with my wife to Northumberland—meeting at our store there—where we heard Mr. Hunt deliver an excellent sermon on love. A great number of people there. Mr. Hunt proceeded on his way to Hanover, and has promised to endeavour to send Mr. Davies this way on his return northward.

"December, 1760.—Mr. Caldwell, afterwards barbarously killed in New Jersey, preached repeatedly both in Lancaster and Northumberland. Thursday, December 25.—Went to meeting,—heard Mr. Caldwell, who gave us the best sermon ever heard in these parts on Christmas day,—several seemed much engaged, and more so than I have observed for some time. The text was from Matt. i. 23. Saturday 27.—Went to meeting, heard Mr. Hunt deliver a very good sermon, 1st Peter iv. 18; a great number of people. At night Mr. Caldwell preached a sermon here,—about seventy or eighty negroes were here,— text Revelations ii. 4, 5. Blessed be God these are comfortable times. Sunday 28.—Went with company to the meeting-house, but it rained most all day, so that we had few there except those that had received tokens, and not all of them. There were fourty-four communicants, several of our friends being sick, and winter time. I adore my blessed Lord I never had more comfortable a sacrament. May the love of God be shed abroad in all our hearts, that God may be glorified, and by our light shining before men. Sermon by Mr. Hunt, Matt. xxii. 4. Monday 29.—Went to meeting,—Mr. Caldwell gave a most excellent sermon, 2 Timothy ii. 19. I ordered Scipio with my chaise and horses to wait on Mr. Caldwell to Bawler's ferry, as his leg was sore. Mr. C. is a great orator. Blessed be God we have had comfortable times. May what we have heard make a lasting impression upon us, and make us delight in the paths of true religion and virtue. Tuesday 30.—Went with David Hening to William Doget's,—found him sober,—then I desired him to walk out with me, which he did; I then discoursed with him as well as I could about his preventing his wife and daughter from meeting at the Lord's Supper after they had received tokens, and several other matters. He confessed his error, and promised amendment of life, which may God grant him grace to perform.

"Thursday, March 12th, 1761.—Yesterday heard the disagreeable news of the death of the Rev. Mr. Samuel Davies. Never was a man in America, I imagine, more lamented. The Christian, the gentleman, and the scholar appeared conspicuous in him. Virginia, and even Lancaster I hope has great reason to bless God for sending such a minister of the gospel amongst us. But he that sent him can send another, and his labour be attended with as much success. But I am afraid our country is too wicked for such comfort. Thursday, 19th—The militia was called on to proclaim King George the Third, which was done in pretty good order. The officers joined and gave the men about fifty or sixty gallons of punch.

"Sunday, April 19th, 1761—Went with my wife and family

to meeting to hear Mr. Hunt's farewell—1st John, 27th. Signed a call for him.

"Sunday, May 3d, 1761—This day Colonel Selden read a sermon in the meeting-house and John Mitchell prayed, but few there, as they were not acquainted with it. Sunday, 17th—Colonel Selden read a sermon, and on the next Sabbath Mr. Criswell read a sermon and prayed, at the meeting-house. Friday 29th—Sent some help to raise Northumberland meeting-house, as Mr. Smith intends getting it up to-morrow. Sabbath 31st—Mr. Criswell read and prayed at the meeting.

"Saturday, June 13th, 1761.—Two Guineamen arrived at York for Mr. Wm. Nelson. Tuesday, 16th.—Another Guineaman came in with about 140 slaves. Friday 19th.—Went to Court. Negroes sell very high, £63 at Hobbs hole. Tuesday, 26th.—Went with Mr. Dale Carter to the Court House,—then went to Colonel Selden's about a glebe for Mr. Hunt, but Colonel Selden could not get the glebe completed.

"July, Friday 24th, 1761.—Fast;—Saturday—Preaching. Sabbath.—The communion service; twenty new communicants, and fifty old ones. Wednesday, 29th.—I went to Colonel Selden's to visit Mr. Hunt, and let him know that there were several subscribers to our meeting. Did not like some of his proceedings, and seemed to prefer Mr. Caldwell to him. We had much conversation with a freeness on both sides,—but with great uneasiness to him.

"Monday, August 3d, 1761.—Speaking of Mr. Hunt,— he does not seem fit for us, in my opinion,—the most of our great men are very forward to have him settled. On this day Mr. Hunt was at his house. I had long and full conversation with Mr. Gordon on the subject. Friday, August 7th.— Yesterday Mr. Criswell wrote to Mr. Todd about Mr. Waddell. Monday, 10th.—Called in Messrs. Dale Carter, Thos. Carter, John Mitchell, and John Wright, and told Mr. Hunt, with them, we wanted to hear Mr. Waddell. Mr. Hunt very earnestly desired to have the matter brought to a conclusion; and expressed a disinclination to remain unless the congregation were unanimously in his favour, and a day was appointed for the subscribers to meet and determine the matter. Wednesday, 12th.—Went with Mr. Hunt in our chaise to the meeting-house to meet the subscribers there,—so few met, nothing was done to what was expected. Mr. Hunt will not stay except we are unanimous. No high debate among us. Sunday, 20th.—Mr. Hunt bade farewell to the people: and gave notice that Mr. Todd or Mr. Waddell would preach in two weeks. I am very much reflected on, and in short the whole of Mr.

Hunt's going away is laid upon me,—but I trust the Lord will give me strength to bear it."

Mr. Todd visited the Northern Neck in the fall, and spent the last Sabbath of October, (25th) and the first Sabbath of November (1st) and administered the sacrament of the Supper. Of the sermon on the latter Sabbath, Colonel Gordon says,— "I never heard a sermon, but one from Mr. Davies, that I heard with more attention and delight,—O, if the Lord would be pleased to send us a minister of as much piety as Mr. Todd." About seventy communicants, black and white, though the day was rainy.

"Sunday, January 31st, 1762.—At home with my family. Molly said all the Shorter Catechisms; James fifty-six of the Larger; and Molly Hening, one hundred and six.

"Saturday, April 3d, 1762.—Mr. Criswell set off for the Presbytery. Colonel Selden could not; James, his son, being dangerously ill. On his return, Mr. Criswell brought news from the Presbytery, which held its meeting at the Byrd, in Goochland, that Mr. Waddell was appointed to visit the Northern Neck; and on the 16th of April, Sunday, the Colonel makes the entry above quoted,—'May the Lord be praised, I at last have had the comfort of going with my wife and family to meeting, when Mr. Waddell performed to admiration.'"

On Sunday, May 30th, the congregation made out a call; on Sunday, June 6th, Mr. Todd administered the sacrament to about one hundred and three communicants; and on the Monday following Mr. Gordon offered Mr. Waddell the call, which he refused to accept, but promised to return and visit the people. On the 16th of the month, as has been noticed, Mr. Waddell was ordained by a committee of Presbytery, at Harris's Creek, Prince Edward.

At a meeting of the Presbytery, held at Providence, in Louisa, October 7, 1762—Mr. Waddell accepts of a call from Lancaster and Northumberland counties, in which the Presbytery heartily concur. No preparations were made for the installation services; nor does it appear that they were ever performed.

Mr. Waddell continued the acceptable pastor in the Northern Neck till about the year 1778, when, on account of ill health and the inroads of the revolutionary war, he removed to the Valley of the Shenandoah. Col. Gordon tells us that on June 30th, 1762, a lottery was drawn for the advantage of the congregation,—and in a satisfactory manner; for which he says "blessed be God." He does not tell either the amount raised or the plan of the scheme.

February 13th, 1763—Sunday.—"Went with my wife and family to meeting;—as we went, found Mr. James Ewell and his wife on the road, walking, as they could not get their horses over, the wind blew so hard. We had a pretty full house to-day. Mr. W. preached from the 4th of Zechariah, 7th, a fine discourse. He named ten persons whom he proposed for elders; Col. Selden, Dr. Robertson, Mr. Chichester, Dr. Watson, Thomas Carter, Dale Carter, John Mitchell, Mr. Belvard, Mr. Wright, and myself,—and I desired the people, if they knew any thing against our characters,—before this day fortnight, to acquaint him with it." The Dr. Andrew Robertson mentioned in this appointment of elders, was a surgeon and physician of great eminence. Born at Inverness, Scotland, in 1716,—graduated at Edinburgh,—he entered the army in Flanders, and was in the battle of Fontenay, in 1745. With Braddock's army, in 1755, he escaped with the remains of his regiment, twenty in number, living on acorns for many days. On his return to Great Britain he resigned his commission, and with his wife and son emigrated to America. Landing at Indian Banks, Richmond county, Virginia, he was entertained most kindly by a Scotch merchant, Mr. Glasscock. Having taken his residence in Lancaster, he soon took the lead in medical practice in the Northern Neck. A gentleman in his feelings and manners, and a man of enterprise, his influence was great; and uniting with Colonel Gordon, he contributed not a little to the prosperity of the Presbyterian Church in the Northern Neck. He died March 1, 1795, aged seventy-nine years. Some of his descendants are in Washington city. On the appointed day six of the persons named, Messrs. Chichester, the two Carters, Mitchell, Gordon and Selden, were ordained elders, the others declined the office.

The seating of the meeting-house in Lancaster was, as usual, a source of anxiety. "Friday, March 25th, 1763—Went to the meeting-house and agreed with Mr. Atkinson to have more double seats and less single ones in the meeting-house. I understand the people are displeased with the single seats, which we thought would be more convenient for the people, as they faced the minister when they sit. But as it is disagreeable to some, especially Mrs. Miller and some other women, and as it is cheaper to have them double, thought it proper to have more of them made; but I have reason to fear there is much more pride among us than piety, and even in those I could not expect it.

"Monday, April 11th, 1763.—Mr. Waddell set off for Williamsburg to take the oaths agreeable to law." It is evident the rigour of the courts was much relaxed, as in this case, and in the case of Mr. Henry, mentioned under date of September 21st, 1759, the dissenting ministers were permitted to exercise their ministry so long before the requirements of the statute were complied with. It was not till Friday, May 20th, 1763, when the Colonel says—"Mr. Waddell, Mr. Hening and Mr. Span went to court with me"—that "Mr. Waddell read the articles of religion this day before Mr. Currie and Mr. Minis, which they certify. Mr. Minis was probably the author of Minis's play.

On Sunday, April 24th, 1763, the sacrament was administered to ninety white and twenty-three black communicants. "Monday, 25th,—Went with my wife and family to meeting to hear the young people say their catechisms. Mr. Waddell gave us good advice and exhortation how to bring up our children, and how comfortable religion was, &c. Molly Hening answered the best, and all the Larger Catechism. James Gordon answered ninety questions in the Larger Catechism: Molly said all the Shorter."

Mr. Whitefield visited the Northern Neck in 1763. "August, Friday, 26th,—This evening I had the comfort of receiving a letter from the Rev. George Whitefield, who landed this day at Urbanna. Saturday, 27th,—Mr. Waddell and I this day set off in our boat about 7 o'clock for Urbanna, got there about ten, and Mr. Whitefield and Mr. Wright, who came with him, readily agreed to come with us, so that we set off about eleven, and got home about two. We are very happy in the company of Mr. Whitefield. Sunday, 28th,—Mr. Whitefield preached from 1 Corinthians, iii. 11, a most affecting sermon to a great number of people. My wife would venture out though in such a condition. Monday, 29th,—At home with Mr. Whitefield— rained. Tuesday, 30th,—Mr. Whitefield, Waddell and Wright went to dine at Colonel Selden's. Wednesday, 31st,—Went with Mr. Whitefield to meeting, where he had a fine discourse to a crowded assembly. Friday, September 2d,—Sent for Colonel Selden and bought his chair horse for £47. 10s. for Mr. Whitefield. Mr. Whitefield much pleased with his horse— preparing to set off to-morrow. Saturday, 3d,—I have been much fatigued this day with fitting out Mr. Whitefield, but Mr. Wright being so unwell, and it rained so, they could not set off to-day. Sunday, 4th,—Mr. Whitefield, Mr. Waddell and Mr. Wright went with me to the upper meeting, where Mr. Whitefield preached from Matthew, xxv. 10, to a crowded house. Mr. Waddell was obliged to make the negroes go out to make room for the white people. Carried our dinner with us; and we dined at the Old Store House, much to the satisfaction of Mr. Whitefield. They set off about 4 o'clock for Dr. Flood's. Mr. Waddell returned to my brother's with them."

On the next Sabbath, September 11th, the sacrament of the supper was administered to about one hundred and fifteen white, and thirty-five black communicants.—" O these delightful and comfortable opportunities, may they make our hearts glow with love to that God who has been so gracious to such blind ignorant creatures, who have lived in stupidity and security so many years. Monday, 26th—Went to the examination of young people, when about fifty or sixty were examined much to their improvement; and afterwards, a sermon was preached which very much affected both young and old."

Great efforts were made to give permanency to the congregation. "Friday, November 18th, 1763—Went to our court with Mr. Waddell,—have got £600 in bonds toward a fund for the maintenance of a Presbyterian minister, which the Almighty seems to bless. O what cause have we to praise the Lord's goodness to us in this congregation! Friday 25th —Went with Mr. Waddell to the glebe to see Henry Hinton, Jr.; could not get finished to-day. Saturday 26th—Finished the survey to-day and got home to dinner." For the cultivation of the glebe, as the labourers in the Northern Neck were almost universally Africans, Colonel Selden presented the congregation with his "negro man Toby."

After the sacrament on December 25th—he says "a comfortable time, blessed be the Lord, who is so kind and benevolent to such dust and ashes as we are who are so unworthy of the least favour. O Lord, what are we that thou shouldest be so mindful of us, in sending the gospel to shine among us in such a remote part of our world. O, Almighty God, give us grace by thy Holy Spirit to improve these delightful scenes to thy glory and our salvation. Monday 26th—Mr. Waddell set off for the Committee in Hanover, where Mr. Rice is to be ordained, and Mr. Criswell comes on his second trials. Saturday 31st—Mr. Waddell got safe home to-day. Blessed be the Lord for all his mercies to us this year. O may our minds be more and more engaged in his service, and begin the new year with new hearts, and with sincere minds give up ourselves to him."

[*Thus ends the fragment of the journal.*]

Of Mr. Whitefield's visits to the Northern Neck there are some pleasant traditions. The widow of Lewis Stevens, of Stevensburg, Newtown, who was a Miss Hening from the county of Lancaster, used to tell with interest, many circumstances, remembered by her friends respecting Whitefield. She described his appearance as he is represented by the wax figure in the museum of Princeton Theological Seminary,— with wig—gown—bands for the neck and wrists;—as fastidious in his dress when about to appear in public;—as cheerful in his private intercourse,—and playful with children. He would sometimes amuse his friends with the history of his narrow escapes from assaults made on him while preaching.

"Come here my little girl," said he to me—and lifting up his wig and taking my hand,—"here, put your finger in that gash—there, is where the brickbat hit me."

From the journal of Colonel Gordon, it appears the clergy of the established church opposed his gathering a school,— that one of them made a farce in ridicule of the Presbyterians,— that the clergy wrote severe letters to Mr. Davies on his visits there,—and that many were for a time prevented from attend- ing the Presbyterian meeting from the ridicule thrown upon them by influential men. That the clergy should feel and ex- press dislike to encroachments on their flocks was both natural and to be expected; and had they been true to their office, and faithful to their church, inroads would, in all probability, have never been made, or would have been comparatively harmless. The united testimony of history and tradition is entirely against the spirituality of the established clergy. Dr. Hawks says, p. 120—"It must be owned, that as a body they were any thing but invulnerable; and the opportunity for censure afforded by their conduct was too inviting to be overlooked by their antagonists. The leading laymen looked around and saw almost every parish supplied with an incumbent of some sort, while the state of religion was in their view, far from flourish- ing; they did not hesitate to impute this condition of things to the clergy themselves, and the people at large were ready enough to lend a willing ear to the charge." The people both saw, and heard, and did not hear;—they saw them on the race field, at the cock-pit, at cards, and drinking riotously and to drunkenness;—they heard their conversation, their ridicule of experimental religion as bigotry and fanaticism,—and they did not hear those gospel truths which are life to the dead, unless they searched for them elsewhere than in the public ministra- tions of the gospel in the established church. And is it won- derful that men who did not value the peculiar holy doctrines of the gospel, joined with those, who both believed and felt their purifying influence, in declaring their want of conviction of the sufficiency and efficiency of this part of the colonial con- stitution? Serious minded people looked on with sadness,— the pious mourned for the house of God,—while the thought- less were left unawakened, and the profane and dissolute be- came worse and worse. "Who is there?"—said a clergyman on the Middlesex side of the Rappahannoc, aroused before the dawn of Christmas morning, by a company knocking at his door. "We have brought a criminal from the other side of the river." "Bring him in, said he"—after he struck a light— "Who is he, and what has he been doing?" "It is I"—said a man staggering into the room, with a laugh and a shout—"it is I." It was a brother clergyman from the Neck, who in his excitement from Christmas eve potations, had crossed the river and had been disturbing the slumbers of peaceable citizens. "Ah, is it you?· What are you here for, this time of night?" Provoked at losing his rest he added—"Well, you shall pay your fine or take your stripes as the law directs." These men had often caroused together till all sense of sobriety was gone. The fine, however, was paid before the delinquent recrossed the river. This was stated by a gentleman of veracity and high standing in Northumberland, not in anger, or the appearance of pleasure in calling up past misdoings, but in sober sadness, as the prevailing cause of past and present evils in the community. "I remember well"—said a gentleman of Richmond county, who served in our navy—a member of an influential and wealthy family—"when a little boy, of seeing Parson G. at our house, and after dinner, he was put in the gig by the servants, and by the orders of my father tied in, and a servant went along to lead the horse and conduct him home, as he was unable to take care of himself from his indulgence at the table, to which he had been invited after church service on Sabbath."

The records of court in the capital, in the case of Jones's heirs, state the fact, that a wealthy widow having intermarried, and lived with, a parson for many years, found after his death, that there was then living a previous undivorced wife in England, who had long mourned her husband as dead in the distant colony.

These and such like events are incidental to our lost world and may occur in all states of society as facts;—but in Virginia the power of redress was so distant and so slow in its exercise, that the evils were unredressed. Is it wonderful if many thought the established order in religion was calculated to destroy all piety?

Mr. Waddell was not cast into prison or fined, or called before the magistrates for preaching the gospel; but was assailed from the pulpit and by the press, legitimate weapons both of attack and defence, and from quarters and by means he could neither retaliate or notice. His capability of defending himself can be seen in one of the few productions of his pen, that escaped the conflagration to which he condemned his manuscripts a little before his death. This having been printed is preserved, and is a specimen of style and manner as inimitable as that of Junius. Passing through Richmond county on a certain occasion, he went to the upper church in the parish of Rev. William Gisberne. For some cause Mr. Gisberne did not attend that day; and by especial invitation Mr. Waddell preached the gospel to a deeply interested audience. The impression made by the oration and the truth was so pervading, that Mr. Gisberne thought it necessary to take public notice of it, and preached from the words "*contend earnestly for the faith once delivered to the saints.*"   In his discourse he took occasion to say many things of Mr. Waddell, calling him "pickpocket, dark-lantern, moonlight preacher, and enthusiast;" and read a *hue and cry*, for the arrest of "the new-light, instigated by folly, impudence and the devil, and bring him to the whipping post."   Mr. Waddell on hearing of his sermon, addressed him through the Virginia Gazette.

"*To the Rev. Mr. W. G., Rector of Lunenburg Parish in Richmond.*

July 21st, 1768.

Rev. Sir—There are few so passive as quietly to submit to the misrepresentations of ridicule, or silently to bear the false charges of prejudice and arrogance.   A mistaken prudence may silence some, and fearfulness others: for my part I think I am under the influence of neither.   As a member of civil society, I am protected, while I behave well, by the laws of my country; and as a Presbyterian minister, I discharge the duties of my office under the same protection.   I therefore consider myself more upon a level with my fellow subjects than will be, perhaps, pleasing to you; and enjoying the privilege to remark on your hard speeches with the same freedom and impunity which a seemly reply from you will deserve.

As a Presbyterian, I approve the doctrinal articles of the established religion according to the act of toleration—and as a minister, I preach agreeable to them.   An occasional sermon of this kind, in compliance with a request, might be allowed any where in our province, without any abuse of law or offence to men.   Such I preached by invitation at your upper church, when I attended to hear you.   My being there, and your not coming, seemed both altogether casual.   In your pulpit I was the advocate of virtue and friend of Christianity: I reflected on no one, nor descended to any peculiarity of sect or party. Yet you chose to represent me in sundry discourses on several Sabbaths, as a composition of all sects which were least known to your hearers, or most likely to be hated by them.   Like a cowardly boy that would rather waste his passion by giving nick-names, than risk a battle, you called me a pickpocket, dark-lantern, moonlight preacher, and enthusiast.   However, if you are pleased with this childish sport, I do not mean to rob you of the pleasure.   A moonlight preacher, I suppose, signifies one that shines with a borrowed light, as the plagiary does. But, if we may believe you, I cannot be suspected of being one. And lest any of your parishioners should be influenced by the example of my stated hearers and friends to respect me, you attempted, regardless of what is most esteemed by the gentleman and the Christian, to sully their reputation, and bring them and me into disrepute together. Do you use such weak and unhandsome methods to prevent them coming to hear me, from a persuasion that their coming would hurt their character. They must certainly be obliged to you for being so much more regardful of their character than you seem to be of your own. Or do you think my doctrine or example endangers their happiness? They are the best judges of that. And you ough to consider that though they be obliged to pay you, they are not obliged in the same sense to hear you.

In one of your Sunday orations, you published, I understand, a "hue and cry," directed to "all well disposed persons who were lovers of the faith and truth," requiring them "to apprehend a certain illiterate new-light preacher, who instigated by folly, natural impudence, and the devil, had taken the advantage of your indisposition and entered your pulpit, which was to be kept sacred, and then belched out his nonsense and ignorance for an hour, to the laughter of some and contempt of others, and to bring the vagrant to George Jerker's, at the publick whipping-post of the county, to be dealt with according to law.

You might be greatly pleased with the beauty of your own thoughts and elegance of expression in the piece—but however great its merits may be, on both accounts, I think it was not very fit to make a part of a sermon, at the head of which stood these words, "Earnestly contend for the faith once delivered to the saints." I do not mean, sir, that there was any impropriety in making it a part of your discourse. I only mean that it could not be connected with your sacred text, or delivered in the way it was, without profaneness in the author, abuse of the pulpit, contempt of the Sabbath, and an affront to the Christian audience and to God. You might have used Dr. Sherlock's sermon on that text, against the Popish recusants, which is written with his usual judgment and decency, without being chargeable with any unusual inconsistency; but perhaps you thought his method of treating the enemies of his religion, of his king and country, was too genteel for my demerit. I must here beg leave to clear your parishioners of the reproachful indecency of laughing in church, with which you have charged them. Sensible that they were hearing a sermon very different from what you intimate, they were in general grave, and of better manners than their parson. If any smiled, it was more from custom, I believe, than from any disrespect to me.

These hints will suffice, I hope, to show you how little I regard the rhodomontade of the Æolian family. If you had been apprised of this in time, you certainly would have suppressed some windy preachments, which have done no honour to your reputation as a defender of the faith, although you might, through an unhappy mistake, view them with emotions of uncommon joy, as proofs of genius and trumpeters of your glory.

I will now venture to recommend to your perusal the seventy-fifth canon of your church, which besides other particulars to be noticed by you, requires that you should endeavour to profit the Church of God, having always in mind that you ought to excel all others in purity of life, and be an example to the people to live well and Christianly, under pain of ecclesiastical censure, to be inflicted with severity. Some would be so rude as to interrogate you here; but I rather beg leave to add the fifty-third canon to the former, which orders "that above all things you should abstain from bitter invectives and scurrilous language against any persons whatsoever." Finding you thus condemned by the voice of kings, and by all the lords spiritual of Great Britain, and signing your confession of guilt, I bid you a cordial farewell, assuring you, sir, that in this, and in other things wherein you think me your enemy,

I am your friend and most humble servant,

JAMES WADDELL."

The interesting and successful career of labour, run by Mr. Waddell in the Northern Neck, was brought to a close during the early stages of the Revolutionary war, principally by two causes—the emigration of leading persons in his congregations to the mountainous regions of Virginia,—and the inroads upon his health and constitution by bilious attacks, to which the climate predisposes the inhabitants of the river banks near the bay,—and the incursions of the British cruisers. The concentration of trade, by which the cities in Virginia were formed, was greatly accelerated during the war, and enterprising men in the Northern Neck sought other locations for trade, for fresh lands, and for health: of consequence the first to emigrate were Mr. Waddell's friends. From being compelled himself to seek the upper country a part of the year, either to avoid the annual attacks of fever in some of its varied forms, or to recover from its effects, he followed the tide of emigration, and sought the mountains as a residence for his family. The congregations of Opeckon and Cedar Creek, in whose bounds Colonel Gordon owned valuable lands, put in a call for him April 14th, 1774; this favourable location he saw fit to decline. At Timber Ridge, May 1st, 1776—"A call from the Tinkling Spring congregation, for Mr. Waddell, was given into the Presbytery, and by them presented to him, which he takes into consideration for one year." In the year 1778, he removed his family to a place called Spring Hill, a few miles above Waynesborough, on the

South Fork of the Shenandoah. Here he remained for about seven years. For some time his labours were confined to the Tinkling Spring congregation; and afterwards were divided between that congregation and Staunton.

A few of the subscription papers for the support of the pastors in the Valley, at an early period, are still preserved; one in the hands of the Rev. James Morrison, taken for the benefit of Mr. Brown, at Timber Ridge, and one in the hands of Rev. B. M. Smith, for the use of Mr. Waddell. From these can be estimated the comparative value of salaries in the congregations in the Valley of Virginia at an early period and those now given. It appears there were subscription papers circulated in different parts of the congregations, to obtain the requisite sum for Mr. Waddell's support. The following is a copy of the one in the hands of Mr. Smith—"We the subscribers in the congregation in Tinkling Spring do promise to pay the Rev. James Waddell the sum of one hundred pounds current and lawful money of Virginia, for the whole of his labours for one year; and we moreover promise to pay the above one hundred pounds in clear merchantable wheat at three shillings per bushel: or in corn or rye of like quality at two shillings per bushel, or in other commodities he may want at said rates; or if we cannot spare said commodities or grain we will pay the current prices of such articles at the times of payment. The payment of one-half to be made in the middle of the term and the other at the expiration of it. In witness whereof we do hereunto set our hands this first day of May, 1779. N. B. The grain to be lodged by the subscribers at two or three convenient places in the congregation.

	£.	s.	d.		£.	s.	d.
John Ramsey,	1	6	0	Ben. Stuart,	1	10	0
Thos. Turk,	1	0	0	Robt. Thompson,	1	16	0
John Ramsey, jr.	1	16	0	A. Thompson,	1	0	0
Wm. Black,	0	15	7	Thos. Stuart,	1	10	9
Wm. Guthrey,	1	8	4	James Bell, senr.	3	0	9
John Collins,	0	5	0	Charles Bookins,	2	8	9
John Caldwell,	0	10	0	Walter Davis,	1	0	0

The subscription for 1783, was £40 in cash, for half the time and ministerial services of Mr. Waddell; the other half of his time was bestowed upon Staunton, for a compensation the amount of which is not known. Notwithstanding the plain living of the productive Valley, this salary was small, for an increasing family, and implied the possession of means, or capacity to labour for their support, not dependent on the congregation.

Embosomed in the beautiful Valley of the Shenandoah, the

pastor of Tinkling Spring was not an uninterested spectator of the thrilling, though distant scenes of the Revolution. Removed from the seat of war, his congregations sent forth their sons to mingle in the bloody strife. The call of General Greene for aid, on his memorable retreat from Cornwallis, seconded by the authorities of the State, aroused the Valley-men to come out of their quiet abode, with the habiliments of war. The hope of Greene, that after securing the retreat of Morgan into Virginia, with his prisoners, from the victory at the Cowpens, he should there meet reinforcements sufficient to enable him to turn upon his pursuer, were fully realized. Campbell, immortalized at King's Mountain, came with his volunteers from the extreme south-west, and McDowell and Moffitt rallied the volunteers of Augusta and Rockbridge and Botetourt, and joined the anxious general on the Dan. Before their departure for the camp, Waddell met the company assembled at Midway, or Steele's tavern, and preached to them the great principles of the gospel, and delivered the pastor's farewell to those of his charge going to risk their lives for wives, and children, and brothers, and sisters, and all that men hold dear. With what interest would that sermon now be read! With what notes did that silver voice call upon the patriots around him to defend their native or adopted land from violation, and their houses from such plundering as has been witnessed by his friends in the Northern Neck! How far he fanned the flame in their breasts, we cannot tell; but certain it is, that in the ever famous battle of Guilford Court House, the Valley-men stood conspicuous, and none fought more bravely than the men from Waddell's charge. The Valley-men were posted on the left to meet the advancing right of the enemy, were early in the action, and constantly advancing or retreating, and almost perpetually engaged, they maintained their post till orders from the commander-in-chief directed them to seek safety in flight, and rally at the appointed place. Hitherto the Valley-men had escaped in a wonderful manner; though exposed to frequent vollies, the fire of the enemy, owing to their position in a gentle ravine, passing over their heads, while the Rockbridge and Augusta rifles made sad havoc with the opposing forces. They knew not how to retreat; they fled. Lee's light-horse were not near to cover their confusion; Col. Washington was elsewhere employed. In their flight they lost more than in the battle; fortunately the enemy was not prepared to pursue their foe, and the butchery was soon over. Many families in Augusta mourned the slain of that day; and some of the congregation of Tinkling Spring carried numerous scars from that retreat to old age. The last

survivor of the wounded in that battle presented in his face the
marks of numerous deep wounds from horsemen's swords.
Left for dead, the mutilated soldier revived and returned to his
friends a hideous spectacle of wounds.   In his old age he boasted of them as his marks of honour.

  Various causes combined to enlist the feelings, influence and
the judgment of Waddell and his amiable lady, in favour of a
location at the eastern base of the Blue Ridge, where they purchased a plantation.   The two branches of the Gordon family
had taken possession of their fertile lands in that section; and
a society that was very congenial was forming, that had need of a
minister of the gospel, at the lower end of Albemarle, embracing
a corner of Orange and Louisa counties.   To this neighbourhood he removed, and took his residence in Louisa, near Gordonsville, about the year 1785, after a residence of about seven
years in Augusta.   The division of Hanover Presbytery into
Hanover and Lexington Presbyteries, took place the next year.
He named his plantation Belle Grove.   There he resided till his
death, and there his remains were interred.   His preaching
places were Hopewell, near Gordonsville, the D. S. meeting-
house, about five miles from Charlottesville, on the road to Rockfish Gap, at the Brick Church, near Orange Court-house, and in
other neighbourhoods occasionally.   There were undoubtedly
many advantages attending this change of residence and labour ;
and there were some disadvantages.   While his mind was in its
meridian vigour, his body weakened by the repeated attacks of
fever in the low country, from which it had never recovered,
showed those signs of decay he did not mistake, and was oppressed by the ministerial duties of his extensive charge in the
Valley ; and less was required or expected of him in his new
residence.   And the education of his numerous family was more
easily accomplished in Albemarle than it could have been in his
situation in Augusta.   Besides, this section of country was destitute of a minister of the gospel, and likely to continue so
unless supplied by him whose physical energy was more com-
mensurate to the labour there required than in the congregations
west of the Ridge.   His congregations gathered from his own
neighbourhood, were necessarily limited; those at D. S. were
circumstantially larger, but composed of plain unpretending
people, not fond of show or parade.   The smallness of his
meeting-house near Gordonsville, and its unfinished condition,
together with the fewness of the auditors, made, on the minds
of strangers, an impression unfavourable to his fame and usefulness as a preacher.   After hearing him in this unfavourable
position, the inquiry would force itself on the heart,—" Does
nobody here know what an orator James Waddell is ?"

  For the advantage of his own family, Dr. Waddell opened a

classical school in his own house, over which he presided, with a becoming reputation.

The great affliction of Dr. Waddell's life was his blindness. Its slow, gradual, and sure advance, with the dimness of vision, cast a gloom over his heart, which at times he could not resist. Pre-eminently happy in his domestic relations, the shutting out of his wife and children from his sight, like the total eclipse of the sun at midday, came on him with a cold shudder; his sensibilities were pained while his faith bowed in meekness. "From my earliest recollection"—says a son—"my father was deficient in eye sight." This deficiency increased from month to month, and ended in cataract.—"He was also very tremulous in his hands, which for some years previous to his blindness deprived him of the use of the pen. Having always been devoted to books, after he became blind, my mother and other members of the family spent some hours daily in reading to him. Owing to this circumstance his powers of mind were not weakened by his loss of sight. He retained his usual flow of animal spirits, which, at times, when he had agreeable, intelligent society, arose to hilarity. He possessed the powers of conversation to an extraordinary degree." People were willing to listen to him; they forgot for the time that they were only listeners. He never made set speeches to his friends, or seemed to have set subjects; he talked to them. He never declaimed in the pulpit; he talked his sermons in the purest English, with his melodious voice and no apparent gesture; every motion of his body was in accordance with his subject, and whether by the fireside or in the pulpit, his listeners felt his mellifluous strains to be resistless. It is impossible for such a man to suffer blindness without unutterable pangs. Could he have been always employed in conversation and preaching, and in hearing from choice authors, the weight had been less oppressive at the heart. But the necessary and protracted intervals in his employments gave ample space for the strong conflicts between that knowledge and those affections that walk by sight, and that faith that walks as seeing things invisible. "During his blindness he was in the habit of preparing his discourses for the pulpit, by calling on some one of his children to find the text, and to read the context: and after examining Cruden's Concordance for analogous passages, and consulting various commentaries, the heads of discourse were written down; all which were afterwards read over to him." For hours he would lie at full length upon his back, his right arm thrown carelessly over his head, his long fingers moving in measured beats noting both the vacuity and fulness of his thoughts, and the passage of time. That tapping of those fingers, like their gentle swing in the pulpit, was full of feeling and eloquence. The man of power was listless, or in a reverie, or his checked feeling was seeking some fit expression for a glowing thought.

In the year 1798, the suffering man visited Fredericktown, Maryland, for the purpose of submitting to an operation for cataract. The immediate effects of the skill of the oculist were less encouraging than had been anticipated, and Dr. Waddell returned to his family with scarce the feeblest hope of ever seeing them, and the sweet light of heaven, again. After some time, upon removing the bandages from his eyes, he thought he saw, with some distinctness, the divisions in the window-sash, and called one of his daughters to pass her finger along the divisions of the window. By trial, he became convinced that he saw the outlines of objects correctly, though dimly. The excitement in the family was great, as the word flew from child to child, "*father can see!*" The servants caught the excitement, and "*master can see*" passed swiftly from mouth to mouth. He caused them all to pass in review before him, that he might refresh his heart with a dim sight of those he had ever been used to look upon; and might gain some faint image of those who had been added to his household after the doors of vision had been shut, and of those too whose young bodies were rapidly increasing with their years. That was a day of rejoicing at Belle Grove. The eyes gradually recovered the power of vision sufficient for the ordinary purposes of life, and to enable him to read with properly fitted lenses. But this visit of the blessed light of heaven was of short continuance; the cataract returned.

Soon after Dr. Waddell's removal to Louisa, came on that spirit of investigation in religious matters which received its peculiar cast from France, and pervaded the whole country, exercising in some places unbounded influence; every where throwing the truths of the gospel into doubt, and in some places into entire disbelief. Ministers of the gospel were every where opposed; their usefulness circumscribed, and for a time their influence lost. Every article of Christian faith was questioned and discussed; and nothing relating to religion and revelation admitted but on the fullest evidence again and again brought forth and pressed on the judgment and the heart; and the Bible, stripped of all the factitious influence of tradition and national enactments, stood alone on the imperishable foundation of God's government and man's necessities, an exhibition of the one and a supply for the other. It is not easy to comprehend or imagine the fearful contest that awaited the ministers of the gospel, when the political and religious notions peculiar to France swept over us like a stream of lava from the revolutionary volcano of Paris. The unwary were swept away;

the timid fled. Waddell losing his sight,—becoming actually blind,—stood at his post, like the true minister of Christ, and with the few prepared, by previous investigation, for the contest, breasted the shock, and to an excited public, hesitating whether Christ were divine, and therefore true,—or human only, and therefore false,—proclaimed the true and proper divinity of Jesus Christ and salvation by his cross.

MR. WIRT'S DESCRIPTION OF JAMES WADDELL—AS IT APPEARS IN THE BRITISH SPY.

"It was one Sunday, as I travelled through the county of Orange, that my eye was caught by a cluster of horses tied near a ruinous, old, wooden house, in the forest, not far from the roadside. Having frequently seen such objects before, in travelling through these States, I had no difficulty in understanding that this was a place of religious worship.

"Devotion should have stopped me, to join in the duties of the congregation; but I must confess, that curiosity, to hear the preacher of such a wilderness, was not the least of my motives. On entering, I was struck with his preternatural appearance; he was a tall and very spare old man; his head, which was covered with a white linen cap, his shrivelled hands, and his voice, were all shaking under the influence of a palsy; and a few moments ascertained to me that he was perfectly blind.

" The first emotions which touched my breast, were those of mingled pity and veneration. But ah! how soon were all my feelings changed! The lips of Plato were never more worthy of a prognostic swarm of bees, than were the lips of this holy man! It was a day of the administration of the sacrament; and his subject of course, was the passion of our Saviour. I had heard the subject handled a thousand times—I had thought it exhausted long ago. Little did I suppose, that in the wild woods of America, I was to meet with a man whose eloquence would give to this topic a new and more sublime pathos, than I had ever before witnessed.

" As he descended from the pulpit, to distribute the mystic symbols, there was a peculiar, a more than human solemnity in his air and manner which made my blood run cold, and my whole frame shiver.

" He then drew a picture of the sufferings of our Saviour; his trial before Pilate; his ascent up Calvary; his crucifixion, and his death. I knew the whole history; but never, till then, had I heard the circumstances so selected, so arranged, so coloured! It was all new: and I seemed to have heard it for the first time in my life. His enumeration was so deliberate, that his voice trembled on every syllable; every heart in the assembly trembled in unison. His peculiar phrases had that force of descrip-

tion that the original scene appeared to be, at that moment,
acting before our eyes. We saw the very faces of the Jews: the
staring frightful distortions of malice and rage. We saw the
buffet; my soul kindled with a flame of indignation; and my
hands were involuntarily and convulsively clenched.

"But when he came to touch on the patience, the forgiving
meekness of our Saviour; when he drew, to the life, his blessed
eyes streaming in tears to heaven; his voice breathing to God,
a soft and gentle prayer of pardon on his enemies, 'Father,
forgive them, for they know not what they do'—the voice of the
preacher, which had all along faltered, grew fainter and fainter,
until his utterance being entirely obstructed by the force of his
feelings, he raised his handkerchief to his eyes, and burst into
a loud and irrepressible flood of grief. The effect is inconceivable. The whole house resounded with the mingled groans,
and sobs, and shrieks of the congregation.

"It was some time before the tumult had subsided, so far as to
permit him to proceed. Indeed, judging by the usual, but fal-
lacious standard of my own weakness, I began to be very uneasy
for the situation of the preacher. For I could not conceive how
he would be able to let his audience down from the height to
which he had wound them, without impairing the solemnity and
dignity of his subject, or perhaps shocking them by the abrupt-
ness of the fall. But—no; the descent was as beautiful and
sublime, as the elevation had been rapid and enthusiastic.

"The first sentence with which he broke the awful silence, was
a quotation from Rousseau,—'Socrates died like a philosopher,
but Jesus Christ like a God!'

"I despair of giving you any idea of the effect produced by
this short sentence, unless you could perfectly conceive the
whole manner of the man, as well as the peculiar crisis in the
discourse. Never before did I completely understand what Demosthenes meant by laying such stress on *delivery*. You are to
bring before you the venerable figure of the preacher; his blindness constantly recalling to your recollection old Homer, Ossian
and Milton, and associating with his performance the melancholy grandeur of their geniuses; you are to imagine that you
hear his slow, solemn, well accented enunciation, his voice of affecting trembling melody; you are to remember the pitch of passion and enthusiasm to which the congregation were raised; and
then, the few minutes of portentous, death-like silence which
reigned throughout the house; the preacher removing his white
handkerchief from his aged face, (even yet wet from the recent
torrent of his tears,) and slowly stretching forth the palsied hand
which holds it, begins the sentence,—'Socrates died like a philosopher'—then pausing, raising his other hand, pressing them
both clasped together, with warmth and energy to his breast,

lifting his 'sightless balls' to heaven, and pouring his whole soul into his tremulous voice—'but Jesus Christ—like a God!' If he had been indeed and in truth an angel of light, the effect could scarcely have been more divine.

"Whatever I had been able to conceive of the sublimity of Massillon, or the force of Bourdaloue, had fallen far short of the power which I felt from the delivery of this simple sentence. The blood, which just before had rushed in a hurricane upon my brain, and in the violence and agony of my feelings, had held my whole system in suspense, now ran back into my heart, with a sensation which I cannot describe—a kind of shuddering, delicious horror! The paroxysm of blended piety and indignation to which I had been transported, subsided into the deepest self-abasement, humility and adoration. I had just been lacerated and dissolved by sympathy, for our Saviour as a fellow-creature; but now, with fear and trembling, I adored him as—' a God!'

"If this description give you the impression, that this incomparable minister had any thing of shallow, theatrical trick in his manner, it does him great injustice. I have never seen, in any orator, such a union of simplicity and majesty. He has not a gesture, an attitude or an accent, to which he does not seem forced, by the sentiment which he is expressing. His mind is too serious, too earnest, too solicitous, and, at the same time, too dignified, to stoop to artifice. Although as far removed from ostentation as a man can be, yet it is clear from the train, the style and substance of his thoughts, that he is, not only a very polite scholar, but a man of extensive and profound erudition. I was forcibly struck with a short, yet beautiful character which he drew of our learned and amiable countryman, Sir Robert Boyle: he spoke of him, as if 'his noble mind had, even before death, divested herself of all influence from his frail tabernacle of flesh;' and called him, in his peculiarly emphatic and impressive manner, 'a pure intelligence: the link between men and angels.'

"This man has been before my imagination almost ever since. A thousand times, as I rode along, I dropped the reins of my bridle, stretched forth my hand, and tried to imitate his quotation from Rousseau; a thousand times I abandoned the attempt in despair, and felt persuaded that his peculiar manner and power arose from an energy of soul, which nature could give, but which no human being could justly copy. In short, he seems to be altogether a being of a former age, or of a totally different nature from the rest of men.

"Guess my surprise, when, on my arrival at Richmond, and mentioning the name of this man, I found not one person who had ever before heard of James Waddell! Is it not strange, that such a genius as this, so accomplished a scholar, so divine an orator, should be permitted to languish and die in obscurity, within eighty miles of the metropolis of Virginia?"

This description, like the poems of Homer, immortalizes the writer and his hero. It graphically presents a veritable, living man, preaching to his little flock, utterly unconscious of the presence of strangers, of talent, or notoriety. His blindness had wrought his tender heart and literary taste to more refinement and intellectuality; and whether the many or the few came to hear, he poured forth gospel truth in strains of elevated piety irresistibly charming. Men admired if they were not convinced. Waddell was not so unknown in Richmond as the last sentence of Mr. Wirt seems to imply. The father and mother of President Madison were his hearers, especially on communion seasons, and not improbably were present at the scene described by Wirt. The Gamble family knew him, as did all families of Presbyterian origin. The Legislature knew him in one of those strong papers presented by his Presbytery on the subject of religious liberty and the management of religious concerns. But years of continued absence from a city, covers a preacher with oblivion's mantle.

But was this an extraordinary effort of the preacher? or was it one of his varied efforts to set forth gospel truth? Was this refined intellectual sort of appeal, his peculiarity? or could he, did he, address the hearts of all men and move the plain and simple as well as the refined? Was it the effect of his blindness?—or did he in former days find the hearts of his hearers and open the fountain of tears? In reply to these very natural questions some entertaining traditions may be given. It was the habit of Colonel Gordon to encourage the sailors, that frequented the river, to attend public worship whenever convenient. The invitation was generally very gladly received by these neglected men. One day the Colonel having conducted a crew to attend sermon, Dr. Waddell preached from the words "Simon son of Jonas lovest thou me?" The sailors became greatly interested in the progress of the discourse; some of them were in tears. In the midst of the sermon the Doctor put the inquiry—and what does Peter say?—An old sailor, by that name, rising from his seat, with tears running down his cheeks, supposing he spoke to him, as he looked so intently at him—replied—"Lord, thou knowest all things, thou knowest that I love thee."

An old gentleman reared in Dr. Waddell's congregation in Lancaster, used to relate the impressions made on his youthful mind by the graphic powers of his minister, which no influence of succeeding years could efface. The brazen serpent raised in the wilderness an emblem of Christ, won his heart; it seemed to him that like a wounded Isrealite he saw the serpent,

—and as a sinner he saw Christ crucified for sin. From these it appears that graphic descriptions was a powerful weapon in his hand, in his early ministry, as well as in the time of his blindness. It was evidently a characteristic of his preaching through life and formed a part of the charm with which he held his audience in sweet captivity.

A miserly man, that used to hear him at Tinkling Spring, in giving an account of the influence of one of his powerful sermons, on the love of God, upon himself—said—"the snow flakes had been falling pretty freely around the house—but had any one told me that guineas lay as thick as the snow flakes, I could not have gone out to gather any till he was done. The author of the British Spy was not the only man that had felt the power of his mellifluous tongue.

Says one, who knew him well, in describing his appearance —"He was tall, thin—spare,—very spare as he grew older,— had a long visage,—his forehead being high,—his nose and chin long,—his face thin,—his eyes a light blue—and his complexion fair. He wore long white top boots,—small clothes buckled at the knee—a long loose strait-bodied coat,—and a white wig. He was seldom vehement in delivery;—often excited, never boisterous,—often deeply pathetic in tone and manner,—very courtly in his manners,—and used much gesture with both hands." A very old lady in the Valley, speaking of him, in 1844, said she "went to hear Dr. Waddell at Tinkling Spring, being urged to do so by a young friend. When she arrived he was at prayer;—he spoke with a low, sweet voice, very distinct; and seemed to use great familiarity with God in prayer, often using the words '*do thou*' in reference to promises and desires which God only could fulfil. In preaching his voice was the same,—if the people were still, all could hear him. He used much gesture, with his right hand particularly."

One circumstance during his residence in Louisa caused him much perplexity. A widow lady in his neighbourhood, was, under some peculiar circumstances, permitted to teach his daughters minuets. A report was spread abroad, charging the Doctor with being an advocate of fashionable amusements. He repelled the charge, asserting that the members of his family never engaged in what were called fashionable amusements, though he thought it expedient to cultivate their manners to fit them for enlightened genteel society. Still the report was spread, and much feeling was excited. The Doctor maintained his position, and did not hide his indignation at the injury done him by imputation of improprieties and actions derogatory to the minister and the Christian. His increasing infirmities had also prevented his regular attendance on the meetings of

Presbytery. This failure in ministerial duty was misunderstood, and was used to give weight to the scandal, that all was not right with the protege of Davies, in his old age. Many consultations were held by the brethren of the Presbytery about the best method of bringing this matter to a favourable issue; a committee was appointed, and a paper issued from the pen of J. B. Smith: a number of letters passed; and the whole subject became more perplexing. Mr. Todd was understood as defending his old friend and co-presbyter, and consequently was involved in the same difficulties. It was determined at last to have a special interview with Dr. Waddell. During the sessions of the Presbytery in May 1794, at Hopewell, an adjourned meeting was held at the Doctor's house on Friday evening. The members present were all greatly the Doctor's juniors, but men of influence, and some, in after years, of notoriety. After supper the Presbytery was called to order, and the business frankly and respectfully introduced.

The following minute is on the Presbytery book, viz. "Dr. Waddell's, 7 o'clock, P. M.—The Presbytery had an interview with Dr. Waddell, and a conversation of a considerable length took place upon the charge against him, and the letter to this Presbytery, which by a resolution of July 26th, 1793, had been referred, for advice, to Synod. And having had a detail of his conduct, and the motives for such conduct, the Presbytery was of opinion that there was no ground for further process against him,—and that the minute making the reference be hereby revoked." Mr. Turner used to describe this meeting in his frank and humourous way, as one presenting the extremes of gravity and ridiculousness, of incensed dignity and anxious rashness: that he and some others had gone with expectation of compassionating the humiliation of an old man for a dereliction of duty; that he soon found that they were the objects of commiseration; and that he never was so glad to get clear of any thing in his life, and was very happy to get to bed. That Friday night, May 2d, 1794, was never forgotten by the company assembled at Dr. Waddell's.

Says one who well knew—"never were children more blessed in parents, than were we; and what was defective in one was supplied in the other. Our morals were carefully watched over by both, and to example there was added precept, inculcated with all the energy which affection could dictate. On Sabbath evenings we were assembled, and after being catechised, received an exhortation from my father which seldom failed of affecting us deeply.

"I never left home for —— but I received a word of serious exhortation from my father; and when at home my admonitions were repeated, and every advantage taken of place and circumstance to render them abiding. Remember—he would say—when I am dead and gone, and you will have none to advise you,—your father told you *this*,—or the *other*,—beside this gate,—or tree,—or whatever we were near,—so that almost every object served to remind me of his instructions."

His servants appeared greatly attached to him as a man and as a minister: and some of them were consistent members of the church. One of them, taken by a member of the family to Philadelphia was set free, in what appeared to be favourable circumstances. In a few years she found her way back to Virginia and sought a member of the family with whom to spend the remainder of her days in cheerful service, affectionate attachment, and the exercise of religious duties and privileges. In his will Dr. Waddell directed that his body should be taken to the chosen place of burial, by his servants. Faithful in life, they performed this last service with reverence and grief.

His last illness, the consequence of a severe cold, in the fall of 1803, was protracted to September, 1805. "His decline was very gradual and he anticipated his end with Christian serenity and joyful expectation of future happiness. He took great pains to prepare us all for the event, which I could not well realize; for I then, as well as in childhood, seemed to look upon my father as almost superior to death. But his end came; and his last words were those of the dying Stephen—Lord Jesus receive my spirit."

An affectionate tribute to the worth of the wife of Dr. Waddell will close this sketch.

" December 11th, 1848.

"*Dear Sir:*—Our mother was the daughter of Colonel James Gordon of Lancaster county, Virginia, and called after her mother, Mary. Her mother was Mary Harrison, daughter of Nathaniel Harrison, of Surry, whose ancestor, as of the large connexion of that name in Virginia, was Benjamin Harrison, of Surry, who died in 1712, and whose tombstone may be seen with its inscriptions at Cabin-Point, of that county. The Harrisons have been distinguished by the terms Berkeley and Brandon, two family seats on James River, the first in Charles City and the other in Prince George. Our mother was of the Brandon descent. She was born in 1752; married when sixteen years of age; was the mother of ten children; and died in 1813, at Staunton.

"Our grandmother, in the early period of her marriage was of the High Church of England, and very bigotted,—so much so, that she refused to hear Mr. Davies preach, although he was a favourite with her husband, Colonel Gordon. Being visited however with protracted illness, a sermon was preached in their house, by this distinguished minister, which she heard from her bed; our grandfather being represented as setting open the door of an adjoining room to afford this opportunity. This sermon was blessed to her awakening and conversion. She lived an exemplary Christian and good Presbyterian, and so died. This was before our father had become acquainted in Colonel Gordon's family, and is only mentioned to show the hand of Providence in preparing the way for that acquaintance and for his after marriage.

"At what time our mother became pious we have no means of ascertaining, probably soon after the event just mentioned, experiencing the Christian counsels of both parents. It is enough for her children to know, and with gratitude, that her life, character, example, counsels and prayers, were those of a meek, devoted, affectionate and pious mother. Her meekness and gentleness were characteristic. This writer never remembers to have seen her angry. Cheerfulness and contentment were depicted on her countenance; and when removed by sorrow or affliction, resignation would quickly take their place.

"The youngest of us remember well her careful reading of the Scriptures and strict observance of the Sabbath,—her place of private prayer,—her catechising hour for the children,—her tenderness and solicitude for them,—her mild and winning modes of addressing them,—and unwearied efforts for their comfort and happiness.

"Our mother was a great reader; the habit was increased during the blindness of our father, from her assiduity in administering to his comfort in this respect. She was low in stature. Expressive black eyes lit up a benignant and cheerful face. As she lived so she died. This is penned by her youngest living child, who has wept while the present duty has freshened his recollections of the best of mothers.

Your Friend."

CHAPTER XVII.

LOG COLLEGES.

The infancy of the Presbyterian Church, in the United States, and particularly in Virginia, was the time of Log Colleges, and disabilities from government for conscience' sake, and exposure to the hard service of a frontier life. It was a healthy infancy; and before the church had reached the stature of youth, it had strangled some strong enemies of freedom of conscience,—and before manhood had come, it rejoiced, with the country at large, that in America the mind and conscience were as free as property and the body, all being under the protection of good laws administered by the legitimate authority, calling civil offences to a human tribunal, and referring purely religious ones to the bar of Almighty God.

In the year 1718, the ardent, devoted, and well instructed, William Tennent, an emigrant from the Episcopal Church in Ireland, joined the Synod of Philadelphia; and, after visiting a number of the inviting fields of missionary labour, settled on the Neshaminy not far from Philadelphia, and opened a famous school, which was generally known as the "Log College"—or "Tennent's Log College." For leaving the Established Church and joining the Presbyterian he gave the following strong reasons, viz.—

"1st. Their government by Bishops, Archbishops, Deacons, Archdeacons, Canons, Chapters, Chancellors, Vicars, wholly unscriptural.

"2d. Their discipline by Surrogates and Chancellors in their Courts Ecclesiastic without foundation in the word of God.

"3d. Their abuse of that supposed discipline by commutation.

"4th. A Diocesan Bishop cannot be founded *jure divino* upon those Epistles to Timothy or Titus, nor any where else in the word of God, and so is a mere human invention.

"5th. The usurped power of the Bishops at their yearly visitations, acting all of themselves, without consent of the brethren.

"6th. Plurality of benefices.

"Lastly. The churches conniving at the practice of Arminian doctrines inconsistent with the eternal purpose of God, and an encouragement of vice. Besides, I could not be satisfied with their ceremonial way of worship. These have so affected my conscience, that I could no longer abide in a church where the same are practised."

The reasons for the Log College were plain and forcible;—a pure and efficient church requires a learned ministry,—the ministry must be raised up, in, and by the church,—the church must educate her sons to be citizens of intelligence or society must deteriorate,—society can never educate the church, but the church must educate society,—and the standard of education in the church is the standard of education in society. He looked around among the settlements in the provinces of Pennsylvania, Delaware, and New Jersey, and saw no college or high-school for the instruction of youth in the languages and sciences, and his heart prompted him to build his *Log College*.

Here young men were taken through a classic and scientific course; and those who wished, through a course of theological reading. His students were fitted to enter upon professional studies of law or medicine, or public life, or the ministerial office. This school soon became the most approved place of education, south of Yale College, and North of William and Mary; and, with this last mentioned venerable institution, gave the youth of the middle and southern provinces, their only chance for an extensive and thorough training; and was the only one in all the south, where Presbyterian discipline prevailed. This private enterprise was entirely successful in its efforts to supply, on a limited scale, a well trained and pious ministry, and eminent professional men for posts of honour and profit in civil society, in what are now called the Middle States.

That great revival which commenced about the year 1740, in New Jersey, and spread north and south to the extent of the provinces, was commenced and cherished by the labours of men reared in the Log College on the Neshaminy. For a time, the influence of the Tennents, the father and sons, was paramount in the religious world. The father was wearing away, and John had just gone from the dawning revival to the world on high,— but William and Gilbert were in their prime. Gilbert traversed New England with long hair, and flowing robe girded about his loins with a leathern girdle, and by his commanding figure and powerful voice arrested the attention of the multitude, while he preached with great plainness and wonderful power, the doctrines of the Reformation. Fruits of his ministry were found in all parts of New England, New Jersey and the settled parts of Pennsylvania.

The Log College gave rise to what may be termed a school, or peculiar kind of preachers, whose attainments were remarkably acceptable to the people generally. Their traits are still discernible, and meet with favour wherever recognized. Didactic,— exhortatory,— plain,— impassioned,— often vehement,— they used the strong doctrines of Scripture as facts for illustration, or weapons to subdue the heart,—and fearless of man in the cause of God, they pressed on to run with speed their race. Accustomed to debate, they were at home with the pen, and ready for their message, armed at all points, whether to preach from the plain desk, the well-arranged pulpit, or in the barn, the school-house, or the shade of the forest. The man that first preached the gospel with the Presbyterian forms of worship, in Hanover county, Virginia, was licensed at Neshaminy,—William Robinson, of whom Davies says—"that man of God, who did much in a little time." Warm from the revival in Jersey, he entered the Valley of Virginia, and passing along the frontiers to Charlotte, he proclaimed, in burning words, the everlasting gospel of Christ to the Presbyterian emigrants in the wilderness. They hung upon his lips. And the citizens of Hanover sent for the man—"fearfully and wonderfully made,"—and trembled and wept, and bowed down in agony, as he delivered his message. The impress of his footsteps remain to this day.

When William Tennent began to wear away with age, Samuel Blair, a pupil and disciple and a leading man in the great revival, a burning and shining light through life, opened a school at New Londonderry in Pennsylvania, on the same plan as the Log College—a school for classics, for the sciences, and for theology. This was conducted on the responsibility and principally by the labours of one eminent minister—but that one, among the most eminent of his day. He visited Virginia and preached with great acceptance. From his school came out the man that has been truly styled the *Apostle of Virginia*—Samuel Davies, a man with whom, in Virginia is associated what is pure in politics and excellent in religion. It is now (1848) just one hundred years,—in the spring of the year—that the two young preachers stood before the general court in Williamsburg, to ask of the Governor and Council that Rodgers might stay and preach with Davies in the congregations gathered by Robinson,—the Blairs—Roan—the Tennents —and by Davies himself—a constellation of great men, that laid the foundation of a Presbytery—the mother of Presbyteries. The Governor said—"take the credentials"—the Attorney General said—"not till I have had an argument;"—an argument on what! Whether a young man claiming the protection of a law made for his protection, provided his creed rendered that law necessary for his protection in the quiet performance of his duty. The rights of conscience were unheeded that day. How changed the scene in a year or two, when young Davies came again to that court and answered the Attorney's argument, and gained some advantage for the rights of individuals in matters of conscience. The simple question was—have the citizens of Virginia a right to build a house for the worship of God in any fitting place. The General Court in 1748 said no; Davies said yes—by the laws of nature and by the Act of Toleration as understood in England. And long ago the whole Virginia public has said—all men are free to worship God. Under the exhortations of the same young man, in that alarming period immediately succeeding Braddock's defeat, the first volunteer company was enrolled for the defence of the frontiers. "In the name of the Lord"— said he—"lift up your banners: be of good courage and play the man for the people and the cities of your God, and the Lord do what seemeth him good."

Rev. Samuel Finley opened a log college at Nottingham, Pennsylvania, about the time the school at New Londonderry was closed by the death of Mr. Blair. This gentleman visited Virginia during the troubles attending the gathering the churches in Hanover; and ultimately died President of Princeton College. From this school proceeded many eminent men, among others, Waddell, commonly known as the *Blind Preacher of Mr. Wirt*, whose influence in Virginia is still widely felt.

While these log colleges were pouring out streams to make glad the city of God, Alison was cherishing a school which was matured into the University of Pennsylvania; and Dickerson and Burr fostered the incipient college now known as Nassau Hall, or the College of New Jersey. From the school of Samuel Blair, at New Londonderry, went Rev. Robert Smith, who opened a school at Pequa, and reared two sons, Samuel Stanhope, and John Blair Smith, the two stars of Prince Edward. These finished their education at Nassau Hall, which had, by the united help of England and America reared her head above the private schools, and invited youths from every quarter to her classic bowers. From Nassau Hall the Smiths came to Virginia to commence log colleges in the "Ancient Dominion.,'

By the year 1771, the Presbyterian congregations in Virginia, the emigrants and those gathered from the old Virginia stock, the people in the Valley of the Shenandoah, and those along the base of the Blue Ridge eastward to the tide water, began to feel the necessity of classic schools of a high order for the education of their youth. When Samuel Stanhope Smith passed through the country as a missionary, he saw the necessity of some man like Tennent, or Blair, or Finley, or Dickerson, or Burr, or like his father, to commence a log college. West of the Blue Ridge was a classic school in the bounds of New Providence, carried on under the care of the Rev. John Brown, which had been in existence for many years. East of the Ridge had been a school conducted by Rev. John Todd, with the patronage of Samuel Davies, in which James Waddell had been teacher on his first residence in Virginia. These were undertaken by individuals with the concurrence of their congregations and the approbation of the community. Other institutions had a temporary existence.

But the schools of learning most interesting to the Presbyterian Church, and to a large portion of the State, as most convenient and efficient, and for a long time the only ones above tide water, were Liberty Hall, now Washington College, in Rockbridge, and Hampden Sidney College in Prince Edward. The origin and progress of these two institutions form an important chapter both in the history of the church, and in the annals of the State. They were the consequence of the principles of freedom of conscience, and an accelerating cause of that entire freedom of conscience in matters of religion which is the glory of the State.

CHAPTER XVIII.

HAMPDEN SIDNEY COLLEGE.

THE Rev. Samuel Stanhope Smith, a licentiate of New Castle Presbytery, may be looked upon as the projector of Hampden Sidney College. Visiting Virginia as a missionary he both saw the necessity of literary institutions in Virginia, and sympathized with the Presbytery of Hanover in her efforts to call them into being. By his recommendation, the Presbytery having, in 1771, taken up the subject of education, and in 1772, having deferred action, and, in 1773, having located it in Staunton, and in 1774 having determined to locate the school in another place, appointed Rev. William Graham the tutor under supervision of Mr. John Brown of New Providence, and directed the Seminary to be carried on near Fairfield, where Mr. Brown had been conducting a classical school.

In the meantime he had been preaching in the counties of Prince Edward, Cumberland and Charlotte, and stimulating them to do something for the youth in that portion of State. If the measure of his popularity is to be determined by the amount of influence exercised in the self-denying efforts to build up an institution for the welfare of the community, he was the most popular young minister in Virginia, at that day.

At Cub-creek, October 14, 1774, the Presbytery having appointed Mr. Graham tutor of the Academy in Augusta, and also appointed committees to raise funds for its immediate endowment,—and having agreed to meet at the house of Colonel William Cabel, on the second Wednesday of November—" to remonstrate against a bill entitled—a Bill for extending the benefit of the Act of Toleration to his Majesty's subjects dissenting from the Church of England in the colony of Virginia,"— The Presbytery taking into consideration "the great extent of the colony, judge that a public school for the liberal education of youth would be of great importance on the south side of the Blue Ridge, notwithstanding of the appointment of one already made in the county of Augusta, and having been favoured with the company of Mr. Samuel Smith, a probationer of New Castle Presbytery, in Pennsylvania, a gentleman who has taught the languages for a considerable time in the New Jersey College, with good approbation, and with pleasure, finding that if properly encouraged he may be induced to take the charge of such a Seminary, we therefore judge it expedient to recommend it to the congregations of Cumberland, Prince Edward and Briery, in particular, and to all others in general, to set a subscription on foot to purchase a library and a philosophical apparatus, and such other things as may be necessary for the said purpose, and on the supposition that proper encouragement shall be given, and Mr. Smith, or any gentleman properly qualified may be induced to take the superintendency, we shall gladly concur to establish and patronize a publick Seminary in Prince Edward, or in the upper end of Cumberland; but if not we reserve to ourselves the power at any time hereafter to fix on any place at or below the mountains, that we shall judge best, and the subscriptions taken in consequence of this order, shall be void as to those who desire to withdraw them." The business was pressed with great spirit and excitement, and the efforts to raise subscriptions were successful beyond all anticipation. "February 1, 1775.—The Moderator (Mr. Leake) being informed that the congregations of Cumberland and Prince Edward had succeeded, beyond expectation, in taking subscriptions for the establishment of a Seminary for the education of youth—thought it expedient to send a circular to the several members appointing a Presbytery *pro re nata*, at Captain Nathaniel Venable's, in the county of Prince Edward, on Wednesday this first day of February, 1775. Being met according to appointment, Mr. Rice opened the Presbytery by a discourse from Heb. xi. 6,—'But without faith it is impossible to please him; for he that cometh to God must believe that he is, and that he is a rewarder of them that diligently seek him.' *Ubi post preces* present the Rev. Messrs. Sankey, Rice, Leake, Irwin and Wallace. Mr. Sankey was chosen moderator, and Mr. Wallace clerk.

"The Presbytery, upon inquiry find that there is above £1300 already subscribed for the purposes above mentioned, and considerable additions are expected. The Presbytery proceed to consider how it would be most expedient to lay out these monies, and when to establish an Academy.

"Ordered that £400 be applied to purchase such books and mathematical and philosophical apparatus, as are most immediately necessary ; and considering that the present non importation agreement may continue a considerable time, we intrust Mr. Samuel Stanhope Smith, to purchase said books and apparatus, in our northern provinces, by and with the advice and concurrence of the Rev. Robert Smith, and the Rev. Robert Davidson, and Mr. John Bayard merchant of Pennsylvania; and the Rev. Dr. John Rodgers, and Mr. Samuel Brown merchant of New York; or any two of them. And we also intrust the visiters and managers, hereafter nominated, and Messrs. Joseph Morton, James Allen, William Smith of Cumberland, Warren Walker, William Morton, and Robert Good, to collect £400, or to borrow it upon interest, and transmit it to Philadelphia, to the said Samuel Stanhope Smith, before the first of May next."

On the next day—"The Presbytery, after viewing several places shown them, by the gentlemen of the part, agree to build an academy-house, and a dwelling-house for the superintendent, and other necessary houses, as far as the subscriptions will admit, at the head of Hudson's Branch, in Prince Edward county, on an hundred acres of land, given for the use, by Mr. Peter Johnson; and we entrust Mr. Peter Johnson, Col. John Nash, Jr., Mr. James Allen, Capt. John Morton, and Capt. Nathaniel Venable, or any three of them, to draw plans of the houses, and let them to the lowest bidder, of which they shall give timely notice to the publick. And we also intrust Col. John Nash, Jr., Mr. James Allen, Capt. John Morton, and Capt. Nathaniel Venable, or any three of them, to have the above-named hundred acres of land measured and bounded, and the title secured for the purposes, for which it was given.

" And as several members of this Presbytery lie at too great a distance from each other frequently to meet together, and consult on the affairs of this Academy, we appoint the Rev. Messrs. Richard Sankey, (of Buffaloe), John Todd, (of Louisa), Samuel Leake (of Albemarle) and Caleb Wallace (of Cub Creek), together with Mr. Peter Johnson, Col. Paul Carrington, Col. John Nash, Jr., Capt. John Morton, Capt. Nathaniel Venable, Col. Thomas Read, Mr. James Venable, Mr. Francis Watkins, and the superintendent *ex officio*, trustees of the Academy. Seven of the trustees shall be a quorum. They are to collect the subscriptions, expend the money, and conduct all the concerns of the Academy, in behalf of the Presbytery; also they are to keep a fair book of accounts, and all the transactions relating to the Academy, to be preserved on the records thereof.

"The Presbytery reserve to themselves the liberty, forever, of choosing the Superintendent, the Trustees, and the Assistants.

"On February 3d—Presbytery chose Mr. Samuel Stanhope Smith, Rector of the Prince Edward Academy, and we entrust the said Smith, and the Rev. Robert Smith of Pennsylvania, and William Charles Huston, Professor in Princeton College, or any two of them, to choose an Assistant. And we also agree that tuition be fixed at £4 per annum for each scholar; 20s. of which shall be paid on the day of entrance; and we also agree that the tuition money shall be divided between the Rector and the Assistants, at the discretion of the Trustees, until they shall find it expedient otherwise to regulate the matter.

"Mr. Sankey having obtained permission to go home, Mr. Rice was chosen Moderator in his room." The Presbytery then proceeded to take steps to have Mr. Smith settled as a preacher as well as teacher, according to the spirit of the Log College in Pennsylvania, which had been so rich in blessings on Virginia. "The united congregations of Prince Edward and Cumberland, having applied to us for permission to present a call to Mr. Samuel Stanhope Smith, a probationer of New Castle Presbytery, it is cheerfully granted. And as we find it would be very inconvenient for any of our members to be present in the congregation when the call is signed, we take the opportunity to assure the Rev. Presbytery [of New Castle,] that we have sufficient information that they are unanimous for Mr. Smith, and we earnestly pray that you may concur in encouraging him to take the care of one of our important vacancies."

The Presbytery then proceeded to make the following manifesto.—"The Presbytery having for a long time had the liberal education of youth, in these upper parts, much at heart, and having succeeded so far in our endeavours to promote it, as to do something considerable towards erecting an academy in Prince Edward county, where we trust every necessary branch of human literature will be taught to good advantage, on the most catholic plan—and whereas some gentlemen who are unacquainted with our sentiments, may encourage this Seminary with reluctance because it is to be under the guardianship of this Presbytery, we take this opportunity to assure the publick, that though the strictest regard shall be paid to the morals of the youth, and worship carried on, evening and morning, in the Presbyterian way; yet, on the other hand, all possible care shall be taken that no undue influence be used by any member of this Presbytery, the Rector, or any assistant, to bias the judgment of any; but that all, of every denomination, shall fully enjoy his own religious sentiments, and be at liberty to attend that mode of publick worship, that either custom or conscience makes most agreeable to them, when and where they may have an opportunity of enjoying it."

This meeting of the Presbytery appears to have been one of those very important ones, whose influence extends to coming generations, and whose actions with its actors ought to be remembered through all time.

The call for Mr. Smith having been laid before his Presbytery, and by it put into his hands, on the 27th of October, at Rockfish.—"Mr. Samuel Stanhope Smith preached a sermon on Eph. ii. 8, "*For by grace are ye saved, through faith, and that not of yourselves, it is the gift of God,"* previous to his ordination, with which the Presbytery are well pleased. Mr. Smith having applied for admission into this Presbytery, informed us that he had neglected to bring a dismission and recommendation from New Castle Presbytery; nevertheless, being well assured of his good standing as a probationer of that Presbytery, and seeing that a call from the united congregations of Cumberland and Prince Edward has been presented to him,—and he being encouraged to receive it by said Presbytery, which amounts to a dismission and recommendation, we judge it safe to receive him; but recommend it to him to procure a dismission, and to produce it to this Presbytery as soon as he conveniently can. The Presbytery then proceeded to ordain Mr. Smith to the sacred work of the ministry by the imposition of hands and prayer. Mr. Smith now takes his seat as a member of Presbytery together with his Elder, Mr. James Venable."

On Wednesday, November 8th, 1775, "Mr. Smith informs, that the gentlemen, not being able to collect or borrow the four hundred pounds, for the purpose of purchasing books, &c., did transmit a letter of credit to him last spring, for three hundred pounds, and twenty in cash, which he has laid out in purchasing of books and mathematical and philosophical apparatus, agreeably to the directions of Presbytery; and that he has purchased on his own credit, in behalf of the Presbytery, to the amount of forty pounds, which are all safe come to hand. The letter of credit and the forty pounds above named, together with the package and portage of the books and instruments, the gentlemen appointed to collect the four hundred pounds are desired to pay out of the collections they have made, or shall make of the subscriptions.

" The gentlemen inform us that ninety-eight acres of land are measured, bounded and secured by deed, from Mr. Peter Johnson, for the use of the Academy.

" The gentlemen appointed inform us, that they have drawn plans, and let an academy house, and a dwelling house for the Rector, at the sum of six hundred and ninety-four pounds; for which the undertaker is to take subscriptions for payment, upon the condition, that such as are found to be insolvent, be made good with the other subscriptions;—and that they have let a kitchen and a smoke house, which are to be valued when the work is done, and paid as above.

" The Presbytery are informed that the gentlemen who were chosen Trustees have signified their acceptance;—and the Rev. David Rice, Colonel Patrick Henry, Colonel John Tabb, Colonel William Cabel, and Colonel James Madison, jr., are now added to the number. Mr. Todd is appointed to write to Col-

onel Henry and to Col. Madison; Mr. Rice to Colonel Cabel,
and Captain Morton to Colonel Tabb, and to solicit their acceptance."

On Thursday, November 9th, 1775, Rev. Samuel Stanhope Smith was installed pastor of the united churches of
Cumberland and Prince Edward. "Mr. Smith informs that
agreeably to the commission of Presbytery he has engaged two
assistants of liberal education, Mr. J. B. Smith and Mr.
Springer."

These efforts for an Academy were made at the time the agitation and distress preceding the Revolution were at their
height; the war had actually commenced, though the declaration had not yet been made in form by the Continental Congress. The distress of community was such that the Presbytery say on the 9th of November, 1775,—"We judge it incompatible with our circumstances, for any of our members to
attend at the next Synod, with our Presbytery book: we
therefore appoint Mr. Todd and Mr. Rice to write to the
Synod, and plead our excuse, until Providence shall put it into
the power of some of our members to attend.

"At Timber Ridge, Saturday, May 4th, 1776, Mr. Samuel
S. Smith informs that Mr. John B. Smith came according to
agreement, and is now in the service of the Academy, as his
assistant; but Mr. John Springer having been providentially
detained, he has on the emergency employed Mr. Samuel
Doak, as second assistant; and the number of students increasing beyond expectation, he has also employed Mr. David
Witherspoon as third assistant. The Presbytery on being
certified of their good character and liberal education, do approve and confirm the choice." Mr. John B. Smith became in
a short time the head of the institution, and one of the most
distinguished ministers that ever graced the Virginia church.
Mr. Samuel Doak in a few years, 1778, was in Tennessee, building a Log College for the rising Presbyterian population of
that now populous State. He took the first library across the
Alleghanies, carrying it on pack horses, in sacks, to endow his
rising College, the first in the great West.

On Monday, May 6th, besides attending to the location of
the Augusta school, the records say,—"As by the death of the
Rev. Mr. Leake there is a vacancy in the Board of Trustees of
the Prince Edward Academy—now known by the name of
Hampden Sidney—the Rev. Archibald McRoberts is chosen
Trustee in his stead.

The affairs of Hampden Sidney went on prosperously, notwithstanding the convulsions of the Revolution, increasing in
reputation and usefulness. On the 28th of October, 1779, at
Prince Edward Court House, after the ordination of his brother

John Blair Smith to the full work of the gospel ministry— "Mr. Samuel Stanhope Smith having had an invitation from the Trustees of the New Jersey College, to accept of the Professorship of Moral Philosophy in that institution, asked a dismission from this Presbytery, from the congregations of Cumberland and Briery, and also from the Presidency of Hampden Sidney. *Resolved*, that the request is reasonable, and he is dismissed accordingly. The Presidency of Hampden Sidney being now vacant, Presbytery appoint Rev. John Blair Smith to succeed his brother, the late President, in that office."— Under this gentleman the institution rose to a degree of popularity and usefulness, as a Log College, both in the theological, and the literary department, which has never been surpassed in its most palmy of succeeding years. In the month of April, 1780, the President accepted a call to become the pastor of the churches of Cumberland and Briery, made vacant by the removal of his brother; and thus from the first united the pastoral office with the duties of the Presidency of the College, and the Professor of Theology, embracing what is properly the labour of three men; and giving a Christian spirit to the efforts for the education of youth, which are never more successful than when conducted in the fear of God, and the love of Jesus Christ the Mediator. With him, men of the greatest probity, and of the highest public estimation and private worth, were associated in the direction of a seminary where the purest sentiments of religion and patriotism were inculcated in a most efficient manner. The names of such men as Morton, Venable, Nash, Watkins, Allen, Henry, Carrington, men honoured for their patriotism, and religion, sound well in conjunction with the two patriots of England, Hampden and Sidney, whose names were early and significantly united to indicate the principles that should be taught there and to give it a name.

It is worthy of observation, that about the same time that the Presbyterian settlements in Virginia were endeavouring to rear their Log Colleges, the one west and the other east of the Blue Ridge, their brethren in Mecklenburg, North Carolina, put up their Log College at Charlotte, and named it Queen's Museum. The king having annulled their charter,—and they having, in the month of May, next succeeding the founding of Hampden Sidney, issued their Declaration of Independence,— the name was changed to Liberty Hall, expressive of the principles and spirit of the men. A full account of this institution may be found in Sketches of North Carolina. It will form a conspicuous chapter in all future histories of that State.

Before we pass by the time of the first President of Hampden Sidney, some scraps gathered from various sources will throw light upon the condition of the country, and the infancy of the Institution. The Academy, or Log College, was opened January 1776,—with the President were associated—J. B. Smith, first teacher, and Samuel Doake and David Witherspoon, assistants. In the course of the summer there were as many as one hundred and ten students under instruction at one time. At the first meeting of the Trustees, of which there is any record, on the 26th of September, an order was passed allowing Messrs. N. Venable and P. Carrington to build cabins for their sons. This was done on account of the difficulty of obtaining board and lodging for the great number of students that came in from all quarters.

At the opening of the school, "Capt. Philemon Holcomb engaged with the Trustees to act as steward for the small sum of £8 per year for diet—for washing and.bed £3; provisions at that time very cheap and plenty. Capt. Holcomb continued as steward until 1st January, 1777, when he resigned, having given the Trustees previous notice thereof, and Mr. William Bibb was then chosen for one year at the price of £11."

Mr. George Craghead, from whose letter to Mr. Watkins the above is taken, who was himself a member of the school, says: "In May, 1776, the walls of the Academy were about three feet high, and on account of scarcity of room for the students to study in, they obtained leave from the undertaker, Mr. Coleman, to erect little huts with the shingles that were intended to cover the Academy. They were packed like a sugar loaf, with a plank for three or four boys to sit upon; and in the night a candle being placed in each hut, there being eight or ten, it showed how intent the inhabitants were in studying till 9 or 10 o'clock at night. That year the students devoted their time to study; very little was spent in recreation or amusement. About the first of July Mr. Hockley, a student, about twenty years of age, universally beloved, was taken with a fever, and in a few days died."

As the declaration of national independence spread through the country, the youth were aroused, and offered themselves as soldiers to redeem that pledge of—"*our lives, our fortunes, and our sacred honour.*" Busy as the students were in their studies, their hearts were full of patriotism; and with the arts and sciences of academic life, they would learn the rudiments of the art of war. Mr. Craghead says—"Mr. John Blair Smith was chosen captain of a company of the students about sixty-five in number, over sixteen years of age,—Mr. David Witherspoon lieutenant,—and Mr. Samuel Venable, son of Nathaniel, was chosen ensign. The students wore uniform, viz. a hunting shirt died purple, and every student, although under sixteen years of age, was mustered every month."

Mr. James Mitchell was employed as a teacher during this

summer. A half a century afterwards this devoted minister of the gospel was moving among his brethren, a patriarch in the Synod. Mr. Doak left the Academy the latter part of the year 1776; and ultimately went to Tennessee, the pioneer of literature in the west. Mr. John Springer, who had been engaged the year before but had been hindered from coming, succeeded him as tutor. On the 11th May, 1777, the Board was called by particular request of Mr. John Springer, who told the Trustees that he had been drunk and did gamble at New London, on one occasion. In consideration of his candour the Trustees only suspended him. He was succeeded by Mr. James Willson.

"In 1777,"—says Mr. Craghead—"about the first of September, there was a requisition from the Governor for one company of militia from Prince Edward county to march to Williamsburg to oppose an expected invasion from the British: all the students, over sixteen years of age, immediately, with the advice of the President, exchanged their numbers for No. 1 with the militia in the county, and marched to Williamsburg, under the aforesaid officers; and after remaining a few days at Williamsburg, were discharged by the Governor; and as the vacation was about to take place, they returned to their expected homes. Several of them never returned to the Academy,—some entered into the United States army as officers, and others enlisted as common soldiers." In the close of this same year, on account of the great depreciation of the money in circulation, the steward, Mr. Bibb—"very abruptly quit about the 25th of December, without giving the Trustees previous notice to appoint a successor. The Academy was likely to have been discontinued, but Mr. Nathaniel Venable, Mr. James Allen, senr., and I believe Captain John Morton united and agreed to furnish provisions for twelve months, and employed a Mr. Young with his family, to attend to the cooking, &c. for the sum of £20 only per student: they acted faithfully until the end of the year of 1778, but lost very considerably on account of the depreciation of paper money. For the next year of 1779, I was informed, that the students found themselves chiefly with provisions and employed cooks, &c., (a poor business I expect). How they were supplied afterwards I do not recollect, as I was taken from the Academy in November, 1778, and was sent to Washington Henry Academy in Hanover county.

"I am satisfied,"—continues Mr. Craghead—"there never was as many students at Hampden Sidney after the year 1776. I often heard the then steward, Captain Holcomb, say that he boarded seventy-five that year; the rest boarded in the neighbourhood, and some few boarded at home. The names of the students, at first, were placed in three classes, No. 1, 2 and 3; at the examination it was usual to say, white, yellow, black.

Those who had been very studious and distinguished themselves before the Examiners, were publicly applauded by the President before the students were dismissed, and those who had been negligent were also named with disapprobation. With respect to the yellow list nothing was said, pro or con. The President always informed the students, that there was a roll constantly kept, wherein were recorded the names of every student, the time of their entry and departure, their place of residence, but above all, the manner in which each had conducted himself; that at a future day it would appear at the Academy, whose conduct had been approved of, and whose had been censured; which ought, he said, to stimulate every student, who had any regard for his future character. There were two societies at the Academy in 1776, one was denominated the Cliosophic (I believe) and the other, Tully Whitefield; which last was changed and called The American Whig Society. They kept records of all their proceedings, and I never knew a single sentence to be expunged."

In May, 1778, Mr. James Willson left the office of tutor, and was succeeded by Mr. Charles Wingfield, of the first class. From this we learn the estimate the President had of the proficiency of the advanced classes, and of that young man in particular, as institutions aim at rearing their own tutors as early and entirely as practicable.

From the foregoing short notices are distinctly seen the difficulties the first President, Samuel Stanhope Smith, surmounted; and also the enthusiasm he excited on the subject of education. The difficulties from the Revolutionary war, however, pressed more heavily on his brother, who succeeded him, and also on himself for a few years after his removal to Princeton. John Blair Smith succeeded to the Presidency in times very inauspicious, except in the trials and perplexities which prove great men and crush small ones. And to have carried an infant college through the scenes and difficulties that surrounded and pressed upon him, is proof of no ordinary mind, and of the presence of that Divine hand that shows itself, in days of calamity, for the cause it loves.

After the battle of the Cowpens, on the 17th of January, 1781, the excitement in the southern country was great. This second victory, in such quick succession to the famous battle of King's Mountain, roused the sinking hopes of the patriots. A few more such triumphs of the American arms would annihilate the British army. Morgan retreated most rapidly, with his prisoners, towards Virginia: Green covered his retreat, himself retiring before Cornwallis, unable to resist an army whose progress he could only retard. His pressing calls for reinforcements brought out the militia from North Western Caro-

lina, and from all the contiguous counties of Virginia, and
the southern sections of the Great Valley. Captain William
Morton, of Charlotte, in two days, raised a company of his
neighbours to join the army of Greene on the Dan. Hearing
of his intentions, the President of the College set out to join
him. On overtaking the company in Halifax, the Captain earnestly entreated him to return to Prince Edward, that he could
serve the cause more at home by his exciting patriotic speeches
than by his presence in camp. Worn out by fatigue, rather
than convinced by his friend, he returned to College.

A company of dragoons had been previously raised in the
counties of Prince Edward, Amelia and Nottaway, and made a
part of Lee's famous legion, whose deeds are so romantically
detailed in his Memoirs of the Southern War. Lieutenant Eggleston was from Amelia, and appears to have been a favourite
of Lee; he was afterwards member of Congress for many
years. On this alarming and pressing call from Green, a company of militia dragoons was raised in Prince Edward, under
the command of Thomas Watkins. Philemon Holcomb, Charles
Scott and Samuel Venable, were the other officers. Among
the privates was the famous Peter Francisco. This company
was attached to Colonel Washington's command; it is said Captain Watkins offered himself and company to Lee, who refused
them because they were not "*fine enough dressed.*" This company signalized itself in the battle of Guilford, in that famous
charge made on the Queen's Guards. Lieut. Holcomb used to
relate the circumstances of that terrible charge upon the Queen's
Guards, in which this troop bore a part. Leaping a ravine, the
swords of the horsemen were upon the heads of the enemy, who
were rejoicing in victory and safety; and before they suspected danger, multitudes lay dead. The strong arm of Francisco levelled three of the enemy during one charge, and eleven
before the fight was over. When this company was formed,
the students, already greatly lessened in number by the calamities of war, pressed forward to the ranks. Peter Johnson,
about sixteen years of age, the son of the donor of the land on
which the College stands, offered himself, and was rejected, as
under age and under size. He nevertheless procured a horse
and offered himself to Lee, and was with some hesitation
received. He served during that momentous campaign with
great honour, taking a part in several actions, besides the decisive one of Guilford Court House. He was in after life a Judge
of eminence in his native State; and has left a posterity to
rejoice in his patriotism.

When the war was over the College was in a depressed state.
The enthusiasm for education was somewhat abated among the
people at large; objects of ambition and speculation engrossed

multitudes. The more thoughtful patriots felt the immeasurable importance of the universal dissemination of knowledge and true morality and religion for the preservation of that political liberty that had been acquired. The friends of Hampden Sidney applied for and obtained from the Legislature in 1783 a charter for the Academy under the legal name of College, with all proper privileges and powers.

The last act of the Presbytery in the management of the College, before the charter, was to appoint some additional trustees. New Providence, October 24th, 1782—"As it appears to the Presbytery that the Trustees of the Academy of Hampden Sidney in Prince Edward, have failed to discharge their duty, through the distant situation of some whose attendance was necessary, upon motion of Mr. Smith, the Presbytery agreeably to the original constitution of that Academy, appoint Messrs. James Allen, Charles Allen, Samuel W. Venable, William Booker, William Morton of Charlotte, Joseph Parke, and Colonel Thomas Scott, in addition to those who already act in that capacity." This act of Presbytery was entered on the minutes of the Trustees on the 19th of December, 1782. The next spring the charter was obtained. Its preamble says —"Whereas it is represented to the present General Assembly, that an Academy has been founded in Prince Edward, and which hath been supported by the generous donations of a few public spirited citizens for several years past; but that in order to make the advantages arising therefrom more permanent and diffusive, certain privileges are essentially necessary for conducting the same in future to greater advantage; and this Assembly, warmly impressed with the important advantages arising to every free State by diffusing useful knowledge amongst its citizens, and desirous of giving their patronage and support to such seminaries of learning as may appear to them calculated to promote this great object,"—enact, &c.

After enacting that the Academy "shall obtain the name and be called the College of Hampden Sidney," the following persons are named Trustees,—Rev. John Blair Smith, Patrick Henry, William Cabell, senr., Paul Carrington, Robert Lawson, James Madison, John Nash, Nathaniel Venable, Everard Meade, Joel Watkins, James Venable, Francis Watkins, John Morton, William Morton, Thomas Reade, William Booker, Thomas Scott, senr., James Allen, Charles Allen, Samuel Woodson Venable, Joseph Parke, Richard Foster, Peter Johnson, the Rev. Richard Sankey, the Rev. John Todd, the Rev. David Rice, and the Rev. Archibald McRoberts. As so large a portion of these were ministers, elders, and members of the Presbyterian Church, and all named by the Presbytery in her previous lists of Trustees, but three, the apprehensions of the Presbytery, expressed in the resolutions that gave birth to the institution, must have subsided, and given place to entire confidence in the Trustees that the College should never be perverted from its original design. In the third article of the charter it is enacted,—" And that in order to preserve, in the minds of the students, that sacred love and attachment which they should ever bear to the principles of the ever glorious Revolution, the greatest care and caution shall be used in electing such professors and masters, to the end that no person shall be so elected unless the uniform tenor of his conduct manifest to the world his sincere affection for the liberty and independence of the United States of America." The oath of office is,—" I do swear (or affirm) that I will to the best of my skill and judgment, faithfully and truly discharge the duties required of me by an Act for incorporating the Trustees of Hampden Sidney."

The literary degrees conferred, under the charter, were first bestowed September 22d, 1786; when the degree of A. B. was awarded to Kemp Plummer, David Meade, James Watt, Ebenezer McRoberts, Thomas McRoberts, Nash Legrand, and John W. Eppes. The last two distinguished themselves in after life, the one as an evangelist, and the other as a member of Congress. In April of the next year, the same degree was conferred on William Baker and Clement Read of the class of 1786. The first diploma of A. M., or the second degree, was conferred on a gentleman that was never a member of that or any other college. "The Rev. Henry Pattillo of North Carolina being proposed to this Board as a gentleman upon whom it would be proper to confer the degree of Master of Arts—*honoris gratia*—it is unanimously resolved to compliment him with that testimony of respect." This diploma, written most beautifully on parchment, in large and small German text and Saxon letters, by the hand as is supposed of that unrivalled calliographist, Drury Lacy, bearing date April 25th, 1787, is still in existence, preserved by the descendants of Mr. Pattillo. It is signed by the President, John Blair Smith—and John Nash, Arichibald McRoberts, James Allen, Francis Watkins, Thomas Scott, Richard Foster, Richard Sankey, Charles Allen,—Trustees.

The College was now in a flourishing condition.—" After the siege of York"—says Dr. Hill—"and the capture of Cornwallis and his army, the male inhabitants, who had been generally kept in the army, returned home, and more quiet times ensued. The congregations which had been almost deserted, collected together again, and public worship was maintained afterwards without further interruption. Students also returned to College, and Dr. Smith entered *de novo* upon his various and responsible duties. The number of students continued to increase, until the rooms in College were as full as they well could contain." During the years 1787 and onwards there was a great revival of religion in the College and congregations and surrounding country, in which a large number of youth made profession of religion. Many of the students were embraced in this revival, that, afterwards, became eminent in the church as ministers and elders. The revival extended into the Valley of Virginia, and many of the students of Liberty Hall became hopeful converts. The influence of the ministers of the gospel that came into the sacred office under the influence of Presidents Smith and Graham, during this revival or in consequence of it, had a controlling influence in the Virginia Synod for half a century, made a part of the active ministry of Kentucky, and threw their influence over the whole Presbyterian Church. The particulars of this revival will more properly be given in the sketches of the two Presidents Smith and Graham.

The labours of President Smith being highly prized, he was called almost incessantly, during the revival, to the duties appropriate to his sacred office. The sphere of his active exertions was bounded only by his physical strength; and as the excitement continued for years, the demands upon him in his two offices, as pastor and president, became too onerous for his feeble constitution. In July 1788, he informed the Board that he designed leaving the College grounds and removing to the neighbourhood. The Board requested him to continue President, although removed from the College; and appointed Rev. Drury Lacy, who had been educated principally by President Smith, to be Vice President, to reside in the College and thus relieve Mr. Smith of part of his labours. In September following, the Board conferred on Mr. Lacy the degree of A. B., "*Causa Meriti.*"

On the 16th of November, 1789, a Trustee was appointed to fill the vacancy occasioned by the death of Rev. Richard Sankey. The appointment was made by the Board without any official reference to the Presbytery, but was, in this case, as in the following years, in accordance to their well known wishes. At the same meeting the Board went into an investigation of the rumour that the faculty—"use unfair methods to proselyte the students to a particular sect,"—and examined several students to ascertain the degree of credit to be attached to it. After investigation, the Board reported the rumour to be without foundation, and directed their report to be published.

In the September of 1789, Mr. Smith resigned the Presidency of the College and gave himself entirely to the work of the ministry. Mr. Graham, of Liberty Hall, having visited Prince Edward some time previous to the resignation, and preached with great acceptance; his character as a successful preacher and teacher standing pre-eminent, and it being understood that causes were in operation to render a removal desirable, efforts were made by the Trustees, during the years 1790, 1791 and 1792, to have him transferred from Lexington to Prince Edward. The matter was finally brought before the Synod in 1792, by two commissioners from the Board, with the consent of Mr. Graham, for their advice and counsel. These commissioners, in October, reported that Mr. Graham declined the invitation. By a committee of the Board appointed for the purpose, the neighbouring congregations had been requested to unite in efforts to obtain the services of Mr. Graham, and had sent him a call. As these efforts failed, the attention of the Board was turned by the Vice-President, to Rev. Archibald Alexander, a member of Lexington Presbytery, recently licensed to preach the gospel, a pupil of Mr. Graham. He was invited to unite with Mr. Lacy in the government and instruction of the College, with equal authority and emolument; and the Committee of the Board invited the neighbouring congregations to unite in employing these two ministers as their regular supplies. An arrangement was made by the congregations, by which Messrs. Lacy and Alexander were to preach in succession alternately at Cumberland, College, Briery, Buffaloe, Charlotte Court House, and Cub Creek: Mr. Alexander declined being connected with the College. These brethren entered on their laborious and extensive circuit towards the close of the year 1794: but finding the arrangement very inconvenient, the charge was divided, and Mr. Lacy confined himself to Cumberland and the College, and Mr. Alexander to Briery and Cub Creek.

In the year 1796, Rev. Drury Lacy having presided over the College, as Vice-President, for about seven years, resigned his office and devoted himself to the work of the ministry at the College Church and Cumberland. The Rev. Archibald Alexander was then chosen President, and accepted the office on condition the faculty should be agreeable and a proper provision made for their support. The latter part of the year he entered upon the duties of the office, and had for tutors John H. Rice, who had been elected by the Trustees in October, and Conrad Speece, selected by himself. Here were associated three young men bound together by strong bonds of friendship through life, stimulated and stimulating in their turns by each other's progress, and each exercising an influence on the Virginia Synod, and felt throughout the Presbyterian Church. Graham in Lexington was surrounding himself with alumni of Liberty Hall of uncommon excellence, and looked with mingled emotions at the progress of Hampden Sidney, as she rose under the fostering care of his pupils, in usefulness and public confidence. These two institutions have exercised a not unhappy rivalship from their commencement. First, Hampden Sidney seemed to get the start in the race of popularity and excellence—and then Liberty Hall appeared to have the advantage—then Hampden Sidney took the lead for a time—and then Washington College, into which Liberty Hall was merged, appeared evidently foremost in the race—but Hampden Sidney is now striving hard to regain all that has been lost, and be at least equal to her competitor. May they both flourish.

Upon the removal of Dr. Alexander to Philadelphia, the Rev. Moses Hoge was chosen President. He became the Professor of Theology by the appointment of the Synod of Virginia. In this double capacity he was the means of preparing for usefulness a large number of ministers, of whom it is not proper now to speak particularly, as they are many of them living monuments of the grace of God, and of the excellency of the institution. Others have within a few years gone to their rest, their memorials are among the churches, and their deeds in the recollection of all. Dr. Hoge died in Philadelphia, in the year 1820.

Mr. J. L. Cushing succeeded Dr. Hoge. During his presidency, the present beautiful college buildings were erected. He was cut down in the prime of life. His successor, Rev. D. L. Carroll, continued in office a few years, struggling with many difficulties on account of the smallness of the funds. His successor, William Maxwell, Esq., laboured under great difficulties from the same source. Vigorous efforts having been made by the Trustees, which have been attended with great success, funds have been secured, that have put the College on a favourable footing, and under the presidency of Rev. L. W. Green, Hampden Sidney is rising like a phœnix from her ashes. God has blessed the College, and the congregations around, with a precious revival of religion. May the College be a fountain of life.

CHAPTER XIX.

REV. JOHN BLAIR SMITH AND THE REVIVAL OF 1787—8.

The Rev. Robert Smith was blessed of God to rear a family of sons, that were an honour to their father and a blessing to the church and the world. Born in the year 1723, in Ireland, in Londonderry, the very scene of the triumph of the Protestant succession to the English crown, won by the valour and sufferings of the Irish Presbyterians; he came with his parents to America in his eighth year. His firsɩ years, in the land of his emigration, were passed on the head of Brandywine; and at the early age of fifteen, under the preaching of that eminent minister, George Whitefield, during his first visit to America, he professed conversion. On his entrance into manhood he commenced a course of studies preparatory to the ministry, which he pursued under the instruction of the Rev. Samuel Blair, at his Log College, the *Alma Mater* of Samuel Davies and John Rodgers. He was licensed by Newcastle Presbytery in 1750; and in 1751 ordained pastor, at Pequea, Pennsylvania, over a congregation that remembered the province of Ulster as their motherland. Here he opened a classical school; and as Log Colleges were giving way to the regular College of New Jersey, he prepared students for that institution. Three of his sons received their early education from him preparatory to the ministry; Samuel Stanhope, William and John Blair; the fourth Robert was educated and became a physician; the sixth son died in infancy. Two of his sons, Samuel Stanhope, and John Blair became eminent as ministers and teachers; and both became president of two colleges. Having preached the gospel almost half a century he went to his everlasting rest in the year 1799. As a preacher he excelled in knowledge of the human heart,—in strong and convincing appeals to the conscience,—and in the tenderness with which he led the penitent soul to its true rest, and abiding hope.

John Blair Smith, the fourth son, was born June 12, 1756, and received his name from a maternal uncle, his mother being the sister of the Rev. Messrs. Samuel and John Blair. During his boyhood he was noted as being ingenuous and warm-hearted and apt to learn. At the age of fourteen he was hopefully converted during a revival in his father's school; in his sixteenth year he joined the Junior Class in New Jersey College, then under the presidency of Dr. Witherspoon; and he received his diploma September, 1773. A great awakening among the students was felt while he was a member of College, which resulted in the hopeful conversion of many; and among others, of a class-mate, Lewis Feuileteau Wilson, afterwards the ornament of North Carolina. Of the twenty-nine graduates of the Class of 1773, twenty-three became ministers of the gospel; and three Governors of States—Henry Lee of Virginia,—Morgan Lewis of New York,—and Aaron Ogden of New Jersey. Of the ministers, four became Presidents of Colleges; William Graham of Liberty Hall, Virginia,—Jacob Dunlap of Jefferson College, Pennsylvania,—John McKnight of Dickinson College,

Pennsylvania,—and John Blair Smith, of Hampden Sidney, Virginia, and of Union College, New York.

The elder brother, Samuel Stanhope, who was graduated at Princeton 1769, having become the head of the rising institution in Prince Edward, Virginia, under the care of the Presbytery of Hanover, the attention of Samuel Blair was turned, by this brother, to the same institution, in the summer after the Presbytery had declared formally its existence and location. On the 9th of November 1775, the day Samuel Stanhope Smith was installed pastor of Cumberland and Prince Edward, Presbytery was informed that two assistants had been engaged, agreeably to their order, John B. Smith, and John Springer, a graduate of Princeton of the Class of 1775. In the May following, on Saturday 4th, 1776—Presbytery were informed that Mr. John B. Smith had came on according to engagement, and was then engaged in teaching; and as Mr. Springer had been detained from entering the work, Mr. Samuel Doak, his classmate, had been employed in his room.

While filling the station of tutor, Mr. Smith pursued his studies preparatory to the ministry under the direction of his brother. On the 18th of June 1777, at a meeting of the Presbytery of Hanover, at Concord, Bedford county, he offered himself as a "probationer for the gospel ministry;"—"and producing a certificate from Newcastle Presbytery recommending him to our care, we therefore take him under our care for further trials." On the next day he read an Exegesis on a subject assigned him by a member of Presbytery—"*An supplicum apud infernos set æternum;*" which was approved. The Presbytery then gave him for further trials a Homily on Regeneration, a Sermon on Rom. iii. 24, and a Lecture on Daniel ix. 24th to 27th. The records of the Presbyterial meetings at which these parts of trial were exhibited, are lost. On Tuesday the 29th of April, 1778, at Tinkling Spring, Mr. Smith opened Presbytery with a popular sermon on 1 John iii. 1,—and on the evening of the same day at the house of the pastor Mr. James Waddell—"the Presbytery having now taken a full view of his whole performance, and being well satisfied therewith, do agree to license the said John B. Smith to preach the gospel as a probationer, and he is licensed therefore accordingly." On the 26th of October 1779, at Prince Edward Court House—"Mr. John Blair Smith, having delivered a sermon on the subject assigned him at our last (*the record of that meeting lost,*) previous to his ordination, the Presbytery proceeded to set him solemnly apart to the sacred work of the gospel ministry, by the imposition of hands and prayer. This done he now takes his seat with us as a member of Presbytery."

At the same meeting of Presbytery, October 28th, the President of Hampden Sidney College having received an invitation to the chair of Moral Philosophy in Princeton College, asked leave to resign the Presidency of the College, and requested a dissolution of the pastoral office. Upon deliberation, Presbytery granted both requests; and immediately appointed John Blair Smith President of the College. April 25th 1780, at Tinkling Spring, a call from the congregation of Cumberland and Briery, was given in to be presented to Mr. J. B. Smith; which he now accepts of." The time of his installation is not given in the records of Presbytery.

About this time he was united in marriage with Miss Elizabeth Nash, daughter of Colonel John Nash of Templeton, Prince Edward, one of the most accomplished ladies of her day, whose piety became as eminent as her personal charms; and both combined rendered her the ornament of society. She bore him four sons and one daughter.

The Rev. William Hill, D. D., of Winchester, one of the few surviving persons that attended on his instructions in College, from whose manuscript recollections of him large quotations will be made, partly in his own words, and partly condensed to suit the limits of this work,—says—"There was more fervour and animation in his preaching than was common in those days,—for he was always a very attractive and popular preacher, and drew crowds after him, for it was one of his peculiar properties to put out his strength in every thing he undertook, and to do nothing by halves. But still for some years his preaching seemed to take no effect, there was no awakening of sinners—arousing of cold professors, nor reclaiming of backsliders,—as the visible fruits of his labours. The troubles of the Revolutionary war were waxing worse and worse, and were drawing nigher and nigher,—so that the British army was now in the midst of his people committing desperate outrages;—and at length caused a suspension of public worship in his congregation and broke up entirely the business of the College."

Patrick Henry, the first Governor of the State under the new constitution, issued a requisition for militia for the defence of the State. The students of the College with full consent of the President, volunteered to answer this call of the Governor, one of the Trustees, and marched with their tutor J. B. Smith, a student of theology, as their captain, to the defence of the capital. With compliments from the Governor, he was sent back after the alarm was over—as able to aid more effectually in the College than in camp—while some of the students were encouraged to enter the service and others to return to their studies.

When General Greene, covering the retreat of Morgan, with his prisoners, after the battle of the Cowpens, entered Virginia in the early part of 1781, Captain William Morton of Charlotte, in about two days, called a company of his neighbours, and set out for Greene's camp. President Smith felt it his duty to offer his services, by way of encouragement to his parishioners, and joined the company in Halifax, on the evening of the first day's march. The captain, his friend, and elder in the church, with much difficulty persuaded him, exhausted in body and with blistered feet, to refrain from the fatigues of the camp, and return to cheer the families of his charge with his presence and counsels.

It is also reported that when news of the depredations of the British forces on the Chesapeake reached Prince Edward, a short time previous to the arrival of Greene, he prepared for a campaign. When Cornwallis invaded Virginia the services of the College were for a time suspended; and all able to bear arms in Prince Edward and the surrounding counties sought the camp. In this state of things it was decided that Smith should remain with the people left at home. After the capture of the invading general at York, the men returned to their homes, the College studies were resumed, and the congregations became more regular.

"The demoralizing effects of the war"—says Dr. Hill—"left religion and the church in a most deplorable condition. The Sabbath had been almost forgotten, and the public morals sadly deteriorated. A cold and lukewarm indifference was manifest in all the ministrations of the gospel throughout all that region of country, without exception, as far as known. Hampden Sidney College alone appeared to revive, and the number of students continued to increase until the rooms were as full as they well could contain." Mr. Smith's impressive manner of preaching drew after him large audiences, but with little apparent effect till about the year 1787, when—"some degree of seriousness appeared to prevail, without any extraordinary efforts, or peculiar instrumentalities, calculated to produce a general awakening, beyond the ordinary means of grace. There were very few Baptists, or Methodists, or any other religious denomination of Christians in these regions, besides Presbyterians." About this time also the Methodists and Baptists began to visit the country. James O'Kelly, a popular Methodist preacher of original genius, from North Carolina, made some appointments not far from College. One of the students by name of William Spencer became a convert, left College and commenced preaching. But his eccentric character, added to his slender abilities and small literary attainments, prevented his usefulness. His uniting with the Methodists produced no

good effect on the College students; it rather excited disgust.
O'Kelly gained some followers; but their character and standing were not such as to produce any very general effect. About
this same time Mr. John Williams, a Baptist, preached extensively in the counties of Mecklenburg, Lunenburg and Charlotte. He was possessed—" of genuine talents, ready utterance
and great fluency of speech, and was in fact a very pleasing,
impressive and popular preacher, and gentlemanly in his manners and deportment. His preaching in Lunenburg and Charlotte, bordered upon the congregation of Briery, and several
young persons became impressed under Mr. Williams' preaching." This called the attention of Mr. Smith more particularly
to that part of his charge; his meetings were more frequent
and his addresses more earnest and pungent. No general
effect was produced further than increased seriousness in the
congregation; and more prayer was offered for blessings from
on high.

The state of things in College, during the year 1787 was
peculiarly interesting; the flax was smoking; and soon burnt
into a flame. While a few children of pious parents treated
the subject of religion respectfully, yet—" of all the students
in College, about eighty in number, there was not one who was
known to be any way serious and thoughtful upon the subject
of religion; they were generally very vicious and profane, and
treated religion and religious persons with great contempt and
ridicule; though attentive to their studies and the acquisition
of knowledge." While there were none known to be " serious
and thoughtful," there were many really so—and as is usual in
such cases, each thought himself alone in his exercises, experiencing that deep feeling of solitariness which usually accom-
panies conviction of sin and danger. " I was"—says a venerable clergyman now living, one of the few that heard J. B.
Smith in Prince Edward and survive—in a letter to F. N. Watkins of Farmville—" I was born in the year 1772; I was myself seriously and deeply exercised on the subject of religion
from a child, through the instrumentality of my parents who
were pious. But I saw nothing, heard nothing like an awakening among the people, till I was a student at Hampden Sidney
a while. I went there at the age of fourteen years, the only
serious boy amongst sixty or eighty students, and was often
laughed at on account of my religious principles; but by the
grace of God, I was never ashamed on that account; but re-
proved them for their want of reverence for the authority of
God. At that time I did not think I had religion, but was
much engaged in the use of all appointed means to obtain it.
After I was there one or two sessions, I saw and heard of, for
the first time, a seriousness and deep concern in Briery congre-

gation; and about the same time, in Cumberland congregation.
Christians became greatly quickened, and awakenings amongst
the dead in sins multiplied in quick succession."

The precise time is not known of the formation of a prayer-
meeting, by Mr. Smith, consisting of the elders of the church,
but one was formed in 1786 or 1787, to meet and pray for a
special outpouring of the Spirit of God.   Many difficulties were
encountered in its formation; some plead they could not, were
not fit to pray before others, especially their minister; others
that they could pray in a small meeting, and not in a large.
But under the exhortations of their minister, and their own
sense of duty and privilege, the Elders' prayer-meeting became
a delightful place; and from holding a private meeting, they
began to hold praying circles, as they were called, in different
parts of the congregations where a few could assemble.   The
spirit of prayer and inquiry increased together.   "During the
progress of the revival in Cumberland"—says the letter to
F. N. Watkins—"in the time of vacation at the College, Messrs.
Cary Allen and William Hill went on a visit to their relations,
who had become subjects of the work of grace, and they were
deeply impressed with a sense of their lost condition, and exposure to the wrath of God."   This was in September 1787.
This visit resulted in the conversion of Allen, and ultimately in
the conversion of young Hill.   The circumstances of Allen's
awakening will be given more appropriately in the sketch of his
life.   It is necessary to state at present nothing more than, he
had been brought up correctly, was a moral youth, of eccentric
feelings and peculiar talents; that his convictions were deep,
and in fact overwhelming, and resulted in the possession of a
hope.   On his return to College to renew his studies he carried
his profession of conversion with him.   The President—"was
exceedingly fearful it was all a delusion, and put him through
the most rigid examinations, set him to reading Bellamy's True
Religion delineated and distinguished from all counterfeits, and
his Paulinus and Theron."   Allen read and bore examination
on his experience, and held to his profession of religion—and,
says Dr. Hill—"was the first student who made any public
pretensions to religion in College."

"There was another student in college"—says Dr. Hill—
"whose mind had been serious for some months before Allen
professed conversion; but who kept it a profound secret from
any one, for fear of persecution and ridicule from his wicked
associates; for he had been as wicked as any of them.   No one
had spoken to him a word upon the subject of religion, and yet
he was under deep conviction from the strivings of God's Spirit.
A pious mother who had brought him up most carefully, and
instructed him in religious things most earnestly, had been

taken from him in his twelfth year. She had taught him the necessity of attending to the salvation of the soul, had prayed with him, and for him—and after praying with him would often lay 'her hand upon his head and bless him, and would say she had strong hopes he would be a minister of gospel, at some future day.' After her death his religious instruction was neglected, and he become thoughtless, and was very careless for a time while in College. But his 'mother's counsels and admonitions would occur to his mind in the most vivid recollections. It would often be suggested to him—is this your mother's little minister, which she often prayed for? After some acts of wickedness, the thought that if his mother could be the witness of his conduct, what must she feel, would wring tears from his eyes and send him to his knees in private to pray for forgiveness for his sins.' But like many another, he would go from his knees to join again with his companions, fearing lest they should know his seriousness. Having no Bible, and wishing to read in that book he had neglected for five or six years, upon inquiry being made in a round about way, he could not hear of a single Bible among all the students. He then went to Major James Morton, the steward, and on the promise of returning it before night, got the loan of the only Bible in his house, the family Bible. This was on Saturday morning; he carried the Bible into the thick woods; and commenced reading the Gospel according to Matthew, and paused not till he had perused the whole; and near sunset, returned the Bible to Major Morton, having spent the time without refreshment, in reading and pondering the words of life. His resolution to seek God was made more firm, but he resolved to do it secretly for fear of his fellow students, unprepared to take the stand of Allen.

"There was a small boy, some years younger than myself" —says Dr. Hill—" whose father lived about six miles in the country; this youth is now the Rev. William Calhoun, living near Staunton, and I supposed then cared nothing about religion. His father was esteemed a pious elder in the church; and had several single daughters who were professors of religion. William went home every Saturday and returned to College every Monday morning. As he was setting off home, I requested him to ask his father to send me some good book upon the subject of religion, for me to read, and it should be taken care of, and returned. He delivered this message to his father, in the presence of the family. His sister Peggy, who possessed more than usual piety and intelligence, instantly replied, I have the very book he should read. Monday morning he brought me an old rusty black covered book, probably little less than a hundred years old, which was brought from Ireland, with the Scoth-Irish immigrants who settled in this part of Virginia. But a book more adapted to my case was never printed. It was *Joseph Alleine's Alarm to the Unconverted.* I did not wish that my fellow students should see me using this old rusty book, but carefully locked it up in my trunk till I had a good opportunity to read it privately. Next Saturday all my room-mates went from home, and left me alone in charge of the room." One young student, anxious for his own soul, waits on another more excited on the subject of religion, and yet neither knew the mind of the other, or ventured to speak on the subject. These youths exhibit the difficulty persons have in beginning religious conversation, even when they might conjecture that the subject would not be unwelcome. Having shut himself in his room, the young man began to read the old book with sighs and tears. His desire for food gave way to his interest; he was not seen at dinner. Repeated raps had been made at his door, and he remained in silence. At length a violent thumping at the door induced him to see who was there; and to his amazement he found an anxious soul.

"A full grown student from North Carolina walked in, and went to my bed where I had been sitting and picked up the old book I had left upon the bed, and opened and saw what it was—and stunned said—why Hill, have you been reading such a book as this? Here was one of the most critical periods of my whole life. At first I knew not what answer to give. I thought if I confessed the truth it would expose me to the contempt and ridicule of the whole College. I never was more strongly tempted than to turn the whole matter into ridicule, and treat the subject with levity; which if I had done, it would have quenched the good Spirit, which was powerfully at work with me at the time, and most probably been the leading step to my being abandoned of God, and given over to ruin. At length I replied, yes Blythe, I have been reading that good old book with deep interest, and I must confess I have neglected the subject too long, and am now determined to attend to the subject of religion more for the future. Blythe instantly blubbered into a loud cry, saying—Hill, I envy you; you may get religion;—but I never can. Would you believe it,—before I left North Carolina, I was a professor of religion and a member of the church;—but when I came here among these wicked students I locked up my Bible in the bottom of my trunk,—abandoned my profession,—forsook my God and turned my back upon my Saviour;—there can be no forgiveness for such a sinner as I am;—your state is infinitely better than mine. Conviction seized upon his mind, and he set out like the prodigal to seek his Father's forgiveness;—and lived consistently with these good beginnings. This young man was

James Blythe, afterwards the distinguished Dr. Blythe of Kentucky."

These three, Allen, Hill, and Blythe, soon found a fourth student, Clement Read, a resident graduate, who was deeply interested for his soul's salvation. They associated for conversation and exhortation, and resolved to spend a part of every Saturday afternoon in religious exercises. As yet, neither the President nor the three Professors, all of whom were members of the church, and two of them licentiates, were aware that any student was seriously inclined except Cary Allen. "Our first meeting was held near a mile from College, in a thick unbroken forest. We had a Bible with us now. Our plan was for each member to give out and sing a hymn, and read a chapter, and pray, in turns. We were raw lads at the business. Blythe, a short time before his death in my house, in alluding to this our first meeting in the woods, said jocularly, referring to myself—I heard this man make the first prayer he ever made before any other person in his life; and I much question whether the Lord ever heard such another prayer from any other person. It was literally a day of small things."

"Our next consideration was to fix the place of our next meeting; and as it might rain and prevent us from meeting in the woods, we determined to meet the next Saturday afternoon in one of our rooms in College. Procuring a room to ourselves we locked our door and commenced. Although we sung and prayed with suppressed voices, not wishing it should be known what we were about, we were overheard by some of the students, when it was noised about through every room in College, and a noisy mob was raised, which collected in the passage before our door, and began to thump at the door, and whoop, and swear, and threaten vengeance, if we did not forbear and cease all such exercises in College for the future. We had to cease, and bear the ridicule and abuse of this noisy riot, which could not be quieted until two of the Professors interfered and ordered them all to their rooms. Information of this riot was given to Mr. Smith. In the evening the College was rung to prayers. When the prayers were ended, Mr. Smith demanded the cause of the riot, and who were the leaders in it. Some of the most prominent leaders stepped forward and said, there were some of the students, who had shut themselves up in one of the rooms in College, and began singing and praying and carrying on like the Methodists, and they were determined to break it up. We had nothing to say; we were not absolutely certain that we were justifiable in introducing such exercises in College without first obtaining permission to do so."

What a scene was this! here were some youth anxious to flee from the wrath to come,—here were others in their thoughtless sinfulness determined to put an end to all unusual effort to be saved,—here was an anxious President of a College, in quelling a riot and inquiring out its cause, discovering the long sought object of his prayers, a company of praying youth among his thoughtless students. "The President's eyes"—Mr. Hill goes on to say—"filled with tears;—it was the first intimation he had that there was such seriousness in College. After a short pause he said—And has it come to this! Is it possible! Some of my students are under religious impressions !—and determined to serve their Saviour! And is it possible that there are such monsters of iniquity, such sons of Belial in College, who dare set themselves against such things ! who will neither serve God themselves, nor suffer others to do so! Then turning to the serious students, who had been the innocent occasion of all this disturbance he said to them—I rejoice, my young friends, that you have taken the stand you have;—you shall not be interrupted in your meetings for the future. Your appointment next Saturday afternoon shall be held in my parlour; and I will be with you,—conduct your meeting for you,—and render you all the assistance you may need."

The brightness of this unexpected triumph, was somewhat clouded, in the opinion of the young men, by the condition of their prayer meeting being in public. But their hearts did not fail in their trembling; they went at the appointed hour and found the parlour filled, and as they were called on in succession, each led in prayer. The President followed with a most impressive exhortation from a heart full to overflowing. "The next Saturday afternoon nearly the whole of the students came out, and many from the neighbourhood around, so that the parlour and other rooms were crowded. As the neighbourhood generally got word of what was going on in College, they all wished to attend; so we had to appoint the next meeting in the large College Hall, which was filled upon subsequent occasions. Within two weeks or thereabout, fully half of the students in College appeared deeply impressed, and under conviction for their sins. Deep impressions and concern were generally made through the neighborhood."

Prayer meetings were set up by the elders in all parts of the congregation; and the pastor, Mr. Smith, was fully employed in preaching, holding meetings for exhortation and prayer, and in conversation with persons under deep exercise of mind. Drury Lacy, a young licentiate, one of the Professors in College, entered into the work most heartily, and with thrilling tones and excited feelings urged the great truths of salvation home upon the consciences and judgment of all. Every other business appeared for a time forgotten in the all-absorbing interests of religion. The awakening in the congregations received a great impulse in every direction. Allen and Hill went, for the Christmas holidays, to visit their connexions, on Great Guinea, in Cumberland, where they had been raised; and took some of their serious, and newly awakened companions along with them. In the neighbourhood were several elders and many members of the church, belonging to the Cumberland church. The young men spent their time in holding religious meetings in the different families of their acquaintance. "To their great surprise while these meetings were going on, one of their companions in College, a resident graduate, Nash Legrand, made his appearance unexpectedly among them. He had hitherto been known only as one of the wildest and most dissipated students, and it was not known that he ever felt a serious impression of any kind. He had never broken his mind to any of us; but conviction for sin had got deep hold of his heart, which gave him no rest, night or day. It was this hidden fire which induced him to follow his fellow students to this neighbourhood." During one night at a prayer meeting at Nathan Womack's, he became hopefully converted, and was as full of joy as Cary Allen. A short memoir of his life will be necessary to give completeness to the Sketches of Virginia, and will be given in another chapter.

Similar scenes were witnessed in different directions from the College; and by the commencement of the year 1788, there was a general awakening in Prince Edward, Cumberland and Charlotte counties. The professors of religion awaked as from a sleep, and put on the armour of godliness; some declared themselves convinced their former profession had been a lifeless one, and professed conversion anew. The news of these interesting matters spread; and many came from a distance to witness the wonders God was working among the people in a large section of country of which the College was the centre, and Smith appeared the controlling mind.

"The Rev. Henry Pattillo, a venerable minister, who had been a pupil and associate of Samuel Davies, in his youth, and who now resided in Granville county, North Carolina, hearing of this work, came over to Virginia, bringing a number of his young people with him, to spend a week or two in Prince Edward and Charlotte, who caught the infection, and carried the sacred fire home with them, from whom it was communicated to others, and a glorious revival broke out in Granville and Caswell counties, North Carolina.

The Rev. James Mitchell, who had been tutor in College, and was now the successor, as well as son-in-law of Rev. David Rice, came from Bedford to witness and join in the work of grace. He became the instrument of a like precious work that spread through Bedford and Campbell.

Rev. William Graham, President of Liberty Hall in Rockbridge county, went over by invitation to attend a communion season in Briery, and took with him two students, Archibald Alexander and Samuel Wilson. "On the Saturday evening," —says Mr. Calhoun, in his letter to Watkins—"of the communion Sabbath, Mr. Graham arrived at old Mr. Morton's, a house in which many Christians usually lodged on such occasions; and on that night, or next morning led in family prayer. The apparent tone of his feelings did not exactly suit the ardour of some of the young converts, and they requested Mr. Smith not to let him preach." Not the first instance of hasty judgment in young professors, who may be truly Christians; under the influence of excitement, and with their warmth of feeling on a new subject, the young converts sometimes feel as if old Christians needed converting over again. Mr. Calhoun tells an interesting case of this kind. "Mr. James Allen, afterwards an elder in Briery, told me he had lived without religion till after he was the head of a family, having a wife and some children. When it pleased God to open his blind eyes, and show him his lost condition, his convictions were awful; and increased to such a degree that his spirits were dried up, and his bodily frame greatly weakened. When it was morning he expected to be in hell before night; and when night came he had no expectation of seeing another morning, anticipating the most fearful doom. At length in the use of appointed means of grace, it pleased God by his Spirit to give him understanding in the Scriptures, which exhibit Jesus Christ the Son of God, as the only and all-sufficient Saviour of helpless, ruined man. When he was enabled to believe understandingly his joy was as great as his terror had been. After a day or two of much comfort, he began to think of his old father, and fearing he had never been converted, though an elder in the church for many years, he resolved to go and tell him his experience, hoping his old father would thereby be led to see how far he came short of real piety. Accordingly he went to his father's house, and after taking him into a private room related his experience. While he was relating his exercise of mind, he saw the tears running down his father's cheeks, from which he hoped the old gentleman was coming under convictions. When he ended his statement, his father asked him if he had finished his narrative. He said yes. The old patriarch said to him—My son, I hope God has in his great goodness and mercy converted your soul;—but you are only a babe in Christ,—you have much to experience and learn yet. He then gave his son a sketch of his conversion in early life,—and his Christian experience down to old age. While the father was relating his own experience, the son was filled with the utmost shame and mortification, that he should have thought of teaching his old father, who, he now saw, knew a hundred times more about religious experience than he did."

As great a change took place after hearing Mr. Graham a few times. "As soon"—says Dr. Hill—"as Mr. Graham saw the state of things, and entered into that atmosphere, his heart caught fire; and during the occasion he exhibited from the pulpit some of the great and happy efforts of which he was capable."—Mr. Calhoun relates—"After the communion services were ended, Mr. Graham preached from Isaiah xl. 1st and 2d, Comfort ye, comfort ye my people, saith your God. Speak ye comfortably to Jerusalem, and cry unto her that her warfare is accomplished, and her iniquity is pardoned." Like Lacy's sermon in the grove in Lexington, this was talked of while the generation, that heard it, lived, unwritten, unwritable, but ever to be remembered by Christians. Mr. Graham returned with an overflowing heart; the two young men also deeply interested; and was rejoiced to see in a little time the work of grace in his own charge which spread through the congregations in that part of the Valley. It is reported, that, previous to his time, the two Presidents had felt something of the spirit of rivalry, which they could not entirely conceal; but after this meeting, like true yoke-fellows they set themselves to the work of God in the gospel. The following letters give some interesting particulars of the revival.

Extract from a letter from the Rev. John B. Smith, of Hampden Sidney, Virginia, to a Lady in Philadelphia, dated October 6, 1788.

"The old gentleman, my father, will give you some account of God's gracious kindness to me and my congregation. We have had an unmerited work of God amongst us. Young and old have been generally excited to attend to the great salvation. Many sweet young disciples, ten and twelve years old, seem affectionately engaged in God's service. Some old sinners have deserted the camp of Satan in all appearance; one, fifty years old, a violent opposer of religion all his days. Another, who for thirty-five years which he had lived, had never so much as attempted to pray but once; and several deistically inclined, are with us, monuments of God's amazing grace. I find my heart enlarged, and my soul engaged in God's service; but have often reason to be astonished at my wretched unfruitfulness in my own exercises. Yesterday we had the Lord's supper administered, and God was with us. I felt his power, I think, and glory to his name for his unmerited grace. Mrs. Smith is very lively. Our young Christians, however, I think, begin to complain much of inward corruptions which they did not suspect at first. God's way is to try us with light and shade in turn. O may you be always in the light, more and more, till the shadows flee in perfect everlasting day. God bless you, my dear madam, and be your strength and stay in the decline of life, and open your way at last, comfortably and clearly, into everlasting rest. This is the earnest prayer of yours, affectionately,

JOHN B. SMITH."

Copy of a letter from the Rev. Robert Smith, of Pequea, to the same Lady, dated October 26, 1788.

"*Dear Madam*—A few days ago I returned from Virginia, where I preached five Sabbaths, one at Alexandria, and four for my son, besides several week days.

The half was not told me of the display of God's power and grace among them; no, not the tenth part. I have seen nothing equal to it for extensive spread, power, and spiritual glory, since the years '40 and '41. The work has spread for an hundred miles, but by far the most powerful and general in John Smith's congregations, which take in part of three counties.

Not a word scarcely about politics; but all religion in public and private. They run far and near to sermons, sacraments and societies. They have six or seven praying societies, which meet every Wednesday and Saturday evenings, and at College on Sabbath evenings also. Numbers of the students have been convinced, and several of them hopefully converted.

We ordained two of them to the work of the ministry, who have been preachers, and took two more upon trial. Clever fellows, indeed. Others are preparing for the work, among them a young man, an apprentice to my son Robert, the doctor, a cousin to Betsy Smith, a praying lad. Betsy Smith and her father, Colonel Nash, grow apace in piety, and some of the Colonel's negroes. Poor things, they have the best of masters. The blessed work has spread among people of every description, high and low, rich and poor, learned and unlearned, orthodox and heterodox, sober and rude, white and black, young and old; especially the youth, whom it seems to have seized generally. Two hundred and twenty-five hopeful communicants have been added to the Lord's table among John Smith's people, in the space of eighteen months, chiefly of the young people.

When they go to sermons or societies, they commonly go in companies, either conversing on spiritual subjects or singing hymns. When they arrive at the place of worship, they enter the house and sing hymns till the minister enters.

Such sweet singing I never heard in all my life. Dear

young Christians, how engaged, how heavenly, how spiritually and innocently they look and speak. I have seen an hundred wet cheeks, some deeply penetrated with convictions, some fainting with love-sickness as it were, in the Saviour's arms, and others rejoicing for the day of God's power and grace, all under the same sermon. The rejoicings were much among some old disciples.

We dispensed the sacrament of the Supper at each of my son's congregations.

The Presbytery met the week before the last sacrament. We were eight in all, including the two that were ordained at that time. All tarried till after the Sabbath, and most of the ministers were exceedingly engaged in their work. Every week-day we had two sermons besides other exercises. The concourse of people on the Sabbath was large. Beside the morning sermon and serving the tables, which lasted till near sundown, they had sermon almost all day out of doors. O, it was a most sweet, solemn, and powerful day.

I shall just mention one particular which was very striking and pleasing to me. After the tables were served, I stepped a few perches below the meeting-house, where there was a cluster of black communicants standing, weeping and rejoicing, and an old negro man, addressing them in such strains as these : "We poor negroes were miserable, wretched creatures, taken captives and brought from our country in bondage here to men, and what was worse, slaves to sin and the devil. But, O ! the goodness of God to us poor black folks. He has made us free men and women in Christ, joint heirs with his own Son. He has sent his servant to preach this gospel to us, who takes us to the Lord's table with himself, and calls us his brothers and sisters in Christ ! O ! the love of Christ to us poor black folks ! Our colour is black ; but his blood washes our souls whiter than snow ! We shall live among the redeemed forever with the Lord. O ! the love of Christ to us poor black people ! O ! his service is sweet ! it is very sweet. Hold on in it, hold on till you get the prize."

When I heard and saw, my head was a fountain, and I stood astonished. Indeed, I could wish frequently to see such a sight, and hear such an address.

So far as I had an opportunity of conversing and discovering, the exercises of people appear to be lively, pure, clear and spiritual.

When I went and heard, and saw, I felt richer in my mind than if I had seen my son mounted upon a throne ; yet I confess I felt several pangs for my beloved child, lest he should wear his life to an end too soon. He had certainly the work of three men to do. All the time of College vacation he will be riding to sacraments, and preaching every where. For the importunities of the people are pressing, and his desires are as strong."

The character, extent, and effects of this revival—the first of any extent in Virginia after the time of Davies, are matters of more than usual importance in the history of the Virginia Synod, and the other Synods south and west, that may trace their origin to Hanover Presbytery.

1. THE CHARACTER.— President Smith's preaching, says Dr. Hill,—" was of the most animating, pungent, practical character, feeling close for the conscience, and applying truth home to the heart. His appointments were very frequent, not only on the Sabbath, but during the week-days also. He never would permit the least noise or disorder or crying out in the worship of God, although it was with difficulty sometimes he could repress it. If at any time there was something of the sort commenced, he would instantly stop speaking and say—'You must compose your feelings, my brethren. God is not the author of confusion, but of peace in all his churches.' Often upon such occasions he would give out a verse or two of some hymn for the people to sing, till silence and composure was produced, and then go on with his discourse. When it became generally known that he would not suffer such things, the most powerful impressions were suppressed and held in. It has often occurred that when the congregation was dismissed, several would be seen fastened to their seats, unable to arise, through the overpowering effects of either joy or distress, and had to be assisted away by their friends. If the least encouragment had been given, he could readily have had as much outcrying, shouting, and things of the kind, as is often seen. In that part of his charge in Guinea, in Cumberland, there was some disorder in worship, particularly when Mr. Smith was not present. The Methodists had much preaching in the neighbourhood, and encouraged the expression of feelings by outbursts; and here also Allen and Legrand had experienced their extraordinary conversion; and the preacher that supplied them most, Mr. Lacy, was then young in the ministry, and not so completely at home in the matter as President Smith, and for a time hesitated about the proper course to be pursued. But the tendency to outbreaking of passionate feeling and all violent exercises were carefully checked by Mr. Smith. They never had credit in the Virginia Synod, which was formed during this revival, and took its immediate impression from Smith and Graham and the standard of feeling by them approved, as it did its more remote from that eminent servant of God, Samuel Davies.

Of the instruction that gave character to the revival, Mr.

Calhoun says—"Mr. Smith instituted prayer-meetings, preached often, and with great zeal. His method was plain, practical and very fervid; but perfectly free from ranting. The Calvinistic doctrines were conspicuous in his sermons. He varied his subjects as occasion required. Sometimes he preached the terrors of the law. But dwelt more on the love of God to a lost world, as manifested by the gift of his Son to die for our redemption. When on this subject he would make powerful appeals, to all the generous and noble feelings of human nature, to induce the careless part of his audience to close in with the gracious purposes of their God towards them. And to encourage the convicted and desponding sinner, he would set forth, in an alluring manner and glowing colours, the pity and compassion of Christ, his benevolence, his readiness to forgive sins, the efficacy of his atoning blood, the perfection of his righteousness for their justification, and his successful intercession in heaven as their High Priest, in their behalf. Sometimes he preached very searching and trying sermons to guard his people against delusion. He was lucid in his exposition of the Scriptures, and exhibited the doctrines clearly and in a practical manner. His address was good."

Dr. Hoge, who was President of Hampden Sidney, some years after Mr. Smith, speaks of him as a minister—in page 414 of his printed sermons—"Remember your Smith, a name dear to thousands in our country, and still dear to numbers in this audience. He was indeed a burning and a shining light. And it was the privilege of some of you to rejoice in his light —to live under his efficacious ministry; and this must have been a distinguished privilege. I have, if I mistake not, heard greater orators,—preachers of more profound meditation, of a more brilliant imagination, and superior to him in any particular qualification, unless the fervour of his piety be an exception. But a preacher possessing every ministerial qualification in a degree so eminent, I have never known. Nor do I ever expect again to hear a preacher, whose discourses will be equally calculated for the learned and the unlearned, the rich and the poor, the devout Christian and the abandoned profligate—in a word every character and description of man. I need hardly observe to this audience that he was the most distinguished instrument in promoting the late glorious revival in our church. A revival which is said to have begun under his ministry, and the fruits of which are still visible in our churches. Methinks I still see him stand the accredited ambassador of the great King of kings and Lord of lords, while every feature and every muscle of his face, every word and action, as well as the lightning of his eyes, seem to bespeak a soul on fire. Remember them which have the rule over you, who have spoken unto you the word of

God, whose faith follow, considering the end of their conversation."

The manner and character of Mr. Smith's preaching has been stated in giving the character of the revival, because it is well known that the character and manner of the preacher— taking manner in its widest sense—who is the leader or principal instrument in a revival, give tone and character to the revival, for good or for evil. The Tennents in Jersey, the Blairs in Pennsylvania, Robinson and Davies in Virginia—and then again Smith and Graham in Virginia, stamped their own impress on the work of God. Mr. Smith was extraordinary in possessing all ministerial qualifications in a happy medium, and no one qualification in an absorbing degree, consequently there were no mannerisms in the revival, or among his pupils. Calvinistic in his doctrines according to the Confession of Faith, he made the grand doctrines of the gospel speak in men's ears an alarming message, which the Holy Spirit sent to the heart. Retentive in memory, strong in argument, powerful in persuasion, having Scripture at command, he was a ready preacher, feeling what was fitting the occasion. Open-hearted, liberal and compassionate, easy in deportment, with friends often facetious, sometimes witty, he was slow in making friendships, and still slower in abandoning friends of his choice. Mr. Calhoun says—"he was lean, of a middling stature, his hair very black, his mouth large, his cheeks lank, his cheek bones visible but not protruding much; I think his chin projected forward, and was broad not sharp—his eyes strongly expressed the emotions of his mind." A lady now living who was a convert under his preaching—says "his eyes were blue when in conversation with you; but when aroused in speaking they appeared dark and piercing." His heart was so set upon his work that he often overtasked his body. Mr. Smith had—says Dr. Hill—"but a slender frame, and was of a very feeble constitution, and exerted himself beyond his strength; and would often go into the pulpit when some of his best friends said he ought to be in bed. Once he ruptured a blood-vessel and fell in his pulpit, and had to be taken and carried home. At another time he was preaching in a private house, standing by a large open window in warm weather, when he ruptured another vessel, and putting his head out of the window, he discharged so much blood, that none of his congregation expected ever to hear him preach again. His physicians and friends seriously advised him to quit preaching; but in a few weeks he pursued his former course as though nothing had occurred. The ardency of his pursuits, and the buoyancy of his nature gave such an elasticity to his feeble frame as soon overcome common dangers and frailties." Those who remember how much we are influenced by small things will know how to give their proper weight to these small matters respecting Mr. Smith, as he was standing forth God's chosen instrument for a great and good work for generations of men.

"He was very careful to supply those who were recently awakened with books suitable to their occasions,—such as— Alleine's Alarm, Baxter's Call, Doddridge's Rise and Progress, Boston's Fourfold State, Bellamy's True Religion delineated and distinguished from all counterfeits, and his Paulinus and Theron, Dickerson's Letters, Willison on the Shorter Catechism, and Sacramental Meditations, and especially Edwards on Religious Affections. There were few of his young members who had not read more or less of these authors; and some of them the whole of them.

"He advised those who were awakened not to be too hasty in professing conversion; and urged them to examine the foundations of their hopes well before they entertained a hope they had made their peace with God, stating it was a dreadful thing to be deceived in a matter of such importance. Generally months, and in some instances a year or more was suffered to pass before they were received into the church. No anxious seat, nor inquiry meetings were used or thought of in those days: but no opportunity was suffered to pass by without talking to such persons in the most plain and faithful manner. In these days nothing was talked much about but religion, and whenever friends met, the first thing they said was—How are you coming on?—what difficulties do you find in your way?

2. THE EXTENT OF THE REVIVAL.—It has been stated that all the congregations in Cumberland, Prince Edward, and Charlotte, were revived. The awakening was very general throughout those counties; and the congregations were enlarged to cover a great portion of the whole country. These counties were supplied mostly by the officers of College and Mr. Sankey. By the instrumentality of Mr. Mitchell, it extended to Bedford and Campbell, and was felt extensively in those counties where there are still remaining some of the subjects of the work. Mr. Graham was blessed in carrying on the good work in Liberty Hall, and seeing it spread over Rockbridge very generally; and Legrand spread it through nearly all the counties up and down the Valley. Mr. Pattillo rejoiced in its influence in Granville and Caswell counties, North Carolina, among people, some of whom had emigrated from Virginia, and had been hearers of Davies. James McGready on his way to Carolina, tarried a while in Prince Edward, and went on his way with a burning heart to Orange and Guilford, and witnessed there a great display of God's grace. "Persons of all ranks in society, of all ages, both old and young, became the

subjects of this work"—says Dr. Hill speaking of part of Cumberland, of Charlotte, and Prince Edward—"so that there was scarcely a magistrate upon the bench, or a lawyer at the bar in Prince Edward and Charlotte, but became members of the church. Young men and women were generally heartily engaged in the work, so that it was now as rare a thing to find one who was not religious, as it had been formerly to find one that was. The frivolities and amusements once so prevalent, were all abandoned, and gave place to singing, serious conversation, and prayer-meetings—very few comparatively, who appeared to become serious, afterwards lost their impressions, or apostatized; and the cases which did occur were chiefly those who never became members of the church. An apostate member of the church was a rare instance indeed. Among the number who did profess religion, no instance is recollected of extravagance or fanaticism, or which exhibited any of the wild and visionary symptoms which have so often attended other revivals, and brought them into contempt. This was attributable to the great caution, vigilance and judgment displayed by Mr. Smith in conducting the revival."

It is remarkable that the congregations on the north side of James River, the theatre of Robinson and Davies, were not visited in this awakening. There is no record of a single neighbourhood revived; on them there was no dew; but preacher and people, who had seen wonders in former days, were left in their barrenness and desolation, and wastings and decay.

In the upper end of the Valley of Virginia, the work in its main features was such as has been described in Charlotte, Prince Edward, and Cumberland. Some of all ages and classes were brought into the fold of God; of this, an account will more properly be found in the memoir of Mr. Graham.

In Bedford and Campbell, there were neighbourhoods of which a similar account might have been given. The case of James Turner of Bedford, requires a special memoir.

The influence of the revival in North Carolina was as cheering and extensive as in Virginia, as may be seen by the Sketches of North Carolina.

3. THE EFFECTS of this revival were precious, incalculably precious, in the great numbers brought into the church, and the consequent good influence on society;—and in the number of ministers it brought into the Lord's vineyard, by whose means the wide bounds of the Virginia Synod received important accessions of churches, especially in the wide regions of beautiful Kentucky. The influence on the churches has never been lost; succeeding revivals and refreshings have perpetuated the good feeling and piety, and the estimated standard of religion

fashioned and reared in those times of excitement. Very few of the individuals, then gathered into the church, remain in the land of the living; and many of their descendants have emigrated to the great South and West; but the traditions of the wonderful doings of God for the salvation of sinners in the years 1788, 1789, are interwoven with the recollections of the people, who, sharing the blessings of grace in their youth, in that favoured time and place, lived to old age adorning society and the church, by the exhibition of Christian character, the more lovely as the gates of heaven drew near. " It is not an uncommon thing"—says Dr. Hill—" after a great excitement on the subject of religion in any place, for it to be followed by a season of deadness and declension, and a falling away of many. It was not so here;—there were no long protracted meetings, in which ministers and members exerted themselves to exhaustion, and then had to relax, to recruit their strength, while the fowls of the air were plucking up the good seed which had been sown. The efforts here used were common means, diligently and judiciously employed, and perseveringly pursued, without relaxation or abatement. It is confidently believed that the subjects of no revival, especially one embracing so many, ever lived more consistently with their profession, and persevered more tenaciously to the end of their days. This gave a character to the Presbyterian Church to the south for vital, exemplary piety, which has pervaded several States, and given a tone to religious exercises far and wide."

A number of young men, members of College and subjects of this work of grace, entered the ministry. From Hampden Sidney came William Hill, Nash Legrand, Clement Read, Cary Allen, James Blythe, and William Calhoun, into the Presbyterian Church, two of whom are still living, and all of whom have memorials; Mr. Charles, leaving the College without making a profession, afterwards became a minister in the Episcopal Church; and Mr. Abner Erly, without uniting with the church in College, afterwards became a minister in the Methodist Church. Others that were members of College at the same time became elders in the Presbyterian Church, as Dr. James Jones, of Nottoway, and Mr. Stephen Trent of Cumberland, and probably others. Many young people not connected with the College became office-bearers in the church, and some entered the ministry.

The names of those that during, or in consequence of this revival, as it was conducted by Mr. Graham, entered the ministry, are more properly given in connexion with the memoir of that man. They are inscribed in the records of the Presbyterian Church; their doings are entwined in the noblest efforts of God's people for about half a century.

With the close of this revival, which continued in his congregations between two and three years, the labours of President Smith, in connexion with the College, closed; and his unwearied pastoral duties were drawing to an end. His multiplied appointments to preach, in his extended charge, requiring frequent and long absences from home, necessarily drew off his attention from the duties of College. Complaints at length reached his ears. Preferring the work of the ministry in such delightful circumstances, and unwilling to be the cause or object of complaint, in July 1788, he informed the Board of Trustees that he designed removing to the neighbourhood to live upon a farm he had purchased for a residence. The Board requested him to continue President of the College, although removed from College grounds; and appointed Drury Lacy, who had been his alumnus, Vice-President. Not feeling satisfied with his connexion with College, he in the year 1789 resigned the Presidency and gave himself entirely to the work of the ministry, after having served the College more than thirteen years, about ten of which he was its laborious presiding officer; on whom devolved much of the labour of instruction.

During the trying scenes of the Revolution, every man was irresistibly drawn to engage in politics; in the domestic circle, the principles and acts of government were discussed; and the sacred desk uttered the principles of law and justice drawn from the divine word. Ministers felt themselves called upon to cheer their congregations in their efforts for liberty, by the strong truths of Revelation, and bear up their sinking spirits by confidence in God's kind and overruling government. If the Presbyterian ministers sometimes dwelt less upon the peculiarities of the gospel of mercy, than upon God's sustaining the cause of truth, in the persons of an oppressed people, they plead the distress of the times, and found an apology, in the hearts of their congregations. Mr. Smith, it has been stated, took an active part in the warlike scenes of the Revolution; he also gave his opinion on political subjects. In the memorable doings of Hanover Presbytery, in her various memorials to the Legislature, he was a leader; of some portion of the papers, he is supposed to be the penman; in all of them, he fully agreed; they will remain forever monuments of patriotism and intellect.

When the bill to provide for the support of religion, commonly known as the General Assessment Bill, was engrossed for its third reading in 1784, there was every prospect that it would become the law of the land. It was advocated by great talents and splendid oratorical powers. Patrick Henry exerted himself to carry it through the House, and made it many friends. Before the final decision in 1785, Mr. Henry became

Governor of the State. When the bill was taken up in the committee of the whole, Mr. Smith appeared as one of the committee of the Presbytery of Hanover, and desired to be heard
on a memorial from the Presbytery against the bill. Permission was granted, and Mr. Smith addressed the committee, and
took part in the discussion which was continued for three days.
When the question was called the bill was lost in the committee
by a majority of three votes. Dr. Hill says—"Alexander
White, a lawyer of great intelligence, who was a delegate from
Frederick county,—and who afterwards filled high offices of
trust under Washington,—declared—"when he returned that
he thought that debate on the part of Smith one of the ablest
and most interesting that he had ever listened to; and that he
thought Smith deserved the victory he had gained." In. this
case the minister had the same advantage over his adversary,
that Patrick Henry had over his, when he plead his famous
cause in Hanover, the popular feeling and voice. One petition,
before the House, in opposition to the bill, had two thousand
names attached. And one opponent, James Madison, was himself a host. Yet to have triumphed in any debate against
Patrick Henry, was no mean honour.

Mr. Smith and Mr. Henry had hitherto been friendly; Mr.
Smith had been swayed by his powerful oratory; and probably
their friendship was not injured by this collision. But a circumstance afterwards occurred which separated these great
men. In September 1787, the Federal Constitution was sent
out for the consideration of the people. The States acted independently in their vote upon the ratification. The Convention of the State of Virginia, which determined that question,
met in Richmond, June 1788. Patrick Henry opposed its
adoption with all his powers. While the subject was before
the people, Henry declared himself a candidate for the Convention, and appointed a day to meet the people of Prince
Edward at the Court House, and address them on the imperfections of that instrument and show the ground of his fears.
Mr. Smith resolved to be present, as the Court House is but
about a mile from the College, and confront him, by defending the proposed Constitution. On the given day, Mr. Smith
was summoned to visit a dying lady in his congregation, and
could not attend. An immense concourse of people assembled, and listened to the powerful attack of Mr. Henry; there
was no reply. A young gentleman, a member of Mr. Smith's
family, took down the speech in short-hand. In a short time
there was public speaking in the College Hall; as usual, there
was a large assemblage; among others Mr. Henry came to
listen and encourage. One of the best speakers, without any
previous announcement, delivered Mr. Henry's speech, at the

Court House, on the Federal Constitution; his respondent delivered a speech prepared by Mr. Smith, in defence of the Constitution, and in reply to Mr. Henry's objections.   Mr. Henry was taken by surprise, and offended; and complained to Mr. Smith, at the conclusion of the exercises, for the unjustifiable advantage taken of him on the occasion.   Mr. Smith contended there had been no advantage, unless the speech had been incorrectly reported; in that case he would make amends. Mr. Henry complimented the correctness of the stenographer, but complained of the abrupt introduction of the subject, the tartness of the reply, and the appearance of an attempt to expose him before that large audience.   Mr. Smith replied, that the speech at the Court House was made to the public, and that it was well known a reply was intended.   If a correct report of the Court House speech had been presented, there could be no complaint lodged against the reply.   Mr. Henry was not satisfied; and from being a regular hearer of Smith, withdrew entirely from his auditory.   How far this alienation had influence to bring about the discontent with the President, or led to the investigation in the succeeding year, whether improper means were not used to proselyte students to a particular sect, may not be of much importance now to inquire.   But this is evident in the life of the great statesman and orator, that his acquaintance with religious truth, and eminent ministers, was greater than his biographer has very distinctly set forth, probably for want of documents; and although he may have felt something of the influence that went over the country in consequence of the French Revolution, yet, in the closing scenes of life, youthful impressions under Davies, manly emotions under Smith and Waddell, were ripened into deep, and we trust, saving convictions of the truth and excellency of the gospel as the word of God.   "Here"—said he, holding up the Bible—"is a book worth more than all the other books that were ever printed:— yet it is my misfortune never to have found time to read it with the proper attention and feeling till lately.   I trust in the mercy of heaven, that it is not yet too late."   A letter to his daughter under date of August 20th, 1796, as given by Mr. Wirt, his biographer,—he says—"I have long learned the little value which is to be placed on popularity, acquired by any other way than virtue; and I have also learned, that it is often obtained by other means.   The view which the rising greatness of our country presents to my eyes is greatly tarnished by the general prevalence of Deism; which with me is but another name for vice and depravity.   I am, however, much consoled by reflecting that the religion of Christ has, from its first appearance in the world, been attacked in vain, by all the wits, philosophers, and wise ones, aided by every power of man, and its triumph has been complete. What is there in the wit, or wisdom of the present deistical writers or professors, that can compare them with Hume, Shaftsbury, Bolingbroke, and others? and yet these have been confuted, and their fame is decaying; insomuch that the puny efforts of Paine are thrown in to prop their tottering fabric, whose foundations cannot stand the test of time. Amongst other strange things said of me, I hear it is said by the deists that I am one of their number; and indeed that some good people think I am no Christian. This thought gives me much more pain than the appellation of tory; because I think religion of infinitely higher importance than politics; and I find much cause to reproach myself, that I have lived so long, and have given no decided and public proofs of my being a Christian. But, indeed, my dear child, this is a character which I prize far above all this world has or can boast. And amongst all the handsome things I hear said of you, what gives me the greatest pleasure is, to be told of your piety and steady virtue." And how touching is the remark he made of himself in the Court House yard in Charlotte, April, 1799, when a successful candidate for the Legislature, less than two months before his death. An opponent asked the people why they followed Mr. Henry—Mr. Henry is not a god!—"No," exclaimed Mr. Henry, who heard the remark—"No, indeed, my friend; I am but a poor worm of the dust—as fleeting and unsubstantial as the shadow of the cloud that flies over your fields, and is remembered no more." On the 6th of June, Patrick Henry was no more an inhabitant of this world;—but his memory will live with his country.

Of the few papers drawn by the pen of Dr. Smith, there is one in the records of Hanover Presbytery, that may be read with interest for its own worth, as well as the circumstances in which it was written. Briery, April 2d, 1791.—"Whereas reports have prevailed that many irregularities are tolerated in the churches under our charge on the north side of James River, which we conceive to be incompatible with the purity of the Christian religion,—*Resolved, &c.* (that a committee of enquiry consisting of McRoberts and Lacy be appointed).

"*Resolved*, that Mr. Smith prepare a resolution to be laid before Presbytery, respecting the objects of discipline as necessary to be attended to by us, with particular reference to these reports; and that he produce it on Monday.

"Monday, April 4th, 1791.—Mr. Smith produced the folresolution, which being approved was adopted by the Presbytery:

"The Lord Jesus Christ, the great Head of the Church, having given himself for it that he might sanctify and cleanse it, and present it to himself a glorious, unspotted church, holy and without blemish, hath instituted means and ordinances to effect this gracious design; published his will in sacred laws, by obedience to which his people are distinguished as his chosen, peculiar people, separate from the world lying in wickedness, and zealous of good works; ordained a strict and holy discipline to be observed as a check on all false professors of his name; and appointed officers to superintend the execution of his gracious plan until he come. This Presbytery, therefore, impressed with an awful sense of their duty, as servants accountable to their great Master, and with a tender concern for the immortal souls committed to their pastoral care, do hereby unanimously resolve, that they will steadily adhere to that discipline which the word of God hath enjoined and our church adopted in its native strictness and simplicity; that they will neither hold Christian nor ministerial communion with those who acknowledge Christ in name only, whilst in works they deny him. Nor is this resolution intended to operate merely against the more atrocious and profligate works of darkness, but also against the equally dangerous and ensnaring wickedness, a more specious form of politeness and liberality of sentiment,—against the indulgence of the fashionable follies and amusements of life,—against gaming and playing at cards and hazard, that vice of covetousness which is idolatry,—against horse-racing and its concomitant dissipations, so contrary to that redemption of time enjoined upon Christians,—against those meetings for mirthful follies and dancings prohibited under the name of revellings, in the New Testament,—and against those levities in equipage, fashionable visitings and dress, which are condemned as the pride of life.

"Upon the whole, therefore, as we are commanded not to be conformed to the world consisting in the lust of the flesh, the lust of the eye, and the pride of life, but to live soberly, righteously, and godly, and to come out and be separate from the men of this world, and from its opinions, fashions, maxims, follies and habits,—we do hereby solemnly declare it to be our resolution to exclude from our communion those graceless church officers and graceless church members who indulge themselves in any of the practices above referred to, or who neglect the sacred observance of the Sabbath, or the duties of family religion. It was ordered that a copy of this resolution be read in the congregations of each individual minister."

Mr. Smith soon left the Presbytery; but the inquiry instituted did not end for some years. The ministers on the "north side of James River," were Todd, Waddell, Irvine, and Blair. After some letters had passed, in the year 1794, the Presbytery received explanations which satisfied the brethren to drop the inquiry.

In the spring of 1791, Mr. Smith was sent from Hanover Presbytery as delegate to the General Assembly, which met in Philadelphia. During his stay in that city he preached in the Presbyterian church in Pine street, which was then vacant, with great acceptance; an unanimous call was immediately made out for him to become their pastor, and met with encouragement from Mr. Smith. The news filled his congregation with consternation; the people could neither believe the fact, nor imagine the cause of his wishing a removal. The Presbytery of which he was a leading member listened to the call with great unwillingness. At a meeting at Concord, Campbell county, July 29th, 1791, the records say—"A call directed to Mr. Smith was delivered to Presbytery, from the Third Presbyterian Church in the city of Philadelphia, generally known by the name of Pine Street. And Mr. Smith being acquainted with the import of that call, and the papers accompanying it, applied for advice to the Presbytery. They having therefore spent a considerable time in deliberating upon the matter, deferred the further consideration of it till to-morrow." On the next day Mr. Smith was not present, having on account of the situation of his family returned home. The remaining members, Messrs. McRoberts, James Mitchell, William Mahon and Drury Lacy,— "having seriously weighed the consequences of the call put into their hands by the Third Presbyterian Church in the city of Philadelphia, in order to be presented to Mr. Smith, agreed to present the said call and papers accompanying it, to him for his consideration; but at the same time inform Mr. Smith, that they do not as yet see their way clear to give their approbation or allowance for him to accept the said call, even in case he should see fit to accept of it any future time; but that they are induced to put it into his hands for consideration solely on account of that deference and respect which is due to his own request, and the application of the congregation which has presented their call to him." This decision, or rather minute, was satisfactory to none of the parties concerned; all preferred something more decisive; and the pastor was evidently inclined to the removal. At a meeting of the Presbytery, called for the purpose, held at Hampden Sidney, —"A motion was made for reviewing the minute of last Presbytery respecting the call put into Mr. Smith's hands, from Pine Street Church, as he complained that the limitation in the body of that minute prevented him from determining in what manner to proceed. The Presbytery therefore, upon a review of the subject, agreed to dissolve the limitation, and to commit the call to his consideration without any restriction. The Presbytery then appointed Mr. McRoberts to attend at Briery on the second Sabbath in October to cite Mr. Smith

and that congregation to appear before the Presbytery, at
their next meeting, to show the reasons for or against his
accepting the call from Pine Street congregation. And Mr.
Lacy was appointed to attend at Cumberland on the same day,
to cite that congregation and Mr. Smith for the purposes cited
above." At a meeting of the Presbytery, held at Cub Creek,
October 29th, 1791, the matter came to an issue as by the
following record.—"Mr. Smith and his congregations after
every step had been regularly taken, appeared before Presbytery, and the call from Pine Street congregation, which had
been put in Mr. Smith's hands for consideration, being read,
he declared his acceptance of the same; whereupon the Presbytery having heard the parties agreed that he be translated."

The next record is—"An application was made to Presbytery from Cumberland, Briery and Cub Creek congregations
by their representatives for leave to prosecute a call for the
Rev. William Graham of Lexington Presbytery, in the county
of Rockbridge, which was granted." This was done in compliance with a request from the Board of Trustees, who, upon
the resignation of the President, were looking around for a
successor. Messrs. McRoberts and Legrand were appointed a
committee—"to write to the Rev. William Graham to point
out to him the importance of his accepting the call." As soon
as the tie that bound Mr. Smith to them was dissolved, the
congregations and trustees selected the ablest man in the
Synod for his successor.

On the same day the pastoral relation was dissolved, Mr.
Smith applied—"for a dismission from this Presbytery in order
to join the Presbytery of Philadelphia, which was granted."
He immediately removed to Philadelphia, where his reception
was equal to his worth. His departure from Virginia was an
unceasing cause of lamentation, while any of his flock, who
knew his worth, continued to meet in the places associated with
his presence. But there was a cause for this sudden and apparently strange removal from a place of extraordinary usefulness and undoubted attachment; and this was *debt*. Mr.
Smith's salary from his Presidency and pastoral office, was
small; his family was increasing in numbers and consequently
in expense;—his labours during the revival called off his attention from worldly matters;—and as a consequence his debts
began to accumulate. On his removal from College grounds he
purchased a farm, hoping to get some aid for his family; and
became involved for the purchase money. His elders did not
look into his matters; and he felt unwilling to call attention to
his private affairs; and the inattention of the one and the
delicacy of the other, led to difficulties that caused the separation. There was, in the neighbourhood, a man who had money

at command, professing great friendship for Mr. Smith. He offered him loans in all his straits, and took security which at last opened the eyes of the borrower. He could not pay his debts and keep his farm; and without his farm he could not be sustained in Prince Edward. The offer from Philadelphia met his necessities, and he embraced it as a providential refuge. When the congregation came to know the true state of their pastor's embarrassment, their high estimation of his services, added to a feeling that perhaps they had not sufficiently looked into the temporal concerns of him who was sacrificing all for them, the elders came forward and offered cheerfully and promptly to liquidate the claims against him, and put the pecuniary relations existing between them, on a firmer basis. Having discovered, that—"like many other pious and devoted ministers, his judgment was good in laying up a good foundation for the time to come, but was too inattentive in managing the affairs of this life"—with sorrow for his situation, and distress at their own anticipated bereavement, their heart spoke out in the offers they made to detain amongst them the man whom they called their guide, their spiritual father, a leader in Israel. But Mr. Smith thought he had committed himself too far in Philadelphia, and that a proposed separation between pastor and people was tantamount to an actual one, in which it is almost sure to end; and therefore persevered in his determination to accept the call from Philadelphia, to which place he removed in the fall of 1791.

When the friends of literature and science, as the handmaids of religion, projected the College at Schenectady, New York, Mr. Smith was called to the chair of President; and retaining his love for science, his interest in youth, and fondness for instruction, he accepted the offer, and in the year 1795 removed to the College. The severity of the climate acting unfavourably on his feeble constitution, he listened to the earnest solicitations of his friends in Philadelphia, and in May 1799 returned to the charge of Pine Street Church.

In the month of August he wrote to Dr. Hill of Virginia, and among other things mentioned that a report was in circulation that the yellow fever had again visited the city; but he believed it to be a false alarm; that there were some cases of a malignant fever, in some families, but nothing that should be called the yellow fever. He therefore continued in the city, visiting his flock as usual; and in two days from the date of that letter, fell a victim to that terrible disease, which had returned in very deed, and was sweeping its victims in indiscriminate profusion to the grave. He expired the 22d of August, 1799, and was laid in Pine street cemetery. Over his remains his congregation erected a becoming monument. By his side sleeps a worthy successor in office, in Hampden Sidney College, the Rev. Moses Hoge, D.D., an humble man of an exalted spirit.   Virginia has cause to mourn that so many of her faithful servants and children, whose labours have erected an everlasting memorial in the Church of Christ, sleep not in her soil.   Will she not, at some day, not far distant, when the crowded city shall not reluctantly witness the removal of the honoured dead from the busy streets, to the rural home more fitting those who have done with time, demand her Smith, her Hoge and her Lacy, to rest with Rice and Baxter amid the scenes of their usefulness in solemn lovely quietude.

CHAPTER XX.

REV. WILLIAM GRAHAM—LIBERTY HALL AND WASHINGTON COLLEGE.

WILLIAM GRAHAM, whose name is inseparably interwoven with the history of literature and religion, in the Valley of Virginia, was born December 19th, 1746, in Paxton township, Pennsylvania, and reared by a pious mother. Michael Graham, the father, was an emigrant to Pennsylvania from the north of Ireland ; and had for his second wife, Mary Miller, also an emigrant at the early age of seven years. At the time of the birth of William, the second child, and oldest son, the family resided about five miles from the present seat of government, Harrisburg, in a frontier neighbourhood. From his earliest days, young Graham was accustomed to the toils and exposures of a frontier life, working the farm with his father till his twenty-second year, and being exposed, particularly during Braddock's war, to the depredations of the Indians. On one occasion his life was exposed. One night, while the neighbourhood was unconscious of the approach of any savages, the dogs at Mr. Graham's house appeared unusually excited, and barked much, without exciting the suspicions of the family. After the family had retired, one of the daughters, by a former marriage, left her bed, and listening at the front window, thought she heard whispering in the garden or beyond. The father on being awaked listened, and became satisfied that Indians were lying in wait ; and instantly determined to leave the house. The family were all immediately awaked, the little ones making not the least noise on being roused from sleep, were arrayed in dark clothing, and prepared for flight to the fort erected for the safety of the neighbourhood, about a mile distant. William stepped out first with a loaded musket, the door being directly in view of the place where the Indians were concealed; the family followed, and the father, locking the door, brought up the rear, armed ready for an assault. In silence and safety they passed on to the fort, and gave the alarm; before morning the families of the neighbourhood were all assembled. At day-light an armed party proceeded to Mr. Graham's house, expecting an attack to be made at that hour. All was quiet; the Indians having discovered that the family had deserted the house, departed without depredation. Upon searching by day-light, traces of a large number of the enemy were discovered in the direction from which the whispering came.

While labouring on the farm, young Graham acquired that amount of education which could be imparted by a country schoolmaster on the frontiers. Though blessed with religious instruction and example, it is not known that he experienced any abiding religious impressions till about his twenty-first year. Active in business, and ardent in his pursuits, and social in his feelings, he knew the importance of that religion he did not seek. When about sixteen years of age he became, through the influence of a family in the neighbourhood, extremely fond of dancing and its accompanying merry-making. He carefully concealed from his parents his propensity and indulgence; and even went so far as to endeavour to deceive them by stealing off for this enjoyment, after the family had retired to rest. The effects of this indulgence upon his mind, made him, in after life, oppose it with uncompromising severity, in young people. He thought it one of the most effectual means ever contrived for the destruction of souls. " It was not"—he said—" the mere act of dancing, or the time consumed by it, to which he objected most strongly; but the mind was almost entirely employed in thinking over the dances past, and in looking forward to the next that was to come: and thus all serious reflection was excluded."

About the time he became of age, he was the subject of deep convictions, which ended in his becoming experimentally acquainted with the way of life through Jesus Christ, by the blood of his cross. Such were his views of divine things, that he earnestly desired to be qualified to preach the gospel. His father's narrow circumstances were a great obstacle; his mother's ardent desires that he should spend his life in the ministry were a great encouragement. The father at length agreed to afford all the assistance in his power, and William joyfully commenced the Latin grammar with his pastor Mr. Roan. After a time he removed to the school of Mr. Finley, at

Masherick; and from thence to Princeton College, Dr. Witherspoon being President. His classical course was comprised
in about five years. Owing to his narrow means, he was engaged in teaching the younger classes, while with Mr. Finley,
and in the preparatory academy while in College, thus improving himself and contributing to his own support.

His mother spared no pains or efforts to assist and encourage
him in his literary course; and rejoiced at his enterprise and
his success. While he was a member of College, this excellent
mother was seized with a paralysis, and, after a short illness,
died. With much of that meek and quiet spirit, which in the
sight of God is of great price, she was eminent for that charity
which thinketh no evil, which hopeth all things and believeth
all things. Peculiarly fitted, by her ardent piety and affectionate disposition, to be near the sick and afflicted, no difficulties, by night or by day, prevented her attendance upon those
who desired her presence. By her example and by her precepts she taught her son the great things of the gospel of Christ.
Her religion, not being confined to internal experiences, manifested itself in her temper and the relative duties of life. Mr.
Graham appreciated his mother while living; and mourned for
her when dead. In after life he said—"he had received more
information respecting the nature of practical religion from her
conversation, than from all the books he had ever read on the
subject, except the Bible."

Mr. Graham pursued his studies with the same ardour he had
shown in all his early pursuits; and was graduated with a class
of twenty-nine, in the year 1773. Of that class fourteen
became ministers of the gospel, four Presidents of College, and
three Governors of a State. His reputation for scholarship was
high among his classmates, and in the College. Henry Lee, a
classmate, afterwards so well known in the Revolution, and as
Governor of Virginia, had formed a high estimate of his acquirements. At the approach of one of the examinations,
young Lee requested to review with Graham, in preparation.
Graham declined the opportunity, fearing loss of time; young
Lee pressed the matter with urgency; and Graham consented,
on condition that subjects of conversation should not be introduced. After the examination, Lee came to his room and said,
—"Well, Graham, I have passed a glorious examination, and I
know that I am indebted for it, in a great measure to you.
What recompense shall I make you?" "None at all," said Graham. After some conversation, Lee left the room, and soon
returned, and laying upon the table Belshaw's Lectures on Natural Philosophy, immediately departed. Upon opening the
volume Graham found a black line had been drawn through the

name of Henry Lee, and underneath was written William Graham. The volume is still preserved by Mr. Graham's connexions, in Virginia.

John B. Smith, his companion in labour in Virginia, and almost his rival, and also Lewis F. Wilson, so beloved and honoured in North Carolina and New Jersey, were his classmates. The revival of religion, with which that class in College was visited from on high, could not have been lost on Graham; its fruits have been scattered, by the different members, through the United States.

Upon leaving College Mr. Graham returned to his father's house, and soon entered on the study of theology with his pastor, Mr. Roan, whose ardent preaching had made him notorious in Virginia, and given him a name on their records of Court. While studying with Mr. Roan, his knowledge of farming, and his skill in repairing the necessary tools of husbandry were turned to good account both to himself for exercise, and to his pastor and instructor for assistance; and such habits were cherished as were invaluable to him in his labours in Virginia.

In the fall of 1774, on the recommendation of the Rev. Samuel Stanhope Smith, employed in founding Hampden Sidney College, in Prince Edward, Mr. Graham was invited to engage in a classical school, in Augusta county, under the direction of the Rev. John Brown, pastor of New Providence and formerly of Timber Ridge.

The Presbytery had been engaged for some years on the subject of founding a literary institution, whose location should be in the Great Valley of Virginia. Their councils and efforts resulted first in Liberty Hall Academy, and ultimately in WASHINGTON COLLEGE.

In the month of May, 1771, the Synod of New York and Philadelphia recommended the Academy at Newark—"to the charity of the various congregations within their bounds." In the month of October, the Presbytery of Lexington, the first session of their meeting, at the *Dee Ess* church, "recommended to all their ministers, to lay it before their several congregations, and to use their best influence to promote that design." This turned the Presbytery to consider the necessity of a literary institution within their own bounds, and fostered by their care; and accordingly the next act recorded, is—"Presbytery being very sensible of the great expediency of erecting a Seminary of learning somewhere within the bounds' of this Presbytery, do recommend it to all the members to take this matter under consideration, and report their thoughts at our next, especially respecting the best method of accomplishing it."

In April of 1772, at Rockfish,—"the consideration of the

minute concerning the New York Academy, and a Seminary amongst ourselves, is deferred until our next sederunt." In June, 1773, at Brown's meeting-house—"the Presbytery think it prudent to defer the fixing the particular place of our intended Seminary, until our next stated Presbytery, which is to be at Rockfish, on the second Wednesday of October next." In October, 1773—"the Presbytery agree to fix the publick Seminary for the liberal education of youth, in Staunton, Augusta." In October 1774, at Cub Creek—"the Presbytery resume the consideration of a school for the liberal education of youth, judged to be of great and immediate importance. We do therefore agree to establish and patronise a publick school, which shall be confined to the county of Augusta. At present it shall be managed by Mr. William Graham, a gentleman properly recommended to this Presbytery,—and under the inspection of the Rev. Mr. John Brown, and the Presbytery reserve to themselves the liberty at a future session, more particularly to appoint the person by whom it shall be conducted, and the place where it shall be fixed, which they are induced to do notwithstanding a former presbyterial appointment,—because there is no person to take the management of it in the place first agreed on,—and it is very uncertain whether there ever will be."

To carry this determination into effect, the Presbytery appointed "the Rev. Messrs. John Brown, David Rice, Samuel Cummins, William Irwin and Caleb Wallace to collect subscriptions, in the several congregations annexed to their names, for the purpose of obtaining a library and proper apparatus,— viz.—Mr. Brown in the Pastures, Providence, and the North Mountain,—Mr. Rice in Botetourt, on the south side of James River,—Mr. Cummins in Fincastle,—Mr. Irvin at Tinkling Spring, the Stone meeting-house and Brown's Settlement,—Mr. Wallace in the Fork of James River,—and Mr. Smith at pleasure." It was also agreed that by the terms of subscription the money should be paid—"to the persons or their order, on or before the twentieth day of December next ensuing, in the year 1775."

By the act of Presbytery in 1774, the grammar school, conducted by the Rev. John Brown, or under his supervision and in his charge, became the centre of operations for literary and theological improvement in the Valley. The Rev. Samuel Houston in his letter to Rev. James Morrison tells us—"that shortly before the war, some men whose sons were growing up, felt a desire for having them or part of them educated liberally, chiefly with a view to the ministry of the gospel. Accordingly a small grammar school was formed in the neighbourhood of Old Providence, composed of Samuel Doak, John Montgomery, Archibald Alexander, James Houston, William Tate, Samuel

Greenlee, William Wilson, Ebenezer Smith, and some others, which greatly increased and drew youths from distant neighbourhoods. This grammar school was moved to the place, near Fairfield, called Mount Pleasant; about which time the Presbytery of Hanover patronised it." This school, spoken of by Mr. Houston, was taught, at first, about four miles East of New Providence. Mr. Brown removed it to New Providence, and after teaching there for a time, removed it again to Mount Pleasant, the highest point of the Ridge, about a mile west of Fairfield, and equally distant from his house, which was situated at a like distance from Fairfield, on the same Ridge, the road to the Academy going out from the North end of the town, and that leading to his dwelling from the South end. The school became more prosperous under the tuition of Mr. Graham and the patronage of the Presbytery.

April 12th, 1775, the Presbytery commenced its Spring Sessions at Timber Ridge; on the 13th, it met at the house of Rev. Mr. Brown; present, Rev. Messrs. Todd, Brown, Rice, Leake, Irwin, Waddell, and Wallace, with John Logan, elder. "William Graham having offered himself on trials for the gospel ministry, produced sufficient testimonials of his good standing in the churches, where he lived to the Northward, and particularly from the churches where he was best known, and having been interrogated on his views for the gospel ministry, and also on his acquaintance with practical piety, and on these points having satisfied the Presbytery, he is continued on trials." On the next day at the same place—"Mr. Graham having read a discourse on Galatians, i. 13; and also an exegesis, on this question,—*An Christus qua Mediator sit Adorandus?*—The Presbytery after consideration sustain them as pieces of trial. The Presbytery appoint Mr. Graham a discourse on 1 Timothy, iv. 10; also a homily on this subject —How far knowledge is necessary to salvation—To be delivered at a Presbytery to be held at the De Ess, on the last Wednesday of June, Anno 1775."

At the same meeting, Mr. James Templeton, a graduate of Princeton College, of the Class of 1772, was examined respecting his views of the ministry, and "also touching the grace of God in him"—and having produced testimonials—"in particular from Dr. Witherspoon,"—respecting his character, moral and religious, was received on trial, and pieces according to custom, were assigned him.

"The affairs of the public school are now taken under consideration, and after the most mature deliberation, the Presbytery find that they can do no more, at this session, than recommend it again, in the warmest manner, to the publick to make such liberal contributions as they shall find com-

patible with their circumstances, for the establishing said
school; and the Presbytery, as guardians and directors, take
this opportunity to declare their resolution to do their best
endeavour to establish it on the most catholic plan that circumstances will permit of." On the next day the affairs of
the school were again considered; and—"the Presbytery finding that they cannot, of themselves, forward subscriptions in a
particular manner, do, for the encouragement of the Academy
to be established in Augusta, recommend it to the following
gentlemen to take in subscriptions, in their behalf—viz:—

"The Rev. Mr. Cummins, Colonel W. Preston, and Colonel
W. Christian, in Fincastle,—Colonel Lewis, Colonel Fleming
and Mr. Lockheart, in Bottetourt,—on the south side of James
River, Captain John Boyer, Captain W. McKee, Captain Adlai
Paul, Captain John Maxwell, and Mr. James Trimble,—in the
Forks of James River, Mr. Samuel Lyle and Captain Samuel
McDowell,—in Timber Ridge, the Rev. Mr. John Brown, Mr.
James Wilson and Mr. Charles Campbell of Providence,—Mr.
William McPheeters, Mr. William Ledgerwood and Mr. John
Trimble, in the North Mountain and Brown's Settlement,—
Mr. Thomas Stewart and Mr. Walter Davis at the Tink-
ling Spring,—Mr. Sampson Mathews of Staunton,—Captain
George Mathews, Captain George Maffit and Mr. James Allen
in Augusta congregation. Mr. Brown, Mr. Irvin and Mr.
Wallace are to give the above named gentlemen notice of their
appointment, and to solicit their favour."

The opportunity of visiting the school under their patronage
being so favourable—"the Presbytery repaired to the school-
house, and attended a specimen of the proficiency of the
students, in the Latin and Greek language, and pronouncing
orations; with which they were well pleased."

About this time was made the visit so pleasantly described
by Dr. Campbell of Lexington, in the Literary Messenger in
1838. "I happened at Mount Pleasant during Mr. Graham's
superintendence. It was near the hour of recreation. Here
was seen a large assemblage of fine cheerful vigorous looking
youth apparently from ten to twenty years of age. They
were mostly engaged in feats of strength, speed, or agility;
each emulous to surpass his fellows in those exercises, for
which youth of their age generally possess a strong predeliction.
Presently the sound of a horn summoned all to the business
of the afternoon. The sports were dropped as by magic.
Now you may see them seated singly or in pairs, or in small
groups, with book in hand, conning over their afternoon's
lesson. One portion resorted immediately to the hall, and
ranging themselves before the preceptor in semi-circular
order, handed him an open book containing their recita-

tions. He seemed not to look into the book, and presently closed it; thinking, as I supposed, he knew as well as the book. Of the recitations I understood not a syllable; yet it was highly agreeable to the ear, sonorous and musical; and although more than sixty winters have rolled away since that time, the impressions then made have not been entirely effaced from my memory. I have since discovered that the recitation was a portion of that beautiful Greek verb, *Tupto*, in which the sound of the consonants pi, tau, mu, theta, predominate. It was observable that, during the recitation, the Preceptor gave no instructions, corrected no errors, made no remarks of any kind. He seemed to sit merely as a silent witness of the performance. The class itself resembled one of those self-regulating machines of which I have heard. Each member stood ready, by trapping and turning down, to correct the mishaps and mistakes of his fellows; and as much emulation was discovered here, as had been an hour before on the theatre of their sports in their athletic exercises. During this recitation, an incipient smile of approbation was more than once observed on the countenance of the Preceptor, maugre his native gravity and reserve. This happened when small boys, by their superior scholarship, raised themselves above those who were full grown. This class having gone through, several others, in regular order, presented themselves before the teacher, and passed the ordeal. The business of the afternoon was closed by a devotional exercise. And now the whole number, without delay, issuing from the hall, spread themselves over the area before the door; each conversing with much glee with those nearest to him; then hastening homeward each took off his several way to some of the farm-houses, which furnished them refectories and dormitories;—and the shadows of the evening lengthening fast, I too, hied me home, much gratified and not a little disappointed. The systematic order of the place struck my attention. A signal called the whole school together; a signal announced the hour of recitation; each class was summoned by a signal. These signals were obeyed without delay—and without noise. The students might pursue their studies in the hall or the open air, as pleased them best. Talking or reading aloud was not permitted in the hall, except to the class reciting. The dignity of the Preceptor, and his well known fitness for the station, gave him respectability, and he was respected. Before this day, I had thought the course pursued in this Latin school resembled the common English schools with which I had been acquainted— '*Sic parvis componere magna solebam.*' But now I saw that the order and discipline of the former were essentially different from the noise, confusion and turmoil of the latter."

The writer of this graphic description of his first visit to a

classical school, became himself a pupil of Graham, and learned
by heart that beautiful verb *Tupto*, and was an honour to the
man he honoured.

The Presbytery met at Rockfish, October 25th, 1775—present, Rev. Messrs. Sankey, who was chosen Moderator, Todd,
Brown, Rice, Leake, Irvin and Wallace,—with elders Robert
Johnson, Robert Burkhannon, Robert Mitchell, Alexander
Blair, Captain Thomas Montgomery and John Irvin.   The following minute was made respecting the meeting appointed to
be held in June, viz.—"Messrs. Brown and Leake being the
only persons who found it practicable to meet at the time and
place appointed for our called Presbytery last June, although
they could not constitute a Presbytery, yet proceeded to hear
the pieces of trial assigned to Mr. W. Graham and Mr. Templeton at our last, and also examined them on natural philosophy, and report that they are well pleased with the performance of the young gentlemen. The Presbytery do approve of
the proceedings on the then occasion, and do so far confide in
their judgment as to sustain the performances of these candidates as parts of trial.—They further report that they assigned
Mr. Graham the 11th verse of 3d chapter of the Epistle to the
Galatians, as the subject of a sermon, and to Mr. Templeton a
lecture on Revelations, ii. 1–8.

"Mr. Graham having delivered his discourse to-day, the consideration thereof is deferred."

The next day, October 26th, Mr. Samuel McCorkle, a probationer from the Presbytery of New York, who afterwards held
a conspicuous place among the ministers of North Carolina, was
taken under the care of the Presbytery.   An evening session
was held at the house of Mr. John Morrison: and—"the Presbytery proceeded to hear Mr. Templeton's sermon and lecture,
and having considered them do approve and sustain them as
pieces of trial. The Presbytery further proceeded to examine
Mr. Templeton and Mr. Graham of science and divinity and to
put them on the defence of their theses. Having now taken a
view of their whole trials, and they having promised to subscribe the formula, having acknowledged the Westminster Confession of Faith, and having promised subjection to this Presbytery, in the Lord,—the Moderator, by the appointment of
Presbytery proceeded to license the said Mr. W. Graham and
Mr. J. Templeton to preach the gospel of Jesus Christ, as probationers, and they are licensed accordingly."

The next evening (of October 27th) the Presbytery again
met at the house of John Morrison, and took up the subject of
the School in Augusta.   "We agree that Mr. William Graham
continue to have the care and tuition of said School;—and upon
receiving a proper recommendation, we choose and appoint

Mr. John Montgomery, late from Princeton College, to be his Assistant.

" We request that the gentlemen appointed by the Presbytesy, last spring, still continue to take subscriptions; and finding that the interest of the School requires that a considerable sum of money be immediately laid out in purchasing books and mathematical and philosophical apparatus, we appoint the Rev. John Brown, Mr. Charles Campbell, Mr. Robert Steel, Capt. Samuel McDowell, Mr. Samuel Lyle, Capt. John Bowyer, Mr. William McKee, and Mr. William Graham to collect what money they can from those who have already subscribed, or who may now encourage the design.   And we appoint the said William Graham, on giving bond and security to the Rev. John Brown and Capt. Samuel McDowell for the faithful discharge of the trust, to lay out the sum of £150, in purchasing books and apparatus for the use of the said School.

" Mr. William Graham is appointed to supply two Sabbaths at Timber Ridge, two at Hall's Meeting-House, two on the south side of James River, five in the Pastures, one at Brown's Meeting-House, one at the North Mountain, and the rest of his time at discretion, until our next meeting of Presbytery."

The Presbytery met at Timber Ridge May 1st, 1776;—present Rev. Messrs. Brown, Waddell, Rice, Irvin, Wallace, and Smith; with Elder Charles Campbell.   Mr. McCorkle, a licentiate, preached the opening sermon from Job xxvii. 8—For what is the hope of the hypocrite, though he has gained, when God taketh away his soul?   Mr. Irvin reported that Mr. Leake departed this life December 2d, 1775.   Mr. Brown is chosen Moderator.   On the 3d of May the Presbytery held its session at the Grammar School—and—" proceeded to examine the school under the care of Mr. Graham.   And having attended a specimen of their improvement in their classical studies, and pronouncing orations, the Presbytery highly approve of the proficiency of the students, and the diligence and abilities of the teachers."

On the next day, May 4th, the Presbytery heard, from the Rev. S. S. Smith, the prosperous condition of Hampden Sidney, which gave employment to these teachers, John B. Smith, Samuel Doak, and David Weatherspoon, beside the president or rector.   And afterwards were informed by Mr. Graham—" That agreeable to the commission of Presbytery, he had purchased books and apparatus for the use of the Academy to the amount of £160 10s. 9½d., which he has paid, and £2 4s. which he has lost in change.   Which monies, with the portage of the books, the apparatus, and all other reasonable expenses, the Trustees hereafter to be appointed, are directed to account with Mr. Graham for, and pay him the balance.   Mr. Graham informs, that the gentlemen appointed last fall have collected and paid into his hands about £128, which he will be ready to account for more accurately with the Trustees of the Augusta Academy when they are appointed."

At the opening of this meeting of Presbytery, a call from the united congregations of Timber Ridge, and Hall's Meetinghouse, for the services of Mr. Graham, was handed in; and being put into his hands, he asked time for consideration. On the fourth day of the session he accepted the call,—and,—"our next stated Presbytery is appointed at Concord, on the fourth Tuesday of October next, the time and place of Mr. Graham's ordination, at which Mr. Wallace is to preside, and Mr. Rice to give the charge. Mr. Graham is to preach on Romans iii. 25, 26, previous to ordination." The minutes of this fall meeting are not to be found, and consequently the official record of his ordination cannot be produced.

On Monday, May 6th, 1776, the Presbytery determined to remove the Academy from Mount Pleasant, for want of accommodations, and made the following arrangement for its location, and for its management by Trustees. "The Presbytery, finding, that as the Augusta Academy is circumstanced, it is highly necessary now to fix on the place for its situation, and the person by whom it shall be conducted; and as this congregation of Timber Ridge appears to us to be a convenient place, and they have obtained a minister, whom we judge qualified; and Capt. Alexander Stewart, and Mr. Samuel Houston, each offering to give forty acres of land, for the purpose, convenient to the place of publick worship; and the neighbours offering to build a hewed log-house, twenty-eight by twenty-four feet, one story and a half high, besides their subscriptions, and assuring us of the probability that fire-wood and timber for buildings will be furnished gratis, for at least twenty years,—we agree that the Augusta Academy shall be placed on Timber Ridge, upon those lands; and we choose Mr. William Graham rector, and Mr. John Montgomery, his assistant.

"And we appoint the Rev. Messrs. John Brown, James Waddell, Charles Cummins, William Irvin, and the Rector *ex officio*, in conjunction with Mr. Thomas Lewis, General Andrew Lewis, Col. Wm. Christian, Col. William Fleming, Mr. Thomas Stewart, Mr. Samuel Lyle, Mr. John Gratton, Col. Wm. Preston, Mr. Sampson Matthews, Col. John Bowyer, Major Samuel M'Dowell, Mr. William McPheeters, Captain Alexander Stewart, Captain William McKee, Mr. John Houston, Mr. Charles Campbell, Captain George Moffit, Mr. William Ward, and Captain John Lewis, at the Warm Springs,—*Trustees*. Seven of the Trustees shall be a quorum. They are to collect subscriptions and donations, expend the monies, and conduct all the concerns of this Academy, in behalf of the Presbytery; also they are to keep a fair book of accounts, and all the transactions relating to the Academy,—the Presbytery reserving to themselves the right of visitation, for ever, as often as they shall judge it necessary; and of choosing the Rector and his assistant.

"The Trustees are to meet together statedly, twice in the year, and have the students examined before them at these times. They are to choose their own Chairman, Treasurer, and Clerk, and appoint a Committee who shall have power to call a meeting of the Trustees as often as any emergency shall make it necessary.

"The Presbytery appoint Mr. Samuel Lyle, Colonel John Bowyer, Major Samuel M'Dowell, Mr. Charles Campbell, Captain William McKee, Captain Alexander Stewart, Mr. John Houston, and the Rector, or any five of them, a committee, to have the lands given to the Academy measured and bounded, and the title secured, and to draw the plans, and let the building of such houses as they shall judge necessary for the use of the Academy and Rector. The first meeting of the committee shall be on next Monday, and they are empowered to call a meeting of the Trustees some time before the first of next July." Early in the year 1777, the School was removed from Mount Pleasant to Timber Ridge.

During the year 1776, his office of Rector being made permanent, and his pastoral office entered upon, Mr. Graham was united in marriage with Miss Mary Kerr, of Carlisle, Pennsylvania. Every thing now seemed to promise extended usefulness to the Academy, and the rector and minister. Students were coming from all parts of the Valley and the scattered habitations in the mountains; and Timber Ridge seemed about to surpass Mount Pleasant in the splendour and duration of its glory. To the building for the instruction of the students were added accommodations for the Rector; and a commencement was made for philosophical apparatus and a library. The Log College, twenty-eight by twenty-four, and one and a half stories high, made but a humble appearance in comparison with Washington College, as she now sits, spread out on the hill near Lexington. And the incipient library of valuable books, with the air pump, and electric machine, and sextant, and microscope, and telescope, a set of large maps, and a pair of twelve inch globes, for a philosophical apparatus,—all purchased for about £160,—would be less imposing now than in those days of frontier life. But then the men that came forth from that institution! Like one of the bold springs of the Valley of the Shenandoah, it poured, from the very spring-head, a stream of power. If Liberty Hall did not make so full and complete scholars as the more richly endowed College has done, she laid the foundation for scholarship, and awakened that thirst for knowledge, which precedes eminence in attainments, and may be named with exultation, as the germ,—the strong root from which Washington College sprung.

But the Academy did not long remain at Timber Ridge; and the short time of her sojourn was disturbed by the heavings and tossings of the all-absorbing Revolution. The Declaration of National Independence was made in the July succeeding the May in which the Presbytery resolved upon the removal of the Academy from Mount Pleasant; the war had begun at least a month previous. A greater part of the students were of that age and condition of body required in volunteers and recruits for the hard service of war. The Rector, for reasons both of a political and religious nature, was an ardent supporter of the Revolution; and so far from repressing the spirit of patriotism in his congregations, or the young men under his care, by his precepts and example he inflamed them with a more vehement love of liberty; with Patrick Henry he might have exclaimed, and probably in the hearing of his people did exclaim—*" Give me liberty, or give me death."* In October of the year 1777, the Legislature made a call upon the militia of the State for a draft, or for volunteers, to fill out the proper number of soldiers, required of the State, on the continental establishment. The draft was to be made—"from. the single men of the militia of the several counties, and of the city of Williamsburg, whether officers or privates, above eighteen years of age, who have no child." The proportion for Augusta county was ninety-seven. On or before the second Monday of February, 1778, the militia muster roll was to be examined by the proper officers, at the Courthouse of each county, and—"the names of all the officers and men of their militia who have not a wife or child, and such single men as are in the county and not enrolled, and who by the militia law ought to be enrolled"—were to be taken down and these persons to be assembled, within ten days, at a place named by the officers, and the draft to be made. "And whereas it is of the greatest importance to the American cause to open the ensuing campaign as early as possible, and to render its operations more decisive and effectual, that the army under the command of his Excellency General Washington should be reinforced by an additional number of troops, to be raised for that purpose in this Commonwealth:—Be it further enacted,— that every man who shall voluntarily engage to enter into such service, to continue therein for six months from the time of his arrival at the place appointed for general rendezvous, shall receive, &c.—and be exempted from drafts for six months after being discharged.

By the same Legislature the county of Rockbridge was set off from the counties of Augusta and Botetourt; the county of

Rockingham from Augusta; and the county of Greenbrier from the counties of Botetourt and Montgomery. By the law for drafting the militia—it was ordered—"that where two or more counties shall have been formed into a greater number, the numbers hereinbefore required from the said counties, as they stood before such alteration, shall be added together, and each of the counties into which they shall have been formed, shall furnish a part of the whole number of men, in proportion to the militia it shall contain. By this law, the draft was for a year, and the volunteer was required to serve six months after reaching the place of rendezvous.

Under these two laws, the militia of the new county of Rockbridge, subject to the draft, were assembled a few miles from Mount Pleasant. Mr. Graham attended, and addressed the meeting in favour of filling up the required quota by volunteers. John Lyle, captain of one of the militia companies, stepped forth as a volunteer; and was followed by a few. The little band marched and countermarched in front of the assembled militia, and increased but slowly. Mr. Graham stepped forth and joined the band; in a few moments the required number was completed. In the selection of officers, which immediately followed, Mr. Graham was chosen captain, and immediately commenced the necessary preparations for the expected campaign, conscious of the delicacy of his position, blending as he did in his own person the extreme characters, of a captain in war, and a herald of the Prince of Peace. But he considered the Revolution, then rapidly progressing, as a revolution in religious as well as political matters; and seeking religious freedom he was willing to hazard his life for civil liberty, without which freedom of conscience does not exist. The students of Liberty Hall sympathized with their teacher. The volunteer company was, however, never called into service. The commander-in-chief, duly appreciating the spirit of the Legislature and citizens of Virginia, urged upon his countrymen the necessity of a longer term of service, for the effectual prosecution of the war, which must be of longer duration than the short time contemplated in the law. But the influence of this volunteering was felt in the Valley during the whole succeeding war.

The pecuniary distress that involved the whole country fell with great weight upon the Rector of the Academy. The number of pupils necessarily declining, the income of the Academy was diminished, and the salary of the Rector curtailed; in common with other clergymen, Mr. Graham found his salary as a minister greatly diminished, both numerically and in value; and the land belonging to the Academy was insufficient for the sustenance of his family. In these circumstances Mr. Graham looked around for the means of support, and determining to engage in agriculture, an employment familiar to the days of his youth, he purchased a farm, on North River, five or six miles from the Academy, and near the town of Lexington, laid off by the act of 1777 as the county seat of the new county of Rockbridge. The Trustees resolved that—"the Rector have permission immediately to remove his family to his farm;—and that he visit the Academy every week, and spend two or three days at it, as circumstances may permit. This arrangement, proving too inconvenient both to the students and the Rector, was soon abandoned; and the students generally followed Mr. Graham to the neighbourhood of Lexington. The Academy at Timber Ridge was discontinued sometime in the year 1779. The meeting-house, near which the Academy had been built, was also in due time removed a few miles nearer Lexington; and its ancient site is known only by the old grave-yard, by the road side, with a few monuments to mark the resting place of many of the pioneers of the Valley. The reflections of Dr. Campbell, from whom we have already quoted, on revisiting Mount Pleasant, will in spirit and many circumstances apply to Timber Ridge.—"Fifty or sixty years after this—(his first visit)—and but a few years ago (i. e. previous to 1838)—in passing near to Mount Pleasant, I turned out of my way to see this quondam seat of the muses. The building and grove have entirely disappeared. No hedge or railing encloses the area. It appears an entire desolation. The elevated position, however, affords the same grand and delightful prospect. I felt myself on classic ground. Here Washington College drew its first breath. On this spot commenced the establishment of a seminary of learning. A few obscure clergymen, without political power, without pecuniary resources, other than what might be expected from the voluntary contributions of a newly settled mountainous district; in perilous times, too, when the Indians behind, and the British before, threatened to devour with open mouth; these men began their work, persevered, and succeeded. They have long since slept with their fathers; and were this benevolent work alone known of them, they would merit the grateful remembrance of the present and future generations. The Trustees too were important auxiliaries in the same work. Most of them continued in office during life, some of them I think for more than half a century. They too have gone the way of all flesh. While remaining here, I called to mind the numerous population which once encircled Mount Pleasant, and which, in various ways, contributed to the advancement of the Seminary; and asked myself where are they all now? Where are the Willsons, Blackburns, Browns, Scotts,—the Greenlees, McDowells, McClungs, Pattons and

Pattersons? where are they now?—Of that numerous population, of various ages, characters and pursuits, which once encircled the spot where I now am, a few, a very few, indeed, children of another century, may, by careful inquiry, be discovered, far dispersed from each other, with hoary heads and furrowed cheeks, their steps marked with imbecility and decrepitude, having advanced far down the vale of life, and still progressing with accelerated speed, destined soon to join in the land of silence their former associates.

"The students, too, that lovely band of youth, whom, long since, I saw animating the scenes around Mount Pleasant,—they too have bowed to the king of terrors, yet a single exception to this may even now be found: (James Mitchell, pastor of the churches at the Peaks and Pisgah, Bedford). I wish I could recollect the names of all the students of that primary school. Priestly, Mitchell, Stuart, Blackburn, McClung, the Wilsons, Browns, and Breckenridges, were of the number. These entered on a classical course about the same time, and were contemporaries on the stage of public life. Several of them became practising attorneys; two of them held seats on the bench of justice in the superior courts of law; four have been members of State Legislature; four of the Congress of the United States, and one was called in diplomatic capacity to superintend our national interests at the court of Versailles. Besides, several of these have, at different times, received appointments by authority of the State, to manage special important trusts in behalf of the commonwealth. I think it may be safely said, that not one of these was ever charged, or chargeable with delinquency in their important trusts, either through want of talents, or want of fidelity.—I thought of the brevity of human life composed of a few short periods; youth, maturity, and decay, and these followed by death and dissolution."

Early in the year 1781, Cornwallis advanced from South Carolina, northward, and was pursuing General Greene through North Carolina, with the double purpose of retaking the prisoners captured at the Cowpens, and of destroying the American forces under Greene. In answer to the call on the Valley for aid, a regiment marched from Augusta and the more southern counties, to the camp of Greene, and were honourably engaged in the battle at Guilford Court House. Among those who maintained their ground through the whole action and retreated at last at the command of their General, were some of the pupils of Graham.

In the month of June in the same year, the Assembly, to avoid a visit designed them by the famous Tarlton, adjourned hastily on the 4th, from Charlottesville, to meet on the 7th, in Staunton. On that day, when scarcely in their seats, they were again alarmed by the report of an approaching visit from the same unwelcome person, and hastily left the town. "It happened"—says a writer in the Literary and Evangelical Magazine for May, 1821—"that on that day, Mr. Graham was on his way from his residence in Rockbridge, to the Stone meeting-house below Staunton, on some clerical business. Meeting with some members of the Assembly on the road, they told him what had taken place. He inquired whether the Assembly had adopted any measures, before they separated, to call forth the militia to oppose the enemy? Upon being told they had not, he expressed his surprise;—'but'—said he—'something must yet be done. There are three roads leading from Staunton towards Lexington. Let us disperse, and some of us take each of the roads, and communicate the intelligence to the militia officers in our way, urging them instantly to call out the militia under their command, and march immediately towards Rockfish Gap.'" The three roads were, the Greenville, the North Mountain, and the Middle, or Ridge Road. The Brownsburg has of late in a great measure superseded the two last mentioned. "The plan was adopted, and the call made upon the officers was promptly obeyed. The intelligence spread with great rapidity, and the men began instantly to prepare to march. During that afternoon, and in the forepart of the following night, the great body of the militia from the upper end of Augusta, and the lower half of Rockbridge, began to move rapidly towards Rockfish Gap."

"Mr. Graham arrived at home in the evening, and immediately sent off a messenger to some of the militia officers in his own neighbourhood. A small company of men assembled at his house next morning. With these he set out, and, when they arrived at Rockfish Gap, found the mountain covered with riflemen determined to permit no hostile foot to enter their borders with impunity. Intelligence soon arrived that Tarlton was not advancing, but had left Charlottesville and appeared to be retreating down the country. It being supposed by some that this might be a feint; part of the troops went to another gap of the mountain, supposing that Tarlton might attempt to force a passage there;—part returned home;—and part advanced forward in quest of the enemy. Mr. Graham went with the last mentioned party. They soon joined the Marquis La Fayette below Charlottesville; but finding the campaign was likely to be a protracted one, they did not continue with him very long; and all except one or two returned. During this short time Mr. Graham made it a practice to have evening prayers in the company to which he belonged. It was observed that they were not very well attended excepting on one occasion. An alarm had been given and from a concurrence of circumstances it was believed a battle would soon take place. On that evening, although the men really had less leisure than usual, they generally assembled and appeared to listen to the prayer with great attention." This expedition ended Mr. Graham's military life. He was not fond of warlike parade or desirous of military glory. His being chosen captain in 1778 was a cause of great uneasiness; the office of chaplain would have been more consonant with his feelings and principles. But conscious that many were looking to him for example; and believing the struggle to be for religious as well as civil liberty; and that no privations could be compared with the blessings of the liberty he hoped to gain; and no place of station or dignity would compensate for the loss sustained if the Revolution in America were rolled back; and unwilling to be an idler in a cause that required the help of all; he readily entered upon any labour to which his country called him, and underwent all privations demanded by the public good. Like Davies he believed that the boundaries of human life were set by God; and the path of duty was the path of safety; and that life and death were circumstantially either a blessing or a curse; that to die bravely was better than to live cowardly; and a part of a minister's duty is to teach his parishioners how to value life.

From the time he became member of the Presbytery of Hanover, Mr. Graham had his full share in the memorials that were sent by the Presbytery to the Legislature. Of the one that was sent by the convention of ministers and elders of the Presbyterian Church that met in Bethel, he stands in a near relation. When the bill for a general assessment was brought forward with such an advocate as Patrick Henry, and with the Episcopal Church to support it, it was generally supposed that it would certainly become a law. To those who had been paying to support their own church and another foreign to it, this bill proposed relief; they were to pay only for the support of the church of their choice. As it was a relief from their former burdens; and as the Presbyterian congregations would not be called on to pay more for the support of their own ministers than they would cheerfully give by voluntary subscription, Mr. Graham was agreed with his brethren to send up the memorial which gives their sentiments on the subject of the support of religion, disclaiming all legislative interference; and under the conviction that the law would in some form pass, proposing the least offensive form in which the assessment could be levied.

But when the passage of the bill was arrested, and the attention of the public called for the express purpose of giving an opinion on the principles and working of the proposed law,

Mr. Graham with his brethren then argued the subject on its merits and by the principles of law, and religion, both revealed and natural. Of the memorial sent up to the Assembly that met in October, 1785, from the Convention of the Presbyterian Church at Bethel in the August preceding, Mr. Graham was supposed to be the principal author. Samuel W. Lyle, elder of Timber Ridge church, says, under date of October 17th, 1847—" I have often heard my father, the late William Lyle, elder of Timber Ridge church, say, that he was present when the memorial to the Legislature on the subject of religious liberty was drawn up by a committee of Hanover Presbytery. That the Rev. William Graham drew it up; that he sat near him; that the Rev. J. B. Smith was in the room at the time, and a member of the committee, and proposed some verbal alterations which were adopted."

This memorial was advocated by Dr. Smith before the committee of the whole house, when he made his famous speech against the assessment with ability and effect that surpassed, in the opinion of good judges, the advocacy of Patrick Henry.

About the time the course of instruction in the Academy on Timber Ridge ceased, Mr. Graham made a visit to the churches northward, and travelled as far as Boston. The interest excited, and expressed, in New England, was mutual. His orthodox, classic, argumentative preaching, without notes, was a novelty to those who, while accustomed to good preaching, had always heard their good sermons read. Some pleasant compliments in favour of preaching without notes were passed; and earnest inquiries were made about the condition of religion in Virginia, the method of studying theology, and the subjects of a religious nature that were most discussed from the pulpit and elsewhere. In answer to the inquiry—"from what then do the Virginia clergy obtain their divinity?"—his reply— "*from the Bible*," had a latitude of meaning that can be best understood when his method of teaching theology comes under consideration. After his return from this visit, which resulted in little advantage to the cause of education, for which under the sanction of the Presbytery of Hanover, the members of which supplied his pulpit in his absence, he had made the journey, he commenced a correspondence with the Litchfield Association in Connecticut, the object of which was a more full supply of the vacancies in Virginia, than could be furnished by the churches of Hanover Presbytery. October 26, 1781. " Upon Mr. Graham's report of his correspondence with the Association of Litchfield; the Presbytery agreed to continue a correspondence with that Association, and appointed Messrs. Brown, Waddell, Graham and Scott a committee for that purpose." On the same day the Presbytery licensed Samuel Shannon and James

Mitchell, so long the minister in Bedford; and heard part of the trials of Moses Hoge, afterwards President of Hampden Sidney; heard from Mr. John Montgomery, that he retained the call from Winchester and Opekon, and Cedar Creek, for farther consideration; made the necessary preparations for the ordination of Mr. William Wilson over the Augusta congregation, at the Stone Church; and—"In consequence of the late signal interposition of Divine Providence in the capture of Charles Earl Cornwallis and his army at York, the Presbytery appointed the second Wednesday of December as a day of public thanksgiving in the churches under their care, unless where the different ministers may have received timely notice of another day near it appointed by Government; also two brethren, Mr. W. Irvin, and Mr. Templin were sent on a mission to what is now Tennessee, and Mr. Mitchell urged to go to the western waters. Other young men were in the course of preparation for the ministry. When the circumstances of the country, after a long war are considered, these facts show that the Presbytery was not inattentive to the claims of the widespreading vacancies. As usual they appointed the different brethren of the Presbytery to leave their congregations for a few Sabbaths, and visit the different vacancies in the neighbourhood.

In the year 1782, December 13th, the records say—"As Messrs. Judson and Pamely (Parmelee) came recommended from the Association of Litchfield to this Presbytery; the Presbytery recommended them to supply in our vacant congregations at their own discretion till our next; and they also recommended them to the notice and regard of the vacancies under their care." These young men made but a short visit in Virginia; not finding the field sufficiently inviting they turned their attention to other parts of the wide spread vineyard. There is no record of any other effect produced by the correspondence with the Association; but as the cords of brotherly affection were strenghthened, the efforts were not lost.

After Mr. Graham ceased to visit the school at Timber Ridge, and instruction was discontinued there, the scholars were assembled in his neighbourhood, and taught at his own house by him, and tutors of his selection. There Moses Hoge, D. D. pursued his studies in preparation for the ministry; and there too Archibald Alexander, D. D.—"at an early age commenced his course of classical learning." After the surrender of Cornwallis, the Trustees not being sufficiently prompt in promoting the cause of education, the Presbytery at this meeting at New Providence, October 24th, 1782, having, on motion of Rev. J. B. Smith, appointed additional Trustees to Hampden Sidney Academy, because—"it appears to the Presbytery that the Trustees of the Academy in Prince Edward have failed to discharge their duty through the distant situation of some whose attendance was necessary,—upon a similar motion by Mr. Graham, and for similar reasons, respecting the Academy of Liberty Hall, in Rockbridge, the Presbytery appoint the Rev. Messrs. Caleb Wallace, Edward Crawford, Samuel Doak, Archibald Scott, John Montgomery, James McConnel, Benjamin Erwin, William Wilson;—and Andrew Moore, John Wilson, John Leyle, James Trotter, Archibald Stewart, Joseph Walker, and William Alexander, Esqs., to act as Trustees of Liberty Hall." This is the last act of Hanover Presbytery, as originally constituted respecting Liberty Hall.

Application was now made to the Legislature of the State by the Trustees for an act of incorporation; and in October, 1782, "an act for incorporating the Rector and Trustees of Liberty Hall Academy, was passed, declaring that the Reverend William Graham, rector, Arthur Campbell, William Christian, Andrew Moore, William Alexander, Joseph Walker, Alexander Campbell, John Wilson, John Trimble, John Hays, John Bowyer, Samuel McDowell, George Maffit, William McKee, James McCorkle, Samuel Leyle, Archibald Stewart, the Reverend Caleb Wallace, John Montgomery, and William Wilson, and their successors are hereby constituted a body politic and corporate, by the name of the Rector and Trustees of Liberty Hall Academy." By whose suggestion this application was made does not appear. The records of Presbytery make no reference to the subject.

Among the powers vested in the Trustees was—"annually to grant such students, as in their opinion merit the same, testimonials under the common seal, and signed by the Rector and three of the Trustees at least, reciting their literary degrees."

These incorporated Trustees did not attempt to revive the Academy at Timber Ridge, but proceeded to erect a small frame building on an eligible site given by Mr. Graham and two of his neighbours whose lands lay adjoining. Mr. Graham carried on the instruction of the Academy by tutors, as far as suitable ones could be obtained; himself always superintending, and often much engaged in teaching, and sometimes being the sole instructor. The first tutor elected by the corporate Trustees was Mr. James Priestly, in January, 1783. Of him, the Rev. Archibald Alexander, D. D., in his address to the alumni of Washington College, in 1843, says—"I wish to preserve from oblivion the memory of the first tutor in this institution, after it was incorporated, Dr. James Priestly; a man of lively genius and extraordinary attainments in some departments of literature. Mr. Priestly was the son of a poor but very pious man in this county. Mr. Graham having, in catechising the youth of his charge, noticed the readiness and accuracy with which this boy answered all the questions proposed to him, obtained the consent of his parents to take him into his own family, that he might give him a liberal education.   The boy being endowed with a most retentive memory and a vivid imagination, soon became a distinguished scholar, and a tutor in the Academy. His memory was so extraordinary, that in hearing his pupils he had no occasion to take a book into his hands.   His principal attention was directed to Greek literature, in the accurate knowledge of which he greatly excelled.   He sometimes entertained his pupils by spouting with astonishing vehemence the orations of Demosthenes in Greek.   Mr. Priestly devoted his whole life to the promotion of classical literature.   The principal theatre of his labours was Georgetown (District of Columbia), Annapolis, and Baltimore, in the State of Maryland.   In each of the fore-mentioned places he established and superintended schools of a high grade of excellence.

"His fame as a teacher of youth having spread extensively, he was selected as the first President of the Cumberland University, at Nashville, Tennessee.   Here he spent the last years of his life; and though all were impressed with a high idea of his extraordinary learning, and his high qualifications as a classical teacher; yet he did not succeed well in organizing and arranging an infant College.   He was indeed a very eccentric though a very amiable man; and married a woman as eccentric as himself.   Among the peculiar opinions which he fondly cherished, one was, that our future felicity would depend very much upon the degree of intellectual culture bestowed on the mind as well as on its moral improvement—an opinion which has been ingeniously maintained by a writer in one of our popular periodicals recently.   Dr. Priestly possessed an enthusiastic ardour in favour of education I have never seen surpassed; and he succeeded in inspiring his pupils with something of the same.   From him the speaker derived the first impulse in his literary course, and, therefore, he feels a pleasure in having this opportunity of paying a deserved tribute to the memory of a teacher who was an ornament to this institution in its earliest days."   Though assisted by the ablest tutors that could be procured, and being himself an unrivalled disciplinarian, Mr. Graham often complained of the difficulty attending the government of the Academy, after the Revolution.   Previous to that time profanity and dissipation were unknown; and a diligent attention to their studies characterized the youth.   After the war, he was called upon to repress profanity, card playing, and other dissipations among the youth sent to the Academy.   His being called upon frequently, to exert to the utmost his talent for discipline, so much distressed him, that he frequently talked

of resigning his post. From principle he was a rigid disciplinarian, and resolved—"at every risk authority must be maintained; and when this was by any one resisted, however formidable the student might be in physical strength, or however
many might combine to frustrate the regular exercise of discipline, he fearlessly went forward in the discharge of his duty,
and generally triumphed over all opposition; and often inflicted
severe castigation on the thoughtless persons, who dared to
rebel against lawful authority." These efforts of discipline
were very disagreeable to him; and part of his severity towards
the unhappy offenders may be charged to the indignation he
felt upon being compelled to extraordinary discipline. It was
peculiarly unpleasant to him to be compelled to summon the
Trustees on account of any improprieties of the students; yet
this disagreeable duty was sometimes forced upon him.

Another view of the condition and habits of the youth assembling at the Academy had its influence in turning his heart
away from the employment of teaching, after the Revolution,
as a perplexing and perhaps useless if not hurtful employment.
In seeing the prevalence of dissipation, and tendency to infidelity among the youth, he proposed to himself and others the
inquiry, whether any good was done by educating vicious youth
to become more influential, and consequently more hurtful by
their education. The hope of witnessing a better state of
things still cheered him in his labours, and the encouragement
of his friends prevented his entire despondency, for a time.
One consideration of great weight was before him,—if the
clergy abandoned the education of youth, to whom would that
important office be committed? And if the education of youth
were neglected what would be the destiny of the nation?

The course of study pursued at the Academy was the same
as that pursued at Princeton while Mr. Graham was a student
there. He gave out the manuscript lectures of Dr. Witherspoon
to be copied and studied by the students as a text book. And
although on account of the irregularity of the classes, there was
no regular Commencement; yet in some instances the degree
of Bachelor was conferred, and occasionally in public. Of Mr.
Graham as a teacher Dr. Alexander says, he—"possessed a
mind formed for profound and accurate investigation. He had
studied the Latin and Greek classics with great care, and
relished the beauties of those exquisite compositions. With
those authors taught in the schools he was familiar by long
practice in teaching, and always insisted on the importance of
classical literature, as the proper foundation of a liberal education." He had a strong inclination to the study of natural
philosophy, and took pleasure in making experiments with such
apparatus as he possessed; and he had procured for the Aca-

demy as good an one as was possessed by most of the Colleges. In these experiments much time was employed, on which inquisitive persons, not connected with the Academy, were freely permitted to attend.

"The science, however, which engaged his attention more than all others, except theology, was the PHILOSOPHY OF THE MIND. In this he took great delight, and to this devoted much time and attention. Though acquainted with the best treatises which had been published, his investigations were not carried on so much by books as by a patient and repeated analysis of the various processes of thought as they arose in his own mind; and by reducing the phenomena thus observed, to a regular system. The speaker is of opinion, that the system of mental philosophy which he thus formed, was, in clearness and fullness, superior to any thing which has been given to the public, in the numerous works which have recently been published on this subject. And it is greatly to be regretted that his lectures were never fully committed to writing, and published for the benefit of the world. It was however a fault, in this man of profound thought, that he made little use of the pen. And it was also a defect, that in the latter years of his life he addicted himself but little to reading the productions of other men; and perhaps entertained too low an opinion of the value of books.

"The study of human nature"—says a writer in the Evangelical and Literary Magazine for August, 1821—" in a philosophical point of view, was one to which his thoughts had been frequently turned ever since he left College. Dr. Witherspoon, in an address to his class at the close of his lectures, observed that in moral philosophy there were difficulties which the present state of human knowledge did not enable us to solve; but he had no doubt the time would arrive, and perhaps at no distant day, when these difficulties would be removed, and we enjoy as much certainty and perspicuity in moral as in natural philosophy. Mr. Graham immediately, as he expressed it—felt his heart burn within him. Oh—said he to himself—that I might live to see that day! But I shall not! Difficulties so great as those which rest on this subject cannot be removed in so short a time! A gleam of hope however rose within him, and he devoted much of his thoughts afterwards to the subject. He soon found that man himself was not understood, and that to this source was to be traced much of the obscurity which spread over moral subjects. The first books from which he derived aid on the subject were Bishop Butler's Sermons, and some of the writings of Lord Kaimes. Reed's Essays on the Mind afterwards fell into his hands, where he found the subject treated much at large and with

great ability; but as an accurate observer of human nature, he
thought him inferior to Kaimes, so far as Kaimes had attended
to the subject. But although he obtained considerable aid from
the books just mentioned, his system and opinions were chiefly
formed from his own original reflections and observations; for
originality of thought was one of his distinguishing characteristics. When he had progressed so far in the philosophy of the
human mind as to have formed a system satisfactory to himself,
he began to examine its conformity to Christian experience,
and to the representations of human nature given in the Scriptures,—and their exact conformity gave him great pleasure,
and satisfied him of the truth of his system. The active principles of human nature he found to be very accurately distinguished by the apostle Paul, when he denominates them the
desires of the flesh and of the mind."

In May, 1785, his connexion with the congregations of Timber Ridge and Hall's Meeting-house was dissolved by Presbytery. The following is all the record made of the matter.

"Bethel, Saturday, May 21st, 1785.—Mr. Graham informed
the Presbytery that the churches of Timber Ridge and Hall's
Meeting-house in Rockbridge, of which he has been for several
years the pastor, had come to an agreement with him that the
relations formerly subsisting between them should be dissolved,
and requested the Presbytery to ratify the said agreement;
which was unanimously complied with. These churches were
therefore accordingly declared vacant." This was done at
that meeting of Presbytery in which it was declared unanimously—that the members of the Presbytery of Hanover did
not approve of any kind of assessment by the General Assembly; and a General Convention of the Presbyterian Church
invited to meet at Bethel, Augusta county.

For a time after this event Mr. Graham preached on the
Sabbath in the Academy-house to the students, and others that
choose to attend; and may be considered as giving himself
wholly to the duties of his office as Rector of the Academy and
the spiritual guide of his pupils. But as his place of preaching
was in the bounds of Hall's Meeting-house, from hearing him
in the Academy, the people invited him to their houses, and in
a short time to the meeting-house;—and in 1789 the union of
Timber Ridge and Hall's Meeting-house was dissolved by Presbytery, and Mr. Graham accepted a call, and the relation of
pastor was renewed with the congregation of Hall's Meeting-
house. This congregation was for convenience divided in the
year 1789; one part worshipping in Lexington, took the name
of the place of its worship; the other, worshipping at the old
place of assembling, was, after building a new house, called

New Monmouth. In these two places Mr. Graham continued to preach, statedly, till he left the county. The churches remained united until 1819.

During the interval of Mr. Graham's resignation of the pastoral Charge of the two churches, Timber Ridge and Hall's Meeting-house, and his being constituted pastor of Hall's and the church in Lexington, on the 10th of April, 1787, at a meeting of the Presbytery at Augusta Church—"A call for the Rev. Moses Hoge, and obligations for support were presented from Timber Ridge and Hall's churches. Mr. Hoge takes them under consideration until our next Presbytery." At the next Presbytery, October 23, 1787, at Mossy Creek—"Mr. Hoge resigns the call presented to him for consideration at our last, from Timber Ridge and Hall's churches."

Another event occurring during the same interval annoyed Mr. Graham. His sensibility and self-respect were assaulted; and the punishment for the offence so severe, the judicatories of the church were called upon to protect the offender. An effort was made to erect a State, called Frankland, on the western waters of Virginia and North Carolina. Mr. Graham was applied to, by some of his acquaintances for a draft of a constitution. He produced a paper. Opposition was raised to some of its provisions, in which the Rev. Hezekiah Balch, a member of Abingdon Presbytery, took a part. On one occasion a tumultuous assemblage publicly burned the effigy of its author, with that of its advocate, Rev. Samuel Houston. With the report of this proceeding came also the report of the prominent part acted by Mr. Balch. Mr. Graham addressed him a printed letter, in a pamphlet form, replete with satire keen even to bitterness, which was widely circulated in the south-western neighbourhoods. The whole matter of the political organization was a failure. The action was premature and irregular. But difficulties of a religious nature were connected with it, that were referred to the Synod of New York and Philadelphia. On the 26th of May, 1787, the following resolution was passed—"In respect to the letter addressed to Mr. Balch, through the medium of the press, and supposed to be written by the Rev. William Graham of Rockbridge county, Virginia, the Synod look upon the same as very unchristian and unwarrantable treatment of a brother; and the Synod do order the Presbytery of Lexington to cite Mr. Graham before them, and make due inquiry whether he be the author, and into the reasons of his conduct in that matter, and censure or acquit him as the nature of the case may appear.

"That in respect to political differences in that part of the country which occasioned a mob or riot, the Synod highly disapprove of, and condemn all such tumultuous and riotous proceedings; but as it appears by a paper signed by a number who acknowledge themselves the authors of the tumult, and also from the testimony of Colonel Cook, that Mr. Balch had no hand in that affair, and that he did take some pains to restrain those unhappy proceedings from going so far as they did; therefore, all things considered, we do not think him blameable in the matter."

At their fall meeting the Presbytery gave Mr. Graham a citation to appear at their next, and answer to the inquiries. The discussion of the subject was delayed at the request of Mr. Graham, till the fall meeting of Presbytery in 1789,—when he acknowledged himself the author of the "letter directed to Rev. Hezekiah Balch," which was in question—" and produced several depositions to prove the truth of the facts with which he charged Mr. Balch, and especially of his approving of the conduct of the mob in Frankland in burning the effigies of Messrs. Graham and Houston. The Presbytery, therefore, on mature deliberation agree, that although they could wish that Mr. Graham had been more temperate in his satire, and more gentle in his expostulations, yet that the treatment he met with was so grossly injurious, that they cannot suppose him to merit a formal censure of this Presbytery, on account of said letter." This political difference made some enemies to Mr. Graham, without adding to the number of his friends.

Soon after being connected with Hall's Meeting-house congregation the second time, Mr. Graham persuaded the people to remove their old church which was of wood, to build a new one of stone; and by his zeal and exertions, although the congregation was, after its division, neither numerous or wealthy, the building was speedily erected and fitted up with pews. The congregation in Lexington soon after erected for themselves a brick house, and also fitted it up with pews. At that time the village was very small, and the church stood out west of the incorporated limits, in a beautiful grove. The original limits of the village were very small, and in 1780 contained but four houses. Its name was taken from the battle ground in Massachusetts in 1776.

Mr. Graham's next step was to improve the singing in public worship. His efforts in this were crowned with success. The teacher he obtained, Mr. Lemus Chapin, for a few months, gave great satisfaction, and remained in the county a number of years, occupied in his profession. From him all the knowledge of church music, in Rockbridge and some of the neighbouring counties, for a number of years, was derived.

All these plans of usefulness were necessary for the prosperity of the congregations under his care, and all had a direct bearing upon what Mr. Graham desired as the fruit of all his labours; but they were not that fruit he sought as the ultimate end, the promotion of vital piety. Although he had been the favoured instrument of bringing many men into the ministry, in some cases directing all their studies, and in others but a part, and thus promoting the cause of God, he had not been favoured with any remarkable success in his ministry. This fact troubled him. The old professors were passing away from his charge by death, and their places were not all filled; there were no students of divinity from his charge, neither were there any hopefully pious young men pursuing their literary studies. When he was licensed to preach—" the closeness and depth of his reasoning, and the warmth of his applications, placed him in the estimation of those who heard him, in the first class of pulpit orators; and some who did not duly reflect, that Paul may plant and Apollos water, but it is God who giveth the increase, said,—surely no one can withstand such preaching; every one who hears it must become religious. * * * * Although his preaching was attended with considerable effect, there was not that great and general awakening which is usually denominated a revival." After his connexion with Lexington and New Monmouth, for some years, the effects of his preaching in producing conversions to God were scarcely visible.

The complaint was general throughout Virginia, that the ordinances of God seemed not to be blessed; and the hearts of many were sad. The dawn of a better day was first seen in Charlotte, among the Baptists. In the year 1787, the congregations under the care of J. B. Smith, President of Hampden Sidney, and pastor of the congregations of Cumberland and Briery, began to feel a greater interest in religious things; and in 1788, the whole region south of James River, east of the Blue Ridge, was greatly excited by the preaching of the gospel. The congregations in the Valley and those north of James River were entirely unmoved. The origin and progress of this revival are given in the sketch of J. B. Smith, D. D. Although as yet unmoved, the way was preparing in the heart of the pastor and in the condition of the congregations, for the church to be aroused and enlarged.

Previous to 1788, the amount of time to be given by Mr. Graham to the Lexington congregation, had been left to the discretion of the pastor, and exigences of the occasion: the greater part of the Sabbath mornings being given to New Monmouth. In that year it was agreed that one-fourth of the pastor's labours should be given to Lexington; and for this the subscription for the first year was £22 18s. 6d.; for the next year £17 8s. 6d. In 1789 a call was given by the inhabitants of Lexington and vicinity for one-fourth of Mr. Graham's time, the year to commence in May, and the salary to be not less than £20. Thirty-six names were affixed, with sums varying from £1 5s. to £0 5s.—in all £20 10s. By this arrangement there was regular preaching in the town congregation, on Sabbath morning, one-fourth of the time, and at other times as often as the pastor might find it convenient or desirable.

In this state of things Mr. Graham complied with an invitation from President Smith, and in the month of August, 1789, accompanied by some of his pupils from the neighbourhood, made a visit to Prince Edward, to attend a communion season in the Briery congregation. "On the Saturday evening of the communion"—says Rev. Mr. Calhoun in his letter to F. N. Watkins—"Mr. Graham arrived at old Mrs. Morton's, a house in which many Christians usually lodged on such occasions; and that night, or next morning, led in family prayer. The apparent tone of his feelings did not exactly suit the ardour of some of the young converts, and they requested Mr. Smith not to let him preach. Mr. Smith preached the morning sermon. After the communion services were ended, Mr. Graham preached from Isaiah 40th chapter, 1st and 2d verses. 'Comfort ye, comfort ye my people, saith your God. Speak ye comfortably to Jerusalem, and cry unto her that her warfare is accomplished, that her iniquity is pardoned.' As soon as he commenced it was evident to all that his feelings were of the strong and tender kind. And in evangelical strains he poured forth gospel truth like floods of milk and wine; while the melting eyes and glowing countenances of a large assembly showed that many were eating as friends, and drinking abundantly of the consolations provided for them of their God.—He brought some of his young people with him, hoping that in the midst of the outpouring of the Spirit, they might receive the grace of God. His hopes were not in vain. Dr. Alexander was one of that young company." This sermon of Mr. Graham made an unusual impression. There are still living a few who heard it; and these, after a lapse of about sixty years, speak of the immediate influence, and the abiding impression of that discourse; it was one among ten thousand. Perhaps the influence was greater from the low estimation the congregation had formed of the sermon to be expected from one whose congregation had not been revived. One that accompanied him from Rockbridge says under date of Princeton, August 16th, 1848—"The sermon of Mr. Graham on the text, Comfort ye, comfort ye my people, &c., was the first sermon which he preached on his first visit to Prince Edward, when I accompanied him. It was preached at Briery, immediately after the administration of sacrament; and Dr. Smith said to me, that he had never heard more than one sermon which he liked as well, and that one was

preached by Rev. James Mitchell. I did not hear the first part
of this discourse; for there being a prospect of rain the communion was administered in the house, and the non-professors,
to which number I belonged, were requested to remain under
the arbour and hear sermons from the Rev. Nash Legrand and
Rev. S. Houston. But the rain came on with violence and
drove us into the house, as many as could press in. I remember the peculiarly solemn appearance of the congregation when
I entered the house. The speaker was then addressing such as
were not the people of God, and he commenced every paragraph
with—O comfortless ye!

"During Mr. Graham's visit to Prince Edward, he preached
a number of times, in various parts of the congregation. His
sermons were of a searching, discriminating character. The
revival in Prince Edward was on the decline when Mr. Graham
paid his first visit; but it was at its height in Bedford. After
spending ten days or a fortnight in Prince Edward, Mr. Graham, Dr. Smith, Mr. Legrand and others, went on to a sacramental meeting at the Peaks of Otter. Here both Dr. Smith
and Mr. Graham preached with great power and effect.
Turner had just come out a flaming convert, and moved the
whole country round with his pathetic exhortations. About
thirty young persons came over from Rockbridge to this sacrament. They had heard of the wonderful works of God in
the conversion of notorious sinners, and they came partly
out of curiosity, and partly from a serious impression on
their minds. Most of them were females, and of the best
families about Lexington. Every one of these except one man,
went home deeply impressed. As Dr. Smith had an appointment to preach a funeral sermon at New London, this company agreed to stay another week and attend the meetings
which were kept up every evening. Mr. Legrand remained
with them, and went over to Lexington in their company. A
happier company I never saw; they made the mountains echo
with their songs of praise. Arriving at Lexington in the afternoon, a meeting was immediately proclaimed; and the people
assembled from all quarters. Mr. Graham and Mr. Legrand
addressed the crowded assembly with great fervency and
solemnity; and two young men were called on to pray. This
more than any thing else struck the mind with astonishment,
for no young person for many years had been known to be
serious, or to profess religion in that community. Many at
this first meeting were impressed. But on the ensuing Sabbath
a great congregation was collected at Monmouth; for the news
spread rapidly. Mr. Legrand preached on the text—'Look
unto me all ye ends of the earth, and be ye saved!' After sermon Mr. Graham gave a narrative of all that he had witnessed,

which he followed with one of the most affecting exhortations I ever heard, during which he poured out a torrent of tears ; and very few eyes in the house were dry. The impression on the minds of the assembly was very general. It is probable that one hundred persons were now brought under serious impressions of religion ; but all these did not become true converts. Frequent meetings were now held in town and country ; and at every meeting great solemnity and deep feeling were manifest. Every day new cases were heard of ; and while the convictions of most lasted for weeks before they ventured to entertain a hope, others were suddenly brought out of their troubles and made to rejoice in the light of God's countenance. A number of educated young men were among the converts, who now turned their attention to studies preparatory for the ministry.

" The revival, though it had its seat in Lexington and vicinity, was not confined to that region, but extended to almost every Presbyterian congregation in the Valley. Sacramental occasions were exceedingly solemn, and attended by many from a great distance. Mr. Legrand travelled on a missionary tour to the south-west along the Valley ; and wherever he went had seals to his ministry. But in a few weeks he returned and laboured again in Lexington and the vicinity.

" Some old professors gave up their former hopes and began anew. Among these was a respectable clergyman who attended the meetings in disguise, that he might not be called on to officiate. He took a journey to Prince Edward to see if he could benefit from attending on the preaching of Dr. Smith. He came out clear before long.

"It was not long before Dr. Smith came over to visit the people. An angel would not have been received with more joy and cordiality ; for he still had the pre-eminence as the father of the revival ; and the very sound of his voice thrilled every nerve of those who had heard him before. It was on a second visit, I think, he preached the sermon, a defence of the revival, from the words,—' Behold ye despisers, and wonder and perish,'—in the grove at New Monmouth, immediately after the communion. It was certainly one of his greatest efforts ; and was among the most eloquent discourses I ever heard from the mouth of man. Many of the opposers of the revival were present, and were cut to the heart ; and while some were convinced of their errors, others were the more enraged and gnashed upon him with their teeth. In returning from the meeting I conversed with an old Presbyterian Elder from Oxford congregation, who confessed that he had been in error and prejudice against the revival, but that Dr. Smith had convinced him of his error."—A. A.

The Seceders in Rockbridge were many of them greatly

opposed to the revival; and Dr. Smith, in his famous defence, bore heavily upon them by name, and said—"that from the time they set themselves in opposition to the revival at Kylsith and Cambuslang, the Spirit of the Lord had forsaken them." While some were convinced, others were rendered more vehement in their opposition, and declared they thought him possessed with an evil spirit.

The revival spread through all the Valley congregations, and its effects are felt to this day in Virginia, Kentucky, and Tennessee, and other western and south-western States, though in a less degree, in the labours of ministers and pious people then brought into the church.

A large proportion of the young people of Mr. Graham's charge became hopefully pious; and the heart of the pastor spoke out, when during the revival he said to a friend—"when this revival began I thought that if three young men would become ministers of the gospel, I should be satisfied. Now these three have become hopefully pious, and have turned their views to the ministry; and I feel as far from being satisfied as ever. I believe I shall never be satisfied while there is one left behind." The pastor had long been sowing, and often in tears; but now he reaped in joy; and would gladly have brought all to Christ. This was his harvest.

In consequence of this revival, a new duty devolved on Mr. Graham,—*the instruction of a Class of Theological Students,*—the first ever formed in Virginia. He had in former years directed the studies of young men preparing for the ministry. Other ministers in Virginia had done the same, from Samuel Davies' time to this revival; and Dr. Smith of Hampden Sidney, had trained Lacy and Legrand and others for the sacred office. But the organizing a class, or making the instruction of a number of youth in theology a special business, was first known at Liberty Hall Academy by the agency of Mr. Graham. Dr. Alexamder, in his address to the Alumni, says— "After the great revival which commenced in this Valley, in the year 1789, Mr. Graham had a Theological Class of seven or eight members under his tuition, which was kept up for several years. It was his custom to devote one day in the week to hearing the written discourses of these candidates, and to a free discussion of theological points. In these exercises he appeared to take a great delight; and the students were always gratified and commonly convinced by his lucid statements and cogent reasonings. As most of those who enjoyed the benefit of his instructions, in this incipient theological seminary, are not now in the world, it may not be improper to say, that some of them rose to eminence in the church, and as Professors or Presidents of literary institutions. The influence which he gained over the minds of his pupils, while under his care, was unbounded. Seldom did any one of them venture to maintain an opinion, different from those which he inculcated. Yet he encouraged the utmost freedom of discussion; and seemed to aim, not so much to bring his pupils to think as he did, as to teach them to think on all subjects for themselves. A slavish subjection to any human authority he repudiated; and therefore, never attempted to add weight to his opinions by referring to a long list of authors, of great name; but uniformly insisted, that all opinions should be subjected to the test of Scripture and reason. Some of his pupils have been heard to say, that the chief benefit which they derived from his instructions was, that by this means they were led to the free and independent exercise of their own faculties in the investigation of the truth. Mr. Graham, in his theological creed, was strictly orthodox, according to the standard of his own church, which he greatly venerated; but in his method of explaining some of the knotty points in theology, he departed considerably from the common track; and was of opinion, that many things which have been involved in perplexity and obscurity by the manner in which they have been treated, are capable of being easily and satisfactorily explained by the application of sound principles of philosophy."

Those—"sound principles of philosophy"—Mr. Graham never committed to writing. They have been preserved in the memory and heart of his pupils, and by them have been taught widely. The principles of mental philosophy inculcated at Princeton Theological Seminary, have not been found in such form and connexion, in any printed volumes, as they were enunciated from the Professor's chair, by a pupil of Graham. Perhaps they will not be lost to posterity, as they have not been to this generation.

Much had been expected from Mr. Graham's theological students; and the hopes of the church were not disappointed. Zealous but not superficial, hortatory but not immethodical, they exhibited clearness of perception, strength of argument, closeness of reasoning, and often profound thinking as well as fervent piety. They imbibed much of the habits of mind and the theological principles of their teacher, but imitated him less than has been usual with students that so much admired their preceptor in every thing pertaining to his office. The voice of Graham was not heard to echo, nor was his manner seen in the pulpit labours of any of his pupils.

The Synod of Virginia being in session at Winchester, Sept. 28th, 1791—" Messrs. (Wm.) Wilson, (Joseph) Patterson and (James) Mitchell, Ministers; and Messrs. John Wilson and Thomas Marques, Elders, were appointed a Committee of Overtures, and ordered to make report as soon as they have business ready for Synod."

At the same sessions, Sept. 30th—"Through the Committee of Overtures it was proposed, that the Synod, if it might appear expedient, should institute and encourage some plan calculated to educate persons designed for the gospel ministry, in that way which may be most suitable to fit them for that office.

"The Synod having approved the design of the proposition, appointed Messrs. Joseph Smith, William Graham, John B. Smith, John McMillan, Joseph Patterson, William Wilson and Moses Hogue, a committee to form a plan for promoting the education of persons for the gospel ministry; and to make report before the rising of Synod."

At the same sessions, Oct. 1st—"The committee appointed to form a plan for promoting the education of persons for the ministry of the gospel made report. The Synod having considered the same, and made such amendments and additions as were judged necessary, agreed to it as followeth:

"The Synod highly approve of the proposition contained in the overture, as they are well convinced of the necessity of extending the opportunity of acquiring knowledge, and especially the knowledge of the doctrines of religion, to all who intend to preach the gospel of Jesus Christ to the world.

"Taking this measure, therefore, into serious consideration, the Synod recommend that there be two general institutions for learning, conducted under the patronage of this body—the one to be established in Rockbridge county in this State, under the care of the Rev. William Graham as the President;—The other in Washington county, Pennsylvania, under the care of the Rev. John McMillan. The principles upon which these institutions are to be conducted, are to be as follows:

"1. The learned languages, and the usual circle of the sciences shall be taught in them, to as many as shall be sent there for instruction.

"2. During the course of academical education, and from the first initiation of the students into the seminaries, a course of religious instruction shall be entered upon, and continually adhered to during their residence there, according to the principles of our Church. Books of a practical and doctrinal nature shall be put into their hands at once: catechetical lectures shall be established; and examinations entered into upon their progress in this kind of knowledge from time to time. The attention to these studies shall be kept up during the whole of their academical course, and suited to the capacities and progress of the youth.

"3. The Presbyteries of Hanover and Lexington shall be the Trustees of the Seminary in Rockbridge, to cherish it by their influence, and pointedly to attend to the examinations of the students, either in a collective capacity, or by committees from their respective bodies, duly appointed.—The Presbytery of Redstone shall in like manner superintend the seminary in Washington.

"4. In one or other of these institutions, it is the desire of Synod that all the youths who intend to engage in the ministry of the gospel, within our bounds, shall be instructed.

" 5. As there are many pious youths of promising genius in our country, who might be very serviceable in preaching the gospel; but through want of ability are unable to obtain an education; it is the intention and desire of the Synod that the ministers in the respective Presbyteries, shall seek out such ; and that they, being examined and approved by the Presbytery, shall be placed in the respective Seminaries, at the expense of the Presbytery who approve them.

"6. And in order to obtain the proper supplies for such indigent students, the Presbytery are exhorted to use their influence in their respective bounds, with the pious and benevolent, to raise annual contributions for establishing a fund for this purpose. This fund to be placed in the hands of a Treasurer appointed by the Synod, who is to return annual accounts of receipts and expenditures. And from it the youth upon the foundation are to draw their supplies, by an order from the respective Presidents.—And those youths, upon obtaining their education, at the expiration of one year after being settled in some line of public business, shall begin to refund the expenses of their education to the treasury, in such a time and manner as the Presbytery may direct.

"7. The rules for the Seminaries and the mode of education therein, shall be submitted by the Presidents to the respective Presbyteries for their approbation.

"8. The Synod recommend it to the Presbytery of Transylvania, to institute and patronise a Seminary within their bounds, upon principles similar to those herein laid down, and for similar purposes; or to encourage either of those that are now recommended."

The Synod of Virginia being in session at Winchester, September 29th, 1792,

"Upon motion, Messrs. Graham, Hoge, and Houston, Ministers, and Mr. John Wilson, Elder, were appointed a committee to draft a minute, that may make the plan of education proposed by the Synod last year, coincide with the Act of Incorporation, instituting the Academy of Liberty Hall, and to make report before the rising of Synod."

The same afternoon, "the Committe appointed to draft a minute which may accommodate the plan of education proposed by the Synod to the Act of Incorporation, instituting Liberty Hall, report—that they examined wherein they do not coincide, and find that the following particulars appear necessary for Synod to adopt, in order to put it in the power of the Trustees of said Academy, to devote their property to the purposes proposed by Synod, agreeably to the proposals said Trustees have made in their petition to Synod. 1st. That instead of constituting the Presbyteries of Hanover and Lexington the Trustees of the Academy in Rockbridge, the Synod agree that they shall remain according to the direction of the Act; only that the Board is requested to fill up vacancies out of those two Presbyteries; and to agree to the direction of Synod that these two Presbyteries may attend at the examinations of the students.

"2d. Lastly, that the seventh article in the Synod's plan is wholly provided for in another way in the Act of Incorporation, and therefore, that the Synod do not desire the Trustees of the Academy of Liberty Hall to comply with it."

The Synod of Virginia being in session at Winchester, September 27th, 1793,

"Through the Committee of Overtures a petition was presented from the Trustees of the Academy of Liberty Hall, stating that they had agreed to the conditions on which the Synod proposed last year to patronise said Academy, and stating that, encouraged by this and other favourable considerations, they had contracted for buildings to the amount of £900, which are to be finished by the 1st of December, and praying the active aid and concurrence of the Synod. The Synod approved the vigorous exertions of the Trustees of the Academy, and earnestly recommend it to, and enjoin it upon the Presbyteries of Hanover and of Lexington, to exert themselves and to use their influence to raise money to aid the Trustees in discharging the contracts already made, and to raise the Academy to as great a state of usefulness as possible."

While the Synod was busied in this arrangement for schools of learning,—on the 29th of October, 1791, application was made to Hanover Presbytery,—"from Cumberland, Briery and Cub Creek congregations, by their representatives, for leave to prosecute a call for Rev. William Graham, of Lexington, in the county of Rockbridge, which was granted." On the same day, James Turner, who has been styled nature's orator, was licensed; and William Williamson, one of the five who formed Winchester Presbytery, was received on trials.

The Trustees of Hampden Sidney had made propositions to Mr. Graham to remove to Prince Edward and take charge of their College, immediately after the resignation of Dr. Smith; and in 1791, had urged the congregations mentioned above to unite with them, in the hopes that their united efforts might procure his removal. Mr. Graham referred the call of the congregations, together with the invitation of the Trustees of Hampden Sidney, to the Presbytery, and they considering it a matter of synodical importance referred it to the Synod of Virginia. That matter was laid before the Synod at their meeting in 1792; and two commissioners sent by the Trustees of Hampden Sidney appeared to advocate his removal, as President, and as Professor of Theology. The Trustees of Liberty Hall, and the Presbytery of Lexington opposed the removal. The Synod, after hearing the subject debated fully, determined that Mr. Graham's prospects of usefulness in Rockbridge and Prince Edward were so nearly equal, that they could not with propriety decide; and therefore left it to him—"to do in the affair what should appear to him most conducive to the interests of the church of Christ and his own comfort and happiness." On the next day after this decision of Synod, Mr. Graham reported to Synod—"that he did not conceive it to be his duty to remove from his present charge."

The wooden building which had been prepared for the accommodation of the students of Liberty Hall, having been consumed by fire, the Trustees, stimulated by the action of Synod and the determination of Mr. Graham, proceeded to the erection of new and more spacious buildings for the accommodation of the students of Liberty Hall. In April, 1793, the committee appointed at a previous meeting—"to open subscriptions for the increase of the funds, and to set on foot means for preparing materials for building an academy house,"—made such a report as encouraged the Board to employ workmen to erect and complete the buildings. By great exertions of Mr. Graham, the buildings for the steward and the students were finished by the 25th of December. And on the 1st of January, 1794, the new buildings were occupied.

The studies of the classes had not been intermitted; and after the erection of the new buildings the Academy, for a time, flourished more than at any preceding period. But difficulties arose from the two offices of Mr. Graham, Professor of Theology under the direction of the Synod of Virginia, and President of the Academy under the charter from the State. At this time religion became an object of jealousy throughout the State. During the Revolution the question had first been mooted, whether there should be a State establishment, or whether all forms of religion should be equally protected, and the decision was for equal protection; the next question was, shall the ministers be supported by law or voluntary subscription, and was decided in favour of voluntary subscription. At this time the question finally debated was—is there any truth in the Christian religion? French principles became popular in Virginia. The scientific researches, the political principles, and the infidelity of Paris were indissolubly connected in the minds of most Frenchmen; and their progress in Virginia, more alarming than wonderful, circumscribed religious action to narrow bounds. Ministers of religion became objects of suspicion and ridicule; and many who had been educated religiously, were led away, at least for a time, by the prevailing fanaticism; no bigots for a religious sect were ever more unreasonable in their opposition to others, than were the advocates for the French principles in their opposition to religious worship founded on the gospel. But for the happy influence of the revival of 1788, east of the Ridge, and of 1789, west of the Ridge, in sending in to the ministry that eminent company of young men, Lacy, Allen, Legrand, Hill, Alexander, Lyle, Marshall, Williamson, Turner, Houston, and others, there is reason to fear the churches would in a great measure have been swept away. The desecration of religious things is scarcely to be credited, and not necessary to relate.

One political circumstance added weight; the abettors of certain political notions, popular in Virginia, were supposed to be favourable to the principles of skepticism. The effect was to turn some against those principles, for reasons of a religious nature; and to make others renounce their belief in the gospel of Christ, for their political party. The collision of these two parties was rancorous to a degree not now known in politics. Mr. Graham had freely expressed his principles and views on political subjects, under the deep conviction that it became every patriot, especially at the time when the constitutions and institutions of the country were forming, to express openly and faithfully those connexions and modifications of principles the emergency evidently required. In doing this, he had made some political enemies; and the cry of bigotry and sectarianism was raised against him and the College over which he presided.

There was another circumstance, arising from himself, from which difficulties arose. "Candour requires"—says the author of the address to the Alumni—"that it should be acknowledged, that he sometimes imprudently made enemies of those who might have been efficient friends, by too free an indulgence of satirical and sarcastical remarks; which weapon he could wield with great power. And it must also be conceded, that towards his opponents, he never manifested much of a conciliatory temper, but seemed rather disposed to stand aloof from them, and to set them at defiance." "He had"—says a writer in the Evangelical Magazine, for 1821—"a quick and acute perception of the ridiculous and incongruous in human conduct, and had a strong propensity to satire. Although he doubtless generally restrained this propensity, yet as he sometimes indulged it, it created him enemies who occasionally had it in their power to impair his comfort and diminish his usefulness." From this, the most unamiable trait of his character, some difficulty arose, not of itself sufficient to render his situation unpleasant to him, but in conjunction with others, filled the cup of his trials too full for him quietly to bear.

The fearlessness of Mr. Graham in expressing his opinion, and the danger to which that fearlessness sometimes exposed him, was exhibited at the meeting of the Synod of Virginia in Harrisonburg in 1794. A party of soldiers on their way to west Pennsylvania to suppress the insurrectionary movements of "the Whiskey Boys"—was in the town at the time of the meeting of Synod. As the scene of discontent and insurrection was within the bounds of two of the Presbyteries forming the Synod, Rev. Mr. Hoge proposed an address to the people inculcating obedience to the laws of the country. Mr. Graham opposed all legislation on the subject, by Synod; and maintained there were wrongs to be redressed rather than a rebellion to be crushed; that the circumstances of the discontented had been misjudged. The avowal of these sentiments in Synod was followed by appeals so strong that the motion for an address was lost by a small majority. The excitement among the soldiery was great; violence was threatened to the Synod and particularly to the man who opposed the exercise of military force in adjusting the affairs of west Pennsylvania. The Synod declined receding from their position, under threats of violence from the soldiery or the clamours of an incensed mob. Mr. Hoge went boldly among the soldiers and citizens and exhorted them to quietness, and by invitation preached an impressive sermon from the words "render unto Cæsar the things which are Cæsar's, and unto God the things that are God's." Mr. Graham, by the advice of friends, retired from the scene of confusion. This event added to the number of those who were willing his situation at Liberty Hall should become unpleasant.

The emoluments of the office of Rector had never well remunerated him. During the first sixteen years of the Academy, tuition had been forty shillings the session; after the new buildings were prepared, in 1794, the tuition was fifty shillings the session. From the tuition money the salaries of all the teachers were to be paid. As Mr. Graham had in a great measure the selection of the teachers, they looked to him for their salaries and were of course first paid. Some years he received nothing from the Academy. With a small salary from his congregations, how was his family to live?

All these reasons combined induced Mr. Graham to resign the Presidency or Rectorship. This event took place, in 1796, when he was in his fiftieth year, and was announced by the following letter,—

"September 25, 1796.

"*Gentlemen:*—After long and solemn deliberation, I have been compelled to come to the resolution of relinquishing the care of that infant Seminary which I have so long endeavoured to cherish. After twenty-two years of anxious toil, it would have been one of the happiest events of my life to have seen the Seminary in a condition of permanent and extensive usefulness, and to have aided in its prosperity. But the impracticability of acquiring the conveniences and even the necessaries of life, for myself and my family, whilst my time was spent in the discharge of the necessary duties of an office which brought me no return, has induced me to resign my office and title of Rector of Liberty Hall.

"That you, gentlemen, may be more abundantly successful in your future efforts, is the desire and prayer of

Your humble servant,

WILLIAM GRAHAM.

"The Trustees of Liberty Hall."

Mr. Graham immediately set out upon a journey to the western part of the State, on a plan which he had near his heart. After his return, the Trustees sent him the following answer.

"*Dear Sir:*—At a meeting in October, 1796, we received your resignation. Your absence then prevented any reply. The reasons you assign we acknowledge are weighty. We could not help lamenting that hard necessity, which deprived us of our Rector, whilst, at the same time, as was natural, we felt emotions of gratitude and esteem. We have long been convinced that much time, pains and expense are requisite to fit men for literary occupations; that the business of education is extremely irksome; and therefore that generous encouragement should be given to those who undertake employments of this sort.

"We hoped ere now to have been able to reward liberally the officers of the Academy; but a variety of causes have hitherto conspired to render our efforts in a great measure vain. However, notwithstanding the embarrassed state of our affairs, we have been happy in seeing the Seminary, for many years, eminently useful in disseminating knowledge, and thereby subserving the general interests of literature and piety. This we attribute, under Providence, to your distinguished talents, and that steady, disinterested zeal, which you have uniformly discovered for the prosperity of the Academy. And although pecuniary compensation has been wanting, yet we believe you have the grateful esteem of every good man, and the approbation of Him who knows all our ways.

"That He may go with you through the remainder of life,— that his wisdom may direct and his providence guard you,—and that every blessing may attend you and your family, is the sincere prayer of the Trustees of Liberty Hall.

SAMUEL HOUSTON, *Chairman.*

"The Rev. Wm. Graham.
  "April 20th, 1797."

Before the resignation, the efforts, of which he had been the principal leader, to secure some permanent funds to Liberty Hall, had been successful. Early in the year 1785, the Legislature of Virginia expressed the high admiration entertained for the character and services of General Washington, by a donation of one hundred shares in the James River Company, and fifty shares in the Potomac Company. Washington felt and expressed a delicacy in appropriating the gift to his own emolument, or in declining the gift of the State. General Knox suggested that he might use the proceeds for the benefit of the widows and children of Virginia officers killed in the war; his own mind modified the suggestion of Knox—"to have the product of the tolls arising from these shares applied as a fund on which to establish two charity schools, one on each river, for the education and support of the children of the poor in this country, particularly the children of those men of this description, who have fallen in the défence of the rights and liberties of it." In the fall of the year the Legislature so changed the act as to permit General Washington to apply the proceeds to any object " of a public nature, in such manner and under such distributions as the said George Washington by deed during his life, or by his last will and testament, shall direct." There the matter lay till the year 1795, when the shares about to become productive demanded consideration. Mr. Jefferson suggested the propriety of giving all to an University to be established in the district of Columbia. General Washington, then President of the United States, was favourably inclined to the proposition, and made an endowment of the fifty shares of the Potomac Company, and proposed to the Legislature the consideration of the propriety of bestowing the one hundred shares of James River stock the same way; but— "Presuming it would be more agreeable to the General Assembly of Virginia, that the shares in the James River Company should be reserved for a similar object in some part of that State, I intend to allot them for a Seminary, to be erected at such place as they shall deem most proper. I am disposed to believe, that a seminary of learning upon an enlarged plan, but not yet coming up to the full idea of a University, is an institution to be preferred for the position which is to be chosen. The students, who wish to pursue the whole range of science, may pass with advantage from the Seminary to the University, and the former by a due relation may be rendered co-operative with the latter."—To this the Legislature replied December 1, 1795, with many expressions of respect, commending the erection of a University in the Federal City, and approving of the endowment of it with the fifty shares of Potomac stock—and— "Resolved also, that he be requested to appropriate the aforesaid shares in the James River Company to a Seminary in such place in the upper country as he may deem most convenient to a majority of the inhabitants thereof."

The following extracts from the records of the Board of Trustees of Washington College give the doings of the Rector and Trustees on this important business, of obtaining the proposed endowment.

"January 5, 1796.—The Rector informed the Board that he [had] called them together, to take under consideration some direct information he had received, of the Legislature of this State having resolved there shall be a public Seminary in the upper part of this State, and that the President of the United States was about to bestow his hundred shares in the James River Company, to aid in endowing the same.

"The Board maturely considered the information of the Rector, and agreed to address the President in such a manner as might give him a true view of the state of this Academy, and of the propriety of the donation being conferred upon it.

"On motion the Board appointed the Rector and Messrs. Samuel L. Campbell and Samuel Houston, or any two of them, a committee on behalf of the Board, to send forward such an address to the President, as will contain the things signified by the Board, as proper to be communicated, and that they report a copy as soon as convenient." [Records, Vol. I. p. 144.]

The committee reported the following, viz:—

"The Trustees of Liberty Hall Academy, in Rockbridge county and State of Virginia, to his Excellency George Washington, President of the United States of America.

"*Sir:*—We have lately heard of your generous and disinterested conduct, in refusing as private emolument, the shares in the Potomack and James River Companies, presented to you by the Legislature of Virginia, as a testimony of their approbation and gratitude.

"We have also heard of the wise and beneficent purposes to which you wished to have the profits arising from these shares applied,—the endowment of a Seminary on the waters of each these rivers for the education of youth, and that you referred the appropriation of the hundred shares in the James River Company to the wisdom of the Legislature of Virginia; who after deliberating on the important subject, agreed that the whole should be applied to one Seminary up the country,—but some differences of opinion arising respecting the particular place to which it should be applied, referred the ultimate decision to your Excellency.

"Supposing our information just, we are constrained by the duty we owe the public, as well as the Seminary we have long had the honour to patronise, to address you on this very interesting subject.

"And here we cannot allow ourselves to think it proper to pray you to grant the donation for the support of education in this Seminary, as a matter of honour or emolument to ourselves, or emolument to the neighbourhood where it stands. This would be selfish and invidious and inconsistent with the feelings of that mind, which always overlooks private interest to embrace and secure the public good. We beg leave only to state a few facts for your Excellency's information, that you may be enabled to decide the important question with greater precision.

"From a conviction of the necessity and utility of a public Seminary to complete the education of youth in this upper part of the State; as early as the year 1776, a Seminary before conducted in these parts under the form of a grammar school, received the nominal title of an Academy, and money was collected to purchase the beginnings of a library, and some of the most essential parts of a philosophical and mathematical apparatus.

"The question then was, where should the Seminary be fixed? Staunton was proposed by some, to be the proper place, as the most ancient and populous town, and nearest the centre of population in the upper part of the State as it then stood. But considering that a public Seminary, which was to be of permanent duration and general utility, ought not to be affected by local circumstances arising from temporary causes;—and viewing the extensive lands upon the drains of [the] Holstein to the south-west, and of the Kanawha to the west, we were of opinion that the time was not very far distant when the population upon these lands must equal, if not exceed the population upon the drains of the Potomac to the northeast, upon one of which drains Staunton stands. We therefore considered the waters of James River as forming a kind of natural and common centre. We also felt a conviction, that the extensive and fertile lands upon James River, would at a period not far remote, point out the necessity and practicability of rendering its streams navigable above the mountains, and we have been happy in seeing our expectations realizing every day.

"We therefore concluded that some spot in the tract of country now known as Rockbridge county, would be the proper place. We therefore organized the Seminary, and set it in motion, hoping that the public would one day aid our exertions and enable us to perfect what had been honestly begun.

"Through the calamities of a long and dangerous war, and the deceptions of a paper currency, together with other misfortunes, great obstructions were experienced, but being happy in able and diligent teachers, we were enabled to preserve the Academy in a state of considerable reputation and usefulness until the year 1782, when we were aided by an act of incorporation from the Legislature of Virginia, which was the first granted after the Revolution.

"In 1793 we found it necessary to fix the spot where the building should finally stand, which was determined to be in that fine tract of country formerly known by the name of the Woods' Creek lands, in the Forks of James River, one mile from the navigation of the North Branch, and on an eminence about three-quarters of a mile from Lexington,—so that whilst it enjoys an extensive prospect of the circumjacent country, and a view of the town, it has agreeably to its great design, an undisturbed retirement for study.

"The situation of the neighbourhood for health and fertility as well as pleasantness, yields to no lands in the upper part of the State.

"If our information of the state of the dispute respecting the place, as it existed before the Legislature, be accurate, it went a great way to determine the propriety of our original opinion. It is said that Fincastle on the one side, and Staunton on the other, were the extremes which made any vigorous claims. Fincastle is situated thirty-seven miles south west from Liberty Hall, and Staunton thirty-five miles to the north east. Therefore Liberty Hall is as near the centre as local situation would admit.

"There is one more fact which we would beg leave to state. In 1793, by voluntary contributions, and some sacrifices of private property, we were enabled to erect and finish plain but neat buildings, sufficiently capacious to accommodate between forty and fifty students, and the business of education is now in full train, and the Seminary in as high reputation as could be expected without funds. Many young gentlemen have finished their education here, who are now serving their country with reputation and usefulness, in different professional departments, and a number are now collected from different parts of the country for the same end.

"The buildings and other furniture of the Academy could not be estimated at much less than two thousand pounds. If the seat of the academy is changed, the young gentlemen must be interrupted for some time in their studies, and the buildings totally lost, as they can be applied to no other purpose. The destruction of so much property, procured with considerable difficulty, unless a much greater preponderating good can be secured to the public, will doubtless be seriously weighed. And as the public good is the only object which can influence your determination, it is unnecessary to add any thing further, but fully confiding in your wisdom, we shall entirely acquiesce in your decision.

"That all possible happiness, present and future, may attend your person, and every public blessing your administration, is the desire and prayer of your Excellency's humble servants, the Trustees of Liberty Hall. By order and in behalf of the Board,   WILLIAM GRAHAM, *C. M.*
                                        SAMUEL HOUSTON, *C. B. T.*
January, 1796."

WASHINGTON'S LETTER TO GOVERNOR BROOKE.

"Philadelphia, 15th September, 1796.

"*Sir :*—The Commonwealth of Virginia having manifested their approbation of my design to apply the hundred shares in the James River Company, which they had before put at my disposal, to the use of a Seminary, to be erected in such part of the State as they should deem most proper, and in consequence of this referred to their opinion,—The Legislature having requested me to appropriate them to a Seminary in such place in the upper country, as I should think most convenient to a majority of its inhabitants,—After careful inquiries to ascertain that place, I have, upon the fullest consideration of all circumstances, destined those shares to the use of Liberty Hall Academy in Rockbridge county.

"It would seem to me proper, that this determination should be promulgated by some official act of the executive of Virginia, and the Legislature may expect it for the purpose of general information.

"With due consideration and respect, I am, sir, your most obedient humble servant,

GEO. WASHINGTON.

"His Excellency, ROBERT BROOKE, Governor of Virginia."

The Trustees of Liberty Hall took the following action:

"Washington Academy, April 12, 1798.

"The committee appointed to draft an address to President Washington, respecting his destination of the use of the shares in the James River Canal Company to this Seminary, reported a draft, which being read and considered, was agreed to, and is as follows:

"*Sir:*—It was not earlier than September, 1797, that we were officially informed of your liberal donation to Liberty Hall Academy.

"Permit us as its immediate guardians to perform the pleasing duty of expressing those sentiments of gratitude which so generous an act naturally inspires. We have been long sensible of the disadvantages to which literary institutions are necessarily subjected, whilst dependent on precarious funds for their support. Reflecting particularly on the many difficulties through which this Seminary has been conducted since the first moments of its existence, we cannot but be greatly affected by an event which secures to it an independent and permanent establishment. Convinced as we are that public prosperity and security are intimately connected with the diffusion of knowledge, we look around with the highest satisfaction on its rapid advances in these United States, unfeignedly rejoicing that the citizen who has long been distinguished as the asserter of the liberties of his country, adds to this illustrious character, the no less illustrious one of patron of the arts and of literature. And we trust that no effort may be wanting on our part to encourage whatever branches of knowledge may be of general utility.

"That you may long enjoy, besides the uninterrupted blessings of health and repose, the happiness which none but those who deserve it can enjoy, and which arises from the reflection of having virtuously and eminently promoted the best interests of mankind, is the fervent prayer of the Trustees of Washington Academy, late Liberty Hall.

By order of the Board, SAMUEL HOUSTON, *Clerk.*

"His Excellency, GEO. WASHINGTON,
    late President of the U. S. A."

WASHINGTON'S REPLY.

"Mount Vernon, 17th June, 1798.

"*Gentlemen:*—Unaccountable as it may seem, it is nevertheless true, that the address with which you were pleased to honour me, dated the 12th of April, never came into my hand until the 11th instant.

"To promote literature in this rising empire, and to encourage the arts, have ever been amongst the warmest wishes of my heart.

And if the donation which the generosity of the Legislature of the Commonwealth of Virginia has enabled me to bestow upon Liberty Hall, now by your politeness called Washington Academy, is likely to prove a means to accomplish these ends, it will contribute to the gratification of my desires.

"Sentiments like those which have flowed from your pen excite my gratitude, whilst I offer my best vows for the prosperity of the Academy, and for the honour and happiness of those under whose auspices it is conducted.

GEORGE WASHINGTON.

"Trustees of Washington Academy."

It appears that for some reasons not fully explained, official notice of Washington's donation was not speedily given to the Board of Trustees. But at the meeting of the Legislature next succeeding the letter to Governor Brooke from Washington, making Liberty Hall the recipient of his donation, the Legislature, without the consent or knowledge of the Trustees of Liberty Hall, passed an Act changing the Academy into a College, under a new Board of Trustees. This caused great excitement. The Board held repeated meetings for consultation. Suspicions were afloat that the secret design of this unexpected movement was to take the institution, with its late endowment, from the hands of those who had hitherto cherished it; and a person was named as the intended President, a person of eminence, but not the choice of the former patrons, Bishop Madison. There may have been no ground for these suspicions. On the 7th of February, 1797, the Board declared—"We conceive the said Act to be a singular instance of infringement on the rights of a corporate body, which had not by any act of theirs violated tenure, or given cause for the abolition of their charter." For this opinion they give six reasons, viz:

"1st. A corporation being an artificial person, and the property belonging to this corporation, being held as private property, cannot be at the disposal of the representatives of the people. 2d. Because the law is not only unjust in its nature, but dangerous in its tendency; the same principle, if it be admitted in one case, may be extended to every such corporation throughout the State. Their charter may be violated, and their estates, in whatever way acquired, may be wantonly sported with, just as caprice or folly may dictate. 3d. Because the business of education must be interrupted at this place for a considerable time, and greatly impeded for the future. If the corporation is dissolved, the property being given by individuals, would revert to the original donors, and in future the liberal would be discouraged from contributing to similar institutions. 4th. Because the debts due to and from this corporation cannot be legally recovered after its dissolution, and as several such debts do exist, it would be an act of injustice in the corporation to suffer such dissolution to take place. 5th. Because the property of Liberty Hall having been committed to us in trust, we consider ourselves responsible for the use of the same, and culpable if we suffer it tamely to be taken from us. 6th. Because we are all assured that the late interference of our Legislature, with regard to Liberty Hall, is in a great degree contrary to the wishes of those good citizens, who for the promotion of virtue and literature, gave largely of their estates to this Academy."

On the 19th of April of the same year, the Board took into consideration the state of the Academy; and on the 20th "appointed Messrs. William Willson, Samuel Brown, Benjamin Grigsby, Samuel L. Campbell, and Samuel Houston, or any three of them, a committee on behalf of the Board to send letters of information to other corporations in the State, of the attempt to deprive us of our charter."—The same committee were requested to prepare a remonstrance to be laid before the Assembly. In November the remonstrance was presented to the Board and adopted, and Mr. Brown was required to commit it to the representatives of the county. What effect the remonstrance may have had is not material; the offensive law was repealed.

On the 25th of November, 1797, "Messrs. J. Willson, Benjamin Grigsby, and S. Houston, or any two of them were appointed a committee on behalf of the Board, to wait upon Capt. Johnson, and instruct him to have the title of Liberty Hall Academy changed into that of a College, if he finds it expedient or beneficial in the Assembly. Also that said committee furnish him with all documents necessary to give him information respecting the Academy." The name was changed to Washington Academy, and the charter remained unchanged. In the year 1813, the name of Academy was by act of Legislature changed to College—and that of Rector to President.

The funds of the College were after this increased by the donation of the Virginia Cincinnati Society, amounting to sixteen thousand dollars. Mr. John Robinson, a citizen of Rockbridge gave, by his last will, his whole estate to the College.

Previous to this period the institution stood upon the character and talents of one man, encouraged by his brethren in the ministry. Washington College stands upon the labours and endowment of the first theologian of his generation in Virginia, and of that man who was "first in war, first in peace, and first in the hearts of his countrymen."

Mr. Graham embarked with ardour in a scheme for settling a colony on the western waters. After a visit to Kentucky, he

preferred Western Virginia for the site of the intended settlement of a choice selection of families, who should form a religious and refined society in the western forests. With these,
in possession of a full supply of fertile land, he hoped to pass
his days removed from the collisions he had felt, and the
jealousies he had encountered, as Rector of Liberty Hall. He
had rejoiced in the success of the colonies from Ireland, as they
sat down under the unfavourable circumstances of poverty and
strangeness of climate and country, through Pennsylvania and
the beautiful Valley of the Shenandoah; his spirit was stirred
by the emigrating families that were removing to the "dark
and bloody ground"—and the fertile prairies of Tennessee—and
he fancied a select colony, culled from the Valley of the Shenandoah and the James, that might have all the advantages of
the early colonies and partake of few of their real evils.—That
on the banks of the Ohio, the chosen families might live retired,
in abundance, in Christian intercourse, in the worship of God,
and rear a patriotic, virtuous, healthy, classic, obedient and
religious offspring.

In full confidence of his anticipated competence, and quiet
and meditation, and happy society, he embarked all his property, and removed his family to an almost entire wilderness
on the banks of the Ohio. In Kentucky or Tennessee he would
have been thrice welcome to old acquaintances; but he feared
they would compel him to be President of a College, like Liberty
Hall, built by the labours of a few clergymen, and he stopped
short, and rested in Virginia. His dream of usefulness and
enjoyment beguiled him and vanished. The situation was not
as captivating to the eyes of others as they passed along, as it
had been to his in the exploration; those whom he wished most
to accompany him could not be fired with the enthusiasm of his
bosom, and would not emigrate—and finally the tract of land in
which his whole earthly property was involved, became the subject
of an inextricable lawsuit. He visited Alexandria to make payment for the purchased tract, but the unexpected and unreasonable lawsuit preventing the payment, he loaned, and ultimately
lost the money. He visited Richmond on the legal business,
and there yielded up his life, and left his family pennyless. On
this last sad journey which he made, on horseback, from the Ohio,
along the Kenawha, across the Alleghanies, through the Valley,
and down the James to Richmond, he was repeatedly exposed to
wet—sometimes rode all day in his undried clothes,—and as he
approached Richmond was caught in a shower and spent the
evening with the clothes, upon his side, very damp. On reaching the city, he was speedily taken ill at the house of his friend
Colonel Gamble. Kindly attended, and served by medical skill,
he passed rapidly and silently away, June 8th, 1799. His

tomb-stone may be found near the south door of the Episcopal church on Church Hill in Richmond.

The Records of Lexington Presbytery say—"Washington Academy, October 16th, 1799 :—Presbytery attended the examination of the students until four o'clock in the afternoon; after which they proceeded to the meeting-house, and heard the oration, which conformably to the request of the Board of Trustees of Washington Academy, Mr. Baxter delivered on occasion of the death of Rev. William Graham, the former worthy and beloved Rector of that Seminary."

Says a pupil—"Mr. Graham was of middling stature, of thin habit of body; but active and easy in his motions. His countenance was benignant and solemn, and indicative of profound thought, and also of strong passions. His sensibilities were very lively, but he had acquired great command over his feelings. His eyes were of a dark colour, and when he was unoccupied had a sleepy appearance, but when excited they became brilliant and piercing. As a preacher he was always instructive and evangelical; though, in common, his delivery was rather feeble and embarassed than forcible; but when his feelings were excited, his voice became penetrating, and his whole manner awakening and impressive. And his profound study of the human heart enabled him to describe the various exercises of the Christian with a clearness and truth which often greatly surprised his pious hearers; for it seemed to them as if he could read the very inmost sentiments of their minds; which he described more perfectly than they could do themselves. He visited Prince Edward after he received the call, and preached again at Briery, a sermon on Christian experience, in which he so accurately described the views and feelings of many, that they were filled with pleasing astonishment. James Allen, one of the subjects of the revival, and afterwards an Elder at Briery, is said to have gone to him, and asked him *how long it took him to compose that sermon?* After some moments silence, he said gravely—*about twenty years.*

"When it was his object to elucidate some difficult point, it was his custom to open his trenches, so to speak, at a great distance, removing out of the way every obstacle, until at last they could not easily avoid acquiescence in the conclusion to which he wished to bring them. As a clear and cogent reasoner, he had no superior among his contemporaries.

From a report prepared for the General Assembly and spread upon the records of the Presbytery, April 29, 1793, we may learn his ideas of ministerial public labours.

" 1st. That all our members banish the spirit of the world from their dress, manners, and conversation, and adopt the

plainness, simplicity, self-denial, and holiness of life, so remarkably exemplified in the first and most successful preachers of
the gospel.

"2d. That dry, formal and unaffecting harangues, be
banished from our pulpits, and that the simple truths of the
gospel be addressed to every man's conscience in the sight of
God, with that fervour and solemnity which the dignity and
interesting importance require.

"3d. That our private preparations for the pulpit consist
chiefly in prayer, self-examination, and a practical study of the
Scriptures.

"4th. That we endeavour always to enter on our public
ministrations with a deep sense of the presence of God, and the
awful importance of eternal judgment, in which we and our
hearers must shortly share; and that we have no other object
in view, but to recommend the gospel as the only means of
escape for condemned perishing sinners. That an active persevering zeal, in preaching and exhorting in season and out of
season, be a leading trait in the character of a Presbyterian
clergyman. In fine let us endeavour to know nothing, in our
official character, but Christ and him crucified.

"These appear to us some of the visible means which God
has blessed for reviving religion in every period of the Church;
or at least they are the inseparable concomitants of a revival;
and could they be generally adopted would be either forerunner of a revival, or a certain indication that a revival was
begun."

Mr. Graham left six children. The oldest and youngest
were sons. The eldest, Jahab (which his father said meant
devoted to God) became a Presbyterian preacher; lived a short
time near Petersburg, Virginia; and was carried by a bilious
fever to an early grave. He died in Staunton at the house
of his father-in-law, Mr. Heiskill, and left no child. The
youngest child, William, after the death of his father, was educated by Dr. Priestly, the protege of the father; became a
physician; married a Miss Nash of North Carolina; settled in
the western part of Georgia, and left a family of children.
One of the daughters died young; the eldest married a Mr.
Murdock and resided near Cannonsburg, Pennsylvania; the
second married the Rev. Mr. Bracken, and lived near the same
place; the third married a son of Rev. David Rice the pioneer
in Kentucky and lived in that State; all three reared families.

His friends have ever thought the great error of his life was
in withdrawing from Liberty Hall at the time he did. And to
those who scan carefully the cause of things as they passed along,
looking at the consequences, as well as causes, by the light of
after events, it now seems plain enough that Mr. Graham made

a great mistake in the removal. But it is not so clear, that one, entering into his feelings—considering the collisions of parties, the jealousies and dislikes cherished against him,—taking into consideration the state of his family with his small income—the tide of emigration setting westward,—the great labour of his station, often without any recompense,—would, having been made his confidential adviser, have positively decided against the removal. God in his wise providence permitted the removal, but did not smile upon the projected colony.

The influence of William Graham did not die with his body, nor was it overwhelmed with his temporal losses. It has been spreading like the western waters he so admired. The current grows broader and deeper as it rolls on to the great ocean. We will not say that the large number of eminent men introduced to public life through the instrumentality of education at Liberty Hall, would not have been in public life, or as eminent, had Mr. Graham not been connected with Liberty Hall; but he was the efficient instrument chosen of God for the purpose of introducing these lawyers and political men and ministers into their sphere of life. Without him Liberty Hall was but a name; by him Liberty Hall will live forever, for who can forget her sons? Washington College, with her spacious and stately edifices, has succeeded Liberty Hall with her small frame and stone buildings for fifty students; the endowment of the Father of his Country has changed the name of the institution; but posterity will read on these buildings, a thousand fold multiplied, the bright ever beaming letters, WILLIAM GRAHAM.

CHAPTER XXI.

REV. DRURY LACY.

DRURY LACY was born in Chesterfield county, Virginia, October 5th, 1758. His father, William Lacy, was a moderate farmer in plain circumstances, of English descent, and Norman French extract. His mother, Elizabeth Rice, was cousin to Benjamin Rice of Bedford, the father of the Rev. Doctors John H. and Benjamin H. Rice. In the memoir of Drury Lacy, drawn up by Dr. Alexander of Princeton, and published in the Watchman of the South, January 10th, 1839, which is authority for much contained in this sketch, it is stated—"their connexion, I believe, was with the Baptist Church." This is more probable than any other supposition in the absence of direct testimony, as the Baptist denomination were very numerous in Chesterfield. The memoir says—"I know that two of his brothers older than himself, were ministers in that society, (the Baptists) both reputed to be humble pious men, but very illiterate. On one occasion, while I was his neighbour, they visited him, and were treated by him with great respect and affection." These brothers removed to the west at an early period of Mr. Lacy's life.

When about ten years of age, Drury attended a militia muster. A person, who had loaded his gun so heavily that he feared to discharge it himself, handed the unsuspecting lad the loaded piece with permission to discharge it. The explosion shattered the gun and also the left hand of the poor boy. This unpropitious event decided the future fortunes of the lad; in the calculations of men, poverty and trial were before him; in the providence of God, usefulness and respectability were to crown his sufferings and loss, and the severe discipline of penury and want. His kind father determined to give him what education he could afford as a means of his future subsistence; and sent him to a noted boarding-school kept by a Mr. McRea, an Episcopal clergyman in Powhatan. His attendance on this school was, in a short time, interrupted by the death of his father. Upon settlement of the estate the affairs of the family were found desperate; and the mother, with Drury and a twin sister took their abode in a small cabin in a neighbourhood of poor but honest people, and passed four years of deprivation and toil. The affectionate pious mother, afflicted with chronic rheumatism, was confined to her bed a greater part of the time, and the daughter turned the spinning-wheel incessantly, and the son, with his one hand tended the garden and potato patch, and cut wood with a light hatchet and brought it on his shoulder the distance of a quarter of a mile. "I have learned"—says his son, William S.—"that his afflicted mother was an affectionate, pious, sensible woman, and encouraged him as far as she could in penmanship, arithmetic, and on Sabbath day in reading the Bible. Oh what a treasure that Bible was to that humble family. Its hallowed light cheered the last days of this afflicted saint; the sister became pious and married quite young, a good, poor man; and the humble mutilated boy was doubtless trained by its holy doctrines and precepts, for extensive usefulness in subsequent life. I have reason to know that from early boyhood he was a diligent reader of the Bible, and that during this obscure and humble period of his life he perfectly committed to memory the catechism."

When about sixteen years of age, Drury Lacy was deprived of his mother by death. After this event he was employed, for a time, by his poor neighbours, to teach a small school. "I have heard him remark"—says his son—"that so very limited were his means, that he was under the necessity of walking barefoot to and from the school-house." The covering for his head, a rough straw hat. Who, in riding by his log school-house, would have said of the bare-footed teacher,—"there stands the Vice-President of Hampden Sidney College, Lacy with the silver voice and silver hand?" God's ways are wonderful.

By strict attention to his duties he acquired a reputation with his employers, and by assiduous application to study, in his leisure hours, he increased his stock of knowledge, and prepared himself for greater usefulness. By the time he was twenty-one years of age, he had, without the aid of an instructor, become well acquainted with geography, English grammar, algebra, geometry and surveying, and was employed as teacher in the county of Cumberland, in the family of Daniel Allen, the father of the eccentric Cary Allen, and step-father to Rev. William Hill, D. D., of Winchester, still living, in his eightieth year. In this position he came under the preaching of Rev. John B. Smith, and by its influence was led to make a profession of religion in connexion with the Cumberland church, at about the age of twenty-two. By the assistance of Dr. Smith, after he had taught in the family of Mr. Allen about four years, he obtained the situation of teacher in the family of Colonel John Nash, who resided about six miles from Hampden Sidney College. Here he had but three pupils; and enjoyed the partial instruction of Dr. Smith in commencing his acquaintance with the Latin language, as part of preparation for the gospel ministry. The Doctor was a visiter at the house of Colonel Nash, and devoted an hour, once a fortnight, to Lacy, to encourage and assist him in his course of study. His proficiency in learning Latin was such, that a vacancy occurring in the faculty of the College, he was employed as under-tutor, when in his twenty-fourth year. In this situation he prosecuted his studies, and completed a classical and scientific course and his preparation for the gospel ministry.

At a meeting of Hanover Presbytery, April 27th, 1787, at Providence, Louisa county, one of the preaching places of Mr. Todd—"the Presbytery was informed that Mr. Lacy, a tutor in the College of Hampden Sidney, attended with a view to come under trials for the gospel ministry. Mr. Lacy was then introduced, and upon inquiring into his experimental acquaintance with religion, the Presbytery was so well satisfied with the account that they admitted him to further trial. Mr. Lacy then read an exigesis in Latin on the subject of Justification, which had been assigned to him by Mr. Smith, as a specimen of his abilities, which was received and sustained as a part of trial." At the time of coming under the care of Presbytery he was about twenty-nine years of age. "The first time"—says the memoir—"I ever saw him, was at the house of the Rev. John Todd, of Louisa, where I was spending a few days when a boy. The Presbytery of Hanover held their sessions at Providence; and in the evening Mr. Lacy lodged there. I remember to have been much struck with his appearance and the solemnity of his manner; but more with his prayer, which was uttered with great fervency, in a very clear and sonorous voice." Before Presbytery adjourned "Mr. Lacy was appointed a presbyterial exercise on 1st Timothy, iii. 16; a lecture on 6th chapter of Hebrews, and a popular sermon on 1st Timothy, i. 10, to be delivered at our next."

The next meeting of Presbytery was at Cumberland Meeting-house, September 20th, 1787; present Rev. Messrs. Richard Sankey, John B. Smith, and John D. Blair. Rev. Henry Pattillo, of Orange Presbytery, sat as corresponding member. "The Rev. Archibald McRobert, formerly a minister of the Episcopal Church, in Virginia, but now a dissenter from that church, and a minister of an Independent congregation, a gentleman of good character in the churches, being present, was invited to sit as a corresponding member, and took his seat accordingly. Mr. Lacy then produced and read a presbyterial exercise on 1st Timothy, iii. 16, which was sustained.

"21st. The trials of Mr. Lacy were resumed, and the Presbytery having proceeded some length therein, declined a further examination, till after sermon. Mr. Lacy then delivered a popular discourse on 1st Timothy, iv. 10, which was sustained. Upon a motion that Mr. McRobert, who sat as a corresponding member, should be invited to join the Presbytery, the overture was unanimously agreed to: and Mr. McRobert finding his way clear to join himself as a member of the Presbytery, received the right hand of fellowship, the Presbytery esteeming him regularly ordained, and took his seat as a stated member.

"September 22d. Mr. Lacy read as part of trials a lecture on Hebrews, 6th, which was sustained. After sermon Presbytery resumed and finished the trials of Mr. Lacy, having examined him upon the languages, sciences, and divinity, all of which were sustained. The Presbytery therefore agreed to license Mr. Lacy as a probationer and candidate for the gospel ministry. He then having adopted the Westminster Confession of Faith, and promised subjection to the brethren in the Lord, after admonition and fatherly advice, was licensed to preach the everlasting gospel. Mr. Lacy was appointed to supply at Hat Creek, Concord and Cub Creek, one Sabbath at each place."

According to the fashion of the times and the necessities of the Virginia clergy, Mr. Lacy wrote out but few sermons, and of these few, scarce any remain. "I have"—says his son William—"occasionally lighted on a manuscript sermon, or part of sermon, written by him in the early period of his ministry. I am of opinion, that during the time of his greatest usefulness, and highest reputation as a preacher, he rarely wrote his sermons, or even prepared short notes. He thought most intensely on his subject, and arranged the subject matter most carefully in his mind, and then trusted to the occasion for language and expression. His preparation for the pulpit was exclusively mental and spiritual. I have often when a youth been greatly impressed with the deep absorption and awful solemnity depicted on his countenance when walking in the yard, or in his chamber. Hence, when he reached the pulpit, there was frequently in his preaching a solemnity and pathos, a freshness and vigour, a penetrating, burning, melting eloquence, which I have never known surpassed. And candour compels me also to say, that not unfrequently, there was a dryness, hardness, and confusion, with an utterance hurried and painfully loud, bringing him for the time as far below the average of respectable preachers as he usually rose above them. He was, I have reason to believe, at times subject to deep mental depression, and sore spiritual conflicts. But, for the most part, indeed I may say in a great majority of instances, he enjoyed the presence of his Saviour, and the light of his Father's countenance."

By the records of Presbytery, it appears that Mr. Lacy was candidate for licensure but a few months. At that time the demand for preaching, and consequently for an increased number of ministers was great: the revival then in progress was spreading wide, and the Presbytery felt the necessity of thrusting labourers into the harvest. At Providence, when Mr. Lacy was taken as candidate, the Presbytery said, in commenting upon the revised form of government sent out by the Synod of New York and Philadelphia, May, 1786—"the learned qualifications of the candidates for licensure are too minutely ascertained. It is therefore recommended to the Synod, to leave that matter entirely to the discretion of the various Presbyteries to act as the circumstances of the particular churches under their care may require." On this opinion the Presbytery acted for some time. In April, 1786, the Presbytery again sent up their objection to the prolonged time of study required of candidates. But no change being made by authority, the Presbytery, after some delay, fell into the rule as adopted.

Mr. McRobert, mentioned in the extracts, was highly esteemed for his preaching powers, and as a pious man. At a meeting of the Presbytery at Buffalo, April 18th, 1787—" a small society in the neighbourhood of Walker's Church, formerly considered as an Independent church, and under the pastoral care of Mr. McRobert, appeared by their elder at the Presbytery, and requested to be taken under its care, and considered as a part of the Presbyterian Church in Virginia. They also requested supplies.

" Mr. Lacy was appointed to supply one Sabbath at Concord, two at Walker's Church, one at Hat Creek, and one at Cub Creek. It is also recommended to him to go to the Northern Neck, if he can possibly make it convenient."

At a meeting of the Presbytery at Cumberland Church, October 10th, 1788—" a petition was presented to the Presbytery by the elders and members of Cub Creek congregation, that Mr. Lacy, a probationer under the care of this Presbytery, should be ordained to the whole work of the ministry, for the general advantage of the church. A similar request was presented by the congregations of Hat Creek, Concord, and Walker's Church, for the ordination of Mr. Mahon. The Presbytery agreed to the requests of the above congregations, and ordered that Mr. Mahon and Mr. Lacy be ordained. Mr. Lacy then preached a sermon previous to his ordination, on Heb. x. 14, a subject assigned him by Mr. Smith, which appointment was approved by the Presbytery." October 11th, Mr. Mahon preached agreeably to appointment on 2 Cor. iv. 5—a subject, through the apparent necessities of the church, having been given out to him by Mr. Smith, which for the same reasons was confirmed by the Presbytery.

" Mr. Mahon's and Mr. Lacy's sermons having been considered and sustained, and an ordination sermon preached by Dr. Robert Smith, (a corresponding member from New Castle Presbytery, father of John B. Smith) who was chosen to preside, on John xxi. 15, 16, 17,—the Presbytery proceeded solemnly to set them apart by prayers and imposition of hands to the whole work of the ministry; and they were admitted to take their seats as full members of Presbytery."

Of the agency of Mr. Lacy in that work of God, which was so extensive, Dr. Alexander writes thus:—" About the time that Mr. Lacy entered the ministry, commenced that remarkable revival of religion, which extended, more or less, through every part of Virginia where Presbyterian congregations existed. And although J. B. Smith was the principal instrument of that work, yet the labours of Mr. Lacy were, in no small degree, successful. His preaching was calculated to produce deep and solemn impressions. His voice was one of extraordinary power. Its sound has been heard at more than a mile's distance. His voice was not only loud, but clear and distinct; in the largest assemblies convened in the woods, he could always be heard with ease at the extremity of the congregation. On this account Mr. Lacy was always one of the prominent preachers at *great meetings*. His preaching also was with animation. His address to his hearers, whether saints or sinners, was warm and affectionate. Indeed according to his method of preaching, lively feeling in the speaker was an essential thing to render it either agreeable or impressive. Mr. Lacy was, therefore, a much more eloquent and impressive preacher on special occasions, when every circumstance combined to wind up the mind to a high tone of excitement than in his common and every day discourses; in which he was always evangelical, but sometimes flat and uninteresting. Upon the whole it may serve to characterize his preaching, to say, that it was better suited to the multitude, than to the select few, who possess great refinement of taste; better adapted to satisfy and feed the plain and sincere Christian, than to furnish a feast for men of highly cultivated intellect. He enjoyed the unspeakable pleasure of knowing a considerable number of humble, exemplary Christians, who ascribed their first impressions to his preaching or conversation; for he excelled in the art of conversing on the subject of experimental religion. To inquirers and young converts, he addressed himself, in private, in a very happy manner; which was to them often the means of important spiritual benefits. And on general subjects Mr. Lacy conversed in an agreeable and instructive manner."

In the commencement of the revival Mr. Lacy was not prepared to act decidedly on the subject of the peculiar exercises which in many cases accompanied the influences of divine truth on those convicted of sin, and seeking salvation. Dr. Smith opposed all violent bodily exercises, from the first: Mr. Lacy thought favourably of them, as accompanying circumstances of the Spirit's operation, and feared to oppose them lest happily he should be found fighting against God. But longer observation, and close examination led him to believe that all such exercises as fallings, swoonings, violent agitations, &c., were in the general detrimental to the cause of religion, though they might appear, in given instances, to be both irresistible and harmless, as in the cases of Legrand and Allen.

Mr. Lacy's popularity in conducting meetings for prayer and exhortation hastened his licensure; and his acceptability as a preacher drew forth from Cub Creek, the church of the Caldwells and the charge of Mr. Henry, a request for his ordination as an evangelist. Holding his office as a teacher in the College he preached around in the neighbouring congregations, with great acceptability, wherever there appeared the greatest necessity or the most inviting field.

In the summer of 1789, Mr. Lacy visited Bedford, the scene of labour for many years of the pioneer in Kentucky, David Rice, the birth place of that eminent and much loved man, John H. Rice, D.D., and the pastoral charge of James Mitchell, with whom he held a series of religious meetings in connexion with the sacrament at Pisgah. Mr. James Turner, a very thoughtless man, attended on the Sabbath: and while the services were going on, was amusing himself on the borders of the congregation, which was assembled around the stand in the woods. Mr. Lacy's clear voice attracted his attention: "Well this is a new preacher, let us hear what he has to say," and he drew nigher; and on hearing a little he felt himself inclined to draw nearer still. Mr. Lacy was relating the story, from ancient history, of an accused person on trial for his life, for a great misdemeanor; the evidence was all against him, and sentence was about to be pronounced. A brother who had fought many battles for his country and gained victories, at that moment arose near the criminal, and raised the maimed arm, from which the hand had been severed in gaining a victory. The sight of him in tears, and the recollections connected with that handless arm, so wrought upon the judges, that, for the sake of the brother, they pardoned the criminal they could but condemn. The preacher suited the action to the word, perhaps unconsciously, and raised his own maimed arm in view of the congregation; and as he plead the advocacy of Christ for sinners, Turner's attention was arrested, and he went home from that meeting a deeply convicted sinner. Some years afterwards Mr. Lacy stepping into a church, as he was on his journey, heard Mr. Turner pouring forth the truths of the gospel with his powerful voice and feeling heart, and as he heard and looked he burst into a flood of tears. As Turner saw him weeping— "Ah, have I caught you too"—and launched another truth all sparkling with kindness and love.

A midnight conversation at the house of Colonel Nash, of Prince Edward, where Lacy lodged for a night, sent Nash Legrand, a young man of promise and of irreligion, to prayer and lamentation in the garden, till the morning light appeared, and then to a religious meeting in Cumberland, where he was hopefully converted, and then into the ministry, where his track was glorious.

"That trait in his character"—says Dr. Alexander—"which was most conspicuous, on first acquaintance, and which ever appeared predominant, was honesty, simple hearted honesty; an undisguised openness and candour, which rendered his very heart transparent. He possessed this virtue in as eminent degree as any person, with whom I have been acquainted. If candour can be carried so far as to be in collision with prudence, he might be said to err in that extreme; but it appeared amiable even in its excess. He was a truly humble man. He entertained no high opinion of his own talents, learning or attainments in piety; on the contrary he was ever disposed to esteem others better than himself. He was also of a kind, pacific temper. I never knew him to have any dissension with any person; and for his brethren in the ministry he ever cultivated and exercised cordial esteem. No envy, jealousy, or dark suspicion, ever rankled in his bosom; all such tempers were abhorrent to his nature.

July 3d, 1788.—Rev. J. B. Smith informed the Board that he designed removing to the neighbourhood. The cause and object of this step were the increasing interest and labour of the revival, which rendered it impracticable for him to fulfil the duties he had been performing in College, and meet the demands for time and labour that came from his congregation. The Board requested him to continue President, though removed from College grounds, and appointed Mr. Lacy Vice-President, devolving on him much of the labour which had become onerous, in managing the College. In this office Mr. Lacy continued for some years.

September 29th, 1788.—The Board conferred on Mr. Lacy, *causa meriti*, the degree of A. B. He had not been a regular student, having pursued his studies under the direction of the President, and carried them to that extent as to be qualified to act as presiding officer in the absence of the Principal.

In the year 1789, Dr. Smith resigned the Presidency of the College, and the whole weight of supervision rested on the Vice-President. Mr. Lacy's situation was laborious, difficult, and unenviable. In the want of permanent funds, the income of the College was not adequate to sustain a sufficient number of qualified teachers. The support of the neighbouring congregations, given to the teachers for their ministerial services, was necessary in order to preserve the appearance of a College. The ardour with which the community had embarked in the cause of education was, as usual, somewhat abated; and political feeling, which at that time entered into every thing of a social nature, had an influence unfavourable to the popularity of the College; and even the blessed revival of religion was made to act unfavourably on some parts of the community around, as the officers of the College were accused of sectarianism. The attention of Synod also was more particularly turned to the institution in Lexington, now known as Washington College, as the place where theological students should be trained for the ministry. The efforts to translate Graham to Hampden Sidney failed; and the tide of favour set for Washington College. Some things had occurred, not of permanent interest, that for a time turned away a part of Hanover Presbytery from their own College. As these things were personal and transient, and connected with the President's resigning, they need not be perpetuated in history. The consequence was that Hampden Sidney for a time languished.

The Commission of Synod sent two young men, Benjamin Grigsby, and Archibald Alexander, to visit places east of the Blue Ridge, particularly the congregations of Cumberland and Prince Edward. After the visit of these young men a plan was agreed on by the commissioners from the congregations of Cub Creek, Buffalo, Briery, and Cumberland, to form a union of these congregations, and call two preachers to officiate in rotation at six places, viz: the four churches, and the College Hall and Charlotte Court House. At a meeting of the Presbytery at Cumberland Meeting-house, November 9, 1793—"calls having been put into the hands of Mr. Alexander through Lexington Presbytery, from the united congregations of Cumberland, Briery, Buffalo and Cub Creek, to engage in the pastoral care of the said congregations with Mr. Lacy; and Mr. Alexander having obtained a dismission from Lexington, and come under the care of this Presbytery, the Moderator called upon him to know whether he accepted the said calls; but he having desired longer time to consider of the matter the Presbytery granted it. On motion resolved, that Mr. Alexander supply in the said congregations, in the same manner as if he had accepted the calls." This plan of collegiate labours being found more laborious than advantageous to the ministers, and not likely to be productive of the good intended, was after a little trial abandoned. Permission was also granted, at the same meeting of Presbytery, to the commissioners of the four congregations to prosecute a call for Dr. Smith, to bring him back from Philadelphia. This proved abortive. The congregations then made other arrangements.

At a meeting of the Presbytery, at the house of Dr. Waddell, Friday, May 2, 1794, preparatory steps were taken for the ordination of Mr. Alexander. The sacred ceremony took place at Briery, Saturday, June 7th. Mr. Alexander preached from John xvii. 17, "Sanctify them through thy truth: thy word is truth." Mr. Lacy delivered the ordination sermon from Col. iv. 17, "And say to Archippus, take heed to the ministry which thou hast received in the Lord, that thou fulfil it;" Mr. McRobert delivered the charge.

At the next meeting of the Presbytery, at the Cove in Albemarle, October 22, 1794—"A call was presented from the united congregations of Briery and Cub Creek for the Rev. Archibald Alexander to take the pastoral charge of said congregations. Which call being read and presented to him by the Moderator, was accepted." Mr. Matthew Lyle presented a dismission from Lexington Presbytery, and was received as a candidate under the care of Hanover. "A call was presented from the united congregations of Briery and Buffalo praying Mr. Lyle to accept the charge of said congregations as their pastor. Which being read and presented to Mr. Lyle, by the Moderator, was accepted." By this arrangement, Briery had part of the services of two men; and Cumberland, embracing the area occupied now by Cumberland, Farmville, and College Church, had the services of Mr. Lacy. With Mr. Lacy and Mr. Lyle the arrangement was permanent. For none of these brethren was there an installation service performed; and for Mr. Lacy no call from Cumberland was put in except the one conjointly with Mr. Alexander. By the conventional rules of the Presbyterian Church these things would be, now, irregular. The Presbytery met at the Cove, both in the spring and the fall of 1794, to attend to a case of discipline; and in the journeyings to this place the relation of his early history and experience was given by Mr. Lacy to Dr. Alexander, as stated in the commencement of this sketch.

From the records of the Board of Trustees, it appears the origin of the plan for the union of the four churches was with Mr. Lacy. He proposed to the Board to associate Mr. Alexander, then a very young man, with him in the College, with equal authority and emoluments; and to secure a support proposed the union of these congregations. The Trustees acted on this proposal in November, 1792, and agreeing to it, appointed Mr. Alexander, and directed the committee to make the proposition to the congregations. The congregations agreeing, the call was made out and sent to Lexington Presbytery; and that Presbytery dismissed Mr. Alexander to the care of Hanover. The experiment of preaching in rotation was tried a little time and abandoned; and with it went the scheme of uniting the two ministers in the College. Lacy loved Alexander sincerely, and Alexander had unbounded confidence in the integrity and uprightness of Lacy; but they could not be united in the College for want of funds. Mr. Lacy continued the College exercises till the year 1796, when he became discouraged and resigned his office with the hope that some better arragement should be made, and removed to a farm near College. The offer of the Presidency was then made to Mr. Alexander; and he, after some delay, was removed to Hampden Sidney. About the same time John H. Rice become tutor in the College, and formed with the President an undying friendship. The arrangements for preaching were that Mr. Alexander should retain his connexion with Briery, and be associated with Mr. Lacy, and alternate in Briery College and

Cumberland. This arrangement continued till 1806, when Mr. Alexander removed to Philadelphia.

December 25th, 1789—Mr. Lacy was united in marriage to Anne Smith, eighth child of William and Mary Smith of Powhatan. "In domestic life"—says Dr. Alexander—"Mr. Lacy was a happy man; blessed with a companion in whom he could confide, he left domestic arrangements, very much, to be managed by her, and in his home, and in the midst of his family, you lost nothing of that respect for his character, which arose from seeing and hearing him in public." Mr. and Mrs. Lacy reared five children, three sons and two daughters; all of whom became in early life professors of religion. Two of the sons became ministers of the gospel in the Presbyterian Church, and are now living, the other a physician; each of the two daughters married Presbyterian ministers. Two of his grandsons have also entered the ministry, in the Church which was the choice of their grandfather.

Mr. Lacy continued the occupation of teaching at his place called Mount Ararat, after withdrawing from the College; and supplied the deficiency of an inadequate salary by taking a few boys as boarders in his house, to be taught the preparatory course for College or for active business. He wrote an almost unequalled hand, plain, beautiful, and unvarying; and has left memorials of his calligraphy, in the beautiful copy of the Minutes of Hanover Presbytery, in one volume, from its organization till the Blue Ridge became its western boundary by the formation of the Presbytery of Lexington. He served as Clerk of Hanover Presbytery the greater part of his ministerial life. There was also a volume of letters to a young female relative, as beautiful in friendship and piety and Christian counsel as in penmanship. These letters appeared in the Watchman of the South, a few years since; and with a memoir of their author would form a volume for the reading of young people not unworthy of a place in the literature of the Presbyterian Church. He is one of the few useful and beloved ministers of the former generations in Virginia, that has left manuscripts enough for a readable volume.

As a delegate from Hanover Presbytery, Mr. Lacy repeatedly had a seat in the General Assembly of the Presbyterian Church, and in the year 1809, he filled the Moderator's chair. At this session of the Assembly, Rev. John Lyle, in a masterly and eloquent manner, defended the Synod of Kentucky in his efforts to preserve the orthodoxy of the Presbyterian Church in Kentucky, and aided by Dr. Green of Philadelphia and Dr. Dwight of Yale College, that year a delegate from the General Association of Connecticut, obtained from the Assembly a justification of the Synod's course, and thanks for her "firmness and zeal," with which she had acted, "in the trying circumstances," in which she had been placed, by the irregularities that had sprung up in the great revival, and by the schisms of the Cumberland Presbyterians. At the same meeting the overture for the establishment of a theological school, was received from the Presbytery of Philadelphia, which being matured, was sent down to the Presbyteries, and in the year 1812, resulted in the location of the Theological Seminary at Princeton, and the choice of Rev. Archibald Alexander as the Professor of Didactic and Polemic Divinity. Also an overture was brought in "for the establishment of a religious tract society, for the purpose of distributing through every part of the United States, such tracts as are at once cheap and calculated to do the most good."

On account of his clear, strong voice, and impassioned manner, when excited by a large assembly, Mr. Lacy was a favourite preacher at Synods and Presbyteries, and other large meetings. It has been a standing rule of the Synod of Virginia, and of the Presbyteries that preceded it, to meet on such a day of the week as to permit the ministers to spend the Sabbath together. And religious worship has been a regular part of the business of these meetings; consequently crowds assemble on these occasions, and Christians enjoy a religious festival. At a meeting of the Synod in Lexington, the religious interest rose very high; and Mr. Lacy was called on to preach to a multitude in the grove, in the rear of the church, on the borders of the village. His text was—"Where is the Lord God of Elijah!" As he progressed in the sermon he became excited to the highest degree his mental and physical nature could bear, and his audience were carried along, without resistance, by his silver voice, loud, penetrating and sweet, and his earnest excited manner, till they were entirely at the command of the speaker. Raising his arms, he turned majestically, and looked upward, and cried "Where is the Lord God of Elijah!" The audience started, and gazed with the speaker, as if they expected to see the effulgence of Israel's God burst from among the over-shadowing branches. Could such scenes be prolonged, what enchanting festivals would the meetings of the judicatories of the church be! Alas, how soon they pass! Lacy with the silver voice and the silver hand speaks no more; the venerable grove, trembling with age, has fallen beneath the axe; and here and there only may be found among the living one of the assembled audience of that day, who carries the undying recollection of that Sabbath in the grove.

Some time after this interesting scene, one of the brethren speaking to him, in a complimentary manner, of the excellency of the sermon—"O,"—said he, in the simplicity and truthfulness of his heart—"that I got from little Archy one afternoon, at * * * * when I went to hear him,"—referring to an afternoon exercise of his young and much loved friend Alexander, which he casually attended, and from which he gathered the thoughts he moulded into that charming sermon, which was never forgotten by the vast assemblage. The excitement was of course evanescent; but there remained a strong feeling, and well defined impression, of the necessity and blessedness of the Divine presence in things of religion.

Hampden Sidney College was the centre of religious action for the churches east of the Blue Ridge and south of James River, in connexion with the Presbyterian Church. In the bounds of the same congregation which embraced the College, was a Law School of high standing, in which "free thinking," on the subject of religion, met with no check. The influences flowing from this fountain were a constant source of uneasiness to the pious people of Cumberland and the associated churches, and was an additional reason for their clinging together and using all means in their united power for mutual preservation, and the salvation of the young. The teaching of two such men as Lacy and Alexander was well calculated, under the Divine blessing, to stop the progress of the evil, and guard the rising generation from its insidious effects. This cause of uneasiness awakened in Lacy no bitterness; nor is it known to have aroused against him any personal dislike. The collision of principles and belief was, of course, frequently severe.

Mr. Lacy's death took place in Philadelphia. Pains, which, for a long time, were supposed to be rheumatic in their origin, were at last found to proceed from calculus. The only hope of relief was in a surgical operation. He repaired to Philadelphia, and after consulting the professional men of that city, submitted to their decision, and committed himself to their care and skill. The event was unfavourable. After a few days of weakness and languishing, he expired at the house of his much attached friend, Robert Ralston, November 5th, 1815. When he left his family in Virginia, his wife was in usually good health. During his confinement in Philadelphia, she was seized with a malignant fever, and in a few days breathed her last. On account of his weak state of body, this mournful fact was not communicated to the husband; and, as Dr. Hoge of Hampden Sidney remarked in a letter to Dr. Alexander—"how will the good man, when he enters heaven, be surprised to find his beloved wife there to meet him"—he received in the world of departed spirits the first intelligence of his wife's having "crossed the flood" before him.

Of this excellent lady, no encomium is required beyond the merited eulogium already given from the pen of her intimate friend, Dr. Alexander. Of the family from which she descended, something should be recorded. Her father, William Smith, was from the county of Gloucester, born November 18th, 1710; his grandfather was from England. Her mother, whose maiden name was Mary Smith, was of a Charles City family, born at Olney in Henrico, October 6th, 1726. They were married February 18th, 1742, and soon after took up their residence in Cumberland, now Powhatan, among its earliest settlers. The family residence is in possession of their grandchildren. Says one of his grandchildren, a minister of the gospel—"shortly after their settling here, the Rev. Samuel Davies began to preach in Hanover. They visited relations in Henrico, and were induced to go and hear him occasionally. They were converted under his ministrations, and continued, while he remained, to attend his preaching as they could. The nearest of his churches was about fifty miles distant. They went on horseback, often fording James River; and sometimes each taking a child or two on horseback with them."—Who rides fifty miles to church now?—and carries a child or two on horseback? We are not surprised to hear, that, of the eight children reared by such parents,—"all or nearly all professed religion, and seven of them raised pious families; every one of the children and grandchildren, as far as I can learn, became Presbyterians." One of the daughters married Major Morton, and became the mother of Mrs. John H. Rice, D. D., and Mrs. Rev. James Wharey; another of the daughters married, as has been stated, Rev. Drury Lacy; another married Rev. Dr. Waddell, of South Carolina. "Of my grandfather's descendants and their immediate connexions by marriage, there have been thirteen ministers—Mr. Lacy, two sons and two grandsons,—Dr. Rice,—Mr. Wharey,—Messrs. Hoge and Brooks, sons-in-law of Mr. Lacy,—Dr. Waddell and two sons,—and myself. I never knew one of any other than the Presbyterian Church."

The inheritance of being the only Presbyterian family in Powhatan descended to his son Josiah, the other members of the family being removed on their marriage. In the year 1806 the Rev. Conrad Speece became a resident in his family, and continued an inmate for six years. A church was not organized in Powhatan till about the year 1826, by Rev. D. A. Penick. The members of the Presbyterian Church in that county, previously to that time held their connexion with the Cumberland Church. The Rev. Conrad Speece lamented the death of his host, which took place in January 1819, as of a near relation and true Christian, a guileless upright man.

"I have"—says his grandson—"bills of goods purchased by my grandfather in Liverpool; among the items in which, I note, at one time, one half dozen, and at another, two dozen Doddridge's Friend's Instructor. By which I judge, the old gentleman was not insensible to the value of good books, nor inattentive to their distribution. The charge was at the rate of fifteen shillings the dozen." The History of the Presbyterian Church in Virginia, is an historical argument in favour of distribution and reading religious books,—and the sending pious missionaries to visit destitute neighbourhoods.

Mr. Lacy was tall, above six feet; of large frame and well proportioned; never corpulent, weighing about two hundred pounds without appearing to have a pound of superfluous flesh. Says one who was a child when he died—"his voice when preaching I remember, it was full, and powerful, and yet soft and melodious." Of his family, suddenly deprived of father and mother, while part were very young, God was mindful. In him the orphan has a shield and defence. Three sons and two daughters survived the parents,—not one being then a professor of religion, and some very young. Subsequently, all became connected with the church of Christ. Two of the sons are in the ministry in the Presbyterian Church, the other a physician and an elder. Each of the two daughters married Presbyterian clergymen. Two of the grandsons of Mr. Lacy are now preaching in Virginia.

Little thought the man who gave the over-charged gun to the little boy, that its bursting, which he dreaded, would be one important link in the chain of events, to raise up an honoured minister, the father of ministers.

It remains, only, to speak of his care of the coloured people, the African race, in his charge. In Cub Creek, where Mr. Henry, the first pastor, had been eminently successful among the negroes, Mr. Lacy found many communicants, the number of which was increased by the labours of the successors of that warm-hearted man. In Mr. Lacy's time the number attached to the Church by profession was about two hundred. One wealthy lady, though herself not a professor of religion, had sixty in connexion with the church. She encouraged her servants to attend preaching, and permitted them to leave their work for week-day preaching. Elders were appointed among the negroes, who not only attended to the spiritual conduct of the servants, but exerted such an influence that the mistress dismissed her overseers and entrusted her affairs to her servants. The coloured people were greatly attached to Mr. Lacy. His loud and musical voice were peculiarly pleasing to them. Some years after his death, his son, the Rev. Drury Lacy of Raleigh, preached in his father's preaching places. Some of the old venerable servants were present, and after sermon crowded around him, with "God bless you, dear master

—you preach so much like old Mr. Lacy used to do—and you look like him in your face—and your voice is like his too." Many of the African race will doubtless appear in the crown of his rejoicing.

CHAPTER XXII.

MARY MOORE.

In the burying ground of New Providence, in Rockbridge county, Virginia, there is a grave, surpassing in interest all surrounding graves. It is by the side of the resting place of a man among the first in his own generation, and a man amongst men of all generations, long the pastor of the people that worshipped in the neighbouring church. Its inhabitant once walked by his side a cherished one, through life overshadowed by his greatness,—wept over his grave the tears of a widow and mother of orphans,—and now lies, where of all places on earth she chose to lie, by his side,—overshadowing in death, him in whose shade she used to live, and on whom, in true affection, she used to lean for support. His deep, blue, sunken eye, that flashed so fiercely in moments of indignation or anger, always beamed sweetly into her full jet black orbs, that could do nothing but smile or weep. But those smiles and tears charmed equally the savages in the wilderness, and Christian people of Providence.

The way to this grave can never be forgotten till another people, with other hearts than now beat in American bosoms, take possession of this beautiful Valley. The maiden name of this woman was Mary Moore. The melancholy romance of her early days, and the Christian excellence of her mature and closing years, make her memory immortal. The history of the sombre deeds attending the destruction of the retired dwelling of her father,—the murder of him with two brothers and a sister on a fair summer's morning,—the captivity of her mother and herself, with a brother and two sisters and a hired girl,— the murder of the brother and one sister on the way to the wigwam homes of their captors,—the death by fire and torture of her mother and remaining sister,—the rescue of herself and the hired girl, together with a brother, the captive of a former year, and their return to their relatives in Virginia,—combines in one story all the boding events incident to the savage captivity always impending the immigrant families taking possession of the rivers and valleys of Western Virginia. It is given as a

sample of many captivities and deaths, by savage hands, of
men, women and children, on the frontiers of all the States in
North America. The authorities on which the relation of the
captivity is founded, are in the hands of the Rev. James Morrison, the son-in-law and successor of the Rev. Samuel Brown,
having been collected by him with great perseverance and care.

A certain James Moore, of Scottish ancestry, born in Ireland,
emigrated to America with his brother Joseph about the year
1726, and took their residence in Pennsylvania. In about two
years Joseph died while in a course of preparation for the
gospel ministry. James, some time after his arrival in America, married Jane Walker, also an emigrant from Ireland.
Her father John Walker, of Wigton, Scotland, emigrated first
to Ireland, became the head of a family of seven children, of
which Jane was the fourth, and then, a few years after Mr.
Moore, emigrated to Pennsylvania. After his marriage Mr.
Moore resided in the Nottingham congregation, for a number
of years. His father-in-law, John Walker, having removed,
with the rest of the family, to Rockbridge county, Virginia,
and settled on a creek which bears the family name, Mr. Moore
removed his wife and four children and took his residence with
them, and made a part of what was pleasantly called by the
neighbours, "the Creek Nation." Here six more children were
added to his family, which consisted of five sons and as many
daughters. The sixth son, named after himself, was the father
of Mary Moore, the wife of Rev. Samuel Brown.

This James Moore, the sixth child of the emigrant James,
was married to Martha Poage, by whom he had nine children,
five sons and four daughters. His fifth child, and second
daughter, he named Mary, after his eldest sister, the wife of
Major Stuart who lived near Brownsburg, and the mother of
the late Judge Alexander Stuart. After his marriage Mr.
Moore resided for some years at a place long known as Newell's
Tavern, a few miles south of the Natural Bridge, where his first
four children were born, viz. John, James, Jane and Joseph.
His cousin, Mr. Samuel Walker, on his return from an excursion to the south-western part of the State, to gather ginseng,
gave a glowing account of the beauty and fertility of the valleys,
and their supposed great adaptedness to grazing. Mr. Moore,
dissatisfied with his location, and thinking some of his connexions were less affectionate to him than became neighbours
and relatives, visited the country in company with his cousin,
and charmed with its beauty and solitude, resolved to remove
his family to the lonely mountains of Tazewell. Accordingly,
in company with an English servant, John Simpson, he sought
a valley on the waters of the Blue Stone, a branch of New
River, cleared a few acres of land, put up a log cabin; and in

the fall of the year 1775 removed his family to their lovely, and ultimately bloody home. His chosen home was App's Valley—so named from Apps (Absalom) Looney, a hunter, supposed to be the first white man who disturbed the solitude, or beheld the beauty of the narrow low grounds luxuriating in the pea vine and sweet myrrh,—extending some ten miles in length, by about forty or fifty rods in breadth, and admirably fitted by its position and production for pasturage. The surrounding, and distant scenery partook both of the grand and beautiful. To Mr. Moore the Valley was enchanting; and being out of the track of the savages in their war incursions eastward, it seemed secure equally from the vexations of the civilized and the savage man.

Mr. Looney, the hunter, built his cabin about a mile lower down the creek; Mr. John Poage took up his residence about two and a half miles above; and a number of cabins were scattered about as convenience or fancy dictated. Mr. Moore's highest expectations in raising stock were realized. Assisted by Simpson he soon became possessor of a hundred head of horses, and a large number of horned cattle, which found pasturage sufficient for both summer and winter, with little aid or care from man. His dream of safety was broken. The wily savages discovered the white man's track, and the white man's cabin west of those Alleghanies they resolved should be an everlasting barrier between their residence in Ohio, to which they had fled, and the hated whites that held the corn fields and hunting grounds, of their fathers and their race, between those great mountains and the Atlantic shores.

To revenge this encroachment on their wished for solitudes, the savages commenced their depredations, and compelled these isolated families, summer after summer, to betake themselves to forts and stockades for mutual defence. On one occasion a number of men being at the house of Mr. John Poage, one of them, on stepping out after night-fall, observed to his companions, that a good look out ought to be kept for Indians that night, for he heard an unusual noise, as of the hooting of owls, which he supposed to be the signal of Indians approaching the house from different quarters. About midnight the house was surrounded by savages; but finding the doors secured and the inmates on the watch, the Indians retired without committing any depredations. One of the party in the house seized a gun, not his own, unaware that it was double-triggered, pressed the muzzle through the cracks of the cabin against the body of a savage who was slily examining the state of things within, and in his eagerness to discharge the piece broke both the triggers, and the savage escaped. All was stillness both within and without the house; such was the nature of savage warfare.

Mr. Poage and most of the families now retired from this advanced position to the more secure neighbourhoods in Rockbridge, Botetourt and Montgomery, while Mr. Moore and a few others remained.

Mr. Moore was a man of courage; he fought bravely in the battle of Guilford; he loved the solitude and sweetness of the Valley, and would not retreat through any fear of the hostile Indians. He feared God, and worshipped him in his family; his wife was devoutly pious, and contented to share his lot. They trained their children in the doctrines and truth of the gospel; to live righteously before God. They trusted in God's providence; and looked to him for protection. Perhaps they tempted him in their boldness and security. Five children were added to his family in this Valley, making the number nine. Of these Mary, the fifth child, was born in the year 1777, and passed the first nine years of her life in alternate solitude and alarms. When seven years old she mourned the sudden disappearance of her second brother, not knowing whether he had gone to captivity or a premature grave by savage hands. On the 7th of September, 1784, James, then fourteen years of age, was sent to Mr. Poage's deserted settlement to procure a horse for the purpose of going to the mill about twelve miles distant through a dreary wilderness. He did not return. The anxious search discovered trails of savages. And in time the hopes that he had hidden in the woods or fled to some distant habitation gave way to the sad conviction that his fate, for life or for death, had been committed to the hands of barbarians. This bereavement grieved, but did not subdue the heart of the father; perils by day and by night lost their power to alarm by their frequency. The children slept in security while their parent resolutely, almost stubbornly, maintained his position in the midst of exposure and loss. After some time a letter was received by the anxious father, from Kentucky, giving him information of his lost son, then supposed to be in or near Detroit. Before any effective steps could be taken for his recovery, another and more mournful scene was acted in App's Valley, on a fair summer's morning, awfully contrasting with the grandeur and beauty of surrounding nature, and the domestic peace and piety of Moore's dwelling.

The morning of the 14th of July, 1786, was the last that dawned upon that dwelling. The sun went down upon Moore's dead body, the ashes of his cabin and the captivity of his wife. A party of Indians came up Sandy River, crossed over to the head of Clinch, passed near where Tazewell Court House now is, murdered a Mr. Davison and wife and burned their dwelling, and passed on to App's Valley hastily, before any alarm could be given, and lay in ambush for the family of James Moore.

A little spur puts out from the mountain, and gradually sloping towards the creek, about three hundred yards before it sinks into the low grounds, divides; at the extremity of one division stood Moore's house, and near the other the trough at which he was accustomed to salt his horses. At the time of the greatest peril all seemed most secure. It was harvest time; and there were two men assisting Mr. Moore in his harvest. The guns were discharged on the preceding evening, to be re-loaded sometime in the morning. Simpson lay sick in the loft; the men had repaired early to the wheat field, to reap till breakfast time; Mr. Moore was engaged in salting his horses; his wife busied in her domestic concerns; and two of the children at the spring. Suddenly the savage yell was heard, and two parties rushed from their hiding places on the ridge, the one down the slope to the house, and the other towards Mr. Moore. All at the sudden alarm started for the house. Two children, Rebecca and William, were shot dead near the salt block, on their return from the spring; and the third, Alexander, near the house. Mary rushed in, and the door was shut and barred against the approaching savages by Mrs. Moore and Martha Ivans, a member of the family, just in time to prevent their entrance. Mr. Moore finding himself intercepted by the Indians, at the house, ran on through the small lot that surrounded it, and on climbing the fence paused, and turned, and in a moment was pierced with seven bullets. Springing from the fence, he ran a few paces, fell and expired. The two men in the harvest field, seeing the house surrounded by a large company of savages (the party consisting of about thirty) fled, and escaped unharmed. Martha Ivans seized two of the guns and ran up stairs to the sick man, Simpson, calling on him to shoot through the crevices; but the poor man had already received his death wound, in his head, from a bullet aimed from without the house. Two stout dogs defended the door most courageously, till the fiercest was shot. Martha Ivans and Mary Moore secreted themselves under a part of the floor, taking with them the infant Margaret; but the sobbings of the alarmed child forbade concealment. Should Mary place the child upon the floor, and conceal herself?—or should she share its fate? She could not abandon her little sister even in that perilous moment, and left her hiding place and her companion. The Indians were now cutting at the door, and threatening fire. Mrs. Moore perceiving that her faithful sentinels were silenced, Simpson expiring, and her husband dead, collected her four children, and kneeling down, committed them to God; then rose and unbarred the door.

After all resistance had ceased, the Indians, satisfied with the blood that had been shed, took Mrs. Moore and her four

children, John, Jane, Mary, and Margaret, the fifth, Joseph
being in Rockbridge at school, prisoners; and having plundered to their satisfaction, set fire to the dwelling. Martha
Ivans crept from the approaching flames, and again concealed
herself beneath a log that lay across the little stream near the
dwelling. But captivity awaited her. While catching a few
of the horses, one of the Indians crossed the log, under which
she was secreted, and sat down upon the end of it. The
girl seeing him handle the lock of his gun, and supposing that
he had discovered her, and was about to fire upon her, came
out, to the great surprise of the savage, for he had not seen
her, and to his great apparent joy delivered herself a captive.
In a short time the Indians were on their march with their
captives, and their plunder, to the Shawnee towns in Ohio,
to which they belonged. The two men that escaped, hastened
to the nearest family, a distance of six miles, and as soon as
possible spread the alarm among the settlements. Before the
armed men could reach the spot the ruin was complete, and
the depredators far on their way to Ohio. Mr. Moore was
found lifeless—scalped—but his body unabused,—and was
buried where he fell. His grave may be seen at this day.
The Indians told the captives he might have escaped, had he
not paused on the fence. Of this he was probably himself
well aware, as·it was not the habit of the Indians to shoot at
a person in rapid motion. But the affection for his family,
was stronger than the desire for personal safety. He was a
brave, and tender hearted man; and would not desert his
family to save himself from a danger his perseverance and
daring had brought upon them all. He had retired from the
society of relatives and acquaintances, and what was life to
him among the smoking ruins of a much loved home and
murdered family !

The morning of July 14th, 1786, saw the family in App's
Valley full of life and cheerfulness; the sun went down that
day on smoking ruins, the dead bodies of the father and four
children—and the journeying of the mother with three children, helpless captives, to—they knew not what in the western
forest. After the horrible event of the morning, perhaps the
mother wept not, when the captors, dissatisfied with the delicate appearance and slow travelling of her weak-minded and
feeble-bodied son John, dispatched him at a blow and hid him
from the sight of pursuers. The hours of night passed slowly
and sorrowfully as the four captives, all females, lay upon the
ground, each tied to a warrior, who slept tomahawk in hand to
prevent a re-capture should they be overtaken by the pursuing
whites. Of this however there was no danger; the rapidity of
the retreat forbade all prospects of a re-capture. But on the

third day, a new cup of sorrow was put in the mother's hand. The little infant Margaret, that Mary could not part with, was spared to the mother. The Indians even assisted in carrying it. On the third day, the little one became very fretful from a wound it had received on its cheek; irritated by its crying a savage seized it, and dashing its head against a tree tossed it into the bushes without a word. The company moved on in silence; the sisters dared not, the mother would not, lament the fate of the helpless loved one; perhaps they pitied the living, reserved for, they knew not what, more than the dead whose last bitter cup on earth was drained.

After some twenty wearisome days of travel down the Sandy and Ohio rivers, they came to the Scioto; here the Indians showed Mrs. Moore some hieroglyphics representing three Indians and a captive white boy; this boy, they told her, was her son, they had captured on their expedition, two years before, who had been here with them, and was still a captive. The prisoners were then taken on to their towns called Wappotomatick and Major Jack, near where Chilicothe now stands, and were kindly received. After a few days a council was called, and an aged Indian made a long speech dissuading from war; the warriors shook their heads and retired. This old man took Mary Moore to his wigwam, treated her with great kindness, and appeared to commiserate her condition. In a short time, a party of Cherokees, who had made an unsuccessful expedition in the western part of Pennsylvania, on their return home, passed by the Shawnee towns, and stopped where Mrs. Moore and her daughter Jane were. Irritated at their ill success, and the loss of some of their warriors, the sight of these prisoners excited an irresistible thirst for revenge. While the Shawnees were revelling with spirituous liquors, the Cherokees seized the mother and daughter, condemned them to the torture, by fire, and death at the stake. Their sufferings were protracted through three days of agony. The uncomplaining mother comforted her poor dying child with gospel truth and exhortation, and died with a meekness that astounded the savages. The Shawnees never approved of this gratuitous act of cruelty, and always expressed unwillingness to converse about the circumstances, charging Mrs. Moore's death upon the Cherokees. They evidently felt dishonoured by the deed. About the captivity and death of other people, and about the burning of Mr. Moore's house, and the massacre of himself and children, they spoke freely and with the exultation of savages.

When Mrs. Moore and her children, as captives, left their habitation in App's Valley, Mary took two New Testaments, which she carried through all her wearisome journey to the Scioto; one of them was taken from her by the young savages,

and the other was her companion through the days of her
bondage. The old Indian that showed his kindness on arriving
at the towns, would often call her to his side and make her
read to him, that he might hear "the book speak;" and when
any of the young Indians attempted to hide the book from her,
as they often did, he interposed with sternness, and compelled
them to restore it, and finally to desist from such attempts.
Whether he gained any knowledge from hearing the child read,
or whether curiosity to hear "the book speak" in English
words was alone gratified, must remain unknown till the great
day.

The two girls remained with the Shawnees till the fall of
the year 1788. In respect to their food, clothing, labour, conveniences and discomforts, their situation differed little from
that of the young Indians. They were kept as property of
value, without any very definite object. Contentions sometimes arose amongst the Indians about the right of ownership;
and in times of intoxication, death was threatened as the only
means of ending the quarrel. Whenever these threats were
made, some of the sober Indians gave the girls the alarm, in
time for their secreting themselves. While free from the influence of strong drink, the Indians expressed great fondness for the
girls, particularly for the little black-eyed, golden-haired Mary.

The Shawnees continuing to be very troublesome to the frontiers, in the fall of 1788 an expedition was fitted out to destroy
their towns on the Scioto. The Indians were informed by the
traders, of the design and the departure of the expedition; and
watched its progress. On its near approach, they deserted their
towns, secreting their little property, and carrying their wives
and children and aged ones beyond the reach of the enemy.
Mary Moore revolved in her mind the probable chances of concealing herself in the forests until the arrival of the forces, and
thus obtaining her liberty; and was deterred from the attempt
by the reflection, that the season was late and possibly the
forces might not arrive before winter, and perhaps not at all.
Late in November the American forces reached the Scioto,
burned the Shawnee towns, destroyed their winter provisions
as far as they could be found, and immediately returned home.
After the departure of the forces the Indians returned to their
ruined towns; and winter setting in upon them, deprived of shelter, their extreme sufferings compelled them to seek for aid in
Canada. On the journey to Detroit they endured the extremes
of hunger and cold. It was the time for the falling of the
snow, which came storm after storm upon these shelterless
people. Martha Ivans and Mary Moore, with few garments,
traversed the forests with deerskin moccasins, the only covering
for their feet in these deep snows. Not unfrequently they

woke in the morning covered with the snow that had fallen during the night; once the depth of their snowy covering was twelve or fourteen inches; their only bed or protection, besides the bushes heaped together being their single blanket. On reaching Detroit, the Indians gave themselves to riotous drinking; and to indulge this appetite sold their young captives. Mary was purchased, for half a gallon of rum, by a person named Stogwell, who lived at Frenchtown, near the western end of Lake Erie. Martha was purchased by a man in the neighbourhood of Detroit, and being soon after released, took up her residence with a wealthy and worthy English family by the name of Donaldson, and received wages for her services. The purchaser of Mary neither liberated her, nor expressed any kindness for her, but employed her as a servant, with poor clothing and scanty fare. The circumstances of her redemption and return to her friends in Virginia are related by her brother James Moore, in the narrative of his own captivity and redemption. This gentleman was living in App's Valley, the scene of his childhood and his father's catastrophe, and a few years since (1839) gave the narration to the Rev. James Morrison, the son-in-law and successor of Rev. Samuel Brown.

FROM THE NARRATIVE OF JAMES MOORE.

(This authentic Narrative gives a specimen of Indian captivity.)

My captivity was the first incident in the disasters of my father's family. It took place on the 7th of September, 1784. I was in the fourteenth year of my age. My father had sent me to a waste plantation, about two and a quarter miles up the Valley (Mr. Poage's) to get a horse to go to mill. We being situated twelve miles from a mill, and that in a dreary wilderness,—I frequently had to go to the mill,—and often came home a good part of that distance in the night, when it was often so dark that I could not see my hand before me. Notwithstanding I had been so accustomed to travelling in these lonely circumstances, by myself, I had not proceeded more than half way to the place where the horses were, before a sudden dread or panic came on me. I thought some wild animal in human shape would devour me. I was so alarmed that I went on trembling, frequently looking back, expecting to see it. I would willingly have turned back and gone home, but I knew it would not do to go home with such an excuse.

I came within a few paces of the waste field, where the horses were, when suddenly the Indians sprung out from behind a large log,—and being before alarmed with the apprehension of being devoured, I screamed with all my might. The Indian that took me laid his hand on the top of my head, and uttered

the words *chit, che, chack* in a quick manner, which I understood to mean *hush.* I then looked him in the face, and perceiving he was an Indian, immediately felt relieved of my
former dread and spoke out aloud—"it is an Indian, why need
I be scared;" and I said to myself—"all that is in it is, I will
have to go to the Shawanee towns." There were three Indians
only in the company. Their leader, Black Wolf, a middle aged
man, of the most stern countenance I ever beheld, about six
feet high, having a long black beard, was the one who caught
hold of me. The other two Indians were young, and one of
them the son of Black Wolf, about, I suppose, eighteen years
of age. They were of the Shawanee tribe, and I belonged to
Black Wolf.

We proceeded on to the old cabin (Poage's). Old Wolf
gave me some salt, which from its reddish cast I suppose he had
made at some of the licks as he came along, and told me to
catch the horses. I then went on to do so with a young Indian
until I came near the horse, when he halted and I took hold of
the horse by the bell collar, and then he came running up and
scared the horse away. I then at his request made a second
trial, and he came running up again, and the horse frightened
at him ran off as before. My intention was to have gotten on
the horse, and thus endeavoured to make my escape; and as I
could not get him for myself, I had no disposition to get him
for the Indians.

I suppose it was about one o'clock, P. M. when I was taken.
In a few moments we started on our journey. The Indians
went up into the thicket where their kettle and blankets were
hid, covered up in the leaves, and took them. We travelled
down a creek called Tugg, the north fork of Sandy, that afternoon about eight miles. The walking was very laborious on
account of the high weeds, green briers, logs, and the steep and
mountainous character of the country. At night we lay down
in a laurel thicket, without fire or any thing to eat. The night
was rainy. I lay beside Black Wolf with a leading halter
round my neck and tied very tight, and the other end wrapped
round his hands so as to make it very secure, and so that I
could not get away without waking him. He had also searched
me very carefully to see that I had no knife. Gloomy and
distressing as were my circumstances I slept some that night.
During the afternoon the two young Indians walked before; I
next to them; and Old Wolf followed; and if any sign was made,
he would remove it with his tomahawk, so that there might be
no marks or traces of the way we had gone. I frequently broke
bushes, which he discovered and shook his tomahawk over my
head, giving me to understand that if I did not desist he would
strike me with it. I then would scratch the ground with my

feet. This he also discovered and made me desist; and showed me how to set my feet flat so as not to make any special marks. It then became necessary for me to cease any efforts to make a trail for others to follow. About sun-down Old Wolf gave a tremendous war-whoop; and another the next morning at sun-rise. This was repeated every evening at sun-down, and every morning at sun-rise during our whole journey. It was long, loud and shrill, signifying that he had one prisoner. The custom is to repeat it as frequently as the number of the prisoners. This whoop is different from the one they make when they have scalps.

About day-light next morning, (Sept. 8th) we started and continued down Tugg about two miles, then ascended the main Tugg Ridge, and then descended until we came to Maxwell's Gap. This gap took its name from a man named Maxwell who was there killed by the Indians whilst in pursuit of the wife of Thomas English, of Burke's Garden, who had been taken prisoner by a party of Indians, headed by this same Old Wolf, and was there re-taken. At this place Old Wolf went off and brought in a middle-sized dutch oven which had been secreted during their former expedition ; this was assigned to me to carry ; and I continued to carry it until we reached their towns. At first it was fastened to my back, and after suffering much with it I set it down, and said I would carry it no more : upon this Old Wolf laid down his bundle, and told me to carry it. I found that I could not even lift it. This softened me a little, and I took up the oven. After some days I filled it with leaves and placed it on my head, and carried it with more ease. We continued on the same Ridge for a considerable distance further the same day, and encamped on it that night, without fire or food. In the evening it rained, and the son of Black Wolf pulled off my hat. This I resisted, struck him in the stomach, and took the hat from him. He then made signs and showed me he wished to cover the gunlock and protect it from the rain. I then let him have it; after the rain was over he gave the hat back to me.

The next day (Sept. 9th) we proceeded down the same Ridge until we came to the clear fork of Tugg, and then descended till night, the day being very wet. We encamped for the night under a projecting cliff; and here for the first time kindled a fire. Old Wolf took the precaution of cutting a number of bushes, and bending them outward from our encampment so as to embarrass any one approaching us, if we had been pursued.

On the third day (Sept. 10th) they killed a lean bear, but so very lean that they would not eat of it. So we were still without food. Several times during the days of our fasting, the Indians went to the north side of a poplar, and cut off some of the bark near the root, pounded it, and put it in the kettle, and put water on it : this we drank occasionally, which seemed to have a salutary effect in relieving us from the sufferings of hunger.

On the fourth day (Sept. 11th) in the evening we killed a buffalo, took out its paunch, and some meat, emptied the paunch and shook it a little in the water, cut it up, put it in the kettle, and made broth, and drank heartily of it, not tasting any of the meat. This is Indian policy, after fasting, not to clog the stomach with food hard of digestion. That same night we made another kettle of broth, and eat no meat.

Some few days after we killed a barren cow buffalo, which was very fat, and barbacued as much of the meat as lasted us for several days; still killing buffalo and deer as we stood in need till we arrived (September 29th) at the towns over the Ohio, on the head waters of Mud River, called Wapatomatick, which took us about twenty-two days travelling. I travelled the whole route barefooted; and had at one time three stone bruises on each foot; my sufferings from them were very great. I frequently walked over large rattlesnakes, but was not suffered to kill or interrupt them, the Indians considering them their friends. There were other towns in the neighbourhood, one of which was called Major Jack.

We crossed the Ohio between the mouths of Guyandotte and Big Sandy, on a raft made of dry logs tied together with grape-vines. On the banks of the Scioto we lay by one day, and the Indians made pictures on the trees of three Indians and of me; intended as hieroglyphics to represent themselves and me as their prisoner. These they afterwards showed to my sister Polly, when she was a prisoner; and pointing to my picture, let her know that was for her brother. Near this Old Wolf went off and procured some bullets which he had secreted.

When we were within a short distance of the towns, the Indians blacked themselves, but not me. This was an omen of my safety, for if I had been blacked, it would signify that I was doomed to be burned to death. I was not taken directly into town, but to the residence of Wolf's half-sister, to whom he sold me for an old gray horse. The reason I was not taken directly to the town was, I suppose, because it was a time of peace. Shortly after I was sold, my mistress left me in her wigwam, for several days, entirely alone, leaving a kettle of hominy for me to eat. In this solitary situation, I first began earnestly to pray and call upon God for mercy and deliverance; and found great relief in prayer. I would rise from my knees and go off cheerful, having cast my burdens on the Lord. I had been taught to pray. My father used to pray in his family. I now found the benefit of the religious instruction and examples I had enjoyed.

Once on my journey, I was sent off a considerable distance

to get water, under a steep bank, where I thought I was concealed from view; here I gave vent to my feelings and wept abundantly. The old Indian however had watched me, and when I returned, he showed me with his fingers, on my cheek, where I had been shedding tears, shaking his tomahawk over my head, and letting me know that I must do so no more. I suppose their object in sending me off was, in reality, to see whether I would try to escape, the situation appearing very favourable for this purpose. After this I was no longer fastened with the halter tied round my neck, they being satisfied that I did not intend to endeavour to escape from them.

In about two weeks after I had been sold, the woman who bought me sent me out in company with her half-brother, and others, on a winter's hunting excursion. We were very unsuccessful. My sufferings from hunger and cold were very great; I had scarcely any clothing; the snow was knee-deep; my blanket was too short to cover me; often after having laid down and drawn up my feet to get them underneath my blanket, I was so benumbed that I could not, without considerable exertion, get my legs stretched out again. Early in the morning the old Indian would build a large fire, and send me and all the young Indians, and make us plunge all over in cold water, which I think was a very great benefit to me, and prevented me from catching cold, as is usual under circumstances of so much exposure. At our return from hunting, in the spring, the old man gave me up to Captain Elliot, a trader from Detroit; but the old woman, who had bought me, finding it out, got very angry, threatened Elliot, and got me back. Some time in April there was a large dance held at a town called Major Jack, which was about two miles from where I lived. In these dances the men and women dance separately, each forming a circle and moving round. I have never seen their war dance, which is very different from the dance which I witnessed. I have seen, I suppose, two hundred dancing at once.

Among the Indians there is a religious society called the Powow, composed of warriors of the best character. No mean Indian is allowed to become a member; nor is a woman allowed near the place where they hold their meetings. The husband of my mistress belonged to this society. Shortly after my return from the winter hunt, the Powow Society held this meeting at Wapatomatick. My mistress's husband attended. On his return home, I saw something awful on his countenance, which much alarmed me. After a fire was kindled, he took his seat in the wigwam, and his wife beside him. She calmly asked him what was the matter with him. He told her, that, at the Powow meeting, from the medicine proceeded a spirit, at first, about as large as his hand,—holding it out,—and it grew until it became the size of a boy,—holding his hand to the height of a boy about twelve years old;—it then addressed the Powow Society, denouncing judgments on them for their sins, and reproving them for their wickedness;—that the Great Spirit was angry with them, for they had become proud and lazy, and brotherly love had departed from among them;—that the time had been when their paths were marked by no footsteps but those of men and dogs, but now their paths were marked with no other tracks but those of horses;—that if a brother should come requesting that a brother should walk with him, he would say that he could not, that his horse was at a distance,—that formerly if a brother came destitute of garments when they had no other clothing but skins, it was immediately given to him, without his paying for it, but now if he came naked and destitute, that he must pay for it, or go away without getting anything;—that the Great Spirit was about to chastise them for their wickedness;—that Wapato-matick, Major Jack, and Kismagogee were all to be destroyed; —and you Wapeuttequah,—addressing himself to his wife,— will be punished for your pride. She was very rich, and could clothe herself with garments so full of silver broaches that they would almost stand alone. I was present in the wigwam, and heard the above conversation between my mistress and her husband.

These predictions were all literally fulfilled in the course of three years. Logan from Kentucky made an incursion on account of the thieving and murders of these Indians, and the above mentioned towns were all destroyed. She who had been my mistress fled into the woods almost naked and was reduced to the most abject poverty. She came to the place where I was living, near Detroit, told me her sufferings and asked for a piece of bread. I told Mrs. Ariome that she who had been my mistress, and had been good to me, was begging a piece of bread; she sent her a loaf, which was received with the strongest expressions of gratitude.

I went to the dance above mentioned in company with the Indian to whom I belonged; and there met with a French trader, from Detroit, named Baptiste Ariome, who took a fancy to me on account of my having a resemblance to one of his sons, and bought me for fifty dollars paid in Indian money—to wit, in broaches, crapes, and the like. I also fortunately met with a Mr. Sherlock, a trader from Kentucky, who had been a prisoner with these same Indians; and was the man who had rescued a young man by the name of Moffit, captured by the Indians on the head of Clinch, whose father, an intimate acquaintance of mine, had removed to Kentucky, and was at that time living there. I requested Mr. Sherlock to write a letter for me to my father, and give it to Mr. Moffit, to let him know that I had been purchased by a French trader, and was gone to Detroit. Father, I have reason to believe, received this letter; this I consider a very providential circumstance, in giving comfort to my friends, and particularly to my father and mother.

Mr. Ariome treated me like one of his sons. I eat at his table and slept in a good feather bed with his son. In him and his wife I met with a father and mother indeed. They always gave me good counsel, and advised me, particularly Mrs. Ariome, not to abandon the idea of returning home, but to try and accomplish it. I wrought on his farm with his sons, and occasionally assisted him in his trading expeditions with the Indians. On one of these occasions four young Indians began to boast of their bravery, and amongst other things said—"one Indian could whip four white men;"—this provoked me, and I told them that I could whip all four of them myself. They immediately attacked me; but Mr. Ariome hearing the noise came and took me away. On another of these trading expeditions I first heard of the destruction of my father's family from a Shawanee Indian with whom I had been acquainted when I lived with them, and who was one of the party on that occasion. This information was given me the latter part of the same summer the event occurred. While I was at Detroit, and before I heard of the destruction of the family, I frequently dreamed that I met my mother, sisters Jane and Polly travelling northward, their frocks being cut off at the knees; but after I heard of the disaster I never more met them in these nightly visions.

Some time in the winter after the destruction of my father's family, I heard of my sister Polly's being purchased by a Mr. Stogwell, an American by birth, but unfriendly to the American cause, in short he was a man of bad character and an unfeeling wretch. He treated her badly indeed. At that time he resided a considerable distance from me. I was preparing to go to see her, but I was told by himself that he intended in the spring to remove within a few miles of where I lived. It was then in the dead of winter, and I declined the undertaking. In the spring I heard that Mr. Stogwell had removed into the neighbourhood where I lived, and immediately went to see my sister Polly. I found her in a most abject condition, almost naked, clothed in a few dirty tattered rags, an object of pity indeed. It is impossible for me to detail my feelings; sorrow and joy were combined; and I suppose her feelings on that occasion were similar to my own. Having found my sister in so disagreeable a situation, I was advised to apply to the commanding officer at Detroit, informing him of her treatment, in order to effect her release. I went with Mr. Simon Girty to Colonel McKee, superintendent for the Indians, who had Stogwell brought to trial to answer the complaint against him; but I could not get her rescued from him. It was however decided, that when an opportunity should occur for our return home, she should be released without any remuneration. This was punctually performed on application of Mr. Thomas Ivans.

THE RETURN OF THE CAPTIVES AS RELATED BY MR. MOORE.

Mr. Thomas Ivans, a brother of Martha, was induced to seek his lost sister and the members of Mr. Moore's family that might be still living. Clothing himself in skins, and securing some money about his person, with rifle in hand, he proceeded to the tribes in whose possession the captives had been, and traced their wanderings to their several places of abode. His sister was living with a Mr. Donaldson, receiving wages. Mary Moore was delivered up by Mr. Stogwell, and James Moore by Mr. Ariome. All being at liberty—says Mr. Moore —we immediately prepared to go to our distant friends, and as well as I remember, set out some time in October, 1789; it being about five years from the time I had been taken prisoner by the Indians, and little more than three from the captivity of my sister. A trading boat coming down the lakes we obtained a passage in it for myself and sister Polly to the Moravian towns, a distance of about two hundred miles, which was on our way to Pittsburg. There according to appointment, the day after our arrival, Thomas Ivans and his sister Martha met us. We then prepared immediately for our journey to Pittsburg. A party from some town of friendly Indians was setting out on a hunting excursion and accompanied us about half way to Pittsburg; which was a fortunate circumstance, for a considerable part of our route was through a wilderness, the hunting ground of an unfriendly tribe. While yet in company with the friendly Indians, we encamped one night in company with a large party of the other Indians, and the next morning four or five of their warriors came very early to our camp, painted red, which alarmed us very much. They made many inquiries, but did not molest us, which might not have been the case had we been alone. After this, nothing occurred worthy of notice till we reached Pittsburg. Here Mr. Ivans unfortunately got his shoulder dislocated, in consequence of which we stayed a part of the winter in the vicinity, with an uncle and aunt of his, until he became able to travel. Having expended all his money with the doctor and in travelling, he left his sister Martha, and proceeded with Polly and myself to Rockbridge, to the house of an uncle, William McPheeters, about ten miles south-west of Staunton, near the Middle River. He received from an uncle, Joseph Moore, the administrator of her father's estate, compensation for his services; and afterwards returned and brought in his sister Martha.

A day or two after we set out, having called at a public house for breakfast; whilst it was preparing, my sister took out her Testament and was engaged in reading. Being called to breakfast she laid down her Testament, and when we resumed our journey she forgot it. After we had proceeded several miles, she thought of her Testament and strongly insisted on turning back; but such were the dangers of the way, and such the necessity of speeding our journey, that we could not turn back. Being connected in association with so many trials, and having been the source of so much consolation, the loss of the book was greatly regretted.

Thus far the narrative of James Moore;—and before we proceed to the relation of the succeeding history of Mary Moore, it is proper to state—that James Moore, the first captive, and the author of the preceding narrative—in a few years after his return from Indian captivity, sought the scenes of his youth in Tazewell, and there passed a long life of irreproachable morality and religion. He reared a large family, most of whom, with himself, became members of the Methodist Church; and closed a long life in the year 1848, noted for his tenacious memory, conscientious regard for truth, and love of the gospel of Christ. Martha Ivans married a man by the name of Hummer, moved to Indiana, and reared a large family. Two of her sons became Presbyterian ministers.

The return of the captives to Rockbridge was a matter of intense interest to the numerous relatives and the public at large. There were smiles and there were tears;—there was gladness and there was sorrow. Those who had loved the parents, and mourned their untimely end, rejoiced over the children rescued from barbarians, to which they were fast becoming assimilated. Shortly after her return, Mary Moore went to live with her uncle, Joseph Walker, in Rockbridge county, about six miles south of Lexington, at the place afterwards known as Donihoo's Tavern, now in possession of Mr. Moffit. At the age of twelve years she was baptised and admitted to the ordinance of the Lord's supper, in the Presbyterian church, by Rev. Samuel Houston, pastor of High Bridge and Falling Spring.

In mature years she became the wife of Rev. Samuel Brown, pastor of New Providence, and passed the days of her womanhood in the affections and sympathies of her husband's charge. Of the eleven children, of which she became the mother, one died in infancy, another at the age of fourteen, giving pleasing evidence of piety; the rest survived her. Through life she retained a strong attachment for the wild people of the forest, which no sense of injury, or memory of wrong, could eradicate or blunt. Her children hung with devotion on her lips, when she could be induced to narrate the history of her early life, and wept with her over the melancholy end of her mother and sister, whose death by fire she did not witness, but whose un-buried ashes were pointed out to her by the significant signs of a savage. Her patience, self-denial, and self-possession, acquired in part in her captivity, were preeminent through life. A pious and dutiful child, she was blessed with pious and dutiful children. As they came to years of discretion, they made a credible profession of religion. The sudden death of her hus-band left her a widow with ten children, the youngest but an infant. The moderate means left for herself and family were, by economy and good management, under the kind providence of God, sufficient to rear and educate her children. She was taken from them before the fruits of her maternal care and solicitude were fully ripened; but while the blossoms were fair.

Upon being asked some little time before her death, how it came, that her children so generally as they came to mature years made profession of faith in Christ; she replied, with some hesitation,—that besides the instruction given usually in pious families, and the means used for the conversion of child-ren, she had added but one worthy of notice, and that was—that she and her husband, after her little ones were disposed in their little beds to sleep, used, in the quietness of the night, to bow the knee at their bedside and beg of God to make them his children and faithful servants,—and ministers of the gospel. The former part of this petition was answered before her death, the latter part after she had gone to see her Saviour in heaven. Of her seven sons, all professors of religion, five entered the ministry in the Presbyterian Church; all licensed by Lexington Presbytery. A son-in-law was the successor of her husband, the comfort of her widowhood, and the guide of her young children. She saw her youngest daughter and child resign its delicate frame to the arms of death, in christian composure; and then passed herself, with overcoming faith, to see her God.

Perhaps, in her modesty, she did not see the power of her own example, and the force of her own character, formed as it had been by peculiar providences and moulded by strange cir-cumstances. Perhaps the strangeness of the circumstances, in which she came out upon the stage of life, made her undervalue the excellence they had formed, and led her to doubt that one so different from others in all her training could possess even common excellence. And when her cheering success in training her household was brought up to view, she attributed it to means open to all and used by many. These means are blessed of God abundantly; and the success in times past encourage men to use them in succeeding times with hope. Yet these common means receive much of their power from the habits, and more from the character of those who use them. And the peculiar influence of any individual, in any given place and course, can be fully understood only by acquaintance with the physical, mental, moral and spiritual training, by which the character has been formed, and the capabilities exercised for that peculiar end. Mary Moore was eminently fitted to be the wife of such a minister as Samuel Brown; her friends saw it; the congregation of New Providence felt it. And her fitness was the consequence of trials and sufferings that fall to the lot of few. Her early life was passed in seclusion from the world. In App's Valley she saw nature in her grandeur, and beauty, and wildness; and her fellow creatures in the endearing relation of connexions and neighbours in the wilderness. There was little for her to love in the world but its simplicity, and in the living beings around her, but their kindness and their piety. Of the pomp and splendour of luxurious life she knew literally nothing. The double log cabin was the only dwelling she knew, and the plain food of the mountains all her taste desired. Her clothing was made beneath her father's roof. The employment of Martha Ivans was to assist Mrs. Moore in clothing the family; and Mary knew how to use her fingers for the same purpose. Her education was of a religious character and for a religious end. God was worshipped in her father's family, day by day; and she was taught to read, that she might worship God understandingly, and know how to serve Jesus Christ in a life of faith. Her parents' example taught her to turn away from society to nature and to God; to live secluded and seek for heaven as her abode, when earth and skies have passed away. While the Indians were plundering the house of Mr. Moore, of whatever they wished to preserve from the flames, each of the captives seized on something to bear away with them in their wanderings. Mary took up two New Testaments; one of which was a companion of her three years' captivity, and through her lips spoke to the Indians the unsearchable riches of Christ. In cold, hunger and fatigue, in the wigwam and the travel through the wilderness, she still clung to this relic of her father's residence, this copy of the gospel of Christ.

Her tender affections manifested the law of kindness written on her heart. She had been the companion of her little infant sister, and probably, as the family was situated, her little nurse. When the hour of peril came she would have hidden it with herself and Martha Ivans beneath the floor of one of the rooms of the cabin; but the wailings of the little one, from a wound made in its neck, by some missile from savage hands, threatened to prevent all concealment. Rather than abandon the babe to the barbarians, she left her hiding place, and met the catastrophe in its company in the open room. Her heroic kindness was ill rewarded by the Indian, whose heart was filled with fear by the wailings of the same infant from the same cause. Lest its cries should betray their line of march, he dashed it against a tree; and taught Mary to lose in silence what she had bought with self-denial.

Her forgiveness of injuries according to the law of the gospel was manifested by the feeling she ever exercised towards the Indians from whose hands such multiplied miseries had been dealt out to her early years. She always plead for mild measures towards these poor lost barbarians, whose sufferings in this life were great, and whose prospects in futurity were dismal; and every movement for civilizing and christianizing them met her hearty approbation. The news of the conversion of any of the sons of the forest filled her heart with gratitude to God, who forgets not the outcasts. She could talk to her little ones about her captivity, and relate all she knew of her mother's death, without bitterness of feeling, though in tears.

Soon after her return to her friends, at the early age of twelve years, she asked for the privileges of the church on profession of her faith in Christ. Through sufferings the orphan had been led to God, her refuge and her treasure. What words were— our Father which art in the heavens—dropping from her lips in the wilderness and at the mercy-seat of her ancestors! The word of God says—They that seek me early shall find me,— and, when my father and my mother forsake me, then the Lord will take me up. It has not pleased God to give us the record of her Christian experience in the wilderness, nor to reveal to us the manner in which the Spirit led her into all truth; he has only shown us the desolate place and the forlorn outward circumstances of her seeking God and finding peace. But the event,—the peace she found, the good hope through grace, and the devoted heart, were seen all through her life; her record of experience is found in her family and in the congregation to which her husband ministered; in her keeping a good conscience both toward God and toward man, in her self-denial for the good of others and of her own soul, in her maintaining a godly walk, in her evidently not living for this world, but for God. Alas! how often is it the case that we desire the fruits of godliness, rather than be willing to pass through the sanctifying process by which they are obtained.

CHAPTER XXIII.

THE COMMISSION OF SYNOD.—WITH SKETCHES OF LEGRAND, MARSHALL, AND LYLE.

THE Synod of Virginia held its first meeting, Wednesday, October 22, 1788, at New Providence, Rockbridge county, Virginia. It consisted of four Presbyteries; Hanover, embracing the Presbyterian population east of the Blue Ridge; Lexington, that on the west side of the Ridge, except the congregations on the Potomac; Redstone, Pennsylvania, west of the Alleghany; and Transylvania, the settlements in Kentucky, then a part of Virginia.

In the month of May, 1789, the General Assembly requested the Synods to recommend to the General Assembly, at their meeting in 1790—"two members, well qualified to be employed in missions on our frontiers, for the purpose of organizing churches, administering ordinances, ordaining elders, &c.—and to meet the expense—"it is strictly enjoined on the several Presbyteries to have collections made during the present year." The Synod of Virginia at its second meeting, in the fall of 1789, taking into consideration the state of the vacant congregations, and the new settlements in their bounds, entered upon a plan of missions according to the following resolutions—viz.

"1st. That we will take all proper care to seek for men of knowledge, integrity and piety, who may travel through our bounds as missionaries, to preach the gospel, to catechise and instruct the youth, and to discharge such other parts of ministerial duty as they may be authorized to perform.

"2d. That there shall be a Committee of Synod appointed, consisting of four ministers and four elders, who shall be called *The Commission of Synod*, to receive the recommendations of such men from the respective Presbyteries, to examine into their credentials and fitness for the discharge of such an office, and who shall give them such directions and instructions as the exigencies of different places, in their wisdom, may require; that they shall meet annually and oftener if thought necessary; and that any two ministers, and as many elders of the Commission as shall be convened at the place appointed, shall have sufficient power to proceed to business.

"3d. That it be recommended to the different Presbyteries

to raise such contributions as they may be able, in their
respective bounds, which shall be put into a general fund for
the support of such missionaries.

"4th. That there shall be a treasurer appointed," &c.—His
duties were defined at length.

To carry into effect. these resolutions, Rev. Messrs. William
Graham and Archibald Scott, with elders John Lyle and
John Wilson, of Lexington Presbytery; and Rev. Messrs. John
B. Smith and James Mitchell, and elders Benjamin Rice and
Charles Allen, of Hanover Presbytery, were appointed—"to
constitute the Commission." The Commission commenced their
labours with spirit and success, and sent their missionaries from
the Bay Shore to the Mississippi. The vigour of action was
unabated for a number of years. As the Presbyteries increased
in numbers and in members, the Commission was divided
and acted as two bodies, the one east of the Alleghany and the
other west, with great efficiency. About the year 1807, the
Synod found the work of supplying the extended and extending
western frontiers too extensive for her means, and after a few
years the Synodical Commission ceased, and the General Assembly conducted the work of missions by a Board appointed
for the purpose.

From the records of the Commission, which have been preserved, a few extracts, partly in a condensed form, and partly
verbatim, will be given to illustrate the principles of the Virginia Synod, and some of their doings in building up congregations in the new settlements. A spirit inherited from the
original Hanover Presbytery, which began the work of domestic missions in her earliest days, is visible in all the proceedings.

The first meeting of the Commission was at Liberty, in
Bedford county, April 2d, 1790. All the members present
but Mr. Scott. He declined acting, and the next Synod appointed the Rev. William Wilson in his place. At the first
meeting it was resolved—"that it is the opinion of this Commission, that the preachers should be unordained preachers
whose object should be to preach the truths of the everlasting
gospel." The missionaries were to preach, and catechise, and
commence the gathering of congregations; their compensation
to be, sixty pounds Virginia currency,—two hundred dollars
a-year. Mr. Nash Legrand, a probationer, under the care of
Hanover Presbytery, and a convert of the revival of '87—'88,
whose preaching had been so popular and effective in Lexington and the neighbourhood, was chosen the first missionary.
He was requested to spend half his time as a missionary in
Lexington Presbytery, and half in Hanover, at places the
Commission should direct.

There was a peculiarity in the relation of the missionaries to the Commission. It was directed by Synod—"that those young men who are employed as missionaries, shall be immediately under the power of the Commission, to direct, instruct, and reprove; but in case any of those young men shall be charged with error in doctrine, or immorality in practice, that would expose them to the censure of the church, upon application to the Commission, he or they shall be given up to the Presbytery by which he or they were recommended to the Commission, for trial and censure agreeable to the rules of our Church." The missionaries were recommended to the Commission either by the Presbytery as a body, or by a number of the members individually: and when chosen by the Commission, they were, by act of Presbytery, put under the care of the Commission. When their term of service expired, or they resigned their commissions, they were recommended to their respective Presbyteries, and their reception was made a matter of record on the books of Presbytery.

Mr. Legrand entered upon his office on the 1st of June, and continued to labour with great success till the 1st of October; though strongly solicited to continue, he resigned his commission with intention of accepting a call from Cedar Creek and Opeckon, in Frederick county.

At the second meeting of the Commission, September 21st, 1790—"upon recommendation of Mr. Smith, a member of Hanover Presbytery, Mr. Hill, a probationer under the care of said Presbytery, was chosen a missionary. Mr. Hill being present accepted the office. Mr. Carey Allen, a probationer under the care of Hanover Presbytery, was also chosen a missionary; and Mr. Smith is directed to give Mr. Allen information, and solicit his acceptance. Mr. Robert Marshall, a probationer under the care of Redstone Presbytery, was chosen a missionary, upon condition said Presbytery recommend him to that office. Ordered, that Mr. Smith and Mr. Graham apply to the members of Redstone Presbytery, for such recommendation; and that Mr. Smith apply to Hanover Presbytery, and request their concurrence with the choice of Messrs. Hill and Allen." Application was made to the Presbyteries, and full concurrence expressed, and Messrs. Hill, Allen and Marshall entered on their labours with spirit.

In April, 1791, at Briery, the missionaries gave in their reports. Messrs. Hill and Allen had laboured east of the Blue Ridge, and Mr. Marshall on the west of the same, from the waters of Back Creek, in Berkley, to the head of Green Brier, and "to Hugh Allenson's," on James River. The narratives of the missionaries, which were a diary of their travels, preachings, reception, places of preaching, prospects for congregations, and the apparent success attending their efforts were—"very satisfactory." Ordered—"that Mr. Hill itinerate the districts of Hanover and Lexington, for six months. That Marshall and Allen itinerate in the districts of Lexington, Redstone, and Transylvania for one year." Under this order, Messrs. Allen and Marshall went to Kentucky, in the latter part of the summer. They did not return at the expiration of the year.—April 6th, 1792, at the meeting in Liberty, Bedford county—"a letter was received from the Rev. David Rice, directed to Mr. Graham, informing—that the missionaries, Mr. Allen and Mr. Marshall would not attend the Commission of Synod this spring; that the late period of their arrival in Kentucky, and the severity of the winter, would in a great measure defeat the design of their mission if they returned this spring; that the attention of the people to the word preached, and their desires for the continuance of the missionaries the ensuing summer, had induced this determination. Which determination the Commission unanimously approved." In September, 1792,—"A letter was received from Mr. Marshall informing that he resigned his office as missionary, and requesting a dismission from their body to the Presbytery of Redstone—accompanied with a request to that body to dismiss him to join the Presbytery of Transylvania; and also a recommendation from this Commission. Mr. Graham produced a statement of Mr. Marshall's accounts for eighteen months, with a receipt for the whole of his wages for that time." Mr. Marshall settled in Kentucky. His life and labours will be the subject of a separate sketch. "Mr. Allen gave a very full and satisfying narrative of his itinerations through the districts of Redstone, Kentucky, Lexington and Hanover." Mr. Allen returned to Kentucky, and finally settled there.

At the meeting in Winchester, October 6th, 1791—"The committee having received a recommendation, of Mr. John Lyle, from the Presbytery of Lexington, have chosen him to the office of missionary. Mr. Lyle being present, accepted the office. Ordered that Mr. Lyle itinerate in the neighbourhood of Winchester, on the waters of the Potomac, Jackson's River, Green Brier and Roanoke, until our next meeting." Mr. Lyle finally settled in Hampshire county, and after labouring many years laid his body among the people of his charge in Springfield.

At the meeting in Liberty, 1792, April 9th, Monday morning, 6 o'clock, William Hill, having made report of his mission through the counties of Richmond, Lancaster, Northumberland, Prince William, Fauquier, and Berkley, resigned his commission, and took charge of the congregations of Charlestown and

Hopewell, in Jefferson county. He is still living, having passed his ministerial life in that part of the Valley of Virginia belonging to Winchester Presbytery.

At the same meeting—April 9th, 1792—"Upon motion the Commission elected Mr. Archibald Alexander, a probationer under the care of Lexington Presbytery, to the office of missionary upon condition that the Presbytery recommend him. Mr. Graham and Mr. John Lyle are directed to apply to the Presbytery for such recommendation." Mr. Alexander still lives—having filled the offices of President of Hampden Sidney, Pastor in the Church of Christ, and first Professor of Didactic Theology in the Theological Seminary of the Presbyterian Church, Princeton, New Jersey.

April 28th, 1792—At New Monmouth,—"The Commission proceeded to elect Mr. Matthew Lyle, and Mr. Benjamin Grigsby to the office of missionary; and received a recommendation from the Presbytery of Lexington." Mr. Grigsby was settled in Norfolk, and after a few years of usefulness in the ministry, was suddenly cut off in the prime of life. Mr. Lyle became pastor of Buffalo and Briery congregations in Prince Edward and Charlotte, and filled up a life of usefulness to the church.

The first tour assigned these missionaries was—"Mr. Alexander and Mr. Grigsby to itinerate in company through Amherst, Prince Edward, Nottaway, and Amelia to Petersburg; then Mr. Grigsby, through Lancaster, Prince William, Fauquier, and Loudon; and Mr. Alexander through Nottaway, Lunenburg, Mecklenburg, Halifax, Pittsylvania, Franklin, Henry and Patrick. And Mr. Matthew Lyle to itinerate through Franklin, Henry, Patrick, Montgomery, Wythe, and Washington counties.

At a meeting in Harrisonburg, September 22d, 1792, after hearing the reports of Messrs. Allen, Alexander, Grigsby, Matthew Lyle, Mr. John Lyle, and receiving the letter from Mr. Marshall, mentioned above, the Commission proceeded, on the recommendation of the Presbytery of Lexington, to choose William Calhoun and Matthew Houston missionaries. Mr. Calhoun went to Kentucky with Mr. Allen, on his second trip; returned and settled in Virginia. He is still living, having passed his ministerial life in and near Staunton, Virginia.

The records of the Commission for 1793 are lost. But from the records of 1794, it appears Mr. Samuel Brown had been appointed missionary in 1793. He was afterwards settled at New Providence, Rockbridge county, and lies among the people of his charge. He was a father of preachers. Mr. Adam Freeman, of Lexington Presbytery, was also appointed in 1793, and continued to act in 1794. In May, 1794, Mr. Samuel Rannells, from Lexington Presbytery, received an appointment. He settled in Kentucky. At a meeting, September 20th, 1794, it appears Mr. James Welch had been appointed missionary on recommendation of Transylvania Presbytery;— and the following minute respecting him, shows the principles of the Commission. "The Commission have been informed that Mr. Welch, shortly after he received a commission, married a wife, and thereby rendered it impracticable to answer the designs of the Commission; therefore, unanimously agreed that said Mr. Welch be struck off from the list of missionaries." Information was sent to his Presbytery, with a request—"to consider him in the same standing as when he left them; the Commission having nothing against him, saving only that he did not answer the purposes of the Commission." He was settled pastor of the churches in Lexington and Georgetown; and for several years Professor of Languages in Transylvania University.

In 1795, the Commission appointed Robert Stewart and Samuel Ramsey, on recommendation of Lexington Presbytery.

There were no new appointments in 1796.

In June, 1797, Mr. James Robinson, of Winchester Presbytery, was chosen missionary. He settled at the Cove, in Albemarle, and there closed his life and labours. On 29th of September, Mr. John Lyle "presented a dismission and recommendation from the Presbytery of Lexington, to ride as a missionary," and was received. The next summer Mr. Lyle settled in Kentucky. The prominent part he acted in the affairs of the church in Kentucky, requires a separate notice of his life.

During the years 1798, 1799, 1800, and 1801, the Commission could not obtain new missionaries. Those who had been in their employ, were all settled as pastors. The Commission therefore proposed to Synod, in 1801, a dissolution of the body. Here the file of records stops. The remaining records are probably irrevocably lost. The Commission was continued for some years under the names of the Commission East of the Alleghany, and the Commission West. The records of Assembly show that the Commission was active, and paid attention to the Indian tribes on the frontiers.

NASH LEGRAND.

Nash Legrand was a descendant of the French refugees, or Huguenots, who settled upon the James River, at Manakin town, a few miles above Richmond, the latter part of the seventeenth century. His grandfather was one of these settlers. "His father, Peter Legrand"—says Dr. Hill in his manuscript, which will be freely used in this sketch, sometimes verbatim and sometimes condensed—"removed to Prince Edward, and became possessed of a farm within two miles of Hampden Sidney College, where he lived and died. His mother was sister to Colonel John Nash of Templeton, in Prince Edward, who had been raised in ease and affluence, and was one of the most accomplished ladies of her day, moved and associated with the first circles of society, and became one of the most pious and exemplary Christians to be found." Her husband unhappily fell into intemperate habits; consequently he made poor provision for his increasing family, and became stern, uncourteous, and sometimes rough. This trial she bore as a Christian. Col. Nash had taken under his care the eldest son of his sister, the subject of this sketch, and given him a classical education at Hampden Sidney, then under the Presidency of Rev. John B. Smith.

Young Legrand, at the time the revival commenced in College, under Dr. Smith, in the year 1787, was prosecuting his studies preparatory to the practice of medicine. In his personal appearance he was remarkably handsome; his frame tall, spare, and well proportioned, graceful, easy in its movements; his manners prepossessing; his countenance open; his hair dark brown, and his forehead high; his eye soft and expressive; his voice melodious. In company that pleased him his conversational powers were extraordinary, seldom surpassed for sallies of wit or amusing anecdote. At the same time he had a degree of hauteur and sternness which made him unpopular with the students, excepting those he selected as associates. His capacity for close reasoning and deep research was not of the first order; but subjects he did grasp he could exhibit in a most forcible and prepossessing point of view. But unhappily he was not free from profanity in his language, nor the taint of vice in his habits, and a mischievous indulgence in frolicsome pranks. The good steward of College was heard to say when Legrand professed conversion—"I am in hopes now, I may have hogs which can walk upon four legs."

When the revival began to be seen in prayer-meetings in College and the neighbourhood, Legrand withdrew from company and kept himself at Templeton, devoted to the study of medicine. Reports, however, of what was doing reached him; and the conversion of his college mates rendered him uneasy. The Rev. Drury Lacy, spending a night at Templeton, was put to sleep in the same room with Legrand, of whose uneasy state of mind he was entirely ignorant. The young man could not sleep, but lay tossing from side to side all night. Discovering in the night that Mr. Lacy was not asleep, he inquired if he might put a question. Lacy readily granted leave. "I wish," said Legrand—"to know what would become of a man, who had led a vicious life, and had determined to reform, and had broken off from wicked practices, and commenced to seek religion, but had not yet attained it; if he should die in that state, what would become of him?" Mr. Lacy replied—"if that be all, he must go to hell and be damned with the rest of the wicked world. Many go that far with the stony ground hearers, and never produce the true fruits of faith and repentance. It is not he that seeks religion, but he that gets it that shall be saved; for many in the great day shall seek to enter in and shall not be able." "If that be so"—said Legrand—"there is no time for me to be loitering in my bed." He instantly rose, retired to the garden, and spent the remainder of the night in groans, and lamentations, and prayers to God for pardoning mercy.

This took place about the beginning of the spring vacation of 1788. In that vacation Carey Allen and William Hill had gone to the Guinea neighbourhood, in Cumberland county, and were diligently employed in holding prayer-meetings among their relations and friends in the evening, and conversing by day with the serious inquirers. The morning after the conversation with Mr. Lacy, Legrand took his horse and rode to the house of Mr. Daniel Allen, the father of Carey Allen, and stepfather of William Hill, an entire stranger in the neighbourhood, and known to these young men only as one opposed to the revival, and by his unexpected appearance excited no little surprise. According to the etiquette of the country, the stranger was courteously received and kindly treated, and not questioned as to the cause of his visit. As evening approached the young men informed him that an appointment had been made for a prayer-meeting at the house of Mr. Nathan Womack, distant about two miles; and with hesitation, as he had said nothing of his state of mind, they invited him to accompany them. His prompt acceptance of the invitation surprised them, and excited some suspicion that he was in trouble of mind. They ventured to propose the subject of personal religion; he frankly told all his experience, and declared that religion was the sole object of his coming to visit them. Somewhat incredulous, they treated him as one in earnest. At the appointed place and hour, a large room was filled with serious worshippers. Religious worship commenced; and it was soon visible from his deep drawn sighs, and many tears, that no one present was more in earnest than young Legrand.

As the exercises progressed his distress increased; the meeting being prolonged on account of his condition and that of some others, he gave vent to his feelings in groans and cries of—"what shall I do?"—"what shall I do?" At length he fell prostrate on the floor, silent and apparently insensible. Laid upon a bed he remained without muscular motion till morning light; his respiration feeble, barely perceptible; his pulse very weak, and a little tremulous; his flesh approaching to cold. The young men continued conversing and singing in the room, and also occasionally praying. About the dawn of day he began to move,—set up,—arose,—and began praising God for the great things he had done for him; and seemed full of joy, and overflowing with love to God his Saviour, to his friends, and to all creatures. Looking at the rising sun, he declared it possessed beauties hitherto unseen by him; and all creation was clothed with new charms. He said he never lost his consciousness all the time he lay upon the floor and bed in that apparently insensible state; that his mind was deeply exercised, all the time with terror or with joy.

Sudden conversions were then rather matters of suspicion than desire. Dr. Smith and others placed little confidence in sudden conversions, especially if connected with bodily prostration, and great mental agitation. The young people around him had received a religious education; and there was no fear of proselyting efforts in his charge. He therefore did not hasten his young people to profess religion; but gave them time to ponder the subject well and consider their situation, weigh their hopes, and examine their principles and views, and not hastily to cry "peace, peace," to themselves. He would often try their hopes and joys, by throwing a doubt upon the reality of their experience of the things that were true and great. He tried Allen; and it distressed him exceedingly. He tried Legrand, but could not shake him off from the position—"I know in whom I have believed"—and—"whereas I was blind, now I see."

The change professed by Legrand was a consistent one; it was a change of principle and of feeling and conduct, all consentaneous, and visible. His temper and deportment were that of a Christian; and his professed views of "the plan of a sinner's salvation by the renewing of the Spirit of God, and the atoning blood and righteousness of the Lord Jesus Christ, were as correct as any could give, and were the ground of his joy and rejoicing." The effect of his sudden conversion and great joy, was peculiar, as in the case of Carey Allen, a few months previous. Others desired the same rapturous exercises; and sought the same preceding distressing views of themselves as sinners. "They wished to feel such a load of conviction for sin as would crush them to the earth; and then such a sudden deliverance as would fill them with ecstatic joy and rejoicing. Many were the attempts to throw away all they had experienced before, begin anew, and get religion in the way Allen and Legrand had obtained theirs. But it is foolish and dangerous to set up the experience of any man as a standard for all others; though the work is substantially the same in all, there is in nothing a greater diversity than in the circumstances attending the conversion of different persons. On the other hand it is equally weak and presumptuous to limit the Almighty as to the time required to convert the soul and regenerate the heart of the sinner. In fact, we scarcely find in the New Testament any other conversions than sudden ones, as in the day of Pentecost, the succeeding preaching, in the case of the Eunuch and of Lydia and the jailor. This appears to have been the common mode of conversion in apostolic days. Conversion was precisely the same thing in those days that it is now, and effected by the same agency of the Divine Spirit, and not by miraculous operations. Miracles never yet converted a sinner."

As soon as Mr. Legrand returned from Guinea in Cumberland, to Prince Edward, he threw aside his medical books, and commenced the study of Theology under the direction of Dr. Smith, and pursued it with vigour. At Cumberland meeting-house, October 10th, 1788, "the Presbytery being informed that Mr. Nash Legrand was desirous of offering himself as a candidate for the ministry, he was introduced; and having been examined as to the dealings of God with his soul, his acquaintance with experimental religion, and his motives for desiring to enter upon the ministry, to the satisfaction of Presbytery, he was admitted to further trials." Mr. Clement Read was admitted to trials the same day. William Mahon and Drury Lacy were ordained, the next day, as Evangelists. "The Presbytery having continued Mr. Legrand and Mr. Read on trials, and the necessities of the church apparently requiring despatch, an intermediate Presbytery was appointed to be holden at Buffalo meeting-house in January, for the purpose of furthering them in their trials. Mr. Legrand was appointed to produce at the same time an essay on regeneration, and a Presbyterial exercise on John xiv. 23." At the appointed time "Mr. Legrand read an essay on regeneration, which was sustained." On the next day, January 15th, 1789, Cary Allen was received on trials. Mr. Legrand's Presbyterial exercise was read; and he was appointed a lecture on the 23d Psalm; and a popular discourse on Romans v. 1 and 2, to be exhibited at the next stated meeting of Presbytery.

At a meeting of the Presbytery at Buffalo, April 24th, 1789, there were present, Rev. Messrs. Richard Sankey, John Todd, Archibald McRobert, John B. Smith, William Mahon, and Drury Lacy; Elders, Charles Allen, Bernard Todd, Samuel Graham, and Stephen Petties. Mr. Legrand opened the Presbytery with a popular discourse, on Romans v. 1 and 2 — "Therefore being justified by faith, we have peace with God through our Lord Jesus Christ: By whom also we have access by faith into this grace wherein we stand, and rejoice in hope of the glory of God." Mr. Legrand also read a lecture on the 23d Psalm. On the next day, April 25th, these pieces were sustained as parts of trial. "Presbytery entered upon the examination of Mr. Legrand respecting his knowledge in the learned languages and sciences, and in the doctrines of religion; and Mr. Legrand having produced a diploma from the College of Hampden Sidney, it was considered a sufficient evidence of his learned qualifications; and his answers upon divinity were esteemed a competent proof of his acquaintance with the doctrines of religion. The Presbytery therefore, having received from Mr. Legrand a profession of his accepting the Westminster Confession of Faith as now received by the Presbyterian churches in America, and of subjection to the Presbytery in the Lord, proceeded to license him to preach the everlasting gospel of Jesus Christ." This year that had passed between the hopeful conversion of Mr. Legrand, and his licensure to preach the gospel, was one of intense excitement, in Prince Edward, Charlotte, Cumberland, and Campbell, on the subject of religion. The revival with which this country was visited for some time was at its height of interest. There were calls for preaching in every direction.

Soon after his licensure, Mr. Legrand was prevailed upon by Rev. Henry Pattillo to visit his charge in Granville county, North Carolina. There his labours were greatly blessed. Passing on from Granville he visited Orange and Caswell counties. In the latter county the greatest excitement on the subject of religion was felt, particularly at the Red House, and the Hico settlements. Rev. James McGready carried the work into counties further south, particularly Guilford, and part of Orange, and about this time gathered in a great company of youth.

Mr. Legrand's preaching was more than usually attractive. His sermons did not give evidence of superior learning, deep research, finish of composition, or close reasoning. Many of his contemporaries far surpassed him in these particulars, and yet fell far behind him in the pulpit, both in popularity and usefulness. His disposition, which inclined to taciturnity, and sometimes to a gloomy reserve, was sweetened by the comfort he enjoyed in religion; and the ardour with which he engaged in the work of the ministry carried him so above all impediments that these defects were not seen in his early ministry. He was free from levity in manner or conversation. The comeliness of his person, the easiness of his manners and gestures, and especially the music and modulation of his voice, were admirably fitted to the pulpit, and attracted attention, without any special regard to the subject matter of his discourses; but combined with the import-

ance of the truths which he set forth with clearness and solemnity, few could resist the influence. The deep and all pervading impressions of godliness, with which his soul was imbued
from the time of his conversion, remained with him for many
years without apparent abatement, and created an atmosphere
about him which every one felt that approached him. He lived
near to God, and enjoyed religion more and more uniformly than
is usual; he excelled in prayer, as one who dwelt near the throne
of grace; the presence of his Saviour accompanied him; and in
the pulpit all these things imparted such an unction to his sermons
and exhortations, that few persons could sit and hear him preach
without feeling more or less conviction for sin. He had a peculiar talent for addressing backsliders and arousing the stupid
consciences of lukewarm professors. He was a favoured instrument of awakening professors of religion to the necessity of
living up to their profession. Under his preaching many old
professors were made to doubt the reality of their religion, and
to set out to seek a better and more scriptural hope; and some
hesitated not to say they were convinced they had never had
experienced true conversion before; and some ministers of the
gospel were known to make similar confessions while attending
on his ministrations, and their future course of usefulness confirmed this opinion.

He did not write out his sermons in full, as his talent lay
more in readiness for expressing in the pulpit, the things he
had prepared, than in selecting proper words while inditing
with his pen. His sermons were on common subjects, filled up
with plain truths, delivered in a simple plain style. He was
entirely free from ranting, or loose declamation; was modest,
grave and unassuming, with a heart for his work. This strain
of preaching, with which he commenced, he carried on through
all his active life. None of the ministers licensed during or
immediately after the great revival, among his associates, were
so sought after by men, or as much honoured by God as
Legrand. While this often had an humbling influence on
them, it never seemed to exalt him with pride.

The latter part of the summer he returned from his most successful tour in Carolina, and was present at Briery in August,
when Graham from Rockbridge made his first visit, accompanied with his young people, and delivered his masterly discourse from the words—Comfort ye, comfort ye my people.
To this meeting in Briery, many young people, from Carolina,
came in companies, earnestly seeking salvation; and an intercourse on communion seasons commenced whose consequences
were of great benefit to the cause of religion. When the
Rockbridge company returned he accompanied them to Bedford, where there were religious services protracted for some

days in Mr. Mitchell's charge, then enjoying the revival. James Turner had just professed conversion, and multitudes were inquiring what they should do. The company from Rockbridge were induced to stay some days in attendance on religious services; and Mr. Legrand accompanied them to Lexington. A revival commenced at the meeting held the first evening after their return; and Mr. Legrand proved a most acceptable preacher. Some account of the revival that followed is given in the sketch of William Graham.

In October the Presbytery of Hanover met at Pisgah in Bedford county, in the midst of the revival. At this meeting of Presbytery, William Moore a Methodist minister, was received on trials, and after examination was ordained to the full work of the gospel ministry. William Hill and David Wiley were upon due examination received on trials for licensure. Carey Allen exhibited parts of his trials and was examined on theology. So the two young men, Hill and Allen, on whose religious services Legrand was attending, when he was hopefully converted, were slowly advancing into the ministry while their young friend was preaching with the greatest acceptance. The ministers in attendance at this meeting were Archibald McRoberts, John Blair Smith, James Mitchell, William Mahon and Drury Lacy. William Graham and Samuel Carrick, from Lexington Presbytery, were present. Sankey, Todd, Waddell, Irvine and Blair were absent. On Saturday, 17th, 1789, the records state—" A supplication was presented to the Presbytery from the congregations of Winchester, Opeckon and Cedar Creek for supplies, especially for such preachers as are not already settled in churches. As these congregations are in the bounds of Lexington Presbytery, Mr. Chipley, the Commissioner, informed Presbytery that they would have regularly applied for leave to make their application to this body, but that the present meeting being a week before that of Lexington Presbytery, the congregations were prevented in their intended application. Messrs. Graham and Carrick assured the Presbytery that their brethren would cheerfully acquiesce in the measures that might be adopted on this occasion, for supplying said congregations according to their request. On Monday, 19th— " Mr. Legrand was appointed to supply in the congregations of Winchester and Opeckon and Cedar Creek, during the months of March and April; and the rest of his time, at his discretion till our next." Where he passed the winter is uncertain; probably in North Carolina, as most pressing means were used by Mr. Pattillo and the people in North Carolina to induce him to labour in the counties bordering on Virginia, either temporarily or stately. God blessed his preaching; and Pattillo desired to secure that preaching for the waste places of Carolina.

In the fall of this year, 1789, the Synod of Virginia determined to carry on the missionary concerns in its wide bounds by a Commission consisting of four ministers and four elders. Of this committee the Rev. William Graham was chairman. In the month of April, 1790, while Mr. Legrand was on his visit of supply to Cedar Creek, Opeckon and Winchester, this Commission appointed him their first missionary.

At a meeting of the Presbytery of Hanover at Briery, May 6th, 1790—"a call was presented to Mr. Legrand from the people about Dan River, in Virginia, and on Hico, in Caswell county, North Carolina. Another call was presented to Mr. Legrand, from the united congregations of Winchester, Opeckon and Cedar Creek. Mr. Smith also, in the name of the Commission of Synod, urged Mr. Legrand to accept of their appointment of him to be one of their missionaries. Mr. Legrand took the calls and request under consideration; but desired time before he returned an answer." At this meeting, Presbytery took the necessary steps—"for raising a sum of money for the purpose of sending forth and paying missionaries to preach the gospel in vacant congregations and other places, where they may think proper." This act was in obedience to a resolution of Synod, in order to sustain the Commission of Synod, in their efforts to evangelize the extended borders of Virginia, westward and southward. Individuals were named by Presbytery, for all the churches in its bounds, who should receive the donations for this purpose. This Commission of Synod, during the period of its existence, was energetic and successful.

On Saturday, May 8th, 1790, at the same meeting—"Mr. Legrand was called upon to determine respecting the calls which were presented him; whereupon he accepted the appointment of the Commission of Synod at present; and in the meantime desired to retain the calls for further consideration." On the same day Carey Allen was licensed to preach the gospel.

Of Mr. Legrand's services under the appointment of the Commission of Synod, Mr. Graham, the chairman, reported to the Assembly, in May, 1791,—"Mr. Nash Legrand, a probationer, under the care of the Presbytery of Hanover, was chosen a missionary in April, 1790. He commenced his circuit in the beginning of the following June, and passed through the counties of Bedford, Rockbridge, Botetourt, Montgomery, Augusta, Rockingham and Frederick, an extent of three or four hundred miles, with a marked success in engaging the attention of the old and young, to the concerns of their immortal souls, and in a general attendance on the means of grace wherever he came."

This is the modest account given by the Commission, of their first missionary's tour—a tour important as the first of a series under the care of the Synod's Commission,—and remarkable for success in such measure as seldom falls to the lot of a missionary. The generation that witnessed the extension of the revival under the labours of Legrand, in that missionary tour, have nearly all passed from the stage of life, and few have left any written memorials of the excitement on the subject of religion. But the name of Legrand has always been pronounced with reverence by those Christians who felt the power of his ministry. There are still living a few who heard his voice; to them, the mention of his name recalls the vision of an angel of mercy, whom multitudes will bless forever.

At an intermediate meeting of Presbytery, held at Buffaloe, July 7th, 1790—"Mr. Legrand was called upon, at the request of Mr. Warren, Commissioner for the congregation of Hico, in North Carolina, to return an answer to the call presented to him by those congregations. But being yet undetermined upon that subject, he requested still to retain the call, leaving the said congregation, nevertheless, at full liberty to call any other, whenever they please." On the next day William Hill was licensed.

At the fall meeting of the Presbytery, at the Bird meeting-house, October 18, 1790—"a Commissioner from the congregations upon Hico in North Carolina, and Dan River in Virginia, appeared, requesting an answer from Mr. Legrand to the call which had been presented to him. But as Mr. Legrand, in consequence of a call from Winchester, &c. had agreed to reside there for a term of time, he petitions for supplies." On the same day Carey Allen and William Hill were recommended by Presbytery to the Commission of Synod, as proper persons for missionaries.

From the fall of 1790, for a period of years, Mr. Legrand lived and laboured in Frederick county, Virginia, in the congregations of Cedar Creek and Opeckon. At the time of his visit in the spring of this year, these old congregations, which had been greatly dilapidated, were aroused, the pious enlivened, and very many were inquiring what they should do to be saved. The large Presbyterian population in this beautiful and fertile part of the Valley lying between the North Mountain and the Blue Ridge, awakened to earnestness in religion, prevailed upon Legrand to become their resident minister. Among these people there had been, from the first settlement of the country, much both of the spirit and the forms of religion, according to the Presbyterian faith: and Legrand found much warm piety to cheer him, in gathering in a harvest to the church. Here was a large company of young people who had been religiously brought up, with few hopeful Christians among them; and a number of old professors, some of whom rejoiced in God. Crowds attended on his ministry, and men began to profess faith in Christ under his preaching.

At a meeting of the Presbytery at Briery, April 2d, 1791— "From a representation of the state of the churches about Winchester, where Mr. Legrand has resided for some time, from the desires of the people, as represented by him, to have him ordained to the whole work of the ministry, and from his own desire, for several reasons, to be ordained, as he has a prospect of residing amongst that people for a considerable time, although he does not wish to be installed at present to that particular charge; the Presbytery agreed to ordain him at this meeting and appointed Monday for that business. Resolved, that Mr. Legrand preach on Monday previous to his ordination upon any popular subject he may choose, as there has been no opportunity of assigning him a particular subject; and that Mr. Graham preside and give the charge upon that occasion." The ordination was put off from Monday 4th to Tuesday 5th, when—"Mr. Legrand preached upon John iii. 14th and 15th, previous to his ordination. After which Presbytery having taken a solemn profession of his faith, and of his adopting the Confession of Faith as received in this church, and of his subjection to the brethren in the Lord, proceeded to set him apart to the whole work of the gospel ministry, by prayer and the imposition of hands; and he took his seat as a member of Presbytery. In October, 1791—at Colonel Morton's "Mr. Legrand applied for a dismission from this Presbytery to join the Presbytery of Lexington; which was granted." At the same meeting Dr. Smith was dismissed from his charge, and from the Presbytery, to remove to Philadelphia; Mr. Turner was licensed, and William Williamson taken under the care of Presbytery.

The success attending Mr. Legrand's preaching was great; all three of his congregations were revived, and attention to religion become very general. In Winchester there was a place of preaching, but no organized church; the professors of religion were in connexion with the Opeckon church about three and a half miles from the village. While the congregations of Cedar Creek and Opeckon were harmonious in the revival, that of Winchester was divided. The part opposed engaged another preacher to give them part of his services; and the dissension ran so high, that Mr. Legrand ceased to preach in Winchester and confined himself to the other two congregations, which afforded ample room for the exercise of his ministerial talents. In these he was blessed with success, for a series of years, beyond the lot of ministers of his day. Many whole families became professors of religion; and scarce a family could be found, in the range of his ministerial labours, in which there was not one professor of religion.

In 1794, on the 4th of December, the Presbytery of Winchester held its first meeting according to appointment, in the town of Winchester, having been set off from Lexington Presbytery, in the preceding September. The members were Moses Hoge, Nash Legrand, William Hill, John Lyle, and William Williamson. The history of this Presbytery for the first fifty years of its existence would form a volume of rich materials of interest and instruction. Mr. Legrand, by the testimony of one of the original members, who has long survived him, was the leading character in usefulness, in the early days of the Presbytery.

About the time of the formation of the Presbytery, Mr. Legrand was united in marriage to an accomplished young lady, Margaret Holmes, a member of the Cedar Creek church. One of her brothers became judge in Virginia, and another governor of Alabama. By this lady he had five children, two sons and three daughters. During her life he was happy in his domestic relations, and happy in his ministry. His congregation at Opeckon finding their house of worship too small, removed the log building and erected the stone church in which their descendants now worship. Before it was finished, the report from Kentucky excited a spirit of emigration amongst the youth, and companies sought a home in that "dark and bloody ground." The congregation on the Opeckon was much diminished by the removal of families of enterprise and piety. But the loss to the pastoral charge of Legrand was gain to Kentucky; and the Lord continued to bless the labours of his servant, and he was happy in his charge.

But the current of human things cannot flow with an unchecked tide of happiness even to the laborious servants of God. Legrand must be taught in the school of affliction and learn obedience by suffering. The wife of his bosom was smitten, and withered by his side. The bruised flower gave forth its odour of loveliness, and the husband's heart was beguiled by its sweetness, while the stealthy step of death entered his house. The fifth child was welcomed to the little family; but the joy of that welcome was speedily checked by the departure of the mother and the wife, lovely in life and lovely in death. Sorrow for her loss, and the weighty cares of his family, weighed down a frame already tottering from his ministerial labours. It was thought advisable for him to travel on horseback. He left his charge for a time, and made excursions; but without regaining his strength; till discouraged by his continued weakness, he relinquished the post he had held, with so much approbation, for years, and returned to his native county. In October, 1809, he applied for dismission from the Presbytery of Winchester, and was united with the Presbytery of Hanover, that had ordained him more than eighteen years before. It is no reproach to those worthy ministers that preceded and succeeded him, to say those eighteen years were the best years the congregations of Cedar Creek and Opeckon ever saw.

Mr. Legrand never again became the stated pastor of a congregation. His ministerial labours were given to vacancies and desolate neighbourhoods, as far as his health permitted. In the course of time he was united in marriage with an amiable and pious lady, Mrs Paulina Read, widow of Major Edmund Read, of Charlotte county, whose praise has been in the churches for her piety and benevolence. His residence was afterwards on the estate of his wife, with whom he enjoyed the comforts of an ample fortune.

On a visit to Frederick county to attend to some business, in the fall of 1814, he was seized with sickness which soon prostrated his feeble frame. He lay at the house of Hugh Holmes the brother of his former wife, and was treated with great kindness and medical skill. Feeling his end approaching, he caused his wife to be sent for, and the last fortnight of his life was cheered by her tenderness. In the month of October he breathed his last, in the exercise of that faith, which the searching questions of Dr. Smith, soon after his conversion, could not shake; and over which the despondency of his natural temperament could cast only an occasional cloud. At the time of his death he was about forty-six years of age.

"Thus lived,—and thus died one of the best and most successful ministers of the gospel, Virginia ever produced. His labours had been more extensive in spreading the revival than any other agent employed in the work;—the sinners who were convicted and converted under his preaching, and the number of hopeful additions to the different churches were more numerous than could be ascribed to any one else. He lived fast, and did much in a short time."

The apparent inefficiency of his latter years may be, in a great measure, attributed to the prostration of his health, and his consequent inability to make those great efforts, with which his success had been previously connected. He had previously preached under great excitement. This, in the latter part of his life, he could not bear for any length of time, for want of bodily strength. He had laboured through the disastrous period of the French revolution; and when the baneful influences of French infidelity were withering so much of Virginia, Cedar Creek and Opeckon were flourishing. No other preacher in the State held his people more closely to the gospel standard, or extended his influence farther, or left behind a sweeter remembrance.

REV. ROBERT MARSHALL.

The grave of one of the most interesting men, who ever died in Kentucky, is covered by a marble slab, near the pulpit window, at the west end of Bethel Church in Fayette county. The annals of the American church, from her rich stores, will not present a parallel, in one particular, to the companion of Carey Allen through the wilderness to Kentucky. There is something peculiar in the appearance of Bethel; and the first question that rises to the lips of the observer, finds its answer in the life of this remarkable man, and the history of the most exciting times known in Kentucky and in all the west. The church and the grave are easily found. Passing along the railway from Frankfort to the deep cut, about nine miles from Lexington, about five hundred yards to the left, a passenger may behold two one-story brick buildings, apparently about the same age, of different shapes, of about the same capacity, within a few yards of each other, yet entirely disconnected, and both, evidently at first sight, intended for places of public worship. These are in a great measure the product of one man's spirit, and in part the labour of his hands; and were intended for worshippers of antagonistic creeds. Between these buildings stood, many years since, the original log church put up by the emigrants of the Presbyterian Church from Virginia and Pennsylvania, under the pastoral care of Rev. Samuel Shannon, that man for labour and endurance. When Allen and Marshall visited Kentucky in the year 1791, the people of Bethel united on Mr. Marshall for their pastor; he accepted their call, fixed his habitation near the meeting-house, and after a ministry of forty years laid his bones near his pulpit. Honest, frank, warm hearted and energetic, Marshall began his ministry fresh from the great revival of 1789 and 1790, in the Valley of Virginia, and laboured with acceptance and honour, amid the discouragements of the new settlements in Kentucky till the great revival which spread its influence over all the South and West at the commencement of the nineteenth century. In the excitement of that agitated period, like many before his day and many since, he lost sight of the great principles of his faith, abandoned the Presbyterian church, and became the leader of a new sect, which he verily believed would embrace the world. Those of his charge who embraced his new sentiments, united with him in erecting the brick church nearest the road, more spacious than the old log building by its side, expecting the congregation would soon fill the walls, and unite permanently in the occupancy. The Presbytery exercised the discipline of the church, and the *new sect* rejoiced in their new light, and the blessing of persecution for conscience' sake. Thus far, there have been parallel cases, and may be again. But the next step is peculiar. In the merciful providence of God, Marshall became convinced of his errors; frankly, openly, and without any reserve renounced them, and returned to the communion of the Presbyterian church. Failing to lead back to the church many of those that had gone with him in building the new house, he united heart and hand with the orthodox congregation, and erected the other church, and in it for more than twenty years preached the true gospel with fervency and success. From the time of his return to the Presbyterian church till his death, he was irreproachable in his theology, as he had always been in his morals;—was above all suspicion, loved and respected by his brethren in the ministry as a champion of the truth; and reverenced by his charge, to whom his aberrations would have seemed as a dream, but for that brick pile, over which they often sighed, not in anger but in sorrow, and as they sighed but loved their pastor the more, great in his aberrations, great in his return.

Rev. Robert Marshall was an emigrant with his widowed mother from County Down, Ireland; born November 12th, 1760, he came to America in his twelfth year. The family settled in the Redstone country, in West Pennsylvania, on the borders of Virginia, on the frontiers. At the early age of seventeen he was in the Revolutionary army, and during three years was familiar with the skirmishes, marches, privations and battles of the most gloomy period of the Revolutionary war. He came from the camp unharmed in body, and unsullied in morals. "While in the army," said Dr. Davidson—" he never swore nor drank, although drinking and profanity were common in the camp, and liquor formed part of the rations. When not on duty, he retired to his tent, and devoted himself, like Cobbett, to the study of arithmetic and mathematics. He was in six general engagements, one of which was the hard-fought battle of Monmouth, where he narrowly escaped with his life, a bullet grazing his locks." In the battle of the Brandywine he was often near the commander-in-chief, and repeatedly heard with distinctness his words of command. In the retreat of that day, becoming separated from his company, he was exposed to the fire of a whole regiment of the enemy. As he ran along a high fence, on a hill side, aiming at a gap, at a little distance, through which to escape, afraid to climb the fence lest he should become too fair a mark, he heard the balls whistle, and tap upon the fence, just by his right hand, in quick succession; but escaped unhurt.

When about twenty-three years of age, he commenced preparation for the ministry, having been led, by the instrumentality of Dr. McMillan, to profess his faith in the Lord Jesus Christ. His preparatory course was completed under the direction of Rev. William Graham, of Liberty Hall, and Rev. Dr. McMillan, the father of the College at Cannonsburg. He had been well instructed in early life, in the principles of religion; had been most deeply exercised under the preaching of Dr. McMillan; had maintained a godly walk, in Liberty Hall, among careless students, whose neglect of religion oppressed Graham's heart. During his college course he solemnly reviewed his religious experience and his hope. He was licensed about the time of the revival in the Valley, by Redstone Presbytery, in whose bounds he belonged, and in the year 1790, September 20th, was appointed by the Commission of Missions of the Synod of Virginia a missionary. After labouring with success in Virginia for some six months, he was sent with Carey Allen to Kentucky. These young men laboured with great acceptance, and soon received invitations to become settled pastors.

In the summer of the year 1792, Mr. Marshall asked to be dismissed from the direction of the Commission, and to be recommended to the Presbytery of Redstone, which had licensed him; and requested of that Presbytery to be transferred to the Presbytery of Transylvania. By that Presbytery he was ordained, on the 13th June, 1793, pastor of Bethel and Blue Spring churches. Mr. Marshall was remarkable for his faithfulness as a missionary, and no less so as a pastor. The example of Graham, and McMillan, and Smith were before him, and multitudes of people ready to perish were around him; and his heart was stirred and his faith called into exercise. He rejoiced in his ministry.

The revival of 1800 was hailed, in its commencement and early progress, as the light of God's countenance shining on guilty man. After a time tares in abundance were sown among the wheat; and in some places it seemed as if the tares entirely choked the wheat. Nevertheless, in the mercy of God, a glorious harvest was gathered to eternal life. The moral influences of that revival were felt all over the southern and western country; are still felt; and will be felt for generations; will not be lost in all coming time. God's word was vindicated, and the riches of his grace magnified in the eyes of man, and a savour of godliness cast into the waves of the thickening population in the great Valley of the Mississippi. The subject of religion became all absorbing, the public mind was highly excited, and things apparently small, of a religious nature, would arrest attention. The wildness of speculation and adventure, for a time, yielded to religion, and men congregated in the wilderness worshipped God with the friendship of brothers. A course of reasoning, a relation of Christian experience, a statement of facts, a prayer, an exhortation, religious conversation, and even private meditations, were followed by great effects of a religious nature. In the progress of the work, it began to appear, from tracing effects to their *more ostensible and immediate causes*, that the presentation of truth in a pungent manner was all that was necessary to arrest attention, awaken the conscience, and bring men home to God, under the present dispensation of grace. In an unhappy moment Marshall gave in his adhesion to that error, and joined with five other ministers, of previous good standing and of credit for talents and acquirements, in forming a new sect which they fondly supposed would be speedily acknowledged as the true Church of God. By others the sect was called by different names, Stoneites, Marshallites, or more commonly, New-lights.

"As a preacher,"—says Dr. Davidson—"Marshall was clear, logical, systematic, and adhered closely to his text. His popularity as a leader of the New-lights, was for a time unbounded, thousands on thousands hanging on his lips at their camp-meetings." His morals were irreproachable in the camp of the Revolution, and in the defection of the New-lights. His fondness for metaphysical discussion was visible, but not a passion. He was a sincere man, believing heartily what he professed, and rejoicing in his faith. Enthusiastic in his feelings, he was sometimes rash, and sometimes, in his sermons, severe. But seeing clearly the end he had in view, he strove, by passion and by truth, to stir up men to believe and to act. He could thunder like McMillan, and could persuade like Smith of Hampden Sidney. He seemed always aiming at a purer way of living; in a former age he might have been an ascetic.

The history of the revival of 1800 and onward, in Kentucky, in its excellencies and defects, its melancholy and its glorious consequences, forms an interesting chapter in Dr. Davidson's History of the Presbyterian Church in Kentucky. It must ever form part of the fundamental history of the State. No man knows Kentucky to-day that does not know her in the first ten years of the nineteenth century.

After the public mind had become weary with the disputations and excitement on the subject of religion, and Marshall sated with the novelty and success of his new course, the subject was presented to this erring, but much loved brother, for revision. The brethren that loved the warm-hearted man, had made many efforts to recover him from his delusion, and had never entirely given him up, as a subject of hope and prayer. The instrument he acknowledged as having been, under God, the most effectual with him, was the Rev. Joseph Glass, of Virginia, who corresponded with him, and finally visited him at his dwelling, near Bethel. Marshall had a strong affection for his brother-in-law, Glass, and a high respect for his metaphysical and reasoning powers, together with an unwavering confidence in his piety and honesty. Glass induced him to go over calmly and prayerfully, the whole ground of difference between his former and his later creed. When the truth flashed on Marshall's mind, from behind the clouds of excitement and false philosophy, like Paul, he was not disobedient to the heavenly vision. With the honesty and frankness of his whole life, he confessed his error, and proclaimed his renunciation with bitter tears. When Marshall was reconciled to the Presbytery, Blythe wept for joy. Thompson, who had been Blythe's pupil, erred with Marshall, and came back with him. Over him Blythe rejoiced and wept. The other four ministers either had no one in whom they could confide, or were too closely bound in error ever to be set free; they went from worse to worse in their departure from truth. In 1811, Marshall was reconciled to the Presbytery. In 1812 he received an appointment under the Standing Committee of Missions of the General Assembly of the Presbyterian Church: and soon after was reinstated in his old charge, Bethel. The orthodox congregation, not satisfied with their old log building, and unwilling to leave the ground consecrated to the church, erected a brick building near the old site, and Bethel, divided, worships in two houses, each built for the same pastor, as a new-light and as orthodox.

Marshall was an active man, possessed of a vigorous constitution, of a well formed vigorous frame, of middling stature, of lively spirits. He was never idle. His farm, which was necessary for his family, was his exercise; his ministry was his labour and joy, and the acquisition of knowledge his recreation. The education of a numerous family necessarily occupied a portion of his time; but as other families shared in the instruction, his teaching was a public blessing. Whoever lived with him loved him as a teacher, and preacher, and invaluable friend. His sermons were usually prepared with much care, full of instruction, often argumentative, always clear and abounding with Christian experience. Warm and passionate in his delivery, he often besought with tears. "Here"—he would sometimes say, when he had come to the boundary of human strength, when sensible things must be lost in the spiritual, or spiritual things will be lost in the sensible—"here I made my grand mistake:"—and would weep. As he enlarged on the grace of God as overtopping man's unworthiness, and the influences of the Holy Spirit in recalling man to God through Christ—"here!"—he would exclaim,—"here, was my recovery." So strong was the conviction upon the public mind that Marshall was an upright man, that when, some little time before his death, an innovator in Christian theology, taunted him with being—"an old apostate," the cry of "shame! shame!" burst from a thousand mouths. The able defence made by his sons was esteemed an act of filial respect, rather than of personal necessity. He was a beautiful example how honesty may outlive mistake; and that a bewailed error of judgment, which brought no moral obliquity with it, shall not be brought in judgment against a guileless man.

Beneath the pulpit window at the west end of the church, is a marble slab with the following:—

Memento Mori.
Beneath this monument,
erected
by filial affection,
reposes all that was mortal of the
Rev. Robert Marshall
pastor of Bethel Church,
who died June 16th, 1832,
in the 72d year of his age,
and the 42d of his
ministry.

If in my life I tried in vain to save,
Hear at last, O hear me from the grave.

Around him lie his friends and connexions, members of his congregation, some of whom, like himself, had left the "green isle" of their nativity, and laid the foundation of a flourishing State in the great Valley of the Mississippi.

JOHN LYLE.

The last, though not least, missionary sent, by the Commission of the Virginia Synod, to Kentucky, was John Lyle. As a faithful preacher, a successful teacher of females and a valiant defender of the faith, Davidson's History of Kentucky shows he had few peers, and no superiors in the extent of his labours, and their abiding usefulness. His want of gracefulness, connected with an early deficiency in hearing, his want of polished literary taste, and his limited acquaintance with the knowledge of books, were counterbalanced by the excellencies with which they were interwoven, good sense, honesty of purpose, fervent piety, an earnest desire for the welfare of his fellow men in their conversion to God, his patience of hope and his endurance in labour. Possessed of few books, and called to incessant preaching in the new settlements of his adopted State, he was indefatigable in his study the fragments of time he could command. During his ministerial life, he was, says Dr. Davidson—"in the constant practice of reading the New Testament in the original."

John Lyle was born in Timber Ridge congregation, Rockbridge county, Virginia, October 20th, 1769. He bore the sirname of his father and grandfather, who were both elders in the Presbyterian church. His grandfather, from the north of Ireland, was among the early emigrants to Timber Ridge. The name of John Lyle is upon the subscription paper for the support of Rev. John Brown, for half his ministerial labours, drawn up in 1754, and opposite is the sum £1. 5s. Two subscribers only gave a larger sum, and two others, only, gave an equal amount. This sum, considering the state of the country, and the value of money, was a liberal contribution for the possessor of a farm of moderate size.

The father of Rev. John Lyle,—says Dr. Alexander— "Elder John Lyle, as he was commonly called to distinguish him from others of the same name, was in my opinion a man of eminent piety. In the period succéeding the war of the Revolution, vital piety had sunk very low in the Valley of Virginia; most professors seemed to have little of the genuine spirit of religion; and fell into undue conformity to the world, and its fashions and amusements. But during this time of general declension, John Lyle and his wife stood forth as shining examples of vital godliness, and holy living. When the revival occurred in the year 1789, it was like life from the dead, to this pious couple. They greatly rejoiced in the progress of this gracious visitation of God; and had the pleasure of seeing two of their own sons brought under the converting influence of the Holy Spirit.

John was a delicate child, and in his youth became defective in his hearing. The disabilities that followed the apparent reserve, and the stiffness of manner connected with his deafness, made a deep impression on a spirit too tender to be unobservant, and too honest not to feel indignant. The suppressed laugh and sly joke mortified a spirit that would not indulge malevolence and had not been trained in the school of Christ to bear all things. Andrew, the elder brother, who was a subject of the revival, possessed fine natural endowments of body and mind; and was encouraged by his father, and his pastor, Mr. Graham, to pursue a course of classical study. When his course of study in preparation for the ministry was nearly completed, he was suddenly called to the eternal world to the grief of all, especially his father, who desired greatly to see his son a minister of the gospel. John, from the time of his conversion, expressed a strong desire for an education, believing that

he was called to preach the gospel. His religious experience
was clear, and his hope of acceptance with God strong and
abiding. But there were difficulties in the way. His appearance was not prepossessing, and he had not exhibited
evidence of mental endowments above the ordinary standard,
or displayed any special aptness to learn. Besides, in those
days, a Rockbridge farm, of moderate size, returning to its
owner, for his labour, an ample supply of the necessaries and
some of the luxuries of life, brought in but little money for its
rich products, on account of the long, weary, difficult way to
market. The Rockbridge men might be said to have been
rich in every thing but gold and silver. The same farms, now,
under good management, with the facilities to market, fill the
purses of the prudent owners. Mr. Lyle the father had
expended on his son Andrew so much that he knew not how to
attempt the education of another son, without prejudice to his
other children. John felt himself called to preach; and
greatly preferred the preparatory course at Liberty Hall, for
a minister, to living at home with his parents as the inheritor
of the homestead. The mother said if John had a call to the
ministry it must be obeyed. The father responded, that the
office of a minister of the gospel was the grandest, in his view,
and the most responsible on earth : but he doubted his ability
to give much aid in John's education, and doubted too his son's
fitness for the great work. The neighbours believed the young
man to be pious and devoted, but had small expectations of his
success as a minister. The family felt with the father, and
acquiesced in the mother's opinion. John was educated for the
ministry, and the events of his twenty-eight years' labours have
made the heart of the family glad. Great economy and great
exertions were necessary to accomplish the desired end. John
sometimes taught school; and studied the languages. Mr. Graham assisted him, in the advanced stages of his education, by
employing him as tutor to the younger classes. His reputation
for consistent piety was high among the students, who in their
thoughtlessness made trial of his principles, and his feelings :
and his close application won him a respectable standing as a
scholar. At the close of his preparatory course for the ministry, John had expended all his father considered as his proportion of the estate, and in the final division no provision was
made for him by will. But he was satisfied; and no doubt his
father's estimation was right, as none concerned expressed
disapprobation.

Mr. Lyle was received as candidate for licensure, by Lexington Presbytery, April 21st, 1796, at Liberty Hall, and was
on 21st of April, 1797, at New Monmouth, licensed in company with George Baxter and Robert Wilson to preach the

gospel. His trial sermon surpassed the expectation of his warmest friends. On the 29th of September, 1797, he presented to the Commission of Synod—"a dismission and recommendation from the Presbytery of Lexington, to ride as a missionary." He was employed during the fall and winter on the frontiers of Virginia proper;—and the next summer went to Kentucky. On the 15th of October, 1799, at Washington Academy, Mr. Lyle was received back from the Commission of Synod and recommended to the care of West Lexington Presbytery, by which body he was ordained. In 1800 he took charge of Salem Church, where he remained for some years.

During the great awakening on the subject of religion, which commenced in 1800, and continued for some years, Mr. Lyle gave a happy exemplification of the firmness of his principles and his resolution to bear sacrifices for the truth. When the irregularities, so fully described by Dr. Davidson, began to prevail, Mr. Lyle was in amazement. But remembering that God had said by the apostle, "let all things be done decently and in order;"—and, "God is not the author of confusion"— he took a decided stand against the "exercises," publicly and in private. When he first saw the "exercises" in his own neighbourhood, his spirit was so troubled he forgot to eat his bread. Wandering into the neighbouring woods, in his perplexity he forgot his company of ministers he had invited to dine with his family, and they partook of their meal without him. Was this new thing the work of God? or was it the delusion of Satan and the sympathy of human nature? Many of the ministers who held a high stand in the church believed these exercises to be of God, or inseparably connected with his work; that this was his chosen way of confounding the wisdom of the world. Mr. Lyle could not approve of them in his judgment, delight in them in his heart, or reconcile them to his creed; and he would not tolerate them in practice. "He preached"— says Dr. Davidson—"at Paris a famous sermon from the text—"Let all things be done decently and in order." This discourse gave great offence to some, while others were delighted; and it had a powerful effect in checking the tendencies to disorder. At Danville he called for silence, while he preached from the words—"Bodily exercise profiteth little,"— and silence reigned, though two of Mr. Houston's people from Paint Lick had commenced barking like dogs.

Mr. Lyle was opposed to those departures from the creed and forms of the Presbyterian Church, according to the Confession of Faith and Directory, which resulted in the formation of the Cumberland Presbyterian Church and the new-light schism. The history of these remarkable events are given fully and accurately in Davidson's History of the Presbyterian Church

in Kentucky. A bare compend would transcend the limits of
this sketch, and also be divested of their circumstantial interest.
As early as the year 1801, in the month of June, Mr. Lyle
gave, at Lexington, the marks of true illumination, and exhorted the people to guard against enthusiasm. He prepared
his famous sermon on Order, after long observation, "which we
know"—says Davidson—"from his diary, he had been making
for nearly three years,"—after careful investigation of Scripture and comparison of texts,—and a reference to church history, as full as could be made in his circumstances; and on the
second Sabbath of July, 1803, delivered it at Walnut Hill, with
great effect. Preaching it at other places, he brought the
sedate to sober reflection, and aided much in drawing the line
of division between the supporters of order, and the defenders
of excess. At the meeting of the Synod in Danville, October
1805, the records of the Presbytery of Cumberland were reported on by the committee of review. Facts and doings were
stated which could not be passed in silence. The Synod after
much deliberation appointed a commission "with full synodical
powers, to confer with the members of Cumberland Presbytery,
and adjudicate on their presbyterial proceedings, which appear
upon the minutes of Presbytery." Of this commission Mr.
Lyle was chairman. It held its meeting at Jasper meeting-
house, Logan county, in the bounds of the inculpated Presbytery,
on Tuesday, the third day of December, 1805. Mr. Lyle opened
the commission with a sermon—on the Call and Qualifications
for the Gospel Ministry. The members of the commission
present, eight ministers and five elders, found but one friendly
family in all the region, that of James Reid, by which they
were all hospitably entertained for the space of nine days, the
time the Commission were in session. For a detailed account
of this meeting reference is made to Davidson's History. The
neighbourhood was exasperated, the Shakers who had already
received some accessions, were on the ground in high expectation of greater acquisitions, and sarcastic and malicious ridicule
invented nick-names for all the members of Commission. Lyle
and his brethren possessed their souls in patience, and after a
laborious investigation, proceeded to lay under a solemn prohi-
bition those who had been irregularly licensed by the Presbytery of Cumberland. On the regular members of the Presbytery, McGready, Hodge, McGee, Rankin and McAdam, they
declined passing any sentence, but cited them to appear before
the next meeting of the Synod of Kentucky.

October 21st, 1806. The Synod met in Lexington. "The
minutes of the Commission were read, and their proceedings
sanctioned." The Cumberland Presbytery was dissolved, and
Hodge and Rankin suspended. In May, 1807, the matter

came before the General Assembly in Philadelphia. The case was argued at length, and the impression was made upon that body, that the Synod had been too rigorous. Letters were sent to both parties, in Kentucky, advising a review of their proceedings. At the meeting of Synod in the fall after three days' deliberation, the action of the preceding year was affirmed. The matter did not again come before the Assembly, from the Synod, till May 1809. The state of things in Kentucky had become notorious. The five leaders of the New-light schism had been deposed. All parties were ready to make a full declaration of their creed and designs, only waiting the action of the General Assembly. The question at the west was—should uneducated men, and men disbelieving the doctrinal articles of the Confession of Faith, be brought into the ministry of the Presbyterian Church. In the Assembly the matter was not so well understood. Mr. Lyle, and Rev. Robert Stuart were present, as delegates from the troubled region, in defence of Synod, having come the weary distance over mountain and river, as travellers were then compelled to pass from Kentucky to the seaboard. Drury Lacy, from Virginia, was moderator. He had seen revivals and known the force of disorderly habits. Many able men, in the judicatory, were favourably impressed with the statements made by the Cumberland Presbytery and their friends ; and the array, that fell upon the sight of the Kentucky delegation, was for a time disheartening. On the third day—"the Assembly took into consideration a letter from the Synod of Kentucky, and having carefully reviewed the same, and having also read another letter from their records, which by accident was detained from the last Assembly, were of opinion, that the Synod have, in these letters, exercised their unquestionable right of explaining their proceedings." Mr. Lyle commented on the letters, and explained fully the condition of things in Kentucky, and becoming excited as he usually did in preaching, he lost the dread that had oppressed his spirits, and with tears depicted in glowing language the sad prospects of the Kentucky church, should the Assembly decide against the cause of the Synod. The Assembly was greatly moved. Dr. Dwight of Yale College, attending the Assembly as a delegate from Connecticut, advocated with great power, the cause of the Kentucky Synod. Dr. Ashbel Green, of Philadelphia, plead for the purity and propriety of the Synod's course. The Synod was sustained without a dissenting voice. A part of the members of Cumberland Presbytery made satisfaction and were united with Transylvania Presbytery ; the remainder, on the 4th of February, 1810, united under the name of Cumberland Presbytery ; from this Presbytery has arisen the body called Cumberland Presbyterians. The Assembly in

their record, say of the doings of the Synod of Kentucky—
"and the Assembly think it due to that Synod to say, that they
deserve the thanks of the church for the firmness and zeal with
which they have acted in the trying circumstances in which
they have been placed."

"His faithful, earnest, and affectionate style of preaching,"
says Dr. Davidson, "was very much blessed. On one occasion,
at Mount Pleasant, the Rev. William L. McCalla noted the
names of thirty-three persons impressed by the sermon, thirty-
one of whom afterwards became respectable members of the
church. He had a particular tact for benefiting young
preachers, whom he delighted to take with him on missionary
excursions."

As a school teacher, Mr. Lyle appeared to advantage. A
female academy was established, by his means, at Paris, Kentucky, at which were collected a large company of young misses.
The number sometimes exceeded two hundred. In its most
flourishing condition, the trustees insisted, peremptorily, that
the reading the Bible should be discontinued, and religious instruction dispensed with, under colour of freeing it from all
denominational or enthusiastical tendencies. Consequently,
Mr. Lyle withdrew from the institution; and the sun of its
glory went down, the scholars departing with the teacher.

Mr. Lyle closed his useful life, July 22d, 1825, aged fifty-five
years, nine months, and two days, having been engaged in the
ministry a little over twenty-eight years.

CHAPTER XXIV.

MOSES HOGE, D.D.

THE Rev. John Blair Hoge prepared for the press a beautiful
memoir of his father. The author's death delayed the publication of a work calculated to be greatly advantageous to the
church at large, and particularly to the branch of it in Virginia. While collecting the materials for his work, the Rev.
Joseph Glass writes to him thus,—in answer to a request.—
"In writing his history I should not know how to begin; beginning it, I should not know how to end. It was not that he
was unlike other men, but that he was always like himself; not
that he was zealously engaged in doing good to-day, but that
in doing good he was zealously engaged every day; not that he

performed duty, but that he never tired in performing it; not that he put his hand to the plough, but that he never looked back; not that he knew how to do good, but that he knew not how to do harm; and it was on a foundation composed of these singular materials that he erected the monument of an unspotted life. It is from the top of this monument that his spirit looks down upon the insignificance of conquerors and kings, and proclaims to the world that the love of God is more durable than polished brass."

Dr. Hoge was born in Frederick county, Virginia, February 15th, 1752. His father, James Hoge, was born in Pennsylvania, and emigrated with his parents to Virginia about the year 1735. The grand-parents of Dr. Hoge were William Hoge and Miss Hume (whose Christian name is lost) both emigrants from Scotland. Their acquaintance commenced on ship-board, where Miss Hume became an orphan. After their marriage they resided first at Amboy, New Jersey; then in Delaware; then on the Swetara in Pennsylvania, and finally on the Opeckon in Virginia, where they both died, bearing through life the character of eminently pious people; and leaving children whose descendants have been eminent in both church and state.

The traveller passing along the graded road from Winchester to Staunton, after leaving Middletown, soon sees the spacious mansion and wide possessions of Major Hite, at some distance on the right. As he approaches he passes a smaller residence in the midst of beautifully undulating fields. That is the birth place of Moses Hoge. There he passed his youth, in cultivating these grounds, in the midst of the beautiful prairie valley of the Shenandoah, bounded by a mountainous horizon on all sides but the north-east.

Dr. Hoge discovered a taste for learning far beyond the opportunities of his neighbourhood; and the feelings and habits of his ancestors were not averse to its cultivation. He was sent to a classical school taught by the Rev. Adam Goodlet, of the Associate church in Culpepper, for a short time; and then recalled to the labour of the farm. His eagerness for improvement was manifested in his using every moment of respite from labour, in the improvement of his mind. His elementary books went with him into the fields, and might sometimes have been seen fastened to his plough. Like Rittenhouse, while turning the furrows in the fields, he was sowing the seeds of knowledge for a glorious harvest. A sentiment that fell from the lips of Samuel Stanhope Smith, in an address to the scholars of Mr. Goodlet's school, made an indellible impression on the mind of young Hoge—"that while sanctified learning is the greatest blessing, unsanctified learning is the greatest curse."

In 1778, he repaired to Liberty Hall, and finished his education, both classical and theological, in preparation for the ministry of the gospel. On the 25th of October, 1780, he was received as a candidate by Hanover Presbytery, at Falling Spring, being introduced by his instructer, William Graham. In the latter part of November, 1781, he received his license to preach the gospel.

He left no written account of the religious experience of his early life. But from his conversation, it is known that in early life he was deeply affected with a sense of religion, had a reverence for God, and preferred the society of godly people. " The first book," says his son—"which he found peculiarly instrumental in enlightening his mind, and affecting his heart, was ' Alleine's Alarm.' And a sermon delivered by the Rev. Dr. Waddell was the first religious discourse from which he recollected to have received any unusual impressions." He did not deem it necessary to establish a claim to the Christian character, that a person be able to declare the precise time when he ceased to be irreligious, and when he began to be truly religious. In one of his diaries, kept in after life, he has this short reference to his early days. It was written on the anniversary of his birth, after taking a review of his whole life : " I have found great reason to be thankful for the invaluable blessing of a pious education, and for the co-operating influences of divine grace which rendered the instructions and admonitions of my parents, particularly those of my father, successful, and thus made religious impressions upon my mind very early, which have not yet been effaced."

Mr. James Hoge, the father of Dr. Hoge, after being for a length of time, a member of the Presbyterian Church, and also a ruling elder in the same, attached himself to a branch of the Associate Church in Pennsylvania. Once or twice a year he visited a congregation at some distance from his dwelling, for the purpose of celebrating the sacrament of the Supper. On one occasion his son Moses accompanied him, and was induced to make his first open profession of religion by partaking the sacred emblems, in the church of his father's choice.

Connected with his thoughts of religion, from early life was a desire to be a minister of the gospel ; and this desire never forsook him in the midst of all the discouragements in his path. He determined to wait patiently on God ; and was twenty-six years of age when he became a student at Liberty Hall. While a member of that institution, his mind underwent a change respecting his church connexion, and he applied to Hanover Presbytery for licensure.

After receiving license he was greatly dissatisfied with his own performances, both mental and physical, spiritual and bodily, and was kept from the conclusion that he had mistaken his calling by a remark of Dr. S. S. Smith, advising him to— "persevere in present duty and leave the event to God." His purpose of going to Kentucky was postponed for a time, to visit the people on the South Branch of the Potomac, in the present bounds of Hardy county; and from his attachment to that people it was finally postponed indefinitely. A call was made for him by the congregation in Hardy, which took the name of *Concrete*; and on the 13th of December, 1782, he was ordained at Brown's meeting-house, Augusta. The ordination sermon was preached by the Rev. Archibald Scott, the father of the present pastor of the churches in Hardy, from Acts xx. 28. Benjamin Erwin presided in the laying on of hands.

His first residence in Hardy was with Robert Maxwell, in whose excellent library of theological works he passed all his hours not demanded by ministerial duties. His place of preaching was at the forks of the road, a little above the Court House, on the land now owned by Mr. Vanmeter. There is an old burying ground near the site of the church, where sleep many of the members of his congregation.

On the 23d of August, 1783, he was united in marriage with Miss Elizabeth Poage, daughter of John Poage, of Augusta county; a match of feeling and reason. She was a woman every way worthy of his love, by her endowments of body and mind and the gifts of grace.

The honourable part taken by Mr. Hoge in the cause of religious liberty, is found in the sketch on that subject. His name is enrolled with the strenuous asserters of religious freedom. In a letter now extant, he declares that the final and decisive opinion of Presbytery against all assessments whatever, was according to his previously expressed opinion, when on a former occasion he proposed a committee to draft a resolution to that import, and was dissuaded from pressing the matter, by the assertion of an individual possessed of information on the subject, that some kind of assessment would be established, and he could only choose what kind he would have.

In consequence of protracted sufferings from sickness, which he believed was confined to the neighbourhood in which he lived, he listened to an invitation from Shepherdstown, and in the autumn of 1787 he removed to that place. The prospect was inviting only to a man of his kind disposition, desirous of doing good. In 1775, Dr. McKnight, a member of Donegal Presbytery, organized a congregation on Elk Branch, embracing the country between Shepherdstown and Charlestown. A difficulty arose about the places of preaching. After his removal, it was determined by a part of the congregation, to have preaching regularly in Shepherdstown, and to the invitation from this part

Dr. Hoge acceded.   The other part of the congregation in a few years united with Bullskin, and had the Rev. William Hill for their minister, and their principal preaching place in Charlestown.

While he was contemplating a removal from the South Branch of Potomac—"The Synod being informed that several disorders and disagreeable circumstances have taken place in some of the churches in the western parts, especially within the bounds of the Presbytery of Abingdon, to the great prejudice to the interest of religion in those parts, did appoint Mr. McCorkle, Mr. Scott, Mr. Moses Hoge, Mr. Francis Cummings, Mr. John Smith and Mr. Vance, or a majority of them, with an elder to accompany each, as a committee in the name of the Synod, to meet at Saline Church, on the waters of Nola Chucky, on the second Wednesday of October next, with power to them to call before them such persons concerned in these disturbances as are members or under the care of Synod,"—and to give judgment, &c.   Dr. Hoge attended at the time and place; but no quorum appeared.   The difficulty occupied the North Carolina Synod for years; and finally came before the Assembly.

During the time of his continuance in Shepherdstown his diary is replete with sentiments emanating from a pious man, with an humble heart, and devout soul, zealously engaged in ministerial duties.   The characteristic features are simplicity and godly sincerity.   His son, in his memoir has made copious extracts calculated to edify the humble Christian and encourage the minister of Jesus Christ.

In the year 1793 Mr. Hoge made his first appearance as an author—in a work entitled "Strictures on a pamphlet by the Rev. Jeremiah Walker, entitled the Fourfould Foundation of Calvinism examined and shaken."   In the preface the author writes—"That every blessing, that all happiness in this and in a future world, must be ascribed orignally to God, no professed Christian can deny.   That the interposition of the Saviour, and what he hath done to open the way for the reception of guilty sinners into the Divine favour is owing to unmerited grace, will be generally admitted.   But that a sinner's conversion and perseverance in a Christian life, and all practical religion, ought to be referred entirely to grace is a sentiment which many disclaim and zealously oppose.   Persons of this description, who are fond of exalting our present powers in religion are often distinguished by the term Arminian.   Whereas they who believe that salvation, when taken in its most extensive sense, in its original purpose, purchase, and application, ought to be referred entirely to grace, are frequently denominated Calvinists, and their peculiar sentiments the doctrines of grace. From this statement of the difference between Arminian and Calvinistic tenets, we may see that that the points in dispute between them are not matters of uninteresting speculation; but of real importance in the Christian life. If it be a fact that our salvation is owing entirely to the grace of God, upon his grace alone ought we to rely; and to him all the honour of our salvation ought to be ascribed. Should we then attribute our salvation in any measure to ourselves, it would be resting our eternal interests in a proportionate degree upon a false foundation, and at the same time an arrogating to ourselves a share of that honour which ought to be forever sacred to the author and finisher of our faith."

This volume was considered as presenting a fair statement of the doctrines of grace, of the errors of Mr. Walker, and a vindication of the true doctrines from all aspersions. The pamphlet and its author have fallen into oblivion,—but the volume of Dr. Hoge is such an exposition as would be read with profit by Christians at the present time. His son says—"Dr. Hoge, with advancing years grew less tenacious of some peculiarities of form and expression, but he never suffered his grasp on the doctrines of grace to be unclenched, and with tears of thankfulness for their consolation and efficacy, he laid them rejoicingly as a pillow under his dying head."

Soon after his settlement in Shepherdstown he was urged to listen to invitations to a place of more temporal importance; but he considered himself called of God to Shepherdstown, and forbid any preparations to be made for his removal. On the death of his second son, which soon followed, he writes, after mentioning the circumstances and keenness of his afflictions,—"I shall not forget 2d Thess., 4th, 13th, to the end. And why should I not be resigned? The great Ruler of the universe doeth all things well. I dare not wish our son restored to life again, were such an event possible. I hope he is in a situation which he would not exchange for ten thousand worlds like ours. I scarcely think it any calamity for a child, at an early period, to be removed from a world of trouble and of sin."

About the first of October, 1793, Mr. Thomas Poage, a brother-in-law of Mr. Hoge, a young minister of great promise, newly married, and about to settle, in the neighbouring congregation of Gerrardstown, was suddenly removed by death. The affliction to the congregation, the family, and Mr. Hoge, was alleviated by his happy spiritual exercises, and the sure hope of heaven he expressed, the last day of his life, in conversation with his sorrowing wife. His aged mother, in feeble health, felt the shock of the death of her youngest son, whom she had fondly hoped might be a useful minister of Christ; and in a few weeks followed her son, into the presence of Him whom her soul loved.

On Saturday, the last day of November of the same year, he assisted at the ordination of Mr. John Lyle, at Springfield, Hampshire county. Mr. Campbell preached the sermon on the words—" The prophet that hath a dream, let him tell a dream ; and he that hath my word, let him speak my word faithfully. What is the chaff to the wheat saith the Lord ?" Mr. Legrand gave a "profitable" sermon on Sabbath; and Mr. Hoge introduced the ordinance of the supper. The occasion proved of great interest. By the settlement of Mr. Lyle at this place, Mr. Hill at Charlestown, Mr. Legrand at Cedar Creek, Opeckon and Winchester, and Mr. Williamson at Front Royal, the way was open for the formation of Winchester Presbytery, which took place on the fourth day of December, 1794. Mr. Hoge preached the opening sermon in the old stone church in Winchester from the words—" The kingdom of heaven is like a grain of mustard seed." The course and prosperity of the Presbytery has not been unfitting the strain of the first sermon. Of this performance he says—"I felt very languid, owing, perhaps, to a cold fatiguing ride. Often when I hope to do something more than common I am sadly disappointed. This is no doubt right. But were I as dead to self as I ought to be, such dispensations would not, I imagine, be any longer necessary. O wretched man that I am, who shall deliver me from this body of sin and death ?"

The meeting of the Synod of Virginia, at Harrisonburg, in the month of September, 1794, was signalized by an effort of the military to put down the freedom of debate in an ecclesiastical body. The Synod, at that time, was composed of the Presbyteries of Hanover and Lexington, in Virginia; Redstone, in Pennsylvania; Transylvania, in Kentucky; and Ohio, north of the Ohio River. In Pennsylvania, in the bounds of one of these Presbyteries, that popular outburst, commonly known as the Whiskey Insurrection, had taken place; and the insubordinate, commonly called the Whiskey Boys, were many of them members of Presbyterian congregations. The part of the armed force, raised in Virginia to quell the insurrection, was encamped at Harrisonburg at the time of the meeting of Synod. The town and country were excited. The proceedings of Synod were closely watched. Mr. Hoge, after conference with some of his brethren, proposed—" That the Synod prepare an address to the people under their care, inculcating upon them the duty of obedience to the laws of their country." Mr. Graham opposed the resolution as uncalled for, and as prejudging in an ecclesiastical court the case of a people that felt themselves aggrieved politically by the practical working of a law of Congress, that pressed as tyrannically upon them as the Stamp Act upon the colonies. The proposition was lost by a small majority. The military were enraged, and threatened personal violence. Tar and feathers were hastily provided. An officer of high grade residing in Rockingham sent to the Synod a demand of the yeas and nays on the question, and the reasons for the decision. This was refused by Synod as an assumption of power. The popular rage increased, and the inflamed soldiery were scarcely restrained from violence by the remonstrances of Dr. Hoge, who rushed amongst them, and entreated them to respect themselves, and refrain from acts that could only be detrimental, and bring disgrace upon themselves. So great was the influence acquired by his proposed resolution, and his earnest remonstrances, that a general demand was made for him to deliver them a sermon previously to their march westward. He took for his text,—"Render therefore unto Cæsar the things that are Cæsar's; and unto God the things that are God's," and left upon his audience an impression of delight with the boldness, clearness, simplicity, and piety of the man.

On the 2d of June, 1795, he was called to part with his father, whom he loved as a parent, and reverenced as a Christian. He repeatedly refers to the pious instructions, counsels, and godly example of his father as a means of impressing his tender youthful mind with a conviction of the great importance of religion. There is extant a paper drawn up by this parent, giving, with great simplicity, and in the style and orthography of a plain emigrant farmer, the dealings of God with his soul, from his earliest recollection, till he became a widower with five children. It illustrates the domestic instruction of the family of William Hoge, the first settler on Opeckon, and is an exemplar of the standard of pious feeling and action of the congregation that was worshipping in the house built on his land. The writer of the paper, James Hoge, describes the feelings of a child in his first desires to find Christ—"I thought I would be willing to travel round the world, if it was possible, if I could be sure to meet with Christ and get him to take me in his arms and tell me that he loved me and would save me." And he describes with equal simplicity the overwhelming views of a Christian in his manhood, when he draws near to God. His last days were days of resignation and joy.

In the fall of 1801, the health of Mrs. Hoge having become very delicate, Dr. Hoge, by the advice of the physicians, sought in a more southern climate a refuge from the frosts of winter in the Valley of the Shenandoah. He journeyed slowly through North Carolina into the lower part of South Carolina, every where experiencing the kindest Christian hospitality, and enjoying delightful Christian communion. The open-hearted Carolinians sympathized with this candid, devout minister, and his feeble, suffering wife, lovely in her decline. With the returning spring he sought his home, cheered with the prospect of rapid improvement in the health of his wife. These hopes and prospects were all blasted before he reached Augusta, and as a last resort he sought the aid of the Sweet Springs, which had been beneficial to his suffering companion on a former occasion. Her vital powers were exhausted before reaching the Springs, and she fell asleep in Christ on the 18th of June, 1802. She had enjoyed the presence of her Lord, in an unusual degree in her life. In her sickness, particularly towards its close, she was beset with fears and doubts. Her sorrowing husband, after much private prayer, held with her a time of special intercession for her relief. And while they were yet speaking the light of the Lord shone upon her soul; and her consolations were strong in death. Her husband chose for her burial place an eminence; and standing at the head of the grave preached Christ and him crucified, as the resurrection and the life. The reflections in his diary on this occasion are full of affection and piety.

In October, 1803, he attended the Synod which met at Hampden Sidney College; and before his return to the Valley, on the 25th of the month was united in marriage with Mrs. Susannah Hunt, widow of William Pitt Hunt, Esq., and daughter of Colonel Joel Watkins of Charlotte county. Mr. Hunt was grandson of one of Mr. Davies' elders, and son of the Rev. Mr. Hunt whose narrative of the Rise of the Presbyterian Church in Hanover has been preserved by Dr. Rice. The name of Watkins is familiar in the civil and religious history of southern Virginia. Dr. Hoge and Mr. Hunt had been intimate friends; and this marriage was one of judgment, and affection, and prudence. It proved a source of comfort and usefulness to both parties.

In 1805 Dr. Hoge was induced to open a classical school for the double purpose of adding to his means of support, and the education of his sons who were now of the proper age for the rudiments of a classical course. He had been attending to the education of young men for the ministry as opportunity occurred; and at this time was more deeply impressed with the importance of a course of theological reading under proper guidance to candidates for the gospel ministry. Some of the members of Hanover Presbytery, about this time, commenced gathering a theological library at Hampden Sidney for the purpose of mutual improvement. The advantage of such a library for the instruction of candidates was apparent. In

1806 the Presbytery "resolved to establish at Hampden Sidney a complete theological library for the benefit of students in divinity. 2d. That an attempt be made to establish a fund for the education of poor and pious youth, for the ministry of the gospel. 3d. That the Rev. Messrs. Archibald Alexander, Matthew Lyle, Conrad Speece, John H. Rice, and Major James Morton, Major Robert Quarles and Mr. James Daniel, be a standing committee to manage the business and make report to Presbytery at its annual meeting. 4th. That whatever funds are raised by the committee shall be vested in the Trustees of Hampden Sidney College; the appropriation of all such funds however shall forever remain with the Presbytery." In the spring of 1807 funds to the amount of $2500 were raised for the purposes above mentioned.

While these things were in progress, Dr. Hoge, animated by the example of Franke, was planning a school for training young men for the ministry, on the principle of mutual improvement in science and piety. Believing such a school necessary, and that a location in the Valley of the Shenandoah was favourable, his faith embraced the means as well as the end. " The silver and the gold are the Lord's—was his reply to one inquiring of him where he would find the means of carrying on his Seminary. He believed that faith in the mountains, like faith in Germany, would build the walls.

The Presidency of Hampden Sidney becoming vacant by the removal of Rev. Archibald Alexander to Philadelphia, on the 6th of June, 1807, Mr. Hoge was unanimously chosen to fill the vacant office. The vote of the Trustees was accompanied by pressing letters from the brethren of the Presbytery, and Mr. Hoge, after some hesitation, consented to remove. One letter says—" What I wish to present to you for your serious consideration is the importance of our Theological School. For some years to come the head of the Theological School must be the President of Hampden Sidney College. Now the eyes of all who are at the same time friends to this institution and acquaintances of yours are directed to you as the fittest person in the compass of their knowledge for a Professor of Divinity."

In the month of October he removed to Prince Edward, and during the sessions of Synod was inducted to office, being received with every mark of kindness and hearty approbation. On the Sabbath after Synod he preached his first sermon, in preparation for the communion, on 1 Peter i. 12, and in the beginning of November entered upon the duties of his office.

In 1809, the General Assembly, after discussing the subject of ministerial education, and the propriety of having a seminary or seminaries for the purpose, sent down to the Presbyteries the

inquiry: *Should there be one or more seminaries established?*
The Presbyteries, which sent up an answer, were divided in
opinion.   The Assembly resolved upon establishing a central
one, leaving the Synods and Presbyteries at liberty to establish
one for themselves if they judged expedient.   The Presbyteries
in Virginia determined in favour of synodical seminaries;
and in 1812, the Synod unanimously resolved on establishing a
Theological Seminary,—and also unanimously resolved that
Dr. Hoge should be their Professor.

From this time till his death, in 1820, Dr. Hoge held the double
office of President of the College, and the Professor of Divinity,
under the appointment of Synod.   In the meantime the Seminary at Princeton was established, and Archibald Alexander,
D. D., was made First Professor.   The endowments made by
the Assembly were more abundant than those made by the Synod
of Virginia.   But with all the disadvantages arising from want
of funds, and an experienced Board of Directors, Dr. Hoge
had the pleasure of seeing about thirty of his pupils at Hampden Sidney among the licensed and ordained ambassadors of the
Lord Jesus.   These have travelled widely and laboured faithfully.   Some of them still labour in the gospel; and some have
gone to receive the reward of their exertions and zeal.   With
all his desires to do good, in his largest purposes, in all human
probability he never contemplated the extent of usefulness with
which the Lord finally blessed him.

His patriotic spirit kept pace with his increasing usefulness,
and Hampden Sidney heard from him the same invigorating call
to arms that burst from the lips of his predecessor Smith.   In
the late war with England, the British forces took possession of
Washington, and burned the Capitol and other public buildings.
Rumour of this sad event spread swiftly over the country.   Dr.
Hoge received information by letter on Sunday afternoon, with
the additional rumour that the British forces, in great strength,
were marching upon Richmond.   Postponing the usual service
for the afternoon, in which he was just about to engage, he
announced to the audience the contents of the communication,
and addressed them on the duty of protecting their homes, and
defending their country.   With impassioned eloquence he urged
the able-bodied men to go where duty called.   By noon on Monday Captain Allen's troop of cavalry was collected at Prince Edward Court House.   They had served one tour of duty; and
were now again assembled as volunteers.   By request, Dr. Hoge
met them at the Court House, and from a cart in the corner of
the yard addressed the soldiers, drawn up in hollow square, and
in strains of eloquent patriotism encouraged them to venture
and suffer for their country.   The impression on the soldiers
was deep and enlivening.   One of the troopers, a sprightly

young man of fine memory and powers of mimicry, paid close
attention to the Doctor's address; and in camp would occasionally repeat it in the words, and with the tones and gestures
of the venerable minister. The company ever bore him in the
highest esteem, and hailed with joy a report that he was to visit
their camp.

Dr. Hoge was blessed in his family; while rearing youth for
usefulness, God blessed his sons and made them useful: rejoicing
to introduce pious young men into the ministry, God thrust his
sons into the harvest. In May, 1813, he thus writes in his
diary respecting the licensure of his youngest—"It fell to my
lot to perform that solemn office; never have I observed so
many tears shed on such an occasion. He has gone forth with
the good wishes of all present, and with the prayers of all the
pious spectators of the scene. With the instructions of a father
I united the love of his mother, reminding him of her prayers
and tears, as well as of her instruction and example. Thus I
have lived to see *three of my sons become preachers of the gospel.*" These were James, John Blair, and Samuel Davies.
James is still living in Columbus, Ohio, a worthy son of a
worthy sire. Samuel Davies was afflicted with feeble health
during his whole ministerial course. After preaching accept-
ably for some years in Virginia he removed to Ohio, and
though happily and usefully employed, gradually fell a victim
to disease. He was happily united in marriage with a daughter
of Rev. Drury Lacy; and their son, Moses Drury, is a settled
pastor in Richmond, Virginia. John Blair early gave ominous
symptoms of the disease of his mother, which finally carried
him to his grave. These symptoms were greatly palliated by
a visit to Europe, and the mild air of the south of France
brought back vigour to his lungs. On his return to Virginia
he became the most popular preacher of his day. Possessed of
a fine imagination, strong sense, a great command of words,
with a sweet flow of thought, a kind heart, and tender sensibilities, with a quick sense of right and wrong, of the congruous
and ridiculous, he preached with a fervency and pathos that
drew all classes to hear him. After preaching for a time in
Berkeley county, he removed to Richmond, hoping to find the
winter climate more favourable to his lungs. These at length
gave way, and leaving a widow and two children, he fell asleep
in his native Valley, and lies buried in Martinsburg, the scene
of his former labours. That Dr. Hoge should rejoice in his
ministerial sons was but an evidence of his thankfulness to God
for their existence, and their interest in the covenant of grace,
and his love for all mankind.

The labours of Dr. Hoge's station became more and more
oppressive to him, till his strong constitution began to exhibit

evident marks of decay. The labours of President of a College and Professor of Divinity had become much more onerous than in the days of the founders of Hampden Sidney. The College course of studies was, throughout the United States, becoming more and more extensive, and demanding more time and more labour in the inculcation. Professor after Professor was demanded in languages and sciences; and in theology, the labour was divided and subdivided among numerous teachers. But no measures were taken to lessen the labours of Dr. Hoge. Some complaints pained his ear, that seemed to him to charge him with neglect—of which he said he would as soon have expected to be charged with an intention of suicide. While it was evident to all that something ought to be done, no efficient steps were taken to accomplish what has since been done, by the life and labours of John H. Rice, D.D. In 1819 his strong powers of body gave way. After a long confinement to his chamber his strength was but partially renewed. In the spring of 1820 he was appointed delegate to the General Assembly to meet in Philadelphia. It had been his ardent desire to attend an anniversary of the American Bible Society in New York. He took this opportunity of gratifying that desire; and journeying to New York was present on the occasion of the annual meeting. Returning, he visited the Theological Seminary at Princeton under the instructions of his old friend Dr. Alexander, with Dr. Miller, and was greatly gratified with what he saw and heard. During the sessions of the Assembly he became ill. He attended, with occasional absences, upon the meetings of the brethren. His last public service was offering the invocatory prayer in the prayer meeting of the Assembly. His symptoms becoming alarming, members of his family hastened to his bedside, and witnessing his prevailing faith, soothed the sufferings of his body. His comfort from the truths of the gospel was great; his faith triumphant. On the fifth of July, 1820, at three o'clock, P. M.—"without an indication of distress, and with an expression sweetly placid and serene he slept in Jesus. His body was deposited in the burying ground of the Third Presbyterian Church, Philadelphia, beside the remains of his intimate friend, John Blair Smith. United while they lived, in bonds of the closest friendship, they are now associated in the tomb."

That the Virginia Synod esteemed Dr. Hoge a theologian is evident from the position he held, unsought for and unexpected. Orthodox in sentiment, clear in thought, kind in feeling, fond of reading, given to study, he filled the chair of Professor to the great satisfaction of his pupils, who invariably held him in increasing reverence. His preaching was admired. His discourses were characterized by simplicity in the plan, the thought and the diction. Every thing seemed to be natural. Sound sense, truth and clearness gave a reality to the things he exhibited from the sacred desk. Always fervent, often highly pathetic, he seemed to have but one object in view,—preaching the gospel of the Lord Jesus Christ. Incorruptible in his principles; irreproachable in his moral and religious character, his words had meaning and weight. In the delivery of his sermons he was not in the classic sense graceful. In his early life, his fine moral and spiritual sensibilities were cultivated to exquisite proportion, while his outward man was neglected. His friend and instructor, Graham, attempted at Liberty Hall to improve his manners and soften his awkwardness. After some trial he relinquished the effort, observing pleasantly that it was impossible to remodel him. His arms appeared disproportionably long, and gave an awkwardness where there was no vulgarity. His first appearance sometimes excited a disposition to smile; not at wit or drollery, but an apparent want of fitness. A conviction of this greatly discouraged him in the commencement of his ministerial course. How entirely this passed away from his frequent hearers, may be known from the fact, that on an expected vacancy in the charge of Mr. Graham, the congregation fixed their attention on Mr. Hoge as successor. The people said, this awkwardness is the way of an honest, tenderhearted, upright, noble-spirited man. He has the heart of a gentleman, and there is no vulgarity in him. In ordinary times some two or three sermons were requisite to make the proper impression. Under one of his more impassioned discourses, his hearers would feel the truth of the assertion of John Randolph, himself an eloquent man, "that man is the best of orators." He never purposely made gestures, yet every limb and feature spoke to his hearers. A jerk of his elbow, or a swing of his long arm, was the precursor or accompaniament of a sweeping proposition, an unanswerable argument, or the assertion of a great truth. The turning and twisting of his handkerchief, with both hands, indicated the evolution of some grand truth, or deep feeling, or pathetic appeal. His old acquaintances understood his motions, and felt assured of the richness of his abundant resources of mind and heart. The tremor of his arm would start the expectation of a rich exhibition of truth. The starting tear in his eye would unlock the fountains in their hearts. The hesitation in his speech would make them almost breathless to catch the promised word. As he grew more fervent, the will and affections of his hearers were in obedience to the will and affections of the speaker. The impressions were not evanescent. The words and thoughts remained, and to them adhered the feeling that warmed the soul. It was impossible to print one of his sermons to the satisfaction of his hearers. He seldom wrote a sermon in full; and there are no types to print his actions. From his diary it appears he was seldom satisfied with his public performances. Often when he was desirous of exhibiting some grand subject, he seemed to himself to have done but very little. In this his audience did not always agree with him. But in one thing he excelled. He left no unkind remembrances of hard words or bitter speeches, or unchristian thoughts, or wounds in the soul. The impression left on those acquainted with him, was that of the wisest and meekest of men.

THE END.

INDEX

[All towns, cities, and counties are in Virginia unless otherwise stated.]

A

Abb's (App's) Valley, James Moore family, 507, 508, 510, 511, 513, 523

Abingdon Presbytery, 463, 558

Abington, Pa., 349

Abridgement of Mr. Baxter's History of His Own Life and Times, An, Edmund Calamy, *see* Calamy, Edmund

Accomack (Accawmack, Accomac) County, 12, 17; Francis Makemie in, 40, 42, 43, 44, 51, 56, 57, 60, 63, 64, 74, 357; Presbyterians in, 46, 51

Act for Establishing Religious Freedom, *see* Bill for Religious Freedom

Act of Toleration, *see* Toleration, Act of

Act of Uniformity, *see* Uniformity, Act of

Acts of Virginia Legislature, *see* Virginia, General Assembly; Virginia, laws

Adair, Rev. John, 262

Adams, Alexander, 54

Addison, Thomas, 161

Africa, 156, 287, 290

Africans, 21, 22, 23, 25, 28, 40, 155, 221, 285, 287, 288, 290, 370, 504, 505; as slaves, *see* Negroes; Slaves

Alabama, Governor of, *see* Holmes, David

Alarm to the Unconverted, Joseph Alleine, *see* Alleine, Joseph

Albany, N. Y., 65

Albemarle County, 121, 126, 135, 378, 395, 498, 530; settled, 101-2; Gordon family, 359, 378

Alexander, Rev. Archibald, 214, 500, 501, 502, 503; and Hampden-Sydney College, 407, 408, 499, 502, 563; at Briery Church, 420, 466; and Augusta Academy, 442, 457; on James Priestly, 458-59; on William Graham, 460-62, 469-70; on Drury Lacy, 489-90, 494-

95, 496-97, 499, 500; in Cumberland and Prince Edward counties, 498, 499, as missionary, 529; on Elder John Lyle, 549

Alexander, Earl Mount, *see* Mount-Alexander

Alexander, William, 458

Alexandria, 422, 486

Alison, Rev. Francis, 138, 392; and Philadelphia Academy, 225, 226

Allegheny Mountains, 105, 398, 486, 507

Allegheny River, 281, 525, 526, 530

Alleine, Joseph, *Alarm to the Unconverted,* 294, 416, 427, 556

Allen, Rev. Cary, 491, 495; and revival of 1787-88, 414, 415, 417, 419, 424, 429, 475, 532, 533; as missionary in Ky., 527, 528, 529, 539, 543, 545; examined and licensed, 534, 537, 538

Allen, Charles, 404, 405, 526, 534

Allen, Daniel, 491, 532

Allen, James, 395, 399, 401, 404, 405, 444, 487; conversion of, 420-21

Allen, Capt. Samuel V., 564

Allen, William, 161

Allen family, 102

Allenson, Hugh, 527

Ambler, Richard, 135

Amboy, N. J., 555

Amelia County, 102, 214, 330, 335, 403, 529

America, North America, 6, 7, 15, 65, 67, 69, 71, 80, 81, 84, 85, 86, 120, 155, 221, 227, 258, 264, 271, 274, 281, 299, 303, 319, 321, 324, 326, 334, 337, 365, 381, 392; emigration to 42, 98, 99, 105, 125; Presbyterian Church in, 46, 61, 62, 63, 107, 164, 535; evangelists in, 47, 53; bishop for, 198, 207, 211-12; slavery in, 285, 287; liberty in, 317, 318, 389; immigrants in, 368, 409, 506, 544. *See also* United States

American Bible Society, 566

McCorkle, Rev. Samuel, 446, 447
McCulloch, Mr., 263, 264
McCullock, Capt., 243
McCuthin, Samuel, 332
McDowell, Alexander, 226
McDowell, Maj. Joseph, 377
McDowell, Maj. Samuel, 444, 447, 448, 449, 458
McDowell family, 452
McGee, Rev. William, 552
McGill [Gill?], Rev. Daniel, 356
McGready, Rev. James, 535, 552; and revival of 1780's, 427
McKee, Col. Alexander, 520
McKee, Capt. William, 341, 444, 447, 448, 449, 458
Mackie (Macky), Rev. Josias (John), 45, 46
McKnight, Dr. John, 409, 557
Macky, Rev. John, 45, 46
McLagen, see McClagen
McLaurin, Rev. John, 251, 260, 263, 273
McMasters, Rev. Samuel, 58
McMillan, Rev. John, 471; and Robert Marshall, 545, 546
McNish, Rev. George, 46, 56, 59; preaching license, 53-55
McNutt, Robert, 332
Macoike, Samuel, see Maycock (Macoike), Samuel
McPheeters, William, 444, 448, 520
McRea, Rev. Christopher, 490
McRoberts, Rev. Archibald, 433, 435, 436, 498, 534, 537; and Hampden-Sydney College, 398, 404, 405; received by Hanover Presbytery, 492, 493-94
McRoberts, Ebenezer, 405
McRoberts, Thomas, 405
McWhorter, Rev. Alexander, 142
Madison, James, 384; supported Thomas Jefferson's Bill for Religious Freedom, 328, 329, 345, 346, 348; Thomas Jefferson on, 345; trustee of Hampden-Sydney College, 397-98, 404; opposed General Assessment bills, 431
Madison, Bishop James, 484
Madison County, 123, 156
Maffit, Capt. George, see Moffit, George
Magna Charta, 328

Magnalia Christi Americana, Cotton Mather, see Mather, Cotton
Mahon, Rev. William, 435, 537; ordained, 494, 534
Maiden Head, 172
Maine, Mr., 363
Major Jack (Indian town), 511, 516, 517, 518
Makemie, Anne, sister of Francis, 57
Makemie, Anne, daughter of Francis, 58
Makemie, Elizabeth, 58
Makemie, Rev. Francis, 98, 125, 131, 134, 140, 159, 164, 166, 304, 307, 357, 358; sketch of, 40-58; associates of, 58-61; theological views of, 61-63; N. Y. trial of, 63-82, 170; letter to Lord Cornbury, 83-84; and Scotch-Irish background, 84-85
Makemie, Francis, son of John, 57
Makemie, Francis, son of Robert, 57
Makemie, John, 57
Makemie, Naomi Anderson (Mrs. Francis), 43-44, 57, 58
Makemie, Robert, 57
Makenzie, Mr., quoted, 89
Manakin town (Manakin Town), 123, 156, 530
Manduit, Jasper, 207, 211; and Samuel Davies' trip to Great Britain, 245, 250, 252, 253, 254, 255, 256, 257, 275
Marchmont, Hugh Hume, 3rd Earl of, 260, 261
Margaret of Bristoll (ship), 21
Maring, Mr., 364
Marques, Thomas, 470
Marriage Act, 329-32
Marryat (Marriot), Dr., 267, 275; academy of, 251
Marshall, Rev. Robert, 529; missionary, 475, 527, 528; in Ky., 528; sketch of, 543-48
Marshallites, 546. *See also* New Light
Martin, Alexander, 349
Martin, Rev. John, 221, 363
Martinsburg (now in W. Va.), 565
Maryland, 43, 64, 65, 68, 71, 73, 78, 100, 120, 164, 166, 311, 380, 459; Francis Makemie and associates in, 40 *et passim,* 66, 70, 84,